Stagecoach Robberies
in California

ALSO BY R. MICHAEL WILSON
AND MCFARLAND

*Legal Executions in Nebraska, Kansas
and Oklahoma Including the Indian Territory:
A Comprehensive Registry* (2012)

*Legal Executions After Statehood in Arizona,
Colorado, Nevada, New Mexico and Utah:
A Comprehensive Registry* (2012)

*Legal Executions After Statehood in North Dakota, South Dakota,
Wyoming, Montana, Idaho, Washington and Oregon:
A Comprehensive Registry* (2011)

*Legal Executions in the Western Territories, 1847–1911:
Arizona, Colorado, Idaho, Kansas, Montana, Nebraska,
Nevada, New Mexico, North Dakota, Oklahoma, Oregon,
South Dakota, Utah, Washington and Wyoming* (2010)

*Wells, Fargo & Co. Stagecoach and Train Robberies,
1870–1884* (2010) [by James B. Hume and John N. Thacker;
edited and expanded by R. Michael Wilson]

Stagecoach Robberies in California
A Complete Record, 1856–1913

R. Michael Wilson

McFarland & Company, Inc., Publishers
Jefferson, North Carolina

This book could not have been compiled without the assistance of the California State Archives, particularly Jessica M. Herrick, archivist.

LIBRARY OF CONGRESS CATALOGUING-IN-PUBLICATION DATA

Wilson, R. Michael, 1944–
Stagecoach robberies in California : a complete record, 1856–1913 / R. Michael Wilson.
   p. cm.
Includes bibliographical references and index.

ISBN 978-0-7864-7996-2 (softcover : acid free paper) ∞
ISBN 978-1-4766-1541-7 (ebook)

1. Stagecoach robberies—California—History. 2. Brigands and robbers—California—History. 3. Outlaws—California—History. 4. Stagecoach lines—California—History. I. Title.
HV6661.C2W553 2014   364.15'520979409034—dc23   2014027785

BRITISH LIBRARY CATALOGUING DATA ARE AVAILABLE

© 2014 R. Michael Wilson. All rights reserved

No part of this book may be reproduced or transmitted in any form or by any means, electronic or mechanical, including photocopying or recording, or by any information storage and retrieval system, without permission in writing from the publisher.

On the cover: *Hands Up* artist:
Newell Convers Wyeth, 1906 © 2014 PicturesNow

Printed in the United States of America

McFarland & Company, Inc., Publishers
Box 611, Jefferson, North Carolina 28640
www.mcfarlandpub.com

To the drivers, messengers, and passengers
who were killed or maimed, or who survived
being robbed by road agents

Table of Contents

Preface — 1
Introduction — 3

Stagecoach Robberies by County

Alameda County	11	Mono County	120
Amador County	11	Monterey County	121
Butte County	24	Napa County	127
Calaveras County	29	Nevada County	133
Colusa County	58	Placer County	147
El Dorado County	60	Plumas County	161
Fresno County	68	Sacramento County	167
Inyo County	70	San Benito County	167
Kern County	73	San Bernardino County	167
Lake County	80	San Diego County	169
Lassen County	84	San Joaquin County	171
Los Angeles County	85	San Luis Obispo County	173
Madera County	88	San Mateo County	176
Marin County	93	Santa Barbara County	178
Mariposa County	93	Santa Clara County	183
Mendocino County	98	Shasta County	188
Merced County	116	Sierra County	215
Modoc County	119	Siskiyou County	220

Sonoma County	228	Tulare County	239
Stanislaus County	236	Tuolumne County	241
Tehama County	237	Yuba County	247
Trinity County	239		

Appendix: Stagecoach Robberies Listed Chronologically   261
Bibliography   269
Index   271

Preface

Hollywood has romanticized the iconic stagecoach robbery, and created more than a few myths, but these were thrilling and life-threatening events in the history of America's southwest. Wherever mineral treasure was discovered, road agents would soon appear to "mine" the roadways of gold and silver being taken out as coin, ingots, and dust and to steal payrolls being shipped in. Drivers, shotgun guards and passengers were occasionally wounded or killed, and many a road agent was killed, or captured and sent to prison.

Stagecoaches were robbed throughout the West, but California, with 460 such events, ranks well above any other jurisdiction, with the other fourteen states and territories west of the 98th meridian combined having less. Over nearly six decades between August 5, 1856, and July 25, 1913, there were stagecoach robberies in forty-three of fifty-five counties in California. Twelve counties reported no stagecoach robberies: Alpine, Contra Costa, Del Norte, Glenn, Humboldt, Kings, San Francisco, Santa Cruz, Solano, Sutter, Ventura, and Yolo; and Imperial, Orange, and Riverside counties were formed after a stagecoach robbery was committed. There were a number of robberies where more than one stagecoach was robbed, and many where there was little or nothing stolen—a "water haul." The number of men involved ranged from one road agent in many instances to nearly a dozen in one robbery. Most were conducted at night, but the road agents had to act when the treasure was aboard, so daylight robberies were not uncommon. The following historical record of those robberies is arranged alphabetically by county, and then within each county chronologically.

Introduction

The United States went to war with Mexico in 1846, and after two years the conflict was settled on February 2, 1848, with the signing of the Treaty of Guadalupe Hidalgo. One concession in the treaty was that California was ceded to the United States, and the timing couldn't have been better for the victor: a week before signing, gold was discovered at Sutter's Mill in Coloma, California. It took nearly a year before word of the great riches to be found in California spread worldwide and the gold rush started. On September 9, 1850, California became the thirty-first state, and a year later the first shipment of stagecoaches arrived by ship by traveling around Cape Horn.

Highwaymen became active in California as soon as there was sufficient plunder to justify the risk, but at first stagecoaches seemed immune to the road agents. That changed in 1856 when the first stagecoach "in motion" was stopped and a robbery was attempted. In California's earliest years there was a rapid growth in the number of footpads, those who lay in ambush along trails and pathways waiting to rob unsuspecting travelers. When gold and silver began to accumulate at mining camps, and was then transported to some major community by mule train, gangs began to form to overwhelm the armed guards that accompanied those treasure shipments. Express companies also began to form and function, and the main companies among them were Adams Express and Wells, Fargo & Company, though there were many smaller operations. After Adams Express failed, Wells, Fargo bought out most of its competition and became so pervasive throughout the west that robbers often called for the Wells, Fargo box, not even considering that express could be carried by some competitor such as Pacific Express, Alta Express, or the small operation of Rutherford & Company Express. In one robbery, for example, road agents stole the Wells, Fargo treasure box but left behind the Alta Express Company box, as they doubted it carried any plunder worth the effort to carry it away; and in another robbery they took both the Wells, Fargo box and the Pacific box, but when captured they hadn't even bothered to open the Pacific box.

The Stagecoach

An icon of the Old West, the stagecoach played a key role in opening the western wilderness to settlement, long before the railroads laid track there. Conestoga wagons could take months to make the trip west, but stagecoaches could make it from staging depots along the Mississippi River to San Francisco in less than a month. As roads began to replace trails and traces in California soon after the gold rush, and as these were further improved, stagecoach lines were established. Early coaches lumbered along behind teams of horses or mules, often mismatched in size and appearance. The teams consisted of two, four or six animals, but when a buggy or cart could be substituted, it was pulled by a single horse, mule, or donkey; however, these did not qualify as a "stagecoach." Some of these early animals were so poor that they were referred to as "skeletons covered with horse hide, which the company fondly hoped would make the trip before dying."

Passengers were allowed twenty-five pounds of luggage, two blankets, one canteen, a dust coat and hat, and they were given a cramped space in which to sit, sometimes sharing the interior of the coach with mail sacks, express packages, and an iron safe. The rocking and rolling of the coach could cause passengers to become queasy, and they could be subjected to sand gnats, a lack of bathing facilities, and lack of sleep. There were worse times for some passengers, however, as a stagecoach might be delayed for days due to swollen rivers or road closures.

A coach might be mired in mud, requiring the passengers to disembark and pull out the coach and the horses, and on steep grades male passengers would disembark and walk behind to lighten the load, regardless of the weather. Temperatures could be unbearably hot, or as stage line entrepreneur James O. Grant noted while crossing the California desert in 1870, "it was so cold that it almost froze the driver and passengers." A stagecoach might also careen out of control and roll over or drop off a steep precipice, or some mishap might lead to the loss of the team, the coach, or even the driver. There were even instances where a coach was carried away by floodwaters, or lost in crossing a swollen river when a ferry sank.

The Stage Line

Terms persistently misused often replace the appropriate words, and this was the case with the term "stage." Originally "stage" was a measure of distance as coaches traveled from one place to another in stages of about twelve to fifteen miles, in ideal circumstances, and at each end of a stage was a station, and a stage "line" consisted of as many "stages" as it took to get from the point of origin to the desired destination, so "line" referred to a line of "stages" comprising a route. A stage line operated stagecoaches as public conveyances carrying passengers, express, the U.S. mails, and private shipments. A stage line, excepting in the earliest days of a "boomtown," could not survive on passenger service alone. The express contract made a stage line successful, and the mail contract could make it quite profitable, but private freight shipments were often too infrequent to do more than add a little extra profit now and then.

Stage lines operated on a regular schedule, so when the schedule changed, newspapers gave advance notice, and stage lines operated on an established route which they did not vary without advance notice. Stage lines were established between towns or between a town and a railroad depot or a port or ferry landing.

Stations

There were two types of stations: the "swing" station and the "home" station. At a swing station the horses would be changed, but at a home station the horses would also be changed but the traveler could eat a meal, perhaps spend the night, and might find a saloon, a store, and a livery, and sometimes businesses of every sort sprang up around a station, and a town might be born. Locating a station on a line, or route, depended on finding necessities, and if they were not available they would have to be hauled in by wagon. These necessities included grass for the stock; water for the stock, farm animals, personnel and travelers; game to feed the personnel and travelers; and wood for heating, cooking, and building. In addition, stations stocked grain for the stock and various spare parts and materials for repair or replacement such as kingpins, harnesses, grease, horse shoes and nails, wheels or wheel parts, and the tools needed to keep coaches in good repair and the animals shoed. Stagecoaches traveled at the approximate rate of eight miles per hour, varying slightly by the terrain and weather, so the time between stations generally was less than a two-hour ride, and between home stations a six- to eight-hour ride.

The Vehicles

A stagecoach was any four-wheeled vehicle pulled by horses or mules. A stagecoach would carry passengers, express, mail, and freight, though on any trip the coach might be empty. A "stagecoach" vehicle was a public conveyance run on an established route and on a regular schedule, so even if empty it had to make the trip, as it had to run on schedule and there might be a full or partial load waiting for the return trip. Stagecoach vehicles included spring wagons or dead-axle wagons, surplus army ambulances, celerity coaches or mud wagons, and of course the deluxe Concord coach. The celerity coach was typically used in the mountains and on soft roadways, if there were passengers, as they were lighter and the wheels were three inches wide, as opposed to the Concord's two-inch wide wheels. Selection of the type of vehicle might be determined by availability, by terrain such as mud or soft sand, the weather the owner expected his coach to encounter, and the load to be carried in each direction.

The Team

Teams were made up of two, four or six horses or mules, and hostlers and drivers knew their animals and often had a relationship with a team that lasted many years. They harnessed the animals to get the most efficient, humane, and safest use. They knew their horses well and kept efficient teams intact whenever possible. The animals on the left of a team, furthest from the driver, were called the nigh, or "near," animals, and those on the right, nearest the driver, were called the "off" animals. The front two animals in a team were the "leaders," which were generally the smallest, smartest, and most alert of the animals, while the rear animals in a team were the "wheelers" and were the largest and strongest to give stability nearest the coach. If the team had six animals, the middle two were called "swingers," and these were generally midsized horses so they were easily controlled by the other two pairs as they did their work leading or stabilizing.

The animals changed out at a station one day might be used the following day for the return trip, or if there were sufficient horses or mules at a station, they might sit out one or two trips before they returned to the previous station. Teams often went from one station to another and returned to the previous station for years, and they came to know every detail of that small piece of roadway. The size of a team depended on a variety of circumstances. First it was determined by the type of vehicle used and the terrain to be covered, the weather, and the load, both going to its destination and returning to the head office. In the mountains or on the desert a "six-up" might be employed, while in level country on good roads a four-up might suffice, or where there was a light load a buckboard, ambulance, or other wagon might be used with a two-horse team, as this often did the job. However, if there was bad weather or bad road conditions, the number of animals in a team might be increased or, if already a six-up, would be driven at a slower pace.

The Drivers and Messengers

The primary persons associated with operating stagecoaches were the driver and the messenger, or shotgun guard. Stagecoach drivers were known by many sobriquets including Knight or Knight of the Lash, Whip, Sagebrush Navigator, or by the biblical reference Jehu. Drivers were a hardy lot representing a cross section of the nation's citizenry. Many chewed or smoked tobacco to excess, and some cussed mercilessly, but others were kind and gentle, especially toward the ladies riding in their coaches. Drivers were the "captains of their vessels" and commanded all who boarded. They were always respected, usually appreciated, and often admired. Not every man could handle the ribbons of a four-up or six-up, and many times it was only a driver's iron will and bravado which brought the coach through bad weather, across swollen rivers, over treacherous roads, with poor stock, while surviving attacks by highwaymen, and on the rarest of occasions attacks by Indians.

Shotgun messengers usually sat beside the driver and shared the discomfort and danger, more so in those rare instances of a robbery because the messenger was the first target of a road agent's bullets. Putting a messenger on a stagecoach was a signal that there was substantial treasure aboard because if there was no treasure to guard, a stage line operator would not pay for a messenger. Many lawmen, while engaged in their primary vocation, also worked as messengers.

The Road Agent

The term "road agent" originated with a station keeper. Two men stopped at his station, left but returned a short time later, and then quickly left again. When the stagecoach arrived, a robbery was reported and the description of the robbers matched the two men who had stopped at the station. The station keeper, in his report, referred to the robbers as "agents of the road," and Wells, Fargo & Company adopted the term "road agents." Road agents were also known by such terms as Turpins, highwaymen, robbers, and footpads. Road agents generally followed a formula, or modus operandi, which varied only slightly, except in a few instances. In California there were many loners, but often road agents worked in parties of two to four men, and on a few occasions numbered nearly a dozen men. Even when they acted alone they often made it appear that there were other road agents lying in hiding, by setting the scene or by their language.

One of the advantages in robbing stagecoaches was that the work could be done at some isolated location, allowing the road agents time to flee before a posse could be organized and ride to the scene. The preferred place for a robbery was where the stagecoach would naturally travel at a slow pace, such as when the coach was ascending a steep or long grade, driving across soft sand, crossing a narrow bridge, or where there was a sharp curve in the road. A stagecoach could be stopped by almost anything, or by nothing more than a man stepping in front of the horses, pointing his gun at the driver, and ordering him to halt. Other methods included placing a small obstruction in the roadway such as a log, a brush pile, rocks, a long tree limb propped at waist level, or tying a rope or a strand of barbed wire across the road. In October 1903 the Auburn to Forest Hill coach was "held up" by a party of five kits playing in the road while the mother skunk watched from the roadside. The horses refused to pass, and every cautious effort by the driver failed to drive them off until, after two hours, they tired of their game and scurried off on their own.

Road agents consistently plied their trade afoot, as the back of a horse provided an unstable platform and put the robber in jeopardy, especially if a shot was fired and his horse shied or bolted. This seemed a commonsense approach, and before the first stagecoach robbery in 1856 two of the aspiring road agents tested a stagecoach by riding in front to stop it, then riding along the side of the coach to look in. When Tom Bell's men attacked a coach a week later, they were afoot.

Road agents' weapons included shotguns, rifles and pistols, or some object that resembled a gun, and they consistently used the same weapons on future robberies when they proved persuasive, and this tendency sometimes became a method of identification. A spy might be assigned by a group of road agents to watch the loading of the treasure box at the express office to see if it was heavy, or to watch for a shotgun messenger to board which would signal that there was substantial treasure aboard. At the scene of a robbery, once the driver, messenger, and passengers were covered by firearms, a road agent would order the driver to throw out the treasure box. Sometimes the mail sacks would also be demanded, but often road agents would not want to involve federal authorities and would not molest the mails. Occasionally the passengers would be "stood up" in a line and ordered to "pungle," or produce the contents from their pockets, or a suspicious road agent might search them himself, though women were typically spared this humiliation. If the robbers got nothing for their trouble, it was termed a "water haul," indicating the value of the plunder was no more than water.

The Pursuit and the Legal Process

Often stagecoach robberies were not solved because there was no motivation to pursue the robbers. Lawmen had no budget to pursue road agents so they had to advance the funds to pay for a posse and a pursuit, and therefore there were many instances where a "posse" numbered only a sheriff and possibly one deputy. Lawmen relied on the rewards for "capture and conviction," or the rewards for recovered treasure, to reimburse them their expenses, so if there was no reward, there was no motivation to pursue the road agents. Still, lawmen in California were relatively effective, and if there was a pursuit, the road agents were often caught. However, so many road agents got away that one might observe that "crime does pay" in California. It was quite common in the Old West that, upon being captured, criminals confessed, and often they would "peach," or inform, on their partners in crime. Those who were jailed would then have an examination before a justice of the peace who would weigh the evidence and determine if it was adequate to hold over the prisoners for the grand jury, and bail would be set. The grand jury would indict the prisoner (return a true bill), and the defendants would then be arraigned. Road agents facing overwhelming evidence often pled guilty, which usually, by their cooperation, earned them a lighter sentence. Road agents were sent to prison, and sentences typically ranged from five to fifteen years, and even when the sentence ranged from twenty to fifty years a road agent rarely served more than a dozen years. Often one of the road agents in a case turned state's evidence and testified against his fellow road agents, and they received a reduced sentence or were released after testifying. Stagecoach robbers were not legally executed, but all too often circumstances during a stagecoach robbery led to a cold-blooded murder, and first-degree murder was a capital crime in all parts of the west. On rare occasions, road agents who murdered might be lynched, such as the Ruggles brothers in 1892.

The End of the Stagecoach

During the late 1870s railroads began crossing into the west, and it was thought by many that this would spell the end of stagecoaches; but in fact more stage lines were established because of the railroads. The railroads made it possible to build towns anywhere along a rail line and to develop new areas some distance from the railroads, and stagecoaches were needed between the rail towns and depots and those towns established some distance away. However, while there was a growth in stagecoach operations, the distances they traveled became shorter, and in some cases there were no "stages" at all, as the coach went from its point of origination to its destination without a change of horses. As the new century dawned, new stage lines were still being established, but the automobile wrought the end of "coaches" as the means of public transportation. By 1910 "automobile stage companies" were being established throughout the west, but stagecoach lines continued to operate in some remote areas of California for another decade. When automobile stages began operating, the road agent adapted and began robbing them, and one of the popular places was the road to Yosemite where groups of automobile stages were robbed in 1916 and 1920.

The Domination of Wells, Fargo & Company

Before 1848 express companies were active throughout the east and Midwest, but there was only one small operation on the Pacific coast—C. L. Cady's Express was first announced in the *Californian* on April 24, 1847. The need for express operations changed dramatically when gold was discovered at Sutter's Mill on January 24, 1848. There was an immediate need for expanded express operations to bring mail to the miners in isolated gold camps and to bring out the gold to a place from which it could be shipped. Several express companies sprang up almost overnight, but the Adams Express Company, by 1852, had established itself as the major express company in California and by 1854 dominated the entire Pacific coast. The men behind Wells, Fargo & Company watched the situation in California and finally opened their Pacific coast express business in 1852. Their first public notice appeared in the *New York Times* on May 20, 1852:

WELLS, FARGO & CO. CALIFORNIA EXPRESS
Capital $300,000
A joint stock company.
Office 16 Wall Street

This company having completed its organization as above is now ready to undertake the general forwarding agency and commission business; the purchase and sale of gold dust, bullion and specie, also packages, parcels and freight of all description in and between the City of New York and the City of San Francisco, and the principal cities and towns in California.

A similar notice appeared in the *Alta California* newspaper in early June 1852, before the company had opened an office and even before its representatives arrived on the Pacific coast. Once the company was established it quickly grew and soon adopted a policy of acquiring its smaller competitors. As early as November 1852 they had bought Gregory & Company's Express; in September 1853 they acquired Reynolds, Todd & Company Express; and in July 1854 they added Hunter & Company's Express. That left them with only one major competitor in the west—Adams Express Company.

Many factors led to the state of economic conditions in the mid–1850s, but in California it was lack of water that most affected mining operations during 1854. Water was necessary for placer mining, so, with a drought at hand, many miners sat about idly during much of that year. There was far less gold to be shipped by express, while merchants and financial concerns overextended credit to the miners. Adams & Company concentrated upon their waning express business in association with Page, Bacon & Company, a banking firm which was situated in the same building. The parent bank, in St. Louis, had invested heavily in the Ohio & Mississippi Railroad, and when that venture failed the parent bank was forced to close its doors. The San Francisco branch had just shipped one million dollars in assets to the parent bank, so when word of the St. Louis closure reached San Francisco on February 23, 1855, the local branch was unable to meet the demand during a rush on the bank and so also had to close its doors. Adams & Company at San Francisco followed suit, never to reopen there. When gold and silver were discovered in Nevada, Wells, Fargo & Company, now the dominant express company in the west, added stagecoach lines to their operations. They purchased the Pioneer Stage Line in 1864, and on November 1, 1866, they added the entire Holladay Overland Mail & Express Company. In 1869 Wells, Fargo & Company sold their stagecoach lines and thereafter contracted the handling of express in their "green treasure boxes" on whichever stage lines operated regionally. Wells, Fargo's little green treasure box had become the standard for carrying express, and other companies included making up similar boxes as part of the process of stocking the road. A treasure box measured twenty inches long by twelve inches high by ten inches deep and weighed nearly twenty-five pounds "lean," or empty. At first the boxes were loaded in the office and deposited into the driver's boot or inside the passenger compartment, but the familiar command of "throw down that box" led to its being bolted into the boot by the early 1870s. On some coaches, which often carried treasure, iron safes were bolted inside the passenger compartment or under the driver's seat.

Stagecoach Robberies by County

Alameda County

ALBERT ALFRED TUBBS, JANUARY 5, 1881

On Wednesday, January 5, 1881, a lone road agent brandishing a pistol stepped into the road and stopped the stagecoach traveling from Walnut Creek to Oakland. After the coach was halted the robber told driver Moore, "Give me your money or your life!" Moore thought it was a joke until the robber said, "No taffy now, no taffy; give up your money or your life," and punctuated the demand with the barrel of his pistol. The robber held out his hat, and Moore dropped in the loose change from his pocket. The robber then examined the Wells, Fargo express box but did not touch it, nor make a demand for it, then ordered, "Go on!" Moore continued into Oakland, and the robbery was reported to Sheriff Jeremiah Tyrrel who rode to the scene with detective Fuller, but they could find no clue to the robber's identity nor a trail to follow. On Friday, January 7, a man walked into the sheriff's office and surrendered, saying he was broke and he confessed to robbing the Oakland stagecoach. He gave the name Albert Alfred Carlton, but later it was learned his last name was Tubbs. His behavior raised some concerns, and by January 25 it had been determined he was insane and he was committed to the Napa Insane Asylum.

Sources: *Daily Alta California (San Francisco)*: January 9, 1881. *Sacramento Daily Union (CA)*: January 25, 1881.

Amador County

JAMES DRISCOLL & GEORGE F. TAYLOR, NOVEMBER 17, 1863

At 5:00 a.m. on Tuesday, November 17, 1863, a stagecoach left Fiddletown for Folsom, with no passengers aboard, and had traveled only one mile from Fiddletown when two masked, armed road agents ordered the driver to halt. He reined in his horses, and then the two robbers made him step down. One of them climbed into the passenger compartment with a pick and bars, and he beat and pried at the iron safe for some time before he gave up. The two robbers then ordered the driver to unhitch the team and take them some distance away, and once the coach was clear they packed explosive powder into the locks and hinges and blew open the safe, causing considerable damage to the coach. They took out $2,035 divided between two sacks of gold dust and then told the driver to move along. At the next opportunity the driver reported the robbery, and lawmen from Fiddletown rushed to the scene, but the robbers were gone and left no clue to their identity or their direction of travel. Wells, Fargo, the next day, posted a reward of $1,000 for recovery of the treasure and $500 each for the arrest of the two road agents; the company advertisement ran for weeks without results.

In early March 1864 two men were arrested for a series of burglaries in the communities around Stockton. James Driscoll, an escapee from San Quentin Prison, and George F. Taylor, an ex-convict who had served out a three-year prison term, were arrested and lodged in jail under their aliases Charles W. De Lacy and George De Lacy respectively, alleging to be brothers. After they were behind bars they were interviewed by Chief of Police Burke, who identified them as Driscoll and Taylor, and comments they made suggested they might be the road agents who robbed a stagecoach on November 17, 1863. The driver of the stagecoach was brought in, and he looked at the two prisoners and positively identified Taylor as the road agent who had climbed into the coach with tools and Driscoll as the second man. Driscoll was also identified as the man who had brought the gold dust to Sacramento to dispose of it. Taylor and Driscoll were taken from San Joaquin County to Jackson in Amador County and indicted for stagecoach robbery. Taylor, who then insisted on using the name C. W. De Lacy, was tried in early May, and though he persisted in his claim of innocence, he was convicted and sentenced to serve seven years in prison. On May 24, Driscoll appeared in a Sacramento courtroom and pled guilty, and on May 25 he returned for sentencing and was asked if he had anything to offer as a reason why sentence should not be passed. Driscoll made a long speech in which he tried to exonerate Taylor, saying, "Another party was engaged with me in this business [the stagecoach robbery], who is out of the state now, and consequently it is not necessary to mention his name." The judge then responded, "The crime for which you have pleaded guilty is one altogether too common in California, and one that ought to be severely punished; but the motive which you have alleged as the reason for your confession and plea of guilty, if true, is certainly a very praiseworthy one, and will commend you somewhat in the mercy of the Court. A man, when he undertakes the commission of a crime, can never tell what the consequences will be, either to himself, to his friends, or the community at large, and the statement you have made that an innocent person is now suffering for the offense committed by you shows you this uncertainty. If it be true that this man was innocent, and was not your coadjutor in the commission of the crime, I would not envy you the feelings you must necessarily have when you meet him at the State Prison. Under the circumstances of this case, and the representations made to me by the officers who have ferreted out the matter I will not, as my first intention, inflict upon you the extreme penalty of the law. The judgement of this court is that you be confined in the Penitentiary or State Prison for a term of seven years, to date from this day." Taylor arrived at the prison on March 28, 1864, and registered as prisoner #2716 under the name C. W. De Lacy. Driscoll arrived at the prison on July 27, 1864, and registered as prisoner #2794. De Lacy (Taylor) had been discharged on May 6, 1864, even before Driscoll's statement in court raised doubt as to his guilt. Prison records show that Driscoll died in prison on May 24, 1867. There are, however, some conflicting notations in the prison record for both men.

Sources: *Daily Alta California (San Francisco)*: November 4, 1858. *Sacramento Daily Union (CA)*: November 1, 1858; November 4, 1858; March 5, 1859; March 24, 1859; November 18, 1863; March 22, 1864; May 26, 1864.

Unknown, January 5, 1867

On Saturday, January 5, 1867, the stagecoach traveling between Irish Hill and Forest Home, with Cal Gossin driving, was stopped by two road agents, masked and armed with double-barreled shotguns. They demanded the Wells, Fargo express box and it was thrown down. One robber took it to the side of the road and busted it open using a sledgehammer while the other road agent covered the driver and passengers with his shotgun. There was not a cent inside the box, so after it was returned to the coach the driver was told to move on. The robbers did not ask for the mail, and neither the passengers nor the driver were molested. Lawmen rode to the scene but could find no clue to the robbers' identity.

Source: *Sacramento Daily Union (CA)*: January 7, 1867.

JAMES A. "BIG JIM" FALKENBERRY & GEORGE W. RINGER, DECEMBER 2, 1867

At 7:00 a.m. on Monday, December 2, 1867, the stagecoach started from Ione for Jackson, but after it had traveled only three-quarters of a mile, driver Cal Gossin was ordered to stop by two road agents, one armed with a double-barreled shotgun and the other a revolver. They demanded the Wells, Fargo treasure box and it was delivered, and then one took it to the side of the road and broke it open with an ax. As soon as he saw the contents, he told Gossin to move along. They took from the box a sack containing $8,500 in gold coin sent from the Ione tax collector to the county treasurer in Jackson. The robbers then went to where they had tied their horses, and each man fled to his home, one taking the money and burying it to be dug up and divided at some later time. As soon as Gossin got to Muletown he sent a messenger to Ione to report the robbery, including a detailed description of the robbers, and when Gossin arrived in Jackson he made his own report. Deputy Surface and Constable J. Perrin at Ione organized a posse of citizens and rode to the robbery scene, and soon they were on the trail of the robbers as it had rained that morning and they had left two clear trails of horse tracks. One set of tracks went directly to the house of George W. Ringer three miles from the scene, two miles outside Ione, and the posse then searched about the area until they were satisfied they had the right man. The second set of tracks led straight into Amador City, and again evidence was gathered incriminating a particular suspect—James A Falkenberry. When Wells, Fargo detectives Warnock and Johnson arrived from Jackson they examined the evidence and had warrants issued for the arrest of the two suspects. Falkenberry, an exceptionally large miner, was arrested at Amador City by Deputy Patterson while Constable Love of Lancha Plana rode to the ranch of George W. Ringer, arrested him and brought him into Ione. As soon as Falkenberry was arrested, he confessed, implicated Ringer, and then led the officers and express agent Edwards five miles from Amador City to the place he said he had buried the money. At first Falkenberry walked about and scuffed at the dirt for several hours, finally saying someone must have found and removed the money, but Deputy Johnson told him he had fooled about enough and if he did not produce the money he would face consequences. The prisoner then walked a short distance directly to the burial place and dug up the sack of coins. Falkenberry then told the officers how they had made masks from the black lining of a coat, and he said he had stopped the coach while Ringer broke open the box. The officers recovered all but two $20 gold pieces, which Falkenberry had taken out and spent. The prisoners were taken before a justice of the peace and held over, with Ringer's bail set at $16,000 and Falkenberry's bail set at $500 as a witness against Ringer. Both men were then taken to Jackson and lodged in the county jail, and once in Jackson the district attorney had Falkenberry rearrested. During the first week of February, Falkenberry appeared in the district court for arraignment and pled guilty, and while he awaited his sentencing the grand jury met and he was indicted. As soon as the foreman signed the true bill, a petition was presented for the jurors to sign asking newly elected governor Henry H. Haight to grant Falkenberry a pardon. In late February, Falkenberry was sentenced to serve four years at San Quentin Prison, and he arrived on February 29, 1868, where he registered as prisoner #3755. On April 16, 1868, he was pardoned. There was not sufficient evidence, beyond the word of Falkenberry, to link Ringer to the robbery, and he was released.

Source: *Sacramento Daily Union (CA)*: December 11, 1867.

Unknown, April 19, 1870

At 8:00 a.m. on Tuesday, April 19, 1870, Hill & Taft's stagecoach from Fiddletown to Ione was five miles from its destination when two men, fully disguised and armed, stepped into the road and at the point of their guns ordered the driver to halt. The driver reined in his team, and when the men demanded the Wells, Fargo express box he threw it down. There was one unarmed passenger inside the coach, and they took $15 from him, but when he explained it was all he had one robber returned $2.50. They told the driver to move on, and then they broke open the box and took out $2,500. A posse went to the scene, but without a description or a trail to follow, they had to return to town with nothing but the busted express box.

Source: *Daily Alta California (San Francisco)*: April 20, 1870.

Unknown, August 8, 1870

At 3:00 a.m. on Monday, August 8, 1870, the stagecoach from Volcano to Jackson had only traveled one mile when it was stopped by two road agents. The masked and heavily armed robbers appeared on both sides of the road and ordered the driver to halt, then demanded the Wells, Fargo express box. The box was thrown down, and the driver was told to move on. After the coach was out of sight the robbers broke open the box and took out a bar of bullion worth $5,100, then fled. A posse was formed at Volcano and were at the scene within an hour, but they could do little in the dark. By daybreak it was clear there were no clues to the robbers' identities nor a good trail to follow, so they took the broken box back to Volcano and turned it over to the local Wells, Fargo agent. Wells, Fargo, to encourage the search to continue, offered a reward of $2,000 for the recovery of the bullion and $1,000 each for the road agents "dead or alive," a rare pronouncement in those times. Still, no arrests followed.

Source: *Sacramento Daily Union (CA)*: August 9, 1870.

--- Williams, November 11, 1870

On Friday night, November 11, 1870, the stagecoach from Jackson to Mokelumne Hill had only traveled three miles from Jackson and was climbing a grade when a man ran out onto the road and grabbed the reins of the leaders. He was masked and armed and he demanded the driver to halt, but there was a heavy Wells, Fargo treasure box aboard so messenger James Sullivan sat next to the driver. The driver whipped up his team while Sullivan took aim with his shotgun and fired, aiming high so he would not hit the horses. The road agent did not appear to be hit, and he fired his pistol at the messenger once as he retreated back into the brush, missing his mark in the darkness. The stagecoach then continued into Mokelumne Hill without further incident and the robbery attempt was reported. The road agent was not recognized, and as the treasure was saved, there was no reward posted so there was little motivation for a pursuit, and neither a body nor a blood trail was found at the scene.

Shortly after the robbery attempt a man who gave the name Williams asked a rancher living near the Mokelumne station for shelter and assistance as he claimed to be very sick. Williams was cared for until his death on February 14, 1871. Just prior to his death, however, he admitted he was the man who had tried to rob the stagecoach and had been motivated because he needed the money to return to his family in the east, and he said he saw no other way to get it. After he died, his body was examined, and it was found he had eight buckshot wounds in his breast and shoulders; this along with infection had been the cause of his illness and death.

Sources: *Daily Alta California (San Francisco)*: February 17, 1871. *Sacramento Daily Union (CA)*: November 12, 1870.

Charles "Gumboot Charlie" Tadmen & Unknown, May 1, 1872

At 2:00 a.m. on Wednesday, May 1, 1872, the stagecoach from Jackson to Volcano was near Pine Grove when two masked and heavily armed road agents ordered driver Hipkins to halt. They ordered the driver to step down, unhitch his team, and take them some distance away. One man guarded Hipkins while the other climbed onto the seat and with an ax chopped the seat away so he could get at the iron Wells, Fargo express box bolted under the seat. The robber then hacked away at the iron safe until he managed to peel it open and remove $500 in half-dollar silver coins and two gold bars valued at $9,575. The two road agents then had Hipkins hitch his team, board, and continue on his route while they took their plunder and fled. A posse was organized and rode to the scene, but they could find no clue to the robbers' identities, and even with bloodhounds they could not find a trail to follow for any distance. Wells, Fargo posted rewards of $500 for the arrest and conviction of both men, or half for one, and one-quarter of the value of any treasure recovered. Wells, Fargo also assigned detectives to investigate, and by May 13 they arrested John Boardman at Volcano and charged him with being one of the robbers. On Thursday, November 14, 1872, Boardman was tried at Volcano, and at 2:00 p.m. the jurors, after five minutes deliberating, acquitted Boardman of the charge and he was released. Charles "Gumboot Charlie" Tadman was suspected, but there was not enough evidence to make an arrest.

In early April 1905 Serafino Scapucino, an absentee owner of the old John Sullivan ranch near Volcano, was visiting the ranch to look over the herd of goats he had pastured there. He was concerned because a portion of the ranch had been swept over by fire a year earlier. At the top of one hill he came across a manzanita bush and among the roots he noticed something white and shiny. He investigated and saw it was a small blob of melted silver, and when he dug beneath the blob he found a number of silver half-dollar coins, oxidized and discolored by exposure to the elements. He dug them up and determined by the weight of the blob and the numbers of coins that they amounted to about $500, as most of the coins were intact. The way they were clustered suggested they had been buried in a sack, but it had either rotted away or had been burned away by the fire, so there was no indication of ownership. It was supposed that these were the coins stolen on May 1, 1872, buried because having a large number of silver half-dollar coins would have immediately subjected the owner to suspicion and arrest, and the robbers later could not relocate the place the coins were buried. There is no report of recovery of the gold bars.

Sources: *Amador Ledger (CA)*: April 21, 1905. *Daily Alta California (San Francisco)*: May 6, 1872. *Sacramento Daily Union (CA)*: May 2, 1872; May 13, 1872; November 18, 1872.

Albert P. Hamilton & Unknown, May 3, 1875

At 8:00 a.m. on Monday, May 3, 1875, the down stagecoach from Ione in Amador County to Galt in Sacramento County was four miles below Ione when a lone highwayman stepped from the brush into the road, took his place at the heads of the leaders, pointed his shotgun at the driver, and ordered the coach stopped. A second masked robber stepped from the brush with pistol in hand, pointed it at the driver's head and ordered him to throw down the Wells, Fargo box. When the box lay in the road, the robber asked if there was much in it, and the driver said he thought there was not much. The robber lifted and shook the box and then said he would have to make it up by robbing the passengers. He had the six inside passengers step out, five men and one woman, and he took from the men their money and valuables, including several watches, jewelry, and two pistols. The last passenger, a Mr. Johnson who had been riding atop, appeared to be known to the robber, who said, "Come down; it's your turn now. You've got money and you never travel without it." Johnson said he only had two bits and told the robber, "You ought to catch me when I'm coming up. I never have any money when I'm going down to the bay, but I'm generally pretty flush coming back." The road agent then took his silver watch, but Johnson asked for it back, as it had little value. "I will take it," the robber said, "or I will get nothing out of you." After he had robbed all the men, excepting the driver, he noticed that the Mexican woman was quite agitated, so he said, "Don't be frightened, madame, I don't want your money," and he returned the purse she handed him. The robber then searched the coach expecting to find money or other valuables hidden before he got control of the passengers, and he discovered Johnson's purse which he had dropped in the coach's boot. He asked the driver if it was his and the driver said no, so the robber said, "It must belong to the other man," and commented that he knew Johnson had money. One of the passengers then pleaded for the return of his watch, as it had been a gift from his dying grandfather. The robber replied, "I really can't return it, but I will do the fair thing—I will remember your grandfather as long as the watch remains in my possession." The robber then broke open the treasure box and took out $400, more than expected when he had hefted it earlier. After the robber had all the plunder he could find, he ordered the passengers to board and then told the driver to continue on, and after all were aboard the driver whipped up his team and hurried to the next point where he could report the robbery. Johnson offered a reward of $300 for the capture of the robbers, and the other passengers added $200; and Wells, Fargo was expected to increase that amount considerably. At Galt the driver and passengers described the robbers: "The one that stood at the head of the team had his face blackened, but his hair, whiskers and eyes showed that his complexion was dark. The other wore a gunnysack mask, with holes cut for the eyes and mouth, and through these apertures it could be seen his eyes were blue and that he had a light colored moustache and whiskers—the latter, it is thought, pretty long. His voice was clear and firm, rather high-pitched, but sharp and correct in expression." Lawmen went to the scene but could not identify the robbers nor find a clear trail to follow.

On May 19, Albert P. Hamilton, who hoped to blend into San Francisco's large transient population, was arrested, identified as a prison escapee and returned to San Quentin without being tried for the two 1875 stagecoach robberies. On May 30, 1876, his sentence was commuted to eight years, and on December 3, 1879, he was released on a writ of habeas corpus. While in prison he met Roger O'Meara, who was released one month before Hamilton, and they rendezvoused. (See El Dorado County on May 24, 1880.)

UNKNOWN, JULY 6, 1875

At 9:00 a.m. Tuesday, July 6, 1875, the stagecoach from Fiddletown to Jackson, where it would connect with the Lathrop coach, was stopped by two road agents, one armed with a pistol and the other with an ax. They had hidden behind rocks just beyond a sharp curve in the road, which required the horses to proceed slowly, and as the coach came around they jumped out and the man armed with a pistol pointed his weapon at the driver and ordered him to halt. The driver was unarmed and had no choice but to obey. They took from the coach $7,000 in gold bullion from the last cleanup of the Phoenix Gold Mining Company at Plymouth. Once they had their plunder they ordered the driver to continue, and after he drove off, the two road agents fled. The driver went one mile to the first house he came to and had the farmer ride into Plymouth to report the robbery. A posse from Plymouth went to the scene but could find no clues to the robbers' identities nor a trail to follow because the terrain was so rocky and hard. The sheriff started for Plymouth at 9:30 a.m. the following morning, but he had no better luck. By July 22, Wells, Fargo had posted a reward of $2,750 for the arrest of the two road agents, and one-fourth of any treasure recovered, but it was never paid.

Sources: *Los Angeles Herald (CA)*: July 22, 1875. *Sacramento Daily Union (CA)*: July 7, 1875. *Territorial Enterprise (Virginia City, NV)*: July 6, 1875.

CHARLES "THE SHOEMAKER" PRATT & GEORGE "TEXAS" WILSON, JANUARY 10, 1876

Two men had committed several robberies in Amador County, but they had not attacked a stagecoach nor tried to steal a Wells, Fargo treasure box. On January 10, 1876, the stagecoach from Fiddletown was on its way to Drytown to connect with the stagecoach for Latrobe, but when it was halfway between Fiddletown and Plymouth in Amador County it was halted. One man, masked and armed with a Navy six-shooter of a large caliber, stepped into the roadway and stopped the horses, then ordered the driver to throw down the Wells, Fargo express box, but he did not ask for the mail. A second man was hidden in the brush covering the driver and passengers with another large-caliber Navy revolver, but he did not step out. Once they had the box on the ground they ordered the driver to continue. Had they taken the time to search the stagecoach they would have found an iron safe bolted onto the coach containing $1,500 in gold dust, but instead they got only $60 from the wooden treasure box. As soon as the coach reached Plymouth, the driver sounded the alarm and a posse was organized, but they were unable to overtake the robbers. (See El Dorado County on January 17, 1876.)

UNKNOWN, JANUARY 31, 1876

On Monday, January 31, 1876, the stagecoach from Jackson to Drytown in Amador County was three miles from its destination when two road agents appeared, both with their heads and clothing covered with barley sacks. The horses were traveling at a rapid gait when the order came to halt, so the driver whipped up the team and continued past the road agents. The robbers fired at the stagecoach, one with a shotgun and the other with a revolver, while messenger Thomas McGee leaned over the top of the coach and fired back, and passenger Head leaned out and with his revolver fired four times. The stagecoach at that pace was lurching about so no one was hit, and it continued into Drytown. Posses were organized and rode to the scene, but they returned to town empty-handed.

Source: *Sacramento Daily Union (CA)*: February 1, 1876.

CHARLES "GUMBOOT CHARLIE" TADMAN & CHARLES THOMPSON, SEPTEMBER 11, 1876

On September 11, 1876, the stagecoach of the William Hamilton line, bound for Latrobe in El Dorado County, left Jackson in Amador County with Edward Smith driving. There were passengers aboard as well as the U.S. mail and two Wells, Fargo treasure boxes. When the stagecoach reached Finn's ranch, two road agents stepped out, masked and armed, and ordered Smith to halt. Smith reined in his team and then, on demand, threw down the two treasure boxes. There was no demand made for the mail sacks, nor were the passengers molested. As soon as the boxes were delivered, the road agents told Smith to continue, and he hurried into Latrobe to sound the alarm. The two boxes contained $195—$150 in gold and silver coins and $45 in gold notes. Lawmen went to the scene and recovered the battered boxes. They found a trail and tracked the robbers, but the trail gave out. A description of the two men was circulated, and a man fitting the description of one of the road agents, who gave the name Charles Tadman, but was better known as "Gumboot Charlie," was arrested on September 17 by Constable Hopkins with his deputies Hall and Wiley four miles above Hall's station, near Jackson, and he was lodged in jail. It was not long before he was joined by Charles Thompson, and their examination was scheduled for September 18 before Justice of the Peace H. Goldner. After hearing the evidence, a positive identification by the driver and passengers, and the testimony of co-defendant Thompson, Goldner held over the two men for action by the grand jury, with bail set in the sum of $2,000. Tadman, it seems, had been known to the lawmen as he was suspected of "having got up a job some three or four years since to rob the Volcano and Jackson stage," according to Virginia City's *Enterprise*, and it was robbed on May 1, 1872.

The grand jury returned a true bill (indictment), and the two prisoners were brought into court for trial in early December. Thompson was again the principal witness against Tadman, and both men were found guilty as charged. On December 22, 1876, Tadman was sentenced to serve four years in the state penitentiary. He arrived the day after Christmas and was registered as prisoner #7319. He served out nearly all of his sentence, with only two months being commuted, and he was released on November 15, 1879. Thompson arrived at the prison on January 27, 1877, and in consideration of his cooperation with lawmen and his testimony against Tadman, he had received a sentence of only one year. Thompson was registered as prisoner #7358. He was discharged, by expiration of sentence, on December 7, 1877, and pardoned to restore all his rights.

Sources: *People of the State of California vs. Charles Tadman and Charles Thompson:* Justice Court Records, County of Amador—September 18–19, 1876; County Court Records, County of Amador—December 5–6, 1876; County Court Records, County of Amador—December 22–23, 1876. *Sacramento Daily Union (CA)*: September 18, 1876. *Territorial Enterprise (Virginia City, NV)*: September 19, 1876.

JOHN A. WRIGHT, FEBRUARY 5, 1877

The same road agent had robbed stagecoaches in Calaveras County on December 28, 1876, and February 2, 1877, and in Nevada County on January 16, 1877. On Monday, February 5, 1877, at 8:30 a.m., the stagecoach driven by Clark Stringham had reached a point south of the Spring Mountain House in Amador County when a man, wearing a silk mask as ladies wear at a masquerade, stepped out of the brush and pointed a revolver at the driver's head. Stringham reined in his team and, upon command, threw out the Wells, Fargo treasure box, the lighter of two aboard. The road agent then threatened, "Throw out that other box or I will blow your brains out." Stringham complied and then the road agent went to the window of the coach and demanded that the six passengers surrender their money. One man contributed $12, but when the next offered only $2 he waved it aside and looked to a third man, who said he had several hundred dollars but had no intention of giving it up and reached toward his "pistol pocket." The road agent then stepped back and ordered Stringham to continue on. In all, the robber, described as an American of average height and slim build, got $105 from the box, or a total of $117. The coach hurried on to the next telegraph and contacted Sheriff John Vogan of Amador County, who was soon on the trail but made no arrest. After robbing the stagecoach in Amador County, the road agent returned to Calaveras County and robbed a stagecoach on February 24, 1877. (See Calaveras County on December 28, 1876.)

ALBERT P. HAMILTON & ROGER O'MEARA, MAY 6, 1880

On Thursday, May 6, 1880, one week after successfully robbing the stagecoach from San Andreas to Milton in Calaveras County, Albert P. Hamilton and Roger O'Meara tried to stop the stagecoach from Jackson to Ione in Amador County. However, at the first sign of danger the driver whipped up his team as the "plucky messenger" exchanged shots with the two robbers. The driver managed to drive his stagecoach out of danger and at the next town reported the attempted robbery. No one had been hit during the gun battle, and the posse was not able to follow their trail and returned to town empty-handed. (See El Dorado County on May 24, 1880.)

CHARLES E. "BLACK BART" BOLTON, JUNE 23, 1883

On June 23, 1883, Charles E. Bolton, "Black Bart," stepped in front of the horses and stopped the stagecoach from Jackson to Ione in Amador County, driven by Clinton Radcliffe. Bolton was masked and armed with a shotgun. The treasure boxes and mailbags were thought to contain a substantial sum, as the area was thriving at the time, and the amount taken gave Bolton the opportunity to take a six-month hiatus. (See Calaveras County on November 3, 1883.)

UNKNOWN, APRIL 14, 1885

On Tuesday morning, April 14, 1885, the stagecoach for Sacramento left Plymouth in Amador County, and at 8:00 a.m., when one and one half miles past Forest Home, it was stopped by a lone road agent. The masked robber jumped from the brush into the road in front of the horses with his pistol in his hand and pointed his weapon at the head of driver Ned Perry. The road agent weighed about 175 pounds, wore faded overalls and neat-fitting boots. His head and shoulders were covered with a barley sack with eyeholes cut in it, but Perry could see his eyes were blue. The robber said, "Well, Johnny, why don't you chuck out that express box and mailbag? Be lively about it." Perry replied, "I guess you have struck the wrong cart. We don't carry any express and this don't happen to be a star route. I guess you are left this time." "None of your funny business, young fella," was the response, "but throw out that box." The robber then "peeped around through the bottom of the stage" and convinced himself there was nothing on board. Concerned this was to be a "water haul," he noticed a package on the floor of the boot and ordered the driver to throw it out. Perry complied and was told to drive on, and the road agent fled into the brush with his plunder of six loaves of bread. The robber, apparently frustrated in learning there was no box or mail, failed to rob the driver, who had $100 and a valuable watch and chain. He did not molest the passengers—Forest Home schoolteacher Miss Lillie Kopp riding atop and her four small pupils riding inside. Perry said later, "I believe I would have been robbed had it not been for the cool and determined gaze of the pretty school teacher."

Sources: *Daily Alta California (San Francisco)*: April 15, 1885. *Sacramento Daily Union (CA)*: April 15, 1885.

UNKNOWN, NOVEMBER 19, 1885

On Thursday, November 19, 1885, the stagecoach from Ione to Jackson was five miles from its destination when a road agent stepped onto the road and called for the driver to halt. Messenger Luddy pulled his double-barreled shotgun from the boot and took aim. He exchanged shots with the road agent, who fled into the brush. No one on the coach was hit, and the driver continued into Jackson. The posse that rode to the scene could find no evidence that the robber had been hit, nor a clue to his identity.

Source: *Daily Alta California (San Francisco)*: November 20, 1885.

Unknown, November 12, 1891

On Thursday, November 12, 1891, the stagecoach from Sacramento to Plymouth, with John Cushman driving, was climbing a grade near its destination when a masked road agent brandishing a pistol sprang from the brush and ordered the driver to stop, then demanded the mail. After he had the pouches he ordered the driver to give him all the money he had in his pockets, and he handed over $24.50. The robber asked, "Is that all the money you have?" and Cushman replied, "Every cent!" The robber then said, "Well, here's a dollar," and threw it back. There were no passengers aboard, and either there was no express box or the robber did not ask for it. As soon as the robber had his plunder he ordered Cushman to move along, and the driver whipped up his team and hurried into Plymouth. He reported the robbery, but no clues to the robber's identity were found at the scene. The mailbags had been cut open and the contents rifled, but there was no report of anything stolen; all the mail matter was collected and delivered to the postmaster in Plymouth to be repaired and forwarded.

Sources: *Los Angeles Herald (CA)*: November 15, 1891. *San Francisco Call (CA)*: November 15, 1891.

William Evans, February 16, 1893; June 15, 1893

On Thursday night, February 16, 1893, the stagecoach from Ione to Jackson had reached the foot of Morrow grade, four miles from Jackson, with Wells, Fargo's messenger Mike Tovey walking ahead of the coach. There was considerable treasure aboard, and he was being very cautious at a point he considered perfect for a robbery. He came to length of barbed wire cut from a nearby fence and stretched across the road, obviously intended to stop the horses. He returned to the coach, armed himself, and warned the driver of the barricade ahead. The driver stopped the coach and waited until Tovey returned to the wire and removed it. The messenger then searched the area but found that the robber had fled after seeing that the messenger was now armed with his shotgun, the driver was alerted, and the barrier had been removed. The coach then continued into Jackson without further incident. There were no clues at the scene nor a trail to follow, so no one was arrested.

At 5:00 p.m. on Thursday, June 15, 1893, the mail stagecoach from Ione to Jackson was four miles from its destination, at the foot of the Morrow grade and only yards from the place of the attempted robbery in February, with Clinton Radcliffe driving. Inside the coach were Mrs. Quillei and her son and John Frey, and outside was passenger W. M. Shallenberger riding with the driver and Wells, Fargo messenger Michael Tovey. Radcliffe saw a man with a blackened face hiding among the rocks on the right side of the road, pointing a rifle at the coach, but before he could speak there was a shot fired and messenger Tovey started to topple off his seat onto the roadway. The man had fired without any warning or demand, though passengers later said they heard a warning simultaneous with the shot. The first bullet struck Tovey in the right shoulder and passed through his body piercing his heart, killing him instantly. Radcliffe grabbed Tovey with one hand and managed to keep him on the seat, but the shot had frightened the six-horse team and they took off at a run. The robber, seeing his plunder getting away, stepped into the road and fired a shot at Radcliffe, and the bullet grazed his back, and then he fired two shots at the horses, wounding one animal each time. Still the four uninjured horses, spurred along by the additional shots, carried the coach several hundred yards past the road agent, where Radcliffe stopped and unharnessed the two wounded horses. The robber did not follow, perhaps because Tovey's double-barreled scattergun had remained in the boot of the coach. Two farmers had been working in a hayfield nearby and ran to determine the reason for the shooting, and this may also have served as a deterrent. C. W. Swain then came along, took Tovey's shotgun and walked to the back of the coach, so the road agent ducked into the rocks and took aim. But when Swain did not fire at him, he fled into the thick brush on the south side of the road and headed toward Sunny Creek. Radcliffe took the coach into Jackson with the four remaining horses and arrived at 7:00 p.m. and he informed lawmen of the attempted robbery and murder but could only describe the man as five feet six inches tall. Tovey was taken to the undertaker's parlor, and when he was undressed and examined it was found he had been shot twice, with the second shot entering his right side below his armpit, and the bullet was lodged in his left shoulder. This second wound was from the bullet which had grazed Radcliffe's back. When Tovey's shirt was removed, the first spent bullet fell to the floor and was determined to be .45 caliber Winchester. A large posse was organized and men were sent out to guard every road, and Constable Kelly and Deputy Constable W. Love went to the scene but could find no clues nor a trail to follow.

Warden Aull of the Nevada State Prison contacted Sheriff Ben K. Thorn and suggested the murderer might have been Milton A. Sharp, the stagecoach robber who had escaped from his prison and might have wanted revenge for Tovey killing his partner years earlier. The search for Sharp had waned, but it was renewed, he was captured, and he proved he was not anywhere near the place of the killing. Meanwhile Sheriff Thorn focused his investigation on William Evans, a man of questionable intellect, and he was arrested on July 12 and lodged in jail. Thorn learned that early on the day of the killing Evans had been at the Rooks home; the sheriff ordered their arrest as accessories, and they were in jail by August 5. Thorn's deputies then used every means to get a confession from Evans. They plied him with whiskey and opium, showed him fraudulent newspaper articles that reported Mrs. Rooks had identified him as Tovey's murderer, and they also showed him forged letters from Frank Rooks telling him that he had better confess. He became so angry, and he was kept so thoroughly doped, that he confessed, and as any piece of manufactured evidence was produced, he was directed to identify it to further incriminate himself. He said,

I got the rifle I shot Tovey down with in the valley. I came from near Red Bluff, California, and was stopping with Rooks near Cat Camp in this county; also at Kendall's near Ione, Amador County. I had the rifle which I did the shooting with hidden near Rooks' place when I attempted the robbery and killed Tovey. I had a horse and tied him near the scene of the robbery. I crossed the wire bridge to Comanche both going and coming, and traveled very rapidly to Rooks' house a distance of twelve miles after committing the murder. The mare I rode belonged to Fairburn. I burned the grass around a buckeye bush where I stood when shooting to get blacking for my face.

I did not know messenger Tovey and did not want to kill him. I wanted to stop the stage and secure the treasure. I might have fired four shots, one at the messenger, one at the stage and once or twice at the horses. I stole the gun.

When I got back to Rooks' it was daylight and I told Frank Rooks what I had done. He advised me to go away for a little while, which I did, but I returned the following Friday morning.

I claim that Rooks' influence brought all this trouble upon me.

I was perfectly sober when I did the shooting. I selected this open place for attack because I thought the messenger would be off his guard thereabout.

The rifle at the Rooks home was then taken as evidence—a .44 caliber Winchester. Evans' first trial started in October 1893, but two jurors became ill and the trial was stopped and postponed. Evans' second trial was called on January 22, 1894, and set for March 12. After five days of testimony and one day of arguments the case went to the jury, and after three hours of deliberating, and three ballots, they found Evans guilty of first-degree murder and recommended life in prison. He was then sentenced to hang, but the sentence was quickly commuted to life in prison. Wells, Fargo detective James B. Hume, almost from the time of Evans' arrest, characterized the entire case as the worst injustice he had ever seen, and said Evans was "no more guilty of killing Tovey than Grover Cleveland." However, Evans never retracted his confession nor redacted any portion of it, even after he was out from under the influence of liquor and opium, though he continued to profess his innocence.

Evans arrived at San Quentin Prison on May 14, 1894, and registered as prisoner #15970. After serving sixteen years of his life sentence and persisting in his claim of innocence and trial misconduct, Governor James Gillett paroled Evans in early 1910, and the ex-convict found work as a gardener for Venice City Trustee Elijah Griffith. On March 14, 1910, Evans stepped in front of a Los Angeles–Pacific trolley car in Venice, California, and was crushed to death, but whether this was an accident or the suicide of an ex-convict who could not adjust to his newfound freedom could not be determined.

Sources: *Los Angeles Herald (CA)*: June 16, 1893; August 3, 1893; March 16, 1910. *Sacramento Daily Union (CA)*: February 18, 1893; June 16, 1893; March 19, 1894. *San Francisco Call (CA)*: June 16–17, 1893; August 3, 1893; January 22, 1894; March 1, 1894.

Unknown, February 7, 1899

At 6:00 a.m. on Tuesday, February 7, 1899, the stagecoach from Jackson to Ione, with Peter Podesta driving, left town on schedule. The coach traveled four miles that first hour, to a point along the road where there was a downgrade and both sides were scattered with high rocks. There were no passengers aboard, but there were two company employees—Frank Goss and Joe Ratto—being taken to their work stations, and messenger Reason E. McConnell was along to guard the Wells, Fargo treasure box, though it was only an ordinary treasure shipment day. Suddenly there was the report of a shotgun blast from the left side of the road, which startled everyone on the coach. Two road agents were seen, each with a shotgun, and one also had a rifle while the other had a revolver. It was the one with the shotgun at the ready that fired first, and the second man with the rifle pulled the trigger but it misfired. Two buckshot pellets struck Podesta in his right hand and passed through, causing a painful wound, and the wind whipped open his coat at that moment and eleven buckshot penetrated the coat, and four went through his underwear causing minor wounds on his abdomen and breast. Five buckshot struck McConnell in his left arm and shoulder, and three passed through the forearm and imbedded in the bone, shattering it, and a fourth pellet was lodged between the bones of the left forearm. At the sound of that first shot, the six frightened horses bolted and took off at a gallop, Podesta urging them on with his whip, and the coach was taken beyond danger before Podesta got control of the team. However, as the coach passed out of range, the second robber, with the defective rifle ammunition, took another shot at the coach with his shotgun. McConnell returned the fire, but the stagecoach was rocking along making his aim unsteady, and he was probably out of range when he first fired. The coach reached Martell's station in another two miles, and the driver telephoned back to Jackson the details of the attempted robbery. Frank Goss took over the reins, but as he could not handle a six-horse team, two animals were unhitched, and Joe Ratto followed behind with those two animals. The coach continued on, but when it was within three miles of Ione, Podesta's hand had become so painful and swollen he decided to return to Jackson with two of the stage horses, where he would receive proper medical treatment. McConnell was taken to his home in Stockton for his medical care and recovery. A Mr. Parker had been following a short distance behind the coach in a buggy, and he reported seeing one of the road agents start south afoot toward the Mokelumne river.

Sheriff U. S. Gregory organized a posse of ten deputized citizens and, with two bloodhounds, hurried to the scene and started on the trail of the robbers. The ground had been frozen, so there were no tracks to follow; but the robbers' camp was found among the rocks, and a Winchester rifle cartridge was found, unspent, though there was a mark from the firing pin. A reward of $1,500 was posted, which motivated lawmen to pursue the robbers. By the evening of February 8, two men, described as tramps, had been arrested, and while one refused to give a name the other claimed to be Smith. Both men had been seen at Martell's station the night before as the up stage passed that point on the route. The two then asked permission and were allowed to sleep in the barn overnight, but they did not stay there, and at 8:00 a.m. on February 8, they passed through Jackson on their way to Mokelumne Hill. By the following day the general belief was that they were the wrong men, and the search for the guilty pair continued with renewed enthusiasm. Deputy Parker and Constable Kelly returned to the scene and among the rocks found a stash of old clothes and rags and an old eight-pound sledgehammer. The rough handle suggested it had probably come from some nearby ranch, so they began a search for its source but that investigation led nowhere. The two men in jail were cleared and released, and the case went cold until March. Sheriff Gregory had been watching an ex-convict named Fred Wilson, and on March 19 he arrested Wilson at Woodland and lodged him in jail. The robber had signed several receipts for items he collected after the robbery, using orders he found in the treasure box, and these were sent to Gregory. The sheriff had Wilson sign his name several times, and after comparing the signatures he was convinced Wilson's claim of innocence was legitimate and he was released and no one else was arrested.

Sources: *Los Angeles Herald (CA)*: February 8, 1899. *Sacramento Daily Union (CA)*: March 20, 1899; March 28, 1899. *San Francisco Call (CA)*: February 8–9, 1899.

UNKNOWN, MARCH 10, 1903

On Tuesday afternoon, March 10, 1903, the stagecoach from Ione to Jackson had reached the intersection of the Buena Vista and Ione roads, a mile below Miller's station, with substantial treasure aboard including the payroll for the Keystone mines. There were a dozen passengers aboard, with Dave Phillips driving the four-horse team, and Wells, Fargo messenger R. E. McConnell was riding atop. The stagecoach was following the baggage wagon fifty yards ahead with one passenger aboard, and following behind was another loaded coach, but without a shotgun guard, indicating there was no treasure aboard. Phillips' coach had just rounded a curve where there was a culvert, and he applied the whip to start the horses on a brisk pace when a rifle shot was heard. Only one passenger, a lady, had seen the road agent, on the right side of the road on a slight hill, arise from some loose brush just before the shot was fired. She claimed he had ordered "Halt!" twice, though the command was not heard by Phillips or McConnell. The first shot frightened the team and "sent the horses into a furious gallop," and after a brief interval the road agent stepped into the road fifty yards behind the coach and fired a second shot. McConnell's position on the seat prevented him from bringing his shotgun into action, and the coach was quickly taken out of range for a shotgun. As he watched the road agent, he saw that he had his gun pointed downward as if clearing a jam or reloading. Three more shots were then fired before the coach was out of range, and at least two of the five bullets fired struck the off-wheeler, the right side horse nearest the coach, one shot in his hip and the other through his neck, and the off-leader received a grazing shot across his neck. The road agent ran after the coach for some distance firing at the coach until it rounded a curve. The coach reached Miller's station and the wounded horse was removed and replaced, but later died. At Dufrene's station, a mile from the robbery scene, the details were telephoned to the sheriff's office in Jackson at 5:15 p.m. and Sheriff Norman with Deputy Jackson started for the scene. Deputy Jackson found four shells from an improved .30–30 caliber Winchester rifle using smokeless powder. One passenger, a Mr. McNichols, described the road agent as wearing a black mask similar to those worn at a masquerade ball, under average height, and young, but others said the robber was covered in black to his waist. Sheriff Tom Norman and Deputy Jackson found boot tracks leading into the heavy chaparral and followed them for miles toward Jackson Valley, but by Thursday night they gave up the chase and returned to town. Later it was supposed he was the same bandit who had robbed several stagecoaches in Mendocino County, especially the robbery of March 25, 1903.

Source: *Amador Ledger (CA)*: March 13, 1903.

JAMES WILLIAM MARTIN, APRIL 24, 1907

At 7:00 a.m. on Wednesday morning, April 24, 1907, the Butler & Talbot stagecoach from Plymouth to Sacramento, with proprietor W. Butler driving, was four miles from Drytown when a lone road agent, masked with a red handkerchief and armed with a heavy revolver, halted the coach and demanded the Wells, Fargo express box. The driver told him he had no box, as his was a mail coach. The robber checked the boot, found there was no box, and then said he didn't want the mail. He took $13.75 from Butler, all the money he had on him as he had hidden $60 under his seat cushion, and then the robber told him to move on. The Wells, Fargo express coach to Carbondale had passed that point an hour earlier, and it was believed the road agent had simply been tardy. Butler's coach continued into Plymouth, and he telephoned a report of the robbery to Sheriff U. S. Gregory, while Constable Norman Wheeler and his deputy Dan Bona of Drytown immediately rode to the scene. Wheeler and Bona found a trail of foot tracks clearly visible in the newly cultivated fields nearby and followed them by a circuitous route into Drytown. Sheriff Gregory joined them at Drytown where they learned that at 8:00 p.m. a man wearing heavy, wet and muddied boots passed down the main street of town toward the Fremont mine, and within a half hour the three lawmen had arrested a man who said his name was William Robinson. The soles of his boots matched the tracks at the robbery scene, but he had only $1.75 in his pockets and no weapon when captured. He gave a detailed alibi but had no way to corroborate it, and then he asked, "How long a sentence will I get if I own up to it?" After a brief delay, as the prisoner mulled over his predicament, he confessed and told the officers he would show them where he had hidden the money and gun. On Thursday morning Sheriff Gregory and the district attorney took the prisoner to the Fremont mine, and he showed them where he had hidden $12 and a "formidable regulation revolver." On Saturday, April 27, the prisoner appeared before Justice Goldner and was held over, with bail set at $3,000. On Monday, April 29, the defendant appeared before Judge R. C. Rust for his arraignment, said he was twenty-seven years old and his real name was James William Martin, and he pled guilty. His sentencing, was set for May 4 when Judge Rust sentenced him to serve ten years at Folsom Prison. Twenty-seven-year-old Martin arrived at Folsom on May 10, 1907, and registered as prisoner #6707; he was paroled on November 5, 1912, after serving five years, six months.

Source: *Amador Ledger (CA)*: April 26–27, 1907; May 3, 1907; May 17, 1907. *San Francisco Call (CA)*: April 25, 1907.

Butte County

OWEN MARTIN, --- PATTERSON AND UNKNOWN, JUNE 9, 1860

On Saturday afternoon, June 9, 1860, five men stopped at a "stand" on the ranch of Captain Maxey near Chico and bought liquor. That night at 9:00 p.m. the stagecoach from Marysville to Shasta arrived at a gulch seven miles below Chico in Butte County, and suddenly five men, masked and heavily armed, rose up from the gulch and pointed their weapons at the driver and at Wells, Fargo messenger Bowen. One robber commanded the driver to rein in his team, and Bowen reached for his pistol; but seeing that resistance was futile and most probably fatal, he surrendered. One of the men unhitched the horses while the leader of the gang took the Wells, Fargo express box, then took the key from Bowen. He opened the box and took out $15,000 as he stated, "The company is rich, and we have a particular use for this money." Once they had the plunder, and the arms of the messenger, they hitched the horses and told the driver to continue on into Chico. As the coach pulled out, James Y. McDuffie, the only male passenger, pulled out his revolver and shot back at the road agents four times, but apparently missed his mark, and the one lady passenger was frightened but unharmed. Once the coach arrived in Chico, Bowen organized a posse and returned to the scene of the robbery but "could find no clue to his treasure nor the robbers," so he returned to town. Wells, Fargo offered a reward of $7,000 for the recovery of the stolen money and $1,000 for the arrest and conviction of each robber.

A description of the robbers was circulated, and Maxey knew he had served the road agents liquor earlier the day of the robbery, but he had no idea of their identities. In early July, Maxey was in San Francisco when he happened to see one of the road agents, the man thought to be the leader. He reported the sighting to officer J. W. Lees who, with officer Johnson, tracked the man to the Oakland boat and arrested Owen Martin, alias Cassel or Castle, on board. They took their prisoner to jail, but he would make no admissions and hired a slick lawyer named Coffroth. Coffroth tried to get his client released on a writ of habeas corpus on July 19, but the writ was denied. Judge McKune had earlier informed Lees of the situation, and on July 16 he and officer Gay of Sacramento had taken Martin to Chico and lodged him in jail to await his preliminary hearing. Martin's attorney managed to delay the trial for several months and was granted a change of venue from Butte County to Oroville in Plumas County, where his client was tried in mid–October. Coffroth, however, could not get his client off, and he was convicted of robbing the stagecoach near Chico; but he never named the other four men nor told where the treasure, or at least his share of it, was hidden. Officers, however, suspected a man named Patterson, but he had left the country. On March 14, 1862, the *Marysville Appeal* reported that marshal Barkley with officers Doebler and Casad had arrested Patterson and taken him to Oroville for trial. Patterson had confessed, waived his examination, and said he would plead guilty when arraigned. On May 10 he appeared in court at Oroville and pled guilty as agreed, and he was sentenced to serve ten years at San Quentin Prison.

On May 13 an Oroville jail trusty named Leonard was sent for lime so that the prisoners could whitewash the interior of the jail. Leonard managed to hide an ax in the lime, and he delivered it to Patterson. That night Patterson dug his way out, then gave the ax to prisoner Harmon, a notorious horse thief, and he dug himself out. The two released all the other prisoners and then set up an ambush to capture the jailor when he came in the next morning to open their cells. When he arrived, they overpowered, tied and gagged him, but not before he cried out, "Murder!" Sheriff Middleton was close at hand and came with pistol drawn, and then the prisoners tried to get him to open the door and come in to unlock their cells, but he made them crawl back through the holes they had made under threat of being shot. Patterson was soon afterward delivered to his cell at the prison.

Sources: *Daily Alta California (San Francisco)*: July 19, 1860; October 31, 1860. *Los Angeles Star (CA)*: June 16, 1860. *Marysville Appeal (CA)*: March 14, 1862. *Marysville Democrat (CA)*: July 21, 1860. *Sacramento Daily Union (CA)*: June 11, 1860; July 20, 1860; May 10, 1862; May 17, 1862.

UNKNOWN, JANUARY 28, 1876

On Friday evening, January 28, 1876, the Wells, Fargo express wagon in Chico was approaching the railroad depot when the horses came upon a rope tied across the street in an apparent attempt to stop the coach and steal the Wells, Fargo express box being transported to the train. When the horses felt the rope across their chests they became frantic, bolted and broke through, carrying the wagon and driver a distance beyond the road agents who had not yet appeared from hiding. This was declared to be one of the boldest attempts at robbery ever recorded as the railroad depot was near the center of town. There was no clue as to who had tried to stop and rob the wagon.

Source: *Marysville Daily Appeal (CA)*: January 28, 1876.

HENRY "LIVERPOOL" NORTON AND "DOC" JOHNSON, JUNE 20, 1876

On Monday, June 20, 1876, the stagecoach from Laporte to Oroville was stopped and robbed by two masked road agents when at the junction of the Marysville and Laporte Road, thirteen miles from Oroville in Butte County. Wells, Fargo's express box was demanded and thrown out. It was broken open, and though at first it was reported to contain only $20, it actually contained between $600 and $800. As soon as the robbers had the box, the stagecoach driver was ordered to continue into Oroville. The robbery was reported and a posse was organized, but they had found no clue to the identity of the robbers before a stagecoach was robbed the following day. (See Yuba County on June 21, 1876.)

CHARLES E. "BLACK BART" BOLTON, JUNE 21, 1879

After the robbery of the Covelo to Ukiah stagecoach on October 3, 1878, Charles E. Bolton laid low for months, but then on June 21, 1879, he stopped the stagecoach from Laporte to Oroville when three miles west of Forbestown in Butte County. He demanded the express box and mail sacks from driver Dave Quadlin, and he took $50 and a silver watch from the express box; as was the usual case, there was no way to determine what was taken from the mails. Sheriff Yeates made every effort to track down the road agent, but he had to return to town empty-handed when he could not follow the trail or identify the robber. (See Calaveras County on November 3, 1883.)

JOHN BROWN, NOVEMBER 30, 1880

The stagecoach from Laporte in Plumas County to Oroville in Butte County was stopped and robbed on Tuesday, November 30, 1880, by a lone highwayman. The coach was one mile from Forbestown, at a point called Garden Ranch Ravine, when the road agent appeared from the brush, masked and wielding a shotgun. He demanded that the Wells, Fargo treasure box be thrown out, and the driver had no choice but to comply. The box contained only a few hundred dollars, so there was no messenger aboard. There were two passengers, two ladies, but they were not molested, and as soon as the road agent had the box the driver was ordered to continue on. The team was whipped up and hurried to the next place with a telephone, and the robbery was called in to Sheriff Sprague in Oroville. Sprague immediately contacted Captain Aull, a Wells, Fargo detective who happened to arrive in town at that moment, and they started for the scene. They had no luck in trailing the robber, and the following day they were joined by J. B. Hume, chief detective for the express company. Wells, Fargo did not want to spare any expense as there had been a number of robberies in the vicinity recently, but the lawmen were not able to work up a case against anyone for six months. (See Shasta County on April 18, 1881.)

UNKNOWN, MAY 25, 1882

At 8:00 a.m. Thursday, May 25, 1882, W. N. Messer's stagecoach from Chico to Susanville was twelve miles northeast of Chico, at Dead Man's Hill on the Humboldt road, when two men and a boy, masked and armed with rifles and pistols, stepped into the road and ordered driver Ed Nelson to rein in his team. When the coach stopped they ordered Nelson to climb down and had the passengers, two men and Mrs. Messer, step out and form a line. They collected $17 from the men and took Nelson's watch and chain. They did not ask for an express box nor for the mail, but as soon as they had the money they ordered everyone to board and told Nelson to continue on his route. Once the coach was out of sight the men fled. There was no way to identify the men or the boy, and there was no reward posted so there was little motivation to pursue the road agents.

Source: *Chico Daily Enterprise (CA)*: May 25, 1882.

GEORGE LESTER AND BOB CLEMENTS, SEPTEMBER 11, 1884

George Lester, using the alias Lane, with Charles Thurman, Louis J. Dreibelbis and Nat Stover had robbed a stagecoach in Nevada County on July 27, 1873. Lester was arrested, tried, convicted, and sentenced to serve fifteen years at San Quentin Prison. He served his entire term and was released on November 5, 1883. He led a law-abiding life, or at least was not arrested for any crimes he committed during the next ten months, but then he and Bob Clements began planning a stagecoach robbery. On Thursday morning, September 11, 1884, the stagecoach from Laporte, driven by Fred Morse, left Forbestown bound for Oroville, county seat of Butte County, with three male passengers and one female passenger aboard. At 3:00 p.m. the stage was coming down the grade above Smith Hurles' ranch when a masked road agent armed with a shotgun stepped into the road, which blocked the way for the horses, and they stopped. A second road agent, also masked and armed with a shotgun, then stepped out from the side of the road and covered the passengers. The man holding the reins of the lead horses demanded the Wells, Fargo express box; upon being told there was none aboard, he ordered the passengers out. The road agent at the side of the coach assisted Mrs. Rollins in stepping down but assured her she needn't be alarmed. The road agents then told the men to hand over their money, and they collected $150. Robert Hall also had $80 in coin and $1,000 in checks in his pockets which the robbers did not find. Mr. Chapman tried to "pungle" only some silver change, but when his hand came out of his pocket he had three $20 gold coins and five singles. When he asked to keep enough to pay his fare and hotel bill, three dollars was returned to him. Mr. Williams tried the same dodge after producing several twenties—asking to keep $20 to get home to Santa Rosa—but he was told he could borrow the money in Oroville. The two road agents then took the mailbags and ordered the coach to continue on.

Morse whipped up his team and hurried into Oroville to give the alarm. The description given by the driver and passengers fit two men suspected of burglarizing Bell's store in Oroville the previous night. Later, on the same night as the stagecoach robbery, Edward Quinton was driving his team up a grade near Miner's ranch when a masked footpad, armed with a shotgun, stepped out and robbed him of all he had—$11 he carried in a pocketbook. The robber, after removing the money, returned the pocketbook and told Quinton to "drive on." Lawmen were soon on the trail of the robbers, and it was thought all the work had been done by the same two men. Forbestown's Constable Parks went out on the Laporte stagecoach the next morning and soon returned with the stolen mailbag. It had been ripped open with a knife and everything was taken, except for a bundle of newspapers.

Lester was captured by Sheriff McClellan at Ione on September 28; he gave the name George

Jackson, and he was lodged in the county jail to await the arrival of his partner in crime. A dispatch was received on October 24 saying that the second robber was captured in the southern part of the state, but it appears they had the "wrong bird." Lester was tried and convicted under his alias of Jackson, and he was sentenced to serve ten years for the robbery. He was released, upon expiration of sentence, on July 8, 1891. Bob Clements was never captured, and so he was not prosecuted for the robbery and did not serve time in prison for that offense.

Sources: *Oroville Weekly Mercury (CA)*: September 12, 1884; September 19, 1884; October 10, 1884; October 24, 1884.

Unknown, September 25, 1891; September 27, 1891

On Friday, September 25, 1891, a road agent planned to halt Langdon's northeast-bound stagecoach from Chico to Powellton when fifteen miles from Chico, near the Chaparral House. He was in hiding when a constable came along and saw a barrier of limbs blocking the road, and he removed them. Apparently the robber did not want to confront an armed lawman so he fled on foot, and the constable in searching the area found a saddle horse stolen from Charlie Wilson's ranch, and he returned the animal to its owner. On Sunday, September 27, Andy Isenberg of Malaga was driving his buggy on the road northeast from Chico, a short distance ahead of the stagecoach, when a lone road agent, masked and armed with a revolver, hailed him, but he had $200 in his pockets so he refused to stop. When the stagecoach arrived at the same location as the attempted robbery two days earlier, near the Chaparral House, the same masked road agent stepped into the road, and this time he pointed his gun at driver Oats and stopped the stagecoach. He demanded the Wells, Fargo box, and it was thrown down. The robber broke it open and found it contained very little money, so he left the money in the box and returned it to the coach. He did not molest the passengers or ask for the mail, and then he told the driver to continue on. With nothing stolen and no one injured, it was not profitable to post a reward, so there was little motivation to pursue the robber. Apparently his bad luck discouraged him as he did not appear on the road again.

Sources: *Los Angeles Herald (CA)*: September 30, 1891. *San Francisco Call (CA)*: September 30, 1891. *Sacramento Daily Union (CA)*: September 30, 1891.

Unknown, November 15, 1901

At 1:30 p.m. on Friday, November 15, 1901, the West Branch Line stagecoach from Chico in Butte County was driving up the grade between Berdans and West Branch, twenty miles from Chico, when a road agent appeared at the top of the hill. The robber wore a barley sack over his head, with eyeholes cut, and had his feet muffled with barley sacks as he stepped from behind a tree. He pointed his revolver at driver T. W. Finchley and demanded that all valuables aboard be handed down. Instead Finchley made a move to draw his revolver, and the robber fired at him but missed. Finchley then returned fire, and as they exchanged shots the robber retreated down Chico Canyon toward the flume. Finchley continued to fire at the fleeing robber, and his last, sixth, bullet struck the road agent in the right arm and he dropped his revolver. The robber had fired five shots, but afraid to be left unarmed as he fled, he retraced his steps, retrieved his pistol in his left hand, and then disappeared into the canyon, which was particularly rough country for a pursuit. The driver continued to his destination and reported the robbery, and the place he had last seen the robber. Thomas Fleck and John Willis, both experienced mountaineers, started immediately on the trail of the road agent, and a posse of deputies followed that evening. The trail could only be followed a short distance; but it appeared the fugitive was still in the canyon, so deputies were posted to guard the only exit and the opposite ridges in case he tried to climb out. However, by the following day it seemed he had made good his escape and he was not captured.

Source: *San Francisco Call (CA)*: November 15–16, 1901.

UNKNOWN, JULY 25, 1913

On Friday, July 25, 1913, the first of two stagecoaches from Blairsden for Gold Lake and Green Camp was near Gold Lake when two masked road agents, armed with revolvers and rifles, halted the coach. They ordered the ten passengers, including four women, to step out and form a line. They began robbing the passengers and had gotten as far as A. J. Boehmer of San Francisco, who surrendered a gold watch and chain and a sum of money, when the second stagecoach bound for Sierra City arrived driven by "Happy Jack" Harris. Harris took in the situation and immediately drew his revolver, and he began shooting at the road agents. They abandoned their robbery scheme and fled into the brush under a hail of bullets, but no one was hit, and both stagecoaches then continued on their way. Posses were organized at Gold Lake, Blairsden and Green Camp, and they scoured the woods around Gold Lake, but they could find no clue to the robbers' identities nor a trail to follow for any distance.

Source: *San Francisco Call (CA)*: July 26, 1913.

Calaveras County

JOHN "BIG" BROWN, HENRY BROWNING AND DAVID WALDIN, FEBRUARY 17, 1857

On Tuesday, February 17, 1857, the stagecoach from Murphy's Camp was nearing Cherokee Flat in Calaveras County when it was stopped by three men, masked and armed. They demanded the express boxes, one belonging to Wells, Fargo and the other to the Pacific Express Company. The driver threw down both express boxes under threat of being shot, and then he was told to continue on. As soon as he reached Cherokee Flat he reported the robbery, and posses were quickly organized at Angel's Camp, Vallecito, San Andreas and Murphy's Camp. They started out on horseback and afoot scouring the countryside for clues or a trail. One posse of seven men from Angel's Camp, led by Justice of the Peace C. G. Lake, cut the trail of the three road agents and followed it for three miles to a cabin, where two miners were arrested and both boxes were recovered. The Wells, Fargo box had contained $33,000 and the Pacific Express box, which had not been opened, contained $4,600. The robbers had busted open the Wells, Fargo box and removed $28,000 in gold dust and then buried those pouches a few inches deep, wrapped in a handkerchief, in the dirt near the cabin. They left behind inside the Wells, Fargo box $5,000 in small bags of coins and all the letters, drafts, waybills, and other worthless papers. The hatchet used to break open the box lay near where the treasure had been buried, perhaps as a marker. All the treasure was recovered and taken into Marysville, where it was returned to the two express companies. The third road agent, a young man named David Waldin, became frightened by the uproar in his local community, surrendered and confessed. On February 23 the other two men, who gave the names "Big" Brown and Harry Browning, were taken into Angel's Camp where all three had their hearing before Justice Lake, and they were held over for trial on the 26th. Waldin turned state's evidence, pled guilty, and was about to testify against Brown and Browning, but they realized their predicament and, hoping for a lighter sentence, also pled guilty and corrected their names to John Brown and Henry Browning. Justice Lake immediately sentenced the two defendants to serve terms of twenty years at San Quentin Prison while Waldin, because of his youth and cooperation, was released. John Brown arrived at the prison on April 27, 1857, and registered as prisoner #1139. He escaped on August 24, 1857, and was not heard of again. Henry Browning arrived at the prison on June 7, 1857, and registered as prisoner #1164. The record shows that Browning died at the prison on November 8, 1857.

On October 31, 1857, sixty prisoners were working on a wharf near the prison when they commandeered a schooner and escaped. On November 5 a number of prisoners were again working on a wharf where a small ship was docked, and a guard saw behavior he suspected would lead to another similar escape. He had at his disposal a six-pound cannon, and he loaded it with grapeshot; then without warning he fired upon the convicts, killing two and mortally wounding a large number, among them Browning. The wounded were carried to the prison infirmary where Browning died of his wounds on November 8, 1857.

Sources: *Marysville Daily Herald (CA)*: February 23, 1857; February 26, 1857. *San Joaquin Republican (CA)*: February 18, 1857.

"CHEROKEE BOB" AND UNKNOWN, JANUARY 16, 1860

At 4:00 a.m. on Monday, January 16, 1860, the Dillon & Company stagecoach from Murphy's to Stockton was one mile from Angel's Camp in Calaveras County. Wells, Fargo had been informed that the coach would be robbed on that trip, so they arranged to have Sacramento officers Daniel C. Gay and Charles P. O'Neil aboard, and they hid in the boot. The coach was ascending a grade, and the passengers, who had been informed of the threat, were walking one hundred yards behind to lighten the load for the horses. Suddenly three road agents, masked and armed, appeared from the dense chaparral, and one pointed his pistol at the head of the driver and ordered him to halt. As soon as the officers heard the command, they jumped out, armed with double-barreled shotguns loaded with buckshot, and O'Neil shot to death the apparent leader of the band. A second road agent was wounded by a blast from Gay's shotgun, but he arose and the two road agents, seeing their leader fall, fled. The officers followed the uninjured robber into a deep ravine, while the passengers rushed forward and fired promiscuously at the fleeing bandits, but without apparent effect. The dead man was lifted aboard, and the stagecoach continued the short distance into Hawkeye, with the passengers right behind, while the officers stayed at the scene to look for the other two road agents. At Hawkeye a Chinese passenger, finally understanding the threat, summed up the situation by saying, "Melican (Mexican) no good, too muchee shoot!"

Soon after the attack on the stagecoach the dead road agent was identified as the notorious "Cherokee Bob." The investigation revealed that Bob and his two companions had been hanging around Stockton for days, and on Friday the 13th they had taken the same stagecoach, with the same driver, to Murphy's. While in Stockton, Bob's movements were closely watched by officer O'Neil, and his plans were learned by interception of a letter. Wells, Fargo, after ensuring there would be adequate protection aboard, loaded a heavy express box but had replaced the gold with bags of lead shot to induce the robbers to make their attempt. The coach appeared quite vulnerable as it ascended the grade near Angel's Camp with the two officers secreted, the passengers a distance behind, and the only person visible on the coach the driver. There is no record that either of the other two road agents was captured.

Sources: *Daily Alta California (San Francisco)*: January 19, 1860. *Sacramento Daily Union (CA)*: January 17, 1860.

UNKNOWN, NOVEMBER 20, 1865

At 9:00 a.m. on Monday, November 20, 1865, the eastbound stagecoach for San Andreas was traveling through a gulch two miles beyond Valley Springs, a half mile beyond the North American House, when two masked men sprang from the chaparral on the left of the road and took positions in front of the horses, "yelling like wild Indians" for driver Daniel Almy to rein in his team. One man was armed with a double-barreled shotgun and the other a pistol, but Almy was determined to save his six passengers—two Frenchmen, another man, and Rose De Lano inside and two men riding atop—so he whipped his horses and steered around them. The robbers then began firing at the departing coach, six to eight shots, and the first bullet from the pistol killed passenger Eberhardt who was riding on the center of the front seat next to the driver. The passenger riding on the left of the front seat, though the most exposed, received only a buckshot pellet through his left leg and another through his hat. The driver received a grazing shot to his forehead which stunned him, but he kept control of the team and urged them forward at a run until one animal was brought down with a bullet that broke its leg. When the horse fell, the coach stopped, and then three passengers quickly jumped out, which seemed to scare the road agents into a retreat. However, there were no arms on the coach, so the passengers could not have put up a fight if the road agents "had the sand" to discover their vulnerability. The horse was raised to his feet, and the coach was driven back six miles to the Salt Spring Valley House, where the wounded horse was replaced along with a new driver, and the coach was taken into San Andreas at 9:00 p.m.

The body of Eberhardt was left at the North American House, and the wounded passenger was brought into San Andreas and lodged in the Weber House. A posse was organized at San Andreas and rode to the scene, where a clear trail of boot tracks led to where the road agents' horses had been picketed out of sight of the road, and then the trail of horse tracks was followed seven miles before it was lost. As the pursuit progressed, members began to form an opinion as to the identities of the road gents. After the San Andreas posse abandoned the chase, a posse was organized at Jenny Lind, and they took the trail. However, no one was positively identified or arrested for the robbery or murder.

Sources: *Sacramento Daily Union (CA)*: November 23, 1865. *San Andreas Independent (CA)*: November 21, 1865.

UNKNOWN, JANUARY 5, 1867

On Saturday, January 5, 1867, the Sisson stage line coach from Murphy's was four miles from Copperopolis, its destination, when it was halted by two masked road agents. They ordered the passengers to step out of the coach so they could work on the Wells, Fargo iron safe bolted inside the passenger compartment. They had brought along explosive powder but the driver pleaded with them not to destroy the coach, so they relented and went to work with hammer and cold chisel. It took a bit longer than they had planned, but they soon had the safe peeled open and they took out $350. The safe was ruined but the coach was saved. The robbers, whom the driver believed he knew, then ordered everyone to board and sent them on their way. As soon as they reached Copperopolis, lawmen were notified and a posse was organized. They rode to the scene but could find no clues, but it was reported the officers were after them. Within the week, Wells, Fargo had posted a reward of $500 for the arrest of the two road agents and $250 for the return of the stolen money, but none of the reward was paid.

Sources: *Sacramento Daily Union (CA)*: January 10, 1867; January 12, 1867.

Unknown, April 5, 1870

Shortly before 5:00 a.m. on Tuesday, April 5, 1870, the stagecoach running from Murphy's Camp to Stockton had just left Gibson's ranch when two road agents stepped out of hiding and ordered the driver to halt. He reined in his team and the men immediately demanded the Wells, Fargo express box. It was thrown down and the robbers then ordered the driver to move on, without asking about passengers or demanding the mail. As soon as the coach was under way, the two road agents went to work on the box and soon had it busted open, and they took out $2,400 in gold dust before they fled. A posse was organized at San Andreas and they hurried to the scene, but there was nothing to find but the busted box. Wells, Fargo posted a substantial reward—$300 each for an arrest and conviction and $600 for recovery of the treasure—but no clues were forthcoming.

A week after the stagecoach robbery, Ford's store in Grass Valley was burglarized and the Wells, Fargo safe was broken into. Within days two ex-convicts were arrested—Michael Delaney and John Sansome—but the case against them for burglary was weak so they were taken to Stockton where they were seen by the driver, but he could not identify them as the road agents who had robbed him on April 5 and they were released. Sansome would return to prison on May 11, 1871, to serve a term of eighteen years for a burglary committed in Sutter County, his fourth commitment to San Quentin Prison. Delaney would return to prison on July 3, 1871, to serve an eight-year term for a burglary committed in Napa County, his second commitment to San Quentin.

Sources: *Sacramento Daily Union (CA)*: April 6, 1870; April 16, 1870.

Unknown, January 17, 1871

Early Tuesday morning, January 17, 1871, two men, masked and armed, stopped the stagecoach running between Stockton and San Andreas when it was a few miles west of Angel's Camp. There was one passenger aboard, but the road agents were only interested in the Wells, Fargo express box, and after it was demanded and thrown down they told the driver to continue on. As soon as the coach was out of sight they broke open the box and removed the contents, then fled. A posse rode to the scene, recovered the broken box, but could find no clue to the robbers' identities nor a trail to follow.

Source: *Sacramento Daily Union (CA)*: January 18, 1871.

Charlie Cooper, James "Alkalai Jim" Harrington and Ezra W. "Old Bill" Miner, January 23, 1871

Ezra William "Old Bill" Miner was soft spoken and gentlemanly, apologizing to his victim's for any undue delay they suffered while robbing them. He joined with John Sinclair and they began a spree of crimes, but when they robbed ranchman Porter of $80, they were arrested at Woodbridge, tried for robbery, convicted and each was sentenced to serve three years in California's San Quentin Prison. Miner was released on July 12, 1870, and he joined James "Alkali Jim" Harrington, and they immediately began planning a stagecoach robbery, recruiting ex-convict Charles Cooper. On January 23, 1871, Miner waved down the stagecoach at Murray's Creek one and one half miles from San Andreas in Calaveras County and asked for a ride into town. Driver Billy Cutler, when he looked forward again, saw two men wielding shotguns at the heads of his leaders. They demanded the Wells, Fargo treasure box, and it was delivered. Cutler told them there were no passengers aboard, so they went through his pockets and took $5 in coin and his watch, but returned the latter for sentimental reasons. They considered taking the driver's boots, but they were too small. After Cutler continued on to San Andreas they broke open the box and took out $200 in coin and $2,400 in gold dust, and Miner and Harrington took the loot and "skipped out" on Cooper. Miner and Harrington started for San Francisco, where Miner was caught. Harrington went to Mayfield and was captured there. Cooper had been picked up earlier and immediately "peached," or informed, on the other two road agents, turned state's evidence, testified and was released. In mid–June Miner and Harrington were each sentenced to serve ten years at San Quentin Prison. Their attorney fought for a new trial, and this was granted after ten months; but when they got to the San Andreas jail it was found that Harrington had a saw sewn into his pants. They were closely watched, retried and sentenced to thirteen years imprisonment. Miner was released on July 14, 1880, and he went to Colorado Springs, Colorado, to live with his sister, but by September he had returned to California and on the 22nd he robbed the Auburn to Forest Hill stagecoach, alone. (See Calaveras County on November 7, 1881.)

Unknown, January 6, 1872; March 5, 1872; March 9, 1872

Just before 11:00 a.m. on Saturday, January 6, 1872, the stagecoach from Milton to San Andreas, traveling on the Mokelumne Hill road, was a half mile west of the North American House when a lone road agent stepped out of a chaparral thicket, pointed his shotgun at driver McConnell, and ordered him to halt. The masked robber then ordered McConnell to throw out the Wells, Fargo express box, all the while pointing his shotgun at the driver's head. After the box was in the road the robber ordered McConnell to drive on. The robber was not interested in the two passengers aboard and did not ask for the mail. When the coach reach Jenny Lind, a posse was organized and quickly rode to the scene, but all they could find was the broken box and the hatchet used to chop it open, and the box was empty. The amount stolen was believed to be quite large as treasure had accumulated in the mountains during the recent severe storm, and this would have been the first opportunity to ship it to Milton.

Shortly after midday on Tuesday, March 5, the stagecoach between San Andreas and Milton, with McConnell driving, had passed the North American House when a masked road agent ordered him to rein in his team. Once the coach was stopped the road agent demanded that McConnell throw out the Wells, Fargo express box, and as soon as it was on the road he ordered the driver to move along, "and don't look back." The robber did not ask for the mail nor about passengers. After McConnell had driven a short distance, he turned and looked back to see what the robber was doing; he was watching the coach and immediately fired a round, and the bullet whistled just over the driver's head. When McConnell had hefted the box to throw it down, he noticed that it was very light, so the amount inside was quite small, and the robber was expected to reappear soon. A posse from Jenny Lind rode to the scene, but they had no better luck identifying the robber than they had on January 6.

On Saturday, March 9, the stagecoach from San Andreas to Milton had passed Jenny Lind and was nearing the North American House when driver McConnell saw a man hiding in the brush. He turned his coach around and drove back to Jenny Lind, where a large posse of men was quickly organized and rode to the place the man was seen. They found the trail of boot tracks and followed for some distance, and finally overtook the man and surrounded him, but he refused to surrender. He put up a fight and was shot in the head, arm and leg, and the head wound was thought to be fatal. He was carried into Jenny Lind where he admitted he had previously robbed the stagecoach twice and was lying in wait to rob it again, but he would not give his name. He died of his wounds and was buried in an unmarked grave.

Sources: *Daily Alta California (CA)*: March 11, 1872. *Sacramento Daily Union (CA)*: January 9, 1872; March 6, 1872. *Stockton Independent (CA)*: March 6, 1872.

UNKNOWN, AUGUST 18, 1873

On Monday morning, August 18, 1873, the stagecoach between Mokelumne Hill and the Mokelumne station had traveled only one and a half miles when it was stopped by two men, masked and heavily armed. They demanded the Wells, Fargo express box and then broke it open, but there was nothing inside so out of spite they destroyed most of the papers and letters. They then had the passengers get out and form a line, and they had the driver join them. One robber covered the men with his gun while the other went through their pockets, and he took $1,000 from the driver; $1,500 and a gold watch from W. H. Duryea; from M. Davidson he took $50, his watch and a diamond ring; he took $5 from H. Ray; and he got $10 from a Chinaman. Once they were certain they had all the plunder they were going to find they had everyone board and sent the coach on its way. As soon as the robbery was reported, a posse was organized and rode to the scene, but there were no clues to the robbers' identities nor a clear trail to follow. The box and damaged contents were collected and returned to the Wells, Fargo office in Mokelumne Hill.

Source: *Sacramento Daily Union (CA)*: August 19, 1873.

UNKNOWN, AUGUST 8, 1874

On Saturday, August 8, 1874, Sisson's stagecoach from San Andreas to Milton was near the North American House when two masked road agents, one armed with a rifle and the other a revolver, ordered the driver to halt. Once the coach was stopped they demanded that the "treasure box" be thrown down, but that coach carried no express. As soon as they confirmed there was no box aboard they ordered the driver to move along, without molesting the passengers nor asking for the mail. In a brief time Russell's coach arrived at the same place, carrying the express and mail, but they were not molested and passed on safely.

Source: *Calaveras Chronicle (CA)*: August 8, 1874.

UNKNOWN, OCTOBER 21, 1874

On Wednesday, October 21, 1874, the stagecoach from West Point to Mokelumne Hill, with Willard Mead driving, had only traveled two miles when a man jumped out of the bushes and stepped to the side of the coach with his revolver in hand. He pointed the cocked pistol at the driver's head but made no demands, and Mead reined in his team and asked the robber what he wanted. The robber did not answer but kept his pistol pointed, and in a moment a second robber appeared and he climbed aboard and tied the driver's wrists behind and pulled a flour sack over his head, but spoke not one word. The mailbags were then removed, cut open, and the contents rifled. The driver could not tell if anything was taken, but the bags and the remainder of their contents were returned to the coach and then one of the robbers, in a disguised voice, asked if there was any money aboard. Mead said there was none, excepting one or two dollars he had, and the robber told him, "keep that to buy whiskey with." One of the robbers drove the coach a short distance, tied the team to a tree, and told Mead not to untie his hands until someone came along, and then they left. However, as soon as Mead was sure he was alone he worked free of the binding and drove into West Point. He reported the robbery but could give only a meager description of the two men. It was supposed the robbers were after the payroll for the Zactero mine, but it was not on that coach. A posse rode to the scene but could find no clue to the robbers' identities nor a trail to follow for any distance.

Source: *Sacramento Daily Union (CA)*: October 26, 1874.

YSIDRO PARDILLO, JOAQUIN OLIVERA, JOSE LENARIS, ANTONE VALACCA, JOSE MARIA, ANTONE SAVAGE, MITCHELL RATOVICH, MITCHELL BROWN AND RAMON RUIZ, NOVEMBER 7, 1874; MARCH 23, 1875; OCTOBER 12, 1875

In late 1874, Ysidro, sometimes Isador, Pardillo formed a gang consisting of Antone "Red Antone" Valacca, Jose Lenaris, Jose "Kokimbo" Maria, Joaquin Olivera, Antone "Old Joaquin" Savage, Mitchell "Big Mitch" Ratovich, and Mitchell "Little Mitch" Brown. Pardillo divided his gang into two parties and put Joaquin Olivera in charge of the second band, and over the next year they exchanged men freely. They also divided their territory, with Pardillo headquartering near Doty's Flat and Olivera's band quartering at Jackson in Amador County. On November 7, 1874, the gang robbed the stagecoach from Sonora to Milton in Calaveras County, but there was no hard evidence to implicate any of the members. The first confirmed stagecoach robbery by these road agents was the stagecoach from Sonora to Milton on Tuesday, March 23, 1875. The mail stagecoach of Miller & Company, driven by L. Miller, was coming to Milton by way of Reynolds Ferry and was at the summit of Ferry Hill when three masked road agents appeared. Two robbers brandished revolvers, and the third held a Henry rifle. The passengers were walking behind the coach, resting the horses during the climb, and they were ordered to stand while the express box was demanded. All stood about as one robber took the box and broke it open with a sledgehammer and took out the treasure amounting to $6,100. The papers and letters were returned to the box and the busted box was handed back to the driver, the passengers were told to board, and the driver was ordered to drive on. During the robbery one man took his change out of his pocket and prepared to turn it over to the robbers, but one road agent told him to keep it as they did not want their money. Posses went to the scene but could find no clue to the robbers' identities, nor a trail to follow, so the road agents involved were never identified from among the gang members. The passengers did note that the three robbers seemed to be "old hands at the game" and were completely composed during the entire affair, and the newspapers called upon the lawmen of Calaveras County to put a stop to the robberies.

On Tuesday, October 12, 1875, the two sections of the gang joined together to rob the Sonora to Milton stagecoach, and included Pardillo, Olivera, Lenaris, Ruiz, Savage, Ratovich, and Brown. Perhaps the number of robbers, and two leaders at the scene, led to confusion. Only three men stepped into the road and halted the stagecoach, and they demanded the treasure box. The driver told them the express box would be coming on the stage which was following at some distance, so the robbers waved him on. They waited quite a while before they realized there was but one stagecoach on the route that day.

After the bungled robbery, Ruiz struck out on his own, and on the night of December 1, 1875, Ruiz, alone, robbed the Sonora to Copperopolis stagecoach in Tuolumne County. Driver Gibbons gave a detailed description of the road agent to Tuolumne County Sheriff Ben K. Thorn, who recognized the robber as Ruiz. Sheriff Thorn tracked Ruiz to a cabin near Telegraph City in Calaveras County, and on December 9, 1875, the lawman broke in on Ruiz before he could get hold of his pistols. Ruiz, after he was in jail, informed on the gang, and by December 29, Pardillo, Antone Valacca and Jose Maria were behind bars, and soon all of the members of the gang were either killed or were captured, convicted, and sentenced to prison terms. Pardillo died in San Quentin Prison on May 7, 1877. Joaquin Olivera was discharged from prison on November 17, 1882; Mitchell "Big Mitch" Ratovich was discharged from prison on April 23, 1878; Mitchell "Little Mitch" Brown was discharged from prison on October 5, 1885.

Sources: *Calaveras Prospect, (CA)*: September 2, 1899. *Calaveras Weekly Citizen (CA)*. October 13, 1875; September 2, 1899. *Morning Tribune (San Luis Obispo, CA)*: December 13, 1873. *Sacramento Daily Union (CA)*: March 25, 1875. *Union Democrat (Sonora, CA)*: December 4, 1875; June 13, 1997.

Unknown, March 1, 1875

On Monday morning, March 1, 1875, the down stagecoach from Mokelumne Hill to Lodi was a mile and a half past Camanche, near the widow Hill's place, and started up a slight grade when two road agents, masked with handkerchiefs, stepped from the greasewood beside the road, pointed pistols at driver David E. Berry, and ordered him to halt. Inside among the passengers was Dr. James Hepburn, who opened the door and asked, "Well, what in Hell do you want?" They told him to close the door and did not molest the passengers, but instead demanded the Wells, Fargo express box and it was thrown down. One robber kept his pistol pointed at Berry while the other took an ax and busted open the treasure box. Inside was a leather pouch containing an express letter and waybills, and a heavy package containing a chunk of coal, "so neatly done up to look like a heavy piece of amalgam." The robbers, thinking they had struck it rich, put the box and pouch back on the coach and told Berry to drive on. Inside the pouch was $25, which they missed. Berry drove as fast as the horses would go to Soller's ranch to get him to drive the coach to Lodi while he returned to the scene to follow the road agent's trail, but Soller was not at home. Berry then drove back to Camanche and reported the robbery, but the citizens responded, "We have not lost any robbers," and refused to organize a posse.

Berry described the road agents as tall, one quite heavyset, wearing black coats over blue working jackets, dark pants and heavy boots. After the coach started, Berry could see the two robbers heading in the direction of the Chaparral House mounted on sorrel horses with white face and feet, but without a timely pursuit the robbers could not be identified or captured.

Source: *Calaveras Chronicle (Mokelumne Hill, CA)*: March 6, 1875.

Charles E. "Black Bart" Bolton, July 26, 1875; November 3, 1883

On the morning of July 26, 1875, the celerity stagecoach, or "mud wagon," from Sonora in Tuolumne County bound for Milton in Calaveras County carrying ten passengers, and driven by John Shine, was three hours out from Sonora and an hour from Copperopolis. The coach also carried a Wells, Fargo express box and the U.S. mailbags, but the treasure box contained only a few hundred dollars in currency so there was no messenger aboard. The horses were slowly ascending a steep grade, approaching the summit of Funk Hill, when a man suddenly appeared from behind a boulder on the side of the road, stepped in front of the leaders, and crouched to keep the horses between him and the driver and ordered Shine to rein in his team. The road agent was masked with a flour sack with eyeholes cut in it which was pulled over his hat and face, and he brandished a modern-style double-barreled shotgun, but also had a Henry rifle. He pointed the shotgun and said, "Please, throw down that box." Shine struggled with the box, so the road agent called out, "If he makes a move, give him a volley, boys." Shine looked to where the robber had directed his instruction and saw the barrels of two guns pointed at him. Once the box was thrown down the demand for the mail sacks followed, and as they struck the roadway one of the female passengers also threw out her purse. The road agent bowed as he returned it to her, saying, "I don't want your money, only the express box and mail." He then gestured Shine to drive on. A second stagecoach appeared on the road, also bound for Copperopolis, but when the driver told the road agent he had no treasure aboard he was told to continue. A short distance beyond the scene the stage drivers rendezvoused and, with a small party, returned to the scene where they found the gun barrels of the robber's confederates to be a ruse—just sticks positioned to appear as gun barrels. They recovered the broken box and mail sacks cut open with a distinctive "T" shape. They hurried into Copperopolis to notify the authorities and described the robber's clothing as a white hat, short linen coat, and light-colored woolen pants.

There had been several stagecoaches robbed in the vicinity in the recent past, and the northeastern part of the state had been active for road agents for more than a decade, but this was the first robbery for this robber with his unique modus operandi. This road agent wore a distinctive mask and a soiled linen duster over typical miner's clothing, and his boots were muffled to disguise his tracks. He leaped from hiding in front of the horses, and used the leaders for cover so that he was barely exposed to the driver, or anyone else who might be riding atop. He avoided stagecoaches with messengers, which meant his plunder would always be modest. He cut the mail sacks open with a distinctive "T" and was overwhelmingly polite in his remarks to the driver and female passengers. Wells, Fargo agent J. M. Pike notified Calaveras County Sheriff Benjamin K. Thorn and related the details of the robbery, and the lawman was soon on the trail of the robber. He found evidence at the scene, including a twelve-gauge shotgun—a breech-loading side-hammer with barrels cut to twenty-four inches—a close-range weapon of formidable firepower. There was nothing, however, to identify the robber nor a trail sufficient to track him. Within a week Wells, Fargo issued a reward poster stating that the road agent had gotten only $160 from their box, but offered a reward of $250 for his capture and one-fourth of any money recovered. Between July 26, 1875, and November 3, 1883, Bolton would be credited by Wells, Fargo's chief detective James B. Hume with robbing twenty-seven stagecoaches, but one robbery was left out and two added incorrectly so that the correct count was twenty-six.

Just after sunrise on November 3, 1883, the stagecoach from Sonora in Tuolumne County to Milton in Calaveras County, driven by Reason E. McConnell, left Reynolds Ferry and within an hour was making its way up the Funk Hill grade. Just before reaching the summit, Bolton stepped into the road in front of the horses, wielding his customary shotgun, and reenacting the exact scenario he had used during his first outing on July 26, 1875. When told that the box was bolted inside the coach, Bolton ordered the driver to dismount and unhitch the horses. There were no passengers aboard, but a young man from the ferry had hitched a ride and shortly before the robbery had dismounted and taken his rifle into the hills to hunt deer. McConnell, stalling for time, said the brakes were bad and the stagecoach would roll backward, but the robber ordered him to block the wheels with rocks. McConnell suggested the robber do it and was surprised when Bolton placed rocks behind the wheels. McConnell then got down, unhitched the horses, and led them up the road while Bolton started working on the metal treasure box. After traveling two hundred yards, McConnell saw the lad from the ferry, James Rolleri, and summoned him. McConnell explained the situation, took the rifle, and the two men started back down the hill. When they were still one hundred yards from the stagecoach, Bolton spotted them and started to run. McConnell fired twice, missing his mark. Rolleri then took his rifle and, just before the road agent entered the brush, fired once, deeply grazing the left hand of the robber. They followed a trail of letters the robber dropped and found several spotted with blood, but the robber had managed to hold on to the sack containing his shotgun, $550 in coin, and twenty pounds of amalgam (or retort gold), for a total value of $4,713. Rolleri then said that he was certain it was the same man who had stayed at the Reynolds Ferry Hotel the previous week, a man who had inquired about stage line schedules. This proved to be the case, and for the first time lawmen had a detailed description of "Black Bart." McConnell hitched his team and hurried into Copperopolis, where he reported the robbery.

A posse of citizens was headed for the scene within an hour; Sheriff Benjamin K. Thorn was at the scene before dusk; and James B. Hume, Wells, Fargo's special agent, was on his way. The sheriffs of San Joaquin and Tuolumne Counties were notified and were asked to watch for the robber. Even though the posse had contaminated the scene and obliterated most of the boot tracks, Sheriff Thorn began to collect evidence: a black derby hat, size 7 1/4; an old leather valise which contained a variety of items including bags of food items stamped with a logo from an Angel's Camp store; but most importantly a handkerchief. On the handkerchief was a laundry mark, "F. X. O. 7." The proprietor of the Angel's Camp store gave a detailed description of the man who had purchased the food items, and it tallied with the description of the man who had stayed at the ferry hotel. Thorn tracked the robber to the cabin of trapper Thomas Martin, a mile from the robbery scene, but the trail was lost there, though Martin confirmed the description once again.

The robber traveled as fast as he could and finally, to speed his escape, hid his shotgun and the amalgam, keeping only the coin. He went to Sacramento, then to Reno, Nevada, before returning to San Francisco on November 10. James Hume had also returned to San Francisco, and there he turned over all the evidentiary items to Harry Morse, an ex-sheriff of Alameda County hired specifically to work on the Black Bart case. Morse compiled a list of the ninety-one laundries in San Francisco, the place he decided to start his investigation, and canvassed them trying to match the laundry mark. On November 12, Morse learned that the laundry mark was from the Ferguson & Biggs California Laundry and was a mark used by their agent Thomas Ware, who operated a tobacco shop and laundry service. Ware identified the mark and said it was assigned to Charles E. Bolton. Morse said he was a mining man and wanted to meet Bolton, a man well known as successful in the mining business, and Morse wanted Ware to introduce them. Ware told him that Bolton lived at the Webb House, 37 Second Street. Detectives were dispatched from the police station to watch for Bolton while Morse went to Ware's shop and requested he accompany him to the Webb House to make the introduction. Ware locked his shop and the two men started, but they met Bolton on the street after walking a short distance. Bolton agreed to accompany this "fellow mining man" to discuss a mining matter, and they walked to the Wells, Fargo office, where Bolton was introduced to detective Hume. Bolton kept his composure as he was questioned, then became somewhat flustered when confronted with inconsistencies, became evasive, and finally refused to answer any further questions. After some coaxing, Bolton began answering questions again, and after several more hours of questioning, and many inconsistencies, the Wells, Fargo agents and a police captain took Bolton to his room in the Webb House and found a large body of incriminating evidence. In the room was also found a bible, inscribed with the prisoner's true name—Charles E. Boles. Questioning continued, and by midnight Bolton, who now refused to answer any further questions, was arrested and jailed.

The next morning Bolton agreed to accompany them to Calaveras County. He was officially in the custody of police captain Appleton W. Stone. John N. Thacker, accompanied by Morse, joined the party as they took the boat to Stockton where they were met by Sheriff Thorn, who had come to the city with trapper Thomas Martin to identify "Black Bart." Martin immediately picked out Bolton from a large crowd of curious citizens who had gathered at the dock. Bolton was jailed overnight, and the next day the party started for Milton where they would meet stage driver McConnell. The driver could not identify the man by sight, as the road agent had been masked, but when the two men were introduced, McConnell positively identified Bolton's voice.

Bolton was next taken to San Andreas and lodged in the county jail. Although everyone was exhausted by a full day of travel, Morse decided to begin a course of relentless questioning, confronting the prisoner with a chronological list of the evidence against him. Bolton filibustered, talking about everything from his mining successes to his civil war experiences, until 1:00 a.m. when he suggested he might make a confession in return for some concessions. Morse offered to charge him with a single robbery, and if he cooperated with a detailed confession and returned the plunder, he would receive a reduced sentence. However if he did not cooperate, Morse threatened, he would be tried with as many offenses as could be proved and receive maximum, consecutive sentences on each. Bolton offered restitution if he could escape a prison sentence, but Morse told him that could not happen. Morse then brought in Sheriff Thorn and Captain Stone, and Bolton confessed to the Funk Hill stagecoach robbery of November 3, 1883, and he agreed to take them to the hidden treasure. They took their rented buggy and started for the scene of the final robbery, and on the way Bolton began relating the details of his other stagecoach robbing adventures.

On November 16, Bolton appeared before San Andreas Justice of the Peace P. H. Kean for his examination and entered a plea of guilty to the November 3 stagecoach robbery. He was held over for trial in the Superior Court, and the following day he waived a jury trial, again entered a plea of guilty, and was sentenced by Judge C. V. Gottschalk to serve a term of six years in San Quentin Prison. Bolton arrived at the prison on November 21 and registered as prisoner #11046. On January 21, 1888, Bolton was discharged, by expiration of sentence, after being credited with good time as required under the Goodwin Act.

Sources: *Amador Dispatch (CA)*: June 30, 1883. *Calaveras Chronicle:* July 31, 1875; November 9, 1883. *Calaveras Weekly Citizen (CA)*: November 17, 1883; November 24, 1883. *Daily Alta California (San Francisco)*: November 14, 1883. *Daily Appeal (Marysville, CA)*: December 16, 1881. *Daily Evening Expositor (Fresno, CA)*: August 6, 1889. *Evening Mail (Stockton, CA)*: November 24, 1883. *Marysville Daily Appeal (CA)*: December 15–17, 1881. *Mendocino Democrat (CA)*: August 10, 1877; October 4, 1878; July 23, 1880; January 27, 1882; June 16, 1882. *Mountain Messenger (Sierra Co., CA)*: November 24, 1883; December 1, 1883. *Transcript (Nevada City, CA)*: December 30, 1875; December 29, 1881. *Oroville Weekly Mercury (CA)*: July 26, 1878; August 2, 1878; June 27, 1879; July 14, 1882. *Plumas National (CA)*: August 3, 1878; June 28, 1879; July 15, 1882. *Sacramento Daily Union (CA)*: July 27, 1875; September 2, 1880. *San Francisco Call (CA)*: November 16–21, 1883. *San Francisco Chronicle (CA)*: January 6, 1884. *San Francisco Examiner (CA)*: April 3, 1887; December 3, 1888. *Shasta Courier (CA)*: November 1, 1879; September 4, 1880; November 27, 1880; October 15, 1881. *Yreka Union (CA)*: June 3, 1876; September 18, 1880; September 3, 1881; September 23, 1882.

UNKNOWN, JULY 22, 1876

At 10:00 a.m. on Saturday, July 22, 1876, the stagecoach from San Andreas to Angel's Camp was halted by a lone road agent, masked and armed with a double-barreled shotgun. He demanded that the Wells, Fargo express box be thrown down, but the driver told him, "There is no box aboard; we don't have a contract with Wells, Fargo." After he climbed up and confirmed there was no box, he took $75 in gold coins from the driver and told him to drive on. The driver hurried into Angel's Camp, reported the robbery, and the lawmen who went to the scene could find no clue to the robber's identity nor a trail to follow.

Source: *Sacramento Daily Union (CA)*: July 24, 1876

JOHN A. WRIGHT, DECEMBER 28, 1876; FEBRUARY 2, 1877; FEBRUARY 24, 1877

On December 28, 1876, the down stagecoach from Murphy's to Milton, driven by Reason E. McConnell, was stopped at dawn when it was near Altaville in Calaveras County. The lone road agent was masked and wielding a shotgun as he stepped into the road in front of the horses, pointed his weapon at the driver, and demanded the Wells, Fargo treasure box. The road agent's sudden appearance startled the team; one of the leaders became "fractious," and then the entire team became unruly. McConnell, with difficulty, gained control and halted the coach. The box was handed down, but unknown to the robber it contained only letters and waybills as the treasure was safely locked in an iron safe bolted to the floor of the coach's interior. As soon as the box was on the ground, he ordered McConnell to continue. There was one passenger riding inside, and the robber, according to the driver, acted as if he was concerned the passenger might shoot him.

On January 16, 1878, the stagecoach from San Juan to Marysville was robbed when three-quarters of a mile below the bridge over the South Yuba River in Bridgeport township, in Nevada County. On February 2, 1877, the down stagecoach from Murphy's to Milton in Calaveras County was robbed by the same road agent at the same place and in the same manner as the robbery on December 28, 1876. Again the robber got very little for his risk, so he moved away from the route between Mokelumne Hill and Ione, and on February 5 at 8:30 a.m. the Jackson to Ione stagecoach was robbed at a point south of the Spring Mountain House in Amador County. Then, on the morning of February 24, 1877, the stagecoach from Sonora to Milton was ascending the Reynolds Ferry Hill Grade, south of Stanislaus, when a lone road agent masked in black stepped out of the brush and pointed his revolver at the head of driver Sam Smith. The coach halted, and the demand was made for the treasure box. Smith told him there was nothing in the box, but he was ordered to throw it down anyway. Passenger Louis Darling was walking behind the coach and had time to hide his money and watch before reaching the coach. A Chinaman and a colored woman who had remained inside were not molested, but the robber stuck his pistol close to the face of Milo Hoadley when he made his demand and Hoadley grabbed the muzzle and tried to wrestle it from the robber. The robber won the tussle, and Hoadley then surrendered his purse containing $83. The road agent then ordered Darling to board and told Smith to continue on. From the box he got $81, bringing his total plunder to only a bit more than $160.

In the afternoon of the same day a man walked across a field to the ranch of Jackson Eproson, five miles from Milton, and asked for food. He acted very uneasy, and when the food was ready he refused to go into the house to eat but asked that the meal be brought to him. After he ate he left, and soon afterward a horse was missed, with tracks heading toward Farmington. Eproson rode into Milton and reported the stolen horse to Constable H. G. Davis, and his description of the man fit exactly the road agent. The lawman formed a posse, and they rode hard to Farmington in San Joaquin County, expecting to overtake the fugitive on the way. At Farmington the posse was just sitting down to breakfast when the man they were after, who later gave the name John A. Wright, walked in and joined them. The moment he saw Eproson he turned and tried to leave, but Davis got the drop on him. He first reached for his pistol but then surrendered without a fight. Wright was arrested and taken to San Andreas on Sunday, where he was lodged in jail. He was searched and found to have the exact amount of money taken in the robbery, but he was allowed to retain the money. On Monday, February 26, he had his examination before Justice Reddick, and with Hoadley positively identifying him, he was held over to answer to the grand jury; after being indicted his trial was set for April 17 before Judge Ira H. Reed. The jury was empaneled on the morning of April 18; he was tried, convicted, and ordered to return on April 25 at 10:00 a.m. for sentencing. The motion to set aside the verdict and grant a new trial was denied, and Wright was sentenced to serve fifteen years at San Quentin Prison. He arrived at the prison on May 1, 1877, registering as prisoner #7550. On September 30, 1880, he was transferred to Folsom Prison where he registered as prisoner #195. On October 1, 1886, Wright was discharged from Folsom after serving nine years and five months.

Milo Hoadley applied for the return of the stolen money and for reimbursement for three trips to Calaveras County to testify, a total of nine hundred sixty miles of travel as well as accommodations. It appears that most the money found on Wright when arrested went to his attorney, a small portion was spent for clean undergarments, and $30 was given to the district attorney, by law. Hoadley's claim was refused, and he was instructed that he had to seek a remedy in civil court against Wright, but that the time for such a claim had expired.

Sources: *Calaveras Chronicle (CA)*: December 30, 1876; January 6, 1877; February 2, 1877; February 10, 1877; March 3, 1877; April 21, 1877; April 28, 1877; May 12, 1877. *Weekly Appeal (Marysville, CA)*: January 19, 1877.

JAMES BENSON, JOHN BENSON, DANIEL PARKS AND AB BRYAN, AUGUST 3, 1877; AUGUST 31, 1877

On Friday afternoon, August 3, 1877, the southbound stagecoach from Milton to Sonora was four miles below Copperopolis, still in Calaveras County, and had just reached the summit of a long grade when three armed, masked men stepped into the road and ordered driver Sam Smith to rein in his team. Smith tried to stand them off by telling them, "There isn't a double dashed cent in the box, anyhow," but one of them replied, "You can't play us this time, Sam. You won't get no watch out of this job." They told Smith to get down and unhitch his team, and one of them assisted him in doing that; then they ordered the two passengers out. They marched the driver, passengers and horses a short distance away and left one man to guard them. Two road agents returned to the coach and first took down the wooden Wells, Fargo express box and broke it open, but found nothing inside. Next they went after Wells, Fargo's iron safe bolted inside the passenger compartment and using sledges and cold chisels soon broke it open and took out a bag containing $600 in silver and other money totaling between $400 and $600. The two then called to the third man, and he herded the driver, passengers, and horses back to the coach, had the passengers board, assisted Smith in hitching his team, and ordered him to drive on. Smith looked back as he topped the hill and saw the three robbers seated in the middle of the road dividing the plunder. Lawmen went to the scene but could find no clue to the robbers' identities nor a trail to follow. Wells, Fargo's chief detective, James B. Hume, was put on the case, but by August 6 he had determined there were no workable clues and waited for some break in the case.

On Friday, August 31, 1877, the down stagecoach from Milton to Sonora, driven by Sam Smith, was halted by three masked road agents when it was four miles beyond Copperopolis in Calaveras County. They stepped into the road in front of the horses and pointed their arms at Smith, who reined in his team. The road agents then had the passengers disembark and march a short distance away, where one robber stood guard, while Smith was required to unhitch his team. They made short work of the wooden Wells, Fargo express box, but there was nothing inside. They next tackled the iron safe bolted inside the passenger compartment and had brought with them the necessary hammers and cold chisels. Once the safe was opened they removed $1,200 in coin, including a sack containing $600 in silver coins. The two road agents who worked on the safe then helped Smith hitch his team while the other man brought back the passengers, who were ordered to board the coach. As soon as all was in readiness the three men ordered Smith to drive on. As the stagecoach passed out of view, the three men could be seen sitting in the middle of the road dividing their plunder.

As soon as the alarm was sounded, ex-sheriff Benjamin K. Thorn went to the scene and took up their trail. He was joined by Wells, Fargo's chief detective James B. Hume, and by the following day they had identified two of the road agents as the Benson brothers, James and Patrick, of Central Hill. When express messenger Thomas Magee heard of the warrant, he enlisted the help of G. F. Wesson and they arrested the Bensons at Junction and the prisoners were taken to San Andreas and lodged in jail, but Patrick quickly proved an alibi and was released. The same day, Saturday, September 1, two men were arrested near the Stanislaus River, eight miles from Modesto, by Hume, Calaveras County undersheriff Garvey, and Stanislaus County undersheriff Lane. The prisoners gave the names W. H. Odum and John Benson, another brother of James Benson. They were brought to San Andreas and they joined James in jail, but Odum was soon cleared and released.

Hume continued his investigation and soon identified a third man believed involved in the stagecoach robbery—Ab Bryan of San Andreas. He went to Carson City, Nevada, with a requisition for Bryan, and a warrant was issued for his arrest. Douglass County deputy sheriff J. C. Lupton received word of the warrant, and on September 6 he found Bryan and arrested him. On September 8, Hume started for San Andreas with his prisoner, and two days later he joined the other two prisoners in the San Andreas jail. Meanwhile Thorn, who was then in the employ of Wells, Fargo, trailed a fourth man to St. Louis, Missouri, and, with a requisition from Governor William Irwin, arrested Daniel "Dave" Parks and returned him to San Andreas. Parks was well known to Thorn, as he had been sent to prison in 1864 for ten years for a robbery in Calaveras County.

The prisoners had their examination in San Andreas and were held over to answer to the grand jury. On Friday, November 2, the Sonora to Milton stagecoach, driven by J. D. Gibbons, was hailed by one man, who looked inside at the single passenger and then summoned two others to join him. After a brief discussion they sent the stagecoach on its way. The actions and comments of the men suggested they were looking for those who had testified against the Bensons, Parks and Bryan at their examination, but none of the witnesses were aboard. The intentions of these three "road agents" was never determined.

In early December each of the men was indicted, arraigned and given until December 6 to plead. They pled not guilty and trial was set for December 7 for Parks, Bryan, and John Benson and December 8 for James Benson, but they all asked for, and were granted, separate trials. Ab Bryan turned state's evidence in time for the trial of John Benson, which commenced on schedule. John Benson's trial took four days, and on the fifth day, December 13, the jury returned a guilty verdict. On Monday, January 11, 1878, Judge Ira H. Reed set the date for sentencing John Benson at January 26 and also permitted James Benson to withdraw his not guilty plea and plead guilty. On the date of sentencing, John was given a term of sixteen years and James a term of twelve years at San Quentin Prison. The brothers arrived at the prison on January 30, John registering as prisoner #7990 and James registering as prisoner #7991. James Benson was pardoned by Governor Washington Bartlett on May 3, 1887, and he was discharged. John Benson was pardoned and discharged on May 5, 1887, serving just two more days than his brother.

The cases of Bryan and Parks dragged on until the next court session in April. The trial of Daniel Parks finally commenced on Thursday, April 18 and concluded on April 20, with the Benson brothers and Bryan testifying against him. The jury returned a guilty verdict the following day and sentencing was scheduled for April 27. Bryan, in consideration of turning state's evidence, had his case continued and was released on his own recognizance, never to be tried for the robbery. Parks was finally sentenced to a term of eighteen years. He arrived at the prison on April 29, 1878, and registered as prisoner #8188. Parks was discharged on June 29, 1889, serving just over eleven years.

Sources: *Calaveras Chronicle (CA)*: September 8, 1877; September 15, 1877; October 5, 1877; November 17, 1877; December 8, 1877; December 15, 1877; January 8, 1878; January 11, 1878; January 19, 1878; February 2, 1878; April 6, 1878; March 30, 1878; April 20, 1878; April 27, 1878; May 4, 1878. *Marysville Weekly Appeal (CA)*: August 6, 1877. *Sacramento Daily Union (CA)*: August 6, 1877; August 8, 1877.

Unknown, February 22, 1879

On Tuesday, February 22, 1879, the Mokelumne Hill stagecoach was one mile above Camanche when two masked road agents, one armed with a shotgun and the other a revolver, stepped into the road and ordered the driver to halt. They demanded the Wells, Fargo express box and one box was thrown down from the driver's seat; but they did not demand the other box nor try to break open the iron safe bolted inside the passenger compartment, and they were not interested in the passengers or the mail. As soon as they had the one box, they ordered the driver to continue, and he whipped up his team and hurried into Camanche to report the robbery. A posse was quickly organized and they rode to the scene, but the robbers had already fled, leaving behind the broken box and the worthless contents. There was no clue to the identity of the robbers, nor a trail to follow, so the box and contents were recovered and taken into Camanche to be forwarded to the Wells, Fargo office. The amount in the box was not reported, but it was thought to be quite small as there was no messenger aboard, and the contents of the second box were not revealed.

Source: *Sacramento Daily Union (CA)*: February 27, 1879.

ALBERT P. HAMILTON AND ROGER O'MEARA, APRIL 29, 1880

Albert P. Hamilton met Roger O'Meara in prison and the two planned to get together after they were both released. O'Meara was released in early November 1879, and Hamilton was released on a writ of habeas corpus on December 3, 1879. As soon as Hamilton was freed he rendezvoused with O'Meara and they began planning stagecoach robberies in Calaveras County. At 8:00 a.m. on April 29, 1880, the two masked, armed road agents stopped the coach from San Andreas to Milton and demanded the Wells, Fargo treasure box. They broke it open and took out the contents, took the driver's boots, and then disappeared into the brush. Posses were organized but they could not find the robbers. (See El Dorado County on May 24, 1880.)

DAVID THOMPSON, MAY 24, 1880

David Thompson, who used the initials "U. D.," was no stranger at San Quentin Prison. He had served three terms there—two for grand larceny and one for burglary. In 1880, after being free for three years, Thompson was staying at the home of Patrick McCoffery but not doing well in adjusting to the life of a law-abiding citizen. About the middle of May he told several people that he was "going to make a raise or go back to my old quarters." On May 24, 1880, at sunrise the stagecoach from Murphy's to Milton in Calaveras County, driven by "Colonel" Lovelace, was stopped by a masked road agent armed with a shotgun. He ordered Lovelace to throw down the Wells, Fargo treasure box and, while under the threat of being shot to pieces, the driver did so immediately. As soon as the box was on the ground the road agent ordered Lovelace to move on, and when the coach was out of sight, Thompson broke open the box and removed all the money inside—$3. Lovelace hurried into Angel's Camp and told Constable J. B. Meyers of the robbery, and his description of the road agent matched Thompson. Meyers went to the McCoffery house and arrested Thompson without resistance, and the prisoner quickly confessed every detail of the robbery. He was taken into town and examined by Justice Tait, and he was held over for action by the grand jury. There had been some confusion about the robbery because another pair of road agents had been active on April 29 and May 8, and Thompson was questioned. He denied any part, and eventually Albert P. Hamilton and Roger O'Meara would properly be credited with those robberies.

Thompson was anxious to return to San Quentin and did not want to wait for the grand jury to convene, so on May 26, by agreement, he was arraigned on an information and pled guilty to the robbery. Judge C. V. Gottschalk ordered Thompson to return to court on June 3, and just ten days after stopping the stagecoach, Thompson was sentenced to serve five years. Thompson arrived at San Quentin Prison on June 15 and registered as prisoner #9381. He served out his entire term and was released, by expiration of sentence, on January 15, 1884.

Source: *Calaveras Chronicle (CA)*: May 29, 1880; June 5, 1880.

EZRA W. "OLD BILL" MINER, STANTON T. JONES, BILL MILLER AND JIM CRUM, NOVEMBER 7, 1881

Ezra W. "Old Bill" Miner left Colorado Springs, Colorado, to look for some opportunity in crime but returned to Colorado in early September 1880 where he met Arthur Pond, who adopted the alias Billy Leroy. The two men teamed up to rob the Barlow & Sanderson stagecoach near Ohio City on September 23, 1880, but they got only $50, so they robbed another stagecoach near Slum Gullion Pass on October 7, 1880, but got only $100. A week later they stopped the Alamosa to Del Norte stagecoach near Banshee station and this time found nearly $4,000. LeRoy had assumed command, which irked Miner, so they split their take and ended their relationship.

Pond would recruit his brother to continue his stagecoach-robbing enterprise, and they would be captured and lynched at Del Norte on May 23, 1881.

After going broke in Michigan, Miner returned to Colorado and partnered with Stanton T. Jones and Charles Dingman. On February 4, 1881, they robbed the Del Norte stagecoach but found nothing aboard. They were pursued and Dingman was captured, while Miner and Stanton fled. On April 28 the two fugitives were captured, in the company of their new partner Jim East, while riding three stolen horses. The lawmen searched the prisoners but failed to find a .32 caliber pistol in Miner's boot, so at 1:00 a.m. he and Jones made their escape by wounding two of the officers. Fearing the same fate as the Pond brothers if caught in Colorado, Miner and Jones fled toward California, arriving in the fall of 1881.

Miner and Jones recruited Bill Miller and Jim Crum. The four road agents stopped the Sonora to Milton stagecoach, driven by Clark Stringham, near Angel's Camp in Calaveras County on November 7, 1881, as it was toiling up a steep grade. Miner, again in control, called out numbers for his men, and they took up assigned positions. One covered the driver while another took control of three passengers, who were ordered out. Two wooden Wells, Fargo treasure boxes were delivered on demand, and they, along with the iron safe bolted inside, were broken open with a sledgehammer brought by Miner. The robbers took $3,300 from the box and a little more than $500 from the passengers. Stringham then asked if he could leave, saying he did not want to miss his connection with the train at Milton, and Miner waved him on, saying, "Ta-ta, my boy." A massive manhunt began and Miner, Crum and Miller were tracked to Miller's ranch in Yolo County, but Jones went his own way and was not seen again. As lawmen surrounded the ranch house, the three fugitives made a run for it. Crum was captured, but Miner and Miller got away. Miner and Miller were seen the following day near Sacramento and, after a thrilling chase, were captured and lodged in the jail at Sacramento. They were tried and convicted, and on December 17, 1881, Miller and Miner were sentenced to serve terms of twenty-five years in San Quentin Prison, while Crum received a sentence of twelve years. In 1884 Miner made a feeble attempt to escape by having his cell mate put a dummy in his bed while he hid in one of the shops, planning to scale the wall after dark, but the plan was discovered and he was found. In November 1892 he again tried to escape, this time with J. Marshall, but the guards learned of the plan and set up an ambush. Marshall was killed by a shotgun blast, and Miner, badly wounded, managed to crawl back into his cell. Miner was released on June 17, 1901, after serving nearly twenty years.

While in prison Miner learned that trains now carried the treasure, and he learned how to rob a train. He robbed several trains in the northwest and then moved his operations into Canada, where he robbed several more trains. He was captured, convicted, and sentenced to a long prison term, but he escaped and fled south. On February 22, 1911, three masked men, well armed, flagged the New Orleans to New York Southern Express at Sulphur Springs near Gainesville, Georgia, but Miner was soon arrested. After his conviction, Miner was put on a chain gang, but he was so feeble he was moved to the state prison farm at Milledgeville, Georgia. He escaped into the Georgia swamps several times, and the last escape took such a toll on his health that he died on September 2, 1913.

Sources: *Daily Alta California (San Francisco, CA)*: August 7, 1863. *Daily Evening Bulletin (San Francisco, CA)*: February 4, 1871; February 6, 1871; February 11, 1871; November 11, 1871. *Daily Evening Herald (Stockton, CA)*: January 24, 1866; February 22, 1866; March 12, 1866; January 23, 1871. *Daily Independent (Stockton, CA)*: February 7, 1871. *Daily Patriot (San Jose, CA)*: January 27, 1871; February 1, 1871; February 27, 1871. *Denver Republican (CO)*: June 7, 1881. *San Francisco Chronicle (CA)*: September 18, 1879; November 8, 1881. *San Francisco Examiner (CA)*: May 21, 1892; November 30, 1892. *San Juan Prospector (Del Norte, CO)*: May 28, 1881. *Rocky Mountain News (Denver, CO)*: October 15, 1880. *Weekly News (Milledgeville, GA)*: September 5, 1913.

WILLIAM SMITH, DECEMBER 29, 1881

At 2:10 p.m. on December 29, 1881, the stagecoach from Milton to Sonora, driven by Clark Stringham, was approaching the top of a steep hill, the steepest on the road and about four miles beyond Copperopolis in Calaveras County, when a lone road agent wearing a black mask and armed with a breech-loading shotgun stepped out and ordered the driver to rein in his team. The robber then demanded the Wells, Fargo treasure boxes. The horses were exhausted from the climb, and Stringham had no choice but to comply. As soon as the coach halted, the passengers were ordered out, and these included Madeline Cuneo, an Italian lady from San Francisco, and H. S. Cohn, a "Jew peddler" whom the coach had stopped to pick up along the road. The road agent ordered the driver to open the box, offering a hatchet he had brought along, but Stringham refused saying he had to care for the horses. The road agent then broke open the boxes, removed the valuables, and then went for the mailbags. He cut open all but one bag and mutilated the letters, the one bag containing a large sum of money was not molested because the sound of a wagon's wheels were heard, and the road agent dodged behind a large rock. The wagon was driven by Dick Martin of Copperopolis, who was "sparking his girlfriend," and the robber got the drop on them. He then ordered Stringham to break open the iron safe, but Stringham said, "There is nothing in the box, and I can't open it anyway." The road agent then threatened to shoot the driver, and Stringham replied, "Shoot and be damned. I'll not open the box." The road agent then hacked away at the iron box until his hatchet gave out and then he gave up. He next went through two trunks, but when he found nothing he left the remainder of the baggage unmolested. He ordered Stringham to "pungle," and the driver dropped his money in the mud, where the robber left it. The driver and his passengers were ordered to board, and Stringham was told to continue on. Dick Martin and his sweetheart were not molested and they followed the stagecoach from the scene. The entire robbery took nearly two hours.

Stringham hurried into Sonora and sounded the alarm, and Sheriff Benjamin K. Thorn went to the scene the following day and found the tracks of the robber and his horse. The animal's hoof prints were peculiar, and Thorn followed the trail to Milton. There he enlisted the help of Constable Devin Henderson, and they continued on to Linden. The next day the trail was lost, so they went to Stockton and reported the matter to Sheriff Thomas Cunningham and Deputy Sheriff Oscar F. Atwood. Thorn and Henderson went north while Cunningham and Atwood went south. Cunningham and Atwood cut the robber's trail at French Camp and followed it into Lathrop. At the livery in Lathrop, Atwood found the robber's horse and soon found the road agent having a meal at the Shannon House. Atwood went in while Cunningham, who might be recognized, covered the exit. With his pistol drawn, Atwood captured the road agent without resistance. The prisoner was handcuffed, and the deputy took from him two loaded revolvers, a Bowie knife, a black mask, and a very sharp chisel, but he said he had discarded his shotgun along the trail. The prisoner was taken to Stockton and lodged in jail. His eye was blackened, which he claimed was from a fall from his horse, but the officers believed it was from his hatchet bounding back when he tried to break open the iron safe. The twenty-three-year-old German gave his name as William Smith. The horse he was riding had been stolen from Martin Duffy of Camanche on Christmas Day. Sheriff Thorn took Smith to San Andreas and lodged him in the Calaveras County jail. The prisoner confessed to the December 29 robbery and waived his examination. He was held over for the grand jury, which convened in June, and he was indicted. When brought into court he pled guilty and was sentenced to serve five years at San Quentin Prison. He arrived on June 27, 1882, and registered as prisoner #10220. He was released, by expiration of sentence, on August 17, 1885.

Sources: *Daily Evening Herald (Stockton, CA)*: December 30, 1881; January 6, 1882. *Independent (Helena, MT)*: July 29, 1881. *San Francisco Examiner:* August 18, 1885.

Burton Greeley, February 26, 1884

On Tuesday morning, February 26, 1884, the down stagecoach from Sonora to Milton, driven by Joe Mulligan, was stopped a half mile above Angel's Creek by a lone highwayman armed with a shotgun. Once the coach was halted he made the driver unhitch the team, then ordered the only passenger, the Reverend B. F. Rattray of Alameda, to climb down as well. "Now, you lay down on the ground and don't you move a hand or bat an eye," he said, and the Reverend responded, "But, my kind sir, it is cold and I might be made sick by the exposure." The road agent told Rattray, "Cold be damned! You get down on that ground or I'll make an angel of you damned quick, d'ye hear?" Rattray was persistent and said, "But I am not only a minister of the Gospel, but it is awful cold, and you are blue in the face yourself. Please don't insist on the sacrifice," and then he "clasped his hands as if in prayer and rolled his eyes beseechingly." The robber relented and told the preacher to walk down the road a good distance and stand with his back to the stagecoach.

The road agent then spent a considerable time trying to break into the iron safe bolted inside the passenger compartment of the coach, but failing to gain entrance, he broke open the wooden treasure box. There was nothing of value inside so he told Mulligan to hitch up his horses and continue on, picking up his passenger when he got to him. The coach proceeded to a point two miles beyond Angel's Creek when two more road agents sprang from behind a bush and again halted the stagecoach. They were armed with a rifle and a revolver. These road agents also had Mulligan unhitch the horses and, along with Rattray, take them some distance down the road and await a signal, a whistle, before returning. From their position in the road they could hear the robbers banging on the iron safe for fifteen minutes before giving up and leaving, without giving the signal to return.

After Mulligan and Rattray tired and had heard no sound from the coach for a while, they returned and found that the two road agents had managed to break off the outer lock but had had no luck in breaking into the interior of the safe. The stagecoach then continued on its way. Rattray said, "My friend, this is a little bit rough to be stopped twice in one morning," and Mulligan replied, "That is nothing on this road."

As soon as they began driving they came to a man walking on the road, and he pulled his hat down and bowed his head as they passed, but Rattray immediately recognized him as the first road agent. They continued on to the first farm and told the men of their experience. The farmers organized a posse and started after the road agent, but they did not find him. Sheriff Benjamin K. Thorn and Wells, Fargo detective James B. Hume struck the trail of the first road agent at Burus' Ferry where he had crossed the Stanislaus River at 10:00 a.m. the morning of the robbery, traveling on foot. At the Crimea House they learned he was heading toward Sonora, but they soon lost the trail. Thorn with Sheriff McQuade headed south, leaving Hume behind to watch for the fugitive. At Chinese Camp the two sheriffs cut his trail again and learned their man had crossed the Tuolumne River at Don Pedro's Bar and headed toward Fresno. When two miles from Enterprise, they learned that the robber was in a store at Fresno Flats. They drove their wagon to the store as quickly as they could, dashed through the front door, and rushed upon the fugitive so quickly that he could make no resistance. The prisoner did not question his arrest until they had already traveled many miles from Fresno Flats, and when told it was for a stagecoach robbery he made no attempt to deny the charge. They took their prisoner to Mariposa Creek and spent the night and then took him into Sonora, a trip of some sixty miles, where he was lodged in jail.

When the party arrived in Sonora, several men came forward to identify the prisoner, who had since given his name as Burton Greeley, as a man they had seen about town a few days before the robbery, and some said he had previously used the name Jack Donovan. Mulligan, the driver, identified him as the first of the road agents and the man who had passed him on foot just after the second halting of the stagecoach. A representative of the *Union Democrat* was allowed to interview the prisoner, and he reported that Greeley was from South Carolina, about thirty-five years of age, medium height, with a muscular and rawboned build, black hair and eyes. He had been mining at Indian Creek but was returning to his home at Fresno Flats, penniless, when the stagecoach was robbed, and he claimed he was innocent. On March 14, Sheriff Thorn transferred his prisoner to San Andreas in Calaveras County for trial. On March 17, Greeley was taken before Justice P. H. Kean, and the date for his examination was set for the March 27. Kean bound him over to await action by the grand jury. Greeley, now aware of the overwhelming evidence against him, confessed to the stagecoach robbery and agreed to plead guilty. In consideration of his cooperation and lack of a prison record, he was sentenced to serve five years at San Quentin Prison.

He arrived on April 1, 1884, registering as convict #11200. Greeley died in the prison hospital on July 20, 1886, possibly from consumption which was epidemic in the prison during those years.

Sources: *Calaveras Chronicle (CA)*: March 1, 1884; March 15, 1884; March 22, 1884, March 29, 1884.

UNKNOWN, OCTOBER 17, 1884

On Friday, October 17, 1884, the southbound stagecoach between Milton and Sonora, while still in Calaveras County, was stopped by a lone highwayman, masked and armed. He took the Wells, Fargo box and broke it open, then told the driver to continue and fled into the brush. Calaveras County sheriff Benjamin K. Thorn and T. J. Mullerson of Murphy's Camp went to the scene and followed the robber's trail. They overtook and captured the robber on October 20 and took him into Milton to wait for the driver to identify him. While he was behind bars his clothing was examined, and the mask he wore during the robbery was found sewn into the lining of his coat. The prisoner was a young man, quite large, and was known to have been employed making shingles in the mountains, but his name was not offered to the press. After he was positively identified by the stagecoach driver, he was taken to San Andreas for his hearing, but there is no further record of prosecution.

Sources: *Amador Dispatch (CA)*: October 20, 1884. *Sacramento Daily Union (CA)*: October 21, 1884.

ALBERT "BERT" ALDRIDGE, LEONARD "LEN" ALDRIDGE AND JAMES LYNCH, DECEMBER 19, 1884

On Friday, December 19, 1884, the northbound stagecoach from Sonora to Milton, with no passengers aboard, was near the Reservoir House in Calaveras County, still eight miles from its destination. Suddenly two masked robbers, each armed with a shotgun, appeared on the road and ordered the driver to halt. One robber kept the driver covered while the other got into the passenger compartment and worked at the iron safe, but he could not get it open. They didn't ask for the wooden box nor for the mail. Sheepherders and their flocks were coming closer to the coach, so the two robbers abandoned the robbery and fled. The driver continued into Milton and reported the robbery, and officers rode to the scene but could not immediately identify the robbers. After investigating for several days, suspicion focused on the Aldridge brothers, thirty-two-year-old Albert and twenty-three-year-old Leonard, and Jim Lynch. The three men were arrested and lodged in the San Andreas jail while evidence was building against them. They were arraigned on December 23 and held over for trial, with bail set at $2,000 each. The Aldridge brothers were tried in late January 1885, with Lynch testifying against them, and on the 30th they were convicted of stagecoach robbery. Lynch, because of his cooperation, was released. On February 3, 1885, they appeared in court, with Albert using initials A. E. and Leonard using initials C. A., and the Aldridge brothers heard their sentences—nine years each to be served at San Quentin Prison. The Aldridge brothers arrived at the prison on February 18, 1885, with A. E. Aldridge registering as prisoner #11585 and C. A. Aldridge registering as prisoner #11586. Both brothers were released on January 18, 1891, after serving five years ten months.

Sources: *Daily Alta California (San Francisco)*: December 23, 1884; February 3, 1885. *Sacramento Daily Union (CA)*: December 13, 1884; January 30, 1885.

UNKNOWN, FEBRUARY 2, 1885

On Monday morning, February 2, 1885, the Sonora to Milton stagecoach was climbing Funk Hill four miles from Copperopolis when two road agents, masked and armed, appeared and ordered the driver to rein in his team. Once the coach was stopped, one of the robbers covered the driver with his gun while the other climbed into the passenger compartment, and soon he had the Wells, Fargo's iron safe opened and took out $1,800. They told the driver to continue on and disappeared into the heavy brush. A posse rode to the scene but could find no clue to the robbers' identities.

Source: *Daily Alta California (San Francisco)*: February 3, 1885.

UNKNOWN, MARCH 26, 1885

At 8:00 a.m. on Thursday, March 26, 1885, the stagecoach from Sonora to Stockton was near Milton in Calaveras County when a lone road agent, masked and armed with a double-barreled shotgun, stepped into the road and ordered driver Kelley to halt. When the coach came to a standstill the road agent demanded that the Wells, Fargo box be thrown down, and it was. There were no passengers aboard, and the robber did not ask for the mail. As soon as he had the box he told Kelley to continue into Milton. The driver whipped up his team, hurried into town to report the robbery, and gave as good a description of the robber as he could. Lawmen rode to the scene but could find no clue to the robber's identity. Wells, Fargo did not disclose the amount in the box, but it must have been small, or possibly even empty, as there is no report of a reward posted for recovery of the treasure.

Source: *Daily Alta California (San Francisco)*: March 27, 1885.

MARTIN RYAN, AUGUST 19, 1885

On Wednesday, August 19, 1885, the stagecoach from Sonora in Tuolumne County to Milton in Calaveras County had crossed the county line when a lone, masked road agent stepped out armed with a double-barreled shotgun and ordered the coach to halt. He demanded the Wells, Fargo express box, and it was thrown down. The robber then told the driver to continue on, and he hurried into Milton to report the robbery. The robber did not molest the passengers or ask for the mail. Wells, Fargo detectives were soon on the robber's trail, and by the following day they had tracked him to Oakdale and arrested Martin Ryan, a forty-year-old Irishman, and they recovered the mask and shotgun for evidence. On Saturday, August 22, they took their prisoner before the magistrate in Milton, and he was held over for action by the grand jury, bail set at $3,000. Ryan could not make the bail amount so he was lodged in jail at San Andreas. Ryan was tried and convicted of stagecoach robbery on October 28 and was sentenced to serve three years in prison. Ryan arrived at San Quentin on November 5, 1885, and registered as prisoner #11902; he was discharged on March 5, 1888, after serving two years four months.

Source: *Daily Alta California (San Francisco)*: August 24, 1885.

UNKNOWN, JANUARY 12, 1886

On Tuesday, January 12, 1886, the up stagecoach from Milton was ascending Funk Hill when two masked road agents suddenly appeared, one from each side of the road. The driver whipped up his team and drove the coach out of danger while messenger Banks fired one barrel of his shotgun at each road agent, but he did not know if he hit anyone. The surprised robbers did not fire until the coach had passed them, and several of their seven shots struck the trunks on the hind boot, but none of the three passengers was hit. The posse that rode to the scene could find no clue to the robbers' identities nor a blood trail.

Source: *Sacramento Daily Union (CA)*: January 13, 1886.

C. A. KENT, NOVEMBER 20, 1886

On Saturday morning, November 20, 1886, the San Andreas stagecoach was one mile from Valley Springs when the lone passenger threw out the Wells, Fargo express box and jumped out after it. He waved his pistol and told the driver to move on, then busted open the box but found nothing inside. A party of men saw the robbery and hurried to the scene, but the man fled into the thick chaparral and hid until they managed to drive him out of his hiding place, and he was arrested by Jeff James. The prisoner gave the name Kent and said he had been employed as a carpenter at the Union mine until recently, and at 2:00 p.m. he arrived in Valley Springs, along with the busted box, and he was lodged in jail. At his examination he was held over for action by the grand jury, indicted, and tried in early January 1887. He was convicted of robbery, and because of the odd circumstances, he was only sentenced to serve one year in prison. Twenty-nine-year-old C. A. Kent arrived at San Quentin on January 31, 1887, and registered as prisoner #12390; he was discharged by expiration of sentence on November 30, 1887, after serving ten months.

Sources: *Daily Alta California (San Francisco)*: November 21, 1886. *Los Angeles Herald (CA)*: November 21, 1886.

UNKNOWN, APRIL 1, 1889

On Monday morning, April 1, 1889, the stagecoach from Murphy's Camp to Milton was near Angel's Camp when a lone road agent, masked and armed, stepped in front of the horses and ordered the driver to halt. The robber then demanded the Wells, Fargo express box and the mail, and the box and the way-pouch were thrown down but the pouch containing the registered packages was pushed back under the driver's seat and saved. There were five passengers aboard but they were not molested, and as soon as the robber had his plunder he told the driver to move on. The driver whipped up his team and hurried into Angel's Camp where he reported the robbery, but the posse that rode to the scene could find no clue to the robber's identity nor a trail to follow.

Source: *Los Angeles Herald (CA)*: April 2, 1889.

CHARLES "THORN" DORSEY AND GEORGE SHINN, JULY 31, 1889

On Wednesday, July 31, 1889, the stagecoach from Sonora to Milton had reached Funk Hill in Calaveras County when two road agents, masked and armed, stepped out of their hiding places and halted the coach. They had the passenger disembark and move away from the coach, and then they blew open the Wells, Fargo iron safe using black powder, and they broke open the wooden treasure box. They then went through the passengers collecting $57, and once they had all their plunder they had the passengers board and told the driver to continue on. Officers went to the scene but could find no clue to the robbers' identities nor a trail to follow.

In October 1890 two San Quentin Prison escapees were captured in Chicago, Illinois, and returned to California, but before being delivered to the prison, George Shinn, the Cape Horn Mills train wrecker, gave a detailed description of their crime spree over the past three years, and this included the robbery of the stagecoach on July 31, 1889. (See Placer County on April 7, 1890.)

CHARLES BROWN, JULY 14, 1890

Late Saturday night, July 13, 1890, a masked road agent lay in ambush on the road between Mokelumne Hill and Valley Springs. Just after midnight the road agent, armed with a Winchester rifle, two revolvers, and a dirk, stepped into the road and halted the coach. He demanded the Wells, Fargo express box, and it was thrown down; he then demanded the mail sacks and three were thrown out, but he did not ask about passengers. Once he had his plunder he told the driver to move on, and as soon as the coach was out of sight he ripped open the mail sacks and went through the mails but found nothing of value; then he broke open the box and found there was no money inside. He left everything where it had been flung in searching and just walked off. The driver reached Valley Springs where lawmen were notified of the robbery. Sheriff Benjamin K. Thorn rode to the scene, gathered up the mail and box, and then started on the trail of the road agent. There was a clear trail of footprints, and the sole of the right boot made a very peculiar impression making the trail easy to follow. Thorn saw that the robber was heading into San Joaquin County. Thorn followed for several miles and then notified Sheriff Thomas Cunningham, and meanwhile rewards totaling $1,600 had been posted. Sheriff Cunningham, with Constable Deal, got on the trail and followed it directly to the robber, and they arrested twenty-four-year-old Charles Brown on Thursday night, July 17. They took their prisoner to the San Joaquin County jail where Sheriff Thorn arrived and took his prisoner back to Calaveras County. Brown acknowledge his guilt but said he was driven to "the act by want." Brown pled not guilty, was tried and convicted, and on August 27 was sentenced to serve eight years at San Quentin; he was delivered to the city jail that night to await transfer to the prison. Brown arrived at San Quentin on August 28, 1890, and registered as prisoner #14253. His sentence was commuted by Governor H. H. Markham to 149 days on January 24, 1891, and he was released the following day.

Sources: *Daily Alta California (San Francisco)*: August 28, 1890. *Los Angeles Herald (CA)*: July 22, 1890. *San Francisco Call (CA)*: July 25, 1890.

UNKNOWN, JANUARY 7, 1892; FEBRUARY 7, 1892

Early on Thursday morning, January 7, 1892, the stagecoach from Mokelumne Hill to Valley Springs had only traveled three miles from Mokelumne Hill when a lone road agent, masked and armed with a double-barreled shotgun, halted the coach. The road agent stayed behind a large pine tree as he pointed his shotgun at the driver and gave his command to throw down the Wells, Fargo express box, but the driver said it was inside. The robber then had the driver climb down, remove the box from the empty passenger compartment and place it in the road. The next command was for the driver to turn out his pockets and place his money on the box, and he deposited $5. The robber then told the driver to board and drive on. The report of the robbery was sent back to Deputy Goodwin who, in turn, telegraphed Sheriff Benjamin K. Thorn at San Andreas including the description, "having an old slouch hat, red bandana over face, wearing a long overcoat with a large rent on the side." Goodwin hurried to the scene and found the broken box, which had been empty, one hundred yards from the road, and nearby he found the hammer and wedge used to break the lock and a few provisions left behind by the robber when he fled. However, there were no clues to his identity, nor a trail that could be followed for any distance.

On Monday, February 7, the stagecoach from Mokelumne Hill to Valley Springs reached the place where it had been robbed a month earlier when the same road agent stepped into the road and halted the coach. He was masked with a gunnysack, dressed in dark clothing, and he carried what appeared to be the same shotgun. He demanded the Wells, Fargo express box and it was thrown down, and the driver recognized his voice from the January 7 robbery. There was one passenger aboard and the robber asked him how much money he carried, but he made no demand and told the driver to move along. The driver whipped up his team and hurried to the next place from which the robbery could be reported, and Deputy Goodwin at Mokelumne Hill organized a posse and rode to the scene. They searched the area, but all they could find was the express box, busted open at one end with a large stone. The box was taken into town and turned over to the Wells, Fargo agent.

After investigating for more than a month, suspicion fell upon Felix McClelland, and on February 13 he was arrested, lodged in jail and closely questioned. A case could not be made against McClelland and he was released, and no one else was arrested for the robbery.

Sources: *Los Angeles Herald (CA)*: January 9, 1892. *Sacramento Daily Union (CA)*: February 8, 1892. *San Francisco Call (CA)*: January 8, 1892; February 14, 1892.

UNKNOWN, APRIL 30, 1892

On Saturday, April 30, 1892, the eastbound "mud wagon" stagecoach from Stockton in San Joaquin County to San Andreas in Calaveras County was five miles from the Sheep Ranch mine and on a downgrade when a masked road agent hiding behind a large boulder, elevated above the coach, gave the order to halt. The driver, Babe Raggio, tried to rein in his team but was having difficulty with the horses. Michael Tovey, the messenger, was seated next to Raggio on his right. Behind the driver and messenger in the second seat were the Rodisino girls, and behind them in the third and last seat was Mrs. Loyed. When the coach failed to stop as ordered, the robber fired one load of buckshot from his shotgun, presumably at the two men on the driver's seat. Four buckshot pellets struck driver Raggio, two in his chest penetrating a lung and two in his left shoulder, and the chest wounds appeared to be mortal. Buckshot pellets also hit passenger Jennie Rodisino twice in her head and once in her body. Tovey was also wounded in his right arm between the elbow and shoulder, but it was not a dangerous wound. Louisa Rodisino, frantic at seeing her sister wounded but not yet knowing she was dead, got out of the wagon and ran up the hill in the direction of the road agent and was the only one to get a close look at him, but she could only say he wore dark clothing and a light mask. Several buckshot narrowly missed Mrs. Loyed when they struck the bow directly in front of her. Raggio, when hit, pitched forward, but he was caught by Tovey before he fell from the stagecoach and the messenger strapped the driver to the seat. Tovey reined in the team and then jumped to the ground, shotgun in hand; but the road agent had already fled so Tovey called Louisa Rodisino back to the coach and then he boarded and took the reins. At the first dwelling house Raggio was taken in and doctors were summoned, but the dead body of Jennie Rodisino was kept aboard and taken to the Sheep Ranch. From the Sheep Ranch, Rodisino's remains were shipped to El Dorado accompanied by her sister, and she was buried on May 4. On the day of Rodisino's funeral, Raggio rallied, and he later recovered from his two very serious wounds.

The robber was apparently well informed and was after the payroll bound for the Sheep Ranch mine, $4,000 in gold coin forwarded by J. B. Haggin. When the coach reached Sperry's ranch, word was sent ahead of the attempted robbery, and Calaveras County sheriff Benjamin K. Thorn organized a large posse and took to the field to scour the countryside for the murderer. The posse found a trail leading northwesterly from the murder scene, toward Mokelumne Hill, and they found tracks going up Sheep Ranch Road. However, it rained very hard Saturday, so after six miles the tracks were completely washed out. Deputy Getchell, in following the trail, when three miles from the scene, found a giant powder cartridge dropped by the robber in making his way through the dense chaparral, apparently to be used to blow open an iron safe if needed. At Sheep Ranch the coach was examined, and eight buckshot were found imbedded in the wood. Wells, Fargo's chief detective James B. Hume was then involved in the case, and he mistakenly formed the opinion that the robber was Milton A. Sharp, a Nevada prison escapee, believing that the attack may have been in retaliation for Tovey's killing of his partner Jones years earlier. However, by May 4, Hume had visited the scene and decided the road agent was a "green hand." The robber had taken up a position that would have required him to cross fifty yards of open country if he had to flee, and that was something, Hume felt, no experienced stagecoach robber would do. Only the confusion caused by the dead and wounded served him in his escape.

Rodisino's uncle, John Rodisino, posted a reward of $2,000 for the capture of the road agent, and Wells, Fargo and the state each added $300. The search for the murderer continued, and on May 29 Sheriff Thorn took Ed Connelly, a burglar arrested four days earlier, to two hiding places; in the second place he found fuse and powder, and this hiding place was very close to where the trail of the road agent was lost. However, after spending considerable time investigating and interrogating the prisoner, Connelly was cleared of the murder. No further clues or suspects surfaced and the case went unsolved.

Sources: *San Francisco Call (CA)*: May 1, 1892; May 3–5, 1892; May 31, 1892.

Unknown, June 17, 1892

On Friday afternoon, June 17, 1892, the stagecoach from Valley Springs to San Andreas, driven by Fred Wesson, was near North Branch when a lone road agent, wearing a black mask and brown overalls and armed with a double-barreled shotgun, ordered the coach halted. There were two lady passengers aboard, both riding atop, but they were not molested. The robber called for the wooden Wells, Fargo express box, and it was thrown down. There was an iron safe bolted inside the coach, but either the robber did not know of it or was not prepared to open it as it was ignored. He did not ask about the mail and told the driver to move on. At San Andreas the robbery was reported and Sheriff Benjamin K. Thorn, with several deputies, rode to the scene and recognized it as near the place the stagecoach was robbed on January 7 and February 7 that year, and though there were similarities, Thorn could not be certain it was the same man. They could find no clue to the robber's identity nor a trail to follow for any distance, so they returned to town.

Sources: *Sacramento Daily Union (CA)*: June 18, 1892. *San Francisco Call (CA)*: June 18, 1892.

John Keener, W. E. Dowdle and Amos Bierer, March 7, 1894; April 16, 1894; May 2, 1894; May 6, 1894; May 19, 1894

At 5:00 p.m. on Wednesday, March 7, 1894, two masked and armed road agents stopped the stagecoach from Milton to Angel's Camp on the Carmen Hill grade of Bear Mountain, three miles from Elkhorn station in Calaveras County. They ordered the driver to throw down the Wells, Fargo treasure box and broke it open with a hatchet, but there was little inside so they went through the passengers and took all their valuables. While they were at work a stagecoach from Neely's stables came up and it was stopped and the passengers robbed. A single rig came next, but the passengers guessed what was transpiring and hid most of their valuables. As soon as the road agents had all their plunder, they sent the two stagecoaches and the single rig on their way. It seemed apparent to all that these road agents were "green" as the only tool brought was the hatchet, and they did not even try to open the iron safe bolted inside the passenger compartment of the first coach. Even if they had opened that safe they would have gotten little as there was no messenger aboard, and the company policy was that when there was less than $300 aboard, no messenger was assigned. Lawmen went to the scene to investigate, but there were no clues to the identities of the two robbers.

On Monday, April 16, the stagecoach from Angel's Camp, driven by Fred Wesson, was three miles from Altaville near Crossett ranch when a lone highwayman, masked and armed, stepped onto the road and stopped the coach. He ordered the passengers to climb out and stand with their backs to the coach while he climbed in and cut the band off the iron safe. He then cut off the lid with a cold chisel. As he worked, one of the passengers tried to look around, but the robber said, "Turn away or I will blow your head off." Once the safe was opened he took out two sacks of silver coins. As he prepared to leave, he told Wesson to have the agent fix the box at his expense, then added, "Fred, I will see you in Angel's in a day or so, and we will take a drink on this." Neither passengers nor the mail were disturbed. The robber, once he had his plunder, had everyone board, and he told Wesson to continue on. The road agent was so cool about the work that everyone was certain there were more road agents covering them from hiding. He was described to lawmen, and they were sure he was one of the men who had robbed the coach on March 7. At first it was reported that he had secured $2,000, but the Wells, Fargo agent said that there was less than $300 in the safe. The road agent apparently had become comfortable in his role, and there was no sign of being "green" during this robbery. Deputy Sheriff De Camp organized a posse of eight men and went to the scene, but they could find no clues to the robber's identity nor a trail to follow.

On Wednesday, May 2, the highwayman moved to the stage road between Milton and Sonora, still in Calaveras County, and stopped the down stagecoach. He was masked in black and carried a Winchester rifle as he yelled out, "Halt!" He then ordered the driver to step down and the passengers to disembark and move a distance away from the coach, and he had them turn their backs to him with the warning not to turn around. He entered the coach and, using giant powder, blew open the safe, and in the process he blew to bits a valise and a sealskin sack belonging to a lady passenger. There was nothing in the safe so he ordered the passengers to board and then told the driver, "Move on and don't look back for five minutes," and the driver did as told. After the stagecoach reached Sonora, passenger Barr began making comments about the robbery and robber. Lawmen went to the scene but could find no clue to the robber's identity nor a track to follow.

On May 6 the stagecoach from Angel's Camp to Milton was just rounding a curve on the Carmen Hill grade when driver Fred Wesson heard the command, "Halt!" He reined in his team when the tall man in a black mask, wielding a Winchester rifle and standing beside the road, "drew a bead" on Wesson, and the coach stopped so suddenly that the four passengers were thrown from their seats. "Throw off the box, lively," was the next command, and Wesson threw down Wells, Fargo's iron safe. As it hit the ground the road agent stated, "And I'm the man that stood up the Sonora and Milton stage last week. Now, then, drive right ahead for five miles and don't look back." Before Wesson could start, the robber handed him a package to be shipped from Sonora, saying that it contained articles he took from the Sonora stage the previous week, and he seemed to be in a joyous mood as if making a joke. Minutes after the coach left the scene,

Wesson and his passenger heard the loud report of an explosion. The stagecoach continued into Milton where the robbery was reported to Wells, Fargo detective John N. Thacker. When Wesson examined the package handed him, he found a note tucked under the strings which read, "Some advice to you, Mr. Barr, and all other good detectives besides, is let me rob and let your notices slide. Mr. Whiteings, Croe Creek, Buzard Lake." This prompted the *San Francisco Call* to respond, "APES BLACK BART ... The rascal sends a threatening note to a victim." Mr. Barr had been a passenger on the Sonora stagecoach on May 2, and the robber took exception to the statements made by Barr afterward. Wesson described the road agent as "6 feet high, has light short hair, large forehead and weighs about 190 pounds." The *San Francisco Call* then reported that "detectives are swarming over the countryside looking for a clew without success," and noted, "neither have they picked up a handkerchief with the robber's laundry mark. Until he drops this important clew to his identity the robber will not be Black Bart's equal."

On May 19 the road agent returned to the same spot on the road as the March 7 robbery, at Carmen Hill three-quarters of a mile from Pool's ranch, twelve miles from Milton. At 11:00 a.m. the down stagecoach from Angel's Camp to Milton, with four male and two female passengers and messenger William "Billy" Hendricks inside, was halted by two road agents. The second man, who usually stayed hidden with a third man, made himself visible because the coach finally carried enough treasure to justify a messenger. One of the lady passengers told Hendricks, "There is a robber," as the command to halt came to driver Wesson. Hendricks immediately leaned out the left side and fired one barrel of his shotgun at the robber on that side of the coach, then called out to Wesson to keep moving. No order was needed, however, as the horses had been moving at a lively gait, and when the first shots were fired they bolted into a dead run. The robber who was shot collapsed but tried to raise up on his elbow, so Hendricks shot him with the second load, each load consisting of sixteen buckshot, which filled his body and limbs with pellets and killed him instantly. The robber on the right, who had remained hidden in the brush, then returned fire, hitting the coach with twenty-two buckshot and severely wounding Miss Bunny of Almaden with three buckshot lodged in her face, and slightly wounding T. T. Hume of Murphy's Camp with several buckshot in his shoulder. The body of the dead road agent was later taken into Angel's Camp. After the coach reached Milton, passenger Mrs. Lillie Stoll of Angel's said that the dead robber had fired one shot before he was killed with two loads of buckshot, and it was then the second robber had fired.

At the scene lawmen found the hat of the second robber, who had lost it in his haste to flee. Several parties then came forward and said they did not know the dead robber's name, but he and his partner were gamblers who had been "laying around Angel's Camp for two or three weeks." By the following day the dead road agent, the tall man, had been identified as John Keener from Visalia. Upon examination the robber had thirty-two wounds in his head, body and legs, and one buckshot had crushed the bone in one leg and another was lodged in his right foot, so every one of Hendrick's buckshot struck the robber. Miss Bunny was recovering from a buckshot pellet which struck her on the forehead above the right eye and entered her head at the right side of the nose, passing downward and through near the left ear. The other two buckshot wounds were not serious, and the doctors reported she would recover fully and retain her eyesight.

Detective John N. Thacker arrived the following day and joined route agent Tice, who had been investigating the series of robberies, and they were certain they knew the identities of the man who fled and the third man believed to be involved. They notified lawmen in the area, and on May 29 W. E. Dowdle was arrested at Copperopolis hiding in a chicken coop, and he was taken to Angel's Camp and lodged in jail. On June 12 Deputy Sheriff Graves arrested Amos Bierer near Angel's Camp, charging him with being the third man at the robbery of May 19. Dowdle had his preliminary examination on June 13 and Bierer had his examination soon afterward, and both men were held over for action by the grand jury. On June 23, Bierer confessed, so on June 24 Dowdle also confessed to the robberies and admitted he was the man who fired on the stagecoach on May 19. They were tried in early August 1894, convicted of "assault to rob," and both defendants were sentenced to serve fourteen years in prison. Twenty-five-year-old A. S. Bierer and twenty-one-year-old W. E. Dowdle arrived at Folsom Prison on August 16 where Bierer registered as prisoner #3222 and Dowdle registered as prisoner #3223. Dowdle was paroled on June 29, 1902, after serving seven years ten months, and he was "restored" June 15, 1903. Bierer was "restored" on June 15, 1903, after serving eight years ten months.

Sources: *Decatur Daily Review (IL)*: May 4, 1894. *Los Angeles Herald (CA)*: March 8, 1894; April 17, 1894: June 13, 1894; June 24, 1894. *Sacramento Daily Union (CA)*: April 17, 1894; May 8, 1894; May 21, 1894. *San Francisco Call (CA)*: April 17, 1894; May 8, 1894; May 21, 1894; June 13, 1894; June 24–25, 1894.

UNKNOWN, AUGUST 31, 1895

On Saturday, August 31, 1895, the down stagecoach from Angel's Camp to Milton was nine miles from Angel's Camp, ascending Palafos Hill two miles from Elkhorn station, when a masked road agent wearing a long linen duster pointed his rifle at driver Fred Wesson and ordered him to halt. Once the coach was stopped, he told Wesson, "Throw down that box!" Once the box was on the road he ordered the two male passengers to step out, and he handed a large hammer to one and told him to break open the box. It only took a few blows to open the box and they determined there was nothing inside. He had the passenger put the busted box on the coach and then had both men board before he told Wesson to drive on. There was no clue to the robber's identity, nor a good description, as he had been completely disguised by the mask and long duster.

Sources: *Los Angeles Herald (CA)*: September 1, 1895. *San Francisco Call (CA)*: September 1, 1895.

UNKNOWN, SEPTEMBER 30, 1897

Before noon on Thursday, September 30, 1897, the first of two stagecoaches, or carryalls, from Angel's Camp in Calaveras County going to Milton, with Lewis driving, had reached the downgrade of Kossuth Hill, eight miles south of Angel's Camp, when they came upon a pile of rocks in the road. Suddenly a masked man, thoroughly disguised with sacking over his clothes and armed with a .44 caliber bulldog revolver, jumped out and startled the driver and passengers, and he told everyone to raise their hands. Another road agent, masked and armed with a shotgun and disguised in a similar manner, appeared on the other side of the road at that time, and all hands were raised. However, the man with the shotgun stayed partly concealed behind the rocks and allowed his partner to do all the talking, and his first order was, "You drive over there and tie up." A second similar stagecoach, driven by Louis Raggio, followed closely and the road agent told the driver to drive up behind the first coach and tie onto it, and the driver did as told. The driver and passengers were ordered out and told to line up and keep their hands raised as one robber searched them for valuables, and they were covered by the man with the shotgun. The robber with the pistol pushed it against the stomach of each man as he robbed him, and the first man robbed was the driver of the first coach. When the robber went next to L. Blewett, one of three passengers in the first coach, the driver turned his head to watch and the robber warned, "Keep your face the other way!" The robber next went to Blewett's wife and her husband said, "She has no money." The robber said, "You shut up," and then searched along her arms for a purse and felt her pockets, and finding nothing said, "Maybe you have some money in your stocking," and then made a search but found nothing. The road agent collected $70 and then ordered the passengers and drivers to board and told them to sit still under penalty of death. The large stagecoach driven by Al Schwoerer, with six male and one female passenger aboard, had been twenty minutes behind the first two coaches, and in a few minutes it appeared at the top of the hill. When the coach was two hundred yards from the other coaches, the man with the pistol charged toward it, brandishing his weapon, and he ordered the driver to halt. The driver was in an animated conversation with a passenger and did not see the robber nor hear the order, so the robber yelled again as a passenger yelled out that there was a road agent, and the robber fired his pistol. This frightened the team and they took off at a run and the robber yelled out, "Hold up there!" The driver could not control the team, so the man with the shotgun called out, "Shoot the horses." At that command the road agent fired three shots from his pistol into the near leader, and all three shots were within a foot of the animal's heart; then he fired one shot into the nigh-wheeler. The horses continued to run so the robber fired two shots at the coach, and one bullet penetrated the side and struck Abraham Aloff, an Arabian peddler riding on the front seat inside the coach, in his right wrist but passed entirely through and then passed through the front wall of the coach and struck Angel's Camp jeweler Charles Ackerman, who was riding atop, in his side. The horses carried the coach forward one hundred yards before the leader collapsed, so the passengers quickly piled out and four men started over the hill, but Aloff was captured before he could flee. His peddler partner Mike Nasrelli had also jumped from the coach, fell to the ground, and was run over by one of the rear coach wheels. After capturing Aloff, the robber with the pistol first ran to Nasrelli and went through his pockets, taking $120, and then returned to Aloff and took $75 from his pockets. The woman passenger could not run as fast as the men and was captured, and she had to surrender $150. The robber with the pistol then yelled out to his partner, "Let's get the box!" and both started for the coach, the man with the shotgun carrying a short-handled rusty ax. They lifted down the Wells, Fargo treasure box and quickly broke it open, took out the contents, and started over the hill, but no one tried to follow. As soon as the robbers fled, the passengers from the first two coaches went to the large coach to help those who were wounded, and the passengers who had fled were called back. The two dying horses were cut loose and the other two, one wheeler and one leader, took the coach into Milton. The two wounded men were examined at St. Luke's Hospital, but both men had to catch the 3:40 p.m. train for San Francisco, so the bullet was left lodged in Ackerman's side to be extracted upon his arrival there. Wells, Fargo agents insisted that there was little of value in their treasure box, the reason there was no messenger aboard, so all the robbers got was what they collected from the passengers. That evening Sheriff Thomas Cunningham talked with Wells, Fargo messenger Reason E. McConnell and other officers, and they were split on a theory, some thinking the two were the same two men who had left Stockton two days earlier while others thought they were the same two men who had robbed the Ukiah to Booneville stagecoach in Mendocino County on September 28. However, after months of investigation, the case went cold and the robbers were not identified.

Sources: *Sacramento Daily Union (CA)*: October 1, 1897. *San Francisco Call (CA)*: October 1, 1897.

ROBERT MURPHY AND HERMAN "HENRY" WESTFALL, MARCH 24, 1899

On Friday afternoon, March 24, 1899, the stagecoach for Angel's Camp left Stockton with two passengers and messengers F. Jackson and Reason E. McConnell aboard riding inside, with Frank Washburn alone on the seat driving. At 8:45 p.m. they reached a point a half mile south of Altaville, where there was a large clump of brush in front of the Keystone mine. Two masked men suddenly stepped out and told Washburn to stop. The man doing the talking held a single-barreled shotgun loaded with #4 buckshot while the other, who took a position behind the coach, was armed with a .38 caliber Colt rifle. When the driver reined in the team, McConnell raised his shotgun, but Jackson said, "Don't fire, Mac; those men want to get on the stage. This is the place where Lee Hendricks and another man usually get on and ride to Altaville." Neither messenger had seen the two men as the curtains were partially drawn closed. In a moment Jackson realized he had been wrong, as the robber standing in front of the coach commanded Washburn to throw out the Wells, Fargo express box. Washburn reached for the box, but stalled so the messengers could react, and McConnell pointed his shotgun at the robber and pulled the trigger but it only snapped. The robber asked, "Why in Hell don't you throw the box out?" Jackson then threw himself across McConnell's knees but the curtain obscured Jackson's view of his target, and he fired his rifle once but the bullet went through the robber's hat. The robber turned and ran, but Jackson's second bullet struck the road agent in the small of his back and passed through, coming out the front. It had been so spent that it was deposited inside his clothing and was later recovered. The second robber was twenty feet behind the coach and he then fired at the driver but missed. After being shot at, Washburn whipped up his team and ran the coach seventy-five yards, stopped to check on the passengers and messengers, and finding all uninjured he then proceeded into Altaville.

The wounded road agent did not fall nor slow down his flight so the messengers thought they had missed their mark, but they learned later that night that the wounded robber had crawled to the nearby house of William Brumer and asked for assistance. Once Brumer saw the wound and heard of the robbery attempt, he sent for the authorities and the man was arrested. The prisoner gave the name Robert Murphy and said he was just nineteen years old, and he identified his partner as nineteen-year-old Henry Westfall, sometimes Westhall, a weak-minded youth who was easily led. The wound to Murphy was thought to be mortal and he could not be moved, so Justice of the Peace Cooley went to the Brumer home, held a preliminary examination, and Murphy pled guilty and was held over on a bond of $5,000. As soon as Murphy named Westfall, he was arrested at his cabin on the Selkirk property, and the next morning he appeared before Justice Cooley, pled guilty, and was also held over on a bond of $5,000. Westfall confessed and said that Murphy had tried to get him to help in robbing the Milton stagecoach two weeks earlier, but he had refused. Murphy, it was known but never proved, had for some time been pilfering the wagons of peddlers which stopped near the Selkirk property. Murphy was removed to the county hospital on March 26, and he had sufficiently recovered by April 5 to appear in court. Judge Gottschalk accepted the guilty pleas, and for their cooperation and because of their youth, he only sentenced them to serve four years at San Quentin Prison. Both men arrived at the prison on April 10, 1899, and Murphy registered as prisoner #18165 while Westfall registered as prisoner #18166; both men were discharged on April 7, 1902, after serving three years.

Sources: *San Francisco Call (CA)*: March 26–27, 1899; April 6, 1899.

PETER MORO, MARCH 12, 1900

On Monday, March 12, 1900, the stagecoach from San Andreas to Mokelumne Hill, with William Colton driving, had traveled halfway and was climbing a grade when a masked road agent, pistol in hand, jumped out of the brush in front of the horses. The robber pointed his pistol at the head of Colton, who was unarmed but recognized the robber as twenty-five-year-old Peter Moro and said, "Moro, take that handkerchief off your face." When the robber made no move, Colton said, "Take off that handkerchief; that's you, Moro, I know you." The robber then walked to the hind wheel of the coach and removed his mask and then tried to convince Colton it had all been meant as a joke. Colton whipped up the team and drove into Mokelumne Hill, where the attempted robbery was reported. Neither the postmaster nor the express agents wanted to accept that Moro, who had built a bad reputation since a shooting scrape a few years earlier, had been joking, but apparently no charges were filed, or the charges did not result in a prison sentence.

Source: *San Francisco Call (CA)*: March 15, 1900.

JAMES E. STARR, MARCH 19, 1900

At 5:00 p.m. on Monday, March 19, 1900, the stagecoach between Milton and Copperopolis was nearing the mining camp of Hodson when a masked road agent with a double-barreled shotgun stepped out from the side of the road. He ordered the driver to halt, and then he demanded that the driver and three passengers hand over their money and other valuables. He collected $17, but he did not ask for the mail, and that line did not have a contract to carry a Wells, Fargo express box. Sheriff Benjamin K. Thorn was telegraphed the details and a description of the robber and he rode to the scene and began his investigation. Two days after the robbery, Sheriff Thorn arrested James E. Starr at Copperopolis and lodged him in the county jail at San Andreas. By the following day, after the sheriff explained the evidence against his prisoner, Starr weakened and confessed. He said he would plead guilty and throw himself on the mercy of the court. Starr had his examination and was held over with bail set at $3,000. At his preliminary hearing on March 28 he pled guilty and confessed to the judge and was held over for trial with bail increased to $4,000. On April 30 he appeared before Justice Cooley and again pled guilty, and seventeen days later the judge sentenced him to serve one year in prison. Twenty-year-old Starr arrived at San Quentin on April 11, 1900; he was "restored" February 11, 1901, after serving ten months.

Sources: *Amador Ledger (CA)*: April 6, 1900; April 20, 1900. *Los Angeles Herald (CA)*: March 29, 1900. *San Francisco Call (CA)*: March 20, 1900; March 23, 1900.

UNKNOWN, AUGUST 9, 1901

On Friday morning, August 9, 1901, the stagecoach from San Andreas to the Sheep Ranch, with Louis Cassenelli driving, had traveled quite a distance from town when a masked road agent stepped out from a clump of bushes, leveled a double-barreled shotgun at the driver, and commanded, "Your money or your life!" The robber, who seemed quite nervous, was wearing a mask made from a heavy sack with eyeholes cut in it. Cassenelli threw out the few dollars he had in his pockets and the robber then demanded the express box, but the driver assured the robber there was nothing of value aboard and he carried no passengers. The robber did not inspect the coach, told the driver to move on, and disappeared into the brush. There was onboard one valuable package addressed to Mrs. G. H. Mastick of San Francisco, but the driver had saved it. At Sheep Ranch he reported the robbery, but the men who rode to the scene could find no clue to the robber's identity and the meager description of the road agent was no help.

Source: *San Francisco Call (CA)*: August 10, 1901.

Colusa County

JAMES W. FINLEY, JULY 20, 1902; JULY 6, 1903

At 6:30 p.m. on Sunday, July 20, 1902, the stagecoach bound for Bartlett Springs driven by John Williams was near Leesville, still eighteen miles from its destination and nearing the top of Brim grade, with nine passengers aboard. Suddenly a man, covered from head to foot in gunnysacks, stepped into the road and ordered the driver to rein in his team. He pointed his shotgun at the driver's head, but the shotgun and his revolver were also partially concealed by gunnysacks. As soon as the coach was stopped he ordered the passengers to step out and form a line and then appointed one passenger, a young man, to pass along the line, search pockets, and collect their money, but telling the man to leave watches and jewelry. The only woman aboard, Hattie Ogden, surrendered her money, but when she started to hand over her diamond ring it was refused. As soon as the robber had the $300 the man had collected, he ordered the passengers to board and then told the driver to move on. Sheriff Shearer and district attorney I. G. Zumwalt went to the scene and looked for clues, then began scouring the countryside for a trail, but the terrain was too rough and a trail could not be followed for any distance. They managed to locate a camp where the robber had burned his gunnysacks and several of the purses that had been collected, but the trail ended there and they had to abandon the chase.

On Monday evening, July 6, 1903, the stagecoach from Colusa was on its way to Bartlett Springs when it was stopped by a lone highwayman on the Brim grade. Driver John Williams was thrilling his passengers with a tale of the robbery that occurred a year previously, and when they reached the same spot where the stagecoach had been halted in July 1902, the same road agent, wearing a dark mask, stepped into the road in front of the horses and leveled his shotgun at the driver. The road agent yelled out, "Driver, stop the team and hold them tight, and I want the passengers to get out and line up on the side of the road." Thirteen passengers followed the instructions while Williams controlled his team, and the robber then walked back from in front of the leaders, sweeping the barrel of his gun along the line as he told them to advance one at a time and place their valuables in the center of the road. Mrs. Helm had only $5.50 and the robber asked her if that was all she had, then ridiculed her for traveling with so little money. When she explained she was only going to Upper Lake, he told her to keep her money, as she would need it there. Once all the others had contributed, he told them to board, then said, "I will camp here until dark and will shoot the first man that comes back," and then he told Williams to move along. The robber had collected only $150. Williams started his team and arrived at the station beyond the hill in minutes. From the station a man was sent to Leesville by horseback, by another road, to telephone Sheriff Shearer. The sheriff immediately organized a posse, and they left for the scene. The description of the road agent led the sheriff to believe it was ex-convict John Lemos, aged twenty-seven, five feet nine inches, blue eyes and medium dark hair, size 9 shoes with buckskin shoestrings, with hands and arms tanned to the elbows.

It was soon determined that Lemos had no part in the robbery, so the search for the road agent continued for a month until late July when driver Williams and Constable Parker followed up on a slight clue. They traveled all night Friday and on Saturday, August 1, they found their man, who proved to be an innocent who slightly resembled the description of the road agent. They returned to town and announced that they had abandoned the chase. In early September Joseph West was acquitted of a burglary at the Capitol Hotel in Fairfield, but he was being watched in Suisun by detectives who suspected he was the Bartlett Springs road agent. West was seen at 11:00 p.m. on September 3, but when Wells, Fargo's detective John Thacker arrived the following day he could not locate the suspect. West had, apparently, slipped out of town overnight and could not be located.

In October 1905 there was a breakout at San Quentin Prison and thirty-nine-year-old James W. Finley, who was serving a life sentence for a murder in Mendocino County in 1904, had made a murderous attack upon one of the guards. While he awaited trial on the new murder charge he confessed to many crimes for which he had never been suspected. He claimed to have robbed the stagecoach to Bartlett springs on July 6, 1903, and again on July 20, 1904, but he had his dates wrong. Finley was convicted of first-degree murder when his plea of insanity failed, and on December 28, 1905, Judge Hart sentenced him to hang. He filed appeals and in March 1908 and July 1913 he was resentenced to hang, but his sentence was commuted to life in prison on October 11, 1913.

Sources: *Los Angeles Herald (CA)*: July 22, 1902; July 8, 1903. *San Francisco Call (CA)*: July 23, 1902; July 8, 1903; September 5, 1903; December 28, 1905. *Sausalito News (CA)*: July 11, 1903.

El Dorado County

Unknown, August 5, 1856

On Monday, August 5, 1856, a stagecoach was traveling on Coloma Road one half mile above Waukesha House when two men on horseback rode up to the coach with guns drawn, and they ordered the driver to rein in his team. They next looked into the coach and realized there were quite a number of passengers aboard and, perhaps fearing resistance, quickly put spurs to their horses and rode off at a gallop. The coach then continued on to the next station, and at the first opportunity the driver reported what he believed to be an attempt to rob the stagecoach. No pursuit followed, so no one was arrested.

Source: *Sacramento Daily Union (CA)*: August 5, 1856.

Unknown, November 10, 1863

Early Tuesday morning, November 10, 1863, the stagecoach from Georgetown to Folsom was ascending a hill near Greenwood and was nearing the summit when two road agents ran out from hiding and halted the coach. One grabbed the reins of a leader while the other climbed up and put his pistol to the head of driver James Orr and asked if he was armed. Orr said he was not armed, so the road agent told him, "Put your foot on the brake and keep it there." The robber then got down and went to the door and ordered out the three male passengers: a German, a Portuguese, and a Chinaman. He demanded that each man give up his money, and the first two did without resistance but the Chinaman objected, so he was pistol-whipped over his head until he handed over $20, all he had. In all the robbers took $100 from the passengers, but they did not molest the driver who had another $100 in his pockets. The robber who had climbed onto the coach had seen there was no express box, and when he checked the passenger compartment he found there was no iron safe. He then told the driver to drive on. As soon as the coach reached the next station a man was sent to report the robbery, and the road agents were described as "one tall, the other short and stout." A posse was organized at Fiddletown and sent to the scene, and they found a sledgehammer and crowbar that had been left behind when the robbers found nothing to break open, perhaps because they did not want to carry away such heavy, incriminating tools. However, the posse did not find a clue to the robbers' identities nor a trail to follow.

Sources: *Daily Alta California (San Francisco)*: November 11, 1863. *Sacramento Daily Union (CA)*: November 11, 1863.

Unknown, June 7, 1864

At 4:00 a.m. on Tuesday, June 7, 1864, the stagecoach bound for Georgetown was nearing its destination when six road agents, five armed with double-barreled shotguns, pointed their weapons at the driver and demanded that he halt. As soon as the coach stopped they went to work on the iron safe bolted inside the passenger compartment; they filed and then blasted for an hour until they opened the safe and found it was empty. As they departed, one of the robbers told the driver, "Tell Wells, Fargo that the next time they send an empty safe, leave it unlocked." Wells, Fargo offered a reward of $500 for the arrest and conviction of the six robbers, but none were captured. Three weeks later a band of six men, representing themselves as Confederate Army soldiers, would rob a stagecoach in the same county, but when they were captured they would not admit to being the men who attempted to rob the coach on June 7.

Source: *Sacramento Daily Union (CA)*: June 9, 1864.

Rufus Henry Ingram, George Baker, John Bouldware, John Clendenning, Alban H. Glasby and Thomas B. Poole, June 30, 1864

Rufus Henry Ingram had experience as a guerrilla and bushwhacker under William C. Quantrill during the early years of America's Civil War. After the raid on Lawrence, Kansas, Ingram, known in Missouri as the "Red Fox," fled into Mexico. In 1864 a Californian named George Baker was traveling through Mexico on his way east to join the Confederate army, and he told Ingram that there was a large body of secessionists in California but they lacked leadership. Ingram convinced Baker to return with him to California, where they could do more good for the Confederacy by organizing California's secessionists and commandeering treasure to finance the southern forces. In Santa Clara County, Ingram joined a contingent of the Knights of the Golden Circle, a long-established secret society whose mission was to create and unite slave states in Central and South America and in the Caribbean. He recruited Jim Grant, George Baker, John Bouldware, John Clendenning, Alban Glasby and Thomas B. Poole to rob one of the treasure-laden coaches heading east and use the money to finance his California forces so they could obtain further treasure to ship south. When Grant compromised their efforts at reconnaissance in Placerville, he was ejected from Captain Ingram's Partisan Rangers, and the plan was changed to have an all-out raid on San Jose, similar to the raid at Lawrence, Kansas. When Santa Clara County sheriff John H. Adams learned of the raid, he prepared an ambush, but Ingram learned of the preparations and abandoned that plan and began planning a stagecoach robbery.

In late June two stagecoaches left Carson City, Nevada, bound for San Francisco, California, on the Placerville route, with fourteen passengers in each coach. At 10:00 p.m. when the coaches were fourteen miles from Placerville, a mile east of the Thirteen-Mile House, and rounding a curve in the road, they were stopped by six road agents, armed but not masked. Eugene Blair was driving the first coach, and Charley Watson was driving the second a short distance behind. When the first coach came round the bend, someone yelled out, "Hold on or I will fire!" and Blair reined in his team. Soon the second coach arrived, and the person repeated the command. He then told the drivers, "We won't detain you but a moment; all we want is Wells, Fargo's treasure." He then assured the passengers that no harm would come to them so long as they remained quiet and did not interfere. The robbers, each armed with two pistols and at least one with a shotgun, took three sacks of bullion from the boot of the first coach. The leader then told the first coach to proceed, and at that moment a shot was fired. As the first coach pulled out, the robbers surrounded the second coach and some men made remarks that they should shoot everyone, but Watson told them that no shot had been fired from his coach, "so no harm should reach to my passengers." When Watson heard that first shot, he warned his passengers not to shoot, as they were on a grade and a second shot could cause the horses to bolt and send the coach over the edge where "all will be dashed to pieces." One man stepped out from the robbers and announced he was the captain and said, "Gentlemen, I will tell you who we are. We are not robbers but a company of Confederate soldiers. Don't act foolish. We don't want anything of the passengers. All we want is Wells, Fargo and Company's treasure to assist us to recruit for the Confederate army." Watson then threw out two sacks of bullion, but a robber said it was not all and another robber climbed up and took out another sack and the Genoa express box; he also grabbed another small box of express freight that he deemed valuable by its weight. One of the women in the second coach was a girl of seventeen, and she engaged the captain and several others in conversation for some time. Finally, the robbing done, the leader handed Watson a receipt for the treasure:

June 1864

This is to certify that I have received from Wells, Fargo & Company the sum of $___, cash for the purpose of outfitting recruits enlisted in California for the Confederate States Army.

R. Henry Ingram, Capt. Com'g Co., C.S.A.

Ingram then told the driver to continue into Placerville. After the coach was under way the girl was asked why she had engaged several robbers in such lengthy conversations, and she said it was so that the passengers could hear their natural voices and later might be able to recognize them accordingly.

The robbers, after the second coach was out of sight, mounted and started for the Somerset House, but along the way they buried most of the treasure, taking only two bars of bullion and some coin. Posses were organized from Placerville, with Sheriff William Rogers taking a dozen men along the Placerville road while sending three deputies toward the Somerset House. On July 1, Ingram's men were in the Somerset House when they were discovered by El Dorado County deputy Joseph M. Staples, Constable George Ranney, and Deputy J. D. van Eaton. Staples and Ranney burst into the room where Ingram, Glasby, Bouldware, and Poole were having a conversation, in the hope they could surprise and arrest them without a fight. However, in the exchange of gunfire that started immediately, Poole and Ranney were badly wounded and Staples was killed. Ingram, thinking that a wounded Poole would slow down their escape and possibly believing his wound mortal, left him behind while the other five men fled. Deputy van Eaton had been sent to cover the opposite side of the house to prevent an escape by that route, and he played no part in the gun battle. Poole was arrested, and he informed on the gang, naming them all as well as key members of the Knights of the Golden Circle. Meanwhile Ingram led his four men back into Santa Clara County and hid in a secluded house, partly hidden by a thicket, until July 15, when he and his men tried to rob the New Almaden Quicksilver Mine a mile and a half from San Jose. Sheriff Adams was soon on their trail with a posse including Marshal Potter and deputies Scott, Brownlee, Bowman, Reynolds, Senter, Gould, Morris and Willis. They surrounded the house, only a mile and a half from town on the Almaden road. The fugitives, realizing they were surrounded, rushed out and began firing at the posse, and a bullet struck Sheriff Adams in the breast, but it was deflected by his watch and caused only a flesh wound. Brownlee received two bullets in his leg, also flesh wounds, and a robber first identified as "Creel," who was actually Bouldware, was shot several times, died, and his body was taken into town. Clendenning was shot by Sheriff Adams and his wounds were thought to be mortal, but he managed to flee into the chaparral. Glasby was captured and he confessed, and he agreed to turn state's evidence against the others. A fresh party went out and found Clendenning, brought him to town, and he lived just long enough to confess. Ingram and Baker managed to slip out of the house, and under cover of the thicket they escaped, with Ingram fleeing back to Missouri and Baker fleeing from California to points unknown.

As a result of Poole's confession, all of the buried bullion was recovered. Poole, Glasby and Hodges were indicted for Staples' murder, along with George Cross, Henry Ignacius Jarboe, John A. Robertson, William Wallace Clendenning, Joseph W. Gamble, H. H. Gately, and John Ingram. They were arraigned before Judge S. W. Brockway, pled not guilty, and asked for separate trials. Poole's trial began on August 24, 1864, lasted three days, and he was convicted of the murder of Staples after fifteen minutes of deliberations and was sentenced to hang. Preston Hodges was tried in September 1864, convicted of second-degree murder, sentenced to serve twenty years in prison, and he arrived at San Quentin on September 13, 1864, where he registered as prisoner #2820. The state supreme court ordered a new trial for Hodges, but before it could begin Governor Frederick Low granted a pardon on February 25, 1865. The charge of treason against all the defendants had been set aside. All of the others had been released in early 1865 when they proved they were in another part of the state when the robbery and murder occurred, and the charge of being accessories before the fact could not be proved.

The motion for a new trial for Poole was denied, and then a series of appeals followed, including a deluge of letters from prominent and involved citizens, but Governor Low refused to intervene. Finally the date for Poole's execution was set for September 29, 1865, and the gallows was erected in the jail yard in Placerville. His last words before being led to the scaffold were, "I am no murderer. I feel as if now for the first time, I am about to be tried before a court of justice." Placerville's *Mountain Democrat,* on September 30, described the execution:

> EXECUTED: Precisely at 12 o'clock yesterday, Thomas B. Poole, implicated in the stage robbery and the killing of Deputy Sheriff Staples, in this county, in July 1864, suffered the extreme penalty of the law. He calmly ascended the scaffold, pleasantly conversed with the officers having him in charge, and the Rev. Mr. Wallace, cordially shook each by the hand, and fearlessly resigned his spirit to its God. He smiled on all, and seemed perfectly resigned. He made no public address. While the cap was drawn over his face and his arms and legs were being pinioned, he stood perfectly composed. He died almost without a struggle and in a few seconds.

Sources: *Daily Alta California (San Francisco)*: July 2–3, 1864; September 10, 1864. *Pacific Sentinel (Santa Cruz, CA)*: October 7, 1865. *Placerville Mountain Democrat (CA)*: July 2, 1864; July 9, 1864; July 23, 1864; August 6, 1864; August 20, 1864; September 30, 1865. *Sacramento Daily Union (CA)*: July 2, 1864; July 9–10, 1864; July 13, 1864; July 17, 1864; July 19, 1864; July 21, 1864; August 23–26, 1864; September 9–10, 1864.

JAMES E. G. "KENTUCK" WATKINS, NOVEMBER 28, 1871

On Tuesday, November 28, 1871, the stagecoach from Georgetown in El Dorado County to Auburn in Placer County, driven by William H. Hill, was stopped by a lone highwayman when halfway between Georgetown and Greenwood, about three miles from each place. The road agent had piled brush in the roadway, and this stopped the horses long enough for him to step out and demand the Wells, Fargo treasure box. Hill thought it was someone in disguise playing a joke, and he replied, "You go to the devil!" However, the masked robber pointed his revolver at Hill and again demanded the treasure box, and it was thrown down. He then motioned for Hill to continue, and the driver wasted no time in whipping up his team. He hurried into Greenwood and sounded the alarm, and by 3:00 p.m. stage line owner Frank Page and Sheriff James B. Hume left Placerville for the scene. For their trouble they only managed to recover the empty treasure box, found broken open about one hundred yards from the road. The contents, $1,000 in gold dust and $60 in coin, had been taken. They followed tracks for some distance, but a storm obliterated the trail and they lost it and returned to town Thursday evening.

Hume took charge of the investigation and published a story that the lawmen had not a single clue to the identity of the robber. In fact the stolen gold dust, or at least a portion of it, was quite distinct, so he sent letters to thirty Wells, Fargo agents asking them to contact all gold buyers in their region to watch for the plunder and say nothing of the affair. Hume made it appear that all his efforts were abandoned. Nothing surfaced until late February when the gold dust was sold at Michigan Bluff in Placer County. As soon as Hume received the telegram he sent a deputy, with several men who could identify the gold dust, to Michigan Bluff. They got a good description of the man who had sold it and learned that the man, who was known as James "E. G." Watkins, had fled into Nevada. A case could not yet be made against Watkins for stagecoach robbery, so a California warrant was issued charging the fugitive with "the crime of feloniously receiving, having, concealing, and keeping, money and property obtained by robbery." Governor Newton Booth issued a requisition to have Watkins returned to California and sent it with Sheriff Hume to Carson City to be delivered to Governor Lewis R. Bradley. Upon receipt of the requisition in early March 1872, the order was issued for the arrest of Watkins, and efficient Nevada lawmen soon had him behind bars. The prisoner was delivered to Hume who took his prisoner to El Dorado County and lodged him in the county jail on March 20. He was then identified as the road agent and charged accordingly. Watkins had his examination, where he pled not guilty, but he was held over for action by the grand jury on the new charge of being the road agent, rather than just receiving the stolen property. He was indicted on March 23, and when brought into court on April 4, he withdrew his not guilty plea and entered a plea of guilty, supposing he would get a reduced sentence for his cooperation. He was correct, and Watkins was sentenced to serve a term of only four years at San Quentin. He arrived at the prison on April 10, 1872, and registered as prisoner #5231. Watkins, after serving a little more than three years, was pardoned by Governor Romualdo Pacheco, with all rights restored, and he was discharged on May 6, 1875.

Sources: *Mountain Democrat (Placerville, CA)*: December 2, 1871; February 24, 1872; March 30, 1872; April 6, 1872.

CHARLES "THE SHOEMAKER" PRATT, JAMES P. "OLD JIM" SMITH AND GEORGE "TEXAS" WILSON, JANUARY 17, 1876

Two men had been committing robberies in the region of Amador and El Dorado counties, but they had not attacked a stagecoach nor stolen a Wells, Fargo treasure box until January 10, 1876. After Charles Pratt and George Wilson secured $60 from the express box on January 10, they recruited James P. Smith, all ex-convicts, to help them with their next stagecoach robbery. On January 17, 1876, the stagecoach from Georgetown bound for Auburn was halted when it was near Greenwood in El Dorado County. The only male passenger was robbed, but the two females aboard were not molested, and the three road agents shared $105 from Wells, Fargo's treasure box. The description of two road agents, Pratt and Wilson, matched the road agents who had robbed the Fiddletown to Drytown coach a week earlier. Miss Ella Marlett of Grass Valley, one of the passengers on the Auburn coach, was riding atop with the driver and reported that "the pistols used by the robbers looked very large."

James B. Hume, chief detective for Wells, Fargo, recognized the description of the men who had served many terms in prison and had recently been released: Pratt had been in San Quentin Prison five times, Smith three times, and Wilson twice, so Hume knew them as desperate men. Hume called upon Stephen Venard to join him in a search for Charles "the Shoemaker" Pratt, James P. "Old Jim" Smith, and George "Texas" Wilson. Hume and Venard enlisted the help of Len Harris, a Sacramento lawman, and after ten days the three lawmen located the robbers hiding in the house of "a colored family" near Folsom. Folsom's constable I. W. Kimble joined the posse and they had a warrant of arrest issued on January 27, and the following day early in the morning they surrounded the house. Hume and Harris went through the back door, but Smith and Wilson heard them coming, grabbed their revolvers and fled out the front door. They were met by the cocked revolvers of Venard and Kimble but they were about to make their fight when Hume and Harris came up from behind them, and, seeing they had no chance, they surrendered without further resistance. They were taken to Placerville in El Dorado County and charged with the Greenwood stagecoach robbery.

Smith and Wilson were tried together, convicted, and sentenced to serve twelve years in San Quentin Prison. Smith arrived at the prison on February 25, 1876, and registered as prisoner #6903. He was removed to the state insane asylum at Napa on October 7, 1884. Wilson also arrived on February 25, 1876, and he registered as prisoner #6904. Following a commutation of his sentence to ten and one half years he was discharged on September 19, 1883, by expiration of sentence. Pratt had not been at the house when his two partners were captured, but he was soon run to ground and captured in late February. He was tried at Placerville in El Dorado County for the Greenwood stagecoach robbery, and he also received a twelve-year sentence. He arrived at San Quentin Prison on June 15, 1876, and registered as prisoner #7055. On April 28, 1878, his sentence was commuted to ten and one half years, but before he could be released he died in prison on March 22, 1883.

Sources: *Amador Dispatch (Jackson, CA)*: January 29, 1876; February 5, 1876; February 24, 1876. *Amador Ledger (Jackson, CA)*: February 5, 1876. *Folsom Telegraph (CA)*: February 5, 1876. *Los Angeles Herald (CA)*: January 12, 1876. *Placer Herald (Auburn, CA)*: January 22, 1876; February 5, 1876. *Sacramento Daily Record-Union (CA)*: January 29, 1876.

ALBERT P. HAMILTON AND ROGER O'MEARA, MAY 24, 1880

On Thursday, April 29, 1880, Albert P. Hamilton and Roger O'Meara robbed the Milton stagecoach in Calaveras County, and then on Thursday, May 6, they had been driven off by gunfire from the messenger on the stagecoach between Jackson and Ione. However, they were still determined to make a big haul, so on Monday, May 24, the two road agents stopped the stagecoach from Georgetown to Placerville in El Dorado County, but there was no Wells, Fargo express box aboard. They went through the pockets of the one passenger and took $65 in coin before they fled. Later that night a posse of four men came across the two robbers on the grade near Greenwood, and the two fled into a thicket under a hail of bullets and Hamilton was wounded in his left arm. The next day a hatless Hamilton appeared at a cabin four miles from Greenwood and had his wound dressed, then ate a hearty meal, was given an old chip hat, and he headed southwest. When his host realized he had cared for the road agent, he notified the authorities and described him as thirty years old, five feet nine inches tall, light complexion, sandy moustache and beard, a bald spot atop his head, wearing a dark coat and pants with overalls over the pants, a dirty white shirt with a calico shirt over it, holes cut at the ankle bones in his boots, and carrying a double-barreled shotgun. On Thursday, May 27, a man discovered the second road agent, O'Meara, and fired at him, but he fled into the chaparral and headed toward Mormon Island. He was described as thirty-two years old, five feet six inches tall, with dark eyes and complexion, dark hair and moustache, dark clothes and hat, with his right index finger noticeably deformed.

Both men, now well know and the subjects of an intensive manhunt, fled from California. Hamilton, after several prison terms and two serious arm wounds, gave up the road agent business and apparently lived out his life as a law-abiding citizen, or as a criminal under an alias, but he was not heard of again in California. O'Meara was more persistent and he was arrested on a charge of burglary in St. Louis, Missouri, and even though he was identified as a wanted man in California, after receiving a stiff sentence he was not extradited and was never prosecuted for his part in the stagecoach robberies.

Sources: *Daily Transcript (Nevada City, CA)*: April 17–18, 1875. *Mariposa Gazette (CA)*: November 28, 1874. *Marysville Weekly Appeal (CA)*: May 7, 1875. *Sacramento Daily Union (CA)*: April 17, 1875; May 4, 1875; May 31, 1880. *Santa Cruz Sentinel (CA)*: April 4, 1874; May 2, 1874. *Visalia Delta (CA)*: September 11, 1874.

UNKNOWN, MARCH 26, 1885

At 10:15 a.m. on Thursday, March 26, 1885, the stagecoach from Placerville to Shingle Springs was near the Mountain House, still three miles from its destination, when a lone highwayman stepped into the road and pointed his revolver at the head of driver Clarence Crippin. The road agent told Crippin, "Halt!" and as soon as the coach came to a stop he yelled, "Throw out the Wells, Fargo and Company box!" Crippin replied, "I've got no box," but the robber said, "I will shoot if my order is not obeyed, throw out that box." Crippin then told him, "It's bolted into the coach, you must come and get it out yourself." There were four passengers aboard and the robber was getting nervous, so he ordered Crippin to drive on and turned and walked into the brush. Crippin hurried into Shingle Springs and reported the robbery, and he described the robber as a tramp who was "a short, thick-set Irishman." Sheriff Seth Loveless organized a small posse and rode to the scene, but he could find no clue to the identity of the road agent.

Source: *Sacramento Daily Union (CA)*: March 27, 1885.

GEORGE STARLING, OCTOBER 14, 1887

On Friday afternoon, October 14, 1887, the eastbound stagecoach from Auburn had traveled four miles and was two and a half miles inside El Dorado County climbing the American River hill on the south fork when a lone highwayman stepped out and halted the coach. He was masked and carried a Winchester rifle, and he had a revolver in his holster. He demanded the Wells, Fargo express box but was told it was an iron safe bolted into the boot of the coach. The robber had the driver get down and then he worked on the safe, but he did not have the right tools and could not open it. He next had the passengers step out and form a line, but since they had ample time to hide nearly everything of value, he collected only $20 and a few items of jewelry. He then told the driver to continue on, but he only went a short distance before turning around and hurrying back into Auburn, where he reported the robbery and gave a detailed description of the road agent. The road agent had headed west after the robbery and was seen rowing a boat across the river, and he was followed right into Auburn. He was watched as he hid his rifle under the water tank on the edge of town, and then he was followed to his room in a boarding house where he left his revolver before going to a theatrical show. His rifle was recovered and turned over to the authorities, but when his room was checked his revolver was missing. Officers, including lawmen from El Dorado County, then went to the theater and arrested their man, who gave the name George Starling and confessed to being the robber. He was lodged in jail at Auburn; Wells, Fargo was notified of the robbery and arrest; and all the plunder was recovered. When it was clear that the case against him was ironclad, Starling decided to do all he could to get a lighter sentence, so when he was brought into court at Placerville on November 14, he pled guilty. When it came time to sentence Starling on the robbery charge, the judge, after learning he was twice an ex-convict, gave him twenty years to be served at Folsom. Nineteen-year-old Starling arrived at the prison on November 17, 1887, where he registered as prisoner #1538. Though he was young, the record showed he had already served two terms in prison under the name James Riley. Starling was transferred to San Quentin on March 31, 1888, but no other information is recorded.

Sources: *Daily Alta California (San Francisco)*: November 19, 1887. *Los Angeles Herald (CA)*: October 16, 1887. *Sacramento Daily Union (CA)*: October 17, 1887.

CHARLES "ORMSTEAD" THURMAN, SEPTEMBER 8, 1890

On Monday, September 8, 1890, the stagecoach from Georgetown to Auburn had reached Greenwood when a lone road agent, masked and armed, stepped out onto the road with gun in hand and ordered the driver to halt. He called for the Wells, Fargo express box to be thrown down, and as soon as it was in the road he told the driver to continue. The coach had only gone a short distance when passenger Thomas Stevens borrowed a pistol from another passenger and went in pursuit of the robber, but he failed to overhaul the road agent. At Placerville on September 11, El Dorado County undersheriff Winchell arrested Charles "Ormstead" Thurman, an ex-convict with a thirty-four-year history of imprisonments. Wells, Fargo detective James B. Hume went to Placerville to identify the prisoner, and as soon as Thurman saw Hume he broke down, confessed, and said he would plead guilty.

Sources: *Chronicle (Auburn, CA)*: September 8, 1890. *Los Angeles Herald (CA)*: September 9, 1890. *San Francisco Call (CA)*: September 17, 1890.

GEORGE J. A. HOYMAN, J. C. COLLINS AND PERRON LEE, DECEMBER 17, 1896; DECEMBER 18, 1896

At 4:00 p.m. on Thursday, December 17, 1896, the stagecoach from Auburn to Georgetown had passed Penobscot when the coach was stopped by a lone road agent, masked with a barley sack and armed with a muzzle-loading shotgun. The road agent demanded the Wells, Fargo express box, and as soon as it was thrown down he told the driver to move on. The robber broke open the box and found there was nothing of value inside. The driver hurried to the next place from which he could report the robbery and said the robber was five feet eight inches tall, weighed 160 pounds, and was wearing a black hat and dark pantaloons. Sheriff William C. Conroy with Deputy Mitchell of Placer County met Sheriff J. H. Hilbert of El Dorado County at the scene of the robbery, and they searched the area. Conroy found the broken box with the waybills still inside, and from these he determined that the box had contained nothing of value. The officers could find no clue to the robber's identity nor a good trail to follow, and a posse from Greenwood had spread out through the countryside to watch for the road agent but had no better luck. Sheriff Conroy took the box back to Auburn and delivered it to the Wells, Fargo agent and the chase was abandoned as they waited for some break in the case, but they didn't have to wait long.

On December 18 at 5:00 p.m. the stagecoach from Auburn to Georgetown was stopped at the same place as the day before by the same road agent, masked with a barley sack and carrying a muzzle-loading shotgun. He again demanded the Wells, Fargo express box and it was thrown down, and then the robber told the driver to move along. The box was broken open but again there was nothing of value inside. It was then supposed that the robber had somehow received faulty intelligence that there was to be a large valuable shipment to the mines of El Dorado, and after missing it the day before he had been sure it would be sent the following day. The posse that rode to the scene could find no clue to the robber's identity, but Sheriff Conroy was determined to find the culprit and he began to build a case against three individuals.

Early Tuesday morning, January 5, 1897, Sheriff Conroy and Deputy Mitchell captured George J. A. Hoyman near Bernie Hill in El Dorado County. Hoyman was chopping wood as the lawmen approached and he started for his coat, but the sheriff warned him to stop. Upon securing the coat the sheriff found a Bowie knife and a fully loaded six-shooter in the pockets. They next went to the cabin and found a fully loaded Winchester rifle and took that along when they lodged their prisoner in the El Dorado County jail. Hoyman was soon joined in jail by J. C. Collins and Perron Lee, who were charged with being Hoyman's accomplices, but Hoyman "peached," or informed, on his partners and turned state's evidence. Hoyman was held over at his examination, and his trial began in late March. On the night of March 27, Hoyman was found guilty of "highway robbery" and sentenced to serve eight years at San Quentin Prison. Collins' trial began after Hoyman was sentenced, he was convicted of complicity in the December 17 robbery, and on April 2 he was sentenced to serve eight years at Folsom Prison. Lee's trial was set for April 10 but there was not enough evidence to implicate him in either robbery as an accessory, so he was released. Hoyman arrived at San Quentin Prison on May 30, 1897, and registered as prisoner #17242. Collins arrived at Folsom Prison on April 3, 1897, and registered as prisoner

#4061. Hoyman was discharged on July 28, 1902, after serving five years and two months; and Collins was discharged on July 28, 1903, after serving six years and two months.

Source: *Los Angeles Herald (CA)*: December 19, 1896.

UNKNOWN, NOVEMBER 14, 1904

On Monday morning, November 14, 1904, the stagecoach from Georgetown to Auburn, with Bert Day driving, was a few miles east of Cool when a lone road agent, wearing a black mask and carrying a rifle, halted the coach. He called for the registered mail pouch, and when it was thrown out he told the driver to move along. He did not ask for an express box nor about passengers. The coach hurried into Auburn where the robbery was reported, and the driver was certain the road agent was new at the business as he seemed very nervous. Still, the robber covered his tracks well and the posse could not track him, nor find a clue to his identity.

Source: *San Francisco Call (CA)*: November 15, 1904.

UNKNOWN, JULY 10, 1906

On Tuesday, July 10, 1906, the stagecoach bound for Tahoe was near Pacific House in El Dorado County when two masked men, armed with shotguns, appeared and ordered the coach to halt. They had the passengers step out and relieved them of their money, amounting to $35, then had them board and told the driver to continue on his route. The Lemmon-Meder automobile party was seen nearby, and at first they were suspected; but when they reached Carson City, Nevada, they and their automobile were searched and they had only $8.75 among them. Lawmen went to the scene but could find no clue to the robbers' identities.

Source: *Carson City Appeal (NV)*: July 12, 1906.

Fresno County

TIBURCIO VASQUEZ, CLODOVEO CHAVEZ AND UNKNOWN, FEBRUARY 26, 1873

In early February 1873 Tiburcio Vasquez formed a new gang with his first recruit Clodoveo Chavez, and then he recruited Abdon Leiva, Teodoro Moreno, Romulo Gonzales and several others. His first plan was to rob the store at Firebaugh's Ferry on the San Joaquin River. On February 26, 1873, Vasquez and his force of eight to ten men, all masked but their leader, descended on the store at dark and captured everyone inside. Vasquez ordered all to lie down and keep quiet, and under the threat of cocked revolvers they complied. The robbers began a systematic search for money and valuables when the Gilroy to Firebaugh stagecoach arrived, surprising them. Two of the robbers went out and took control of the driver and the Wells, Fargo express box, hoping to find a rich payroll for rancher Henry Miller, but they were disappointed. They then continued to ransack the store and took from George L Hoffman $250, from the driver they took $20, and from a man named Allen they stole $27. They then made Hoffman, the Wells, Fargo agent at the station, open the safe, and they took out $100. Finally they gathered up $100 in clothing and fled into the night with their meager plunder. No one was killed, but in August at Tres Pinos that would change. (See Kern County on February 25, 1874.)

Sources: *Fresno Weekly Expositor (CA)*: March 5, 1873. *Sacramento Daily Union (CA)*: February 23, 1873.

JOHN M. HERBERT AND HARVEY H. LEE, MAY 7, 1884

The first toll road into Yosemite Valley opened in mid–June 1874 and two other toll roads were in operation within a month, but people had been traveling into the valley for two decades on horseback to take in the beauty of the scenery. Once the roads were in operation, stagecoaches began to operate, and they carried rich tourists and occasionally an express box. On May 7, 1884, two road agents, masked and heavily armed, stepped out and halted the stagecoach from Fresno to Yosemite when it was still in Fresno County, twenty-three miles from Madera. They went through the passengers but found only a cheap silver watch and a $5 gold coin, though some later reports said they found $60 and three watches. They were nervous and ordered the coach to continue, without thinking to ask for a treasure box or mail sacks.

The two road agents fled to San Jose while the driver hurried into Madera and sounded the alarm. The following day Fresno County deputy sheriff Witthouse went to the scene to investigate; but first he circulated the detailed descriptions provided by the driver and passengers, and the road agents turned out to be Harvey H. Lee and John M. Herbert. Santa Clara County sheriff Benjamin Branham, upon receiving the descriptions, started looking for the two men and found Lee early on the morning of June 7, and by that evening Herbert had joined him in a San Jose jail cell. Branham notified Witthouse, and the prisoners were transferred to the Fresno jail on June 11 to await their examination.

On June 24 the two prisoners had their examination before Justice of the Peace S. H. Hill and they were held over for the grand jury, bail set at $5,000 each. They were indicted and at their arraignment pled not guilty, and their trial began in early September. Though they mounted a vigorous defense, they were easily convicted on September 8 by overwhelming evidence. Lee, it appeared, had stayed out of trouble for a decade before robbing the Yosemite coach, and it could not be shown that they were involved in the robbery of August 13, 1883, so they were only charged with that later robbery. Each man received a sentence of twenty years, and on September 19 they arrived at San Quentin Prison. Herbert registered as prisoner #11385 and Lee as prisoner #11386. Herbert was transferred to Folsom Prison on March 1, 1890, and his sentence was commuted by Governor Henry Markham to ten years on May 12, 1892, and one week later he was discharged. Lee was discharged, with good time credits, on June 18, 1897.

By August, Lee had found a partner in twenty-three-year-old Charles Williams. Like many an imprisoned stagecoach robber, Lee found that coaches rarely carried treasure by the late 1890s, so the two men decided to rob a train, capitalizing on what Lee had learned during his recent years imprisoned with train robbers. They robbed a train in Oregon on September 25, 1897. On October 8 Lee pled guilty and tried to exonerate Williams, but they were sentenced to serve terms of thirty years and seven months. On July 16, 1906, Lee managed a pardon and release, and he died penniless, a ward of the county in Fresno's County Hospital, ten years later at the age of sixty-nine.

Sources: *Fresno Weekly Expositor (CA)*: June 18, 1884. *Fresno Weekly Republican (CA)*: May 9, 1884. *Mariposa Gazette (CA)*: August 18, 1883; August 25, 1883. *Oregonian (Portland, OR)*: September 26–28, 1897; October 9–10, 1897. *Red Bluff Beacon (OR)*: February 6, 1862. *San Bernardino Guardian (CA)*: October 22, 1870. *San Jose Herald (CA)*: June 12, 1884. *San Jose Mercury (CA)*: December 27, 1866; May 2, 1867; June 8, 1884.

Inyo County

YSIDRO PARDILLO, JOAQUIN OLIVERA, JOSE LENARIS, ANTONE VALACCA, JOSE MARIA, ANTONE SAVAGE, MITCHELL RATOVICH, MITCHELL BROWN, RAMON RUIZ AND UNKNOWN, APRIL 28, 1875

Ysidro Pardillo, sometimes Isador Pardillo, formed a gang and divided it into two sections, each with its own area to work. Pardillo's band consisted of Jose Lenaris, Red Antone, and Kokimbo. They robbed the Sonora to Milton stagecoach on November 7, 1874, and again on March 23, 1875. On Wednesday, April 28, 1875, a stagecoach had just reached Yellow Grade, three miles from Cerro Gordo, when four men appeared in the road with shotguns and covered the driver, while six more men stepped out of the brush and quickly unharnessed the team. They had the passengers step out and tied their wrists and ankles, while the driver was ordered to step down on the opposite side and take a seat on a rock. They went through the pockets of the passengers and took all their money and valuables, took the mail pouches and Wells, Fargo express box and tied them onto a stage horse, and then they started off with the team. One of the stage horses broke free, but the robbers did not waste time trying to catch him, so the driver was able to catch him and he rode in Cerro Gordo with news of the robbery. While the citizens organized a posse, word was sent to the army at Darwin, and soon posses were scouring the countryside from Cerro Gordo and Darwin to Lone Pine. Four of the robbers, all Mexicans, were recognized by the driver and he joined one posse, but they all returned to their respective towns empty-handed. (See Calaveras County on November 7, 1874.)

UNKNOWN, FEBRUARY 10, 1877; FEBRUARY 14, 1877

On February 10 the stagecoach from Mojave to Darwin in Inyo County, driven by Billy Balch, was attacked by several masked Mexicans at daybreak. The messenger managed to arrest one of the party and saved the treasure. On February 14 at daybreak the same coach, Billy Balch again driving, was approaching the same location twelve miles south of Darwin, with passenger John T. "Jack" Lloyd riding on top next to the driver. It was the day for a messenger and the treasure box to be aboard, and Lloyd's position next to the driver gave the impression he was the messenger and confirmed for the road agents that there was treasure to be taken. In fact, there was no treasure nor a messenger aboard.

One road agent, without warning or command, fired at Lloyd just as the coach passed, and nearly the entire load took effect in the back of Lloyd's head, killing him instantly. Lloyd slumped forward but did not fall off the stagecoach, and Balch, who had one buckshot pellet pass through his coat sleeve, again whipped up his team and took it into Darwin. The local deputy sheriff organized several posses and led the main force to the scene of the killing to take up the trail of the murderers, but to no avail. The remains of Lloyd were turned over to the Odd Fellows Lodge at Darwin for burial, and his lodge at Palisade was notified by mail.

Source: *Silver State (Winnemucca, NV)*: February 19, 1877.

UNKNOWN, NOVEMBER 29, 1880

Just after midnight on Monday, November 29, 1880, the stagecoach from Bishop Creek to Independence was stopped by a lone highwayman, masked and armed. He demanded the Wells, Fargo express box, and it was thrown down. He did not ask about passengers, and there were none aboard, and he did not call for the mail pouches. As soon as he had the treasure box he told the driver to move along, and the driver hurried into Independence to make his report. The posse which rode to the scene could find no clue to the robber's identity, though just twelve days later another stagecoach would be robbed in Inyo county; but Charles Baker would not admit any involvement in this earlier robbery.

Source: *Sacramento Daily Union (CA)*: January 1, 1881.

CHARLES BAKER, DECEMBER 11, 1880

Charles Baker was twenty-four years old when he served his first sentence at California's state prison for embezzlement. The ten months he spent behind prison walls served as an opportunity to learn from California's worst desperadoes, worst because they were failures at their chosen trade—apprehended and convicted. Still, Baker listened with interest, and after his release he spent a few months acclimating to his newfound freedom before taking up arms and stopping a stagecoach. On December 11, 1880, Baker, working alone and masked, stepped onto the road between Benton in Mono County and Darwin in Inyo County and ordered the driver to halt. He demanded the Wells, Fargo express box, and the driver had no alternative but to deliver. Baker was soon captured and was tried in March. He was convicted of robbery and sentenced to serve ten years in San Quentin Prison, registering as prisoner #9842 on April 5, 1881. Baker was released in February 1885, and soon he was interested in holding up another stagecoach. He found a willing partner in Charles Manning, and on January 25, 1886, they stopped and robbed the stagecoach from Cloverdale to Mendocino City, at Anderson Valley. (See Mendocino County on January 25, 1886.)

T. C. "BUD" HARNISS, ARLIE F. MAIRS AND LOUIS "LEW" SCHALTEN, DECEMBER 27, 1883

On Thursday night, December 27, 1883, the express box from the stagecoach traveling between Bishop Creek and the railroad station in Inyo County, driven by Louis "Lew" Schalten, was reportedly stolen by two masked, heavily armed road agents. On board the coach were passengers Arlie F. Mairs and T. C. "Bud" Harniss, a Bishop Creek saloon keeper, but neither man was molested. According to the three men aboard, as soon as the robbers had the express box they ordered Schalten to continue on. The box contained $680.

Wells, Fargo's special agent John N. Thacker was put on the case, and with the assistance of messenger Mike Tovey they began to carefully put together a chain of circumstantial evidence, each link pointing to the driver and two passengers as the robbers, and the two detectives finally swore out complaints against the three men. Sheriff Gregg arrested Schalten and Harniss at Bishop Creek while Undersheriff Crough arrested Mairs at Independence. They were jailed and confronted with an "indisputable chain of circumstances surrounding them, and they 'fell down.'" On February 14 Schalten provided a detailed confession:

> I got up the night the stage was robbed about half past one; there was a light in Bud Harniss' saloon and I called or knocked at the door. One of them got up and let me in. We had a drink, and Bud Harniss says to me, "Is there any money going out in the stage to-night?"
>
> I says, "You heard what Charles Levy said at the supper table to-night," and he says, "I don't' remember."
>
> I said that he said that there would be about $900 to-night in the box and he wanted me to act as messenger. I says to Charles Levy, "How much is there in it?" He says, "$3."
>
> Bud Harniss says, "We can make more than that out of it," and says, "Arlie, let's take it in."

He (Arlie) says, "Dry up; you don't mean what you say." Bud says, "I am in for it," and says, "Get up and put on your boots." Bud then says to me, "Come on, Lew."

I hesitated, and he says "What are you afraid of? They can't catch us. We three can swear to the same thing and all hell can't catch us." I says, "Boys, this is a scaly piece of business and we all know the consequences."

We then got to the bar and had another drink, and Bud then says, "Hurry up, as we have not much time to spare." and he said, "Where can we get an ax?"

I says, "If you fellows want to rob the stage you can get an ax at Dunn's wood pile or at George Gill's."

"All right," says Bud; he then says, "You go and get the ax and Arlie and I will go to the barn and hitch up."

I went and got an ax at George Gill's, put it in the wagon and went and helped them. I got out at the office and put the box in. Arlie says, "Let me drive." I let him drive and on the road about 300 yards Bud says, "Lew, you break the box open, as you know how to get into it easier than I do." I got in on the back seat and took the box in between the two seats and smashed her in, took out what money there was in it and put it in my pocket. When we came to the bridge they pulled up and I said, "All right, boys," so I jumped out of the wagon and packed the box about 40 yards from the road, and came back and got in, and drove on to the depot. When we got there Mairs went on to Independence and Bud and I came back to Bishop. We went into the saloon and burned the way pocket and waybills and money sacks. Bud had the handling of the money, some time after he gave me $20 and then $80. That is all that I have received of it. The ax I took back to Geo. Gill's wood pile.

On Friday, February 15, at 2:00 p.m. the prisoners had their examination before the magistrate and within an hour and a half had been held over for trial in the Superior Court, an information has been filed, they had pled guilty, submitted their statements to the court, and had their date set for sentencing on Monday, February 18. The *Inyo Independent,* on February 19, reported that Schalten was primarily responsible for the robbery and that the other two men believed the driver's suggestion to take in the stage was just "drunken joshing." The newspaper's editor observed that the driver, the trusted agent of the express and stage companies, conceived and executed the entire scheme, took and broke open the box, and disposed of the contents. The editor insisted that Harniss and Mairs, longtime residents of Bishop Creek, were entirely innocent but had protected Schalten because of their longtime friendship. Schalten took offense to the characterization of his part in the robbery and pointed to his confession, and in response the newspaper published the confession in full on February 23.

Also on February 23 the *Independent* reported on the sentencing of the three men. The three defendants had been found guilty of grand larceny, rather than robbery, and sentenced by Inyo's Superior Court judge Hannah to terms of two and a half years in San Quentin Prison. All three men arrived at the prison on February 25, 1884, Harniss registering as prisoner #11152, Schalten as prisoner #11153, and Mairs as prisoner #11154. On February 25, 1886, the three men were discharged after serving their entire sentence, less good time credits awarded under the Goodwin Act.

Source: *Inyo Independent (Independence, CA)*: December 29, 1883; February 16, 1884; February 23, 1884.

Kern County

TIBURCIO VASQUEZ AND CLODOVEO CHAVEZ, FEBRUARY 25, 1874

On February 24, 1874, a traveler arrived at the Coyote Holes stagecoach station with some stock. He spent the night and in the morning he went out to round up his stock, but a mile from the station he happened upon the camp of two Mexicans, Tiburcio Vasquez and Clodoveo Chavez, and they took him captive at the point of their guns. They tied his wrists behind and marched him toward the station, and were met by station keeper Raymond. They bound him and then bound the ankles of the first captive and left both men lying on the ground. They continued to the house and, without any demands, fired fifteen shots into the dwelling, then ordered everyone out and Mrs. Raymond and five others came out. Only M. P. "Old Tex" Shore, an old man already intoxicated, refused, so Vasquez went in and marched him out with the barrel of his Henry rifle pointed at his back. The entire party was then herded up a hill and told to sit and remain there, but Shore refused to cooperate until Vasquez shot him in the leg. The two robbers returned to the station and ransacked the house for valuables. They found a Henry rifle without ammunition and an unloaded shotgun. At 1:00 p.m. the northbound stagecoach from Los Angeles to Owens River, driven by Davis, stopped at Coyote Holes station and was captured by the two bandits, pointing Henry rifles, and with two pistols each in their belts. Passenger M. W. Belshaw was riding atop, and passengers Craig and William Fessenfield were inside. The passengers were ordered out, Davis and Belshaw were ordered down, and they were made to sit in a line. Each man had to deliver his money, though Davis managed to hide a purse containing $40 in gold. Fessenfield handed over $40 in gold and a spyglass, but his silver coin was returned to him, and he managed to hide his watch in his overshoe. Craig gave up a sizeable amount of money, but the exact amount was not reported. Belshaw contributed $20 in gold, a fine silver watch and, after the robbers went through his luggage, a new pair of boots. Once the collection was completed the passengers were herded onto the hill with the others, but Davis was kept back. When the second robber returned from the hill Davis was ordered to unhitch his team, and then to deliver the Wells, Fargo express box and break it open using an iron bar handed him by Vasquez. He found nothing inside, so their total plunder was only $300 and several watches. Two heavy teams from Los Angeles arrived at that time, and the teamsters were captured at the point of Henry rifles and marched up the hill to join the others, bringing the total of captives to fourteen. One of the captives had hidden on his person a pepperbox, or Allen deadless, but felt it unwise to deploy such a small weapon against Henry rifles or heavy revolvers. As dusk neared and nothing further of value was expected to materialize, Vasquez went through the stable and selected the six best horses, led them out, and put them with two other horses he intended to take along. He mounted his horse while Chavez mounted a stage horse, and Chavez led the other seven horses as they rode off in a southeasterly direction. The party on the hill then dispersed, with some going to the house and others searching for the two missing men. The men were found, untied, and all returned to the house, where Shore's wound was treated. Two hours after the road agents departed the down stagecoach arrived at the station, but had the robbers remained they would have been disappointed as none of the passengers had much money.

Prior to Coyote Holes, the gang had descended upon Tres Pinos in August 1873 and killed three men who resisted; on November 10, 1873, they robbed Jones' store three miles from Millerton; and on December 26, 1873, they captured and robbed the entire village of Kingston where bandit Refugio Montejos was killed, Manuel Lopez was seriously wounded, and Chavez was shot in the leg but escaped, and then the gang dispersed. Chavez had healed in time to join Vasquez at the Coyote Holes robbery, but then Chavez struck out on his own. There were many reports of Chavez robbing stagecoaches, but none are confirmed. Instead he terrorized stores, isolated mining camps, stagecoach stations, helpless travelers along the roadways, and teamsters in the areas of Cerro Gordo and Borax Lake. In 1875 Chavez was hiding at the Baker ranch in Arizona, and trying to recruit a young boy, when his childhood friend Luis Raggio killed him to save the youngster from a life of crime.

After Chavez left, Vasquez gathered together the remnants of his gang and recruited a few others, and they committed several robberies. In May 1874 Vasquez hid at the house of Greek George, but Los Angeles County sheriff William Rowland learned of Vasquez' hideout and dispatched a posse to capture or kill the bandit. On May 13 they surrounded the house and Vasquez refused to surrender, but he was brought down with a shotgun blast and captured. By May 27 he was well enough for the trip to the San Francisco city jail. From there he was taken to the jail at San Jose, indicted on a charge of murder during the Tres Pinos affair, tried in early January and convicted. Judge David Belden sentenced him to hang on March 19, 1875; all efforts for an appeal or a commutation of sentence failed, but Vasquez persisted in claiming he was innocent.

On March 19 at 9:00 a.m. a crowd besieged the jail as Father Lerda and Vasquez' brother were admitted. He had spent a quiet night, awoke at 2:00 a.m. for a smoke, then slept until 6:00 a.m. when he was served breakfast. At 9:30 a.m. the priest administered the last rites, and then the condemned man said his last good-byes. At ten o'clock the gallows was tested for the last time, and a half hour later the witnesses assembled in the jail yard and this caused a great stir among the crowd outside. Vasquez' "cousins without number" finally filed out of the jail at 11:00 while outside Sheriff Larue delivered the rope, in which he had tied the knot, to Sheriff Adams and it was tied to the crossbeam so that it would provide the proper drop length. At 12:30 p.m. Vasquez was served dinner and he "ate with relish," and at 1:15 the prisoner was brought into the anteroom where the priest had him kneel while undersheriff Winchell read the death warrant, but the condemned man arose when the reading was half done. The sheriff then asked him if he had anything to say, and he handed him a paper and said, "I am resigned to die. I hope God will have mercy on my soul." The sheriff asked, "Is that your answer to this warrant?" and he replied, "It is." The procession then moved out of the jail and into the yard and reached the scaffold at exactly 1:30 p.m. Deputy Winchell led, with Father Lerda following beside Vasquez, and other lawmen followed behind. Once the prisoner was standing on the trapdoor, the priest said, "For charity's sake let all repeat silently the Lord's prayer as I kneel for the peaceful death of our friend, Tiburcio Vasquez." All three hundred witnesses remove their hats and knelt, while Vasquez stood holding his crucifix aloft and repeated the prayer with the priest. Vasquez then removed his coat and tie, and deputies Winchell and Sellman bound the prisoners' wrists and arms, thighs and ankles. Without delay, or a chance for the prisoner to speak again, the noose was cinched in place, the black hood was pulled over his head, and at 1:38 p.m. the restraining cord was cut and the trapdoor was sprung. The body dropped six feet six inches and there was not a movement of any kind. Drs. Brown, Cory, Thorn, and Todd monitored his pulse and in thirteen minutes they announced that the prisoner was dead. The priest then looked through the open trapdoor and asked, "Are you sure he is dead?" and one doctor replied, "Yes, sure." The priest then muttered a prayer, gathered up his robe and retired. The body hung for seven minutes more before the undertaker cut the rope and took the body to a nearby room for an examination by the doctors, and they determined that Vasquez' neck had been dislocated and then signed the death certificate. Once the examination concluded, the body was placed in the elaborate coffin provided by his family, and family members carried it to the hearse parked outside the jail yard. The body was driven to the home of Garcia in Santa Clara for burial in the Catholic cemetery the following day.

Sources: *Daily Alta California (San Francisco)*: February 28, 1874. *Los Angeles Herald (CA)*: March 3, 1874. *Sacramento Daily Union (CA)*: March 7, 1874; March 20, 1875. *Visalia Delta (CA)*: March 5, 1874.

S. A. "Ned" Allen and Charlie Williamson, January 15, 1875

On January 15, 1875, the stagecoach from Lone Pine to Bakersfield was stopped by two road agents after leaving Havilah near Stark's station in Kern County, California. Following the robbery the road agents fled to San Francisco, with Sheriff Bowes and Deputy H. Bludworth close on their trail. The lawmen captured the two fugitives, and by February 27 they were on their way to Bakersfield. The two prisoners arrived by stagecoach on Sunday, February 28, but their examination was postponed until Wednesday because of the distance one key witness had to travel. At 10:00 a.m., when the court convened, the two men were brought before Justice Wilkinson and gave their aliases Ned Allen and Charles Williamson. They were arraigned and waived examination, whereupon they were remanded to the custody of the sheriff to await action by the grand jury. While awaiting indictment, Allen agreed to turn state's evidence against Williamson. On March 13 the *Kern County Weekly Courier* reported that Williamson was brought into court and, after pleading guilty, said he was the least guilty of the two men and that "the same offers and inducements were made to me that induced my companion to peach." Williamson was sentenced to serve ten years in San Quentin Prison, and the judge then heard from the district attorney regarding Allen, who said that a conviction of Williamson would not have been possible without his testimony, so the judge ordered Allen's release "but did so with great reluctance." Williamson arrived at San Quentin Prison on March 13, 1875, and registered as prisoner #6430. His sentence was commuted to nine and one half years by Governor William Irwin on April 23, 1878, and he was discharged, by expiration of sentence, on August 6, 1881. (See Plumas County on June 27, 1876.)

Charles Castle and James Wellock, March 17, 1875

On March 17, 1875, the northbound stagecoach from Bakersfield in Kern County to Panamint Springs in Inyo County, driven by W. J. Ladd, was stopped at 3:00 p.m. when two and one half miles beyond Canebreak station, still inside Kern County. On board were two Wells, Fargo treasure boxes, one filled and the other empty. When the two road agents demanded the box, the driver threw out the empty box, and when ordered to move along, he hurried to Coyote Holes station and recruited P. Cline to go with him and arrest the robbers. En route they met two men but had no reason to suspect they were the robbers. At the scene they found many boot tracks from footwear of the type known as "O.K.," with heavy nailed heels, and realized these were the tracks of the two men they had met on the road, who both were wearing "O.K." boots. They were quickly on their trail, but the men had stopped and extracted the "tell-tale nails."

Ladd and Cline hurried on to Coyote Holes station, and in about an hour the two suspected road agents, who had been traveling by a more circuitous route, arrived. Ladd pulled his revolver and put the barrel to the head of one road agent demanding he surrender, and the man said, "Don't hurt me, we didn't hurt you." They were taken into Bakersfield and given their examination before Justice Wilkinson, where they gave the names Charles Castle and James Wellock. The evidence was strong enough to hold them for the grand jury, and the sheriff, concerned for the security of his jail, took them to Visalia and lodged them in the jail there. In May the Kern County grand jury convened, and when Wellock turned state's evidence, a true bill (indictment) was returned against Castle. Castle first pled not guilty, but he was facing the testimony of his fellow road agent, so he soon changed his plea to guilty. When court convened on Friday, Castle was brought in and sentenced to serve ten years at San Quentin Prison. He arrived at the prison on

May 8, 1875, and registered as prisoner #6516. He was removed to Folsom Prison on September 30, 1880, and thirteen months later, on November 8, 1881, he was discharged upon expiration of his sentence.

Sources: *Kern County Weekly Courier (Bakersfield, CA)*: March 20, 1875; March 27, 1875; May 8, 1875.

JOHN M. BRANNAN, OCTOBER 4, 1875

On Monday night, October 4, 1875, the "Omnibus" stagecoach, driven by A. P. Bernard, was on its way from Bakersfield to Sumner in Kern County to connect with the train for San Francisco. On board were the U.S. mails, the Wells, Fargo express box, and five passengers—four men and one woman. At 11:00 p.m. the coach had only gone as far as north Third Street, about four hundred yards beyond the bakery, when a lone highwayman stepped out of the weeds and bushes by the roadside and, wielding a double-barreled shotgun, demanded the treasure box. He was wearing a bandage about his head and the rest of his face had been blackened, but there were three lights on the stagecoach and each shined directly onto the robber. As soon as the box was delivered he ordered the driver to continue on, but Bernard hurried back into Bakersfield and sounded the alarm.

A search was conducted the following day and tracks were found from the scene to the rear of the brewery, and by noon the box was found smashed open and empty, with $324 missing. Suspicion immediately attached to a well-known character about town, known as "Johnny-behind-the-rocks," though his real name was John M. Brannan. His boot tracks were observed and they corresponded exactly in size and design to the tracks found at the scene of the robbery, the tracks trailed to the rear of the brewery, and the tracks about the area of the empty Wells, Fargo box, so he was arrested. He was searched, and though he had been "hard up" he was found to have a $10 coin in his pantaloons, a $10 coin in his coat pocket, $240 in gold coins in his left boot, and $11 in change. In all, $311 of the $324 of the stolen money was recovered.

On Wednesday, October 6, the prisoner was brought before Judge Adams for his examination and it was learned that he had borrowed a shotgun from John Lake after 9:00 p.m. the evening of the robbery, saying he wanted to go hunting in the morning. However, he returned it shortly after 11:00 p.m. saying he did not need it any longer, and the next day he loaned Lake $10. When Brannan had first appeared in town, after the robbery, several persons noticed that he had blackened his face, had partially washed off the black, but had left traces about his eyes. This evidence was deemed conclusive, and Brannan was held over for action by the grand jury, bail set at $1,500. Brannan was indicted and tried within weeks. He was easily convicted by the overwhelming evidence, and at 3:00 p.m. on October 30 he was sentenced to serve fifteen years in California's state prison. He arrived at San Quentin on November 1, 1875, and registered as prisoner #6735, but he was removed to Folsom Prison on August 23, 1880. His sentence was commuted to eleven years by Governor George C. Perkins, and he was discharged upon expiration of sentence on December 4, 1882.

Sources: *Kern County Weekly Courier (Bakersfield, CA)*: October 9, 1875; October 30, 1875.

UNKNOWN, NOVEMBER 30, 1875; DECEMBER 4, 1875

On Tuesday night, November 30, 1875, the northbound Telegraph Stage Line coach was two miles south of Caliente when two masked road agents, armed with double-barreled shotguns, stepped into the road and ordered the driver to halt. They demanded the Wells, Fargo express box and as soon as it was thrown down they ordered the driver to move on, and he hurried into Caliente to report the robbery. The road agents did not ask about the passengers aboard nor ask for the mail. They broke open the box and took out $4.50, all that was inside as Wells, Fargo had sent a sizeable shipment of money by boat.

On Saturday night, December 4, 1875, the same two road agents, masked and armed with double-barreled shotguns, stopped the Telegraph Stage Line coach one mile south of Caliente and again demanded the Wells, Fargo express box. Apparently they were determined to make a good haul, and this time they found $3,000 in the box. They did not ask about passengers nor about the mail. A posse rode to the scene but could find no clues to the identities of the robbers, and apparently after obtaining the large haul they retired as they did not appear on the road again.

Sources: *Los Angeles Herald (CA)*: December 1, 1875; December 5, 1875; December 7, 1875.

RICHARD "DICK FELLOWS" PERKINS, DECEMBER 4, 1875

Richard Perkins, or G. Brett Lytle, used various names at different times, but he was best known as Dick Fellows. After Perkins was released from prison on April 4, 1874, convicted of a stagecoach robbery in late 1869, he stayed out of trouble for twenty months, or at least he was not identified in any crimes committed. But then Perkins learned that a large shipment of gold coin supposed to total $240,000 would be carried by stagecoach from end-of-track at the rail depot in Caliente to a failing bank in Los Angeles, a trip that took an entire day and night. The stagecoach was scheduled to make the trip through Kern County on December 4, 1875, so Perkins devised a plan to rob the coach and recruited another desperado to assist him. The train carrying three Wells, Fargo boxes of gold coin arrived at the Caliente depot at 7:00 a.m. on December 4 guarded by S. D. Brastow, division superintendent for Wells, Fargo, and Jerome Meyers, chief of police in Stockton. James B. Hume, chief detective for Wells, Fargo, met the train, and within an hour the gold was transferred to a special stagecoach and the three men boarded, Brastow and Meyers inside and heavily armed Hume atop with the driver. The stagecoach made the trip and delivered its gold shipment without incident. Perkins had sent his companion, who had a horse, ahead to the spot where they planned to stop the stagecoach. Perkins, who wanted to avoid any premature pursuit that might be started if he stole an animal, went to a nearby livery and rented a horse. However, shortly after leaving town the horse threw Perkins and galloped off. Perkins picked himself up and walked back into town, where he found that the mare had returned to her stall. He missed the special coach, and Perkins' companion had abandoned the scheme when Perkins failed to arrive.

Perkins had wasted many hours and night was approaching, but, since he was again in the business of robbing stagecoaches, he decided to stop the incoming coach. He stole a likely looking animal tied to a hitching post and rode a mile and a half from town. At 9:00 p.m. he halted the northbound stagecoach from Los Angeles by pulling his pistol and ordering driver Duggan to halt. He demanded the Wells, Fargo express box, and as soon as it was thrown down he motioned the driver to continue. He had not brought any tools to open the box, so he decided to tie it on the saddle and carry it to a secluded spot where he could work on it at his leisure. However, the box being lifted onto the saddle spooked the horse, causing the animal to run off.

Perkins was again afoot, now with the heavy stolen treasure box, making his way in the dark. He carried the box toward the rail construction site, but he suddenly fell headlong into a deep ditch, breaking his left foot and ankle. Still determined, he managed to pull himself out of the ditch and pushed the box along in front of him until he found a place to bury the chest, after removing more than half of the $1,800 inside. He made his way to a farm where he stole another horse, but this animal had a peculiar temporary shoe, a mule's shoe on one hoof, and left a track easily followed. By the following morning a well-mounted and well-rested posse caught the injured road agent hiding in a barn, and he was lodged in the Kern County jail at Bakersfield.

Perkins was tried for the robbery, convicted, and sentenced on June 8, 1876, to serve eight years at San Quentin. The following day, Perkins managed to chop through the wooden plank walls of the makeshift, temporary jail and, using a pair of crutches provided by Kern County, escape. For two days he hid in the willows along the Kern River before slipping into a farmer's corral. Using a bit of rope, he tied the only horse to a rail while he went into the barn to steal a saddle, but the horse broke loose and ran away, leaving Perkins to limp away. A $300 reward had been posted, and without a mount to help him escape, Perkins was arrested the next afternoon and returned to jail. The prisoner was put under a constant guard until he could be transferred to prison on June 16, 1876, registering as prisoner #6834.

Perkins was released by expiration of sentence on May 16, 1881, and later that month he registered at a Santa Cruz hotel; a few days later he found a job as an advertising solicitor for the Santa Cruz *Daily Echo*. He declined monetary payment for his services and instead placed an ad, using his real name: "G. BRETT LYTLE, PROFESSOR OF LAUNGUAGES, SEEKING PUPILS IN SPANISH." However, after his recent imprisonment, Perkins made only a token effort at rehabilitation and he was still interested in robbing stagecoaches. (See Monterey County on January 13, 1882.)

UNKNOWN, DECEMBER 7, 1875

On Tuesday evening, December 7, 1875, the Kernville stagecoach was near Walker's Basin when a lone, masked road agent stepped from behind a bush, drew his revolver, and ordered the driver to rein in his team. As soon as the coach was stopped he demanded the Wells, Fargo express box, and it was thrown down. The robber did not ask about passengers nor ask for the mail, but as soon as he had the box he ordered the driver to move on. The driver hurried to the next station and reported the robbery, describing the road agent's distinctive clothing: "He wore polished boots, a white stove pipe hat, and a silk faced overcoat." A posse was organized and rode to the scene, but there were no clues to the robber's identity. The busted box, emptied, was recovered and returned to Wells, Fargo, but the amount in the box was not reported.

Source: *Daily Alta California (San Francisco)*: December 8, 1875.

FREDERICK GILLETT, OCTOBER 12, 1876

On October 12, 1876, after the up stagecoach from Mojave to Darwin passed the Panamint junction it was stopped by a lone highwayman, masked and heavily armed. He stepped into the road and ordered the driver to halt, then demanded that he throw down Wells, Fargo's express box. Once the box was in the roadway the road agent ordered the coach to move on, and the driver hurried to the next station to report the robbery. The scene was investigated but there were no clues reported, so the description of the road agent was widely circulated. On Sunday, October 22, Darwin's ex–deputy sheriff James Wales saw a man whom he recognized as the road agent. Wales tried to make an arrest, but the fugitive went for his revolver and the two men exchanged several shots. Wales was wounded in the leg while the fugitive was wounded in the shoulder, and though neither wound was serious, the shoulder wound was sufficient to disable the robber and he was captured. The prisoner identified himself as Frederick Gillett and he was taken before Judge McManus, who found no cause for the arrest and discharged the defendant. McManus then called for an examination of Wales charging him with being the assaulting party, but the evidence was insufficient and he was also released.

As soon as Gillett was freed he was rearrested by James B. Hume, Wells, Fargo's chief detective, and he took his prisoner to Kern County charged with another stagecoach robbery. Sheriff Passmore and defense attorney H. W. Woods accompanied the prisoner to Indian Wells where, following another examination, it was decided there was insufficient evidence to prove guilt, and he was again discharged. Hume immediately rearrested Gillett and this time took his prisoner to Bakersfield. Hume had another arrest warrant issued after he provided new evidence at an examination in Bakersfield, and Gillett was held over to answer to the grand jury, but the jury was not in session so the prisoner was lodged in jail. On January 2, 1877, the grand jury indicted Gillett for the stagecoach robbery near Panamint Junction, and on January 5 he pled not guilty. His trial was scheduled to begin on January 11, but on January 10 his case was continued to the first day of the next term of the court, and though in early March the prisoner confessed to the Panamint junction robbery, he still pled not guilty. Gillett was tried and convicted of robbing the Mojave to Darwin stagecoach on October 12, 1876, and sentenced to serve ten years at San Quentin Prison. He arrived on March 12, 1877, and registered as prisoner #7442. On September 30, 1880, he was removed to Folsom where he registered as prisoner #204. From that "prison without walls" he tried to escape but failed, and as a result he forfeited the good time he had earned under the Goodwin Act. He was finally released, by expiration of sentence, on March 12, 1887, after serving every day of his ten year sentence.

Sources: *Courier Californian (Bakersfield, CA)*: January 2, 1877; January 5, 1877; January 10, 1877.

FRANCISCO SOTELLO AND SANTOS SOTELLO, JANUARY 6, 1877

The Sotello brothers, Santos and Francisco, came from one of the oldest families in California. Both men had been in trouble during their youth, and to spare the family the shame, these "black sheep" adopted aliases, Santos Sotello taking the name Chico Lugo and Francisco Sotello taking the alias Francisco Olivas. In late 1876 Francisco Olivas was suspected of a first-degree murder, a crime which could bring the death penalty. He could not return home, even after the posse gave up the search, so he and his brother, Chico Lugo, fled northwest past Mojave into Kern County. In January 1877, when Lugo was just twenty-six years old and Olivas was just nineteen years old, the two brothers decided to rob stagecoaches. On January 6, when the stagecoach from Darwin to Mojave was in Red Rock Canyon in Kern County, they stepped out, masked and with guns in hand, and robbed the stagecoach of the Wells, Fargo express box. After getting the box, the two road agents "went through" the passengers, including County Registrar Briggs. The robbers fled into the Tehachapi Mountains, confident that they could not be captured while hiding in that rough terrain. (See Los Angeles County on January 20, 1877.)

UNKNOWN, AUGUST 28, 1896

At 2:30 p.m. on Friday, August 28, 1896, the stagecoach from Kernville to Caliente was four miles north of Havilah when a lone road agent, wearing a mask made from a flour sack and armed with a revolver, stepped from behind a large oak tree and told driver William Sweet, "Hands up!" As soon as the coach had stopped, the robber said, "Throw out that box and be in a hurry about it. Time is precious with me." Sweet responded, "All right," but after a brief delay the robber said, "Then be in a hurry about it." The robber had moved to a little rise where he could better supervise the work and see the three passengers, whom he asked, "Are you armed?" and all three men said no. Ernest Brantiheidt, a mining man who was terribly ill, then added, "I have no gun, but you can kill me if you want to, because I have been thinking about doing it myself," but he was ignored. Sweet tried to throw out the box but found it was fastened to the coach, and he informed the robber. The robber then told Sweet, "Well, then, you had better get a crowbar I have here behind these bushes," pointing in back of him, "and tear it out, for I have but little time to fool here." Sweet got the crowbar and, with the help of one passenger, in ten minutes pried the box loose. The robber then told the passenger to throw it down on the bank where he was standing, but the man said he could not because it was too heavy, so the robber said, "Then drop it into the road and be in a hurry about it." He did not ask for the mail and did not molest the passengers, saying, "I never bother working men, these corporations are what I am after." As soon as the box lay in the road he ordered Sweet to move along. When the coach was under way, passenger Dan Doherty looked back and saw the robber pick up the box and carry it into a thicket by the roadside. Sweet whipped up his team and hurried into Havilah, and he described the robber as thirty-five years old, five feet ten inches tall, and weighing about one hundred sixty pounds, clean shaven with a sandy complexion; wearing a duck coat, blue overalls, and a white felt hat. Passenger Doherty, an old-timer in the area, was certain the robber was a stranger to that region. A posse rode to the scene but could find no clue to the robber's identity nor a trail to follow. The box had contained $2,000 in gold bullion from several cleanups at the mines near Kernville so rewards were posted for the arrest and conviction of the robber and for recovery of the plunder, but they were never paid.

Sources: *Los Angeles Herald (CA)*: August 29, 1896. *Sacramento Daily Union (CA)*: August 29, 1896. *San Francisco Call (CA)*: August 29, 1896.

UNKNOWN, MAY 30, 1901

On Thursday, May 30, 1901, the Keeler stagecoach was between Mojave and the Eighteen-Mile House when a lone road agent, masked with a handkerchief and well armed, halted the coach. There was no mail nor an express box aboard, so the robber took from the one passenger $1.50, then told the driver to move along. The coach hurried to the Eighteen-Mile House and reported the robbery, but nothing was done to try to catch this inept, almost laughable, road agent.

Sources: *Amador Ledger (CA)*: June 14, 1901. *Los Angeles Herald (CA)*: June 1, 1901.

Lake County

UNKNOWN, OCTOBER 9, 1875

On Saturday, October 9, 1875, the northbound stagecoach left Calistoga for Lower Lake on schedule, but when it was four miles south of Middletown, two masked, armed road agents halted the coach. They demanded the Wells, Fargo express box and it was thrown down, but they were not interested in passengers or the mail. After they had the box they ordered the driver to continue into Middletown, and he whipped up his team. He reported the robbery, a posse was organized and rode to the scene, but they could find no clue to the robbers' identities nor a trail they could follow for any distance. The box contained nothing of value, and the entire contents were found with the busted box and delivered to the Wells, Fargo office in Middletown.

Source: *Sacramento Daily Union (CA)*: October 11, 1875.

UNKNOWN, MARCH 23, 1884

On Sunday, March 23, 1884, the northbound stagecoach from Calistoga to Lower Lake was five miles below Middletown when a lone road agent ordered the driver to halt. He demanded the Wells, Fargo express box, and as soon as it was thrown down he ordered the driver to continue. He did not ask for the mail and was not interested in the five passengers. When the coach reached Middletown the robbery was reported, and a posse was organized and rode to the scene. There were no clues to the robber's identity nor a good trail to follow, but the broken box was recovered. Wells, Fargo later reported that there was very little of value in the box.

Source: *Territorial Enterprise (Virginia City, NV)*: March 25, 1884.

WILLIAM ROGERS, NOVEMBER 29, 1884

On Saturday afternoon, November 29, 1884, the Sanderson & Company stagecoach from Cloverdale in Sonoma County northbound for Lakeport in Lake County, when near Tyler's station, was halted by a lone highwayman, masked and armed. He demanded the express box and mail sacks, and the unarmed driver had no choice but to deliver them. The robber then gestured for the driver to move on. As soon as the driver reached Lakeport he sounded the alarm and within the hour posses were in the field from both towns—Cloverdale and Lakeport. However, they were not able to capture the road agent.

It was later learned that the mails had contained nothing and the box contained only $1.50. Still, progress was being made to capture the bold, ineffective road agent, and these efforts were joined by James B. Hume, Wells, Fargo's chief detective, and detective Captain Aull. They happened to be in the area looking for John "Shorty" Hays, a stagecoach robber who had escaped from San Quentin Prison on December 13, and the escapee had been seen in the vicinity of Guerneville. Hays was captured at Los Angeles on January 1, 1885, which allowed the two detectives the opportunity to help track down the Lake County road agent. The fugitive was soon captured and turned out to be William Rogers, well known to prison officials and lawmen as William Root, W. H. Rote, and "Bigfoot." He had previously served two terms in San Quentin—first in 1878 from Tehama County and again in 1879 from Calaveras County, both times for burglary. Rogers was captured in early January, and when taken before the justice of the peace for his examination, he pled guilty, expecting to get a reduced sentence for his cooperation. However, when he was brought before the judge and again pled guilty, he was surprised when he was sentenced to serve a term of thirty years at San Quentin. Rogers arrived at the prison on January 15, 1885, and registered as prisoner #11539. He was released on March 15, 1903, after serving more than eighteen years.

Sources: *Cloverdale Reveille (Santa Rosa, CA)*: December 6, 1884; January 3, 1885.

UNKNOWN, JUNE 23, 1888

At 2:30 p.m. on Saturday, June 23, 1888, the Lakeport stagecoach was stopped by a lone road agent, masked and armed, near the Bradford mine in Lake County, twelve miles from Calistoga. The Wells, Fargo treasure box was demanded and delivered, but neither the mail nor the passengers were molested. The robber was never identified.

Source: *Territorial Enterprise (Virginia City, NV)*: June 25, 1888.

JAMES E. BIRK, JOSEPH MOONEY AND UNKNOWN, JUNE 25, 1890

At 8:30 a.m. on Wednesday, June 25, 1890, the northbound stagecoach from Napa to Harbin Springs was stopped on the Lowley toll road near Calistoga by three masked road agents. They ordered driver J. Halmer to climb down and "hand over the box," but there was no box. They then ordered the passengers to come out and form a line, and from Leon Bine of San Francisco they took $245 and two gold watches, one belonging to his wife, and they took the driver's gold watch and $8. They did not molest Mrs. Bine, nor did they take any of the $500 in jewelry carried by Mrs. Maguin. In their haste and nervousness, the one holding the plunder dropped

$150 as they fled, and this was returned to Bine. The stagecoach continued on into Middletown, near Harbin Springs, and the driver reported the robbery. Sheriff George S. McKenzie of Napa County organized a posse and went in pursuit. They scoured the countryside around St. Helena Mountain, but they could not find the road agents. The fugitives said later they could hear the posse as they searched and managed to avoid them, waiting until dark to make their escape. The road agents started out at about dusk but they were seen by a man who reported to Sheriff McKenzie that their men were heading for the Knight's Valley road, and from their direction they were expected to appear a few miles north of Calistoga. The sheriff and his posse then rode rapidly to the road and set up an ambush at the summit between Napa and Knight's Valley, six miles from Calistoga. The three road agents had struck the road and sat down to rest, but when they arose they left behind a bundle, so one man returned while the other two continued on. At midnight two men were seen coming toward the posse and they were ordered "Throw up your hands," and when they raised them only slightly they were ordered, "Throw them up higher." The men were searched and they had $27.50 and two of the stolen watches in their pockets. While the capture was commencing, the third man was coming along the road, unseen by the posse, and he heard and saw the situation so he dropped the third watch in the road, fearing if he was captured it would identify him as one of the road agents as the other two watches had done for his companions. He fled taking along $80 of the plunder, and the third watch was found and all three watches were returned to their owners. The next morning Sheriff McKenzie organized a fresh posse and began searching for the third road agent, but to no avail, and the prisoners would not inform on him.

Deputy Sheriff Howard, of St. Helena, delivered the two prisoners to the Napa County jail the following day, and they identified themselves as James Burkley, sometimes Berkley, age thirty of Boston, Massachusetts, and thirty-nine-year-old Joe Morgan of Pennsylvania. They confessed and said they had been put out of work by a strike and were desperate for money when they stopped the stagecoach. They had passed through Calistoga the night before and went out on the Lowley toll road, then stopped the stagecoach thinking it carried the express and mail. On July 7 they were brought into court for their arraignment and charged with stagecoach robbery, and they pled guilty, correcting their names to James Birk and Joseph Mooney. The judge then wasted no time in sentencing each man to serve ten years at San Quentin Prison. Both men arrived on July 8, 1890, with Birk registering as prisoner #14207 and Mooney registering as prisoner #14208. Both men were "restored" on January 8, 1897, after serving six years six months.

Sources: *Daily Alta California (San Francisco)*: June 27, 1890. *Los Angeles Herald (CA)*: June 27, 1890. *San Francisco Call (CA)*: June 26, 1890; July 8, 1890.

WILLIAM BRAWN, OCTOBER 11, 1894

On Thursday, October 11, 1894, the stagecoach from Lakeport was stopped and robbed by a young man, apparently "green" at the business. He demanded the Wells, Fargo treasure box and it was delivered, and the robbery was reported as soon as the driver got to his next destination with a telegraph. A posse was organized by Lake County sheriff Johnson, and from the scene they tracked the robber so effectively that he had not had time to open the box. He was arrested and identified himself as William Braun, he confessed that this was his first crime and hunger had driven him to commit the robbery, and he said he was willing to accept his punishment. The following day Braun was taken into Lakeport and lodged in jail to await his examination. C. P. Adams, the Wells, Fargo agent at Lakeport was in the posse, and he recovered the treasure box, opened it, and found all the contents intact including $20.70. In Lakeport Braun corrected the spelling of his name to Brawn and pled guilty, and he was immediately sentenced to serve seven years at Folsom Prison. Brawn arrived at the prison on October 15 and registered as prisoner #3290, and he was discharged by expiration of sentence on July 15, 1899.

Source: *San Francisco Call (CA)*: October 13, 1894.

Lawrence B. "Buck" English and R. N. Breckenridge, May 7, 1895

On Tuesday afternoon, May 7, 1895, the stagecoach from Calistoga to Lakeport had reached a point one and a half miles from Mirabel in Lake County when two masked road agents stepped from the bushes with large revolvers in hand, and a second large revolver holstered, and ordered driver Al Palmer to halt. They called for the Wells, Fargo express box, and it was thrown down. One of the robbers then covered the driver and passengers with his pistol while the other broke open the box, but there was no money inside. The five passengers were then ordered out of the coach and told to form a line at the side of the road and raise their hands. The smaller, younger robber covered them with his pistol while the older, tall robber went through their pockets, collecting about $1,000 in money and watches. Only a Chinaman resisted, and he was badly pummeled and then robbed of his money and all his papers. While the robbers were at work, two teams drove up, each wagon with only a driver, and the drivers were called by name and told to get down. When the robber doing the searching felt he had all the plunder he was going to find, he ordered everyone to board and sent the coach and wagons on their way into Middletown, while the two robbers fled in the opposite direction. Two hours later they were seen, still traveling afoot, passing through Adolph Sutro's place and heading toward Oak Hill. At Middletown the passengers described the robbers: one was five foot ten inches in height; the other five feet eight inches; both wore long ulsters, old shoes, and masks but their clothing was hidden by the ulsters; and one had a light moustache. As soon as the information was delivered, a posse was organized at Middletown, and Lake County and Napa County lawmen were notified.

Reports came in regularly saying where the pair of road agents had been seen last and where they were going. They had passed Etna Springs on the night of the robbery headed for Berryessa Valley, and early in the morning of May 9 Undersheriff Robert Brownlee learned the pair had camped on P. D Gridley's place all day Wednesday, then had breakfast at Charles Moore's place and told him they were going to take the stagecoach to Napa. The driver of the Napa coach, John Gardner, heard this report and sent word that if he met the pair he would give them a ride.

Brownlee then organized a posse consisting of district attorney Theodore A. Bell, J. N. True, and John Williams, and they boarded a double-seated wagon and started for the summit of the grade en route to Napa, where they planned to set up an ambush. However, the posse wagon arrived at the same time as the stagecoach, 10:30 a.m., and Brownlee saw the taller fugitive seated next to Gardner and said to Williams, "There is the fellow; stand them up." Williams raised his gun at the same time the fugitive raised his, and they fired simultaneously. The robber's shotgun was filled with bird shot, and a few pellets struck Brownlee and Williams in their legs, but the bulk of the load struck the butt of Brownlee's shotgun, and the shock threw him out of the rig. Bell then got off the wagon on the side opposite the stagecoach to get a clear shot at the taller robber, but just then the shorter robber tumbled out of the passenger compartment and started running for the brush. True fired a load from his shotgun at the fleeing youngster and peppered him lightly, and he immediately turned, threw up his hands, and cried out, "Don't shoot! Don't shoot!" While the lawmen were distracted, the taller robber put the barrel of his revolver to Gardner's head and told him to drive fast. The coach had been moving slowly uphill, but Gardner whipped his team into a run. Bell quickly took a knee and carefully aimed at the fleeing robber, and fired. The robber slumped onto Gardner but quickly recovered, and before a second shot could be fired the coach went around a turn. Bell followed on foot for five hundred yards, but by then the other officers had secured their prisoner and brought along the wagon, and they soon caught up with the coach expecting another fight. However they found that the coach had stopped after the robber fainted, and he was handcuffed and put in the stagecoach with Bell and Williams while Brownlee and True brought in the shorter, younger robber in the wagon. The prisoners were lodged in jail and county physician Dr. Springsteen was summoned to give medical care, but he felt the three buckshot wounds to the older man's abdomen were mortal. The officers found among the prisoners' belongings four stolen watches and $116 in cash, as well as papers taken from the Chinaman. The older of the two then identified himself as forty-year-old Buck English, an ex-convict from a notorious family of desperadoes, most of whom had "died with their boots on." As soon as English was able to talk, he asked Brownlee, with a show of pride, "How many of you fellows did I kill?" When told he had killed no one, he seemed terribly disappointed. The younger man said he was twenty-four and gave the name John Smith, but readily admitted it was an alias. The county physician also treated Gardner who had received six painful flesh wounds to his thigh, and he was expected to fully recover. Wells, Fargo had posted rewards of $300 for each man and this had been matched by the state, so the four posse men and Gardner would share $1,200.

On May 22 and 23 John Smith had his preliminary hearing and at the outset admitted his real name was R. N. Breckenridge, and proceedings then continued before Justice Bradford under that name. After two days of testimony, but no defense, Breckenridge was held over for trial with bond set at $10,000. The defendant appeared in court on May 29, and he pled guilty; Judge Ham sentenced him to serve twenty-five years at San Quentin Prison. English's condition had its ups and downs for weeks, but by early July he had recovered sufficiently to appear in court. At his arraignment on July 9 he pled guilty, and Judge Ham sentenced him to serve life in prison at San Quentin. Breckenridge arrived at the prison on May 20, 1895, and registered as prisoner #16359; he was discharged on August 29, 1910. English arrived at the prison on July 10, 1895, and registered as prisoner #16426. He was paroled on February 1, 1912.

Sources: *San Francisco Call (CA)*: May 8, 1895; May 10, 1895; May 22–23, 1895; May 30, 1895; July 9, 1895.

Lassen County

HENRY C. HILL AND UNKNOWN, AUGUST 29, 1889

On Thursday, August 29, 1889, two men robbed a stagecoach near Susanville in Lassen County. Sheriff Frank P. Cady went to the scene and was soon on their trail and followed them to Big Meadows in Plumas County. On August 31 the sheriff came upon the two robbers and a gun battle followed, during which Cady was shot in the right leg three times, and he shot one of the fugitives in the leg, then pistol-whipped him into submission and captured his partner, who gave the name H. C. Hill. Neither robber could give further resistance, as they had emptied their revolvers at Cady. The sheriff recovered the entire $1,000 stolen by the pair and then took his prisoners to Susanville, where Hill was lodged in jail. The following morning Hill had his preliminary examination, during which he confessed and pled guilty to robbing the stagecoach. Later that day Wells, Fargo detective Thacker arrived to look for the robbers, and upon seeing Hill told Sheriff Cady that the prisoner had been employed by the company as a stock tender several years earlier. Hill was sentenced to serve seventeen years at Folsom Prison, he arrived on

September 11, 1889, and registered as prisoner #1981. Hill was discharged on April 11, 1900, after serving ten years and seven months. There is no record of Hill's partner.

Sources: *Daily Alta California (San Francisco)*: September 3, 1889. *Sacramento Daily Union (CA)*: September 4, 1889.

HENRY I. WISE, SEPTEMBER 1, 1890; SEPTEMBER 24, 1890

In mid–August 1884 Henry I. Wise was convicted of grand larceny in San Benito County and he was sentenced to serve five years. He arrived at the prison on August 20 and registered as prisoner #11347; he was released on March 20, 1888. There is no record of crime for Wise over the next twenty-nine months. On Monday, September 1, 1890, the stagecoach from Liegan to Susanville had reached Millford in Lassen County, still five miles from its destination, when a lone highwayman, masked and armed, halted the coach. The robber demanded the Wells, Fargo treasure box, and it was thrown down. As soon as the road agent had the plunder he told the driver to continue into Susanville. Sheriff Frank P. Cady rode to the scene but could find no clue, nor a trail to follow, but he recovered the broken box which had been emptied.

On September 24, 1890, the stagecoach from Lompoc was near Los Alamos in Santa Barbara County when it was halted by a lone, masked road agent and he demanded the Wells, Fargo express box. It was thrown down and the robber then told the driver to move on. The driver hurried into Los Alamos and reported the robbery and four men started for the scene, and from there they found a trail to follow. Soon the trail played out, so the men separated, with each heading toward one of the locations they expected to find the robber. Posse man John Conway, an insurance agent, cut the trail of the robber and followed on horseback for over twenty hours before he captured his man. His prisoner said his name was Harry West, but he later changed that to Henry West. Conway took his prisoner to the county seat at Santa Barbara where he was convicted of robbery and sentenced to serve one year in prison. He arrived on October 1, 1890, and registered as prisoner #14286; he was discharged on August 1, 1891, after serving ten months.

Sheriff Cady continued to investigate the Susanville stagecoach robbery until he was certain that the road agent was convict Henry West. When West was released, the sheriff was waiting at the prison door to arrest him, and on August 3, 1891, they arrived at Susanville. On August 18 West pled guilty and was sentenced to serve ten years at San Quentin Prison. He was taken back to the jail, and on August 21 Cady and his prisoner started back for San Quentin. West insisted his real name was Henry I. Wise, so he was registered under that name as prisoner #14642. Wise, or West, was discharged on February 21, 1898, after serving six years six months.

Sources: *Sacramento Daily Union (CA)*: August 3, 1891; August 21, 1891; October 1, 1890. *San Francisco Call (CA)*: September 3, 1890; August 19, 1891.

Los Angeles County

UNKNOWN, OCTOBER 21, 1869

On Thursday, October 21, 1869, the stagecoach from Los Angeles to San Francisco, with seven passengers inside and Ben Truman riding next to the driver on top, had only traveled a short distance north from the city when it was stopped by four Mexican road agents, masked and armed with revolvers. They demanded the Wells, Fargo treasure boxes, and Truman threw down two boxes while the driver kept control of his team. The robbers then ordered Truman to climb down and marched him to the rear of the coach with a cocked pistol in his back, assuring him that no harm would come to him. They then ordered the other passengers to step out and form a line, and they were searched and robbed of their money, totaling $1,300, and two small pistols. The robbers seemed nervous. During the collection of plunder one robber snapped his pistol at a German passenger he thought was going for a pistol, but it either misfired or the firing pin rested on an empty cylinder; and another robber accidentally discharged his pistol, harming no one. Once they had their plunder they ordered everyone to board and told the driver to move on. They did not ask for the mailbags and missed a fortune, as several hundred thousand dollars in greenbacks had been shipped north in the pouches. After the coach was out of sight, the robbers broke open the treasure box with a cold chisel and removed $500, then fled south to San Diego where they remained for several days to attend the races. The following day the down stage found the broken boxes and returned them to Los Angeles.

A posse from Los Angeles went to the scene and found their trail, and they followed it south to San Diego. The lawmen searched all over San Diego but could not find the four robbers, and they disappeared from town before they could be arrested. In following their trail from San Diego, the lawmen had found that the robbers had paid for lodging and supplies on their way south using bogus gold dust. The stagecoach company offered a reward of $250, the city of Los Angeles offered the same amount, and Wells, Fargo offered a reward of $1,000 for the arrest and conviction of the four and the recovery of the stolen money. The four road agents would travel east and attempt to rob another stagecoach on November 7. (See San Diego County on November 7, 1869.)

Francisco Sotello, Santos Sotello and Jose Tapia, January 20, 1877

Santos Sotello, alias Chico Lugo, and Francisco Sotello, alias Francisco Olivas, were from a prominent California family, but they turned to a life of crime. After they robbed a stagecoach in Kern County on January 7, 1877, they turned their attention to Los Angeles County. On January 20 Lugo and Olivas, with Jose Tapia, appeared on the stage road between Newhall in Los Angeles County and Ventura and robbed the Ventura-bound stagecoach below the boundary. They secured the Wells, Fargo express box and then fled to Elizabeth Lake. The two brothers, with Francisco Romero, made their way over the Tehachapi Mountains and went to Panama, a Mexican settlement near Bakersfield, where they stole a small string of horses, then robbed a Tulare Lake store of $500 and supplies, beating the owner into unconsciousness. The men drove the stolen horses south and, when recognized, engaged in a gun battle with men trying to recover their stock. No one was hurt but their resistance caused a large posse to form and they were soon on the trail, and the three horse thieves had to abandon the horses. The posse kept on their trail for a week but finally gave up and, on their return to Bakersfield, stopped at the ranch of George Reig, where they found him dead and his house ransacked. Next the outlaw brothers were heard of in San Francisquito Canyon, where they bound fourteen Chinese miners and robbed them of $260 in gold dust. A posse led by ex-sheriff Robert H. Paul kept pressure on the two fugitives until finally a tip came which put the two men in a valley in the San Bernardino Mountains. The posse captured Olivas without resistance, coming upon him so quickly he could not make his fight even though he had two fully loaded six-shooters in his belt. Lugo at the time of the capture of his brother was at a celebration in town, but being clean shaven he was not recognized and escaped.

Bob Paul, who at the time was the shotgun messenger for Wells, Fargo between Mojave and Lone Pine, lodged his prisoner in jail. Friends of Olivas tried various legal maneuvers to gain his release and finally obtained a writ of habeas corpus, but driver Briggs appeared and identified Olivas so a warrant was sworn out by Justice Peterson ordering Olivas taken before a Kern County justice for examination. E. Diaz, to counter this maneuver, arrested Paul for "personating an officer," and his examination was held in Lone Pine where he was acquitted. Paul was then deputized to take Olivas before the Kern County justice, and the prisoner was held over to answer to the grand jury. Romero was soon afterward captured at Kern and taken to Tulare County, while Tapia was captured at Darwin and charged in the Los Angeles to Ventura stagecoach robbery. Tapia was held over to answer to the grand jury at his examination.

At trial Tapia pled guilty to the stagecoach robbery and was sentenced to serve ten years at San Quentin Prison. He arrived on March 21, 1877, and registered as prisoner #7463. Tapia's sentence was commuted, and he was discharged on December 21, 1881, after serving only four years nine months. Francisco Olivas (Sotello) was convicted and also sentenced to serve a term of ten years, arriving at San Quentin Prison on May 29, 1877, and registering as prisoner #7602. Olivas was released on November 20, 1883, by expiration of sentence, but he would return to prison on a conviction for grand larceny in 1886. Francisco Romero was charged in the Tulare Lake store robbery, convicted and given a five-year term at the San Quentin Prison. He arrived on June 25, 1877, and registered as #7647. Romero was discharged by expiration of sentence on January 25, 1881.

Chico Lugo (Santos Sotello) once again fled into the Tehachapi Mountains, but by July 19 he had been tracked down and captured. A bold young man had come upon the desperado lounging beneath a tree smoking a cigarette, and he was immediately recognized. The young man, Rafael Lopez, crept up keeping the tree between himself and the bandit and then, suddenly springing upon him with pistol in hand, took Lugo prisoner. He was taken into Los Angeles and later transferred to Kern County, where he was tried and convicted of robbing the Darwin stagecoach on January 6. Lugo talked freely of his exploits and was easily convicted, receiving a term of fifteen years at San Quentin Prison. He arrived at the prison on September 23, 1877, and he was discharged from prison in February 1887.

Sources: *Bakersfield Courier Californian (CA)*: March 8, 1877; March 15, 1877; March 22, 1877; May 13, 1877; June 7, 1877; June 27, 1877. *Calaveras Chronicle (CA)*: February 24, 1877. *Kern County Weekly Courier (CA)*: July 19, 1877. *Los Angeles Weekly Star (CA)*: January 17, 1876; April 29, 1877; May 5, 1877. *Los Angeles Daily Star (CA)*: March 15, 1877; June 17, 1877; July 10, 1877. *Los Angeles News (CA)*: November 7, 1877; November 13, 1877. *Daily Alta California (San Francisco, CA)*: July 13, 1877.

UNKNOWN, MARCH 9, 1877

The stagecoach from Anaheim arrived in San Diego on March 10, 1877, carrying the mail from the north, and the driver reported that the coach had been stopped by a highwayman on the previous night and the driver on the San Juan division had been wounded. One of the through passengers, C. F. Lutgen, then gave the details to the reporter for the *San Diego Union Tribune*. Lutgen reported that it was 9:15 p.m. and the coach was just nineteen miles south of Anaheim in Los Angeles County, four miles north of Rawson's ranch and fourteen miles north of San Juan Capistrano. There was deep sand on that part of the road, so the coach was moving quite slowly. Lutgen was riding on top next to driver George H. Smith, and just as the coach turned a curve a man appeared from behind bushes on the left side of the road and hailed the driver, saying, "Hold on, hold on!" Lutgen said he had been drowsy but the command awoke him fully and he thought that the man only wanted a ride. Smith began to rein in his team just as the man came into clear view, and they saw that he was masked. Smith asked, "What do you want?" and the road agent demanded, "Hand down that box!" and pointed his six-shooter at Smith to emphasize the command. However, the question had been intended to distract the robber and Smith instantly raised his whip, and in the same moment the road agent fired one round at him. The ball grazed Lutgen's knee and struck Smith in the left hand, the hand in which he held the reins. Smith applied the lash and held the reins firmly in his wounded hand while Lutgen fired twice at the road agent. The coach had lurched forward fifteen yards and the horses were already moving at a fast gait, and this ruined the aim of Lutgen so he missed his man. After driving for three or four minutes Lutgen asked Smith, "Are you wounded?" and Smith replied, "Yes, Sir. I'm shot through the hand; can you drive?" Lutgen answered, "Not four horses," and Smith said, "Well then, I must go on so."

Smith "plied the whip and kept the animals at a twelve-mile gait for at least ten minutes, all the while holding the reins with his bleeding and shattered hand, determined to get the stagecoach and treasure box beyond the reach of the highwayman." At last Smith could not hold on any longer, so Judge Egan, a passenger riding inside, was called to the driver's boot while the coach was still in motion and he took the reins. Egan drove to Rawson's ranch where Lutgen dressed Smith's wound. The journey was then continued to San Juan Capistrano, Egan driving with Lutgen and Smith atop. At San Juan Capistrano a surgeon took charge of the wounded driver and treated Smith's wound. A new driver was put aboard and the coach continued on to San Diego.

Lutgen was certain there was more than one road agent, but this conjecture was based on the brazen behavior of the man, as neither Lutgen nor Smith saw other road agents. The man seen was described as medium height, with whiskers but carefully masked, wearing a light-colored hat and coat. He spoke in a "clear, ringing voice and was unquestionably an American." Lutgen "spoke in terms of the highest praise of the cool, steady courage and fortitude of the driver, to whom is due the protection of the passengers and the safety of the treasure box." There were no clues, and without anything stolen, there was no reward posted for the arrest of the robber, and the robber was not identified.

Source: *San Diego Union Tribune (CA)*: March 11, 1877.

JOHN S. BIXLER, AUGUST 27, 1877

The stagecoach bound for Newhall in Los Angeles County from Soledad in Monterey County was waylaid by a lone highwayman at 10:00 a.m. on Monday, August 27, 1877. The Wells, Fargo express box was demanded and the unarmed driver, Frank Shaw, had no choice but to deliver the box. As soon as the box was in the roadway Shaw was told to continue on into Newhall. He hurried into the little town and sounded the alarm, and the following morning Ned Bushyhead, James Russell and driver Shaw started for the scene of the robbery. Bushyhead returned to town that evening and reported that robber J.S. Bixler was well mounted and headed toward Smith's Mountain, but the small posse had not yet overtaken him, and they failed to do so.

Source: *San Diego Union Tribune (CA)*: August 29, 1877.

Madera County

JOHN TATUM, JUNE 18, 1896

On Thursday, June 18, 1896, the Yosemite stagecoach was five miles from Raymond when a lone road agent stepped into the road, masked and carrying a double-barreled shotgun, and ordered the coach halted. Once the coach was stopped passengers reported seeing several accomplices lurking in the heavy brush as the robber called for the Wells, Fargo express boxes, and the boxes for Wawona and Grub Gulch were thrown down. He did not call for the mail but ordered the eight passengers to step out and form a line with their backs to the coach, and he took from them money and jewelry valued at $1,000. He then told everyone to board and ordered the driver to move along. The driver whipped up his team and hurried into Raymond, where he reported the robbery and a posse was quickly organized and deputized. The lawmen rode to the scene and searched the area, but all they could find was a single set of boot prints about the broken boxes, and the boxes were returned to town. The officers were already searching the hills for several fugitives and believed two were responsible for the robbery, but they eluded capture. On June 19 officers arrested men named Littlefield, Robinson, and Baumen and they were lodged in the Raymond jail, but by the following day each man proved an alibi and was released.

Meanwhile officers circling the robbery scene cut a single set of horse tracks of the road agent leading away from the robbery scene, and on June 21 they followed the trail directly to the barn of John Tatum near Pea Ridge. Along the way they found buckskin horse hair clinging to branches where the robber had made his way through heavy brush, and in Tatum's barn they found his buckskin pony which was an exact match for the horse hair they found along the trail. They arrested Tatum and determined his boot soles matched the tracks at the scene, so they took their prisoner into town and lodged him in the Raymond jail. Sheriff R. A. Prouty had suspected Tatum of being one of two robbers who had stopped the Mariposa coach on October 7, 1895, but he could never work up a case. Tatum continued to profess his innocence and at his preliminary hearing before Justice Ayer on June 28 he pled not guilty, but he was held over for action by the grand jury. Tatum was indicted and his trial began on September 25 and lasted three weeks. Though all the evidence was circumstantial, it was overwhelming in its accumulation and on October 13 the jurors convicted him of the June 18 stagecoach robbery. On October 24 Judge Conley sentenced Tatum to serve ten years at Folsom Prison, but he appealed and made bond, and on November 10, 1897, when no one appeared to argue the case, the judgment was affirmed; still it was another year before Tatum was resentenced. Thirty-one-year-old Tatum arrived at Folsom Prison on December 29, 1898, and registered as prisoner #4264. He was "discharged and restored June 17, 1904," after serving five years six months.

Sources: *Los Angeles Herald (CA)*: June 19, 1896. *Sacramento Daily Union (CA)*: June 19, 1896; June 23, 1896; October 15, 1896. *San Francisco Call (CA)*: June 20, 1896.

"BLACK KID," JUNE 2, 1900

On Saturday, June 2, 1900, A. H. Foster, one of the oldest employees of the Yosemite Stage & Turnpike Company, was taking a party of tourists to the Mariposa Big Trees. As his coach reached the top of a small hill near Raymond, two miles from Grub Gulch, he was commanded to halt by a lone highwayman who then, waving his .44 caliber rifle, told him to drive to one side. The passengers were ordered to hand over their valuables, and the robber collected $80. He had held the coach for an hour and a half when two soldiers of Troop F, 6th Cavalry came along, and he covered them with his gun, disarmed them, and had them tie their horses to a tree and they were required to join the others. Soon a Spaniard driving a wood wagon appeared and he was ordered to join the growing crowd. In twenty minutes the first Yosemite stagecoach appeared with Bright Gillespie driving and nine passengers aboard, including two couples. They were ordered to give up their money and he collected $111. The next stagecoach to come along was driven by Tom Skelton, and he was asked if he had arms or a hatchet and when he said no, he was ordered to throw down the Wells, Fargo express box and then join the others on the side of the road. Skelton's coach was followed closely by another stagecoach driven by Ernest Stevens with five Chinamen aboard. Once again the passengers were ordered to hand over their valuables, but one said, "No sabbe talk." The road agent leveled his rifle at the Chinaman and said, "You can't fool me as they did on the Big Oak Flat road." According to the *Los Angeles Herald*, the "Chinamen then heap sabbe," and they turned their pockets inside out, but he only collected $15 from them. All were ordered to join the others, and at that point thirty-two people including five women, two soldiers and three teamsters, four coaches, a wagon and two horses were under the road agent's control. After waiting some time and no one else appearing, he had two passengers mount the soldiers' horses and had the soldiers board one of the coaches, and then he told everyone to board and the drivers to drive on. After the hostages had gone only three hundred yards they met Major Rucker and Captain Wilcox commanding a detachment of sixty-eight men from Troop F, 4th Cavalry, coming from the Presidio in San Francisco. Once informed of the robbery they hurried to the scene, but as the robber was trying to open the treasure box he saw the soldiers and fled into the heavy brush. The area was searched and a sergeant found a sack containing a sweater, hat, box of .44 caliber cartridges, and a pair of large field glasses, and these items were collected for evidence. Driver Skelton described the robber as "a swede, five feet nine inches in height, wearing overalls, a pair of brogan shoes and a black hat; he wore a blue handkerchief as a mask, and his hands were blackened."

The robber, who by his statement about Big Oak Flat road confirmed he was the road agent at that robbery, had handed Foster a card reading "The Black Kid" and said, "I hope we will get better acquainted, old man." Madera County sheriff W. B. Thurman and constable Leonard organized a posse and started for the scene. They could not find any clues to the robber's identity nor a trail to follow. However, in mid–August detectives Ed Gibson and Jack Fitzgerald arrested forty-year-old Tom Moran, and they believed they had captured "the Black Kid," and lodged him in the city jail. There appears no record of Moran being charged with stagecoach robbery, or any other major crime. The "Black Kid" disappeared from the Yosemite Valley stagecoach roads for a while and the case went cold.

Sources: *Los Angeles Herald (CA)*: June 4, 1900. *San Francisco Call (CA)*: May 19, 1900; June 3, 1900; August 18, 1900.

JACK STONE, AUGUST 15, 1905; JULY 7, 1906; SEPTEMBER 2, 1906; JUNE 19, 1907; JUNE 24, 1907

At 2:00 p.m. on Tuesday afternoon, August 15, 1905, the down coach from Wawona to Raymond was halted by a lone highwayman three miles below Ahwahnee, a few miles above Grub Gulch. The robber, with his pistol holstered, pointed his shotgun at the driver and had Walter Farnsworth get down from his seat, searched him for a gun, and then had him direct the eleven passengers, five men and six women, to come out and line up along the roadside. The robber then collected their valuables totaling $95. Many of the passengers, as soon as they realized their situation, had hid most of their money and jewelry. An *Examiner* reporter was aboard and asked for $2 to pay for his room at Wawona, but the road agent refused to return it, but then allowed the reporter to snap his photograph, saying, "Sure, fire away, for no one will know me with this disguise on." He handed back all the watches, remarking, "I have no use for them," and then told the passengers to board. As soon as everyone was seated, he ordered the driver to move along. The road agent stayed at that spot, a popular one for robberies, and when the up coach arrived he repeated the same process. The road agent was described as slender, five feet ten inches tall, with a slouch hat, a linen duster, and linen trousers. A posse was organized at Madera, went to the scene, and found a trail of horse tracks, and they followed it as they picked up empty purses along the way, but eventually they lost the trail. Jack Sweet, who lived near Grub Gulch, fit the description and was suspected, but he proved he was far away at the time of the robbery and was not arrested. No one else was suspected and no arrest was made.

On Saturday afternoon, July 7, 1906, five Yosemite stagecoaches, each traveling minutes behind the next coach to avoid the dust, were near Ahwahnee and approaching a curve in the road. As the first coach passed around the curve, out of sight of the coach following, a lone highwayman with a duster drawn over his head stepped out, pointed a Winchester rifle at the driver, and stopped the first coach. He ordered the passengers to throw out their valuables, and once he had them on the ground he ordered the driver to continue on. The second coach then arrived and the same process was followed; then the third, fourth, and fifth coaches' passengers were robbed in the same manner. After the fifth coach started on its way the road agent collected the valuables from the road and fled into the brush. Sheriff Jones was notified by telephone, and he immediately started in pursuit of the robber. A year earlier Jack Sweet had been suspected of a stagecoach robbery, but he had proved he was absent at the time and was not arrested. The stagecoach robber this time again matched Sweet's description, so on July 8 he was arrested by Mariposa County sheriff R. A. Prouty and Madera County sheriff J. M. Jones and brought into Ahwahnee. Ed Skelton, one of the drivers, looked at Sweet and said he resembled the robber, but upon looking over his Winchester rifle he was positive it was not the weapon used by the road agent as he had taken particular notice of the rifle's pattern of rust. Sweet was freed and, with no one else suspected, the case went cold, though they were certain this road agent was the same man who had robbed the coach in the same vicinity on August 15, 1905. On July 11 Sheriff Jones announced that he had given up the chase.

At 12:30 p.m. on Monday, September 2, 1906, the Yosemite-bound stagecoach, driven by Bright Gillespie, was three miles from Ahwahnee, and just at a sharp bend in the road where the horses had to walk slowly. A masked road agent stepped into the road, pointed his Winchester rifle at Gillespie, and told the driver, "Come on up." The road agent wore a white felt hat, a burlap sack reaching to his knees with eye and mouth holes cut into it, a short-sleeved shirt, brown checkered trousers, and his boots were muffled with black cloth, but the imprint of hobnails could still be seen in the soft dust of the road. Gillespie drove to within a few feet of the robber and reined in his team. The robber then told the passengers to step out, and once they were standing next to the coach the robber told the driver to continue ahead fifty feet. As soon as the coach had pulled ahead, he had the passengers, five men and two women, form a line along the roadside. He had each present their money, but after seeing that the first two men had only nickel-plated watches he did not ask for jewelry. He even included the women in his robbing but did not molest the driver. One of the passengers was a soldier and when they were first stopped he wanted to shoot the robber with his .38 caliber rifle, but the other passengers talked him out of it, concerned that the robber had accomplices hiding or that the soldier might miss. Once the robber was finished with the passengers, he marched them ahead to the coach and told them to board, but three of the men who had cameras to take pictures at Yosemite asked if they could take his picture, and he agreed. Wertemer Bishop of New York, took one picture; A. Formsbee from Brooklyn, New York took two pictures; and R. A. Tuttle took one picture of the robber in a group shot with the other passengers. Once the passengers boarded, the robber told Gillespie to throw down the Wells, Fargo express box and the mail pouches, and he did as told. The robber broke open the box, took out the valuables, and then he went through the mail pouches. Once he was done he told the driver to continue on his route, and after the coach had left he set fire to the worthless contents from the treasure box and then fled. The sheriff organized a posse and went to the scene but could find no clue to the robber's identity nor a trail to follow beyond the boot prints in the dust of the road. Wells, Fargo posted a reward of $250 for the arrest and conviction of the road agent, and they were certain he was the same man who had robbed the stagecoach in the same vicinity on August 15, 1905, and July 7, 1906. Still, the robber could not be found, and no one was arrested.

At 3:00 p.m. on Wednesday, June 19, 1907, two regular Yosemite Stage & Turnpike Company coaches from Raymond to Wawona, the first coach driven by Archie Turner, were approaching the Mariposa line when the horses became skittish. Turner then noticed a man standing on the side of the road pointing a rusty repeating rifle at him, and he called out, "Pull up!" Once the coach was stopped he told the passengers to raise their hands, then asked about the second coach and was told it was following. While he waited he asked why they were delayed six hours and was told there had been a wreck on the railroad, and then he helped himself to some peaches, potatoes, and crackers from inside the coach. He seemed impatient until the second coach driven by Bright Gillespie appeared and was stopped, and then he had all the passengers get out and form a line. He directed passenger Francis S. Eaton to "pass the hat" and collect purses and watches, and had Mrs. Eaton stand behind him to avert any attack from behind. After the collection was completed, and Mr. Eaton had $250 and several items of jewelry, the plunder was tied in a handkerchief and handed to the robber. The robber then demanded Eaton's watch, but he said it was a keepsake and that he would send $200 to any address if he could keep it. The robber then said he could keep it for $25, which would be borrowed from Turner, but the driver only had $20. The robber took the money and returned the watch. He then ordered the passengers to board and told the drivers to move along. He was believed to be the same man who had robbed stagecoaches in the same vicinity three times previously as he was dressed similarly in a slouch hat with a sack over his head and upper body, with eye, mouth and arm holes cut into it, and he carried the same rusty repeating rifle. Everyone recalled the repeated robberies by a man calling himself "the Black Kid" in 1900 and supposed it was the same man returned to the place of his successful adventures. Rewards were posted, and Sheriff R. A. Prouty organized a posse and went in pursuit. Gillespie, driver of the second coach, was sure it was the same man who had robbed him on two previous occasions and described him as five feet six inches tall, 160 pounds, dark complected, and about forty years old.

At 11:30 a.m. on Monday, June 24, 1907, two stagecoaches traveling from Madera to Yosemite, one behind the other, were between Crooks and Grub Gulch thirty-five miles from Madera when a lone highwayman stepped out and stopped the first stagecoach, which blocked the second. The road agent, wearing a white mask and carrying a new rifle, appeared nervous but appeared to be the same man who had robbed the stagecoach near Ahwahnee a few days earlier. He had the passengers step out and ordered them to give up their valuables, and he collected $150 in all, though a great deal of money and jewelry was hidden. Sheriffs from Fresno, Madera, Mariposa, Merced, and Tuolumne counties organized posses and began scouring the countryside for the robber, and by June 27 the posses from Madera and Mariposa counties believed they had trailed the road agent twenty-five miles from the scene of the robbery and had him cornered in the Chowchilla mountains. They were certain from his description that the man they were after was Jack Stone, a former employee of the Yosemite stage company. Apparently the fugitive slipped through the posse and on June 30 he arrived in Madera and took a room at a D Street lodging house. Leaving behind a bundle containing a new black suit, Stone then went to the barber shop and had his moustache shaved off to change his appearance. As Stone left the barber shop he encountered Jerome Martin, an acquaintance, and he was asked where he was going, and the fugitive replied, "Bakersfield, if these damn officers will let me get through." Martin notified undersheriff Hansley who started searching for Stone, but he had retrieved his bundle and was nowhere to be found. Sheriff J. M. Jones returned from the search near Course Gold later that day and he too searched Madera without results. Stone managed to make his getaway and was not captured, and the "Yosemite road agent" disappeared from the region.

Sources: *Los Angeles Herald (CA)*: June 25, 1907; June 28, 1907; August 16, 1905; July 8, 1906; July 10–12, 1906; September 3, 1906. *Merced Express (CA)*: August 19, 1905. *Oregonian (Portland)*: June 28, 1907. *San Francisco Call (CA)*: July 1, 1907; August 16, 1905; June 21, 1907.

Marin County

VICTOR J. COLWELL, SEPTEMBER 19, 1899

On Monday, September 19, 1899, the Bolinas stagecoach was at Cattle Bridge, six miles from San Rafael, when a lone road agent, masked and armed, appeared in the road and commanded the driver to halt. The robber called for the Wells, Fargo express box and it was thrown down, and then he told the driver to move along. The driver whipped up his team and hurried into San Rafael where he reported the robbery to Sheriff Harry Harrison and described the road agent, and the sheriff quickly organized a posse and rode to the scene. They found the broken box and determined the robber had obtained $60 and three gold watches, and there was a clear trail to follow. The trail led to Ross' station where they captured Victor J. Colwell, with the money and watches still in his pockets. He confessed and was taken into San Rafael where he had his examination before Judge Rodden, and he was held over for the grand jury with bail set at $3,000. It was thought Colwell would plead guilty, but he surprised everyone when he hired an attorney and they started to build a defense of insanity through the prisoner's bizarre behavior. Colwell was tried in early February 1899 but his "insanity dodge" failed, and the case went to the jury at 8:00 p.m. on February 10. After only a few hours in deliberations Colwell was found guilty. He appeared before Judge Angellotti on Monday, February 13, for sentencing and the convicted robber heard a summary of the case and evidence against him before the judge sentenced him to serve seven years in prison. Twenty-nine-year-old Colwell arrived at San Quentin on February 21, 1899, and registered as prisoner #18088; he was discharged on November 16, 1903, after serving four years nine months.

Sources: *Sacramento Daily Union (CA)*: September 20, 1899. *San Francisco Call (CA)*: January 26, 1899; February 10–11, 1899; February 13, 1899. *Sausalito News (CA)*: February 25, 1899.

Mariposa County

CHARLES "ORMSTEAD" THURMAN, CHARLIE "STIFFY" BOYLE AND THOMAS R. BRAZIER, MAY 30, 1864

Charles Thurman—alias Charles Thompson, Bill Early, and Ormstead Thurman—had served several terms in San Quentin Prison before 1860: he arrived at the prison on March 7, 1855, to serve a four-year term for grand larceny but escaped on September 4, 1856. He was soon convicted of grand larceny again and arrived at the prison on January 12, 1858, for a two-year term but escaped on July 3, 1859. He was captured two months later, returned to prison, and was released upon expiration of sentence on February 26, 1860. He returned to prison on September 22, 1861, on another grand larceny conviction but was involved in a mass breakout on July 22, 1862, but he was immediately captured and returned to the prison and was released on November 16, 1863. Thurman went to Mariposa County where he lived in the cabin of ex-convict Charlie "Stiffy" Boyle, and they decided to rob the Coulterville stagecoach. Late on the night of May 29, 1864, the two road agents, masked and armed—Boyle with a pistol and Thurman with a shotgun—took up their positions by the side of the road, and at 1:00 a.m. when the stagecoach was still fifty yards away both men commanded the driver to halt and brandished their weapons.

Thurman covered the driver and the passenger riding atop while Boyle demanded that the driver order out the passengers. The driver said they were all Chinese who did not speak English, but somehow he managed to convince the three Chinamen to come out. Boyle ordered the passenger atop, an American, to come down, and he took $500 and a pistol from him, but returned $50 when he whined that it was all he had. Then he took $500 from the Chinese passengers. Boyle next told the driver to hand down the Wells, Fargo express box, and he busted it open and took out $1,500 in gold dust and $150 in coin. Boyle ordered everyone to board, and once everyone was seated he told the driver to continue on. The two robbers returned to their cabin, split the money, and Boyle gave the stolen pistol to Thurman since he had one of his own. Over the next two weeks the pair committed a number of robberies but left stagecoaches alone, and then they split up. Thurman went to Sonora using the alias Bill Early, and he gambled away a large sum in gold dust and coin, which raised suspicions he might be one of the road agents. He was lodged in jail and the lawmen found that his revolver was inscribed with the name of the stagecoach passenger. Thurman quickly confessed and "peached," or informed, on Boyle, and to fend off a possible lynching he implicated Thomas R. Brazier, and the naming of a second confederate seemed to satisfy the mob. Thurman related that they had been closely watching for treasure being shipped from the McAlpin vein and thought it was aboard the stagecoach that left Coulterville on May 29. However, the box was light so after they finished at the stagecoach they headed toward Chinese Camp expecting to intercept the mine's owner with the treasure, but they missed their chance and only managed to stop a guard returning to Coulterville. They tied him to a tree and took $20, and the guard might have died there if a Chinese man had not come by and cut the ropes, thus avoiding a murder charge. Boyle and Brazier soon joined Thurman in jail and on Monday the three prisoners were loaded into a wagon and started for the city of Mariposa for trial, but Thurman managed to escape. While Thurman was free, Boyle and Brazier were tried and convicted and Boyle was sentenced to serve ten years while Brazier was sentenced to serve five years. Boyle and Brazier arrived at San Quentin Prison on August 3, 1864, and Boyle registered as prisoner #2816 while Brazier registered as prisoner #2817. Brazier was released on October 19, 1868, after serving four years two and one half months. Boyle was released on October 14, 1872, after serving eight years two and one half months.

Thurman was arrested at Placerville in January 1865 and he was returned to Mariposa County, tried, convicted of robbery, and sentenced to serve ten years in San Quentin Prison, and on April 8, 1865, he registered as prisoner #2994. During this prison term Thurman and several other prisoners began planning an escape, but it was discovered and foiled. Thurman was certain that fellow prisoner Frederick Engles had informed on them and on May 20, 1865, he murdered Engles in the prison yard, but all the witnesses to the crime were convicts, who, at that time, were prohibited under law to testify in the courts and so he escaped punishment. Thurman was discharged by expiration of sentence on June 9, 1873, and he wasted no time planning another stagecoach robbery, this time in Yuba County. (See Nevada County on July 27, 1873.)

Unknown, August 13, 1883

At 11:00 p.m. on Monday, August 13, 1883, the stagecoach from Wawona to Yosemite, driven by Ernest Stevens, was near Inspiration Point when three masked road agents stepped out onto the road and pointed their six-shooters at the driver. After he reined in his team they unhitched the horses and, with several shots in the air, drove them off a good distance. Once the coach was stranded they ordered the passengers out and had them form a line along the side of the road, then one robber searched the four men and took $900 and some jewelry, but they did not molest the three women passengers nor the driver. They did not ask for the Wells, Fargo express box, perhaps knowing there was none aboard, nor did they ask about the mail. Once the robbers had collected all the plunder they expected to find, they just walked off into the heavy brush. The driver and male passenger then rounded up the horses, which took considerable time and gave the robbers ample time to travel some distance, hitched the team and continued into Yosemite. Posses were organized at Big Trees and at Mariposa, but neither could find any clues to the robbers' identities nor cut a trail. Wells, Fargo would not post a reward as it had no box aboard, and neither did the state or the stage line so the chase was abandoned.

Source: *Los Angeles Herald (CA)*: August 15, 1883.

CHARLES MEYERS AND WILLIAM "WILLIE" PRESCOTT, MAY 22, 1885

On Friday morning, May 22, 1885, a stagecoach left Madera for Yosemite in Mariposa County with ten passengers aboard. Late that morning the coach was ten miles west of Clark's station, a heavily wooded area that affords the perfect location for highwaymen, when two masked road agents with their clothes turned inside out stepped out from behind large trees on each side of the road. One road agent pointed his double-barreled shotgun at the driver while the other pointed the muzzle of his weapon at the passengers, and the man with the shotgun ordered the driver to halt. While one road agent stood back covering all with his shotgun, the other climbed up onto the seat and took down the Wells, Fargo express box, then ordered the passengers to step out, form a line, and he went through them for money and jewelry, including the earrings from the lady passengers. As soon as he had all the plunder he could find he called the driver by name and told him to whip up his team. As the stagecoach pulled out the two robbers, carrying the treasure box, fled into the heavy timber. When the passengers began to account for their losses they determined that the robbers had gotten $1,300 in currency, in addition to the value of the jewelry, but the Wells, Fargo box on that run carried little money and nothing else of value. As soon as the robbery was reported a reward of $1,200 was posted for the capture of the road agents, and four sheriffs organized posses and began combing the countryside for tracks or clues. The robbery took place in the loneliest part of the country and any "stragglers would be noticed immediately and carefully scrutinized."

Within a week Charles Meyers and a man named William "Willie" Prescott had been arrested and charged with the robbery, and though the plunder had not been found, officers believed they had hard evidence these were the right men. They took their prisoners to Fresno Flats for an examination and on May 29 they were held over for trial with bail set at $20,000 each, and the prisoners were then taken to Fresno and lodged in jail. On June 23 the two men were taken into a Fresno court for an examination and were held over for action by the grand jury with bail reduced to $5,000 each. Their trial began on September 1, but strange happenings, such as one juror going insane during the trial, delayed the closing arguments so the case did not go to the jurors until September 23. The jury deliberated for ten hours before finding both men guilty, and on November 2 they were each sentenced to serve twenty years at San Quentin Prison. However, neither man appears in the records at San Quentin.

Sources: *Sacramento Daily Union (CA)*: May 25, 1885; June 24, 1885; September 24, 1885; November 3, 1885.

UNKNOWN, DECEMBER 3, 1885

During the early morning hours of Thursday, December 3, 1885, the stagecoach from Coulterville to Merced was stopped in Pleasant Valley by two road agents. They took the Wells, Fargo express box, but it contained little, and they took the mail. There seemed to be no evidence, but over the months that followed the investigation focused on Douglas Lawson and John H. Martin, and finally in November 1887 they were brought to trial. The case was based upon weak circumstantial evidence and on November 5, 1887, Lawson was acquitted, and the case against Martin, based upon even less evidence, was dismissed by Judge Hoffman.

Sources: *Daily Alta California (San Francisco)*: November 4–5, 1887. *Sacramento Daily Union (CA)*: December 7, 1885.

LEE SYKES, JULY 2, 1888

On Monday, July 2, 1888, the stagecoach from Madera to Hildreth was one mile from its destination when a lone road agent suddenly jumped out from behind a rock. He pointed his shotgun at driver Tom Blocker and Wells, Fargo messenger J. R. Nicholson and ordered the latter to throw his gun out of the wagon. Once the messenger was unarmed the road agent threw a wrench to the driver and ordered him to "unscrew the treasure box" bolted to the floor of the coach, and this was done. The box, containing $10,000 in silver bullion, was thrown out, and then the road agent ordered Blocker to turn his wagon around and not return to Hildreth, the closest place to report the robbery. Blocker, Nicholson and passenger Arthur Mitchell said they could see two accomplices partially concealed behind the rocks, but they wore masks, so they could not describe their faces. As soon as the robbery was reported, Constable Hensley and stage line owner Matt Madill started in pursuit of the robbers, but they did not capture them. On July 23 a man entered the Wells, Fargo office with a saddle and valise to be sent to Hildreth. Agent Alonzo Coons recognized him as the road agent, and he found Sheriff Dallas McCord and Constable Tibbitts and they captured the man at the livery stable. Only then did they realize for sure they had a murderer in custody—Lee Sykes. (See Shasta County for October 21, 1887.)

The robber had apparently hid $8,000 of the bullion, perhaps because of its great weight or difficulty in converting it, and in early 1889 a Negro named Stewart found the bullion but would not turn it over to Wells, Fargo. On June 2 Wells, Fargo filed a suit to recover the treasure or its value from Stewart.

Sources: *Sacramento Daily Record-Union (CA)*: July 4, 1888. *Territorial Enterprise (Virginia City, NV)*: July 4, 1888; June 2, 1889.

UNKNOWN, OCTOBER 24, 1888

At 9:00 a.m. on Wednesday, October 24, 1888, the southwest-bound stagecoach from Coulterville to Merced was nine miles out from Coulterville when a lone road agent, standing 150 yards in advance of the coach, hailed the driver and ordered him to stop. The road agent pointed his rifle, and when driver Andy Reed did not slow, a single shot was fired. The .45 caliber bullet passed between Reed's knees; passed through the dashboard, a valise, and a mail pouch; and lodged in the Wells, Fargo treasure box. Reed reined in his team, and then the road agent, masked and completely disguised in a suit of gunnysacks, ordered him and his only passenger—J. S. Carter who was superintendent of the Red Cloud mine—to step down. He made Carter turn his pockets inside out and took his $39, then made the stagecoach driver bust open the treasure box, but it was empty. He did not molest the mails. The robber then ordered Carter to board and Reed to drive on, while he walked off into the brush and disappeared from view. Reed continued to the next station and reported the robbery, but lawmen could find no clue to the robber's identity nor a trail to follow. The description, due to his disguise, provided no leads.

Sources: *Daily Alta California (San Francisco)*: October 25, 1888. *Los Angeles Herald (CA)*: October 25, 1888. *Sacramento Daily Union (CA)*: October 25, 1888.

FRANK WILLIAMS, DECEMBER 2, 1889

Four days after robbing the stagecoach from Shasta to Redding, the same road agent appeared in Mariposa County, and on Monday December 2, 1889, the Merced to Mariposa stagecoach was six miles above Hornitos going up the Bear Mountain grade when a masked road agent dressed in blue overalls, a brown jumper, with a white handkerchief for a mask called out, "Hold up there!" He presented a .45 caliber six-shooter and asked the driver if he had any arms, and when told no, the robber asked if he had a hatchet. When the driver said he had a hatchet he was told to throw it out with the express box. Once the box was on the road, the robber broke it open and removed the contents. He next asked for the mail, cut open the bags, and took out the registered packages, but he was not satisfied so he looked inside the empty passenger compartment and found a small safe, and he busted that open. At that moment they heard a team coming down the grade, so the robber climbed up on the seat and told the driver to proceed and stop when he reached the wagon, but the driver did not stop as told and the robber pointed his pistol at the driver's head and said, "When I tell you again to stop, do as you are told." Blackmore, who was driving the oncoming express wagon, realized the situation and abandoned his wagon to run a half mile to his house to get his gun. Meanwhile the second man riding on the wagon was captured and an express box was taken from the bed and broken open, and then the road agent ordered each man to proceed in the direction they had been traveling. As soon as the wagon reached a telegraph, the sheriff and deputies of Tulare County were notified, and they started from Merced for the scene of the robbery. They found the robber's overalls and jumper discarded near the scene of the robbery, and they collected the broken boxes and mail pouches along with the contents left behind and took them into Merced. However, they could find no clue to the road agent's identity nor a clear trail to follow. (See Nevada County for December 15, 1889.)

WILLIAM FREDERICKS, MAY 15, 1890

Early Thursday morning, May 15, 1890, the stagecoach from Merced to Mariposa, with Fernando Bevano driving and one female passenger aboard, was nearing its destination when a lone road agent stepped into the road and halted the coach. He demanded the express and the packages be thrown down, and then he had passenger Miss Farnsworth step out and took from her $.40. He told Miss Farnsworth to board and then ordered Bevano to move along, and the driver whipped up his team and hurried into Mariposa. He reported the crime and a posse was organized, and at 5:15 a.m. they left town for the scene, The posse found the express packages torn open and rifled, but nothing had been taken as there was nothing of value being shipped. Posse man James Scofield found a trail and followed it to a sheep cabin eight miles from town, and he arrested eighteen-year-old William Fredericks, a German, without resistance. Scofield took his prisoner into town and lodged him in jail, where he was positively identified as the road agent by Miss Farnsworth and Bevano. On May 24 Fredericks was taken before Justice Temple and held over for the grand jury, but the district attorney filed a bench warrant based upon an information and took the prisoner before Judge Corcoran, where he pled guilty. The judge then, because of the defendant's youthfulness and apparent lack of criminal experience, only sentenced him to serve four years at Folsom. Judge Corcoran lectured Fredericks at length, and the defendant broke down and wept during the presentation and sentencing. Fredericks arrived at Folsom on May 26, 1890, and registered as prisoner #2221. He was "restored May 26, 1893," after serving three years.

Sources: *Daily Alta California (San Francisco)*: May 16, 1890. *Los Angeles Herald (CA)*: May 17, 1890. *Sacramento Daily Union (CA)*: May 17, 1890. *San Francisco Call (CA)*: May 16, 1890; May 25, 1890.

Unknown, October 7, 1895

At 6:30 a.m. on Monday, October 7, 1895, the stagecoach from Merced to Mariposa, with John Smith driving, was three miles from its destination when two road agents, covered from head to foot, stopped the coach and commanded, "Throw out that box." One robber pointed a pistol and the other held a rifle. Smith told them, "The box is empty and will do you no good," and to prove his point he lifted the lid and let them examine the interior. The two robbers stepped away from the coach and had a whispered conversation, then returned and demanded what money Smith had, and he gave them $5. Once they had the money they told Smith to drive on and "don't look back or you will be shot." Smith hurried into Mariposa and reported the robbery, and he said he was certain that neither man had been involved in the Coulterville stagecoach robbery a week earlier.

Source: *San Francisco Call (CA)*: October 8, 1895.

Mendocino County

Charles E. "Black Bart" Bolton, October 2, 1878; October 3, 1878; January 26, 1882; June 14, 1882

On Wednesday morning, October 2, 1878, Alexander Fowler was driving his stagecoach from Arcata in Humboldt County to Ukiah in Mendocino County, and when ten miles from its destination, he was stopped by one man disguised in sacks and wrappings. Charles E. "Black Bart" Bolton held a double-barreled shotgun on the driver as he took a position in front of the leaders, using them as a shield. The robber ordered Fowler to throw down the mail sacks and Wells, Fargo express box, which contained only $40 in coin and a gold watch. Fowler threw out the box and one mailbag, but the robber told him he knew something of the mail going over the road and said, "throw out the other bags." Once he had the box and mailbags, the polite road agent ordered Fowler to move along. Mendocino County sheriff James R. Moore organized a posse and went to the scene, but there were no clues to the robber's identity.

Sixteen hours after robbing the stagecoach near Ukiah, the stagecoach from Covelo to Ukiah, in Mendocino County, driven by Nathan Waltrip, was robbed near Centerville on October 3, 1878, only twenty miles from the robbery the previous day, and from the details reported it was clearly Bolton again. Waltrip tried to lure the road agent closer and lifted the box to the wheel, then told Bolton to come get it, but the driver was told again to throw it down, and Waltrip obeyed. Bolton then called for the mail and it was thrown down next to the box, and Waltrip was told to drive on. Bolton got more than $400 on this outing. After this eighth robbery Wells, Fargo increased their reward to $300 and the post office added another $200, bringing this sum with the state's $300 to a total reward of $800 for the capture of "Black Bart."

After two copycat robberies in Yuba County on December 15 and December 27, 1881, the real Black Bart reappeared on the afternoon of January 26, 1882, in Mendocino County, and he stopped the stagecoach coming from Ukiah to Cloverdale. Bolton stepped into the road in front of the horses only a mile from the toll station operated by J. A. Lance, reportedly wielding a rifle instead of his usual shotgun, but he was masked and dressed in his customary attire and he politely requested the Wells, Fargo express boxes and mail sacks. Driver Harry Forse delivered two boxes and the mails before he hurried to the station. He organized a small posse and returned to the scene, but when they arrived they found only the two boxes broken open, the contents removed, and the mail sacks slashed with a distinctive "T." The posse followed a clear trail for some distance before darkness ended the pursuit, and the following day they lost the trail. Two larger posses were organized but could not capture the road agent. Wells, Fargo reported that the box held only $300, but by then they were inclined to underreport their losses, and there was probably a substantial sum found among the mails.

Bolton took a four-and-a-half month hiatus and then, on June 14, 1882, he stopped the stagecoach traveling from Little Lake, near Willits, to Ukiah in Mendocino County when the coach was three miles from the former place. Bolton, as was his practice, stepped into the road in front of the horses and pointed his shotgun at driver Thomas Forse. When the polite request came to "please, throw down that box," Forse replied that he couldn't because the iron box was bolted down. Bolton had Forse dismount, searched him for weapons, then had him unhitch the team and take the horses a distance down the road. The road agent had brought the correct tools and within an hour he had emptied the iron box and fled. A posse went to the scene, found a trail of foot tracks and followed for some distance, but they eventually lost the trail and returned to town empty-handed. (See Calaveras County on November 3, 1883.)

THOMAS PAUL, OCTOBER 11, 1879

At noon on Saturday, October 11, 1879, the stagecoach bound for Eureka from Ukiah, by way of Little Lake, had only traveled three and one half miles and was near Cal's English in Mendocino County when a road agent called out to driver Thomas Forse, "Hand out that box, quick!" Forse was startled and unsure he had heard correctly, so he asked, "What did you say?" The masked road agent then repeated his demand from concealment and emphasized the urgency by brandishing the twin barrels of his shotgun so Forse could see them. The box was thrown out, and the road agent next commanded, "Drive on seven miles before you stop to speak to anyone." Forse drove on and shortly came to a group traveling in the opposite direction, and he warned them of the road agent ahead, but they continued anyway and when they came to the scene of the robbery they were not molested.

Forse hurried on to the next stagecoach station and reported the robbery to Wells, Fargo's Agent Wheeler and Sheriff James R. Moore. Wheeler and Moore organized a small posse and went to the scene but could find no trace nor a clue to the identity of the lone robber, described only as a masked man heavily armed and of average size. On Sunday the posse discovered the broken treasure box and papers scattered about a bush not far from the scene, and the box, which had contained $942 in gold and silver coins, was now empty. They also found the leg from some knit drawers with eyeholes cut in it, which had served as the robber's mask. Wells, Fargo posted a reward of $600 for the arrest and conviction of the road agent and dispatched detective James B. Hume to Ukiah to investigate. There were other outlaws active in the area and they had murdered two men, and Hume was able, from their descriptions, to identify them as ex-convicts well known to him and recently released from San Quentin Prison.

However, Hume was not concerned with that case and concentrated his efforts on the stagecoach robbery case, and soon he had identified his man as Thomas Paul. Hume circulated Paul's description and in January 1880 the highwayman was captured by Oregon lawmen, and Governor George C. Perkins issued a requisition. The arresting officers were en route from Oregon to Mendocino County when Paul managed to escape and remain free for three days before being recaptured on February 2. Hume, unwilling to take any more chances of an escape, went to Oregon to bring back Paul, and they arrived at Ukiah on Thursday, February 12, where the prisoner was lodged in jail. Paul hired, as his defense counsel for his examination, J. T. Rogers, but the evidence was sufficient to be held over for action by the grand jury. The case did not seem particularly strong against Paul until late February when a man came forward and surrendered property to the authorities which had been stolen during the robbery, and he stated he had received it from Paul. In April, Paul was indicted, and when brought into court he pled guilty, hoping for a lighter sentence; his strategy worked, as he received a sentence of only five years. Paul arrived at San Quentin Prison on May 1, 1880, where he registered as prisoner #9256. He was transferred to Folsom Prison on July 26, 1880, where he registered as prisoner #37. Folsom was not a secure facility and in late November 1882 Paul managed to escape and remain free for several weeks. Freedom as a fugitive did not suit Paul, so he turned himself in to a county officer and asked to be returned to prison. An application was then filed for a pardon and the accompanying letter, dated December 20, 1882, mentioned that he had voluntarily surrendered to authorities to complete his term. This swayed the state executive and Paul was pardoned by Governor George C. Perkins on January 8, 1883, after serving only two years eight months.

Sources: *Daily Humboldt Times (CA)*: October 21, 1879. *Mendocino Democrat (CA)*: February 14, 1880; February 21, 1880. *Mendocino Weekly Dispatch (CA)*: October 18, 1879; February 13, 1880; March 1, 1880; April 30, 1880. *Ukiah City Press (CA)*: October 17, 1879.

Unknown, June 10, 1881

At 6:30 p.m. on Friday, June 10, 1881, the Eureka stagecoach was three and one half miles above Ukiah, with Jack Morrison driving. He heard someone say, "Hold on!" and turned his head to see a masked man holding a shotgun on the side of the road. Morrison whipped up his team and after the coach passed the road agent the man fired both barrels of his shotgun, but without causing any damage or injury. Morrison drove at a rapid gait into Ukiah where he reported the robbery attempt, and a posse was immediately organized. The posse rode to the scene and found the flour sack with eyeholes cut in it used for the mask, and two barley sacks which had been used to muffle up the robber's boots. They followed the foot tracks to the place the robber had tied his horse, and then followed the trail into town. They had their suspicions and believed they had a clue, but they could not make a case so no one was arrested.

Source: *Sacramento Daily Union (CA)*: June 13, 1881.

Unknown, May 5, 1884

At 12:30 p.m. on Monday, May 5, 1884, the northbound stagecoach left Cloverdale for Ukiah. The coach had traveled only five miles, three miles inside Mendocino County, when two men masked in flannel appeared with double-barreled shotguns and ordered the driver to stop, and he reined in his team. They next called for the mail and express box, and four sacks of regular mail and one sack of registered mail were thrown down, and this was followed by the Wells, Fargo express box. One robber broke open the box and was going through the mail when a wagon approached with several men aboard, so he took a moment to join his partner and they waved on the late arrivals with their shotguns. The robber who had been searching for valuables returned to his work while the other continued to cover the driver and passengers with his shotgun. Once they had all the plunder they returned the sacks and broken box to the coach and, without molesting the passengers, told the driver to continue on his route. The driver whipped up his team and hurried to the next station from which he could notify Cloverdale, and soon a posse was organized and on their way to the scene. However, the robbers had left no clues to their identities nor a good trail to follow, so no one was arrested for the robbery.

Sources: *Daily Alta California (San Francisco)*: May 6, 1884. *Los Angeles Herald (CA)*: May 6, 1884. *Territorial Enterprise (Virginia City Nevada)*: May 6, 1884.

WILLIAM CORBETT AND JOHN DWYER, OCTOBER 9, 1884

On October 9, 1884, at 3:00 a.m. the stagecoach from Cloverdale and Anderson Valley to Mendocino City, when three miles from Booneville in Mendocino County, was stopped by two masked, heavily armed road agents. They demanded and received the Wells, Fargo express treasure box and the local mailbag. After the box and mailbag were delivered, the robbers told the driver to continue on, and the box was reported to contain $3,664. The amount taken from the mails was not known, but being only the local mail, it was almost certainly an insignificant sum. The driver hurried into Anderson and reported the robbery. The citizens of Anderson, knowing the sheriff was away electioneering, organized a posse consisting of John Burger, E. K. Jones, Charles Rector, John Ingram, Nute Ornbaum, and Hugh Hereford and they went to the scene of the robbery. They were soon on the trail of the robbers and captured them, and they identified themselves as nineteen-year-old William Corbett of San Francisco and twenty-two-year-old John Dwyer of Missouri. They were captured so soon after the robbery they still had all the plunder with them, and it was recovered to the cent.

At first it was thought that parties from Anderson had lynched the two road agents, but they soon arrived at Ukiah and the prisoners were lodged in jail. By the first week of November the two road agents had been examined, indicted, tried and convicted of the stagecoach robbery. On November 8, the night before they were to depart for the prison to begin their five year terms, they escaped from the jail. Undersheriff Seawell had no notion that the boys were planning or preparing for an escape when he went to supper, but when he returned he noticed that the iron shutter over the barred window of the jail was ajar. On examination he found that the bars had been sawed through and the lock for the shutter had been pried off with one of those iron bars. He checked the prisoner population and found all present excepting the two convicted road agents, and the other prisoners feigned ignorance of the entire affair.

Sheriff J. M. Standley formed a posse and they traced the men to the Seven-Mile House, but the escapees had continued on and were next heard of east of Cloverdale. The men were finally cornered and captured in Napa County on November 13 and jailed there to await transfer to San Quentin. Mendocino officers took their prisoners directly from the Napa County jail to the prison on November 14, 1884. Corbett registered as prisoner #11449 and Dwyer as prisoner #11450. Dwyer had his sentence commuted and he was released on January 6, 1887, while Corbett was released, by expiration of sentence, on June 14, 1888.

Sources: *Territorial Enterprise (Virginia City, NV)*: October 10–11, 1884; October 16, 1884. *Ukiah City Press (CA)*: November 14, 1884; October 17, 1884.

UNKNOWN, DECEMBER 4, 1884

On Thursday, December 4, 1884, the westbound stagecoach from Lakeport to Ukiah was halted and robbed by a lone highwayman after it had passed over the border into Mendocino County. The robber demanded the Wells, Fargo express box and broke it open, but only found $1.50 inside. He then returned the box to the coach and told the driver to continue on his route. The driver hurried into the next station and reported the robbery, and soon the sheriff was on the robber's trail. The sheriff followed the robber's trail for four days, and on December 8 he found the fugitive asleep by a small campfire near Hermitage. He arrested the road agent, who immediately began showing signs of insanity, and took his prisoner to Ukiah for his hearing. There is no record of a prosecution.

Source: *Territorial Enterprise (Virginia City, NV)*: December 11, 1884.

Unknown, January 24, 1885

At daybreak on Saturday, January 24, 1885, the stagecoach from Ukiah to Little Lake was near Willits when it was halted by a lone highwayman, masked and armed. He demanded the Wells, Fargo express box and it was thrown down, and then he told the driver to move on. After the coach had driven out of sight the robber broke open the box and found it was empty. There was no reward posted, but lawmen rode to the scene, determined there were no clues to the robber's identity, and returned to town with the busted box.

Source: *Sacramento Daily Union (CA)*: January 26, 1885.

Charles Baker and Charles Manning, January 5, 1886

In late 1885 Charles Baker, alias Charles or H. W. Hanlon, found a willing partner in Charles Manning. Baker, using his alias H. W. Hanlon, decided to stop both the up and down coaches on the route between Cloverdale and Mendocino City, and Baker chose for their location the point in Anderson Valley in Mendocino County where the two coaches passed. On January 5, 1886, they positioned themselves in the brush along the roadway, within two miles of one another. They were approximately the same size and dressed similarly. When the southbound coach arrived at 10:30 p.m. one of the road agents stepped out and, covering the driver with his gun, demanded the treasure box. As soon as it was delivered the driver was ordered to move along. The southbound coach came abreast of the northbound coach in less than a mile and the northbound driver reported that he had been robbed. The southbound driver then said he, too, had been robbed, and the manner was so similar that it was at first believed to be the same man. The two road agents fled, buried their plunder, and tried to remain inconspicuous for nearly two months.

Sheriff J. M. Standley listened intently to the reports of the two drivers and concluded that the work had to be done by two men, as the two coaches had been stopped almost simultaneously some distance apart. There were no clues at the scene, so he sent out descriptions of the road agents as provided by the drivers and passengers, and in late February he received word that two men matching the description were on the stagecoach from Cloverdale to Anderson Valley. He went out after his quarry and captured Baker, still using his alias, and Manning soon after they had dug up their plunder. He lodged them in the jail at Ukiah and returned the treasure to Wells, Fargo.

There was some delay in getting the prisoners to trial, but in April 1889 they were both convicted of the robbery and sentenced to serve seventeen years in San Quentin Prison. Baker, still using the alias Hanlon, registered as prisoner #13524, and Manning registered as prisoner #13523. They both arrived at San Quentin Prison on April 11, 1889. Manning wanted to escape and he arranged to have guns hidden near a work site outside the prison walls, and the two road agents and one other convict made their move. Their attempt was immediately met with gunfire from rifles and then from the prison's Gatling gun, but they managed to flee three miles before being cornered. The fight went on for hours before the convicts, after being assured they had not killed anyone, surrendered. Baker was involved in another escape attempt in 1891, but it was also foiled. He caused no more trouble and was released on November 11, 1899. Baker did not appear on California's criminal rolls again. Manning was released on the same day as Hanlon, each serving ten years of their sentences, and he also disappeared from the criminal rolls of California.

Sources: *Mendocino Beacon (CA)*: January 12, 1889; March 2, 1889; April 13, 1889. *Mendocino Dispatch Democrat (CA)*: August 15, 1890. *San Francisco Examiner (CA)*: September 6–7, 1891; September 10, 1891; September 26–27, 1891. *San Francisco Chronicle (CA)*: August 12–13, 1890; August 26, 1891; August 28, 1891.

JOHN MARTIN, JANUARY 26, 1886

On Tuesday, January 26, 1886, Sheriff J. M. Standley of Mendocino County was delivering three prisoners to the prison at San Quentin by stagecoach. The stagecoach from Cloverdale in Sonoma County to Ukiah was ordered to stop by a lone road agent dressed in disguised clothing with a false beard and a slouch hat. He waved his shotgun but the sheriff ordered the driver to drive on, and as the coach passed the road agent the sheriff was trying to draw his pistol when he saw, for a moment, the robber pointing the shotgun at him, but he did not fire. After the coach passed, the robber fired at the driver but missed, and the coach was driven out of danger. Sheriff Standley immediately notified his deputies and they organized a manhunt for the road agent, and Standley described him as five feet eight inches high with a gray beard, an old white slouch hat and blue-lined overalls. The sheriff believed he fled toward Lake County.

The day following the attempted robbery a posse led by Peter Shelford and consisting of Y. Allen, Sam Allen, William Frazier, and H. Groshong found the robber, and before he could draw his arms Shelford pointed his rifle at his head and he had to surrender or die. They took from him the shotgun, a bulldog revolver, and a large butcher knife, and found all his distinctive clothing used as a disguise, except for the hat and false beard which he said he threw away. He said he was John Martin, a sailor, and he confessed to the robbery. He insisted that he did not intend to shoot anyone but could not explain why he had shot at the driver after he passed him by. The posse loaded their prisoner into a spring wagon and took him into Cloverdale on January 27, but he was scheduled to be transferred to Ukiah the following day where he would have his examination. In early February the prisoner pled guilty on a charge of "assault to rob," and he was sentenced to serve seven years at San Quentin Prison. Twenty-nine-year-old Martin arrived at the prison on February 14, 1886, and registered as prisoner #12026. He was discharged on November 14, 1890, after serving four years eight months.

Source: *Daily Alta California (San Francisco)*: January 27–28, 1886.

GEORGE THOMAS, SEPTEMBER 6, 1886

On Monday, September 6, 1886, the northbound stagecoach from Cloverdale to Ukiah was halted when four miles from Cloverdale, two miles past the Mendocino county line. A lone highwayman, masked and armed, pointed his weapon at the driver and ordered him to rein in his team, and once the coach was stopped he demanded the Wells, Fargo express box. It was thrown down and the road agent then told the driver to move on. After the coach was out of sight he broke open the box but found little of value inside. He left the broken box by the side of the road and in his haste to flee left behind his gun as he started south for Healdsburg. A posse from Cloverdale consisting of Mr. Dow, William Frazier, Peter Shelford, and Hiram Groshong hurried to the scene and found a clear trail to follow. They tracked their man to Healdsburg, and the following morning they arrested George Thomas. He confessed to the robbery and was turned over to Mendocino County sheriff J. M. Standley to be taken to Ukiah for trial. On September 11, Thomas had his preliminary examination and he pled guilty, and he was sentenced to serve eight years at Folsom Prison. Thomas arrived at the prison on September 13, 1886, and registered as prisoner #1381. He was discharged on January 13, 1892, after serving five years and four months.

Sources: *Daily Alta California (San Francisco)*: September 8, 1886; September 12, 1886. *Territorial Enterprise (Virginia City, NV)*: September 9, 1886.

Unknown, April 19, 1887

On Tuesday, April 19, 1887, the stagecoach from Ukiah to Cloverdale was two miles from Hopland and approaching a well-known redwood tree when a road agent stepped out from behind the tree with a Winchester rifle in his hands. The robber, wearing a barley sack with eyeholes for a mask and barley sacks on his hands and boots, ordered the driver to halt. Once the coach had come to a standstill he ordered the driver to pass down the Wells, Fargo express box, and as soon as it was in the road he told the driver to move along. He did not ask about passengers nor for the mail sacks. After the coach was gone he broke open the box and took out $30, all that was inside. As soon as the driver reached Cloverdale he reported the robbery and William Frazier, Peter Shelford, and William Forsythe rode to the scene, taking along a bloodhound. Even with the well-trained dog they were unable to follow a trail for any distance and returned to town empty-handed.

Source: *Daily Alta California (San Francisco)*: April 21, 1887.

Unknown, November 20, 1888

At 3:00 p.m. on Tuesday, November 20, 1888, the southbound stagecoach, with no passengers aboard, was between Eureka and Ukiah, just nineteen miles from its destination, when a masked highwayman stepped into the road. The road agent pointed his weapon at the driver and ordered him to halt, and the driver reined in his team. The road agent then demanded the Wells, Fargo express box and the mail pouches, and as soon as they were thrown down he told the driver to move on. Wells, Fargo would not comment on anything of value in their express box, but it was thought to be a small amount or nothing as there was no messenger aboard, and no one would place a value on what might have been in the mails. Lawmen could find no clue to the identity of the robber and no trail to follow, so no one was charged for this robbery.

Sources: *Sacramento Daily Union (CA)*: November 22, 1888. *Territorial Enterprise (Virginia City, NV)*: November 23, 1888.

Unknown, December 4, 1888

At 6:00 p.m. on Tuesday, December 4, 1888, the stagecoach from Mendocino City to Ingram, the terminus of the North Pacific Railroad, was six miles north of Ingram when a lone road agent, masked and heavily armed, stepped out and halted the coach. He demanded the Wells, Fargo express box and mail, and the box and three mail sacks were thrown down. The robber immediately told the driver to move along. After the coach had driven out of sight he busted open the box and took out $100, but the value of the mail was not known. A posse from Ingram rode to the scene and found the busted box, but found nothing else that would lead to the robber.

Sources: *Los Angeles Herald (CA)*: December 6, 1888. *Sausalito News (CA)*: December 7, 1888.

Unknown, September 5, 1889

At 1:20 p.m. on Thursday, September 5, 1889, the northbound stagecoach left Ukiah for Cahto, and when it was five miles north of Ukiah it was halted by a lone road agent. The robber was masked and armed, and he pointed his gun at the driver's head and ordered him to throw down the Wells, Fargo express box and the mail. The driver threw out the box and one pouch of mail, which was all he had aboard, and then he was told to continue on. The robber took the box and mail, busted open the box and took out an estimated $1,000, but the value of the mail was not known. On September 6 a man resembling the road agent was arrested and taken from Cloverdale into Ukiah, but he had only $15 in his pockets. He claimed he had been picking hops in the area but did not know the name of his employer. The matter was investigated and his alibi proved out, so on November 10 he was released. There had been no clues at the scene of the robbery, nor a clear trail to follow, so lawmen gave up the chase and no one was charged in the robbery.

Sources: *Daily Alta California (San Francisco)*: September 7, 1889. *Los Angeles Herald (CA)*: September 11, 1889. *Territorial Enterprise (Virginia City, NV)*: September 8, 1889.

UNKNOWN, JUNE 6, 1890

At 2:30 a.m. on Friday, June 6, 1890, the northbound stagecoach from Ukiah had only traveled three miles when one masked and heavily armed road agent stepped into the road and ordered the driver to halt. Once the coach was stopped the robber demanded that the Wells, Fargo express box be thrown down, and as soon as it was lying in the road he told the driver to move along. After the coach was out of sight the robber busted open the box and took out $1,600. The robbery was reported from the next station with a telegraph, and a posse was organized and rode to the scene but all they could find was the busted box.

Source: *San Francisco Call (CA)*: June 7, 1890.

GEORGE W. CUMMINGS, OCTOBER 12, 1890

On Sunday night, October 12, 1890, the Overland stagecoach was eighteen miles north of Ukiah, at "Robber's Ridge" six miles south of Willits in Mendocino County, when a young man, masked and armed with a pistol, stepped from behind a tree and ordered driver Lew M. Daniels to halt. Daniels reined in his team and upon command he threw down two express boxes and several mail pouches. The robber immediately went to work opening the boxes and cutting open the mail sacks, and while he was preoccupied Daniels drew his pistol, pointed it at the robber and pulled the trigger, but it only snapped. The robber fired at Daniels twice but missed, and the shots frightened the team and they took off at a run, leaving the robber to ransack the boxes and pouches. After the coach was gone the robber gathered $80 in gold from registered packages and $10.90 from one express box, and as soon as he had the money he started afoot for Cloverdale, sixty miles distant.

By the following afternoon the road agent had been tracked by Sheriff J. M Standley, who arrested twenty-one-year-old George W. Cummings just as he was about to leave for San Francisco, and once behind bars the prisoner confessed to the robbery. Deputy T. J. Welden then took the prisoner to Ukiah and lodged him in jail, and on October 15 Cummings was turned over to the U.S. marshal. His room at 865 Mission Street was then searched, and officers found ten shares of Mexican mining stock, five European government bonds, and four dime novels, as well as personal papers. The papers indicated the robber was from Galt and his real name was Henry Rivers. He was taken before U.S. Commissioner Sawyer, insisted on using the name Cummings, and was held over for the U.S. grand jury on a bail of $10,000, and in default he was returned to his jail cell. The *San Francisco Call* newspaper, on October 16, speculated, "If the Grand Jury indicts him and he is found guilty in accordance with his confession to the arresting Sheriff the young man will be sent up for life" as required when stealing the U.S. mail. Cummings pled guilty to "robbery of a U.S. mail carrier," but because of his cooperation and his youth he was only sentenced to serve ten years at San Quentin Prison. He arrived at the prison on October 25, 1890, and registered as prisoner #14317. He was discharged on April 24, 1897, after serving six years and six months.

Sources: *Los Angeles Herald (CA)*: October 14, 1890. *San Francisco Call (CA)*: October 16, 1890.

HARRY MILLER, NOVEMBER 15, 1891

At 8:00 a.m. on Sunday, November 15, 1891, the Eureka to Ukiah stagecoach, driven by Charles Lambert, was nineteen miles north of Ukiah making its way up a steep grade when the driver was confronted by a masked road agent carrying a distinctive Ballard rifle. The robber ordered Lambert to throw down the Wells, Fargo express box and the mailbags, and he did so with no hesitation. There were no passengers aboard, but the robber did not seem interested in robbing passengers in any case. The robber then ordered Lambert to move along, and the driver whipped up his team and hurried into Ukiah well ahead of schedule. Lambert notified Sheriff J. M. Standley and described the road agent as "tall and youthful looking, wearing a blue calico mask, drab duster, and heavy stodgy boots." The sheriff had on record that the farmhouse of John Roon, a mile north of Willits, had been broken into on the 13th and a Ballard rifle had been stolen, along with a blue calico dress and a drab duster. He had been investigating the break-in and learned that an athletic young man with smooth face and demi-blond hair had been loitering about the area for several days. Standley, instead of going to the scene of the robbery, went to Roon's farmhouse, took up the trail, and followed it from one lumber camp to another until he was told that the young man was Joe McKay, who had been cutting wood for Henry Willard at Hopland. McKay, Standley learned, had left Hopland on the 11th and returned on the 20th, so the sheriff went to the place he had worked and found a letter addressed to McKay, but it was from his brother George B. Miller and posted at the Hermitage in Oakland Heights. The sheriff went to the home of Joaquin Miller, "poet of the Sierras," but he was not at home, though his son George was there and he unknowingly directed the investigation toward his brother Harry. Standley then returned to Ukiah and found that Harry Miller had been in Cloverdale but left for Santa Rosa, so the sheriff followed by train and when he walked into the Burns' Hotel he found the fugitive sitting in the lobby reading a newspaper, and he made his arrest. Miller confessed and told the sheriff he had not been home in four years when, after a falling-out with his father, he took his father's best horse and rode north into Oregon. He was arrested for housebreaking and sentenced to serve two years at the prison in Salem, but he escaped after five months, then assumed the alias McKay and returned to California.

Miller had his examination on December 10, and he was held over by U.S. Commissioner Sawyer to answer to the U.S. grand jury on a charge of robbing the mail, bail set at $10,000. He was indicted and convicted, and sentenced to serve two years at San Quentin Prison. Miller arrived at the prison on January 9, 1892, and registered as prisoner #14783. He was discharged on September 9, 1893, after serving one year eight months.

Sources: *Sacramento Daily Union (CA)*: December 9, 1891; December 11, 1891.

UNKNOWN, MARCH 9, 1893

On Thursday, March 9, 1893, the stagecoach from Gualala to Ukiah had crossed into Mendocino County when a lone road agent, masked and armed, stepped onto the road and ordered the driver to halt. He demanded the Wells, Fargo express box, and it was thrown down, and then he told the driver to move along without asking about the mail or passengers. At Ukiah the robbery was reported to Sheriff Johnson, he organized a posse, and they rode to the scene. After investigating for ten days the sheriff arrested Patrick J. Randolph at the Gualala River and on the evening of March 19 he lodged his prisoner in the county jail, and the sheriff was confidant he had enough evidence to convict his prisoner. Two days later he arrested Henry, or Harry, Emery at Point Arena, and he joined Randolph in the Ukiah jail. On March 31 the two prisoners appeared in Judge Prage's courtroom for their preliminary hearing, and the judge released Emery but held over Randolph, setting his bail at $2,000. Randolph had tried to prove he was in a logging camp at the time of the murder, but his alibi was disproved. The evidence against Randolph was too weak to obtain a conviction on the robbery charge, but on August 18, 1894, thirty-seven-year-old P. J. Randolph arrived at Folsom to begin serving a five-year sentence for second-degree burglary.

Sources: *San Francisco Call (CA)*: March 20, 1893; March 25, 1893; April 1, 1893.

UNKNOWN, NOVEMBER 15, 1893

At 11:00 a.m. on Wednesday, November 15, 1893, the northbound stagecoach from Ukiah had traveled only five miles when a lone road agent, masked and dressed in blue overalls with a cotton mask covering his entire face, appeared and pointed a double-barreled shotgun at the driver. Once the coach was stopped he called for the Wells, Fargo express box, and it was thrown down. The robber did not ask for the mail and did not molest the passengers. As soon as the box lay in the road he told the driver to move on. After the coach was out of sight the robber busted open the box, but there is no record of his plunder so it must have been light or nothing. The posse that rode to the scene recovered the busted box but could find no clue to the robber's identity nor a trail to follow.

Sources: *Los Angeles Herald (CA)*: November 16, 1893. *Sacramento Daily Union (CA)*: November 16, 1893.

UNKNOWN, SEPTEMBER 14, 1894

On Friday afternoon, September 14, 1894, the northbound stagecoach from Ukiah to destinations in Idaho had only traveled ten miles when a lone highwayman stepped into the road and ordered the driver to rein in his team. Once the coach was stopped the robber demanded the Wells, Fargo express box, and it was thrown down. The robber did not ask for the mail, nor about passengers, and told the driver to move on. After the coach was out of sight the robber broke open the box and took out the contents, leaving the rest, but there was little of value in the box. At the first opportunity the driver sent word of the robbery back to Ukiah, including a description of the masked road agent. Sheriff Frank T. Johnson rode to the scene and took up the trail of two men and followed it until, on Wednesday, September 19, he captured Charles West and W. C. Wilbur four miles north of Cloverdale. On September 20 he arrived in Ukiah with his prisoners and lodged them in jail, but there is no record they were charged with the robbery.

Sources: *Los Angeles Herald (CA)*: September 15, 1894. *Sacramento Daily Union (CA)*: September 20, 1894.

GEORGE W. HILTON AND DAVID OLDHAM, JUNE 15, 1895

At 3:00 p.m. on Saturday, June 15, 1895, the stagecoach from Ukiah to Anderson Valley, with William Russell driving, reached a deep canyon on Robinson Creek, six miles southwest of Ukiah. A lone, masked highwayman, armed with a double-barreled shotgun, stepped out of the brush on the side of the road and ordered the driver to halt. As soon as the coach came to a stop the robber called for the two Wells, Fargo express boxes, and they were thrown down. The boxes contained $1,019.04, the majority of the cash drawn by county supervisor Flanagan to pay road contractors in his Mendocino district. The robber was not interested in the mail nor the five passengers aboard and immediately told the driver to move on. Russell, after traveling a short distance, met an Indian and had him take the news back to Ukiah and report to Sheriff Frank T. Johnson who, with city marshal Alexander Burke, started immediately for the scene. Johnson and Burke discovered a trail leading from the scene and, following it, found a mask, the broken boxes, and a pair of overalls. They followed the tracks to Charles "Slit-Nosed Charley" Stanford's cabin, four miles west of the robbery scene, where the robber had spent Saturday night and in the morning started for Hot Springs, after receiving directions from Stanford's son. Bloodhounds were brought out and they took up a scent, but after two miles they refused to work further.

Johnson and Burke went to the home of Ukiah's Baptist deacon David Oldham, four miles from Ukiah on the road to Lower Gap, to inquire about his hired hand George W. Hilton who matched the description of the road agent, but Oldham provided an alibi for Hilton. Sheriff Johnson returned to Ukiah on June 17 empty-handed but he had a "perfect description" of the robber for Wells, Fargo detective John N. Thacker when he arrived that night. Johnson was not satisfied with Oldham's alibi and his protests and decided to question the deacon, and he learned that Hilton had gone to Whittier Springs in Lake County. Johnson, with Stanford's son, went to Whittier Springs, and Hilton was identified by the boy, arrested and lodged in jail. Oldham was again questioned and insisted that Hilton had been with him making pickets at his redwood camp eight miles north of Ukiah, and Hilton had made 250 pickets the day of the robbery. The camp was inspected and it was found that no new pickets had been made, so Oldham was brought to the sheriff's office and questioned by Johnson, Thacker and ex-sheriff Standley, and he retracted his alibi for Hilton. The prisoner was then brought into the office and Oldham said, "Well, Hilton, seeing the evidence these men have against you, I guess I did not see you Saturday afternoon at 3 o'clock." This statement so upset Hilton that he made a full confession of the robbery, implicating Oldham as the man who planned the robbery and received half the plunder. Hilton told the sheriff where he could find his share of the money, and at Hilton's cabin in Whittier Springs the sheriff found $458 wrapped in half a flour sack hidden in his mattress.

Hilton had his preliminary hearing on June 24 and was held over by Justice Critchfield for action by the grand jury, bail set at $5,000. Oldham, though he protested his innocence, was arrested and he had his preliminary hearing on June 25, with Hilton testifying to every detail of the robbery plot initiated by Oldham, and Hilton testified, "The deacon told me I would find $5,000 aboard the coach." A few weeks before the robbery Oldham went to Booneville with Hilton and pointed out shotgun messenger Jamison so he could recognize him if he was on the coach. Hilton testified that on the day of the robbery he had hid in the brush and looked over the passengers on the coach, saw Jamison was not aboard, and took a shortcut over the mountain arriving at the scene of the robbery in advance of the coach. After Johnson and Burke, and several others, testified, Justice Critchfield held over Oldham for action by the grand jury, setting bail at $1,000. After the two men were lodged in jail, a party of men returned to Oldham's redwood camp and began a thorough search, and in an old stump near the camp they found $500, wrapped in the other half of the flour sack that had contained Hilton's plunder when recovered.

The trial of Hilton and Oldham was held in mid–July, and on July 16 they were convicted of the robbery. On July 18 Judge McGarvey gave a lengthy scolding to Oldham before he sentenced him to serve twelve years at Folsom Prison, and then the judge sentenced Hilton to serve eight years at San Quentin. Twenty-eight-year-old Hilton arrived at the prison on July 19, 1895, where he registered as prisoner #16436. Thirty-two-year-old Oldham arrived at Folsom Prison on July 20, 1895, where he registered as prisoner #3526. In March 1896 the state supreme court ordered a new trial for Oldham at Ukiah, but he was first tried for perjury in his robbery trial. After the jury deadlocked twice, the charge of perjury was dismissed and he was tried for the second time for stagecoach robbery, with Hilton testifying at all three trials. Oldham was convicted, but this time Judge McGarvey only sentenced him to serve eight years at Folsom, and apparently he was returned under his old prison number. There is no record of his release. Hilton lived long enough to testify against Oldham at all his trials, but he died in prison on August 8, 1897.

Sources: *San Francisco Call (CA)*: June 16, 1895; June 18, 1895; June 25–26, 1895; July 19, 1895.

John Schneider, December 31, 1895; January 15, 1896

At 9:30 a.m. on Tuesday, December 31, 1895, the stagecoach from Harris, the northernmost stagecoach station in Mendocino County, to Ukiah, the county seat, had reached Sewards ten miles north of its destination with Theodore Howard driving. There were aboard four lady passengers: Misses Edith and Fannie Rice of Willits, and Mrs. R. D. Cook and her daughter-in-law from Santa Rosa, so when the coach reached the foot of the grade they did not step out to walk behind as men would have. The coach was climbing the grade and had just passed the fork, with the other road leading to Redwood Valley, when a lone highwayman stepped from the brush with his revolver in his hand and ordered Howard to halt. The robber was medium height and weight dressed in light clothes, and his face was covered by a red bandana. He demanded the Wells, Fargo express box, and it was thrown down. When the robber hesitated, Howard prepared to get under way, but then came the demand for the way mail and registered packages but there was no demand for the overland mail. The pouches were thrown down next to the express box, and then Howard was told to move on. As soon as the coach reached Ukiah, Sheriff J. R. Johnson was notified and he headed for the scene with undersheriff Philo Handy and deputies J. L. Johnson and H. T. Hatch, and the sheriff took along his bloodhounds. Ex-sheriff J. M. Standley with Constables Alexander A. Burke and G. W. Hughes started out separately to try to cut off the robber's most likely route of escape, but they had no luck. That evening Handy and Deputy Johnson returned to Ukiah and said the sheriff was continuing on the trail with his bloodhounds, and they were heading toward a point east of Capella. Handy brought with him the broken express box and the mail pouches, all cut open with an ax; the letters, packages and contents of the box had been taken, but all the other papers were recovered. At midnight the sheriff returned and reported that he believed he saw his man go into camp, but his dogs would not work beyond the river east of Capella because of the frozen gravel on the ground. He said they would start again in the morning, fresh and with supplies, to continue the chase, but soon it became clear that the robber had eluded the posse, and the chase was abandoned.

In early January 1896 Sheriff Johnson received a clue to the robber's identity and went to Santa Rosa, but the clue was a false lead and when he returned to his office in Ukiah on January 15 he was met by Justice of the Peace H. R. Spaulding from Covelo, who had been sent by stagecoach driver Theodore "Spud" Howard saying he had been "stood up." The location was a narrow pass two miles north of Capella known as Robbers' Pass, because of previous experiences at that spot. According to Spaulding, Howard had just topped the grade and was about to start down into the pass when he heard a gruff voice from the brush command him to halt and say, "Throw down the Wells, Fargo express box," and Howard then saw a masked man with a cocked revolver in each hand pointed at him. He reined in his team and threw down the express box. Howard was about to proceed when the robber told him to get down and Howard was thoroughly searched, and the reasoning was that there was a rumor after the first robbery that Howard carried a large cache of valuables on his person in case the box was stolen, but his pockets were empty. Howard was ordered to take his seat just as a buggy arrived and the robber ordered the driver to come up beside the coach, and then Theodore Fulwider, a prominent merchant in Willits, was searched but he had only silver change in his pockets. After robbing Fulwider the robber told both men to drive on, and they both hurried from the scene. In a short time Howard met Spaulding on the road, told him the details of the robbery, and asked him to notify the sheriff. It had been raining for twenty-four hours and was still raining when the posse left Ukiah for the scene of the robbery, so bloodhounds would be of no use. Constable Burke and Deputy Nelson McClure rode to the scene as soon as they heard of the robbery, and the sheriff followed soon afterward.

On Friday, January 17, ex-sheriff Standley and Joel Starkey tried to arrest a man suspected of being the road agent, but Standley was shot twice and missed by a third shot before the man escaped. On the night of January 19 word came to Sheriff Johnson that a suspicious-looking stranger was loitering about the Henry place, seven miles north of town, and he took J. L. Johnson and McClure and they went with Finney, the man who brought the news. After scouring the region without success, Sheriff Johnson and McClure started for John Roeder's ranch, but they saw a man afoot and stopped him to inquire if he had seen a man of a certain description, but he said no. J. L. Johnson and Finney then came along and the party of four continued, leaving the man standing in the road. After rounding a curve they all dismounted and, with guns drawn, rushed back upon the man and captured him before he could draw his revolver, as he had been distracted reading a paper as he walked along the road. The man was searched and he had two .44 caliber revolvers on his person, one similar to those carried by U.S. soldiers and the other nickel-plated, and he had $17 in his pockets. The officers feared that their prisoner could be lynched when he reached town, so they took a circuitous route and smuggled him into the jail, but still a crowd of over three hundred gathered at the door within minutes. When told of the fear of a lynching he told the officers, "Give me a good gun and I will make them sick," but no attempt was made to take the prisoner. Once in the jail his revolvers were examined and one had three expended rounds, the number fired at Standley, and later that evening Starkey came to the jail and identified the prisoner as the man who shot the ex-sheriff. The prisoner gave the name John Schneider, pretended not to recognize Starkey, and when asked about the stagecoach robberies he replied, "You will have to prove that on me." Later that evening he agreed to be photographed, but only if the picture was withheld from the press. The prisoner was five feet seven inches tall, one hundred seventy pounds, with a light complexion, round face, blue eyes and a flat nose. Even though no accomplices were seen the search continued as it was believed he could not have eluded capture without help, but none were found.

On January 22 Sheriff Johnson appeared before U.S. Commissioner T. L. Carothers with an affidavit charging Schneider with robbing the U.S. mail on December 31, 1895, a warrant was issued, and U.S. marshal Barry Baldwin authorized the sheriff to serve the warrant. The prisoner was then charged with robbing the stagecoach on January 15 and with shooting Standley. Schneider had his preliminary examination on January 28 charging him with the January 15 stagecoach robbery, and the defendant refused the services of an attorney. After three days of testimony, justice Sullivan held over Schneider for action by the grand jury, bail set at $8,000. Schneider was arraigned on April 14 and his trial began immediately and lasted four days. On April 17 the case went to the jurors, who spent twenty-two minutes deliberating before returning a verdict of guilty for robbing the stagecoach on January 15. His trial for robbing the same coach on December 31 was then supposed to begin, but he pled guilty after consulting with his attorney. He waived time for sentencing and was immediately sentenced to serve fifteen years for the January 15 robbery and five years for the December 31 robbery, to run consecutively. Sheriff Johnson then announced that he believed he had evidence incriminating Schneider in the murder of Sheriff Pasco of Nevada County, and his hearing on the wounding of ex-sheriff Standley was scheduled to begin the next day. He was tried on two counts of assault to commit murder, convicted, and sentenced to serve a term of twenty-five years. Schneider arrived at San Quentin Prison on April 19, 1896, where he registered as prisoner #16721. He was discharged on May 3, 1909, after serving thirteen years.

Sources: *San Francisco Call (CA)*: January 1, 1896; January 16, 1896; January 21–22, 1896; January 29, 1896; January 31, 1896; April 18, 1896.

UNKNOWN, SEPTEMBER 26, 1897

On Sunday, September 26, 1897, the stagecoach from Ukiah to Booneville in Mendocino County was six miles southwest of Ukiah and passing through a heavily wooded area. Suddenly two masked, armed road agents jumped out of the trees and halted the coach while brandishing shotguns, one pointing his weapon at the driver and the other pointing his at the coach. The driver reined in his team and in that moment John R. Barnett realized they were about to be robbed, so he thrust his hand inside his coat to take out and hide his wallet. He managed to pull it out and throw it under the seat, but one of the robbers must have thought he was going for a pistol because he fired the load of one barrel from his double-barreled shotgun. One buckshot pellet struck Barnett in his right shoulder near the base of his neck, ranged downward shattering his spinal column, and killed him instantly. The road agents then demanded that three express boxes be thrown down, and as soon as they were in the road they ordered the driver to move on. They did not search the body nor F. D. Berryhill, the other passenger riding inside. As the stagecoach drove on, the robbers could be seen carrying the treasure boxes into the dense woods. As soon as the coach reached the Elledge ranch, Barnett's body was taken out of the stagecoach and, along with the details of the robbery and murder, was rushed into Ukiah where Sheriff J. R. Johnson organized a posse and took along several bloodhounds. The dogs picked up a scent and followed it through some very rough country, but lost it when the trail reached the road to Cloverdale. Soon after the robbery and murder Fred Donohue and John Crow saw two men, not far from the murder scene, riding toward Geyserville, and they would later learn they fit the description of the robbers. Two days later two men were walking on a road forty miles from the murder scene and they asked for a ride from Mendocino grape grower J. E. Gator, and later he learned that he may have given a ride to the two road agents. On September 30, the same day Gator was giving two men a ride, Sheriff Johnson gave up the search and returned to Ukiah empty-handed.

The investigation continued and on October 12, 1897, Sheriff Johnson arrived at Ukiah with prisoner Charles Meyers, charged with being one of the Booneville stagecoach robbers. Meyers had been arrested at his Kearney Street lodging house in San Francisco and had been tracked there after it was learned that he had suddenly abandoned his job at a Geyserville ranch just before the robbery, and he matched the description of one of the road agents. Fred Donohue and John Crow, who had seen the two men riding toward Geyserville, were summoned to the sheriff's office. Crow arrived first and said that Meyers matched the description of one of the men he had seen, and the officers held Meyers for the arrival of Donohue. However, Donohue said that Meyers resembled the man he had seen the day of the murder but was definitely not him. Interest in the murder of Barnett waned somewhat until January 27, 1898, when Frank Harrington of Alexander Valley was arrested by deputies Leard and Weise and charged with the crime. He would not deny being one of the road agents but merely said he would provide an alibi. "Lish" Finney, a teamster, had reported meeting two men on the road before the robbery, one of whom asked about the Booneville coach, and he said Harrington was one of those men. However, the following day Harrington's employer arrived with his work record ledger and proved Harrington was nowhere near the murder scene on the day of the crime, so he was released. On February 5 Parker H. Barrett was arrested by ex-sheriff J. M. Standley and charged with robbing the Booneville coach and with murder. After Barrett was lodged in jail, officers were trying to connect him with the Keswick store robbery, during which a robber named Sharp was killed, and a German who knew Sharp said that Barrett was a constant companion of Sharp; but Barrett insisted he could prove an alibi for both crimes. J. E Gator then arrived and cleared him of being one of the men to whom he had given a ride, and Barrett proved an alibi for the Keswick affair. After Barrett was released the case went cold, and no one was ever prosecuted for murdering Barnett or for that stagecoach robbery.

Sources: *Daily Californian (Bakersfield)*: February 8, 1898. *Daily Tribune (Salt Lake City, UT)*. September 29, 1897. *Los Angeles Herald (CA)*: February 6, 1898. *Sacramento Daily Union (CA)*: October 1, 1897. *San Francisco Call (CA)*: September 29, 1897; October 13, 1897; January 28, 1898.

John N. Davis and Edgar L. Davis, December 25, 1897

On Saturday night, December 25, 1897, John N. Davis and Edgar L. Davis, brothers, disguised themselves, mounted, and rode to a place two miles south of Willits in Mendocino County, which they had selected for a robbery. When the Ukiah to Laytonville mail coach appeared the brothers called on the driver to halt, but instead he whipped up his team and drove out of danger as the brothers fired at the coach five times. John then rode hard into Willits to beat the coach into town and establish an alibi while Edgar returned home. The driver reported the attempted robbery and said he was sure he had recognized the voice of John Davis, and he was arrested. The investigation quickly focused on Edgar Davis as the second road agent, and he joined his brother in jail. By January 7 both brothers had been moved to the jail at Ukiah, the county seat, and when it was clear that Sheriff J. M. Standley had a good case against them they confessed. They were charged with attempting to rob the U.S. mail, and on January 10 they were taken before U.S. commissioner Heacock. They were held over for trial, but both brothers said they would plead guilty and throw themselves on the mercy of the court. On January 15 they appeared in the U.S. circuit court for sentencing, and Judge de Haven sentenced each brother to serve seven years at hard labor at San Quentin Prison. The sentence was described as "light" because they had pled guilty as promised, and it was their first offense. The brothers arrived at the prison on January 21, 1898, and John registered, under the name J. L. Davis, as prisoner #17603, and Edgar registered, under the name E. L. Davis, as prisoner #17602. Both men were released on October 13, 1902, after serving four years nine months.

Sources: *San Francisco Call (CA)*: January 4, 1898; January 7, 1898; January 11, 1898; January 16, 1898.

Unknown, July 16, 1901; July 23, 1901; August 1, 1901; August 26, 1901

On Tuesday afternoon, July 16, 1901, the Blue Lakes and the Potter Valley stagecoaches left Ukiah, but at 2:00 p.m. they were stopped by a lone road agent, wearing a white mask and armed with a single-barreled shotgun, when they reached a canyon a short distance above Fort Brown. The robber stood on a bank above the road, and as Raymond Hill, driver of the Potter Valley coach, approached, the robber pointed his long barrel shotgun, which appeared to be an old-model Winchester, at Hill and told him, "Stop!" The male passengers were ordered to step out and line up facing the dirt bank while the lady passengers were to stay in the coach but stand up, but the men hesitated. When the second command was given, they knew it was not a joke and the men quickly climbed out. Once they were in place the robber commanded them to take out their valuables and toss them up to him. While they were complying with that order, the Blue Lakes coach approached driven by "Bunt" Bucknell. Hill tried to signal but Bucknell did not understand and drove right up to the scene and brought his coach to a standstill. The road agent then ordered the first group of male passenger to board, and he went through the second party of passengers in the same manner. There were eighteen passengers in all between the two coaches, mostly men. He got $100 from the passengers in the first coach, and though the amount from the second stage was not known, it was thought to be substantial. The parties described the man as five feet ten inches, medium build, wearing a black slouch hat, dark sack coat, blue or brown overalls, and his dark whiskers were seen under the mask but they appeared to be a false beard. When the Potter Valley coach reached its destination, Sheriff J. H. Smith was notified by telephone and he started for the scene, while Deputy Ornbaum started out from Ukiah to search for the robber, and many deputies from outlying assignments joined in the search. Before noon Wednesday, Undersheriff J. R. Thomas arrested Peter W. Shannon at Ukiah, but he presented a good alibi. However, he was not released when two boys, fishing near the robbery scene, said they saw a man afoot and they were certain it was Shannon, who seemed to be on his way to Willits. Shannon, when arrested, had only $52.30 in his pockets and a membership card from the California Cycling Association. Shannon was finally cleared and released

On Tuesday, July 23, the lone highwayman, masked with a bandana and armed with a single-barreled shotgun, moved his operation to the coast region. He stopped the stagecoach between Mendocino City and Cazadero at Dark Gulch, five miles from Mendocino City, at 3:00 p.m. It was supposed he was not familiar with the route as stagecoaches had not carried Wells, Fargo treasure for at least three years, so when he commanded the driver to throw down the express box, he was told there was none. He did not believe the driver and looked into the boot to be sure, then found that the three passengers on the coach were working men and refused to take their money, saying, "You may go. I never rob a working man." He waved his hand for the driver to move along. Unlike the robbery on July 16, this road agent seemed quite nervous, but his description was similar in height and weight. Officers went to the scene, but there seemed little hope that they could catch the robber as the country was wild and rugged, making tracking nearly impossible. On July 25 Deputy W. F. Ornbaum arrested a man named Voss at Comptche and lodged him in jail on suspicion that he was the road agent, but while he was behind bars the same road agent appeared again, clearing him of the charge and he was released.

On August 1, 1901, the northbound stagecoach for Potter Valley was stopped one mile north of Fort Brown, within a half mile of the robbery of July 16. The robber, armed with a single-barreled shotgun, directed driver Raymond Hill to halt and had the passengers step out, form a line, and turn over their valuables. The passengers, after the previous robberies, were prepared, and all they had among them to deliver was $5. The robber was thought to be a man who lived in that area, so when Sheriff Smith received the phone call he started out immediately to investigate. There were a number of arrests of suspicious characters, but all proved to have ironclad alibis and were released.

On Monday, August 26, 1901, the westbound Ukiah to Mendocino City stagecoach, driven by Clay Rennick, was eleven miles west of Ukiah, four miles from Orr Hot Springs, when it was stopped by a lone road agent, masked and armed with a single-barreled shotgun. He ordered the two passengers to step out and relieved them of their money, thought to be substantial as they were vacationers on their way to the springs. He next demanded the Wells, Fargo express box and it was thrown down, and then he told the passengers to board and told Rennick to move on. The westbound coach soon met the eastbound coach and Rennick told driver Joseph Ainslie the details to report in Ukiah, and Ainslie proceeded with great caution expecting to see the road agent at any time, but he was not molested. When he reached the area where the westbound coach had been halted, he saw several hunters walking on the road carrying repeating rifles, and they told him they saw the road agent grab the express box and flee as they approached. Ainslie reported the robbery to Sheriff Smith and, with Deputy Ornbaum, started for the scene, but they could find no clue to the robbers identity nor a trail to follow for any distance.

Sources: *Dispatch Democrat (Ukiah, CA)*: July 19, 1901. *Los Angeles Herald (CA)*: July 28, 1901; August 2, 1901. *San Francisco Call (CA)*: July 18, 1901; July 24, 1901; August 27, 1901. *Ukiah Republican Press (CA)*: July 26, 1901.

JOHN IVANS, DECEMBER 21, 1901

At 6:00 a.m. on Saturday, December 21, 1901, the southbound overland stagecoach was one mile from Willits when a masked road agent, armed with a shotgun, halted the coach and ordered driver George Cook to throw out the Wells, Fargo express box and mail pouches. Cook complied, but as he carefully watched and listened to the robber, he became convinced the road agent was John Ivans, the stagecoach driver between Willits and Fort Bragg. When Cook arrived at Willits he went to Ivans' room and learned that Ivans had arisen before 6:00 a.m. and was not seen in town again until after 7:00 a.m., and Cook then charged him with the robbery. Sheriff J. H. Smith was notified and he started for Willits while the sheriff's son, Charlie Smith, shadowed Ivans until his father arrived and swore out a warrant, and they arrested Ivans. Meanwhile the mailbags had been found, cut open and the contents rifled, but the express box and the shotgun were not found. The sheriff started for Ukiah with his prisoner, and on the way Ivans confessed to robbing the stagecoach and said he would tell where the box and gun were hidden. He said he had not had time to break open the box, and his shotgun had not been loaded, and this proved true when they were discovered later by following the prisoner's directions. The sheriff continued into Ukiah and lodged his prisoner in the county jail, but on December 24, U.S. Marshal Shine took the prisoner to San Francisco to be tried in the U.S. district court for robbing the mail. On January 21, 1902, Ivans appeared before Judge de Haven and pled guilty, and two days later the judge sentenced him to serve six years in prison. Twenty-five-year-old Ivans arrived at San Quentin on January 22, 1902, and registered as prisoner #19382; he was discharged on May 19, 1906, after serving four years four months.

Sources: *Los Angeles Herald (CA)*: December 22, 1901; December 24, 1901. *San Francisco Call (CA)*: December 24, 1901; January 21, 1901; January 23, 1901.

UNKNOWN, FEBRUARY 13, 1903; MARCH 24, 1903

On Friday morning, February 13, 1903, the westbound stagecoach from Ukiah to Mendocino City had traveled twenty-five miles when a lone road agent, masked and armed, stepped into the road and halted the coach. He demanded the Wells, Fargo express box and it was thrown down. He took the box to the side of the road and blew the lock off the box, then stuffed the contents into his pockets before he returned the broken box to the coach and told the driver to move along. He was not interested in the passengers and did not ask for the mail. There was no messenger aboard, a sign that the contents of the box had little or no value. Sheriff J. H. Smith and a deputy rode to the scene but could find no clue to the robber's identity, nor a trail to follow for any distance, so they returned to town and waited for some development in the case.

At 9:00 a.m. on Tuesday, March 24, 1903, J. L. Johnson's stagecoach from Ukiah to Mendocino City had reached the point two miles east of the Halfway House when two shots rang out fatally wounding the two leaders, and there was a call to halt. A road agent had concealed himself behind a tree along the roadside but Wells, Fargo messenger Q. A. Overmeyer could not see him, so he told driver Harry Owsley to whip up the four-horse team and drive them out of range. The road agent, seeing that the coach was not going to stop, fired at the messenger, wounding him mortally. The messenger fell from the coach as Owsley plied his whip and urged his team into a run amid a shower of bullets, several of which became imbedded in the woodwork of the coach indicating that the robber had a repeating rifle. The road agent followed the coach afoot for a quarter mile shooting, until it made a turn and could not be seen by the robber. Owsley reached the Halfway House where the two leaders collapsed and soon died. There were no other horses available, so Owsley took one of the wheelers and rode into Comptche, ten miles further along the route, where he secured a span of horses. He returned to the Halfway House and took the coach into Mendocino at 11:00 p.m. where he delivered the express boxes containing over $15,000 in payroll money. Meanwhile, the supply team from Al Johnson's camp passed the place of the attack, picked up Overmeyer's body, and took it to the Halfway House, and according to Johnson it appeared the messenger had been killed instantly. J. L. Johnson normally went out as messenger whenever there was substantial treasure, but he was not able to make that trip and sent Overmeyer in his place. Overmeyer's body arrived in Ukiah the next day, and the general feeling was that the murderer would be lynched if caught.

Deputy Sheriff Grace and a posse arrived at the Halfway House at 8:00 p.m. the night of the killing, where they waited out a rainstorm and in the morning were met by Wells, Fargo detective John Thacker and messenger Hatch, accompanied by J. L. Johnson. They recruited a number of local woodsmen and with bloodhounds took the trail of the robber and found a camp, which showed he had waited there for days preparing to rob a treasure-laden coach, indicated by a messenger aboard. By the following day the posse with dogs was following the trail while another posse from Booneville was searching toward Anderson Valley. A Mrs. Stevens had been on her way to the Halfway House to catch the coach and she saw the man carrying a rifle walking toward the place the robbery was attempted, but she turned back when she heard the gunshots. She described the man she saw in great detail, and detective Thacker believed he was John A. Lemos, an ex-convict who had been discharged from prison on May 4, 1894. It was later proved that Lemos was not the robber, but officers were convinced that this robber was the same man who had attempted to rob the Ione to Jackson stagecoach on March 10, 1903, due to the similarities in his methods.

At 6:00 a.m. on April 19 deputies William Ornbaum and Ben Melton brought forty-year-old Louis Galeni, or Gleen, into Ukiah and charged him with murder and robbery. He had been staying at an old cabin in a gulch near Wending, where the dogs had followed the trail of the road agent in late March, but the scent had faded so that they did not get as far as the cabin this time. In searching around the area, officers found several hiding places or camps he had prepared. Galeni did not resist when arrested, did not inquire about the charge, but when told, he said he could not say where he was when the robberies occurred. No gun was found, but Ornbaum did find an overcoat which matched the description of the one worn by the road agent in robbing a previous stagecoach. Though his shoe soles did not match those of the road agent, a similar pair was found in one of his other camps. There is no record that Galeni was prosecuted for the murder and robbery, and no one else was charged.

Sources: *Amador Ledger (CA)*: March 27, 1903. *Los Angeles Herald (CA)*: March 25–26, 1903; March 28, 1903; April 21, 1903. *San Francisco Call (CA)*: March 21, 1903; March 25, 1903. *Sausalito News (CA)*: March 28, 1903.

UNKNOWN, JULY 27, 1907

At 2:30 p.m. on Saturday, July 27, 1907, the northbound stagecoach from Ukiah bound for Witter Spring, Blue Lake, and Upper Lake, driven by Clay Rennick, had traveled ten miles and had just rounded a curve when a road agent armed with a rifle and revolver, and masked with a blue handkerchief, halted the coach. Before the robber could line up the eighteen passengers from the first coach, the northbound coach from Ukiah for Potter Valley, driven by George Banson, rounded the same curve and was stopped. He ordered out the seven passengers in the second coach as well and had the twenty-five people form a line, leaving the drivers to handle their four-horse teams. He collected money, watches and jewelry and then had everyone board, and as soon as everyone was seated he told the drivers to continue on their routes. Two freight teamsters were following the coaches, and could not pass on the narrow road with two coaches in front, and after the two coaches were under way they were stood up for their money as well. The coaches both hurried to the next stop with a telephone and reported the robberies to Sheriff R. E. Donohoe, who organized a posse and started for the scene. The man was described as five feet nine inches tall, weight 150 pounds, wearing a long linen duster with gunnysacks tied around his legs. The sheriff had a man under suspicion, but he did not have sufficient evidence to warrant an arrest, so he continued to look for a suspect.

Sources: *Los Angeles Herald (CA)*: July 29, 1907. *San Francisco Call (CA)*: July 28, 1907.

UNKNOWN, JANUARY 15, 1908

On Wednesday, January 15, 1908, the northbound stagecoach from Ukiah for Potter Valley, driven by Neil Stockgoff, had just climbed the grade near Wattenberger's resort, and reached the place called Wool Rock, when a masked road agent with a shotgun ordered him to halt. The robber called for the Wells, Fargo express box, perhaps expecting the payroll for the Snow Mountain Water & Power Company plant on the Eel River, but he was told the stagecoaches on that route did not carry express. He then called for money from the driver and two passengers. Stockgoff threw down his purse containing $6 and the robber returned $2, saying, "I do not need it all." Then from the two passengers he took $3.50 and $2.50. He wished "all good luck" to the driver and passengers and sent them on their way. Thomas Menhall, owner of the Clear Lake bean cannery, watched the robbery take place and he had several hundred dollars in his pockets. As soon as the coach was under way he turned his buggy around and headed for Wattenberger's resort, where he reported the robbery. He had seen a rig tied in the brush just before coming to the robbery scene, and he was surprised when he saw the road agent climb into that rig and follow him down the road. Menhall was sure he knew the man and told Sheriff R. E. Donohoe who he believed he was, and the sheriff began searching for him but could not find his man.

Source: *San Francisco Call (CA)*: January 16, 1908.

UNKNOWN, JANUARY 15, 1908

At 1:00 p.m. on Wednesday, January 15, 1908, the southeast-bound stagecoach from Ukiah to Lakeport had traveled only ten miles and was rounding a curve when a masked man armed with a large revolver stepped into the road and ordered the driver to halt. He then ordered the only two passengers, C. A. S. Frost and Heinz Springe riding atop, to step down. Once the passengers were on the ground the robber ordered the driver to join them, and then he had the driver search each passenger for money. The driver fumbled in the clothing of the two men until he produced $7.50 in silver coin; then the robber said, "But I guess I won't take all your money," and had the driver return a dollar and a quarter to Frost and a silver dollar to Springe. He next demanded the money held by the driver and collected from him $7 plus the $5.25 left from the passengers, but he returned $3 to the driver. The robber then ordered the three men to board, and once they were seated on the box he told the driver to move along. As soon as the coach was under way the robber made a dash down the road in the opposite direction and disappeared into the brush. The driver was able to sound the alarm in minutes, but officers could find no clue to the robber. Both passengers had considerable gold in their pockets and were surprised that the robber did not demand a more exhaustive search, which led them to believe he was a "green hand" at the business, and possibly a local farmhand inspired by several stagecoach robberies that had occurred recently.

Source: *San Francisco Call (CA)*: January 16, 1908.

Merced County

DAN MCCARTY AND EUGENE TYLER, MAY 7, 1877

On Monday, May 7, 1877, the stagecoach from Los Banos to Gilroy in Merced County driven by Paul Reynard was stopped by two masked road agents when three miles east of the

Summit House, or thirty-five miles west of Gilroy. One road agent was white and appeared very young while the other was an older Negro, and the latter directed all the action during the robbery. Each road agent was armed with a six-shooter which they pointed at the driver while demanding the Wells, Fargo express box. The driver told them he had no box, so they ordered him to step down, lay face down on the ground, and put his hands behind him. They tied his wrists and went through the coach, cutting open the express bag which contained nothing, and went through the U.S. mail pouches tearing apart every letter and package. Still, however, their take was negligible, so after forty-five minutes' work they untied Reynard and took from him $2.50, all he had. As soon as the men were through with the robbery they untied the driver and ordered him to board and continue on. Reynard whipped up his team and at his first opportunity reported the robbery. The disguises of the road agents had been ineffective and they were immediately recognized by Reynard, so it was not long before their descriptions were broadcast throughout the region— "One of them is a colored man, very black, named Eugene Tyler; five feet, eight inches high; weighs 180 pounds; and twenty years old. The other is a white man named D. McCarty; about five feet five inches high; light hair; and about twenty years old. He has been working for Donnelly, Dunne & Co." California's Governor William Irwin and Wells, Fargo posted rewards totaling $600 for the arrest and conviction of each road agent.

On May 18 Undersheriff Thomas M. Lane and Deputy H. L. McCoy arrived in town with two prisoners who had been arrested and charged with being the road agents. Earlier that morning a Mr. Boyd had met Tyler traveling along the rail lines with McCarty, and he hurried into town and gave the information to the sheriff's office. Lane and McCoy, with Boyd, hurried to the place where the two fugitives were last seen, each lawman armed with a pocket pistol. The two fugitives had continued on so the lawmen followed them to Hughes & Keys station near Hills Ferry on the San Joaquin River, but the station had burned down recently and the two fugitives were found among the rubble. The lawmen started for the fugitives, handing their reins to a bystander, and as McCoy reached into his pocket, McCarty leveled his Smith & Wesson six-shooter at him. The two parties then discussed the situation for some time, with the lawmen insisting it was their duty to capture the two men "dead or alive," and McCarty insisting he was ready for a fight. Finally Tyler intervened and convinced McCarty to surrender, and both men gave up their weapons, two fine-quality six-shooters. The two prisoners were taken into town and lodged in jail. At their examination they were held over for action by the grand jury; they were indicted, and in August they pled guilty.

The *Gilroy Advocate,* on August 11, 1877, reported, "Eugene Tyler, the Negro, and Dan McCarty, the boy, who stopped the stage in the Pacheco Pass, a few months ago, and robbed Paul Reynaud [sic], the driver, of $2.50, have acknowledged themselves guilty of highway robbery, They now await the sentence of the court of Merced County." They had hopes of receiving a lighter sentence for their cooperation and this worked, as McCarty, because of his youthful appearance, was given a sentence of only one year while Tyler, being considered the bad influence and leader at the robbery scene, was sentenced to serve five years. Both men arrived at San Quentin Prison on August 16, 1877, and McCarty registered as prisoner #7714 and Tyler as prisoner #7715. McCarty was discharged upon expiration of sentence on June 15, 1878. Tyler was pardoned and released on March 16, 1881. (See San Luis Obispo County on May 18, 1882.)

Unknown, February 26, 1890

On Wednesday evening, February 26, 1890, the stagecoach from Mariposa to Merced was a mile from its destination when two road agents, masked and armed, stepped into the roadway in front of the horses. Once the coach was stopped they demanded the mail, and the pouches from Mariposa, Coulterville and several post offices along the route were thrown down. The robbers then demanded the Wells, Fargo express box, and it was also thrown down. As soon as their plunder lay in the road the road agents told the driver to move along, and he hurried into Merced to report the robbery. A posse was quickly organized, but by the time they reached the scene the mail and box were gone, along with the robbers. The posse could not find a clue to their identities nor a trail to follow from the scene.

Source: *Daily Alta California (San Francisco)*: February 27, 1890.

FRANK "TEX" KELLETT, AUGUST 1, 1895; OCTOBER 1, 1895

At 2:00 p.m. on Thursday, August 1, 1895, the stagecoach from Coulterville to Merced, driven by stage line proprietor George Kirk, was four miles past Snelling and running on schedule. He had just rounded a curve and his team was walking slowly, in preparation to climb a hill, when a masked road agent appeared from the side of the road and, waving two pistols, ordered the driver to rein in his team. There was but one passenger aboard, and he ordered Constanso Bartolomo to step out and robbed him of $9; then he demanded the Wells, Fargo express box. Kirk threw it down, but the robber, at the point of his pistol, made Kirk get a sledgehammer from the coach and bust it open. While this was going on, the Minges boy rode up in a cart and was ordered to tie his horse to a telephone pole and then hold the reins of the coach leaders. Once the box was opened the robber took out several packages of coins, and when he finished his work he asked if the Mariposa stagecoach would be along. Kirk told him it came down another road three miles across the mountains, and the robber replied, "I guess I will not have the time to rob that stage today." He ordered the passenger and driver to board and continue into Merced, a distance of twelve miles, and Kirk whipped up his team and hurried into town. All the time the road agent was at work, Kirk could see two men standing on a hill two hundred yards away, watching, and he believed they were accomplices, and as the coach started, the road agent turned and walked toward the two men on the hill. Sheriff Warfield organized a posse and with Constable T. A. Mack, district attorney Ostrander, and several officers rode to the scene and started scouring the countryside for the robber. That night a message came into Merced from Hornitos saying the sheriff believed he had struck a hot trail and was following with three trusted deputies, but they failed to capture the road agent. Rewards were posted by Sheriff Warfield, George Kirk, and the Wells, Fargo company.

On Tuesday, October 1, the stagecoach from Coulterville bound for Merced, with Bert Campbell driving, left Snelling on schedule and had traveled four miles by 2:00 p.m. It was just one hundred yards from the point where the stagecoach was robbed on August 1, and had just rounded a curve preparing to climb a hill, when a man masked in canvas stuck his head out of a culvert and said, "Hold on!" as he pointed a rifle at Campbell. The driver reined in his team and then the three passengers were ordered out. One was an old man and he was herded in front of the leaders and told to stand there, but as he scrutinized the road agent he was told, "I'm not very good looking, anyway. Stand with your back toward me," and the old man turned around. The robber then ordered passenger Jim Cathay to take the reins while he had Campbell throw out the express box, and then ordered the driver to take the coach ax and break it open. Once the lid was smashed he had Campbell turn it upside down and shake it, and among the contents on the ground was a bag of money which the robber picked up, cut open, and put the money in his pocket. Campbell asked if he wanted the box and the robber said no, so Campbell gathered up the other contents, put them back into the busted box, and put the box back on the coach. The robber ordered everyone to retake their seats, without molesting them, and then told Campbell to continue into Merced, which was still twelve miles away. Campbell whipped up his team and hurried into town where he reported the robbery and described the robber as wearing a canvas mask, his clothes were covered in a long waterproof or mackintosh, and he spoke with a German accent, but no horse had been seen. Deputy Ed Stockyard, with constables T. A. Mack and Jim Collins, rode to the scene and arrived less than an hour after the robbery.

Following nearly a month of investigating the robberies, Constable T. A. Mack received word that a man under suspicion, known as Frank "Tex" Kellett, had left Fresno Flats and started for the road between Coulterville and Merced. Mack, with Constable Ed la Tour, first got ahead of Kellett but let him pass, and then followed him to the home of Jim Long near La Grange. Mack quietly went to the front door and suddenly threw it open, and he got the drop on Kellett. Mack ordered him to raise his hands, and he raised the right hand but dropped his left to his pistol. Mack warned him he would shoot, so he raised his left hand and surrendered; at 2:00 a.m. on October 30 Mack delivered his prisoner to the county jail in Merced. The prisoner insisted his name was Smith, but he was known as an ex-convict who had been sentenced to ten years from Fresno County in 1887 for cattle stealing. Mack returned to Jim Long's ranch the following day and brought in the prisoner's horse, saddle and valise. The only incriminating objects among his belongings was a monkey wrench seen during the August 1 robbery and the head of a sledgehammer stolen from Long's blacksmith shop. A pistol and a new Marvin rifle were also brought in. The prisoner was taken before Judge Read on the afternoon of October 31, and the date of his preliminary examination was set for November 11. Kellett was held over for trial at his hearing and his bail was set at $3,000. During the hearing Kirk positively identified Kellett as the man who had robbed him on August 1. Kellett was tried later that month, convicted, and Judge Read sentenced him to serve ten years at San Quentin Prison. He was discharged on July 14, 1902, after serving six years and eight months.

Sources: *Los Angeles Herald (CA)*: October 2, 1895; August 2, 1895. *San Francisco Call (CA)*: August 2, 1895; October 31, 1895; November 1, 1895; November 13, 1895.

Modoc County

CHARLES E. "BLACK BART" BOLTON, OCTOBER 27, 1879

On October 27, 1879, two days after robbing the stagecoach between Roseburg, Oregon, and Redding, Charles E. Bolton robbed the stagecoach from Redding to Alturas in Modoc County. The celerity wagon, driven by Ed Payne, was traveling slowly along a particularly narrow and winding portion of the road twenty-five miles east of Redding, and as it came around a sharp turn he found Black Bart standing in the middle of the road, masked and armed with a shotgun. The demand was made for the mail and express box, and as soon as they were delivered the road agent ordered Payne to continue on. Payne hurried into Millville where a posse of three lawmen was quickly organized. They went to the scene and took up the robber's trail of boot tracks at daylight, but soon lost it in rough country. The treasure box, it was reported, again yielded nearly a "water haul," but the mails were reported to have produce $1,300 in plunder. (See Calaveras County on November 3, 1883.)

CHARLES W. "BUD" HEAP, OCTOBER 1, 1895

On Tuesday, October 1, 1895, thirty-five-year-old Charles W. "Bud" Heap boarded the stagecoach at Chico bound for Bidwell and rode atop with driver Ellery Phillips. When the coach was near Fort Bidwell, Heap demanded that Phillips give him $5. Phillips refused, so the youth declared, "I will have your money and Wells, Fargo's besides." He pulled out a dirk and grabbed Phillips by the throat, but the driver was too quick for him and knocked him off the coach. Phillips whipped up the team, hurried into Bidwell, and swore out a warrant for Heap's arrest. A constable from Bidwell went to the scene, followed the trail of boot tracks, and arrested Heap asleep in a barn not far from where he was pushed off the coach. He was taken into Bidwell and lodged in jail, then taken to Chico. In 1882 Heap had served time for illegal voting, and in 1893 he was sent to prison for twenty-five years for "assault with a deadly weapon" for threatening to kill his wife, but he was discharged on January 31, 1895. On October 14 Heap appeared in the court at Chico and was held over on a charge of attempting to rob the U.S. mail, and he was scheduled to be taken to San Francisco to be arraigned in the federal court. The federal charge could not be proved, as he had made no attempt to rob the mail nor any statement about it, so after a long delay the charges in Modoc County may have been reduced to minor offenses and he may have received a brief sentence to be served in the local jail, or the charges may have been dismissed, as there is no record of Heap returning to prison.

Sources: *San Francisco Call (CA)*: October 2, 1895; October 15, 1895.

UNKNOWN, SEPTEMBER 9, 1912

In 1912 there was a mining boom in the Warner Mountains in northern Modoc County, near the Oregon border, and stagecoaches were being used to bring in payrolls and take out the mineral treasure from the High Grade mining camp. On Monday, September 9, 1912, the stagecoach from Fort Bidwell to High Grade, with "Cyclone" Thompson driving, was at the halfway point when a lone road agent, masked and armed, with his feet muffled in sacking, ordered the coach to halt. Thompson was known as a gunman, and one to shoot on the slightest provocation, but his friends had recently convinced him to go unarmed to avoid trouble, so he was helpless when covered by a loaded firearm. The robber said, "Hand over the leather sack." Thompson believed the robber was after the payroll for the Consolidated Mining Company and replied, "Haven't got it this time." The robber then threatened to shoot at any sign of interference, reached into Thompson's pocket, and removed a small sack containing $150. As soon as the robber had the money he ran into the brush and disappeared, and Thompson continued on to High Grade. Lawmen rode to the scene but could find no clue to the robber's identity nor a trail to follow for any distance.

Source: *San Francisco Call (CA)*: September 11, 1912.

Mono County

UNKNOWN, SEPTEMBER 2, 1889

At 4:00 a.m. on Monday, September 2, 1889, the stagecoach from Bodie to Hawthorne, driven by Fred Fletcher, had just passed the outskirts of Bodie when a lone highwayman, masked and armed with a double-barreled shotgun, stepped into the road, aimed his gun at the driver's head and ordered him to halt. Once the coach had stopped he demanded the Wells, Fargo express box, and it was thrown onto the road. As soon as the box was delivered the road agent told Fletcher to continue on. There were no passengers aboard, and the robber did not ask about them nor call for the mail. Fletcher, when he reported the robbery, said he recognized the robber by his peculiar voice. Will Langerman, the driver in Hawthorne, reported that the box contained

$3,000 in coin and gold bars. The busted box was later recovered near the scene of the robbery and the robber had overlooked an envelope containing "a bundle of greenbacks." Lawmen went to the scene and searched for clues, but apparently there were none and Fletcher could not put a name to the voice, so no one was arrested for the robbery.

Sources: *Territorial Enterprise (Virginia City, NV)*: September 3, 1889. *Walker Lake Bulletin (CA)*: September 4, 1889.

Monterey County

THOMAS BARRY, SAMUEL L. BURNS, BENJAMIN F. CLAUGHTON AND THOMAS SELBY, JUNE 4, 1870

In late May, Thomas Barry was visiting with his cousin Samuel Barns and there were a number of people present, including Benjamin F. Claughton, Thomas Selby, and Samuel L. Burns. They began discussing robbing the mail, and Selby boasted that it was easy and that he had done it previously in Nevada County. In early June the four aspiring road agents were at Stone's store, a Wells, Fargo express office and post office, and they saw the proprietor put up $600 in the express box bound for San Luis Obispo on the Friday stagecoach. When the robbery was proposed again, Burns and Selby said they had no horse fit for the ride, so Barry on a gray and Claughton on a brown horse agreed to do the work but split the plunder equally afterward. They stocked up on supplies and obtained a shotgun, so Claughton gave his revolver to Barry. On Thursday they rode by a long, circuitous route until they overtook the stagecoach some miles south of Plato station the following day.

On Saturday, June 4, 1870, Leavitt's Coast Stage Line coach, driven by C. V. Smith, picked up the mail and express box at Stone's store and continued north toward the Salinas River, with five passengers aboard including driver William Cliff traveling as a passenger and seated atop. Cliff, who was more suspicious than most passengers would be, noted two men ride out from the woods behind the coach when the coach was still seven miles below Plato station, and he noted that they were armed—one with a shotgun and one with a revolver. However, they made no advance on the coach and when it stopped at Plato station they rode past. After a change of the four-horse team, the coach continued, but after traveling eight miles the same two men, unmasked, appeared on the road and commanded driver Smith to rein in his team. The larger man (Claughton) held the shotgun, cocked, and pointed it at the head of Smith and demanded the mailbags. While Smith controlled his team, Cliff was preparing to throw out the mail pouches, but Smith said, "Boys, I don't think you are posted?" The smaller robber (Barry) with revolver in hand said, "Then throw out the express box." Cliff then threw down the Wells, Fargo express box next to the mail pouches. When the small road agent said, "Throw down that second box," Smith replied, "I am satisfied you are not posted at all—that other company has drawn out of the business." The robber acknowledged there should be no second box aboard and then told Smith to drive on. After the robbers finished with their work at the scene they rode northward at a leisurely pace. All along the route men had heard of the robbery and several saw the robbers, who were identified by their horses as well as their clothing and physical descriptions, and there was great interest as this was the first stagecoach robbery reported in the area of San Luis Obispo for some time.

In late July the two road agents, and two others, were in Natividad when they were recognized and a committee of vigilantes captured them and lodged them in jail. As soon as they were behind bars, Barry confessed and informed on Claughton, Burns and Selby. They were taken to San Francisco on July 24 where they were charged with obstructing the U.S. mail. They were arraigned in the U.S. circuit court in August, and trial was set for Wednesday, October 19 for Claughton, the larger man with the shotgun at the scene of the June 4 robbery. Barry, who was but twenty years old, had turned state's evidence and had been promised that he would not receive time at the state prison, and he was the prosecution's primary witness. Claughton was convicted that evening after the jury deliberated only fifteen minutes, and he was scheduled to be sentenced the following Saturday. The trial for Burns and Selby began the next morning and they were also convicted. On Saturday Judge Lorenzo Sawyer sentenced Burns to serve two years at San Quentin Prison and he registered as prisoner #4626; Selby was sentenced to serve two years in prison and he registered as prisoner #4628; and Claughton was sentenced to serve four years in prison and he registered as prisoner #4627. All three men had arrived at the prison on October 27, 1870, and Selby died in prison on June 25, 1871; Burns was released on July 15, 1872, after serving twenty and one half months; and Claughton was released on March 18, 1874, after serving forty-one months.

Sources: *Daily Alta California (San Francisco)*: October 19–20, 1870. *Sacramento Daily Union (CA)*: July 25, 1870.

Unknown, July 14, 1870

At 10:20 p.m. Saturday, July 14, 1870, the northbound stagecoach from San Luis Obispo to Salinas, with passengers bound for San Francisco, was ten miles south of Salinas when the driver saw two men, "mounted and armed to the teeth," at the brow of the hill his coach was ascending. They had their guns drawn and pointed at the coach, and the only way to avoid them would be to veer off the road. It was obvious that "resistance would have most likely resulted in precipitating the coach and passengers down a steep bank and killing all on board." The driver reined in his team, and then the men rode up and told him to throw down the Wells, Fargo express box, while assuring the passengers they were not interested in any money or other valuables they might be carrying. Once the box was in the road the road agents told the driver to continue, but one said to the driver, "If the box is heavy, I will drop you a gold piece." The coach then continued into Salinas and the driver reported the robbery. A posse went to the scene, found the broken box and returned it to town, but could find no clues nor a trail to follow.

Source: *San Luis Obispo Tribune (CA)*: July 16, 1870.

Unknown, May 5, 1871

On Friday night, May 5, 1871, the San Juan stagecoach southbound for Los Angeles was stopped by three road agents, masked and armed, when three miles south of the Salinas River. They demanded the Wells, Fargo express box, and it was thrown down. They broke it open, but there was nothing inside but a letter valued at $50, which they took. When they rifled through the papers looking for money they tore up the Germania Life Insurance Company receipts, perhaps in frustration or haste. There were passengers aboard but they were not molested, and the robbers did not ask for the mail. A posse was organized and rode to the scene but could find no trace of the road agents. Wells, Fargo issued a reward of $100 for the arrest of each of the robbers, but they were never identified.

Source: *Daily Alta California (San Francisco)*: May 7, 1871.

UNKNOWN, APRIL 20, 1872

On Saturday, April 20, 1872, the southbound stagecoach from Gilroy to Hollister, in Monterey County, was nearing its destination when two road agents, masked and armed, stepped into the road and ordered the driver to halt. They demanded the Wells, Fargo express box but there was none aboard, so they demanded the mail sacks and then ordered the passengers to step out and form a line. While one robber covered everyone with his gun the other went through the passengers and collected $150, but he did not molest the driver, who remained on his seat to control his team. They ordered the passengers to board and then cut open the mail sacks and took out everything that looked valuable, and as soon as they had their plunder they ordered the driver to continue on. The driver hurried into Hollister and reported the robbery, and a posse was organized. They rode to the scene but could find no clue to the robbers' identities, nor a trail to follow, so they gathered up the mailbags and the remaining contents and returned to town.

Source: *Sacramento Daily Union (CA)*: April 24, 1872.

UNKNOWN, AUGUST 11, 1874

On Tuesday afternoon, August 11, 1874, the stagecoach from Salinas to Monterey was robbed when it was nearing Johnson's dairy in Monterey. Two road agents, one a thick-set Mexican and the other a tall American with red whiskers, stepped into the road and ordered the driver to halt. They pointed their weapons and demanded the Wells, Fargo express box, and it was thrown down. As soon as they had the box they ordered the driver to continue, and they fled, carrying away the box, which contained $113.75. As soon as the driver reached downtown Monterey he notified Deputy Graves who organized a posse and rode to the scene, but they could not find a clue to the robbers' identities, nor a trail to follow, nor the box. Another posse was raised at the Halfway House and they took to the roads to try to cut off the robbers' escape, but they had no better luck.

Source: *Sacramento Daily Union (CA)*: August 12, 1874.

UNKNOWN, AUGUST 31, 1875

On Tuesday, August 31, 1875, the Soledad stagecoach was stopped when one mile below Lowe's station, and two masked and armed road agents demanded the Wells, Fargo box. It was thrown down, and the robbers told the driver to move on, without molesting the passengers nor asking for the mail. They busted open the box and took out $1,000. It was believed these were the same two men who had stopped the coach on August 11, 1874, so this time lawmen hurried to the scene, but they were not able to identify the robbers nor find a clear trail to follow.

Source: *Daily Alta California (San Francisco)*: September 7, 1875.

UNKNOWN, OCTOBER 22, 1875

On Friday night, October 22, 1875, the southbound Coast Line stagecoach was sixteen miles south of Soledad, at a place called Lost Chance Gulch, when the driver heard the command, "Pass out Wells, Fargo's treasure box, and be quick or I will blow your brains out." The driver threw out the box, and the robber stooped to pick it up. Just then ex-sheriff A. W. Poole, the only passenger on that trip who was walking behind the coach, told the road agent, "Drop it, or you are a dead man." The robber fired at Poole with his pistol and Poole fired back with both barrels of his sawed-off shotgun, and the robber fell over a bank and down into the gulch. Just then a second robber, who had been hidden in the shadows of some brush, fired at Poole with a pistol and then turned and ran. Poole returned that gunfire but did not know if he had hit the second man. Poole returned the box to the stagecoach, and they continued on to Salinas, their destination. A mile further on a lone, masked highwayman was seen, and Poole, then riding on the seat next to the driver, fired at him as he retreated and shot at the coach three times. The next morning a posse rode to the scene of both shootings and at the bottom of the gulch found blood on the dirt and rocks, so it was clear that Poole had wounded at least one of the robbers, but they could not find any of the road agents and returned to Salinas empty-handed.

Source: *Sacramento Daily Union (CA)*: October 25, 1875.

WILLIAM L. EARL AND JOSE M. GIL, APRIL 14, 1877

On Saturday morning, April 14, 1877, at half past one, the stagecoach from Soledad to San Luis Obispo, driven by W. Cambridge, when three-quarters of a mile below Jolon in Monterey County, was stopped by two masked road agents. Each man wielded a double-barreled shotgun, which they pointed at Cambridge, ordered him to halt, and then demanded the Wells, Fargo express box. Cambridge threw it down, and then the road agents ordered him to drive on. They did not ask for the mail sacks, nor did they molest the passengers. Cambridge hurried on to the next station and sounded the alarm.

Posses were soon on the trail of the robbers, and it was not long before they were captured and lodged in jail. They gave their names as William L. Earl and Jose M. Gil. At their examination they were held over for action by the grand jury, and in early July they were indicted on the lesser charge of grand larceny, upon the agreement they would plead guilty to receive a reduced sentence. When brought into court for their arraignment they pled as agreed, and in consideration of their cooperation Earl and Gil were sentenced to serve four years at San Quentin. They arrived on July 13, 1877, Earl registering as prisoner #7661 and Gil as #7662. Both men served out their entire terms, less good time as required under the Goodwin Act, and they were released by expiration of sentence on July 13, 1880.

Source: *San Luis Obispo Tribune (CA)*: April 21, 1877.

GEORGE ADAMS, DECEMBER 3, 1879

On December 3, 1879, the Coast Line stagecoach driven by Jim Myers, when approaching Soledad in Monterey County, came to a line tied across the road with a white handkerchief tied in the middle to make it visible to the horses. Myers pulled up the team, and a voice called out, "Throw out that box." He looked toward the sound and saw the shadowy figure of a man standing among the chaparral, and behind him was the dim light of a campfire. The Wells, Fargo treasure box was delivered, the line was dropped, and the robber ordered the coach to continue into Soledad. After the coach left, the robber broke open the box and took out $167 in money and a check for $140 drawn on a bank in San Luis Obispo. As soon as the coach reached town, Sheriff John C. Franks went to the scene and followed a clear trail through Watsonville and into San Francisco, where he arrested the road agent and identified him as Salinas resident George Adams. Adams was only nineteen years old and had never been in any trouble, but he readily admitted to being the road agent. He said he had no weapon, and was about to run away when the driver threw down the box. The sheriff brought his prisoner back to Salinas by train the following day and lodged him in jail.

The grand jury was in session at the time, so there was no delay in beginning criminal proceedings. Adams again admitted, at his examination, that he was the robber. He was quickly indicted and on December 18, only two weeks after he had stopped the stagecoach, Adams pled guilty. He was sentenced the same day to serve five years at San Quentin and was immediately transported to the prison where he registered as prisoner #9148. Adams served out his entire term and was released, by expiration of sentence, on July 15, 1883.

Sources: *Salinas City Index (CA)*: December 11, 1879; December 18, 1879.

JAMES R. PALMER, MARCH 30, 1880

On Tuesday night, March 30, 1880, the Coast Line stagecoach from San Luis Obispo to Soledad, driven by Jim Myers, was nearing its destination when a masked youth, sporting a shotgun, stepped into the road and ordered the driver to rein in his team. The road agent next demanded the Wells, Fargo treasure box, and it was thrown down. As soon as the box was delivered Myers was told to continue into town, and he immediately whipped up his team. Myers reported the robbery to Sheriff John C. Franks who dispatched a deputy to the scene, the same place the stagecoach had been robbed six months earlier, and he took up the robber's trail. At daylight the box was found on the bank of the river, broken open and rifled of its contents. Sheriff Franks then took up the trail and followed the road agent into Tulare County. He was on the trail five days, the same time it took to capture the previous road agent, and he captured this robber as well. The prisoner gave the name James Palmer and claimed he was only nineteen years old, and he was taken to Salinas and lodged in jail. Franks had earned the $600 reward by the capture, $300 from the state and $300 from Wells, Fargo, and he still had $600 due for his previous capture of a stagecoach robber. Palmer had his examination and was held over to answer to the grand jury, he was indicted in early April, and within a month of the robbery he had his trial, was convicted, and was sentenced to serve a term of seven years at San Quentin. Palmer arrived at the prison April 26, 1880, and registered as prisoner #9248. He was released, by expiration of sentence, on January 26, 1885.

Sources: *San Luis Obispo Tribune (CA)*: April 10, 1880; May 8, 1880.

A. S. GONZALES, JULY 19, 1881

At noon on July 19, 1881, the Coast Line Stage Company's northbound coach from San Luis Obispo to Soledad was robbed near Gonzales in the Salinas Valley. The coach, driven by John Walker with four passengers aboard, was stopped by a lone highwayman a mile beyond R. R. Harris' place near the junction of the new roads over the Cuesta Mountains, just five miles from San Luis Obispo. The first the driver knew of the road agent was his voice from behind a sycamore tree, in Spanish, ordering Walker to halt and throw down the box. As soon as the Wells, Fargo treasure box was in the road the driver was ordered to continue. The mails were not requested and the passengers were not molested. The robber got $10 in coin and a package containing $8. Richard Perkins, then using the name Lytle who was in the area, telegraphed a detailed account to the *Daily Echo*. He was quickly credited with this robbery by Wells, Fargo's chief detective James B. Hume, perhaps in an effort to close the case, but this was an error. In early August, A. S. Gonzales was arrested and at his examination he was held over for the grand jury. Then on August 20 the district attorney, afraid he did not have sufficient evidence for an indictment, filed an information. The defendant was arraigned in early September and his trial was set for September 24, but the case was so weak that it was dismissed and Gonzales was released. No one was ever prosecuted for this stagecoach robbery.

Source: *Santa Cruz Daily Echo (CA)*: July 20, 1881.

Richard "Dick Fellows" Perkins, December 11, 1881; January 13, 1882

Dick Fellows, within months after his release from prison, robbed the stagecoach between Santa Barbara and San Luis Obispo on August 25, 1881. He did not appear on the road for four months, but on December 11, 1881, at 8:00 p.m. he stopped the stagecoach from San Luis Obispo to Soledad in Monterey County when it was a mile from its destination. He wore a white mask as he demanded the treasure box, which was thrown down, and he profited by $60 before ordering the driver to continue. Posses could find no clue to the identity of the robber. He would rob two stagecoaches in Santa Barbara County, one on January 2 and another on January 8, 1882, before returning to Monterey County.

On Friday evening, January 13, 1882, the Coast Line stagecoach coming toward Soledad had been stopped between the Oak Grove Hotel and the Salinas River by a road agent masked with a gunnysack. There had been several passengers aboard but they were afraid the coach would be robbed and laid over at the hotel. The driver, James Myers, was stopped when he was a mile from Soledad, his destination, and ordered to throw out the treasure box. The robber then took the hatchet from the coach and broke it open. He told Myers he would leave the hatchet where he could find it the following day and ordered him to continue. There was $41 in the box.

Detective Charles Aull learned that the road agent had first gone to Santa Cruz, then stayed overnight January 24 at Pescadero, and on Wednesday went to San Mateo. Aull was joined by several more detectives, but before they could take action, Perkins was captured at 4:00 p.m. by C. Van Duren on Couts' ranch on the road to Mayfield in Santa Clara County. Van Duren turned Perkins over to Constable Burke of Santa Clara. On Friday, January 27, Burke telegraphed that he was taking his prisoner to San Jose by buggy, but at Mountain View he boarded the train and arrived at San Jose at 6:35 p.m. The detectives were watching for a buggy, so they were not at the railroad depot. Burke decided to take the streetcar to St. Johns and Market Streets, where he disembarked with his prisoner and started for the jail. Perkins was a congenial sort, and as the two men passed the I. X. L. Saloon, the prisoner invited the lawman to have a drink, and in they went. As soon as Perkins downed his drink he started for the door at a run, with Burke in pursuit, but Perkins was too fleet afoot and escaped. Burke fired at him but missed. The barkeep, Thomas Farrel, joined the chase and briefly gained on Perkins but, not knowing the gravity of his crime, refrained from shooting the fleeing fugitive who was handcuffed and bare-headed. Perkins was spotted several times over the next twenty-four hours, but no capture was made. Sheriff John C. Franks formed a posse, but by January 28 he had given up and a posse of twenty private citizens took up the chase.

On February 3 at 5:00 p.m. Dr. W. F. Gunckel found a man hiding on the second floor of his barn on Stockton Avenue. The doctor went to the second floor to throw down hay to feed his horse, but he smelled the strong odor like bad whiskey breath and believed a drunk or tramp was hiding there. He found the man bedded down behind bales of hay and ordered him out. The doctor summoned a neighbor, and when Perkins came down he kept both hands in his pockets. The neighbor then gave him a hat, and while he was putting it on, the doctor's wife came out and remarked that she thought it was Dick Fellows (alias for Perkins) as the man fit the description of the fugitive. After Perkins left, the bed behind the haystacks was searched and the doctor found empty bottles of porter, food taken from his cellar, and a hatchet, and he also found that his file was missing. It was supposed that Perkins' peculiar behavior suggested he had cut the chain between his cuffs but still had the cuffs on his wrists, so he had hid his hands in his pockets. Lawmen were summoned and the area was searched for hours, but the fugitive could not be found. Perkins was later captured in San Jose, but he also escaped from that jail. He was finally captured by a posse deep in the Santa Cruz Mountains, near Boulder Creek, while he was trying to make his escape to the coast. He was taken to Santa Barbara, tried, and on March 27, 1882, he was convicted of a number of robbery charges.

On March 30 the judge sentenced Perkins to a life term in Folsom Prison. Perkins had one last chance for freedom, so on April 2, 1882, he escaped from the Santa Barbara jail before he could be taken to Folsom. He ran several blocks and found a horse staked out in a vacant lot. He quickly mounted and tried to ride off, but the horse bucked him off and ran away. He was lying in the dirt, stunned by the fall, when he was rearrested and returned to his cell, and only later did he learn that the horse had been eating locoweed for days and was staked out to recover. Perkins arrived at Folsom Prison on April 6, 1882, registered as prisoner #470, and after serving twenty-two years he was pardoned by acting Governor Porter on March 8, 1904.

Sources: *Daily Herald (San Jose, CA)*: January 28, 1882; February 3, 1882. *Los Angeles Daily News (CA)*: December 10, 1869; December 24, 1869. *Los Angeles Star (CA)*: December 11, 1869; January 22, 1870. *Kern County Weekly Courier (CA)*: December 4, 1875; December 11, 1875; January 15, 1876; January 22, 1876. *San Jose Herald (CA)*: January 28, 1882; January 29, 1882; February 3–5, 1882; April 2, 1882; April 22, 1882. *San Luis Obispo Tribune (CA)*: July 23, 1881; August 6, 1881; August 20, 1881; August 26, 1881; September 3, 1881; October 1, 1881; January 7, 1882; January 14, 1882; January 21, 1882; February 4, 1882; February 11, 1882; April 8, 1882. *San Jose Mercury (CA)*: January 28, 1882; January 29, 1882; February 3–5, 1882; April 2, 1882; April 22, 1882. *San Francisco Examiner (CA)*: June 24, 1894.

Napa County

JAMES R. DOLLAR AND WILLIAM RUSSELL, JUNE 12, 1877

Shortly after noon on June 12, 1877, the stagecoach from Calistoga in Napa County to Lakeport in Lake County, pulled by a team of six horses driven by Wash Gwin, was seven miles above Calistoga and "toiling up the grade going north" on the St. Helena toll road near Bradford's station. Suddenly two medium-sized, masked and heavily armed road agents appeared. The two men wore over their heads sacks with eyeholes cut in them, and the sacks went all the way to their waists where they were tied off with string. One, wearing blue overalls, was armed with an army musket while the other, who wore brown overalls, carried a double-barreled shotgun. They pointed their weapons at Gwin, ordered him to halt, and then demanded the Wells, Fargo express box. As soon as the box was handed out the road agents ordered Gwin to continue on. Gwin's coach was filled with many women and children, but none of the passengers were molested.

Gwin had only gone about one hundred yards when he met the Lower Lake stagecoach bound for Calistoga and driven by Budd "Eli" Philpott. That coach had two treasure boxes, one from Lakeport filled with coin and the other from the quicksilver mines which was comparatively light. Wash shouted to Philpott, "Look out, I have just been robbed," but the warning came too late for Philpott to turn around as the grade was much too narrow, so he continued on. As Philpott reached the place where Gwin had been robbed the road agents appeared and shouted, "Halt, or we'll blow your brains out!" Philpott reined in his team, and when the command to hand out the box came, he fumbled about to give himself some time. The robbers became impatient and as one man covered Philpott the other began to climb up onto the boot, so Philpott handed out the light box. The two road agents, being satisfied it was the only one aboard, ordered the stagecoach to proceed. Philpott's coach was filled with Chinamen, but the road agents did not molest them.

There seemed no clue to the identities of the road agents but it was certain they were "green at the business," yet were familiar with the stage route and schedule. They had selected a place where they could rob both stagecoaches within a few minutes and flee. As soon as the down stage arrived at Calistoga, officers were informed and they formed a posse. At the scene they found both boxes "bursted open with an ax," which was lying nearby and was identified as one stolen at Calistoga. There was a trail of boot tracks with distinctive nail marks in the heels and soles, and these tracks led away from the robbery scene. During the investigation which followed, a Mr. Weybright, who lived at the foot of St. Helena Mountain, said that two young men had come to his house for breakfast, saying they had not eaten for a day, and he provided a description. Meanwhile a man named Cherry with Rufus Henson and C. Connor, who lived near Calistoga, followed the foot tracks of the two road agents to a wheat field near Kellogg, only five miles from the scene of the robbery. Henson, on horseback, was following the trail which skirted along the edge of the field and saw that the tracks turned into the field. As he looked toward the field he saw one of the road agents pointing a shotgun at him, so he dropped down on the opposite side of his horse and made his way to a nearby house where he borrowed a Henry rifle. He motioned to Cherry and Connor to join him and the three men gave chase. Cherry fired two shots at one of the fleeing fugitives before he surrendered, and the other robber also surrendered immediately when Connor fired one shot at him. They were handcuffed, taken into Calistoga, and lodged in jail.

The two men were given their examination and they identified themselves as William Russell and James R. Dollar. The shotgun was shown in court, but the musket could not be found and was thought to have been hidden or thrown away. Testimony proved that the robbers had only obtained $25 from both boxes, and $14.50 had been recovered when they were arrested. They had purchased a bottle of whiskey and, when discovered, had just turned into the field to drink their liquor and take a nap. They were held over to answer to the grand jury, and the night of June 13 they were taken to Napa and jailed there. The *Napa Daily Register* noted, "They are the same parties spoken of in yesterday's edition as being under suspicion, and although they deny their guilt, and the evidence against them is wholly circumstantial, yet there is little doubt of their being the robbers, as they have been traced from Calistoga to the scene of the robbery, and from there to the place where they were captured. They account for their actions in running from their captors by saying that they had stolen two turkeys the night before, and thought the farmers were after them. This was so; the turkeys were found in a sack, but this does not acquit them of the stage robbery."

The men were questioned about their identities. Dollar, a man of medium height with light hair and moustache, about twenty-five years old, said he had a wife in San Francisco and had worked in the Lower Lake schoolhouse until it burned down recently. The other man, Russell, was of medium height with dark eyes and hair and about twenty-three years old. Dollar and Russell were tried at the June session of the Napa County court and each defendant was convicted of two robberies—a separate conviction for each stagecoach. Both men were sentenced to serve nine years at San Quentin and both arrived on July 3, 1877. Russell was registered as prisoner #7652 and Dollar as #7653. Governor George C. Perkins commuted Russell's sentence to seven and a half years, and he was discharged on September 28, 1882. Dollar served out his entire sentence and on June 3, 1883, he was released upon expiration of his sentence.

Source: *Napa Daily Register (CA)*: June 14–15, 1877.

UNKNOWN, AUGUST 16, 1881

On Tuesday morning, August 16, 1881, the stagecoach traveling between Aetna Springs and St. Helena was climbing a grade when a bald road agent, fully disguised and with a revolver in his hand, stepped out and ordered the coach to halt. He demanded the Wells, Fargo express box, but there was none aboard so he called for the mail pouches, but there was no mail aboard for that trip. He next ordered the passengers to step out and form a line, and one man and two women followed his instructions. The robber took $25 from the man, but gave back $5, then told them to climb aboard, and once they were seated he ordered the driver to move along. He appeared new to the business and trembled while collecting his plunder. At St. Helena the robbery was reported and a posse rode to the scene, but there were no clues to the robber's identity nor a trail to follow.

Source: *Sacramento Daily Union (CA)*: August 17, 1881.

UNKNOWN, OCTOBER 8, 1885

On Thursday, October 8, 1885, the stagecoach from Lakeport to Calistoga was nine miles from its destination when a lone highwayman, masked and armed, stepped out and stopped the coach. He ordered the driver to throw down the express box and as soon as it was on the ground he told the driver to continue on. He was not interested in passengers and did not ask for the mail. The highwayman busted open the box but found little of value inside, but the box did contain a package containing a silk dress consigned to a woman in Calistoga and a watch and he took those. Shortly after the robbery a young hunter stumbled upon the road agent walking in the woods, carrying the package, and though this seemed odd he did not place any significance on the occurrence until he learned of the robbery, and he described the robber in great detail. Lawmen had gone to the scene but could find no clues until the hunter came forward. The driver had described the road agent as "well dressed, with a strong voice, certainly no tramp," and this description also fit the dapper Michael Donovan. Lawmen received a description of the dress and watch, and they began looking for Donovan.

The girlfriend of Donovan was the addressee on the package containing the silk dress, and Donovan delivered the package. A week after the robbery Donovan moved to Nevada City and his girlfriend followed, and she took employment in a house of ill repute. Donovan was traced to Nevada City and on the evening of October 30 he was arrested by Constable L. S. Cherry and Stephen Venard in the house of ill repute where his girlfriend worked, and the dress was found among her belongings and taken as evidence. The prisoner was taken back to Napa, and on November 2 he was lodged in the county jail. He denied the charge and said he could prove an alibi. His examination was scheduled for November 5, and Wells, Fargo detective John Thacker went to Nevada City and on November 4 brought the girlfriend to Napa to testify. On November 5 the hearing was held and Donovan, as promised, proved an alibi and was discharged. There were no further clues nor suspects and no one else was charged in the robbery.

Sources: *Daily Alta California (San Francisco)*: October 9, 1885; November 1, 1885; November 3, 1885. *Sacramento Daily Union (CA)*: November 5, 1885; November 7, 1885.

UNKNOWN, MARCH 23, 1888

On Friday, March 23, 1888, the stagecoach from Calistoga to the mines had traveled only thirteen miles when a road agent standing on the side of the road ordered the driver to rein in his team. The robber was armed with a Winchester rifle and wore a flour sack with eyeholes cut into it for his mask, and he had blue overalls covering his clothing. He called for the Wells, Fargo express box to be thrown out, and after it was on the ground he told the driver to continue on. The passengers were not molested, and the robber did not ask for the mail pouches. A posse was organized and rode to the scene, but all they could find was the box with the top broken in, and the small amount of money inside was gone but all the other papers remained. It was believed that the robber expected to find the large payroll of coin on the way to the mine, but it went out the following day under guard. A $600 reward was posted, but the robber was never identified.

Source: *Los Angeles Herald (CA)*: March 24, 1888.

Unknown, September 14, 1899; March 2, 1900; August 14, 1901

On Thursday afternoon, September 14, 1899, the northbound stagecoach on the Calistoga and Clear Lake line reached a place near Mrs. Greenlee's ranch known as "Hardscrabble," or "Desperate Bend," where there was a sharp projection of the mountain requiring a sharp turn onto a steep incline, and where the horses had to proceed at a very slow pace. The coach was still a mile and a half from the tollhouse when a lone road agent, waving a double-barreled shotgun, stepped out of the heavy brush and ordered driver Tuck Quigley to halt. The robber then demanded the Wells, Fargo express box, and it was thrown down, but he was not satisfied. He ordered the eight passengers to step out and form a line and told them to "shell out." He had them step out one at a time, pile their money and valuables in the roadway, and then step back, until all had contributed. The Reverend C. F. McCoy gave up $5 and complained that he was a poor man, so the robber gave him back a dollar, saying, "All right pard, here's one simoleon for luck." Passenger Newton Stiff slipped his wallet into his boot and contributed only his loose silver change. William Abbey, an invalid, also made an appeal for generosity and was given $.50. During the time that the passengers were busy piling up their money the mask on the robber's face slipped several times, and the driver and Stiff were sure it was Joseph Weir, a local character. Once the collection was completed the robber told Quigley to drive on. As the coach pulled out the robber gathered up the pile of plunder in the road, grabbed the express box, and ran into a thicket, and in a few moments three shots were heard as the robber shot the lock off the box. Quigley hurried to the tollhouse where he telephoned the report to Calistoga and Napa.

In Calistoga Constable Grauss and City Marshal Nash organized a posse and started for the scene, and from Napa Sheriff D. A. Dunlap started for Calistoga with Constable Allen. At 5:00 p.m. they were joined in Calistoga by Constable Spurr of St. Helena, who brought along his bloodhounds. By the time Dunlap reached the scene Grauss and Nash had arrested Weir and lodged him in the Calistoga jail, but some believed the robber was George Coburn, a Lake County desperado. However, Weir was identified by Quigley and Stiff and the next day bloodhounds were used to follow a scent right to Weir's door, but he persisted in his claim of innocence, even to his mother when she visited. Weir seemed to fit the description given by Quigley: five feet eight inches tall, light hair and complexion, wearing a black hat pulled down over his eyes, blue overalls, and carrying an old-fashioned double-barreled shotgun. On September 23 Weir had his preliminary hearing before justice Chinn, all the evidence was presented and it was found lacking, so the prisoner was discharged. No others were suspected so lawmen had to again wait for some break in the case.

At 12:30 p.m. on Friday, March 2, 1900, the regular mail stagecoach from Calistoga to Clear Lake was six miles from Calistoga climbing the grade at Mount St. Helena, and a mile and a half from the tollhouse near the same place it was robbed in September, when a masked road agent suddenly appeared behind a fence partly concealed by the brush. He ordered driver Albert R. Palmer to halt and pointed his double-barreled shotgun at the driver's head. Palmer stopped the coach and was told to throw down the Wells, Fargo express box. At the same time the robber told Palmer to look away or he would shoot him, and he repeated the command several times. After the box was thrown down he looked into the passenger compartment and found Mrs. Thomas C. van Ness and her daughter, Mrs. C. F. Peterson, and an Italian gardener bound for Harbin Springs. He did not molest the ladies but told the gardener to deposit his money next to the express box, and the gardener stepped out and laid down $4.50, then boarded. After the gardener was seated the robber told the driver to continue on, without molesting the driver or asking for the mail. Palmer whipped up his team and hurried to the tollhouse where he telephoned Napa and Calistoga. All of the passengers were quite agitated by the ordeal, excepting Mrs. Peterson who made a careful examination of the robber and described him as medium height, slightly stooped, dressed in dark clothing, with a red handkerchief over his face. When word reached Calistoga, Constable Grauss and Marshal Nash started for the scene, and Sheriff Dunlap with Napa constables Allen and Secord started for Calistoga. Constable Spurr and Marshal Johnson of St. Helena hurried to Calistoga with their bloodhounds, and as soon as the posse reached the scene the dogs took up the scent and started toward the Oat Hill mine. The box was found one hundred yards from the scene of the robbery, with the lock blown off with some explosive, and $4 had been removed, all that was inside. There the posse divided, with some men going with the dogs toward the Oat Hill mine and others heading into Pope Valley to cut off the robber's route. By the following day the dogs had followed the scent to within four miles of the mine, but there the road agent covered his trail with cayenne pepper, and after the dogs got a few whiffs, they were unable to work any further. A heavy rain began to fall on Saturday so the posse slept the night in the heavy woods, and the following morning some men returned to town with the dogs while several others tried to continue on the trail. On March 5 the sheriff announced that he had given up the chase, and again he waited for some break in the case.

At 11:45 a.m. on Wednesday, August 14, 1901, two stagecoaches left Calistoga bound for Clear Lake with twelve passengers in the first coach and four in the second, including six women. The first coach was five miles from Calistoga at 1:00 p.m. and turning up the Mount St. Helena Road when driver Albert R. Palmer found a lone highwayman standing in the middle of the road twenty-five feet ahead. The robber, masked with a blue handkerchief with eyes holes cut into it, aimed a Winchester rifle at Palmer's head and ordered, "Stop that stage and throw up your hands!" It was the same place the stagecoach had been robbed in September 1899 and in March 1900, the place known as "Hardscrabble" or "Desperate Bend." As soon as the coach was stopped, the road agent commanded the passengers, "Pile out of there, and be lively," and he had them line up on his right. Hardly had the first coach stopped when the second coach came around the curve and the road agent pointed his rifle over the heads of the twelve passengers and ordered driver William Conner to halt and hold up his hands, and then he had the four passengers alight and line up on his left. He took a position where he could watch everyone, including both drivers, and said to the passengers, "Come forward one at a time and shell out." He laid aside his rifle and drew his old fashioned "horse pistol," and the passengers, one-by-one with hands above their heads, advanced and were searched. He checked each man carefully reaching deep into any pocket where he thought there might be some valuable left behind, but he trusted the women to surrender their valuables. Once he had all the plunder from the passengers, he told Palmer to throw down the Wells, Fargo express box and the mail, and once these were in the road he told Conner to throw down his express box, but the second driver replied, "Ain't got any. I'm only extra." And the robber replied, "Well, you've been driving pretty regular lately," showing he had knowledge of the routes and schedules. He then ordered everyone to board and sent the coaches on their way. He had collected $400 and several items of jewelry from the passengers, but it was reported there was very little of value in the express box, and the value of the mail was not known. It was speculated that the road agent had expected to find the payroll for the Copper King mines, but it had been held back for a later coach. The coaches continued a mile and a half to Toll Gate where lawmen were notified by telephone, and Sheriff Dunlap started from Napa while Calistoga's city marshal Nash hurried to the scene and took up the trail. The robber who was seen was described as five feet eight inches in height, dark complected, 150 pounds, wearing a dark slouch hat, linen duster, and heavy working boots, but two boys reported that early in the day they had seen two men lurking about the scene of the robbery. One of those men matched exactly the description of the road agent seen, and the other was "tall and dark," believed to be an accomplice who waited in hiding and kept all covered with some weapon.

Sheriff Dunlap arrived that afternoon and joined the posse with bloodhounds, but all they found was a half-empty mail sack in a gulch a half mile from the scene. It had been gone through quite thoroughly but a great deal of the mail, valueless to the robber, was left behind, gathered up by the posse, and delivered to the postmaster in Calistoga. On August 18 Sheriff Dunlap arrested Clifford Turner, of Putah Creek, on suspicion of being the road agent who was in the road, and he was taken to Napa that evening. However, there is no record that Turner was held over for the grand jury, so the evidence must have been weak.

Sources: *Los Angeles Herald (CA)*: September 15–16, 1899; March 3–4, 1900; August 15, 1901; August 18, 1901. *San Francisco Call (CA)*: September 15–16, 1899; March 3, 1900; March 6, 1900; August 15, 1901.

Unknown, January 3, 1903

At 1:00 p.m. on Saturday, January 3, 1903, the six-horse stagecoach from Calistoga to Clear Lake, driven by William Conner, had reached Dusty Bend on Mount St. Helena, a popular place for robberies, when it was halted by a lone road agent, masked and armed. He demanded the Wells, Fargo express box, and after it was thrown down he ordered the nine passengers to step out and form a line. He collected a small sum from each of the four grown men but took nothing from the woman, the young man, the three small boys, or the driver. The robber then had the passengers board, and as soon as everyone was seated he told Conner to move along. The driver whipped up his team and hurried to the tollhouse, and from there he sent word to Constable Ben Grauss and Officer Ed Powers at Calistoga, who organized a posse and started for the scene. They had a good description from the driver and passengers: six feet tall; dark complexion, hair and eyes; weight about 170 pounds; worn blue overalls with a hole in the right knee tied closed with a string. The posse found the box with the lock shot off and the contents removed, but they had no information on the amount inside, and they collected the box for return to Calistoga. They could find no trail to follow for any distance, so they awaited the arrival of the dogs. At 5:00 p.m. Sheriff D. A. Dunlap and Constable Allen of Napa and Constable Spurr and Marshal Johnson of St. Helena arrived at Calistoga and immediately started for the scene with bloodhounds, but it was doubtful they could accomplish much until daybreak. The search continued the next day, but by then the road agent had too great a head start and was neither captured nor identified.

Source: *Los Angeles Herald (CA)*: January 4, 1903.

Unknown, April 27, 1903

Just after 2:30 a.m. on Monday, April 27, 1903, the stagecoach from Calistoga to Oathill, with proprietor Justin Reed driving, was nearing the summit of Oathill grade seven and a half miles from Calistoga, at the place called "the Cave," when a lone road agent, masked with a gunnysack with eyeholes and brandishing a large revolver, ordered the coach to halt. He demanded that the Wells, Fargo express box be thrown down, and after it was in the road he went through the one passenger, a Chinaman, and took his silver watch. The passenger had dropped his money onto the floor of the wagon and saved it, but the robber took from Reed $2.60, all he had. While the robbing was going on, a traveling butcher named Fickas drove up, was halted, and was robbed of $6. Once the robber had all the plunder he could find he told Reed and Fickas to move on, then took the express box and headed into Schwartz Canyon in the direction of Pope Valley. Reed reported the robbery and described the road agent as five feet eight inches tall, weighing

175 pounds with blue eyes; he wore gunnysacks on his feet so there would be no boot tracks, his hands were dark on the back but white on the palms showing he was not a working man, and he wore a blue shirt with white stripes and black pants.

Sheriff D. A. Dunlap with Deputy Spurr and Constable Allen left Napa for the scene and then continued into Pope Valley while Constable Foff with Deputy Hower went into Knight's Valley to head off the robber's flight in that direction, leaving the rest of their large posse from Calistoga to search the countryside. However, the area was rough and rugged with many hiding places for a lone bandit so the efforts proved futile, and no one was identified or arrested for the robbery.

Sources: *Los Angeles Herald (CA)*: April 28, 1903. *San Francisco Call (CA)*: April 28, 1903.

Nevada County

Unknown, May 3, 1858

On Monday morning, May 3, 1858, the stagecoach from Nevada City had traveled a short distance from town when four road agents stepped into the road and ordered the driver to halt. They were masked and heavily armed, and they pointed their guns at the driver's head as they demanded the Wells, Fargo express box. It was thrown down and then, without asking about passengers nor calling for the mail, one told the driver to move along. After the coach was out of sight the robbers broke open the box and took out $21,000 in gold dust.

As soon as the robbery was reported posses were organized, they rushed to the scene, and soon took up the trail of the robbers. Quickly two men were lodged in jail and lawmen were on the trail of two more. On May 8 Robert Dutton was arrested in San Francisco, and then a second man was arrested on the ferry, and both were taken back to Nevada City where they were lodged in jail with the other two prisoners. Three men denied any knowledge of or part in the robbery, but Dutton said he knew some of the details of the robbery but had no part in it, and he supported the claim of innocence by the other three prisoners. At their examination there was not enough evidence to hold any of the prisoners so they were all released, and the delay allowed the guilty parties to escape justice.

Sources: *Daily Alta California (San Francisco)*: May 4, 1858. *Sacramento Daily Union (CA)*: May 8, 1858.

Robert Finn, George W. Moore and George Shanks, May 6, 1866; May 16, 1866

By 1866 the roads near Nevada City were infested with road agents. They robbed any person thought to have valuables, but they particularly targeted the Wells, Fargo treasure boxes carried on the stagecoaches. The country within a few miles of Nevada City was particularly rugged terrain with steep ravines and gullies, and in May the water in the creek bottoms had been swollen by recent heavy rains. Large boulders perched precariously above the roads and trails, ready to tumble down at any time, and chaparral had grown as high as a man. Black's crossing, later Purdon's crossing, was near the summit on the approach to Nevada City on the south side of the Yuba River, and it was the ideal place to stop a stagecoach, as the horses had to be driven at a slow walk and were tired after pulling the coach up the steep grade. On May 6 the North San Juan stagecoach going to Nevada City, driven by John Majors, was stopped at Black's crossing by three disguised road agents and they found that the only passengers were two Chinamen. One Chinaman was flat broke but the other had $400 in his money belt, and they beat him badly when he resisted. The robbers managed to open Wells, Fargo's wooden treasure box only to find a solid iron box inside, and they were not equipped to open it. Majors said, "Sorry, boys, the company must have been expecting you," and the leader of the robbers replied, "We'll come better prepared in the future." Frustrated by their inability to open the express box, they went a few miles distant and stopped Latta's Washington stagecoach a short distance beyond the Six-Mile House, but found only $50 in the pockets of the passengers. Later the driver of Marker's stagecoach, when near Hunnefauth's, was warned of road agents, but that stagecoach was not robbed. After the two robberies, three men were seen riding through the woods, circling around and heading into Nevada City, but they were not recognized and they were too distant to get a good description.

The road agents began to plan their next stagecoach robbery and on May 14 two of the road agents went into Nevada City to stock up on supplies, including a cask of gunpowder. They made camp six miles north of the city, not far from the summit, and enjoyed cigars and brandy while taking turns of two hours standing guard. Early on the morning of May 16 they positioned themselves in the brush at the summit of the road into Nevada City and prepared to halt the Telegraph Line stagecoach again. At 4:30 a.m. the San Juan coach, driven by Sam "Kalamazoo" Cooper and carrying six passengers, came lumbering over the summit with the horses at a slow walk. Suddenly the three disguised road agents leaped into the road in front of the horses, waving their arms, and ordered Cooper to stop and throw out the Wells, Fargo express box. The driver said, "Hello George, so it's you again," and George W. Moore replied, "Well, don't ever mention my name again. I want nothing to do with you, but I mean to have that box so toss it down. I'm after Wells, Fargo." Cooper had known Moore previously and knew him immediately when he appeared.

When the box was on the road the six passengers were ordered to step out and form a line. Frank McKee and Ned Hatfield were relieved of their revolvers, but there was no further molestation of the passengers. Hatfield, who was known to the robbers, expressed concern that they would take his money, about $3,500 of the money in the box, and one of the robbers said they would but reminded Hatfield that he would be reimbursed by Wells, Fargo, as the money was in their care. One of the robbers watched the seven men while the other two road agents took a crowbar and beat on the box, but that had little effect so they brought out the cask of gunpowder and told the driver, "We came prepared with powder this time," and then announced, "Either we get the gold this time or we'll blow the stage into the Yuba River." They carefully tamped the gun powder into the lock and detonated it, but it had little effect. Next they tamped in a larger charge and this time also tamped around it mud and leaves to form a shaped charge. This blew the lock and the men pulled out $7,900 in gold dust and coin. After the collection was completed the robbers passed around a bottle of brandy among the passengers and enjoyed a cigar while they gathered up and threw the shattered pieces of the box into the coach. They ordered everyone aboard and told Cooper to drive on, and the entire operation had taken just thirty minutes.

The driver wasted no time getting into Nevada City. It was 6:00 a.m. and there was hardly a soul on the street, but he pulled up in front of the sheriff's office rather than the stage office, and this attracted considerable attention. He awoke Sheriff R. B. Gentry and related all the facts of the robbery, and within an hour the sheriff had a four-man posse in the saddle. His deputies included his brother Albert, James H. Lee, A. W. Potter, and Stephen Venard. They rode to the scene and began looking for a trail. Lee and Venard found footprints leading into the brush, and the two men followed. The remainder of the posse went around to the bridge on the opposite side of the trail to wait for the two deputies to come out. When it became too rough for the horses, and it seemed clear that the men meant to come out at Hoyt's crossing, Venard sent Lee around to the bridge with his horse to meet the sheriff and the other two deputies and relate this intelligence, while he continued on the trail afoot.

Venard had just come into Myer's Creek, a mile from where he left his companion, and was about to cross when he realized that one of the robbers was standing right in front of him twenty feet away and about to bring his revolver into play. As Venard brought his Henry rifle to his shoulder he saw that another robber was a short distance above and also pulling his revolver, but he had no time to change targets and fired a single round from his Henry rifle sending a bullet right through the robber's heart and killing him instantly. At the sound of the shot, the second robber scrambled behind a large boulder for cover. Venard took aim and waited and when the robber raised up to fire, Venard put a single round through his brain. The man had snapped his revolver at Venard, but it had misfired. Venard hurried to where the men lay and took their pistols, then searched the area and found the stolen treasure. He covered the bodies and loot with leaves and marked the spot before continuing his search for the third robber. Soon he saw the man sixty yards away trying to climb out of the ravine over a particularly steep side. Venard fired once and the man fell, wounded in his arm, but he immediately arose and began scratching his way up the hill again. Venard took a second longer with his fourth shot, the second fired at this fugitive, and the man dropped in his tracks. The robber rolled over and looked down at Venard before his head slumped, and the deputy knew his man was dead. The robber then rolled down the hill, coming to rest at the bottom of the ravine.

Venard made his way toward the bridge at Hoyt's crossing and when he stepped onto the road he found a large body of men milling about, and they asked what had happened. He learned that the Wells, Fargo's agent Bill Davidson had posted a $3,000 reward for the robbers, dead or alive. "Well, you better all go home," Venard told them; "they are all dead." The sheriff was incredulous, so Venard guided him back to Myer's Creek and showed him the bodies, and while there they collected the stolen treasure. They checked it over and found the loot $20 short. The posse then returned to town, notified the coroner, and by 2:00 p.m. returned the stolen treasure to the Wells, Fargo office. Coroner W. C. Stiles quickly assembled a jury and went to the scene of the killings. After a careful examination of the battleground they recovered the bodies, which took nearly four hours to get them to the nearest point on the road, and at times the bodies had to be dragged. The jury then returned to town for the inquest and to identify the bodies.

The leader of the gang, and the first man killed, was at first identified as Jack Williams, but his real name was George Shanks. He had serve a term in California's San Quentin Prison and later adopted the alias Jack Williams, the name of a desperado hanged in 1856, and became known as "the ghost of Jack Williams." When Shanks' body was searched they found the missing $20 gold piece, so that the entire stolen treasure was returned to Wells, Fargo, and the coroner also found a gold watch and diamond ring taken from Sam Henry in the robbery several weeks earlier. The second man killed was Robert Finn, sometimes spelled Flynn, alias Caton or Katon and Kerrigan. He was a deserter from the army and an escaped convict from San Quentin Prison. The third man killed, and the one requiring a second shot, was George W. Moore. Moore, when his body was examined, was found to have a boot on one foot and a shoe on the other, necessary as he had broken his ankle in a mining accident. When Moore was searched, the coroner found two photographs pinned inside his shirt over his heart, showing his wife and children. One man said he knew Moore previously and that he had also spent a term in California's prison, but did not know the crime he committed or the name he used.

Venard was given a great deal of notoriety as a result of his actions, and he was offered the entire reward. He insisted that he would only take his fifth share, but finally agreed to half at the insistence of the other posse members. He apologized for the wasted bullet and would only take reimbursement for three rounds. Sheriff Gentry appointed him a regular deputy and assigned him to Meadow Lake. Wells, Fargo also presented him with a gold-mounted and inscribed, special-model Henry rifle. Governor Frederick F. Low appointed Venard a lieutenant colonel in the National Guard and cited him "for meritorious service in the field." Venard then took a position with Wells, Fargo as a shotgun messenger and for a brief period served as a guard on the Central Pacific Railroad's pay car. Venard died of kidney disease in the county hospital in Nevada City on May 20, 1891. He was described as a "man of modest demeanor, thoroughly temperate, of the strictest probity and not afraid of anything." He died so poor that his friends had to take up a collection of $70 to pay for his burial.

Sources: *Daily Alta California (San Francisco)*: May 16, 1866; May 18, 1866; May 23, 1866; August 6, 1866; August 8, 1866; August 10, 1866; May 22, 1891. *Los Angeles Herald (CA)*: May 22, 1891. *Sacramento Daily Union (CA)*: May 16–19, 1866; June 1, 1866; May 22, 1891; May 24, 1891. William B. Secrest, "When the Ghost Met Steve Venard," *Old West Magazine,* Fall 1968. "Steven Venard, Nevada County Pioneer," *Nevada (County) Historical Society Quarterly*, vol. 21, December 1967.

Louis Randolph Bonher and Unknown, December 1, 1866

In late November a drover sold a lot of hogs to Cashin & Company in Nevada City for $750. He then sent the money by express to Marysville. There were two boxes sent out of Nevada City, one for Virginia City, Nevada, and the other to Marysville, so they went on separate coaches in opposite directions. The stagecoach for Marysville left Nevada City on schedule on Saturday, December 1, 1866, and after traveling a short distance, two road agents halted the coach and demanded Wells, Fargo's express box. The driver, with guns pointed at him, had no choice but to comply, and he threw down the box for Marysville. One road agent then demanded that he throw out the second box, and when he insisted there was but one the road agent climbed up and found he was telling the truth, so they quickly carried the box away, broke it open, and removed $965. Posses went out to the scene but could find no clue to the robbers' identities. Wells, Fargo posted a reward of $1,000 for the arrest of the robbers and the recovery of the money, but no arrests followed immediately.

In January, Louis Randolph Bonher, alias Snyder, approached two men at Auburn and proposed robbing a stagecoach, and to convince them to join in the project he told them of the robbery of the coach on December 1, details that only a robber could have known. The plan was postponed due to bad weather; and in the meantime Bonher was arrested and charged with the December robbery, and during his time in jail he made several additional incriminating admissions. His first trial concluded on February 21, 1867, when the jury deadlocked six for guilty and six for acquittal. He was scheduled for a second trial and it began on February 24 and concluded the following day, but once again the jury deadlocked. His third trial concluded in May 1867, and once again the jurors could not agree, with nine men voting for acquittal. The problem in all three cases was that the men to whom the incriminating admissions were purportedly made were paid informants of the sheriff, tasked with getting such statements, and they were disbelieved as their interest could have been a share of the reward. Before his third trial Bonher was arrested for stealing a sum of money from the Devil's Gate tollhouse in Nevada, and after his third acquittal he was held in jail awaiting a requisition from Nevada's governor Henry G. Blasdel to be taken there for trial. The records of Nevada's state prison, however, do not show a convict named Bonher serving time in Nevada.

Sources: *Nevada Transcript (CA)*: December 4, 1866. *Sacramento Daily Union (CA)*: February 22, 1867; February 25–27, 1867; May 25, 1867.

Unknown, November 18, 1867

On Monday evening, November 18, 1867, Gregory & English's stagecoach from Lake City to Moore's Flat was one half mile from Backbone House, with McKinney driving, when a lone road agent halted the coach. He was masked and brandishing a revolver with an eight-inch barrel as he commanded, "Stop and put your foot on the brake or I will blow your damned head off." McKinney reined in his team and asked, "What do you want?" The robber replied, "I'm not after you; I want that box," and McKinney responded, "Wade in, if you think you will get it." The robber then said to passenger Kite Robinson and the driver, "I will kill the first one who moves," then had Robinson move aside. He climbed into the passenger compartment and found the wooden box with a hasp and padlock fastened to the coach, and after some hard work he managed to break off the hasp and padlock. He found inside the wooden box a "chilled iron safe" with a combination lock, so he started to work on that box, which contained $400 from Mark's & Company in Lake City sent to Moore's Flat. After he worked for some time on the safe with no effect McKinney said, "if you are going to blow up that box let me get down and get my horses off," but the robber said, "I have no powder." He worked for over forty-five minutes on the two boxes and then climbed out and said, "I guess I'm caught out; drive on." McKinney drove into Moore's Flat at a rapid pace and reported the robbery, but the posse that rode to the scene could find no clue to the robber's identity nor a clear trail to follow for any distance.

Source: *Nevada Transcript (Nevada City, CA)*: November 21, 1867

LOUIS J. DREIBELBIS, GEORGE LESTER, NAT C. STOVER AND CHARLES "ORMSTEAD" THURMAN, JULY 27, 1873

On July 27, 1873, at 7:30 p.m. the Telegraph Stage Company's coach from Colfax driven by Bob Scott was on the stage road five miles below Grass Valley in Nevada County when it was stopped by road agents. The place chosen was at the top of the grade above Morrison's station near Bear River, where the horses would be tired from the long ascent and walking at a very slow pace. Usually two stagecoaches ran over that route, but there were only twelve passengers that day so the other driver, George Britton, was riding along. The coach came to a bend in the road at the lower end of Sheet's ranch about dusk when four masked and well-disguised men, three with muffled feet, stepped through a gate in front of the horses. They were armed with three shotguns and a revolver, and these were trained on Scott and the passengers. The horses stopped of their own accord but nothing was said until Scott asked, "What do you want?" Passenger E. B. Ryan, riding atop, asked, "Yes, boys, what does this mean?"

One of the road agents finally responded, "We want that treasure box," and Scott told him it was on the other stage. There was a long pause until one robber said, "Well, we'll keep you till the stage comes up." After some arguing Scott finally admitted, "It's no use fooling; this is the only stage tonight." One road agent replied, "That's what we thought," and then two road agents began unhitching the horses. Scott told them he could do it better, and he and Britton unhitched the team and tied them to the fence twenty yards away. Next the passengers were ordered to step out, and they were herded thirty paces ahead of the coach where they were guarded by two of the men with shotguns, while the other two robbers went through the baggage. The safe, made of sheet iron, was bolted inside the coach and had two locks—an outer and an inner one. The robbers easily removed the outer lock with a pick and then packed giant powder into the inner lock, lit the fuse, and stepped away. It seemed to take a long time, which led several passengers to think they had made several attempts to blow the safe, but the slow-burning fuse finally ignited the powder with a loud report. The contents of the safe were removed, amounting to $7,578, and the four men retreated through the same gate from which they had appeared.

The passengers returned to the coach and found that it had been shattered by the blast. The lock was torn to pieces, the plate bent nearly double, and the back portion of the top of the coach blown to bits, a hole being made clear through nearly eight inches in diameter. Fragments of the lock were driven through the iron safe and the bottom of the coach. The lining and padding was ripped off all around the inside, the back part being almost gutted. The sides of the passenger compartment were blown out and the woodwork "very much broken." However, the running gear was still intact so the horses were hitched, the passengers boarded as best they could, and the coach hurried into Grass Valley. As soon as the robbery was reported Sheriff Joseph Perrin formed a posse, went to the scene, and began tracking the robbers. They found footprints and carefully measured them, then followed them for half a mile where they found masks, giant powder, and other items left behind by the road agents. At a nearby cabin they arrested two men who were taken into Grass Valley and lodged in jail. On Monday night a third person was arrested, and his examination was set for Friday, August 1.

At the examination before Judge Davidson a variety of passengers, lawmen and the stagecoach driver testified and Charles Thurman, alias Charles Thompson, was identified, partly by his deep-set eyes and by his clothing. The prisoner was held over to answer to the grand jury, bail set at $2,000. A number of men were suspected of being the other road agents and arrested, but each one had an alibi and was released. After Thurman was arrested but before his trial, James Hume, Wells, Fargo's chief detective, captured a man in Coloma whom he believed was one of the road agents. The prisoner had in his possession a small bar of gold bullion from the June 23 robbery and gold coins with powder burns, taken in the robbery of the Downieville stagecoach on July 27. Seeing that the case against him was made, he admitted to being Louis J. Dreibelbis, he confessed to both robberies, and he "peached," or informed, naming Thurman, Nat Stover, and George Lane, whose real name was George Lester, and he also named James Meyers as an accessory. He testified against the four men in separate trials and in consideration of turning state's evidence he was released. Dreibelbis had a long criminal history in California. He had served six years of a twelve-year sentence in San Quentin for a stagecoach robbery in August 1865, so it was stipulated that he would leave the state and he returned to Illinois.

Based primarily on Dreibelbis' testimony, Thurman was indicted, tried, and convicted in late February 1874. Following his conviction he was sentenced to serve fifteen years and he was delivered to San Quentin Prison on March 5, 1874. Thurman remained in prison for more than nine years and was released on August 5, 1883. Stover was captured after being named by Dreibelbis, indicted and tried, and convicted in November 1873. On November 29 he arrived at San Quentin to serve a five-year term. However, less than four years later he died in prison. James Meyers was arrested and tried in November, and he was convicted of being an accessory. He was sentenced to serve a term of ten years at San Quentin Prison and was released on May 29, 1880, and he later died in Grass Valley. The last man named by Dreibelbis, George Lane, was arrested and charged with the July 27 robbery under the name George Lester. He was convicted, primarily on the testimony of Dreibelbis, and sentenced to serve a term of fifteen years. He arrived at the prison on June 5, 1874, served his entire term, and was released on November 5, 1883. Lane, or Lester, if he learned anything in prison it wasn't reform, as on September 11, 1884, he robbed the stagecoach from Forbestown to Oroville in company with Bob Clement. He was captured, tried, convicted, and sentenced to serve a term of ten years at San Quentin, this time for the federal charge of robbing the U.S. mail.

Sources: *Downieville Messenger (CA)*: June 28, 1873. *Marysville Daily Appeal (CA)*: September 12, 1865; September 16, 1865; September 23, 1865. *Grass Valley Daily Union (CA)*: June 25–27, 1873; July 3, 1873; August 2–3, 1873; August 8, 1873; August 14–15, 1873; August 17, 1873; August 19, 1873; August 27, 1873. *Sacramento Daily Record Union (CA)*: June 21, 1864; April 6, 1889. *San Francisco Police Gazette (CA)*: August 19, 1865; October 14, 1865, September 16, 1865.

Unknown, December 17, 1875; December 22, 1875

At 10:30 a.m. on Friday, December 17, 1875, the stagecoach from San Juan to Marysville, driven by Mike Hogan, was four miles above Smartsville and a half hour ahead of schedule, so he had his team slow from a trot to a slow walk. Suddenly a man wearing a mask jumped from behind a bush on the lower side of the road, pointed his rifle at Hogan's head and said, "Stop, and hold up your hands." Passenger Robert Winans, riding next to Hogan, raised his hands, but Hogan kept hold of his whip and reins. The road agent then yelled, "Hold up your hands or I'll blow your brains out!" Hogan immediately threw down his reins and whip and held up his hands, and the robber then said, "Hand out that box and be quick about it." Hogan tried to pull the box free but there was a valise wedged against it, so the robber told him, "Hurry up!" Hogan finally threw down the box and asked, "Will I drive on?" and the robber answered yes. Hogan started his team but kept an eye on the robber as if trying to size him up for later identification, and the robber warned, "Drive on or I'll blow your brains out." The robber did not ask about the passengers which included Winans' brother Henry, James Smith, Miss Wetzler, and a Chinaman. Throughout the entire encounter the robber seemed quite nervous, so Hogan drove on concerned he might be shot on purpose or by accident. After traveling out of sight of the robber, Winans, who had a pistol, got down and cut across country to watch the proceedings at the express box, but he was seen and told to stop. He later reported that there were two robbers at the box, and as he watched they broke it open with an ax, took out all the contents but one paper, and fled. Later the box was recovered and delivered to Timbuctoo. Winans and Hogan described the robber in the road as heavyset, five feet nine inches high, dark complected with dark hair, square faced, blue eyed, wearing a checkered shirt and tongued boots. Hogan was certain he could identify the robber if seen again. Wells, Fargo offered a reward of $250 for the capture of the "robber or robbers," and one-fourth of any treasure recovered.

On Wednesday, December 22, 1875, the stagecoach between Marysville and San Juan was stopped by a lone road agent at about the same location as the robbery of December 17. He demanded the Wells, Fargo box and, finding little inside, went through the passengers. Once he had all the plunder he expected to find he told driver Hogan to drive on. Lawmen at the scene were not able to find a clue to the identity of the robber who appeared, or his partner who remained in hiding.

Source: *Territorial Enterprise (Virginia City, NV)*: December 17, 1875.

CHARLES E. "BLACK BART" BOLTON, DECEMBER 28, 1875

On Tuesday, December 28, 1875, the Marysville to San Juan stagecoach driven again by M. Hogan was halted five miles above Smartsville. Hogan was busy pointing out the spot of the previous robbery to his passengers when he was interrupted by the command, "Halt and throw out the box, quick!" He did as he was told, and then the lone robber told him to drive on. The passengers, five men and two women, were not molested. As soon as Hogan reached town he organized a large posse and they returned to the scene to take up the trail of the robber. The ground was soft from the rain the previous night and this was believed to give Hogan the advantage, and the streams on both sides of the scene were impassable. At the time of this robbery, Wells, Fargo detectives had arrested a large number of questionable characters and lodged them in jail, including "five Spaniards, two Greeks, and one white man." The detectives seemed confident they would be able to convict at least a portion of the prisoners for robbing stagecoaches. In late February there was a spree of robberies and burglaries in Marysville, and officers thought that three men seen walking along the Smartsville Road might also be stagecoach robbers, but there is no record they were caught. Later John "Sheet Iron Jack" Allen was arrested and suspected of being one of the robbers of the coaches near Smartsville, but he was never charged with those robberies. (See Calaveras County on November 3, 1883.)

JOHN A. WRIGHT, JANUARY 16, 1877

On December 28, 1876, at 9:30 a.m. the down stagecoach from Murphy's to Milton was robbed when it was near Altaville in Calaveras County. Then on January 16, 1877, the stagecoach from San Juan to Marysville, driven by M. Hogan, was three-quarters of a mile below the bridge over the South Yuba River in Bridgeport township, Nevada County. Suddenly a lone highwayman, masked and armed with a six-shooter, appeared and halted the coach. He ordered Hogan to get down from the driver's seat and enter the passenger compartment, where the Wells, Fargo express box was stored on that trip, and throw it out onto the road. Hogan threw out the wooden box, but the road agent demanded the iron safe. The safe was bolted into the body of the coach and Hogan told the robber he could not comply. The road agent accepted the explanation and ordered Hogan to drive on, adding, "You will find your box in the road when you come this way again." The robber removed a $5 coin and a watch worth $20, all that was in the box, and left the box in the road as he had said he would before he fled. Hogan drove a short distance but then returned and found the box broke open with a small ax, such as those used by a boy, and it had been left behind. It was an old ax with a new helve and had been recently ground to a sharp edge. The box and ax were brought into Marysville and turned over to lawmen who formed a posse and went to the scene, but they could find no clue. Stagecoaches would be robbed by the same road agent in Calaveras County on February 2, 1877, and February 24, 1877, and in Amador County on February 5, 1877. (See Calaveras County on December 28, 1876.)

CHARLES "THORN" DORSEY AND JOHN C. P. " PATTERSON" COLLINS, SEPTEMBER 1, 1879

On Monday, September 1, 1879, the stagecoach from Eureka to Nevada City was three miles from its destination, nearing Moore's Flat, when two masked road agents halted the coach and had the passengers step out and form a line along the roadside. One robber, armed with a shotgun, covered the passengers while the second man searched them, took what valuables he found, and then went through the express and mail. The last item taken from the coach was a valise containing gold bars worth $6,700 belonging to William F. Cummings, a banker from Moore's Flat. Cummings, seeing his gold being stolen, leaped forward and struggled with the robber, and he was getting the best of him until the man with the shotgun fired a load of buckshot which struck Cummings in his neck, killing him instantly. The robbers then herded the other passengers into the coach and had the driver continue on his route, leaving Cummings' dead body where it had fallen. Besides Cummings' bars of gold, the robbers had only collected $800 in plunder from the passengers' pockets, the express matter, and the mails. As soon as the coach reached Nevada City the robbery was reported and a posse was organized, and they rode to the scene to begin their investigation and search for the robbers. They did not find any clues to the identity of the road agents, nor a clear trail to follow, but soon the best detectives in the state were working on the case and rewards totaling $5,100 were posted to encourage the search and the recovery of the treasure.

Six weeks after the murder Charles Mulvane was arrested at Petaluma, but he proved he had nothing to do with the robbery and was released. After weeks of working up clues Hattie McIntyre, a prostitute working at an inn in Sierra County, reported to Wells, Fargo's chief detective James B. Hume that, under orders from Madame Romargi, she had carried food to two men hiding in an abandoned mine tunnel three miles from her place of employment. She gave a detailed description of the two men and Hume immediately recognized them as Charles Dorsey and John C. Patterson, whose real name was John C. P. Collins, ex-convicts recently released from San Quentin Prison. They were traced to Tombstone, Arizona Territory, in December but then all trace of them was lost. Hume continued to build the case against the two men, and the accumulation of evidence mounted until it was certain he was after the murderers of Cummings. On June 20, 1882, Hume received a letter from the chief of police in St. Louis stating that he had arrested Patterson for burglary, and a man named Roger O'Meara informed him that Patterson was wanted for murder in California, and Hume immediately set to work to extradite the prisoner to California. Meanwhile San Francisco police captain Isaiah Lees and Wells, Fargo's "chief of police" Charles Aull put photographs of Dorsey on circulars and distributed them throughout the west. Once Patterson was in the hands of Hume he "peached," or informed, on Dorsey and said he could be found in Chicago or Union City, Indiana. Lee and Aull first went to Chicago but could find no sign of Dorsey, so they next went to Union City and captured Dorsey on the evening of October 3, 1882. Dorsey, under the alias Charles H. Thorn, had used his stolen money to go into the lumber business, and over the past year he had become a prosperous and respected citizen of the community.

Patterson and Dorsey were taken to Nevada City, and on October 28 they were arraigned and entered pleas of not guilty. Dorsey's trial began in late February 1883 and testimony, including that of Patterson who then insisted his real name was John C. P. Collins, indicated that they had robbed the stagecoach, killed Cummings, and after they reached St. Louis they had the gold bars converted at the mints in Philadelphia and New Orleans. Testimony also proved that it was Dorsey who had fired the fatal shot. After closing arguments the case went to the jury at 8:00 p.m. February 28, and after eight hours in deliberations the jurors returned a verdict at 4:00 a.m. finding the defendant guilty of first-degree murder, with a recommendation of life imprisonment. Dorsey, as he was being led out of court, complained, "That's a Hell of a jury. If they thought I killed that man they ought to have hung me, and if they did not think I did it they should have turned me loose." Dorsey was sentenced to life in prison and on March 14, 1883, he was on his way to his new home. Dorsey would later escape from prison, commit numerous crimes all over California, be captured after being free three years, and be granted parole on December 21, 1911. (See Placer County on April 7, 1890.)

Collins' (Patterson) trial began on March 2 with motions for a continuance to the next term and a change of venue, but both were denied and Collins' trail began immediately. Testimony concluded on March 15, arguments were finished the following day, and the jurors found him guilty of first-degree murder and recommended the death penalty. On March 27, 1883, after a fifteen-minute speech to the judge in which he proclaimed his innocence and blamed the newspapers, the detectives, and the Knights Templar for his conviction and sentence, Collins was sentenced to hang at Nevada City on May 11. On May 3 the construction of the gallows had begun when the *Daily Alta California* newspaper noted that there was a vigorous effort to have Collins' sentence commuted to life in prison, and that this would cause delays. The editor was correct and after many delays the date set for Collins' execution was Friday, February 1, 1884.

As Collins prepared for his execution he was attended daily by Father Meagher and the Sisters of Mercy. During his many months in jail Collins showed no sign of nervousness, but on the night before his execution he tried to commit suicide. Somehow he managed to get a boot shank and ground one edge until it was sharp as a razor, and at midnight he used it to severe the veins in his left wrist, but he had not cut deep enough and the profuse blood flow slowed and finally clotted. Even though his deathwatch guards checked on him regularly throughout the night, the wound, and the large pool of blood he had hidden beneath the bedclothes, were not discovered until 5:00 a.m. The guards then moved him to an adjoining cell and they found the boot shank, following his directions. After it was certain he had no other means to take his life, Father Meagher and the sisters were admitted to console him. As the hour drew near a crowd of two hundred gathered in the jail yard in a driving rainstorm. The prisoner was brought out at 1:15 p.m. being escorted by Sheriff Carter, his deputies, and Fathers Dalton and Meagher. On the scaffold awaiting their arrival was Placer County sheriff Huntley, Sierra County sheriff Mead, and Colusa County sheriff Davis. Collins, once on the trapdoor, was asked if he had anything to say to the witnesses and he made a fifteen-minute speech, blaming especially detective Lees and the Masonic Fraternity for the death of an innocent man, and he said Lees' only interest was in "blood money." He proclaimed his belief in a Supreme Being and after Father Dalton concluded a prayer he kissed the crucifix and announced that he was ready. His wrists and arms, knees and ankles were quickly strapped, the noose was cinched in place, and the black hood was drawn over his head. Just after 1:30 p.m. the trapdoor was sprung and in eleven minutes his pulse ceased and he was pronounced dead. His neck had been broken in the fall and not a quiver nor movement of the body was visible. The rope was then cut and the body was lowered into the coffin waiting beneath the gallows, and given in charge of the coroner for burial.

Sources: *Daily Alta California (San Francisco)*: May 3, 1883. *Eureka Daily Sentinel (CA)*: August 17, 1882. *Los Angeles Herald (CA)*: October 5, 1882. *Red Bluff Sentinel (CA)*: October 11, 1879. *Sacramento Daily Union (CA)*: October 16, 1882; October 23, 1882; October 26–27, 1882; October 30, 1882; February 22, 1883; March 3, 1883; March 15, 1883; March 17, 1883; March 27, 1883; February 2, 1884.

UNKNOWN, JULY 26, 1880

On Monday morning, July 26, 1880, the stagecoach from Spenceville to Wheatland was one mile above Smartsville when a lone road agent, masked and armed with a double-barreled shotgun, ordered the driver to rein in his team. He demanded the Wells, Fargo express box, but it was chained to the coach, and the robber had brought no tools to remove it so it was left untouched. He did not ask for the mail but instead ordered the two passengers to step out. One passenger, a peddler, exited on the side opposite the road agent and took off at a run, saving whatever money he had in his pockets, while the other passenger stepped out and was relieved of $50. The robber then told the passenger to board, and once he was seated the robber told the driver to move along, without making any further demands. At Smartsville the robbery was reported and a small posse rode to the scene, but they returned in several hours empty-handed and without a clue to the robber's identity.

Source: *Sacramento Daily Union (CA)*: July 26, 1880.

UNKNOWN, SEPTEMBER 30, 1880

On Thursday, September 30, 1880, the Nevada City to Marysville stagecoach was three miles from Smartsville when one masked road agent, armed with a double-barreled shotgun, stepped into the road and ordered driver Frank Bailey to halt. He asked for the Wells, Fargo express box, but there was none aboard. He did not ask for the mail, but to avoid a "water haul" he ordered out the one male passenger and had him turn out his pockets, taking $15. He then ordered the passenger to board and told Bailey to continue on, and in minutes the coach arrived at Smartsville. The driver reported the robbery and a small posse was organized and rode to the scene, but they could find no clue to the robber's identity nor a trail to follow for any distance. No rewards were posted, so there was no motivation to pursue the road agent further; but it was suspected he might be the same man who robbed the Wheatland stagecoach on July 26.

Sources: *Los Angeles Herald (CA)*: October 1, 1880. *Sacramento Daily Union (CA)*: October 1, 1880.

UNKNOWN, OCTOBER 30, 1880

On Saturday, October 30, 1880, two road agents tried to stop the stagecoach from Nevada City to North San Juan but at the first call for the driver to halt he whipped up his team and took the coach out of danger. The horses were already traveling at a rapid gait when the men first appeared, but all they could do was stand in the road and watch the coach disappear. They did not fire shots after the departing coach and fled into the heavy brush. No effort was made to track or capture the robbers.

Source: *Sacramento Daily Union (CA)*: November 1, 1880.

UNKNOWN, DECEMBER 10, 1880

At 8:30 a.m. on Friday, December 10, 1880, the stagecoach from Truckee to Sierraville had only traveled four miles when it was halted by a road agent. There were no passengers aboard and the Wells, Fargo express box was light, so it was not broken open and was returned to the coach. The robber, to avoid a "water haul," took $75, a gold watch and a hat from the driver, and he then told the driver to move along. There is no record of a pursuit.

Source: *Sacramento Daily Union (CA)*: January 1, 1881.

UNKNOWN, DECEMBER 27, 1881

Charles "Black Bart" Bolton laid low for four months, allowing time for a copycat robber to appear in the hills north of Smartsville in Nevada County. Although this was the second robbery of the North San Juan to Marysville stagecoach within two weeks, this robber, unlike the first, was unusually polite but let his shotgun speak for him, perhaps being more determined to shift blame to Bolton and using the newspaper accounts of his first robbery as a guide. There was but one confederate aiming a gun barrel at the driver this time, but it was later presumed it was a stick positioned similar to the ruse used on July 26. Driver Mike Hogan delivered the treasure box and mail sacks before he was waved on. He hurried into Marysville and organized a posse. They hurried to the scene and recovered the broken box and mail sacks, cut open with a distinctive "T," but they could find no clue to the robber's identity. (See December 15, 1881, in Yuba County.)

UNKNOWN, SEPTEMBER 23, 1885

On Wednesday, September 23, 1885, a man was riding his mule a few hundred yards ahead of the North San Juan to Nevada City stagecoach when he came upon two men, masked and heavily armed, lying along the roadway awaiting the arrival of the coach. Their appearance frightened the mule and it turned about and ran back to the stagecoach, which carried considerable bullion and had a shotgun guard riding behind. Once all were alerted the coach came on, but the two road agents had lost their nerve and fled. No effort was made to identify or track them.

Source: *Sacramento Daily Bulletin (CA)*: September 24, 1885.

FRANK WILLIAMS, DECEMBER 15, 1889

The same road agent had stopped three stagecoaches: first in Shasta County, then in Mariposa County, and finally on December 12, 1889, in Placer County. On Sunday, December 15, 1889, the road agent moved his operation to Nevada County and stopped the stagecoach from Downieville to Nevada City. He called for the Wells, Fargo express box and the mail, but he was not able to break open the express box. He went through the mail and took five registered letters that looked promising. Concerned that he might be facing a "water haul" he robbed two passengers of $147.50, and as he reached out to take their money in his left hand, while holding his revolver in his right hand, they noted the distinctive diamond ring he wore on the little finger of his left hand. The road agent then told the driver to continue on. The road agent decided it was time for a long rest so he fled to San Francisco, the place he had been hiding after each robbery. The passengers gave the same approximate description as before, except they said the robber was five feet seven inches tall and only about twenty-five years old, rather than middle aged, and they described in great detail the diamond ring.

The road agent, who used the names Frank or Charles Williams or C. W. Moore, had been befriended by police court bailiff Thomas Ryan, as he thought the man suspicious and wanted to see what he was about. Ryan checked at the Russ House and learned that Williams had used several names when registering, and he found the store where Williams had purchased a .45 caliber revolver and a sawed-off shotgun, and ammunition for each. He also found the pawn shop where he had purchased his blankets and his oversized yellow, rubber raincoat. Although the robber was described as stout the storekeeper described the purchaser as "of slight build." During the month that Williams had come and gone several times from San Francisco, Ryan began to put together a case and he had made a point to listen to any updated descriptions provided to detective Isaiah Lees, especially the description of the diamond ring. On December 20 Ryan was walking on Kearney Street when he met Williams, and he noticed the diamond ring on the little finger of his left hand matching exactly the description give by the victims of the December 15 robbery. He told Williams he was then engaged in a "particularly spicy case" at the police court involving a very pretty woman, and the bailiff invited Williams to attend Judge Joachimsen's court to listen to the testimony. As soon as Williams arrived in the court, Ryan and detective Lees arrested him and delivered him to the city jail. The storekeeper who had sold him the guns and ammunition and the pawnbroker who sold him the other goods were sent for and they identified Williams, but the prisoner claimed he had bought the shotgun on speculation but sold it at a loss, and he had bought the other items for a friend in Redding. Several valises were tracked down, and inside each were incriminating items, including a bank book from Helena, Montana, with entries matching the dates of the robberies. On January 14, 1890, four men came from Placer County and identified Williams as the road agent, and one of them was the Forest Hill stagecoach driver Frank Powell. Williams was turned over to U.S. Marshal Long for trial in the U.S. district court.

Williams' trial began on April 12, and on May 2 he was convicted on three counts of robbery. He was sentenced to serve a life term at Folsom Prison, where he registered as prisoner #2212. Williams was determined to escape and he enlisted the help of five other men, all of whom worked in the prison quarry. He also recruited a recently paroled prisoner to smuggle firearms into the quarry. On June 28, 1893, they put their plan into action, captured guard Frank Briarre and used him as a shield. As they made their way up the steep path out of the quarry, Briarre jumped off the trail, taking one of the prisoners with him. There followed immediately a fusillade of gun shots from Winchester rifles and a Gatling gun, and soon two of the convicts, who had managed to hide among the rocks though badly wounded, surrendered. Three other convicts were piled one atop the other, riddled with bullets and dead, and among them was Williams. The convict who had been pulled back into the quarry by the guard was the only escapee uninjured.

Sources: *Daily Alta California (San Francisco)*: December 21, 1889; April 20, 1890; April 23, 1890; May 3, 1890. *Evening Bulletin (San Francisco, CA)*: December 21, 1889. *Fresno Expositor (CA)*: December 23, 1889. *Los Angeles Herald (CA)*: November 30, 1889; December 14, 1889. *Mariposa Gazette (CA)*: May 3, 1890. *Nevada (City) Transcript (CA)*: December 17–18, 1889; December 22, 1889; December 24, 1889. *Placer Herald (CA)*: September 7, 1889; September 28, 1889. *Redding Republican Free Press (CA)*: November 30, 1889; December 14, 1889. *Sacramento Daily Union (CA)*: September 3, 1889; September 17, 1889; September 23, 1889. *San Francisco Call (CA)*: April 17, 1890. *San Francisco Chronicle (CA)*: December 21, 1889; December 24, 1889; January 15, 1890; April 19, 1890. *San Francisco Examiner (CA)*: December 21–22, 1889; April 18,

1890. *San Joaquin Valley Argus (CA)*: December 7, 1889. *Territorial Enterprise (Virginia City, NV)*: December 4, 1889; January 15, 1890.

UNKNOWN, AUGUST 2, 1894

On Thursday morning, August 2, 1894, the stagecoach from Truckee to Tahoe City had only traveled three miles when a lone highwayman, masked and armed with a rifle, fired a shot and ordered the driver to halt. The robber was perched on a bank above the coach, and once it was stopped he ordered the fifteen passengers to throw out their money. As soon as the plunder lay in the road he ordered the driver to continue on, and he did not ask for the express box or the mails. Once during the robbery the robber's handkerchief mask fell away and all could see that he was about twenty-five years old, and he was described later as small of stature and slight of build. After the coach had driven a distance away from the scene the road agent gathered $33 from the dirt and fled. At the scene lawmen could find no clue to the robber's identity, nor a trail to follow.

Source: *San Francisco Call (CA)*: August 3, 1894.

UNKNOWN, OCTOBER 30, 1894

On Tuesday, October 30, 1894, the down stagecoach from North Bloomfield bound for Nevada City had reached Rock Creek, three miles north of its destination, when stage line owner and driver Arthur Meyer saw a masked road agent standing in the road, armed with a revolver, and he reined in his four-horse team. The robber ordered Meyer to step down, but when the driver refused the robber shot twice, with the second bullet going through Meyer's body, killing him, and he collapsed into the boot onto the reins, which kept the frightened horses from bolting. C. H. Bovee, the only passenger and an invalid, crouched down in the passenger compartment. The robber then abandoned his plan to rob the coach and fled, but fired three more shots apparently expecting the horses to take off at a dead run. Farmer Arbogast, who was working in his field nearby, went to investigate the shots and grabbed the reins and calmed the horses, then he took the reins and within thirty minutes the stagecoach was charging down Broad Street in Nevada City. Meyer's body was taken to his hotel room while Bovee reported that the road agent was a short, stout man with a heavy voice, and within minutes of the arrival of the coach a large party of armed men were organizing for the pursuit. They took to the hills and ravines in every direction but all they could find was the robber's mask made from an old coat lining and the robber's lunch, left behind in his haste to depart. The road agent had headed toward the higher mountain ranges, but after following his trail for more than a mile all sign of him was lost. Rewards were posted but there were no clues to the road agent's identity, so they were never paid.

Sources: *Los Angeles Herald (CA)*: October 31, 1894. *San Francisco Call (CA)*: October 31, 1894.

UNKNOWN, SEPTEMBER 15, 1900

On Saturday afternoon, September 15, 1900, the Nevada City to Downieville stagecoach, driven by L. L. Gaffney, made twenty-seven miles to the grade a mile and a half beyond Nigger Tent when a lone road agent called out from the brush, "Halt!" Gaffney reined in his four-horse team when he found the twin barrels of a shotgun pointed at his head. The robber wore overalls, had his boots muffled with sacks, and had a barley sack with eyeholes pulled over his head. Upon the demand the driver threw down the Wells, Fargo express box. Inside the coach was one passenger—W. F. Eschbacher, editor of the *Downieville Messenger*—and he was ordered to step out, and he had $30 taken from his inside jacket pocket. As soon as the road agent was sure he had all the money from the passenger he told him to board, then told Gaffney to continue on. The driver whipped up his team, never giving away the fact that the wooden treasure chest was empty, while beneath his feet was an iron chest bolted to the stagecoach filled with gold. As soon as the coach reached a station with a telephone, Sheriff D. B. Getchell was notified. The sheriff went to the scene but there was neither clue nor track to follow.

Source: *San Francisco Call (CA)*: September 16, 1900.

UNKNOWN, APRIL 11, 1903

At 8:30 a.m. on Saturday, April 11, 1903, the stagecoach for Downieville left Nevada City with Joseph Downey driving. In thirty minutes the coach was three miles from town, near Lake Vera, when a lone highwayman, armed with a Winchester rifle, jumped into the road and ordered Downey to rein in his four-horse team. Once the coach was stopped the robber ordered Downey to throw out the treasure box, but he was told that Wells, Fargo had bolted it into the stagecoach. He then had the passengers—which included six women, two children and one man—climb out and form a line. Once they were all where they could be watched he ordered Downey to get down and hold the reins of his leaders, and the robber climbed up and shot at the padlock three times, smashing it slightly, but it would not open. He then heard a team approaching so he stepped down and demanded money from passenger J. Spencer, who tossed him his purse containing a small sum he carried for his immediate needs. The robber grabbed it and fled into the woods heading north. He was fully masked and his boots were covered with gunnysacks, but he was believed to be a stranger who had been seen loitering about the area for days. The robbery was reported and officers were looking for the road agent, who they believed was heading for Emigrant Gap where he could board the train. The posse could not follow his trail and he did not appear at the rail depot, so no one was arrested.

Source: *Los Angeles Herald (CA)*: April 12, 1903.

UNKNOWN, JUNE 23, 1909

At 5:00 a.m. Wednesday, June 23, 1909, the stagecoach bound for Downieville left Nevada City with five passengers aboard and John Grofette driving. The coach had traveled four and a half miles when a roughly dressed road agent, masked with a handkerchief, stepped into the road in front of the four-horse team, pointed his gun at Grofette and ordered him to stop. He then had Grofette throw down the Wells, Fargo express box and climb down after it, and he called upon the five passengers to step out of the coach. He had the six men line up along the roadside, with hands raised, and then he laid down his gun and began collecting money, but not bothering with jewelry. As soon as he had collected from everyone, totaling $92, he busted open the express box and took out something he thought valuable. He then picked up his gun, ordered the passengers and driver to board, and told Grofette to continue on his route. The coach quickly reached Ferndon, two miles further along the route, and Grofette telephoned the details back to Nevada City. All thought, by the way the man laid aside his gun and his overwhelming confidence, that a second man waited in the brush and had them covered all the while they were being robbed. It was speculated that the robbers thought they might intercept a rich haul coming from the Allegheny mines, which had reported several strikes recently, but they stopped the coach in the wrong direction and there was little in the express box.

Undersheriff Waters and Deputy Martin organized a small posse and rode to the scene, but that area is some of the roughest country between Nevada City and Downieville and there seemed little hope they would capture the robber. When they arrived at the scene they expected to find the express box busted open; but it was nowhere to be found, so the robber, or robbers, had carried it off. Waters and Martin returned to Nevada City that evening and reported that they had found no clues nor a trail but believed the road agent had headed south along the Yuba River, so at 2:00 a.m. Sheriff Walker started out hoping to have better luck. Wells, Fargo sent detectives Lord and Seymour to Nevada City to assist in the investigation, but by the 28th they had abandoned the chase and left, and the posse gave up looking for the robber or the express box. Some supposed that the robber was a local man and he had thrown the box into one of the many abandoned mines in the area after removing the contents, but it was decided that nothing more could be done until the box was found, and it never was.

Sources: *San Francisco Call (CA)*: June 24–25, 1909; June 29, 1909.

Placer County

UNKNOWN, JULY 6, 1858

At 3:00 a.m. on Tuesday, July 6, 1858, the stagecoach from Michigan Bluff to Yankee Jim was nearing its destination when it was halted by road agents, masked and heavily armed. They demanded the Alta Express Company box, and it was thrown down. Once they had the box they ordered the driver to continue into Yankee Jim, and after the coach was out of sight they broke open the box and took out $7,000 in gold dust. The company was notified of the robbery, and their employee, Mr. Ford, started from Sacramento to Yankee Jim to reimburse those who had lost treasure, and to pursue and capture the robbers. A reward of $1,000 was offered for their arrest, but there were no clues to their identities and the gold dust did not turn up in the area, which would have given lawmen a clue, so no one was arrested.

Source: *Daily Alta California (San Francisco)*: July 7, 1858.

JAMES DRISCOLL AND UNKNOWN, NOVEMBER 1, 1858

At 4:00 a.m. on Monday, November 1, 1858, the stagecoach from Rattlesnake Bar in Placer County to Folsom had only traveled one half mile from town and was climbing a small hill when three masked road agents leaped out of the bushes. One of the road agents jumped onto the coach from the right and held his gun to the driver's head while the other jumped up on the left, grabbed the Wells, Fargo express box, and threw it down onto the road. There was also an Alta Express Company box aboard, but they left it under the seat. The third road agent stood in front of the horses and held his gun on the driver. Inside the coach were two Portuguese and two Chinese male passengers, but they were not molested. As soon as the robbers had the box they fled back into the bushes, and the driver turned around and hurried into Rattlesnake Bar where he reported the robbery to the Wells, Fargo agent. The agent started posses in different directions, hoping to cut off the road agents as they fled, and he sent one posse to the scene where they found the busted box a short distance from the scene of the robbery. The driver then started out again for Folsom and arrived later that morning, where he learned that the stolen box contained $4,488. Wells, Fargo posted a reward of $1,000 for the capture of the three road agents. None of the road agents was identified or captured until the afternoon of March 5, 1859, when James Driscoll was arrested by Sheriff Stockton at Horsetown. He was taken to Sacramento and lodged in jail, but then on March 24 the arresting officers took him to Auburn for trial. He was convicted under the name J. W. Driscall and sentenced to serve ten years in prison. He arrived at the prison on September 14, 1859, and registered as prisoner #1698.

Driscoll attempted to escape twice: first in October 1859 and again the following year. On July 12, 1863, Driscoll escaped, with five years yet to serve, and went to San Joaquin where he found partner George F. Taylor, and the two men adopted aliases, with Taylor using the name George De Lacy while Driscoll use the name Charles W. De Lacy, and they represented themselves as brothers. They began a spree of burglaries in the Stockton area, and in early March they shot and killed a policeman at Auburn when he discovered them during the commission of a burglary. In late March the two were arrested and they had an assortment of burglar tools of a peculiar construction, the marks of which matched marks on keys and locks of several burglaries in Stockton. Their base camp was near San Joaquin, and marshal Taber found there a veiled mask apparently intended to be used in some robbery scheme, and a fine ivory-handled, silver-mounted, four-barrel Sharp's pistol and a gold locket stolen in a Stockton burglary. (See Amador County on November 17, 1863.)

Francisco Nunes, Samuel White and Unknown, November 8, 1859

Wells, Fargo learned that there would be an attempt to rob a stagecoach leaving Todd's Valley with considerable treasure in the express box, and the intelligence included the date and the names of several of the road agents. Instead of replacing the treasure with worthless cargo, in case the report proved false, Wells, Fargo had Sacramento officers Daniel C. Gay and Charles P. O'Neil go to Todd's Valley and hide inside the passenger compartment of the coach so that the road agents would move forward with their plan. On Tuesday, November 8, 1859, the stagecoach left Todd's Valley on schedule at 3:00 a.m. with passenger M. J. Fulton riding inside with the officers. The coach had only traveled three-quarters of a mile when four men, masked and armed, rushed out of the chaparral, ordered the driver to halt, and demanded that he throw down the express box. Upon hearing the commands, the two officers, one on each side, fired on the road agents, killing two immediately, and then they stepped down and exchanged nearly twenty shots with the other two road agents as they retreated; one was shot down and thought to be mortally wounded while the fourth man fled into the chaparral unhurt. The officers were not hurt, but the driver received a minor wound when one of the robbers' bullets grazed a finger. The three bodies were lifted aboard the coach, and it returned to Todd's Valley before continuing on its regular run. The following day an inquest was convened by the local justice of the peace, and the two dead road agents were identified as Francisco Nunes, alias Jose Maria, and Samuel White, alias Davenport. The officers testified that Gay had shot Nunes while O'Neil had shot White, and the killings were determined to be "justified." The third man had not died so he was not a part of the inquest testimony, and neither he nor the man who fled unhurt were identified in the record. There appears no record of an inquest for the man mortally wounded, but he must have died as no one was sent to prison for the crime, and the fourth man was not captured though it was believed he was known to lawmen.

Sources: *Daily Alta California (San Francisco)*: November 10, 1859. *Sacramento Daily Union (CA)*: November 9, 1859; November 11, 1859.

Unknown, May 28, 1860

On Monday, May 28, 1860, the stagecoach from Iowa Hill to Sacramento had only traveled a short distance from town when six road agents, masked and heavily armed, halted the coach and demanded the Wells, Fargo express box. One robber held the horses while four pointed their revolvers at the driver and passengers, and the last climbed up and threw down the Wells, Fargo express box. They immediately broke it open and took out $11,000, with $8,300 belonging to Fiske & Company. The robbers then told the driver to move along, and after the coach was under way and they were certain the driver would not turn around, they fled. At the next station a man was sent back to Iowa Hill where a posse was organized, but they could find nothing at the scene but the busted box. Wells, Fargo paid Fiske & Company promptly, and the investigation continued. On June 16 a man was arrested at Michigan Bluff with a bag of gold dust worth more than $3,000, and it was thought to be part of the plunder from the stagecoach robbery. It was reported that two more arrests would follow quickly, but there is no record of any prosecutions and it appears that the man who had been arrested was in possession of his own gold dust.

Sources: *Daily Alta California (San Francisco)*: May 29, 1860; June 17, 1860. *Visalia Weekly Delta (CA)*: June 9, 1860.

JOHN "CONNUB" CLARK, JOHN "SHORTY" HAYS AND EDDIE LEE, SEPTEMBER 12, 1873

John Clark, alias Jake Clark or "Connub," was convicted of a burglary in Butte county in 1869 and arrived at San Quentin on October 9. Over the next twenty-one months he received an extensive "jailhouse" education on the techniques of criminal activity, and he met John "Shorty" Hays, who was serving a term of five years for a grand larceny in Yuba County. The two men also befriended Eddie Lee, alias Thomas Martin, who was serving a term of six years for a burglary in San Francisco County. Lee was pardoned and released on February 22, 1872; Hays was released on October 31, 1872; and Clark was released on June 28, 1873. As soon as all three men were free they rendezvoused and prepared to rob stagecoaches. There seemed to be no reason to delay any further, so within three months they set their ambush along the Forest Hill to Auburn stagecoach route in Placer County.

On September 12, 1873, three masked, heavily armed road agents stepped out and called for the driver of the coach from Forest Hill to Auburn to halt. They demanded the Wells, Fargo express box, and it was delivered without any show of resistance. It had seemed so easy that the three men, as they moved north, easily recruited a fourth man interested in making fast money— and the recently released convict used the name Charles Thompson. The four men made their way to the Yreka to Redding stagecoach route and made camp near Buckeye, just north of Redding in Shasta County in preparation for another robbery. (See Shasta County on October 10, 1873.)

ALBERT P. HAMILTON AND UNKNOWN, APRIL 16, 1875

Albert P. Hamilton had been serving a ten-year term at San Quentin Prison for a stagecoach robbery committed in Santa Clara County, but seven and a half months after his arrival at the prison, on November 15, 1874, he escaped with three other convicts. At 8:30 a.m. on Friday, April 16, 1875, two stagecoaches from Grass Valley to Colfax had just climbed the grade on the Colfax side of the Bear River ditch, in Placer County, when two masked road agents appeared and ordered the drivers to halt. Each man was armed with a Spencer rifle, a revolver, and a large knife, and it was the revolvers that were cocked and pointed at the drivers' heads when the command was given. Once the coaches came to a halt the road agents demanded the keys to the Wells, Fargo iron safe, but they were told there were no keys on board. They then had the passengers step out and line up on the roadside with the drivers, and they took from them $500, two gold watches and a revolver, but declined to rob M. Dodsworth who they said was "a cripple and a hard working man." They took $22.50 from driver Matthew Daily, driving the Nevada stage, and when he asked for half to be returned, the smaller robber replied, "No! The times are too hard," and he took $11.50 from driver Bob Scott, who was driving the Grass Valley stage, but gave him back $1 "to have a drink in Colfax." When the four passengers in Scott's coach and two in Daily's coach had realized the situation, they hid $1,500 in money and some jewelry inside the coach before they were ordered out, and the robbers did not search the coach so they did not find it. As the smaller robber collected the plunder he remarked how he had been looking for work all over the country but could not find a job as "the Chinese are running the country." They then hefted the mail pouch and Wells, Fargo express box, but they were light so they did not open either. The smaller robber found keys in Daily's pocket, but none would open the iron safe, and they had not brought tools nor explosives. As soon as the two men had all the plunder they thought they were going to find, they ordered the passengers to board and then told the drivers to continue on. Both coaches hurried into Colfax, a short drive ahead, and reported the robbery, and the robbers were described: "One road agent was described as a rather large man weighing 165 pounds; with a full black beard and moustache trimmed closely; the upper part of his face was blackened and he wore no mask. The second road agent was 150 pounds and did all the talking and robbing. The smaller robber was cool, but the larger one was very nervous." Posses were quickly organized and rode to the scene of the robbery, but they did not find the two road agents. (See El Dorado County on May 24, 1880.)

Unknown, February 4, 1876

At 4:00 p.m. on Friday, February 4, 1876, the stagecoach from Forest Hill bound for Auburn was one half mile from its destination when two road agents, masked and armed, stepped into the road and ordered the driver to stop. They demanded the Wells, Fargo express box and it was thrown down, but they were not interested in the passengers and did not ask for the mail. They told the driver to continue on, then broke open the box but found little of value inside. The driver hurried into Auburn and reported the robbery, a posse was organized and hurried to the scene, but they could find no clue to the robbers' identities nor a trail to follow for any distance.

Source: *Sacramento Daily Union (CA)*: February 5, 1876.

Unknown, April 5, 1876

On Wednesday, April 5, 1876, the stagecoach from Forest Hill to Auburn was one and one half miles from its destination and just rounding a curve when the driver came upon a masked road agent standing in the middle of the road. The robber had his gun leveled at the driver and ordered him to halt, and he reined in his team. The robber then demanded the Wells, Fargo express box, and it was thrown down. As soon as the box was on the ground the robber ordered the driver to continue as he stepped aside to let the coach pass. After the coach was out of sight the robber busted open the box and removed $1,300, then fled without leaving a clear trail. The driver whipped up his team and hurried into Auburn, where he reported the robbery. Lawmen organized a posse and rode to the scene, but they could find no clue to the robber's identity.

Sources: *Los Angeles Herald (CA)*: April 7, 1876. *Territorial Enterprise (Virginia City, NV)*: April 6, 1876.

Unknown, October 17, 1876

Before noon on Tuesday, October 17, 1876, the stagecoach from Georgetown to Auburn was nearing its destination when a lone road agent, masked and armed, stepped in front of the horses and halted the coach. He demanded the Wells, Fargo express box but there was none aboard. The robber climbed up and looked into the boot and confirmed there was no express box, but there was a box being shipped to A. J. Bailey at Pilot Hill and he took that. He was not interested in passengers and did not ask about the mail. He told the driver to move on and fled into the brush. There is no record of a pursuit, and the contents of the box were not reported.

Source: *Sacramento Daily Union (CA)*: October 18, 1876.

MILTON ANTHONY SHARP AND WILLIAM C. JONES, MAY 15, 1880; AUGUST 6, 1880

In 1866 twenty-six-year-old Milton Anthony Sharp left home and made his way to California and Nevada where he worked as a miner over the next dozen years. He had a penchant for investing in questionable mining stocks but never managed to strike it rich. In 1879, after going broke once again, Sharp was working on the farm of Peter Ahart on the outskirts of Auburn, California, when he met William C. Jones, alias Frank Dow, an ex-convict. Jones managed to convince Sharp to join him in a stagecoach-robbing scheme, and he assured his "green" partner that he had learned the business well. They worked at the Ahart farm a while longer, accumulating a stake, and then disappeared after they had stocked a deserted cabin, and laid low for months. On May 15, 1880, the two men suddenly appeared on the road between Forest Hill and Auburn station, less than one mile from the latter place. They stopped the down coach and made the passengers line up along the roadside and then "went through them" and the driver, taking $150 and several valuable watches, then quickly made their escape into Nevada.

On June 8 Jones and Sharp stopped the Carson City to Aurora stagecoach, with Cambridge driving and carrying seven passengers, when it was in the vicinity of Dalzell's station. Both road agents were masked and held shotguns on the driver while they ordered him to throw out the Wells, Fargo express box. The passengers were ordered out and lined up, and one robber held his shotgun on the passengers while the other searched them for valuables, collecting about $1,000. The road agents delayed the coach for over an hour while working on the express box and finally took out $3,000 before telling the driver to continue on. The driver hurried into Aurora to report the robbery. Wells, Fargo's agent at Carson City, H. L. Tickner, took a shotgun messenger and went to the scene to investigate as soon as he heard of the robbery, but they could find no trace or clue.

On June 15 the pair of road agents stopped the up coach on the Carson City to Bodie run eighteen miles beyond Wellington's station, near Dalzell's station. Cambridge was driving again, and just as the coach came to a bend in the road, which required the driver to slow his team, the same two road agents stepped onto the road and covered the men with shotguns. The coach stopped and the box was thrown out, but this time it carried only $300. The robbers did not molest the driver nor the inside passengers. An hour later the down coach loaded down with bullion passed the same location, but it passed unmolested. The standing reward of $300 per robber was posted by Wells, Fargo for the capture and conviction of the road agents, so several posses were soon in the field, and a large force of Indians was also pursuing the robbers. Wells, Fargo's detective James B. Hume was brought out of Utah and put on the case.

On August 6 the two masked road agents took up their positions a short distance from the Grizzly Bear House, two miles from Auburn in California, and at 6:30 p.m. they stopped the coach from Auburn to Forest Hill as it was climbing the North Fork hill. They ordered the passengers out and lined them up, and one of the robbers held a shotgun on them while the second robber tried to open the iron safe bolted inside the passenger compartment. He could not get it opened so the robbers had the passengers board, the road agent with the shotgun boarding with them, and the other took a seat next to the driver and ordered him to drive his team a quarter mile off the road. Once again they lined up the passengers and then managed to break the safe free from the coach. When it was on the ground they opened the iron box with a hammer and cold chisel and found $1,500 inside. Next they went through the two passengers and then ordered the driver to return to the road and continue on, while they went off in a different direction. The driver, the same man who was driving the California coach which had been robbed on May 15, said later he was certain these were the same men.

On Monday, August 30, 1880, the stagecoach from Belleville to Candelaria, in Nevada, was met by two road agents near Coal Valley station, and driver G. Finley was ordered to halt. Finley ignored the order, and one of the road agents fired at him, the bullet passing between him and a passenger. The sound of the pistol startled the team, and they took off on a dead run, urged on by Finley's whip. The road agents were identified as the same two men who had been working the road from Aurora to Carson City.

On September 2, 1880, the stagecoach from Bodie, California, to Mammoth City, Nevada, on the road between Aurora and Carson City, near the Mammoth Ledge, was robbed by "a man whose face was blackened and tarred after the most improved Digger style." Sharp and Jones were using masks made of black oil cloth such as that used to make buggy tops, and this shiny black material was mistaken for a tar coating to disguise the face of the robber—either Jones or Sharp—while the other road agent remained concealed.

On September 3 at 9:00 p.m. two men stopped the Bodie to Carson City stagecoach near the forks of Hall and Simpson's road nine miles south of Wellington's station, but they were interrupted and fled without getting anything. At 2:30 a.m. the return coach was five miles from the place where the previous robberies had occurred, and shotgun guard Mike Tovey, who rode next to the driver, saw footprints in the roadway traveling in the same direction as the coach and ordered the driver to stop. He lit a lantern and got down to investigate, and then every half mile he repeated the process. When they reached the place the coach had been stopped the night before, Tovey got down and, as before, bent over to examine the tracks. Just then Jones and Sharp appeared out of the darkness, and the first robber, Jones, covered Tovey with a rifle and ordered, "Throw up your hands, you son of a bitch." Sharp was behind Jones and said, "You are trying to sneak up on us, are you?"

Tovey straightened up and, throwing up his hands, said, "Don't shoot; I'll go back and get the box," and Jones replied, "Go back, you whelp, and if you make a move we'll murder every mother's son of you." As Jones spoke, Sharp, also armed with a rifle, stepped around his partner and fired a single shot toward Tovey, but the bullet went into the chest of the nigh-leader. The horse lunged forward several times and then sank to the ground, dead. The others horses began to lunge and rear, but they could not run away because the dead horse held them in place. This distracted the robbers long enough for Tovey to make his way behind the stagecoach, and he was now behind the lamps so that he was in darkness while both robbers were at the dim edge of the light from the coach lamps. Tovey whispered to J. Billings, the division agent who was also riding on top as a guard, "Hand down that gun," and Billings passed down Tovey's double-barreled shotgun. Tovey crouched behind the coach and rested the barrel of his shotgun on the rear wheel, then waited patiently for the robbers to advance on the coach. Sharp moved to the right to flank the coach while Jones came straight forward, saying, "Don't move or I'll murder every last son of a bitch."

Tovey shouted out, "Who's moving?" which covered the sound of cocking his shotgun. Tovey then continued in a tone simulating fear, "You've got the drop on us. Come and get what you want." Tovey's voice must have convinced Jones that he had the upper hand because he lowered his rifle and advanced into the full glare of the lamps. Tovey then said loudly to the driver, "Throw down the box, quick, and let's get out of this." Jones, muttering more about murdering everybody, moved forward again until he was next to the fallen leader and said, "Your heads are level." These were the last words he spoke as Tovey opened up with the right barrel of his shotgun and the load of heavy buckshot took effect in the robber's face, killing him instantly. The dead man fell under the horses and one of the swingers, a middle horse in a six-up, began to rear and lunge, stomping Jones' legs to mush. Within a few seconds, Billings had retrieved his weapon and fired several rounds at Sharp while Tom Woodruff, the messenger riding inside the coach, pulled his six-shooter and also fired at the second robber. Sharp was returning fire when Tovey ran to the rear of the coach and came face to face with Sharp not twenty yards away. Tovey fired one barrel, but without effect, and the road agent returned fire striking Tovey in the right arm, which shattered one of the bones between the wrist and elbow. Tovey dropped his shotgun causing the second barrel, which he had reloaded after shooting Jones, to discharge. Tovey next managed to pull his revolver with his left hand and fire after the fleeing robber twice, but being right handed his shots missed. Tovey examined his wound and saw that he was bleeding profusely, so he called to Billings and Woodruff to take him to Hall and Simpson's house not far off the road. Woodruff, who had pursued Sharp into a stand of willows but lost him there, returned. He and Billings then took Tovey to the farmhouse where the bleeding was stopped and the wound bandaged.

As soon as the three guards were out of sight the driver heard a voice say, "Throw down that box," and he looked back to find Sharp covering him with a Henry rifle. The driver, who was unarmed, threw down the box and Sharp cut it open with a hatchet. He pocketed the few hundred dollars it held but in his haste missed a package of $800 in coin. The robber next asked the driver which way his partner had gone, as Sharp was behind the coach and could not see Jones lying in the road beneath the horses. The driver, who was afraid to speak the truth, said he did not know. Sharp walked off into the darkness while calling to his partner several times. The messengers returned in a short time and were surprised to hear that the road agent had been so brazen as to come back after the treasure. The guards examined the dead robber and saw that the buckshot had struck him in the lower part of his face, taking out the lower jaw; one buckshot had also taken out an eye; and there was blood oozing from several neck wounds. The deceased was tall, dark complected, with a black moustache and probably a goatee, as there were some remnants of a beard on the lower part of the neck which remained. The deceased was dressed in dark clothes, but there seemed little else to determine his identity. The body was carried a short distance off the road and buried deep enough to protect it from scavengers, and the grave was marked so it could be easily found later.

Detective James B. Hume went to the scene and exhumed the dead robber's remains. He returned to Carson on September 10 and told the editor of the *Daily Appeal* that he had cleaned up the face of the corpse and took a long look, but could not identify the body though he had expected to recognize him as a man who worked the roads in California. He had gone through the deceased's pockets for clues and collected the mask he wore, which was made of black glazed oil cloth of the type used in carriage tops. Hume left for California on the next stagecoach. From a bank deposit book and papers Hume found in the dead robber's pocket he learned that the two men shared a room in a Minna Street boarding house in San Francisco. The book also showed that both men had made substantial deposits in the Savings Union on the same day, and that the deceased robber was named W. C. Jones, while the fugitive was "M. A. Sharp." Hume coordinated his efforts with the police in San Francisco, and Chief Crowley detailed detectives to examine the fugitive's room. Detectives Coffey and Jones found, in a valise, the watch and chain belonging to E. B. Shaw, another stolen watch and ring, and material resembling the dead robber's mask. The two detectives remained in the room waiting for Sharp to return, and finally he arrived telling the landlady he had come for his valise. The officers sprang from the room and covered Sharp with pistols, threw their prisoner to the floor, took a new Colt six-shooter from his belt, and put on the handcuffs. Their prisoner had been carrying a roll of blankets when he entered the house, and it contained another six-shooter and a Bowie knife, which the officers collected.

Sharp was then searched thoroughly and the detectives found $1,600 in a money belt tied around his waist and $800 sewn into his coat lining. Sharp gave his correct name but denied knowing anyone named W. C. Jones. He said he had only come to get his property to move to another house, and claimed his partner was Frank Keith, but could not say where he was. The landlady was then given the description of Jones and she confirmed that Jones was the man who shared the room with Sharp.

Hume took custody of the prisoner and returned him to Carson City on September 18. By October 1 the prisoner was lodged in the Aurora jail, and his bail had been set at $10,000. The grand jury had returned seven indictments: four for robbery of Wells, Fargo, one for robbing driver Cambridge, one for robbing Ed Shaw, and one for attempting to kill Mike Tovey. On October 24 Sharp escaped from the jail by making a hole in the east side of the courthouse through a wall three bricks thick. The streets were crowded, so a large posse was soon raised and began scouring the hills. He was soon captured, and his trial, set for October 27, was not delayed. He was convicted on the second robbery indictment on October 30, and trial on indictments three through seven were postponed. He was sentenced to serve twenty years in prison on the first conviction so the other charges were dropped, and on November 12 Sharp was delivered to the Nevada State Prison, where he was registered as prisoner #158. Sharp was never tried for stagecoach robberies in California. Instead, through model behavior, he earned trusty status and managed to escape on August 15, 1889. On June 15, 1893, Tovey was murdered and Sharp was suspected, and the search for Sharp began anew. He was captured on September 28, 1893, he proved an alibi, and was returned to the Nevada prison, but on July 10, 1894, he was paroled.

Sources: *Free Press (Bodie, CA)*: October 10, 1880. *Carson Daily Appeal (NV)*: June 16–17, 1880; June 22, 1880; September 5, 1880; September 9, 1880; September 11, 1880; September 14, 1880. *Carson Tribune (NV)*: June 9, 1880; September 6, 1880. *Belmont Courier (NV)*: September 11, 1880. *Genoa Weekly Courier (NV)*: November 18, 1881. *Nevada City Transcript (CA)*: August 10, 1880. *San Francisco Daily Morning Call (CA)*: September 14, 1880; February 5, 1885; August 17, 1889. *Territorial Enterprise (Virginia City, NV)*: May 16, 1880; June 15, 1880; August 10, 1880; September 7, 1880; September 15, 1880; September 19, 1880; September 21, 1880; September 23, 1880; October 1, 1880; October 26, 1880; November 2, 1880.

UNKNOWN, SEPTEMBER 11, 1880

At 11:30 a.m. on Saturday, September 11, 1880, the down stage from Georgetown to Auburn was stopped by a lone highwayman when one mile from its destination. The road agent ordered the passengers to step out and form a line, and then he went through them for their money and jewelry. Once he had all the plunder he thought he would find, he told them to board and then told the driver to move along. Uncharacteristically, he did not ask for an express box nor for the mail. A posse rode to the scene but could find no clues, and without a substantial reward from Wells, Fargo or the postal service, the chase was quickly abandoned.

Source: *Sacramento Daily Union (CA)*: January 1, 1881.

UNKNOWN, SEPTEMBER 22, 1880

James B. Hume, Wells, Fargo's chief detective, reported that Ezra W. "Old Bill" Miner, after a trip to Colorado, returned to California and on Wednesday, September 22, 1880, took the Wells, Fargo express box from the stagecoach traveling between Auburn and Forest Hill in Placer County. The road agent acted alone, which would have been quite a departure from Miner's usual modus operandi. Just as this road agent finished robbing the stagecoach, Judge Frank Page came up in a buggy and was relieved of a valuable gold watch and $280 in coin. The robber went to Colfax that night and paid a brakeman $5 to stow him away in a boxcar. At Reno the same man bought a ticket to Denver, and there he pawned Page's watch for $65. If this was Miner, Hume reports that he was soon joined in Denver by Stanton P. Jones, and Hume continued that together they robbed a stagecoach in Sagauche County, Colorado. They were pursued three hundred miles by Sheriff Bronaugh and a deputy, and after their arrest one of the prisoners got possession of the sheriff's pistol, shot the sheriff breaking his wrist, and seriously wounded the deputy before escaping. Miner's road agent activities with Jones, however, came at a later time in his career. Also, it seems unlikely the Placer County, California, stagecoach robbery could have been conducted by Miner as he was in Colorado on September 23, 1880, robbing a stagecoach with Arthur Pond. The real road agent was never identified. (See Calaveras County on November 7, 1881.)

Unknown, November 1, 1880

At 12:30 a.m. on Monday, November 1, 1880, the stagecoach from Georgetown to Auburn was one and a quarter miles from its destination when a small man, masked and armed with a Winchester rifle, ordered the driver to halt. Once the coach was stopped the robber went to work on the Wells, Fargo iron safe bolted to the coach and soon had it opened. He took out $2,159.30 in coin and $285 in gold dust, told the driver to continue on, and after the coach was under way, fled. Wells, Fargo posted rewards but there had been no clues at the scene and no one was arrested.

Sources: *Pacific Rural Press (CA)*: November 13, 1880. *Sacramento Daily Union (CA)*: November 2, 1880.

Thomas Tracy and Charles "Schwartzwalter" Wilson, May 27, 1881

On May 27, 1881, the stagecoach was returning from the Dutch Flat rail station to the town of Dutch Flat when two masked and armed road agents stepped out and stopped the coach. They demanded the Wells, Fargo express box and as soon as it was delivered they sent the driver on his way, and he hurried into town and sounded the alarm. The two road agents smashed open the box and took out less than $25, then fled, leaving behind an old pistol and their masks. Lawmen could find no clue to the identity of the robbers and there was no reward posted, so there was little motivation to pursue the matter, or the robbers.

On Saturday morning, June 11, the pay wagon for the New York Hill mine was ascending Massachusetts Hill, just beyond the Black Lead hoisting works, when two road agents appeared and ordered the driver to halt. Both men wore flowing black masks which concealed their features, and one sported a double-barreled shotgun. At first the two men aboard the wagon were incredulous, as they were close to town and the mine, with residences nearby. Soon, however, they realized the demand was in earnest, and the driver reined in the team. Once stopped, one of the robbers positioned himself at the head of the horses while the other went around and lifted out the sack of coins, which had been made up at Campbell's store and contained $8,000. He was apparently aware of the money aboard and went directly to it. He next waved his gun indicating the driver should continue. No words were spoken after the initial order to halt, and the wagon hurried forward to the mine to sound the alarm. George Johnson, mine superintendent, immediately dispatched men to intercept the robbers if they went south while another man went to Boston Ravine and then to town to report the robbery. Within an hour Deputy Sheriff William Reynolds and Constable Peters, with a posse of citizens, took the field, and later that day famed road agent killer Stephen Venard arrived to join the pursuit.

Some arrests were made but these proved to be the wrong men, and rewards totaling $2,000 were posted. Two men, who identified themselves as Thomas Tracy and "Smith" were arrested at San Juan Ridge and taken into Grass Valley for an examination. They proved an alibi, but as soon as they were released they were rearrested by Constable Peters for the Dutch Flat stagecoach robbery. Tracy soon confessed his part, clearing Smith though he was held in jail, and Tracy identified his partner as Charles Wilson, alias Schwartz or Schwartzwalter. Railroad detective Len Harris worked up a case against the prisoners for robbing several stagecoaches in the area recently and learned the two men were on their way to Camptonville in Yuba County to rob another stagecoach when Tracy was arrested. The prisoners were turned over to Sheriff John C. Boggs of Placer County and lodged in the county jail at Auburn. On Tuesday, June 21, Wilson was arrested between Colfax and Dutch Flat, and he joined Tracy in jail. Smith, who up to that time was still thought to be one of the robbers and was a well-known San Quentin resident, was cleared and released.

The case against Tracy and Wilson, though mostly circumstantial, was strengthened by several admissions, and the two men, when brought into court for their examination, pled guilty hoping to get a lighter sentence. However, when the prisoners returned to court in late June they were sentenced to serve fifteen years at San Quentin Prison, and both men arrived at the prison on June 29, 1881. Tracy was registered as prisoner #9967 and Wilson as #9968. Wilson was released on July 9, 1891, after forfeiting seven and two-thirds months of good time credit. Tracy was released, by expiration of his sentence, on November 29, 1892, after two years of good time credit was forfeited for bad behavior.

Sources: *Placer County Herald (CA)*: June 4, 1881; June 18, 1881; June 25, 1881; July 2, 1881.

UNKNOWN, MAY 9, 1883

At 1:00 a.m. Wednesday, May 9, 1883, the stagecoach driven by George Secord from Dutch Flat to the rail station, a distance of a mile, had just left town when three masked and armed road agents stepped into the road and ordered Secord to halt. Instead Secord pulled his pistol and fired at the three figures as they quickly retreated, and at the same time he whipped up his team and took the coach to the depot safely. One of the messages telegraphed reached Wells, Fargo detective John N. Thacker who was aboard a train bound for Butte, Montana, and information developed at Dutch Flat suggested that the three aspiring road agents were on the same train. Thacker enlisted the help of Constable Leach, and they arrested three suspicious characters. Two of the men surrendered meekly, but the third showed resistance until Thacker displayed his Bulldog pistol in a manner that showed he knew how to use it; and then all three prisoners walked to the jail. Thacker telegraphed for Secord to come to Butte and identify the three men, and the stagecoach driver started on the morning train. It appears that the three prisoners were not the road agents, and no one was prosecuted for the attempted robbery.

Source: *Territorial Enterprise (Virginia City, NV)*: May 11, 1883.

UNKNOWN, APRIL 5, 1887

On Tuesday, April 5, 1887, the stagecoach from Auburn to Forest Hill was going up the grade two miles from its destination when a lone road agent, masked and armed with a double-barreled shotgun, stepped into the road and ordered driver Cornelius Reese to rein in his team. The robber demanded that the Wells, Fargo express box be thrown down, but the driver told him it was fastened to the coach. The robber checked and found that it was. He then gave up on the box, which contained $1,500, and called for the mail sacks and the driver's purse, which was empty, and the purse and mail pouches for Butcher Ranch and Forest Hill were delivered.

The robber then told the driver to move along without asking about passengers, and as soon as the coach was under way the robber took the purse and mailbags and disappeared into the brush. The driver, in his haste to get to town, ran over and crushed a wheelbarrow being used by a road repair crew a quarter mile from the scene, and as soon as he reached Auburn he reported the robbery. The sheriff took several deputies and rode to the scene, but the road agent was gone from the area and had left no clue to his identity nor a trail to follow for any distance.

Sources: *Daily Alta California (San Francisco)*: April 6, 1887. *Los Angeles Herald (CA)*: April 6, 1887.

JOHN SANSOME, AUGUST 11, 1887

On Thursday morning, August 11, 1887, the stagecoach from Michigan Bluff to Auburn, with Jim Murray driving, had only traveled three-quarters of a mile to El Dorado Canyon when a lone road agent appeared in the road and ordered the driver to halt. He demanded the Wells, Fargo express box and the mailbags, and the bags were thrown down; but the box was attached to the coach and had to be pried loose before it could be thrown down. The robber then told the driver to move on without asking about passengers. After the coach was out of sight the robber carried away the box, which contained $265, and the mailbags. It was not a regular gold shipment day, which accounted for the small amount in the box. A posse rode to the scene from Michigan Bluff, but they could find no clues. Soon after the robbery a packet of thirty letters was found wedged under the railroad tracks, and a gun was found lying nearby, and the postmaster determined that $286.40 had been removed from twenty-nine of the letters.

On Friday, August 26, two men broke into the home of Mrs. May in Colfax and stole a valuable watch and chain. It was not long before the two burglars were seen, and one was captured while the other escaped. The captured burglar was lodged in the Colfax jail and as soon as he was behind bars he "peached," or informed, on his partner whom he knew as William U. "Bill" Austin, and he told how Austin had bragged about robbing the stagecoach on August 11. Soon afterward Austin was captured on the Sacramento train a mile and a half from Clipper Gap and lodged in the Colfax jail, and Wells, Fargo detective James B. Hume was summoned. As soon as Hume saw Austin he identified him as John Sansome, an ex-convict with a long record of convictions for grand theft and burglary, including the burglary of a Wells, Fargo office in May 1875, and Sansome had been free only since he was pardoned on June 29, 1886. Sansome was tried in early February 1888, and on February 16 he was found guilty of the stagecoach robbery. On March 6 Judge Meyers sentenced the defendant to serve a life term at San Quentin Prison. Forty-six-year-old Sansome arrived at San Quentin Prison on March 9, 1888, for his sixth term and registered as prisoner #12889, but the last notation on his prison record was that he was "taken out on a writ of probable cause Oct. 29, '89," when he appeared before the state supreme court. The supreme court overturned Sansome's conviction and ordered a new trial, which was scheduled at Auburn for July 1890. He was retried and it was determined that there was no new evidence beyond that which had already been reviewed and overturned by the high court, so on July 25, 1890, Sansome was discharged.

Sources: *Daily Alta California (San Francisco)*: August 12, 1887; March 7, 1888. *Los Angeles Herald (CA)*: August 12, 1887. *Sacramento Daily Union (CA)*: August 12, 1887; August 29, 1887; July 28, 1890.

UNKNOWN, JUNE 15, 1889

On Saturday, June 15, 1889, the stagecoach from Auburn to Forest Hill had only traveled two miles when a masked road agent stepped into the road and halted the coach. He demanded the Wells, Fargo express box, and once it was in the road he ordered the driver to move along.

He was not interested in passengers nor the mail. Once the coach was gone he pried open the box, but there was nothing of value inside. He fled the scene leaving the box, which was found by the posse, but they could find no clue to the robber's identity nor a trail to follow for any distance.

Source: *Sacramento Daily Union (CA)*: June 16, 1889.

FRANK WILLIAMS, SEPTEMBER 2, 1889; SEPTEMBER 16, 1889; DECEMBER 12, 1889

On Monday, September 2, 1889, the stagecoach from Auburn to Forest Hill had just reached the top of a new grade five miles from Auburn, referred to as the Forest Hill or Noyo grade, when a lone highwayman stepped into the road and ordered the driver to halt. He then demanded the Wells, Fargo express box and broke it open, removing $300. He placed a note in the box addressed "compliments to J. B. Hume" and containing a sort of sarcastic rhyme, reminiscent of "Black Bart." There were six passengers aboard, five women and one man, but they were not molested, nor did the robber ask for the mail. As soon as the driver could reach a telegraph, he reported the robbery to Sheriff John Butler of Placer County, the constables of the cities, and to the Wells, Fargo office in San Francisco. Wells, Fargo's chief detective James B. Hume was assigned to the case, but he could find no clue to the identity of the robber, nor his whereabouts.

On Monday, September 16, the same lone highwayman appeared near the same place and halted the stagecoach bound for Auburn. He demanded the Wells, Fargo express box and broke it open, but there was nothing inside so he returned the box to the coach and ordered the driver to continue into Auburn. He did not molest the passengers nor ask for the mail. Again there were no clues to the identity of the robber, nor a trail to follow, but lawmen believed the man had returned to Auburn.

After the second robbery the matter seemed closed until the strange actions of Henry Williamson aroused the suspicions of lawmen in Auburn, and Williamson's voice, manner and size tallied exactly with the road agent. It was decided to arrest him and see what could be developed during questioning, but Williamson disappeared from Auburn and lawmen thought their intentions had been discovered, and this added to their suspicions. When there was no trace of Williamson, Auburn's constable H. L. Fick believed he had gone to Sacramento. Williamson had, in fact, gone to Sacramento with a group of Placer County residents to attend the fair, and there was nothing nefarious about his disappearance from Auburn. Fick went to Sacramento but he could find no sign of Williamson, so he gave up the chase and returned to Auburn empty-handed and frustrated. On September 22 Fick was strolling down J Street and was about to cross Eighth Street when he came face to face with Williamson, who had come to town for the fair. He arrested his man and lodged him in jail, but no case could be made and Williamson was released.

A road agent had robbed stagecoaches in Shasta and Mariposa counties, and then on Thursday, December 12, 1889, the Auburn to Forest Hill stagecoach was stopped by the same road agent five miles from its destination. The masked highwayman again appeared above average height and quite stout as he pointed his .45 caliber revolver at driver Frank Powell and ordered him to halt and then throw down the Wells, Fargo express box. However, there was no express box aboard that coach, so the robber asked for the mailbags and they were thrown down, but he was not interested in the passengers. Once he had the mail he told the driver to continue on. Lawmen rushed to the scene and found the mailbags, which had been cut open and the contents rifled, but only one registered letter could not be accounted for. There was no clue to the robber's identity so the investigation continued. (See Nevada County for December 15, 1889.)

CHARLES "THORN" DORSEY AND GEORGE SHINN, APRIL 7, 1890

On Monday afternoon, April 7, 1890, the stagecoach from Michigan Bluff to Auburn was stopped when one and one half miles from its destination. There were two masked road agents; the smaller road agent was armed with a revolver while the other robber was armed with a shotgun. They called for the Wells, Fargo express box to be thrown down and then ordered the passengers to come out and line up, and the man with the shotgun covered the five passengers while the man with the pistol began collecting valuables from them. However, a passenger named Muir refused to give up his valuables and advanced on the man with the shotgun, daring him to shoot. The smaller robber became so agitated that he dropped his pistol, but he picked it up before ordering all the passengers to board, leaving Muir unmolested, and then gave the command to continue into Auburn. After the coach was some distance away the men broke open the express box and took out the small plunder inside, including forty letters, and added it to the $30 taken from the four passengers. In their haste and confusion they had missed a large sum of money carried by a Chinaman, and they refused to take a $200 check from another passenger. There were no clues to their identities after lawmen examined the scene. Muir concocted a story of the utmost bravery on his part, but later it was exposed as "pure bosh," and road agent Dorsey after his arrest said he was about to shoot Muir down as he had murdered a man named Cummings years earlier, but Shinn had talked him out of committing another murder.

On August 30, 1881, George Shinn and four others wrecked a train at Cape Horn Mills, California. Shinn was captured, tried, convicted and sentenced to serve a twelve-year term at San Quentin Prison. Shinn, through model behavior, gained outside trusty status and on December 1, 1887, he drove his cart through the gate during a heavy rainstorm, which kept the guards indoors, and he had Charles Thorn, alias Dorsey, under the tarp. Thorn was serving a life sentence for a murder committed during the robbery of a stagecoach at Moore's Flat on September 1, 1879. The two men moved about California for some time, then went to Chicago. In October 1890 James B. Hume was notified that the two prison escapees were in Chicago, and he went there to make the arrest. He had been interested in the two men for nearly three years because he was certain they had been returning to California to commit crimes, at least some involving Wells, Fargo treasure. Once the prisoners reached California, Shinn was interviewed by Hume and several other officers, knowing that Thorn would never talk to them. Shinn told them of dozens of crimes the two men had committed during the past three years, including three stagecoach robberies: the Sonora to Milton stagecoach on July 31, 1889; the Quincy to Oroville stagecoach on September 10, 1889; and the Michigan Bluff to Auburn stagecoach on April 7, 1890. Shinn and Thorn were returned to San Quentin on October 26, Thorn under his old prison number, 10487, and Shinn under his old prison number, 10760. However on October 31, to keep him away from Thorn, Shinn was transferred to Folsom and registered as prisoner #2284. Neither man was charged with any of the crimes they committed over the three years they were free. The record shows that Shinn "was restored" on December 24, 1893. Thorn was paroled on December 21, 1911.

Sources: *Daily Alta California (San Francisco)*: September 11, 1889. *Sacramento Daily Union (CA)*: September 11, 1889. *San Francisco Call (CA)*: April 9, 1890.

UNKNOWN, APRIL 10, 1890

On Thursday, April 10, stagecoach wagon driver Ira Burke stopped his six-horse team near Auburn and got down to have a drink of water. Suddenly a small man with a flour sack over his head, with eyeholes cut into it, stepped out of the brush with a pistol in his hand. He demanded Burke's money, and though the driver had $85 he handed the robber $5. The robber said he knew that Burke had more money, but the driver told him if he wanted more he should go under the wagon cover and take the coin out of the treasure box. The robber climbed into the wagon under the cover, so Burke jumped onto the singletrees and whipped up the team. The robber called out frantically for him to stop, and when he didn't the robber fired through the seat twice, thinking the driver was there. The shots only frightened the horses and drove them on at a faster pace, and after running the team a mile and a half Burke stopped and searched the wagon, but the robber had dropped off, and Burke thought it had been about a half mile back. He continued into Auburn and reported the attempted robbery, but the robber could not be found. After two good scares it seems that this road agent gave up the work and moved on.

Source: *Sacramento Daily Union (CA)*: April 11, 1890.

UNKNOWN, JULY 3, 1901

On Wednesday, July 3, 1901, the Forest Hill to Auburn stagecoach was near Dodd's place, twelve miles from its destination, when a lone road agent wearing a mask, with his feet muffled with barley sacks and carrying a double-barreled shotgun, called out to driver Henry Crockett, "Halt!" Crockett replied "in a jocular way" so the command was repeated, and Crockett yelled, "I'll be cussed if I'll stop." The road agent then shot the horse nearest him, which brought the coach to a halt. The robber commanded the five passengers to throw out their wallets and told Crockett to throw down the Wells, Fargo express box. The passengers tossed out $20, and after he picked up the money he took the box and disappeared into the brush. The box contained $50 in money billed to J. G. Dodds at Westville. Crockett got down and cut loose the dead horse, and then whipped up the remaining three and hurried to the next station, where he telephone lawmen in Auburn.

Sheriff Kenna was ill, so deputies Coan and Dependener rode to the scene while Undersheriff May was on the telephone advising lawmen in all communities of the robbery. The next day a load of bullion came from Forest Hill to Auburn, but there was a Wells, Fargo messenger on board, as was the policy, and it made it into Auburn unmolested. There was no clue to the robber's identity nor a clear trail to follow, so no one was arrested.

Sources: *Los Angeles Herald (CA)*: July 4, 1901. *San Francisco Call (CA)*: July 4, 1901.

UNKNOWN, AUGUST 3, 1901

On Saturday evening, August 3, 1901, the stagecoach from Colfax to Forest Hill was stopped by a lone road agent, masked and armed. He demanded that the Wells, Fargo box be thrown down, but there was no express box on board. He did not ask for the mail but instead ordered the three passengers, drummers on their way to Forest Hill, to climb out and line up, and he relieved them of $20. He then had the three passengers board and told the driver to move along, and the coach hurried into town where the robbery was reported. The posse that rode to the scene could find no clue to the robber's identity nor a clear trail to follow for any distance.

Source: *Los Angeles Herald (CA)*: August 4, 1901.

Plumas County

EDWARD BUGBEE, CHARLES W. WATSON AND --- AUSTIN, FEBRUARY 25, 1857

It was raining very hard at 3:00 p.m. on Tuesday, February 25, 1857, as the California Stage Company coach from Marysville to Rabbit Creek in Plumas County stopped at the foot of Eagle Bird Hill, thirty miles north of Marysville, to let out three passengers to lighten the load for the horses on the steep grade. When the coach reached the summit, three rough-looking characters emerged from the brush and the leader pointed a double-barreled shotgun at driver Ned Winchell and pulled the trigger, but his powder had been soaked by the rain and the firing pins only snapped. Another road agent then drew his six-shooter and emptied it at Winchell, "perforating the stage near the driver's box," and Winchell drew his six-shooter and fired back five times. Neither the driver nor any of the robbers were hit, but the sudden sound of gunfire frightened the horses and they took off at a run, carrying the coach out of range and out of danger. The third man did not appear to have a weapon, and all three road agents then retreated and disappeared into the brush. After traveling a short distance Winchell got his team under control and stopped to wait for his passengers, and as they passed the spot of the attempted robbery the three men did not reappear, perhaps being out of ammunition and fearing the passengers were armed. There was no money aboard the coach, but the driver believed the men were after the four horses. Winchell described the leader, with the shotgun, as tall with red hair and beard, while the other two were "ordinary looking, with no particular marks by which they could be recognized." That night three rough characters checked into the St. Louis Hotel in Marysville and lawmen were alerted. They went to the room and arrested Bugbee and Watson who had escaped from San Quentin Prison, and a man named Austin. Watson had escaped on June 6, 1856, and had remained free for seven months, and he was joined by Bugbee who escaped on January 14, 1857. While they were suspected of the attempted stagecoach robbery, they were not charged. They were returned to the prison on March 4, 1857, to continue serving out their sentences, now even longer because of their escape. Watson escaped again on December 6, 1857, and was not heard of again. The prison records do not include a date of discharge for Bugbee. Apparently Austin was the man without a weapon, the other two men were blamed for the attempt to halt the stagecoach, and he was not prosecuted for the crime.

Sources: *Daily Alta California (San Francisco)*: February 27, 1857. *Sacramento Daily Union (CA)*: February 27, 1857

UNKNOWN, AUGUST 17, 1875

On Tuesday evening, August 17, 1875, the Oroville stagecoach was returning to the city from Quincy with six passengers aboard—two men and two women inside and two men seated on top with the driver. The coach was ascending a steep hill with a bank on one side and a declivity on the other, seventeen miles from its destination, when the coach suddenly stopped as all heard the command, "Throw up your hands!" The two women crawled under the seats while the two men on top raised their hands, along with the driver, and one cried out, "Don't fire!" Colonel A. W. von Schmidt peered out of the coach and saw only one masked road agent armed with a double-barreled shotgun, the barrel aimed at those on the outside seat. He told the others, "I am going to make a fight of it," and suddenly sprang out of the coach and had the drop on the robber with his large revolver. The robber swung his shotgun in the direction of von Schmidt and the driver saw his opportunity; he whipped up the team, the coach lurched forward with the horses at a run, and he drove away leaving behind the robber and von Schmidt. The road agent could not change the direction of his aim or he might be shot, and von Schmidt commanded, "Drop that gun!" and sprang toward the road agent. The robber was so surprised that he dropped the shotgun, turned, and ran into the brush. Von Schmidt did not follow, as he believed the man had at least one accomplice, though none were seen, and perhaps the man who fled had another gun on his person, the brush was quite heavy, and it was getting dark. The colonel then examined the ground and realized that the robber, to prevent leaving distinguishable boot marks, had been in his stocking feet. The coach, which was carrying $9,000 in gold dust and $2,500 in other treasure, returned in a few minutes and von Schmidt boarded, and they continued into Oroville without further incident. Since no one was hurt and nothing was stolen to warrant a reward, which would finance a pursuit, none was initiated.

On September 11, 1875, Wells, Fargo's general superintendent John J. Valentine presented von Schimdt with a fine Jurgensen watch and a letter of commendation in recognition of his bravery in protecting the company's treasure.

Sources: *Daily Alta California (San Francisco)*: September 12, 1875. *Sacramento Daily Union (CA)*: August 19, 1875

S. A. "Ned" Allen and James "Texas" Jones, June 27, 1876

After robbing a stagecoach in Kern County on January 15, 1875, S. A. "Ned" Allen, alias Sol White, stole a treasure box from a stagecoach on March 30, 1875, which was not a robbery but a grand larceny, and he was arrested. However, Allen escaped after a murderous assault on jailor Ross and he fled leaving Ross for dead, but the jailor recovered so Allen avoided a murder charge. Allen then robbed the stagecoach traveling from Oroville in Butte County to Laporte in Plumas County on June 27, 1876, possibly to find a stake to move his operations into Nevada.

On October 3, 1876, at 9:30 a.m. the stagecoach from Aurora in Esmeralda County to Carson City in Nevada was one mile from Kilgore's station and the Mountain House when two masked road agents armed with double-barreled shotguns and six-shooters halted the coach. They demanded the Wells, Fargo express box and sawed it open, taking out $228, checks and papers. On board were five passengers and nine bars of gold bullion, but the robbers did not molest the passengers nor take the bullion, perhaps because of its great weight. Wells, Fargo's chief detective James B. Hume was soon on their trail and traced them to Jackson, California, where they were arrested within a week following the robbery. Hume was familiar with both men and identified one as California stagecoach robber S. A. "Ned" Allen. The other road agent, also well known to Hume, was identified as James "Texas" Jones, a man involved in a number of robberies from Chinese workers. He took his prisoners to Sacramento where he booked passage on the stagecoach for Carson City. On October 13, 1876, the men were lodged in the Douglas County jail at Genoa, they had their preliminary examination that same day and were held over to answer to the grand jury. They were both indicted, held for trial, and in December they were convicted of stagecoach robbery. Allen arrived at the Nevada state prison on December 19, 1876, sentenced to serve eight years. He served out his entire sentence and was released on December 5, 1883. Jones was sentenced to serve five years and arrived at the state prison on December 20, 1876. Jones escaped from the prison in December 1880, at the age of 64, and was not heard of again. Allen was never tried for the robbery of the stagecoaches in California.

Sources: *Kern County Weekly Courier (Bakersfield, CA)*: February 27, 1875; March 6, 1875; March 13, 1875. *Territorial Enterprise (Virginia City, NV)*: October 4, 1876; October 14, 1876.

Charles E. "Black Bart" Bolton, July 25, 1878; July 30, 1878

On Thursday, July 25, 1878, the stagecoach from Quincy to Oroville was a mile from the Berry Creek sawmill when it was stopped by one man, masked and wielding a shotgun, who stood in front of the leaders. He demanded the Wells, Fargo treasure box, and the driver threw it down. There were three passengers aboard but they were not molested, and the road agent did not ask for the mail pouches. Once the robber, Charles E. Bolton, had the treasure box he told the driver to continue, and the driver quickly whipped up his team. At the next stop the driver reported the robbery and lawmen hurried to the scene, but they could find no clue to the robber's identity nor a track to follow except that the robber had failed, for the first time, to muffle up his boots and they were determined to be between size 6 and 8. He left a poem, the second and last he would leave, and he obtained from the box $379 in coin, a silver watch worth $25, and a diamond ring worth $200.

On July 30, 1878, just after sunrise, Bolton, or "Black Bart," halted the stagecoach traveling from Laporte to Oroville, driven by Dan Barry, when it was just six miles from Laporte and still in Plumas County. Bolton stepped out of heavy timber in front of the horses and followed his familiar pattern of robbery. Wells, Fargo reported he got only $50 in gold nuggets and another cheap watch. Sheriff James H. Yeates organized a posse and went to the scene, but found only a few boot tracks he thought to be size 8. There were no further clues, and the road agent was not identified or captured. (See Calaveras County on November 3, 1883.)

Unknown, January 14, 1879

Just after dark on Tuesday, January 14, 1879, the stagecoach from Quincy to Oroville, with seven passengers inside and one riding on top, was running a little late when it reached Dry Creek, one mile from its destination. As the coach started up a slight grade two masked men jumped out of the brush on each side of the road, and the "short, stout man" tried to grab the reins of the leaders, while the "tall, boney chap" leveled his rifle at driver Joel Meacham and ordered him to "Halt!" The man trying to grab the reins of the leaders frightened the horses and they plunged to the side of the road away from him, then started off at a dead run, and Meacham encouraged them on with his whip. As the horses started off the tall robber fired his rifle at the driver, and the bullet narrowly missed the head of passenger J. N. Turner, seated next to Meacham. One passenger inside, Dr. Lucas, tried to get his pistol, but by the time he had it in hand the coach had been driven out of danger, and out of range, of the robbers. The coach hurried into Oroville and from there Wells, Fargo messengers were sent in pursuit, but they could not find the robbers, who would have gotten very little from the Wells, Fargo express box.

On Sunday evening, February 16, Meacham was summoned to the express office to pick up a package. When he arrived he was surprised to find nearly a dozen men present, he accepted the package, and when he opened it he found inside a Morocco watch case with a gold watch inside. The watch was inscribed, "To Joel Meacham, for gallant conduct in saving treasure-box from highwaymen near Oroville, January 14, 1879. Wells, Fargo & Company." The watch was accompanied with a letter of commendation from company superintendent John J. Valentine.

Sources: *Marysville Daily Appeal (CA)*: January 18, 1879. *Oroville Mercury (CA)*: January 17, 1879.

George Higgs and William Jose, October 11, 1886

On Monday, October 11, 1886, the stagecoach from Gibsonville in Sierra County bound for Reno, Nevada, had reached Gimletville in Plumas County when two masked road agents dressed as tramps, armed with pistols, halted the coach. They ordered the passengers to step out and form a line, then went through them taking from one passenger $5. During the time that one robber was collecting the meager plunder the other stood back and covered them with his pistol, and he was so nervous he accidentally discharged his revolver, hitting General D. W. H. Day in his side. The wound was serious but not fatal, so the robbers had the passengers board and then called for the Wells, Fargo express box, and it was thrown down. One of them hefted the box, then shook it, and finding it light put it back onto the coach without opening it. They did not ask for the mail and told the driver to continue on.

Soon after the robbery and shooting, Sheriff Dean of Plumas County arrested two men he believed were the road agents. When police captain Appleton W. Stone arrived at the county seat of Quincy he took the two prisoners to the bedside of Day, who "declared positively that neither of the prisoners was the right man." After the two prisoners were released, Stone was detailed to pursue and capture the two robbers, and he started searching in the direction of Gibsonville, where Wells, Fargo agent Walker maintained the only provision store in the vicinity. However, Walker said he had not seen the men described by Day and the other passengers, so Stone circulated their descriptions and the notice of reward throughout the region. Seven days after the robbery, Stone met a small boy on the road, and he told of meeting two tramps carrying a flour sack and making their way through the snow ten miles north of Gibsonville. Stone returned to Walker's store and checked his books, and they found the sale of a sack of flour and other supplies to two men less than a week after the robbery. A Chinaman then came forward and said that two men, matching the description of the road agents, had been camped in St. Louis Ravine, a few miles from the store. Stone recruited the local constable and a number of citizens and on the morning of October 18 they made their way through a foot of snow to a hill overlooking the ravine, and from the first cabin they saw smoke rising from the chimney. They rushed upon the cabin and found the fire burning in the fireplace, and the remnants of the supplies, but the two men had fled. There were two sets of boot tracks, each of one man, leading away from the cabin so the posse men stayed until nightfall, hoping the two would return. After dark they gave up the ambush and went back to Walker's store.

Meanwhile Walker's clerk Hankins and Eugene Squire met the two fugitives making their way toward Oroville through another ravine in back of Gibsonville. The fugitives had been walking in the creek at the base of the gorge near Crescent Mills so that they would not leave tracks in the snow, and when they realized they had been seen they tried to flee. There was a lively chase through shallow water, over rocks, and through heavy brush, but finally Hankins and Squire overtook the two fugitives and captured them at the point of their rifles. The prisoners gave the names William Jose and George Higgs, they said they had been working in the timber country since the previous last summer, and they denied stopping any stagecoaches. They were marched back to Gibsonville and secured, and when Stone returned from the St. Louis Ravine cabin he took charge of the prisoners and took them to the county seat at Quincy and lodged them in jail. They had their examination on October 20 and were held over for trial, and when they were brought into the district court on October 28 for arraignment they pled guilty, tried to correct their names to James Higgs and William Jess but were refused, and waived time, so each defendant was immediately sentenced to serve three years at San Quentin Prison. The reason for the light sentence was the testimony of Day that he was shot by accident, the youth of the two men, and the circumstances leading to the robbery—that they had just arrived from England and were destitute and desperate. Higgs and Jose arrived at San Quentin Prison on October 31, 1886, where Jose registered as prisoner #12300 and Higgs registered as prisoner #12301. Both prisoners were released on February 28, 1889, after serving two years and four months.

Sources: *Daily Alta California (San Francisco)*: October 12, 1886; October 30–31, 1886.

WALTER A. ARRISON AND UNKNOWN, DECEMBER 4, 1886

On Saturday, December 4, 1886, the Oroville to Quincy stagecoach was near Bidwell's Bar when two masked road agents, one armed with a breech-loading shotgun and the other a muzzle-loading shotgun, halted the coach. They demanded the Wells, Fargo express box and once it was thrown down they wasted no time breaking the lock using a new hammer and cold chisel, and they removed a bar of silver worth $955 sent from Spanish Ranch in Plumas County. They also demanded the mail and went through the bags carefully, removing anything that looked as if it had value. They returned the mail sacks to the coach along with the busted treasure box, and one robber then sent his regards to Wells, Fargo's chief detective James B. Hume before sending the driver on his way. They were described as

> an American, five feet nine inches tall, stout build with square shoulders and about 170 pounds, with brown hair and moustache, and about twenty-five years old; he was disguised with a mask made of slate colored canvas, fit tightly to his head and shoulders with eyeholes bound with braid, and he wore blue overalls and new rubber overshoes over his boots. The other was an American five feet seven inches tall with medium build, dark hair, and eyes showing considerable white; he wore a dark moustache, has a large nose, white teeth, and looks like a Jew or Frenchman; he wore a short navy-blue coat, brown vest and dark pants with white stripe, greenish-gray plaited woolen shirt with bright brass buttons; his hands and complexion were dark.

Wells, Fargo posted a reward of $300, the state matched that amount, and the U.S. government added $200.

On December 5 the two fugitives were reported at Kentucky Ranch and after breakfast they headed south, but it took several weeks before the first clue surfaced. The silver bar had been broken into pieces and sold, and one piece was bought by John North. When he tried to spend the nugget it was recognized as part of a bar, and he was arrested. North said he had bought the silver nugget from a man named George Henderson, and Henderson was soon arrested. At their examinations North and Henderson pled not guilty and were held over for trial. As Henderson's trial neared he insisted his name was actually George Alonzo Harrison, but he was tried as Henderson. He was charged with robbery, and on March 16, 1887, at 9:00 p.m. the case went to the jury. After seven minutes in deliberations the jurors found the defendant guilty, and he then insisted his name was Walter A. Arrison for sentencing. Judge Freer, on March 26, sentenced Arrison to serve fifty years in prison. Two days later North was tried for receiving stolen property, convicted, and sentenced to serve two years in prison. The search for the second road agent continued and on May 13 Dan F. "Little Al" Raymon was arrested and charged as the second road agent, but following his examination on May 20 he was released for a lack of evidence and the second robber was never identified. Twenty-seven-year-old Arrison arrived at San Quentin Prison on March 28, 1887, where he registered as prisoner #12472. He had served a prior term under #1157 but had been "pardoned and restored" by Governor George Stoneman on September 21, 1885, and released.

Just before 3:00 p.m. on Monday, May 18, 1896, convict James Walter Ellis, alias Bob Kelly, went to the cell of Arrison. Arrison, during the previous eleven years, had worked his way into the position of "cell tender," and in that capacity he had free access to the corridors, and the door to his cell was kept open. When Ellis entered Arrison's cell, Arrison struck him with an iron bucket. Ellis then pulled out a makeshift knife and stabbed Arrison several times, one a mortal wound. Arrison called out for help and guards arrived, overpowered and disarmed Ellis, and locked him in solitary confinement. Arrison was rushed to the hospital where he lingered in agony until shortly after 6:00 p.m. when he died. Ellis, who had served eighteen months of his sentence for a burglary committed in Los Angeles County, was tried twice for the murder of Arrison.

Sources: *Daily Alta California (San Francisco)*: March 20, 1887; March 27, 1887; May 13, 1887. *Sacramento Daily Union (CA)*: December 7, 1886; March 27, 1887

CHARLES "THORN" DORSEY AND GEORGE SHINN, SEPTEMBER 10, 1889

On Tuesday, September 10, 1889, the stagecoach from Quincy to Oroville was seven miles from its destination when it was stopped by two road agents, masked and armed. There were four passengers aboard, two men and two women, and they were ordered to step out. The robbers demanded the express box and it was delivered and broken open, and inside was a gold bar worth $731 but the other contents of the box remained unreported. They robbed the male passengers, collecting $23 from one man and $12 from the other, but they did not molest the ladies nor did they ask for the mail. They then ordered the passengers aboard and told the driver to continue on. On September 15 officers arrested Antoine Schneider at Greenville, and he was lodged in jail, suspected of being one of the stagecoach robbers. He was soon joined by Michael Dunlevey who was arrested at Crescent. When Schneider was arrested he had a shotgun and a roll of blankets, and inside the roll were four new grain sacks, while Dunlevey had a roll of blankets and a red comforter, and inside the roll was an XL pistol, a miner's single-hand hammer, and a miner's candlestick. Schneider had a $5 gold piece and a small nugget in his pocket, and Dunlevey had two $5 gold pieces. They had their examination before Judge Ketchum at 3:00 p.m. on the 16th and were released due to a lack of evidence.

In October 1890 two escapees from San Quentin Prison were captured in Chicago, Illinois, and when they were returned to California George Shinn related their criminal activities over the past three years, and this included the robbery of the stagecoach on September 10, 1889. (See Placer County on April 7, 1890.)

MARTIN MEYERS, FEBRUARY 16, 1895

At 6:30 a.m. on Saturday, February 16, 1895, the stagecoach from Oroville to Forbestown had traveled only three miles when it was stopped by a lone road agent, masked and armed with a shotgun. He had been hiding behind an oak tree near the road, and as the coach neared he "popped out" and poked his shotgun at the head of driver Fred Moore as he commanded, "Halt!" After the coach was stopped the robber ordered the two passengers to step out, and he collected from them $180, consisting of twenty $5 bills and $80 in $5 and $20 gold pieces, and a gold watch and chain. After they boarded he called for the Wells, Fargo express box and then told the driver to continue on his route, but he did not ask for the mail. The robber broke open the box and took out $240. Moore hurried to the next station and reported the robbery, and the road agent was described as tall with long white whiskers. A posse was dispatched to the scene, but all they could find was the busted express box. The description, however, led Wells, Fargo's special messenger George Hackett to believe he was looking for the sixty-five-year-old ex-convict Martin Meyers, aliases Tom Connors and Durant, who had been living in a cabin eighteen miles north of Oroville. Hackett, with J. L. Tucker and Marshal Maben, got onto Meyers' trail, and on February 18 they found him on the Knights Landing train at Palermo and arrested him without incident. He was headed for Davisville with a ten-pound sack of flour among his luggage, and in the bottom of the sack they found the stolen money, watch and chain. Meyers would not say where he had hidden his shotgun, even though he confessed to the robbery. The officers took him to Marysville and lodged him in jail, and the following day he was taken to Oroville for his examination but he pled guilty and was immediately sentenced to serve a term of life in prison. Meyers arrived at San Quentin Prison on February 20, 1895, and registered as prisoner #16241. Meyers died in prison on May 14, 1905.

Sources: *Sacramento Daily Union (CA)*: February 19–20, 1895. *San Francisco Call (CA)*: February 17, 1895.

Sacramento County

UNKNOWN, SEPTEMBER 2, 1902

At 8:00 p.m. on Tuesday, September 2, 1902, the stagecoach from Sacramento to Walnut Grove, with Ed Bryan driving, had traveled sixteen miles and was near Courtland when a lone road agent masked with a gunnysack, and brandishing a revolver, halted the coach. He ordered the driver to get down and then told the two passengers to step out, and he had the three men form a line with their backs to the coach. He went through the pockets of Joseph Fisher and took out $16, then went through Bryan's pockets and took $4.50. When he came to Henry F. Isham, he resisted and grabbed the robber's pistol. As they struggled the pistol was fired into the air before Isham wrested it from the robber's grip and tried to strike him on the head, but Isham missed and struck the robber's shoulder. The man turned to run and Isham grabbed him and struck him another blow, but the road agent pulled free of Isham's grasp, slipped into the underbrush, and escaped. Isham tried to fire the pistol at the fleeing robber, but it was "an old-fashioned affair" and would not work after the first discharge. During the struggle the mask was displaced and Isham said he was sure he would recognize the man if he saw him again, but it had been very dark and apparently he never came in contact with the man again as no arrests followed.

Sources: *Los Angeles Herald (CA)*: September 4, 1902. *San Francisco Call (CA)*: September 4, 1902.

San Benito County

UNKNOWN, JULY 31, 1893

On Monday, July 31, 1893, Al Leonard's mail stagecoach operating between San Benito and Hernandez Valley was halted by three masked, armed road agents. They took everything of value and then sent the coach on its way. Leonard went in pursuit of the three robbers and overtook them, but they got the drop on him and he had to retreat. He went for Sheriff E. E. Holbrook and they started together after the robbers, but they had fled out of reach and there was no clear trail to follow.

Source: *San Francisco Call (CA)*: August 2, 1893.

San Bernardino County

B. F. CLARK AND RICHARD JOHNSON, AUGUST 29, 1874

On Saturday at 10:00 p.m. August 29, 1874, the stagecoach westbound for Los Angeles had left Spadra in San Bernardino County and traveled only four and a half miles when a man suddenly sprang from the brush and tried to grab the harness of the off-leader, the right front horse. At the same time he yelled to driver Tommy Peters, "Halt!" The horses were at a trot, and the fast gait prevented him from getting hold of the harness. Next the road agent fired a shot at the horse, attempting to drop him and thereby stop the stage, but this "spooked" the horses and they continued on. Peters yelled at the horses, whipped up the team, and dropped into the boot just as the road agent took the second shot at him. As Peters proceeded toward town he saw, from the labored breathing of the off-leader, that the horse was seriously wounded, so he pushed the team to get as close to town and as far from the road agents as he could before the horse fell. The stagecoach was just at Fabron's place, on the outskirts of San Bernardino, when the horse collapsed and died of loss of blood from a neck wound. None of the passengers—two men, three women and two children—were injured by the shots or the harrowing rush toward town. It was only conjecture that the target was the Wells, Fargo express box; but it was empty, so had the road agents stopped the stage, they would probably have gone through the passengers to avoid a "water haul."

As soon as the coach reached town the alarm was sounded and deputies Mayfield and Yager formed a posse by deputizing James Stewart, Eugene Lander and Gus Starke. They hurried to the scene of the robbery and found a clear trail of boot tracks from two men. As soon as there was enough light, Mayfield, Yager and Lander took up the trail of footprints and followed it toward the Cajon Pass. The trail was circuitous but the lawmen were tenacious, and after following the tracks all day they came upon the fugitives at Vincent's house in the pass, fourteen miles from the scene of the robbery, where they had just ordered something to eat. They were disarmed, arrested without resistance, and placed under guard. The posse was very tired, so they decided to start back the next morning.

Lander was put on guard during an early hour, and one of the prisoners, patiently awaiting his opportunity, made a desperate attempt to escape by attacking him. Somehow he managed to get possession of his own pistol, taken from him when arrested. The prisoner pointed the cocked pistol at Lander, but "quick as thought," Lander jumped him and a terrible struggle ensued. The prisoner managed to fire one round but missed Lander, and the bullet struck Yager in the hip causing a minor grazing wound. Yager then rushed to Lander's aid and received a severe blow to the head. The prisoner was finally overpowered and again disarmed. The prisoners, who gave the names B. F. Clark and Richard McMahon, were taken into the city of San Bernardino the following day at 10:00 a.m. and lodged in jail to await their examination. On Tuesday, September 1, the prisoners were taken before Justice Mathews where bail was set at $1,500 for Clark, who had tried to escape, and $1,000 for McMahon who had not. They were remanded to the custody of the sheriff and returned to jail to await action by the grand jury, which was then in session. On September 19 Mr. Pridham, agent for Wells, Fargo in Los Angeles, went to San Bernardino and summoned Tommy Peters to the local office to make a presentation:

> Office of Wells, Fargo Express,
> San Francisco, September 11, 1874.
> Mr. Thos. Peters, San Bernardino, Cal.
>
> Dear Sir:
> Your recent action in protecting the express is in such marked contrast to the nerveless timidity which has manifested itself in some drivers under similar circumstances, that we beg leave to testify our appreciation of your merit.
> Accompanying this, by express, we send a first class gold watch, chain, and key, with the following inscription:
> "Presented to Thos. Peters, in recognition of his courage and resolution in protecting the express from highwaymen near San Bernardino, Cal., Aug. 29, 1874.
> Wells, Fargo & Co."

Please accept, with our best wishes for your prosperity and happiness.

Very truly yours,
John J. Valentine, General Sup't.

The grand jury returned true bills (indictments) against the two prisoners, and then McMahon insisted his true name was Richard Johnson, and they were tried together in early October. Both men were convicted, Clark of an assault to murder and rob and Johnson of attempted robbery only. Johnson was sentenced to serve six years and arrived at the prison on October 15, 1874, and registered as prisoner #6200. During his transportation to the boat in San Francisco, to be taken across the bay to the prison, he tried to escape. He had filed off one of his shackles the previous night and would have gotten away from his guard except for the presence of a San Francisco policeman. Johnson, who had been in San Quentin three times previously, was discharged, by expiration of sentence, on December 14, 1878. Clark was sentenced to serve a term of twelve years, he also arrived on October 15, 1874, and registered as prisoner #6199. Clark had served one previous term at San Quentin for attempting to rob the U.S. mail in 1870. He was discharged, by expiration of sentence with good time credits under the Goodwin Act, on June 15, 1882.

Sources: *Daily Alta California (San Francisco)*: August 31, 1874. *Los Angeles Herald (CA)*: September 20, 1874. *San Bernardino Guardian (CA)*: September 5, 1874; October 24, 1874.

San Diego County

Unknown, November 7, 1869

On October 21, 1869, four Mexican bandits robbed a stagecoach north of Los Angeles, then fled south to San Diego. Lawmen followed, but the robbers had left the city before they could be arrested and traveled east. At 8:00 p.m. on Sunday, November 7, 1869, the westbound stagecoach from Fort Yuma to San Diego had traveled sixteen miles, and was near Seven Wells, when the same four Mexican road agents appeared and halted the coach. The road at that place was narrow, and the brush on both sides of the road was quite heavy, so they were able to surprise the driver when they stepped out suddenly, "armed to the teeth and stripped to the buff." One man stepped in front of the horses while the other three surrounded the coach, but when the team was not stopped immediately, the robber in the road shot the off-wheeler. As soon as the first shot was fired, passenger W. Bichard, who had brought his shotgun, fired a load of buckshot into the abdomen of the man in the road, and he cried out, "My God, I am shot!" This began a gunfight with the other three robbers, who had the passengers outgunned as those in the coach only had three revolvers and Bichard's shotgun. Still, they drove off the other three road agents empty-handed, while passenger Davis got only a slight flesh wound on his leg. Before the coach got under way the area was searched and the robbers' coats and spurs were found hanging on the bushes, and these were collected. Posses were organized and rode to the scene, and the following day they found a horse tied near the robbery scene, apparently left by the other three robbers in case their partner had only been wounded and made good his escape. The countryside around the robbery was vigorously searched but the other three road agents could not be found, and it was supposed after the gunfight and loss of a man they had fled south of the international border. The dead man could not be identified, so there was no clue to the identities of the other three road agents.

Sources: *Daily Alta California (San Francisco)*: October 23, 1869; November 13, 1869. *San Diego Union (CA)*: November 11, 1869.

Unknown, February 22, 1875

At dusk on Monday, February 22, 1875, the stagecoach from San Diego to the mines near Julian was seven miles from its destination when two masked, armed road agents appeared near the top of the Coleman grade and ordered the driver to rein in his team. Once the coach was stopped they demanded the Wells, Fargo express box, but the driver refused to deliver it and said, "If you want it you will have to take it from me." One man was armed with a double-barreled shotgun and he aimed it at the driver's head while the other robber, with pistol in hand, climbed up and took down the box. There were four passengers on board, but at the foot of the grade three stepped out and walked some distance behind to reduce the weight of the pull for the animals, but the fourth man was an invalid and he remained in the coach. Without waiting for the three passengers to catch up, the robbers told the driver to continue on, and he drove ahead. As the driver left the scene he could hear the blows being struck on the box, they busted it open and took out $1,000, but they did not disturb anything else in the box. The robbers expressed no interest in the passengers nor in the mail. The coach went a distance and then returned for the three passengers, and the box was recovered with all the contents intact but the money. The robbery was reported at the first opportunity and a posse was soon at the scene, but they could find no clues to the identities of the robbers nor a clear trail to follow. Wells, Fargo posted a reward of $750 representing $250 for the arrest and conviction of each road agent and one-fourth of the treasure recovered, but the reward was never paid.

Sources: *Daily Alta California (San Francisco)*: February 26, 1875. *Los Angeles Herald (CA)*: February 26, 1875. *Sacramento Daily Union (CA)*: February 24, 1875.

Charles A. Bush, March 6, 1877

In February 1877 a superintendent of the California & Arizona Stage Line learned that several men were planning to rob one of their stagecoaches, and they assigned detective John Mantle to infiltrate the gang, learn their plans, and arrest those who committed the robbery if they proceeded. Detective Mantle joined William "Poker Bill" Bloodworth who was leader of the group, Charles A. Bush, C. C. Hatch and Frank Lee as they began planning the robbery. They went to Ehrenberg in the Arizona Territory to reconnoiter the road and pick the best place to stop the coach, but they had a falling-out and Hatch and Lee withdrew and went north to Prescott. Bloodworth and Bush then continued on to Walker's station, not far from Indian Wells in California, and they chose their spot for the robbery one mile from Indian Wells station. Mantle went along, but he was not to be part of the robbery nor share in the plunder. However, Bloodworth was arrested for some prior crime, taken to Los Angeles, and lodged in jail. Bush then included Mantle in the robbery plan, and he recruited Frank J. Gibson as his "sentinel," or lookout. On Tuesday night, March 6, 1877, Bush and Mantle stopped the stagecoach and demanded the Wells, Fargo express box, and as the box was passed down Bush's mask fell away and the driver got a good look at his face. After the express box and mail sacks were in the road they ordered the driver to continue on, and Bush and Mantle carried away their plunder. They broke open the box and took out the contents—$315 in money and $9,500 in Army drafts—then they rifled the mail sacks and burned some of the valueless mail for light to examine the other letters and packages, but the amount they obtained is not reported. Bush took the army drafts as his share and gave $315 to Mantle to divide with Gibson, but Gibson was never paid a share. Bush said he was going to leave California, but Mantle convinced him to accompany him to San Bernardino to purchase horses. Bush buried the drafts in a secret location before they departed. In San Bernardino Mantle contacted the authorities and arranged to have himself, Bush and Gibson arrested, and they were lodged in jail together at Los Angeles. Mantle continued to work the case and managed to convince Bush to give him a diagram, or map, to the buried drafts, and all were recovered. Mantle was then released, and he returned to Arizona as an undercover detective working up a case against Thomas Brophy and John Sutton, who robbed a stagecoach on May 12, 1877.

Bush and Gibson were taken to San Francisco and indicted by the federal grand jury for robbing the U.S. mail. Bush was tried in July, and on the 30th he was convicted and sentenced to serve eight years at San Quentin. Gibson's trial began immediately after Bush was convicted, and on August 1 he was acquitted of being an accessory to the robbery. Bush arrived at the prison on August 15, 1877, and registered as prisoner #7712. He was pardoned by U.S. president Rutherford B. Hayes on November 9 and discharged on November 26, 1880, after serving three years three and one half months.

Sources: *Daily Alta California (San Francisco)*: July 30, 1877; August 1, 1877; August 3, 1877. *Sacramento Daily Union (CA)*: March 8–9, 1877; March 13, 1877; July 17, 1877; July 30–31, 1877; August 2, 1877.

UNKNOWN, AUGUST 28, 1877

On Tuesday morning, August 28, 1877, the southbound stagecoach from Los Angeles to San Diego was stopped by a masked, armed lone highwayman when it was near Ellinitos, south of the county boundary. He demanded the Wells, Fargo box, it was thrown down, and he immediately broke it open. He took out the valuables, returned the box to the coach, and told the driver to continue south. As the coach pulled away the driver saw him mount a "splendid horse" and start out northeast for the mountains. As soon as word reached San Diego, Deputy Bushyhead started for the scene and took the robber's trail into the mountains, while Sheriff Coyne was delayed organizing a posse, and he was soon following Bushyhead's markers. However, the lawmen were not able to overtake the road agent, and there was no clue to his identity.

Source: *Sacramento Daily Union (CA)*: August 30, 1877.

San Joaquin County

JAMES CASEY, EUGENE MURPHY AND PETER SMITH, OCTOBER 23, 1884

On October 23, 1884, at 7:00 a.m. the southbound Ferry Hill stagecoach, driven by Frank Grimes, was approaching a small bridge on the road between Banta in San Joaquin County and Grayson in Stanislaus County, which required the coach to move at a slow pace. The driver noticed three men, roughly clad, lounging near the bridge, but they were not masked so he paid them little attention. As the coach neared the group, one of them, who had been carelessly leaning over the railing of the bridge, straightened himself and commanded the driver to halt. At the same time the other two emphasized the command by aiming their guns at the driver. One of the men was armed with a double-barreled shotgun while the other two men had six-shooters. There was but one passenger aboard, J. J. Sweeney, who was riding atop with the driver, and he was covered by the shotgun while the other two men pointed their revolvers at Grimes and demanded the Wells, Fargo express box. After the box was delivered one of the men, noticing Sweeney's watch and chain, asked him to hand it over. Sweeney later claimed that he replied the watch was a present from his mother and the robber, if he wanted it, would have to "take it from my dead body." Sweeney said that the robbers apparently did not want to go to that extreme over a watch, so they ordered Grimes to move on. Grimes drove a mile and a half to Kasson's ranch, and from there messengers were sent to San Joaquin City where Constable Finch and Joe Nye were notified of the robbery. From there telegrams were sent to the Wells, Fargo office in San Francisco and to San Joaquin County's Sheriff Thomas Cunningham. Grimes had reported that the robbers were apparently "green at the business" as they were terribly nervous and could not hold the muzzles of their guns steady; and he gave a good description of the three men.

By noon of the same day the sheriff had left Stockton to investigate the robbery and track the road agents, and he was joined by Wells, Fargo's detective John N. Thacker. The robbers had been trailed by Deputy Sheriff Fulkerth from the scene of the robbery to Gerlach's ranch in the mouth of Lone Tree Canyon, eight miles distant. The three men stopped for lunch at noon and then left for Ingram Canyon, where they stopped at the ranch of a widow and had another meal at 3:00 p.m. Instead of striking into the foothills they continued to skirt along the edge of the valley and arrived at Ed Thomas' ranch at 6:00 p.m. where they ate supper. After eating their third meal in six hours they went down the canyon a short distance, found a haystack, and settled in for the night. Fulkerth found them asleep in the haystack and captured them without resistance.

Sheriff Cunningham and detective Thacker were but a mile and a half away when the three road agents were captured by Fulkerth, having been delayed when their horses gave out and they could not obtain fresh animals. When they joined the deputy and his prisoners, Thacker questioned them and they admitted their guilt. They declined counsel and gave their names as James Casey, Peter Smith, and Eugene Murphy. Murphy said of Sweeney's story, of refusing to surrender his watch, "He is a liar. He sat on his seat as limp as a rag and almost scared to death." They said they had missed a "water haul" by ten cents, all that was in the box excepting three letters written in Chinese. They said, as their excuse, that they were motivated to rob the stagecoach "out of hunger."

The prisoners were taken to Modesto and lodged in jail, and their examination before Judge Treatwell was scheduled for Monday, October 27. When they appeared they waived examination and were held over for the grand jury, bail set in the sum of $5,000 each. Their arraignment was set for 3:30 that afternoon in Department 2 of the Superior Court, but was delayed to the following day when they pled guilty, and each defendant was sentenced to serve five years in San Quentin. They arrived at the prison on October 29, 1884, only six days after robbing the coach: Casey registering as prisoner #11434, Murphy as #11435, and Smith as #11436. Eugene Murphy was the first to leave the prison when he was pardoned and released on August 19, 1886; James Casey was also pardoned, and he was released on December 31, 1886; Peter Smith served out his entire sentence and was released upon expiration of sentence on May 29, 1888.

Sources: *Stockton Daily Independent:* October 24, 1884; October 26, 1884; October 28–29, 1884.

UNKNOWN, JUNE 5, 1886

On Saturday afternoon, June 5, 1886, the stagecoach from Hills Ferry to Banta was one and a half miles from its destination, in San Joaquin County, when a masked, armed road agent stepped into the road from hiding and ordered the driver to rein in his team. The driver halted, and then came the demand for the Wells, Fargo express box and it was thrown down. The robber did not ask about passengers nor the mail and immediately ordered the driver to continue on. After the coach was out of sight the robber broke open the box and found it was empty. Lawmen went to the scene and recovered the busted box but could find no clues nor a trail, and with no rewards posted there was no motivation to go in pursuit.

Sources: *Daily Alta California (San Francisco)*: June 12, 1886. *Territorial Enterprise (Virginia City, NV)*: June 10, 1886.

MICHAEL CUCOVICH, JULY 22, 1892

On Friday, July 22, 1892, the southwest-bound two-horse stagecoach from Stockton to Robert's Island, driven by Jimmy Hooper, had only traveled three miles when a lone road agent, armed with a Winchester rifle, stopped the coach expecting to find large payrolls for the great ranches south of the city. There was no express box aboard, nor any of the treasure he expected, so he ordered Hooper to get down and had passengers Reuben May and Isaac Pledger step out, turn out their pockets, and throw their money on the ground. Each man was careful to hide most his valuables, so that the robber got only $2 and a gold watch from the driver and a total of $4 from the two passengers. After the robber had obtained his meager plunder he told everyone to board and ordered Hooper to continue into town. The robber started off afoot across a grain field, and Hooper went a short distance where he tied off his team and borrowed a saddle horse to follow the robber. One passenger stayed with the coach while the other rode into town to give the alarm. Sheriff Thomas Cunningham soon arrived with a posse of deputies, constables and citizens totaling more than a dozen men, but armed only with pistols. The road agent turned and fired periodically at his pursuers so they would keep their distance, but he was driven toward Stockton and finally surrounded in a field between the hospital and the fairgrounds, near the Slough House east of the city. It appeared he intended to make a fight of it to the death, and he pumped rounds into his rifle and continued to fire to keep his pursuers at bay until he had fired twenty-six bullets and seemed to be out of ammunition. He had been hiding among the tules in a creek bed, but he stepped out with his arms raised and surrendered. During the gunfight Constable James P. Carroll received a severe gunshot wound below the elbow of his left arm, shattering the bone, but the bullet had been deflected by a memorandum pad and then by his watch, which saved his life. The first man to reach the fugitive was detective Simpson and the fugitive tried to slash him with a Bowie knife, but the man was overpowered by officers Sawyer and Marshal and Deputy Black, disarmed and ironed, and taken to the jail in Stockton. It was discovered that he had an entire belt of ammunition, and there were several rounds still in his rifle when he gave up. He gave the name Tracy Nick and he knew several of the officers by name, but he was not recognized by them. It was not long, however, before the prisoner was identified as Michael Cucovich, who had been committed to the insane asylum in January 1890 and was discharged as "cured" six months later.

The investigation revealed that a week before the robbery Cucovich had purchased the new repeating rifle and the Bowie knife, and the day of the robbery he went to French Camp and waited for the coach. It was not long before the prisoner had an examination by doctors, and he was adjudged insane and returned to the asylum. On November 15, 1893, Cucovich was assisting an attendant in delivering laundry when he suddenly bolted and "started off like a deer." Several attendants hurried after him, but they could not overhaul the desperate escapee, and he does not appear in the record again.

Sources: *Sacramento Daily Union (CA)*: July 23, 1892; November 16, 1893. *San Francisco Call (CA)*: July 23, 1892.

San Luis Obispo County

UNKNOWN, MAY 28, 1875

On Friday, May 28, 1875, the southbound stagecoach from Soledad for Paso de Robles had reached Naciemento, eighteen miles north of it destination, when a lone, masked road agent stepped from behind a tree, aimed a double-barreled shotgun at the driver, and ordered him to halt. Once the coach was stopped the man demanded that the driver throw down the Wells, Fargo express box, and as soon as it was in the road he ordered the driver to continue on. There were eighteen passengers aboard, but they were not molested. The coach drove off and the man picked up the box and fled. Wells, Fargo posted a reward of $300 for the arrest and conviction of the road agent, but it was never paid.

Sources: *Los Angeles Herald (CA)*: June 10, 1875. *Sacramento Daily Union (CA)*: May 29, 1875.

RICHARD "DICK FELLOWS" PERKINS, AUGUST 25, 1881; DECEMBER 29, 1881

On August 25, 1881, Richard Perkins, alias Dick Fellows, possibly encouraged by a July 19 road agent adventure in which he took no part, robbed the Coast Line stagecoach between San Luis Obispo and San Jose when it was three miles south of San Luis Obispo. He took only the treasure box, which contained $268 in coins, but did not request the mail or molest the passengers. He did not appear on the road for four months, but then he robbed the stagecoach between San Luis Obispo and Soledad on December 11, 1881, when it was one mile from its destination.

On December 29, 1881, Perkins returned to San Luis Obispo County and closed out the year by stopping the stagecoach from Santa Barbara to San Luis Obispo, driven by Townsend, when seven miles from Arroyo Grande. He was wearing a handkerchief for a mask and brandishing a six-shooter as he commanded the driver to halt and throw out the treasure box, and as soon as the box lay in the road he ordered the driver to continue on. Once the coach left, he broke open the box and took out $46.50. The posse that went to the scene could not find a trail to follow nor a clue to the identity of the road agent. (See Monterey County on January 13, 1882.)

DAN MCCARTY AND JOHN WEISENSTEIN, MAY 18, 1882; MAY 25, 1882

Dan McCarty had robbed a stagecoach in Merced County on May 7, 1877, and spent a year in San Quentin Prison. After his release he stayed out of trouble for five years, or at least he was not identified as involved in any crimes, but in early 1882 he met John Weisenstein and the two men decided to rob stagecoaches. On April 27, 1882, they robbed the stagecoach traveling from Hills Ferry to Banta when it was still in Stanislaus County, but their plunder was meager so they decided to move their operation to the coast roads. On May 18 when at the foot of a mountain four miles from San Luis Obispo, the two masked and armed road agents stepped into the road and halted the coach. They demanded and received the Wells, Fargo express box and then ordered the driver to continue on, and he hurried into San Luis Obispo and reported the robbery. Sheriff Oaks was notified of the robbery at 6:00 a.m., and he went to the scene but could find no clue to the identity of the road agents, except confirming that there were only two men involved. Following this second "water haul," McCarty and Weisenstein, early on the morning of Thursday, May 25, tried to stop the same stagecoach when it was about to ascend the small hill near Bean's place. However, two masked men suddenly leaping into the road frightened the horses, and they took off at a dead run, carrying the stagecoach out of danger. Later that same day John Hanson found the treasure box from the robbery of May 18 under a small bridge near his home, where it had been cut open with an axe, and all the contents—a pair of ladies' shoes, a pair of boots, and one letter—were lying nearby. From that place there was enough of a trail and other clues to track the road agents, and it was not long before McCarty and Weisenstein were lodged in the San Luis Obispo jail. The two men had their examination, and the evidence, though mostly circumstantial, was strong enough to hold them for the grand jury. Weisenstein, who had no previous prison record, pled guilty and agreed to turn state's evidence to get a reduced sentence, and he was sentenced to serve five years. He was received at Folsom Prison on December 15, 1882, registering as prisoner #543. Weisenstein was taken out of prison on December 21, 1882, to testify against McCarty, and he escaped from the Salinas jail with McCarty on February 24, 1883. Weisenstein was recaptured and returned to Folsom Prison on March 5, 1883, but he escaped from that prison on December 8, 1884, and was not heard of again.

McCarty pled not guilty, and while awaiting his next court appearance he escaped from the Salinas jail on February 24, with several other prisoners including Weisenstein. McCarty separated from the others and stole a horse and buggy, arming himself with a six-shooter. When overtaken by the sheriff's posse that same day he attempted to fight them off but was seriously wounded in his right side and had to surrender. He was returned to his jail cell and, being in no condition to escape again, he pled guilty to the robbery of the Soledad to San Luis Obispo stagecoach, hoping to get a lighter sentence by cooperating. However, McCarty had a prison record for robbing a stagecoach in 1877, so he was sentenced to serve twelve years. He arrived at Folsom Prison on April 3, 1883, and registered as prisoner #572. He was discharged after serving seven years eight months.

Sources: *Gilroy Advocate (CA)*: May 12, 1877; May 26, 1877; August 11, 1877. *San Luis Obispo Tribune (CA)*: May 27, 1882. *Stanislaus News (CA)*: May 25, 1877.

L. C. CUFF AND N. G. STUTZMAN, JULY 21, 1888; MARCH 12, 1889

At 9:00 p.m. on Saturday, July 21, 1888, the stagecoach from Templeton to San Luis Obispo with six passengers aboard was five miles north of its destination, in San Luis Obispo County, when a six-foot-tall, slender and masked highwayman stepped out onto the roadway and stopped the coach. He waved his revolver at the driver as he called for the Wells, Fargo express box and the mail pouches, and they were thrown down. However, this did not satisfy him and he had the passengers step out, line up, and he went through them for money and jewelry. He then told the driver to continue on, and after the coach was a distance away, his partner, who had been concealed in the brush aiming his shotgun at the coach, joined him and they broke open the box and cut open the mail pouches, sorting through the packages and letters and removing everything of value. When the coach reached town the driver reported the robbery, the sheriff and district attorney organized a posse, and they rushed to the scene to gather clues and pursue the road agents. However, it was to no avail, and they returned to town with the empty box and the mail pouches.

On Tuesday evening, March 12, 1889, the stagecoach from Gilroy to Santa Margarita was seven miles north of San Luis Obispo climbing a hill near Borondas, just two miles from the place of the July 21 robbery, when a six-foot-tall, heavyset and masked road agent stepped into the road and stopped the coach. He called for the Wells, Fargo express box but showed no interest in the passengers or the mail. The box was thrown down just as the second six-horse stagecoach came up and, seeing the box lying in the road, stopped. The robber pointed his pistol at the second driver and told him, "Drive on," and as soon as the second coach passed, the robber told the driver of the first coach to move along. After both coaches were out of sight, the robber was joined by his partner and they broke open the box, perhaps expecting to find $3,000 which was supposed to be on that coach, but they only found $32.90, a shawl and jewelry. They took out their plunder and fled. During the robbery the wind blew aside the robber's mask several times and his features were clearly seen, and he was described as having gray whiskers.

Detective Oates sent word to lawmen to watch for the road agents, as he was certain they were in the area, and on March 16 Constable Bennett of Gilroy obtained a clue that led him to suspect two men staying at the Railroad Hotel. Bennett, with officers McDuffee and Ban, went to the hotel and called for the man in one room to surrender, but when he refused, one of the officers climbed through the transom and captured his man still laying in bed. They next went to the room of the other suspect and arrested him in his bed as well. The first man, six feet tall and slender, identified himself as twenty-six-year-old L. C. Cuff who said he had come to Gilroy from Arkansas less than a year ago. The second man said he was twenty-six-year-old N. G. Stutzman who had come to Gilroy a year ago from Kansas. Both men at first insisted they were innocent and could prove an alibi, but in Stutzman's room the officers found a distinctive, valuable shawl and jewelry taken from the express box on March 12. Once it was clear that the evidence was mounting and conclusive, both men confessed, said this was their first criminal offense, and therefore refused to confess to the July 21, 1888, robbery. They said they were just trying to get enough money to travel east to their homes. They admitted that they had devised the plan to rob the stagecoach and left Gilroy on March 11 and reached Santa Margarita later that day. At the scene Stutzman stayed in the brush and covered the coach while Cuff did the work of halting the coach and calling for the express box, and after getting their plunder, they walked to Templeton. They were lodged in the Gilroy jail, and the following day detective Oates took them by stagecoach to San Luis Obispo. On March 19 they appeared in court for their arraignment and they pled guilty to stagecoach robbery, and each defendant was immediately sentenced to serve fifteen years in San Quentin. They arrived at the prison on March 21, 1889, with Cuff registering as prisoner #13484 and Stutzman as prisoner #13485. Both men were "restored" on October 21, 1892, after serving three years and six months.

Sources: *Daily Alta California (San Francisco)*: July 21, 1888; March 19–20, 1889. *Los Angeles Herald (CA)*: March 13, 1889. *Sacramento Daily Union (CA)*: March 13, 1889; March 18, 1889.

San Mateo County

Thomas Brison and Joseph Smith, April 16, 1885

At 9:30 a.m. on Thursday, April 16, 1885, the U.S. mail stagecoach left San Mateo for Pescadero. The coach had traveled only thirty minutes, about four miles, when the lead horses stopped at a rope stretched across the road, not far from San Felix station and near Crystal Springs. Two road agents, masked and armed with double-barreled shotguns, stepped out of the brush and demanded the Wells, Fargo express box, and it was thrown down. The robbers were not interested in the passengers, nor did they call for the mail pouches. One robber covered the driver while the other dropped the rope, and then they told the driver he could continue; but before he could whip up his team the two robbers grabbed the express box and carried it into the brush. As soon as he could, the driver reported the robbery, and the county sheriff rode to the scene. He searched the area and found the box with the padlock pried off, but all the contents—a COD bill for Pescadero—was still in the box. The sheriff continued to search for any clue to the robbers' identities or a trail to follow but finally returned to San Mateo after 8:00 p.m. with only the busted box to show for his efforts.

Nearly a year would pass before two men were charged with the robbery, and the evidence against them was overwhelming. Twenty-four-year-old Thomas Brison turned state's evidence and testified against his partner Joseph Smith, and on March 19 at Redwood City, Judge Head sentenced Brison, because of his cooperation, to serve two years at San Quentin Prison. The following day Judge Head sentenced eighteen-year-old Smith to serve five years at Folsom Prison, and the defendant's only complaint was that he expected to go to San Quentin, and as a result his destination was changed to San Quentin. Brison arrived at San Quentin Prison on March 20, 1886, and registered as prisoner #12073; and Smith arrived the following day and registered as prisoner #12075. Brison was discharged on November 19, 1887, after serving one year eight months; and Smith was discharged on October 20, 1889, after serving three years seven months.

Sources: *Daily Alta California (San Francisco)*: April 17, 1885. *Sacramento Daily Union (CA)*: April 17, 1885.

UNKNOWN, JUNE 22, 1896

After 1:00 p.m. on Monday, June 22, 1896, the stagecoach from Half Moon Bay was nearing the Spring Valley dam five miles from San Mateo when a road agent, with a white handkerchief for a mask, wielding a "horse-pistol" and carrying a rifle, slid down a pile of rocks into the brush along the side of the road and leaped out in front of the horses. The robber ordered driver Ed Campbell to halt, but his sudden appearance frightened the horses and they swerved to the right and took off at "a blind gallop for several miles." Campbell whipped up his team to hurry them along and left the robber standing, dumfounded, in the roadway. The robber fired four shots after the coach, but he did not hit any of the three passengers, a man and woman inside and another man riding atop, nor the coach. The shots seemed to motivate the horses even more, and Campbell had nearly reached San Mateo before he slowed the team to a trot. Campbell reported the attempted robbery, but neither he nor his passengers could give any description of the road agent. Sheriff Elroy was notified at Redwood City and he organized a posse and started for the scene, but he could not find any clue to the robber's identity.

Sources: *Sacramento Daily Union (CA)*: June 24, 1896. *San Francisco Call (CA)*: June 23, 1896.

UNKNOWN, AUGUST 17, 1905

At 9:00 a.m. on Thursday, August 17, 1905, the Davis' brothers stagecoach from Half-moon Bay to San Mateo was on the Crystal Springs road three miles from its destination when a road agent, with a revolver in hand and masked with a black handkerchief, halted driver Edward Campbell. On the seat next to Campbell was O. Olsen and inside were J. C. Santos, Peter Jule, Ralph Roosen and Miss A. J. Johnson. The order was given to throw down the express boxes and the mail sacks, and the boxes of Wells, Fargo and Levy Brothers were thrown out. The driver hesitated to throw down the mailbags, and the robber then ordered Santos to remove his hat and pass it among the inside passengers to collect their valuables. Santos did not understand the order at first, and when he hesitated the driver was also threatened with death. An express wagon driven by E. Bertelotte then came around the bend, and the robber told Campbell to continue without taking Santos' hat. The road agent was upset at the interruption by the second coach so he took a shot at Bertelotte but missed, so the driver jumped down and ran up the road with the robber following, and he shot at Bertelotte twice more, missing. The road agent then returned to the boxes, broke them open, and took out $225 in valuables, though both companies said there was nothing of value in their boxes. Another wagon then appeared and the robber left the broken boxes in the road but took the unopened mail sack and ran into the heavy brush along the roadside. Bertelotte then returned and both wagons continued into San Mateo. Wells, Fargo's detective John N. Thacker was put on the case, and Sheriff Joseph Mansfield organized a posse to ride to the scene. The robber was described as five feet seven inches tall, one hundred eighty pounds, wearing a long black overcoat, blue overalls, and a tight-fitting black cap. The posse recovered the broken boxes and returned them to town, but they could not trail the robber beyond his foot tracks near the scene and he was never identified.

Sources: *Los Angeles Herald (CA)*: August 18–19, 1905. *San Francisco Call (CA)*: August 18–19, 1905.

Santa Barbara County

Richard "Dick Fellows" Perkins, Late 1869; January 2, 1882; January 8, 1882

After robbing a lone rider near Los Angeles, G. Brett Lytle moved northward. In late 1869 the Coast Line stagecoach from Los Angeles to Santa Barbara, when near its destination, was stopped by a lone highwayman. The road agent was soon tracked down, arrested, and insisted his name was Richard "Dick" Fellows. Fellows, whose real name was Lytle but who used Richard Perkins as an alias, was tried for the stagecoach robbery in Santa Barbara County, convicted, and sentenced to serve eight years at California's San Quentin Prison. He arrived on January 31, 1870, and registered as prisoner #4378. As soon as Fellows arrived behind the prison's walls he began a campaign to gain an early release. He represented himself as being well educated and then convinced the prison officials to place him in the library, an "elevated trusty" position given only to those favored by the staff. He was then in the position to contact a great number of prisoners, so he next established Bible study classes and positioned himself as the religious spokesman for all the convicts. All his efforts convinced the warden and other officials that he had been thoroughly reformed by their influence and by the prison experience, and they recommended an early pardon. On April 4, 1874, Governor Newton Booth granted an unconditional pardon, which restored all his rights. Fellows had served less than half of his original sentence, and for the next twenty months he managed to stay out of trouble, or at least was not caught for any crimes he committed. He robbed a stagecoach in Kern County on December 4, 1875, and was sent to prison again and released on May 16, 1881. He then robbed three stagecoaches, one in Monterey County and two in San Luis Obispo County.

On Monday, January 2, 1882, Fellows attempted to stop and rob the Telegraph Stage Company's coach going from San Luis Obispo to Santa Barbara when at the old adobe house two miles beyond Los Alamos in Santa Barbara County. The driver, George Richmond, drove near the old house to avoid dead sheep scattered along the roadway. He was trying to make up time and the horses were at a trot when a voice from the house shouted, "Stop! Box!" and a shot was fired. One passenger, a blacksmith named Dorsey riding atop, said the bullet whizzed within inches of their heads. Richmond applied the whip and, as two more shots were fired at them, drove the coach out of danger and into Los Alamos. The two passengers riding inside were not harmed. A posse went to the scene but could find no clue to the robber's identity nor a clear track to follow.

On Sunday, January 8, Fellows succeeded in stopping the same stagecoach from San Luis Obispo bound for Santa Barbara, when five miles from Los Alamos, and took the Wells, Fargo express box. Richmond, again driving, saw a horseman in the road acting suspiciously, making a complete circuit of the stagecoach and inspecting the passengers, before he rode up and presented his six-shooter. The robber, masked with a gunnysack with eyeholes, ordered Richmond to halt, then dismounted and tied his horse to a tree. He demanded the treasure box and told Richmond, "The next time I order you to stop, I guess you'll mind. God damn you!" Richmond threw out the box, and Fellows then continued, "I understand that you carry a pretty good watch. Just drop it out in the sand. I want it to time you by, you son of a bitch." Richmond dropped his gold hunting-case watch, valued at $250, and was then ordered to continue. There were two passengers aboard, one man and one woman, but they were not molested. A party went to the scene and found the box where the road agent had burned a hole in one corner, but the box had been empty. There was no clue to the robber's identity nor a clear track to follow.

On January 9, Wells, Fargo dispatched detective Charles Aull to capture the road agent who had been so active on the roads of Santa Barbara County. He started his investigation in the city of Santa Barbara and, from the descriptions, knew that it was Dick Fellows, alias Richard Perkins. He had been a turnkey at San Quentin for several years and knew Fellows quite well. He sent out dispatches and tried to track his quarry, but he had no clues until Monday, January 23, following the robbery of a stagecoach ten days earlier. (See Monterey County on January 13, 1882.)

UNKNOWN, OCTOBER 18, 1869

On Monday, October 18, 1869, a stagecoach was stopped by one road agent, masked and armed, when near Santa Barbara. As the robber concentrated on the driver, a passenger drew his revolver and shot the robber twice, once in the arm near his shoulder and once in his head. The robber, uttering a string of oaths, retreated into the heavy brush, mounted his horse and rode away empty-handed. On October 27 a man appeared at a cabin near the scene of the robbery, confessed he was the road agent and surrendered, saying he would die soon of his wounds. He would not give his name, and after he died he was buried in an unmarked grave.

Source: *Sacramento Daily Union (CA)*: October 29, 1869.

UNKNOWN, MARCH 26, 1877; MARCH 31, 1877

On Monday night, March 26, 1877, the Coast Line stagecoach bound for Santa Barbara was still fifty miles west at Oak Grove, near La Graciosa, when a lone road agent halted the coach and demanded the Wells, Fargo express box. He had disguised himself and carried a double-barreled shotgun, and he spoke in broken English "as a blind," and there was nothing about him that reminded anyone of a local resident. He showed no interest in the passengers and did not ask for the mail. As soon as the box lay in the road he ordered the driver to continue on. A posse was organized and rode to the scene, but there was no clue to the robber's identity, and no clear trail to follow for any distance. Wells, Fargo would not disclose the contents of the treasure box, but it was thought to be quite small as there was no messenger aboard the coach.

On Saturday night, March 31, 1877, the same stagecoach was one mile from the place it was robbed on Monday when the same road agent, similarly disguised and armed, stepped from behind a bush onto the road and ordered driver Dick Smith to halt. He called for the Wells, Fargo boxes and Smith threw down one, and the road agent asked, "Is that all?" Smith replied, "Yes," and the robber told him to continue on without checking. Smith looked back after he had driven a short distance and saw the man strike a light to work with while breaking open the box. The box had been quite light and may not have had anything of value inside, as the box from San Luis Obispo had been sent to Santa Barbara by steamer and arrived at its destination the previous night. The posse that rode to the scene was again frustrated. However, after two "water hauls" the road agent seemed to retire from the business, as he did not appear along that stretch of the route again.

Sources: *Daily Alta California (San Francisco)*: March 28, 1877. *Sacramento Daily Union (CA)*: March 28, 1877; April 3, 1877.

JOHN RUTHERFORD AND JAMES THOMPSON, SEPTEMBER 22, 1884

At 7:15 p.m. on Monday night, September 22, 1884, the stagecoach for Guadalupe in Santa Barbara County, driven by seventeen-year-old Wesley Froom, left the rail depot at Santa Maria and was moving at a slow pace due to heavy fog. As the coach approached the graveyard near Guadalupe at 7:45 p.m. Froom heard two shots fired in quick succession, followed by the command, "Halt!" Next came the order, "Throw out the treasure box," but Froom replied that he could not as it was too heavy. He was then commanded to exert himself and, if needed, get the aid of a passenger, though there was only one passenger, a drummer, aboard. Froom glanced toward the voice and saw two horses, and behind each was a man with a pistol pointed in his direction. He then applied himself and managed to get the box over the edge of the boot and let it tumble to the ground. As soon as the box lay on the road the road agents ordered him to continue on, and "not look back under pain of death." Froom whipped up his team and hurried into Guadalupe to report the robbery. The town became quite excited, and within minutes there were several bands of armed men scouring the surrounding countryside. C. W. Merrit, acting agent for Wells, Fargo at Guadalupe, with Deputy Sheriff T. C. Nance and Constable Lierly hurried to Santa Maria. At 9:15 p.m. two riderless horses came into town, and fifteen minutes later two men came in afoot from the east and went directly to Graves' Saloon. These men were already suspected, as they had been making daily trips to the stage depot in Santa Maria, and their absence at the time of the robbery added to the suspicion. Nance and Lierly, after deputizing Merrit and a man named Cook, arrested the two men without incident, and they gave their names as James Thompson and John Rutherford.

In Santa Maria on the night of the robbery James Thompson had been so intent on watching the loading of the box that he was conspicuous, and Rutherford was nearby leaning on a rail. They saw that the box, when loaded on the stagecoach at Santa Maria, was very heavy. Immediately after the box was loaded Thompson and Rutherford were looked for in Santa Maria and missed. Horses belonging to the Tunnell brothers, James and Henry, also went missing, and these were the two riderless horses which came into town an hour and a half after the robbery. The saddles showed wear, and one saddle had bluish paint marks similar to the color of a treasure box. Lawmen were sure that the road agents had taken the box some distance from the scene of the robbery and hidden it, so on Tuesday morning, September 23, parties were sent out to look for the treasure box. Two men saw where a fence had been cut recently and followed two sets of horse tracks to a field of haystacks. Late in the afternoon, Lark Thornburgh and J. B. Darden found the box in one of the haystacks within two hundred yards of the place where the robbery occurred. The box was taken into town and opened, and all of its contents were found intact including $1,860.

The two prisoners had their examination on Tuesday, September 30, and each prisoner claimed to have an alibi, and each said he could prove they were at the "disreputable house" when the robbery occurred. However, at the hearing Louis Hertz said he was responsible for delivering the box at the depot and he saw both defendants there. He checked the waybill and contents and locked the box, and he delivered it to the stagecoach. After the box was recovered it showed signs of hard use, and then it was entered into evidence. Stagecoach driver Froom testified that "on the road near the graveyard two men stopped me, they had cut through the field and when I turned the corner they were in front of me. I saw that one had a light roan and the other a darker horse, but I could not see the men." James Tunnell then said he had hitched his dark roan to the rail and when he returned the horse was gone. When it returned it was very tired, the saddle was cut or worn, and there was blue paint, like the treasure box, on the saddle; and Henry Clay Tunnell said about the same of his light roan horse and saddle. Hugh Graves testified that the defendants were in the habit of spending their evening in his saloon, but did not arrive on the night of the robbery until 9:30 p.m., they had eaten and then were arrested. Deputy Sheriff Nance said he had taken one pistol from each man and each pistol had one round fired recently. N. H. Rose then testified to boot tracks and matched them to Rutherford's boots. Charles De Witt testified he was on the road ahead of the stagecoach and saw Rutherford, and another man he did not recognize, riding hard for Guadalupe just before the robbery. After several recesses and motions to dismiss the case, the defendants were held over for trial with bail set at $6,000. The prisoners were tried in the Superior Court and convicted of the stagecoach robbery in December 1884. Rutherford was sentenced to serve twelve years and Thompson was sentenced to ten years, and both men arrived at San Quentin Prison on December 16, 1884. Thompson registered as prisoner #11495 and was released, by expiration of sentence, on June 16, 1891. Rutherford was registered as prisoner #11494 and was released, by expiration of sentence, on August 16, 1892.

Sources: *Santa Maria Times (CA)*: September 27, 1884; October 4, 1884. *Territorial Enterprise (Virginia City, NV)*: September 28, 1884.

UNKNOWN, NOVEMBER 3, 1888

On Saturday, November 3, 1888, the two stagecoaches from Santa Barbara to Los Olives were stopped by road agents, who were masked and heavily armed. They broke open the Wells, Fargo express boxes but found nothing, and they went through the mails and packages with similar results. To avoid a "water haul" they robbed the Santa Barbara–bound passengers of $50. Once they determined they had all the plunder they were going to find they told the drivers to continue on to Los Olives. There were no clues to their identities, so no arrests followed.

Sources: *Territorial Enterprise (Virginia City, NV)*: November 4, 1888. *Janesville Daily Gazette (WI)*: November 6, 1888.

HARRY MILLER, DECEMBER 4, 1896

At 10:00 p.m. on Friday, December 4, 1896, the mail stagecoach from Los Alamos to Lompoc had just passed the Stuart post office when, according to sixteen-year-old driver Harry Miller, a tall road agent masked and wearing a large sombrero, pointed at him what Miller believed to be a gun. On command Miller halted the coach and then the robber came forward and Miller saw the man had only a club, but he said he was too frightened to resist when the robber went through the mailbags. Once the robber was through rifling mail he told Miller to continue on, and the boy whipped up the team and hurried into Lompoc to report the robbery. Deputy Nick Foxen organized a posse and rode to the scene of the robbery, but he could find no tracks whatever. Postal inspector Flint issued a reward:

> Sheriff Hicks, Santa Barbara County: Stage robbed last night between Los Alamos and Lompoc. Government offers a reward of $500.

The lack of any sign of a robbery at the scene led officers to believe that Miller had rifled the mail sacks, and by the following day, under close questioning, he confessed that he thought there was money in the registered packages, decided to rob the mail, and "fixed up" the story of the road agent. He was taken to Los Angeles, charged with robbing the U.S. mail, and at his preliminary hearing in the Federal Court he was held over with bail set at $1,000. On December 28 Miller appeared before Justice Wellborn, pled guilty, and was sentenced to serve one year in the Santa Barbara County jail.

Sources: *Los Angeles Herald (CA)*: December 13, 1896; December 29, 1896. *San Francisco Call (CA)*: December 6–7, 1896.

UNKNOWN, MARCH 5, 1898

At 9:00 a.m. on Saturday morning, March 5, 1898, the stagecoach from Santa Barbara to Los Olives was eight miles from its destination, climbing a small grade, and as the coach rounded a sharp curve at the summit a voice called out, "Halt!" A small man, masked with a gunnysack and with a revolver in each hand, appeared at the side of the road. He called for the Wells, Fargo express box and it was delivered, but he did not ask for the mail. He ordered the three passengers to step out, and he collected their loose change and some loose change from the driver, totaling $10. After he had collected their coins he heard a second coach approaching so he told the passengers to board, and once they were seated, he told the driver to move on. The two male passengers and the driver had between them several hundred dollars, but the robber did not have time to search them and made no attempt to rob the woman passenger. The robber fled into the brush just as the second coach rounded the curve so the driver of that coach, who was alone on the seat, did not see the road agent. The agent at Los Olives reported that the box contained only one package valued at $5. From Los Olives, Sheriff Hicks was telephoned at Santa Barbara with the details of the robbery, and within an hour he had sent two deputies to the scene to investigate. By March 7 deputies Storni and De la Cuesta had tracked their man to the summit of the mountains near Santa Ynez but lost the trail there. Storni recovered the box, busted to pieces, some distance from the road and returned it to town. The deputies also reported that a man matching the description of the road agent had been seen at Goleta, so the sheriff sent two men there, but when they could not find him they supposed the robber had boarded a train south for Mexico. No arrests followed.

Sources: *Los Angeles Herald (CA)*: March 6, 1898. *Sacramento Daily Union (CA)*: March 6, 1898. *San Francisco Call (CA)*: March 6, 1898; March 8, 1898.

Unknown, June 4, 1898

On Saturday, June 4, 1898, the stagecoach from Santa Ynez to Santa Barbara, with Frank Cook driving, was nearing Red Gate when a lone road agent, masked and armed with a double-barreled shotgun, was seen crouching at roadside. As the coach passed, the road agent rose up, pointed the shotgun at the driver, and ordered Cook to stop. Cook reined in his team but when the coach was stopped the man made no move, so Cook asked, "What do you want?" The robber replied, "Throw out the box," and Cook replied, "There is none. We haven't carried a box since we were robbed in March." The robber then ordered the three passengers to step out—two men and a boy—and he told them to turn their pockets inside out. The men complied, but Charles Mattel was so frightened he was frozen in place. Frank Stowell contributed $55 and H. H. Scovel added another $10 to the pile of plunder. The robber told them to board, and as soon as all were seated he told Cook to move on, then gathered up his plunder as the coach departed. The sheriff and a posse, with bloodhounds, went to the scene and took up the chase, but there is no record of an arrest.

Sources: *Sacramento Daily Union (CA)*: June 5, 1898. *San Francisco Call (CA)*: June 6, 1898.

Unknown, February 9, 1899

At 5:00 p.m. on Thursday, February 9, 1899, the stagecoach bound for Santa Barbara was twenty-five miles from its destination, on the San Marcos Rancho, when a lone masked road agent hiding behind a fallen tree aimed his shotgun at the driver and ordered him to halt. He had the two passengers—a Mr. Paddock and J. W. Armstrong—step out and surrender $40, then told them to climb aboard and ordered the driver to move on, with the comment, "Tell Hicks I shall never bother him again." The driver and passengers described the robber as short, stout, with brown hair wearing blue overalls and a jumper. Sheriff Nat Stewart took Deputy Peter Storni and rode to the scene, and they spent the next three days tracking the robber through the

Santa Ynez Mountains. They traversed the roughest trails, searched every cabin, and followed up every clue but without any positive result. The sheriff believed it was a local wood chopper, either a Negro disguised as a German or one of the many German wood choppers residing in the area, but he was never able to identify the robber.

Sources: *Los Angeles Herald (CA)*: February 10, 1899; February 12, 1899. *Sacramento Daily Union (CA)*: February 10, 1899. *San Francisco Call (CA)*: February 14, 1899.

Santa Clara County

JAMES GRANT AND JAMES WILSON, JULY 6, 1864; JULY 9, 1864; AUGUST 5, 1864

James Grant had been one of Rufus Henry Ingram's first recruits for Captain Ingram's Partisan Rangers, but after he compromised their reconnaissance at Placerville in preparation for a stagecoach robbery, he was criticized by the other five members. He threatened to kill several members so he was ejected from the band, and he decided to strike out on his own robbing stagecoaches for his own gain rather than to aid the Confederate army. He recruited James Wilson as his partner, as he believed he needed two to do the work. On Wednesday night, July 6, 1864, the southbound stagecoach for Los Angeles was twenty-two miles below San Jose, on the Salinas Plains, when two highwaymen stepped into the road and ordered the driver to halt. Each was masked, one armed with a shotgun and the other a pistol. They told the passengers to step out and then collected $60 before they ordered them to board. The robbers then told the driver to continue on, without asking for the express box or the mail.

At 1:30 a.m. on Saturday, July 9, 1864, the northbound stagecoach for San Jose was within one hundred yards of the place it had been robbed three days earlier when the same two road agents appeared. The coach had been traveling at a high rate of speed for some time but had just come to a sandy part of the road near a cluster of trees, and the soft roadbed required the horses to slow their pace. The masked road agents suddenly sprang from behind the trees, one with a shotgun and the other a pistol, and one yelled out, "Stop your horses," and the other said, "Give us your express." The driver, seated next to the express agent, threw down the box, saying, "There it is." The man with the pistol then pulled back the curtain on the passenger compartment, waved his pistol at the eight male passengers and said, "Come out with your money, men." Instead of getting out, the first man, Hollister, handed over his purse containing $10, but the second man said, "I am sick and have no money," and then each passenger parroted the same excuse. He asked Joseph Patton for his money, and again he gave the excuse he was sick. The robber next ordered H. Goldstein out of the coach, and Goldstein quickly dropped $40 in gold into his boot, and then after he was standing outside he handed over $2.50 in silver saying it was all he had. The robber had Goldstein turn out his pockets and found there was nothing more inside. The robber scolded him, saying, "You have no business to travel this road without money." When the robber was distracted for a moment Goldstein dropped his gold watch in the sand, and he later recovered it after walking back two and a half miles from the station. After Goldstein had given up his silver coin, the second robber, with the shotgun, came up and asked how much money Goldstein had, and when he was showed the silver he told the first robber to return it but was told, "No, we better keep it; we will need it on the road." They next asked for the express box, and it was thrown down, but then the express agent asked if they would return the letters inside the box, and the road agent said, "Certainly we will accommodate you at once." He carried the box fifty yards and broke it open with a hatchet, rifled through the contents, and then returned the box to the driver. The driver asked, "Did you get much money out of the express?" and he replied, "Not a damned cent." The driver then asked if they got as much money as they did when robbing the passengers on Wednesday night, and the robber said he did not and he did not get much either time, and then he said they were a damn poor crowd. The express agent offered them a drink from his flask and after they had imbibed they pointed their guns at the coach and said, "Boys, you can go ahead now; we will not trouble you anymore; it don't pay us to come here—you carry too poor a crowd." Later the road agents were described as one looking like a soldier with belt and cap and of medium size, while the other was larger and heavier and did not have the look of a soldier. Once the coach was under way the robbers mounted and followed for a mile before they turned off onto the San Jose to Watsonville Road.

The robbers must have meant it when they said it did not pay to rob on that road, because on the night of August 5 they moved their operations to the road where they would find the Visalia-bound stagecoach. The coach had reached Pacheco's Pass when the two road agents, again armed with a shotgun and a pistol, stepped out and halted the driver. They had him step down and then had the three passengers step out and form a line. They did not trust the passengers but searched them and took $80 from Redfield, who had hidden several hundred dollars in the coach when first stopped; $15 from Criswell; and $18 from the driver, but the third man had only "a trifling sum." They then brought down the express box, but it felt light so they shook it, then returned it to the coach without breaking it open. They told everyone to board the coach, and then it was allowed to continue on to Visalia.

Each time a posse went to the scene and returned to town empty-handed, but after the last robbery, and based upon the descriptions and information received from the Placerville stagecoach robbery informants, lawmen believed they were looking for James Grant. They stationed men to keep watch on the house of a girl in whom Grant had showed great interest, and eventually he showed up. They ordered him to raise his hands, but instead he turned to run and a load of buckshot struck him in the back. He was arrested and this led to the arrest of his partner, Wilson. As soon as Wilson was behind bars he confessed and turned state's evidence, and in February 1865 they were still in a Sacramento jail awaiting transfer to the Santa Clara County jail for their trial on a stagecoach robbery charge. Grant's trial began about the first of April, the charge reduced to grand larceny, with Wilson the prosecution's main witness. Grant was convicted and sentenced to serve a term of two years at San Quentin Prison, and he arrived on April 3, 1865, where he registered as prisoner #2982. He was discharged on December 20, 1866, after serving one year, eight and a half months.

Sources: *Daily Alta California (San Francisco)*: February 23, 1865. *Los Angeles Star (CA)*: July 23, 1864. *Sacramento Daily Union (CA)*: August 15, 1864.

Tiburcio Vasquez, Bartola Supulveda and Crocopolo Mauriata, August 11, 1871

In August 1871 there was an active Mexican gang operating in Santa Clara County including Tiburcio Vasquez, Bartola Supulveda, Crocopolo Mauriata, Pancho Galindo, and John Doe Bacitos. On August 11 the first three selected a place along the Visalia to Gilroy road near Soap Lake, eight miles from Gilroy, and broke away a fence. When Democratic candidate Moore arrived in a buggy, they captured him and made him drive through the break in the fence into a field and out of sight of the road. They bound and blindfolded him and stole $55. It was not long before the two-horse stagecoach arrived, with four passengers aboard, and they captured it at gunpoint, took it into the field, and bound and blindfolded the four male passengers and driver. Inside the coach was Miss Murphy of San Joaquin who had the presence of mind to push the Wells, Fargo express box beneath her seat and cover it with her dress. After the robbers searched each man, they checked the stagecoach boot and concluded there was no express box aboard, and they did not molest Miss Murphy. They warned, "Don't make a move till we come back, or we'll murder every one of you." They left but returned shortly with a picket teamster, tied and blindfolded him, and went through his pockets. They gave the same warning again, but after they did not return for an hour and a half the driver convinced Miss Murphy to untie him, he untied the others, and everyone headed into Gilroy. They described the robbers as young Mexicans, "well dressed and splendidly mounted."

After the three road agents left their captives they overtook an old man named Grewell and stole $6. Grewell soon met Billy Brown, who was armed with a Kentucky rifle, and he agreed to go with Grewell in pursuit of the robbers. They were coming upon them when they were seen, and the robbers waved their pistols and fled toward the mountains. Brown fired once without effect, and Grewell, in his excitement, snapped and cranked his Henry rifle about fifty times before he realized he had forgot to load his weapon; by the time he realized his mistake the robbers were out of range. They continued into the mountains and robbed a sheepherder named Patterson of $2.50, but missed $100 he had hidden in his boot, then they made for the mines near Los Angeles. In Gilroy Deputy Sheriff Harry Woodruff organized a posse and went to the scene, and from there they followed the robbers' trail. The following day the posse was joined by Sheriff Harris and they kept after the robbers for several days, but finally they abandoned the chase and returned empty-handed, though they had at least identified the three road agents.

Sources: *Daily Alta California (San Francisco)*: August 12, 1871. *San Jose Patriot (CA)*: August 12, 1871; August 18, 1871.

UNKNOWN, NOVEMBER 14, 1871

On Tuesday, November 14, 1871, the northeast-bound stagecoach from Visalia to Gilroy, in Santa Clara County, was nearing its destination when masked road agents stepped into the road and ordered the driver to halt. He reined in his team, and they immediately demanded the Wells, Fargo express box, then told him to continue on without asking about passengers or the mail. After the coach was out of sight they broke open the box and removed $500, then fled. The posse from Gilroy went to the scene but could find no clues nor a trail to follow, so no one was arrested for the robbery, even after the usual rewards were posted by Wells, Fargo.

Source: *Sacramento Daily Union (CA)*: November 15, 1871.

ALBERT P. HAMILTON AND PETER CARR, APRIL 1, 1874; APRIL 28, 1874

Albert P. Hamilton, alias Henry Tarlton, had a fair education as a youth, but before he turned eighteen he left his home in Ohio for California. The promised opportunities for fame and fortune did not materialize, so the disillusioned youth joined the army. After a few months, however, he realized that a military life was not for him and he deserted in August 1867. He made his way to Tulare County where he "uttered" a false order for goods at a Visalia mercantile, stole a horse, and fled into Inyo County. A tenacious lawman tracked him, made the arrest, and charged him with grand larceny. Hamilton gave his name as Henry Tarlton when he was taken to the Tulare County jail, and after the army refused to pick up the deserter, he was prosecuted in the district court. Tarlton (Hamilton) was easily convicted of the charge and sentenced to serve six years at San Quentin, where he disclosed that his first name was actually Albert, but he persisted in using Tarlton for his last name. In prison Tarlton continued his education, but of a different nature, and when he was released on September 28, 1872, by expiration of sentence, he considered himself a much improved outlaw.

Hamilton did not come to the attention of lawmen for eighteen months, but by late March 1874 he had partnered with Peter Carr and they planned to rob a stagecoach. Hamilton took an honest job for a few weeks to earn a stake to support their plan, and after receiving his first paycheck, he absconded with his employer's shotgun. The two aspiring road agents selected a steep grade near the summit above Santa Clara Valley, in Santa Clara County, where the horses would walk slowly and passengers, if any were aboard, might disembark and walk behind to lighten the load. During the late afternoon of April 1, 1874, the two men stretched a rope across the road as a barrier and hid in the brush. Hamilton wore a mask and carried the shotgun, the only weapon they had, so Carr was to remain in hiding. The four-horse celerity wagon from Santa Clara bound for Santa Cruz, driven by J. P. Smith, reached the rope barrier just before 3:00 p.m. and Hamilton rose up, pointed his shotgun at Smith, and demanded Well's, Fargo's express box. The driver said there was no box aboard, and after a brief argument he threw out two mail pouches. Hamilton refused to molest the U.S. mails and then went through the passengers, ordering them to throw out their money. The occupants began throwing out bills and coins, and then Hamilton returned the mail pouches to the driver's boot before ordering Smith to continue on. Once the coach was under way, a passenger looked back to see the road agent groveling in the dirt, collecting the bills and coins totaling less than $45.

Four weeks later a Concord coach, driven by W. E. McFarland, was stopped again at almost the same place. It was nearly 2:00 p.m. when two masked men, both now armed with shotguns and wearing dark hats pulled down, stepped from the same side of the road and into the path of the team. Once the stagecoach was stopped, Hamilton walked to the rear of the coach while Carr held the horses. Hamilton walked to the opposite side before poking his shotgun into the window and demanding that everyone hand out their wallets. The men began handing him coins, so he again demanded their wallets. The horses were becoming restless, so Hamilton allowed McFarland to continue on to Santa Cruz after collecting less than $10. In Santa Cruz the driver reported the robbery to Sheriff Bob Orton, and several posses were soon in the field.

One posse consisted of deputies Jackson Sylva and Frank Curtis, and they followed up a lead which took them to the cabin of "Mountain" Charley McKiernan. He claimed to have seen two men hunting squirrels the previous day, and their descriptions matched the two road agents. McKiernan joined the two lawmen as they searched the area, and they discovered the two fugitives hiding in an old barn. They exchanged several shots before McKiernan wounded Hamilton and both men surrendered. The lawmen recovered the stolen money and took the men to jail. In May they were tried for the April 1, 1874, stagecoach robbery and convicted, and both men were sentenced to serve ten years at San Quentin Prison; they both arrived on May 26, 1874. Carr registered as prisoner #6021 and after serving four years, two months and two weeks he was pardoned by Governor William Irwin on August 15, 1878; but he would commit a burglary in San Francisco in early 1879 and return to prison for another five years and would be released again on September 4, 1882. Hamilton registered as prisoner #6020, but he escaped from prison on November 15, 1874, in company with his three cell mates. He hid for five months, but on April 16, 1875, he would rob another stagecoach in Nevada County. (See El Dorado County on May 24, 1880.)

Isaiah Pierce and Harry Edwards, April 28, 1874

At 2:30 p.m. on Tuesday, April 28, 1874, the northwest-bound stagecoach from San Jose to Santa Clara had reached Lexington, sixteen miles south of Santa Clara, when two masked road agents stepped into the roadway, pointed cocked double-barreled shotguns at the driver, and ordered him to halt. They demanded the Wells, Fargo express box, but the driver told them he did not carry an express box on that route. The robbers then said they would rob the passengers and ordered the two men and two women to step out and form a line. The older robber ordered the passengers to hand over their money and watches, and he collected $150, one inexpensive silver watch and one gold watch worth $100. The older robber excused the women from being robbed while the younger, noticeably a nervous robber, covered everyone with his shotgun. The collecting was done carelessly so that every man retained a portion of his money. The robber doing the collecting then ordered the driver to come down so he could go through him, but the driver argued that it would be a waste of time as he carried no money. The robber decided not to rob the driver and told everyone to board, and then he told the driver, "Git up and dust, damn you!"

As soon as the coach reached the first station the report was sent to Sheriff John H. Adams. The description of the older man seemed to match the lone robber who stopped the stagecoach on April 1 (Hamilton), but this mistake would have no bearing on later developments. The older man was described only as heavyset while the younger man was described as "light complected, slight build, small hands and feet, and both were dressed in new, fashionable dark clothing." Sheriff Adams organized a small posse of three men at San Jose, and they rode to the station operated by "One-Eyed" Mountain Charley near the scene of the robbery. Mountain Charley told them that he was returning from hunting that evening and met two men, who he thought might be the two men being pursued, and was about to capture them when he realized he had only one cartridge in his Henry carbine. He had to let them go, but he joined the posse and they spent the night scouring the countryside in all directions. At 10:00 a.m. the posse came upon the two road agents hiding in a hog pen next to an old deserted building twelve miles from Lexington, eight miles from the road. The robbers were badly fatigued and were completely surprised at being discovered, but they showed fight. They fired twice without effect as the posse was beyond the range of their shotguns, and they were out of range for most of the posse who were armed only with revolvers. However Mountain Charley, one of the best shots in the region, had his Henry carbine, and he and A. Newell returned fire from one hundred fifty yards off; Mountain Charley's second bullet struck one of the robbers in his arm, causing a minor wound. This, however, was enough to convince the pair of fugitives to surrender, and they hung out an old hat as a signal that they gave up. They were arrested and taken to San Jose by Sheriff Adams, and that afternoon they were lodged in the county jail. All the plunder was recovered from their pockets, and they gave the names Isaiah Pierce and Harry Edwards, from Stockton. They confessed, saying they were after the express box and did not know that all express went by rail from Santa Clara and San Jose to Santa Cruz. On April 30 they waived their examination and Justice May set their bail at $3,000 each, and they were held over for the grand jury. They were tried, convicted and sentenced to serve long prison terms at San Quentin, but their records do not appear in the archive.

Sources: *Daily Alta California (San Francisco)*: May 1–2, 1874. *Sacramento Daily Union (CA)*: April 29–30, 1874.

UNKNOWN, APRIL 29, 1905

At 6:00 p.m. on Saturday, April 29, 1905, two stagecoaches were climbing Mount Hamilton and were between Smith's Creek and the observatory at a place known as Sandy Point when a lone road agent, masked in black cloth and armed with a double-barreled shotgun, accosted four passengers who had tired of riding and were walking ahead of the coaches. Just then the first coach driven by Al Jamison came up and was halted. The robber told the passengers to get out, join the other four, and form a line. In a moment the second coach, driven by Al Parron, arrived and was stopped in the same manner, and his passengers joined the others. Following closely behind the second coach was a double-seated carriage with two women and two boys aboard, and they were stopped and told to join the line, and in all the robber had twenty-five persons under the twin muzzles of his shotgun, with two drivers still on their seats handling their teams. Once all were in a line the robber pulled out his old-fashioned revolver, then laid aside his shotgun and robbed each passenger with the barrel of his pistol pressed into their abdomen to prevent resistance. The robber felt each man's pockets and when he felt or heard the jingle of coins he had the man deliver his money, but all he collected for his trouble was $30 and several rings and watches. While the robber was about his work he pointed to a bluff, a short distance away, where he said his partner sat with a shotgun pointed at them. As soon as the robber made his collection he walked into the brush and whistled to his partner to join him. The coaches continued into Mount Hamilton and the driver telephoned Sheriff Frank H. Ross at San Jose with the details of the robbery and a description of the robber: thirty years old, five feet nine inches tall, 160 pounds, slim with bony hands, a scar over his left eye near his nose, slouch hat, dark gray coat, blue overalls, and heavy shoes. Sheriff Ross with Deputy Starbird stocked up for several days on the trail and rode to the scene, where they determined that only one man was involved based upon boot tracks. They searched the area that night and the next day before they gave up the chase. There was a man who was under suspicion, but he was not captured.

Sources: *Los Angeles Herald (CA)*: April 30, 1905. *San Francisco Call (CA)*: May 1, 1905.

Shasta County

Unknown, August 10, 1859

On Wednesday, August 10, 1859, the stagecoach from Angel's Camp to San Andreas in Shasta County was stopped by one man, masked and armed, and he demanded the treasure boxes. A Freeman & Company shotgun guard was aboard, and he fired at the robber three times with his pistol but missed his mark each time. The robber retreated and the stagecoach driver whipped up his team and continued into San Andreas, where the attempted robbery was reported. Lawmen went to the scene but could find no clue to the road agent's identity.

Source: *Daily Alta California (San Francisco)*: August 10, 1859.

John "Jake" Clark, John "Shorty" Hays, Eddie Lee and Charles Thompson, October 10, 1873

After robbing a stagecoach in Placer County on September 12, 1873, John "Jake" Clark, sobriquet "Connub," John "Shorty" Hays, alias James F. Costello, and Eddie Lee, alias Thomas Martin, moved north into Shasta County and recruited ex-convict Charles Thompson. On October 10, 1873, the four road agents stopped the southbound stagecoach from Yreka to Redding and, after securing the Wells, Fargo express box, made the passengers step out and line up. They went through them, including a reporter for the *Sacramento Record* who later complained, "Here I want to enter a protest against green men undertaking such close work. Their hands trembled so I was fearful they would shoot accidentally and hurt someone." The robbers went through a total of eight passengers, all men, and from five Chinamen they took a total of $1,460 and from the other three they got $460—a total of $1,920. They next broke open the box and took out $2,000. As soon as they had all the loot they fled south. The passengers quickly boarded and the coach hurried into Buckeye to report the robbery.

The four men separated, with Lee and Thompson deciding to stay in Sacramento. After a few days Thompson was arrested and he quickly "peached," or informed, on his fellow road agents. Hays and Clark had gone to San Francisco and, not knowing that they had been identified and described, made little effort to remain inconspicuous. Hays, well known to lawmen in the city, was next to be arrested. He had used $800 of his share of the plunder to buy an interest in a restaurant at the foot of Jackson Street on the wharf, and that is where he was found and captured, and San Francisco's *Daily Alta California* newspaper reported that Hays was wanted in Shasta County on a charge of robbery. Clark was soon in custody and he joined Hays in the San Francisco County jail, but Lee managed to elude the authorities for several weeks.

The three men first arrested, Clark, Hays and Thompson, were taken to Shasta County and charged in the robbery of the stagecoach near Buckeye. They were indicted on a large body of evidence; but, on December 14, 1873, the three men were in the jail's exercise room without supervision just before supper. They pried open a door and armed themselves. When their food arrived they captured the undersheriff and cook and locked them in a cell. As they worked on their shackles the sheriff arrived and was also captured and locked in a cell. Hays could not break his chains, so when the three men were outside, they separated. Hays hid near the jail while the other two men went into the nearby woods, and soon Clark and Thompson were captured and led back to their cells. Once the lawmen were occupied with the two fugitives they had captured, Hays fled into the woods and made his way south, walking through deep snow as he followed the railroad tracks. After several days he went to a cabin to warm himself and was nearly captured, but he managed to pull his gun and warn off his attacker. He went on to Red Bluff and, breaking into a blacksmith shop, finally broke off his chains. In ten days he made it to Marysville and on Christmas eve he walked into the United States Hotel and had his first good meal since his jailbreak, then bedded down and was sleeping soundly when arrested. Hays was returned to jail and, with his two confederates, was tried in February 1874 for the October stagecoach robbery. Each man received a sentence of twenty-one years to be served at San Quentin Prison. Thompson received no credit for informing on his fellow stagecoach robbers. The men were taken together to the prison, arriving on February 16, and Hays was registered as prisoner #5884, Thompson as #5885, and Clark as #5886.

Hays and Clark were taken out of prison on March 7, 1874, by court order to be tried in Placer County for robbing the Forest Hill to Auburn stagecoach on September 12, 1873. They were both convicted and sentenced to serve terms of thirty years. They were returned to the prison, Hays now prisoner #5929 and Clark prisoner #5930. Hays escaped from prison twice—once in May 1876 and again in December 1884 and he lost 137 months of credit toward his release, but it was later restored and he was discharged on October 17, 1891. Clark escaped from prison on January 14, 1881, and was not heard of again. Thompson had his sentence commuted and all rights restored by Governor George C. Perkins, and he was discharged on September 24, 1881.

Eddie Lee was captured a few weeks after the other three road agents were first jailed, but a case could not be made against him in Shasta County. He was taken to Placer County and charged with the robbery of the Forest Hill to Auburn stagecoach on September 12, 1873. He was indicted, tried, and convicted of the charge in early March 1874 and sentenced to serve a term of only four years. Lee arrived at the prison on March 21, 1874, and registered as prisoner #5933. He was discharged, upon expiration of his sentence, on August 13, 1877.

Sources: *Daily Alta California (San Francisco, CA)*: October 31, 1873. *Daily Morning Call (San Francisco, CA)*: June 5, 1881; January 9, 1885. *Marysville Appeal (CA)*: December 25, 1873. *Sacramento Record (CA)*: October 11, 1873. *Sacramento Bee* [CA]: November 13, 1873. *San Francisco Chronicle (CA)*: October 31, 1873. *San Francisco Examiner (CA)*: October 18, 1891; November 1, 1891. *Shasta Courier (CA)*: January 20, 1877. *Yreka Journal (CA)*: February 18, 1874, June 7, 1876. *Yreka Union (CA)*: June 10, 1876.

WILLIAM CHANDLER AND H. S. HUNT, FEBRUARY 16, 1875; OCTOBER 24, 1876

Barlow & Sanderson's mail stage left Shasta for Redding, in Shasta County, every evening at 7:00 and returned at 2:00 a.m. On Tuesday, February 16, 1875, the stagecoach, driven by Jerry Culverhouse, rushed back into Shasta at 8:00 p.m. only one hour after departing, and it was driven by passenger Charlie Fife. The stagecoach stopped in front of the Empire Hotel and on board were the U.S. mails, the Wells, Fargo express box and several passengers, who reported that an attempt had been made to stop the coach. They said that just as the coach was descending the grade below Lower Springs three masked road agents jumped into the road from behind a bush and pointed their weapons, including at least one double-barreled shotgun, at the driver and ordered Culverhouse to halt. The coach was nearly abreast of the robbers when they appeared, so Culverhouse whipped up his team and drove past them, then turned to look back just as the man with the shotgun fired both barrels. The buckshot struck the coach and Culverhouse's head, face and back, but instead of causing the coach to halt, the explosion frightened the horses and they "struck out at high speed." Culverhouse, though severely wounded, kept control and reined in his team after they were out of danger from the road agents. He let passenger Fife, who had been riding inside, take the reins and they returned to Shasta. The sheriff was summoned and he organized a posse. They went to the scene and investigated before taking the trail of the three robbers. Eight buckshot were removed from Culverhouse, and the reporter for the *Shasta Courier* counted forty-three buckshot in the canvas cover just behind the driver's seat. He said, "It is evident that the shot which struck there glanced upward, striking Culverhouse after their force was partly spent," and had the load taken effect directly the driver would have been killed. One buckshot struck the driver's right eye and it was feared it might have penetrated the eyeball, so on February 27 he started for San Francisco to consult an oculist.

By February 20 officers arrested Charles D. Burch, a man who had served a term at San Quentin for a burglary in El Dorado County, but Burch proved an alibi and was released. Within a month two more men were behind bars charged with the robbery attempt—one named William Chandler but better known as "Wild Bill," and the other named H. S. Hunt. Both men were examined and held over for the grand jury, but there was not enough evidence to bring an indictment so they were released, and the third man was never identified. However, it was generally believed that it was Hunt who fired the load that wounded Culverhouse. In June 1876 Burch and James Demerest committed a store burglary at Trinity Center, and when Constable Bell from Anderson station tried to arrest them, they resisted and Burch was killed. On April 17 the *Courier* welcomed Culverhouse's return to Shasta and remarked that "we are glad to see him well and hearty" and observed that he had "undergone a severe operation" on his eye. The following year Culverhouse was working as a deputy sheriff and operating his own stage line between Yreka and Shasta by way of Scott Valley when he announced on March 18 that he was going to operate an express from Trinity Center to Cinnabar. He hired H. C. Tickner to run the operation and P. G. Strickland as Yreka's agent.

On Tuesday, October 24, 1876, the stagecoach from Shasta to Weaverville in Shasta County was coming down the mountain, thirteen miles from its destination shortly after noon. As the stagecoach rounded a short curve a lone road agent jumped from behind a bush and covered John McNemar with a Spencer rifle before the Wells, Fargo messenger could pick up his shotgun. He demanded the treasure box and it was thrown down, and the robber then ordered the driver to continue as he started for the side of the road with the treasure box. McNemar, as soon as they were out of sight of the road agent, had the driver stop the coach, and he got down and walked back to the scene of the robbery. Just as he arrived the road agent was finishing his work, having easily opened the box with a pick. He had the contents of the box, $6,800 in gold, in his hands as he looked up and saw McNemar. The messenger fired one barrel from his shotgun and this knocked the robber down, but he sprang up and started to run. The road agent was about to pass over a ridge fifty yards distant, which would have concealed him, when McNemar fired the second load from his double barrel shotgun, which killed his man. The messenger gathered up the deceased, the box and treasure and carried it to the coach. The stagecoach then continued on to the Tower House where he left the body and continued into Shasta. Shasta County's coroner William P. Hartman went to the Tower House with an inquest jury to "inquire into the death of an unknown person found dead in the woods, ... by gun shot wounds, said shots being delivered from a gun in the hand of John McNemar (Wells, Fargo & Co's Messenger)," and the jurors concluded that the death was justified. The description of the dead road agent was circulated, and it was soon determined that he was H. S. Hunt.

Sources: *Los Angeles Herald (CA)*: February 18, 1875. *Sacramento Daily Union (CA)*: February 17, 1875. *Shasta Courier (CA)*: February 20, 1875; February 27, 1875; April 17, 1875; March 18, 1876; July 1, 1876; October 21, 1876; October 28, 1876.

UNKNOWN, OCTOBER 19, 1875

On Tuesday, October 19, 1875, the northbound stagecoach from Redding to Yreka and destinations in Oregon, with John Reynolds driving, had traveled only fifteen miles when two masked and armed road agents stepped into the road and ordered Reynolds to rein in his team. One of the robbers pointed his gun directly at Reynolds, so the driver brought the coach to a halt, and the robber demanded the Wells, Fargo express box. The second road agent stood silently watching as Reynolds told the man making the demand, "It is in the bottom of the boot, and hard to get at." The robber took careful aim at Reynolds' head and fired, but when Reynolds saw the movement he dropped into the boot, and the shot frightened the horses. The team "galloped away at a lively rate," but Reynolds still had hold of the reins and managed to keep control and then spurred them on with his whip. The coach was driven out of danger, leaving the road agents behind and saving the express box and the several passengers he had inside his coach.

Source: *Los Angeles Herald (CA)*: October 21, 1875.

CHARLES E. "BLACK BART" BOLTON, JUNE 2, 1876; OCTOBER 25, 1879; SEPTEMBER 1, 1880; OCTOBER 8, 1881; OCTOBER 11, 1881; SEPTEMBER 17, 1882

Charles E. "Black Bart" Bolton had taken a vacation from his stagecoach robbing for several months before reappearing on Friday, June 2, 1876. This time he stopped the stagecoach from Roseburg, Oregon, to Yreka in Siskiyou County, California, when it was five miles north of Cottonwood. His modus operandi was the same, excepting this time he worked at night for the first time, but he chose a night with bright moonlight to aid in his work. Driver A. C. Adams was ascending a steep grade, driving his six-up at a slow pace, when a masked road agent stepped in front of the team; hidden by the leaders, he pointed his shotgun at Adams and politely demanded the express box and mail sacks, then waved him on. The stagecoach hurried into Cottonwood, and at first daylight a posse went to the scene. They were joined by Deputy Sheriff John Halleck, but he could find no clue nor a trail to follow. The state added $300 to the reward of $250 offered by Wells, Fargo, but no one came forward to collect. Wells, Fargo refused to quantify their losses, so the amount taken was never documented, though it may have been substantial as Bolton took off an entire year.

On Saturday, October 25, 1879, the stagecoach from Redding left for Roseburg, Oregon, at dusk. As the team ascended the grade to the summit of Bass Hill, near Buckeye, Bolton suddenly appeared from the roadside and ordered driver James Smithson to rein in his team. When the express box was demanded, Smithson told the road agent that he could not throw out the box as it was chained inside the coach. Bolton ordered the driver to dismount and hold the leaders' harness. He ordered the only passenger, a woman, to step out and move away while he broke open the box and removed the contents, which proved to be nearly a "water haul," but the robber then went through the registered mail which, newspapers reported, contained more than $1,000. Bolton then had the passenger and driver board and continue on.

At 2:00 p.m. on Wednesday, September 1, 1880, Bolton stopped the stagecoach from Weaverville in Trinity County to Redding, driven by Charley Creamer, after it crossed the line into Shasta County and was climbing Trinity Mountain, but before reaching Last Chance station, ten miles above the Tower House. He demanded and received the wooden treasure box and the mail sacks, but then demanded the second box. Creamer told him it was bolted inside the coach and made of iron. Bolton ordered out the only passenger, a woman, entered the coach and tried to chop open the second box with an ax, but finally he had to give up. He had the woman board and sent the coach on its way. He kept the wooden box, broke it open and removed $100, but the amount found in the mail was unknown. As soon as the coach reached town a posse was organized, and they followed the robber's trail for some distance before losing it. Once again lawmen returned to town empty-handed.

On Saturday, October 8, 1881, Bolton returned to Bass Hill, near Buckeye in Shasta County, and stopped the stagecoach from Redding to Yreka driven by Horace Williams. After the mail sacks were thrown out he learned that the treasure box was bolted inside the coach, so he had the three passengers get out and walk some distance down the road while Williams was ordered to hold the leaders. Bolton broke open the box and got just enough loot to avoid a "water haul," about $60. He then had Williams board and drive on, picking up his passengers along the way. The posse that rode to the scene again found no clue and returned to town empty-handed.

On Tuesday, October 11, three days after robbing Horace Williams, Bolton found driver Lewis Brewster, who was driving south from Lakeview, Oregon, to Redding, already stopped two miles north of Round Mountain and engaged in making some repair. The road agent made him climb aboard, throw out the mail sacks and Wells, Fargo express box, and then had the coach continue on. Brewster stopped after traveling a short distance and returned to the scene with rifle in hand, but Bolton had already secured his booty and fled.

Bolton did not try for another stagecoach for two months, but on Sunday, September 17, 1882, he set up his operation fourteen miles from Redding where he planned to stop the down stage from Yreka. Driver Horace Williams, whom he had robbed two years earlier, delivered the Wells, Fargo express box and mail sacks before continuing on to his destination. Again the posse came up empty-handed. (See Calaveras County on November 3, 1883.)

John "Sheet Iron Jack" Allen, John A. Toney and Frank Chapman, November 3, 1876; November 6, 1876; November 8, 1876; November 11, 1876

John "Sheet Iron Jack" Allen, although his real name was probably John D. Gundlack, had been sent to prison in early 1875, but after a few months imprisonment he was granted a new trial, convicted of "assault," sentenced to pay a fine, given credit for time served, and released. In late 1876 he rendezvoused with John A. Toney, a man he met during his brief stay in prison, and Frank Chapman, a man with no criminal record. Allen was planning several stagecoach robberies, and on Friday, November 3, 1876, three masked men, heavily armed, stopped the mail coach between Reid's Ferry and Buckeye. They demanded the Wells, Fargo express box and mail sacks. They smashed open the box and took out $1,100, then slashed open the mail sacks and took a considerable amount of money from the registered mail. Allen would not take part in any further robberies, but he did the planning and had Toney and Chapman do the work at the scene while demanding an equal share.

On Monday, November 6, 1876, the stagecoach from Shasta to Weaverville, when near Redding, was stopped by two road agents, masked and wielding shotguns. They appeared suddenly from a stand of willows near the road, pointed their weapons at the driver, and called for the coach to halt. They demanded the Wells, Fargo express box, and it was thrown down. The coach was then allowed to continue on, but when the box was opened the two road agents found it was empty. On Wednesday, November 8, the same two road agents, Toney and Chapman, determined to overcome their "water haul" from two days earlier, stopped the same coach at approximately the same place and this time took $1,100 from Wells, Fargo's express box. On November 11 two road agents stopped the stagecoach traveling between Yreka in Siskiyou County and Redding when it was near Ross' station, though three road agents were reported. Their faces were blackened and they were well armed, so when the demand was made for the Wells, Fargo express box it was thrown down immediately, and then the coach was ordered to move on. Deputy Sheriff Whiting and Constable Eckles went to the scene and recovered the treasure box, but they could find no clue to the identities of the robbers, nor a good trail to follow. The box, it was later learned, was empty.

Allen doubted the men were telling him the truth about their lack of plunder on two robberies and felt certain they were cheating him out of his share, so he went to local lawmen. He intended to "peach," or inform, on them and take his cut from their rewards, but in order to explain how he knew the details of the robberies and identities of the road agents he had to confess to his part in planning the robberies. Allen was arrested and, since his part came before the robberies, he was charged as a principal as if he had been at the scene, rather than as an accessory. Chapman was arrested at Chico on November 16 and lodged in the Shasta jail with Allen. Toney was arrested by Undersheriff Robert Kennedy and Constable L. D. Bickford at Rising River in Hat Creek Valley on November 18, and he joined his two fellow road agents behind bars. On December 2 the grand jury indicted the three road agents. On December 12, while awaiting trial, Toney, Chapman and Allen, with two other prisoners, tried to dig their way out of jail but were discovered just before they broke through the wall, and thereafter they were heavily ironed. On December 23, 1876, Allen pled guilty to three robbery charges and was sentenced to serve eight years on each charge, or twenty-four years in total. He arrived at San Quentin on Christmas day and registered as prisoner #7313. His term was conditionally commuted to ten years by Governor George C. Perkins, and after agreeing to leave the state, he was discharged on June 25, 1883. Allen not only reneged on his promise to leave California but committed a grand larceny in San Francisco County and was returned to prison on April 22, 1884, to serve six years on a new commitment.

Toney had been in prison twice previously, and on December 23, 1876, he also pled guilty to three stagecoach robberies and was sentenced to serve seven years on each conviction, a total of twenty-one years. Toney arrived at San Quentin on Christmas day 1876 and registered as prisoner #7312. He served thirteen years and was released on November 25, 1889. Chapman had no prison record in California, so he was allowed to turn state's evidence and testify against the other two men. He pled guilty to three robbery charges and was sentenced to serve sixteen months' imprisonment on each conviction, or four years total. He arrived at San Quentin on Christmas day and registered as prisoner #7314. Chapman was conditionally pardoned by Governor William Irwin and discharged on May 4, 1877. He was required to leave the state and lost no time in booking passage to return to England.

Sources: *Daily Alta California (San Francisco)*: November 19, 1876. *Republican Free Press (Redding, CA)*: April 5, 1884. *San Francisco Examiner (CA)*: September 17, 1882; September 27, 1882. *San Francisco Chronicle (CA)*: April 1, 1884. *Shasta Courier (CA)*: November 11, 1876; November 18, 1876; November 25, 1876; December 23, 1876; December 30, 1876. *Yreka Union (CA)*: November 11, 1876.

THOMAS BROWN, JOSEPH BROWN AND DAVID TYE, NOVEMBER 3, 1876

Thomas Brown, alias Tom Foster; Joseph Brown; and David Tye were stealing horses in central California in 1874. Thomas and Joseph were caught, lodged in the Sutter County jail, tried, convicted on separate charges, and sent to prison. After he was released Thomas partnered with Dave Tye, and by the end of October 1876 his brother Joseph had escaped from San Quentin and the three men rendezvoused and decided to rob a stagecoach. They set their sights on the stagecoach running from Yreka in Siskiyou County to Redding in Shasta County, but they missed the coach on November 1 and 2. On November 3 they stopped the stagecoach and demanded the mail sacks and Wells, Fargo express box before ordering the driver to continue on. From the mail sacks the three men took $1,230 in currency, a gold bar valued at $275, and $130 in gold notes; and from the treasure box they got $1,060 in gold dust and $45 in gold notes. The brothers were disappointed with Tye's performance throughout the robbery and decided to find another man to replace him for their next robbery—Charles "Red" Frazier. (See Yuba County on November 13, 1876, and Shasta County on May 27, 1877.)

SAMUEL HART AND JOE HENDRICKS, JANUARY 22, 1877

James B. Hume, Wells, Fargo's chief detective, reported that after some limited success as road agents in San Luis Obispo and Santa Barbara counties in 1876 and 1877, Samuel Hart and Joe Hendricks moved their operations to Shasta County. They were credited with six stagecoach robberies in those two counties, but no record of those robberies can be found, nor is any explanation given why these two men would pull up stakes where they had been successful and travel 350 miles to resume the same criminal activity. On Sunday, January 14, 1877, Hart and Hendricks bought shot and powder at Grotolend's store in Redding, and then on January 19 they burglarized Breslauer's store at Redding where they stole blankets and other items. On Monday, January 22, as the Shasta stagecoach was nearing Redding, the two men covered themselves with blankets in a poncho-like manner to disguise their clothing, and with handkerchiefs tied over their heads, they stepped from the brush onto the roadside, pointed their weapons at the driver, and ordered him to stop. One man was armed with what appeared to be a revolver, but this later turned out to be a wooden gun blackened with soot, while the other carried a double-barreled shotgun. The next command was to throw down the Wells, Fargo treasure box, and the driver tossed out the wooden box immediately, assured that all the treasure he carried was locked safely in the iron box bolted inside the passenger compartment. The robbers knew there was another box and one of them wanted to bust open or "blow the stuffing" out of the inside box, but the other road agent talked him out of it so they got very little for their risk.

The following day Sheriff Hull and Special Officer Douglas went to the scene and cut the trail of the road agents. They tracked them to Anderson station, where they found them waiting for the train to "the lower country," and they still had with them the property stolen from Breslauer's store. On Wednesday, two days after they robbed the stagecoach, the two men were lodged in the Shasta County jail. Justice was swift, as the two men had their examination within days and were held over for action by the grand jury. They were indicted, and when brought into court for arraignment they pled guilty. On February 20, 1877, Judge Hopping sentenced each man to serve ten years in San Quentin. They arrived at the prison on February 23, where Hendricks registered as prisoner #7402 and Hart registered as prisoner #7403. Hendricks was only in prison twenty months before he died on October 30, 1878, possibly of consumption (tuberculosis) which was epidemic in such close quarters. Hart was removed to Folsom Prison on August 23, 1880, and was pardoned and released by Governor George Stoneman on June 2, 1883.

Sources: *Shasta Courier (CA)*: January 27, 1877; February 24, 1877.

TOM BROWN, TOM CONNORS AND MARTIN MYERS, MAY 27, 1877

Tom Brown, who had been convicted of a stagecoach robbery in Yuba County, was taken out of prison to testify against Charles "Red" Frazier, and on April 24, 1877, while in the Marysville jail, he managed to escape. He headed north and met two old friends—Tom Connors and Martin Myers—and they robbed the stagecoach between Roseburg and Redding in Shasta County on Sunday night, May 27, 1877. Brown fled into Oregon with Deputy Sheriff John Hendricks and Wells, Fargo messenger John Reynolds close on his trail, and they captured him at Ashland, Oregon, when he stopped to replace a horseshoe. Their prisoner was first taken to the jail at Yreka and then on to Redding, where he was tried and convicted of stagecoach robbery. The judge sentenced him to seventeen years, and on September 22, 1877, Brown arrived at San Quentin. He was once again brought to Marysville to testify against Frazier where again he nearly escaped from the jail by digging a tunnel. Brown was returned to prison after testifying against Frazier but was once again taken out, this time in April 1878 to testify against Connors. Again he made several attempts at escape, and upon his return to San Quentin he was quickly transferred to the more secure facility at Folsom. He became a model prisoner for several years, but all the better to find another opportunity to escape, and this came on June 15, 1886. Brown "stepped out for a smoke" and took off at a run. He hid for the rest of the day and then spread pepper on his trail to foil the dogs, and he made his way to Ione before heading to Big Trees in Calaveras County. County Sheriff Benjamin K. Thorn was on his trail and captured the fugitive after knocking him semi-conscious during a desperate struggle, and by mid–July Brown was back in prison. He once again tried the "model prisoner" dodge, and this time it worked only because he got his good time credits restored and was discharge on April 3, 1891, before he could execute another escape plan. Tom Brown was not heard of again on California's criminal roll.

Thomas Connor was found guilty of robbing the stagecoach in Shasta County on April 27, 1877, and was sentenced to serve seven years at San Quentin. He arrived at the prison on April 25, 1878, and registered as prisoner #8173. Connor was released, by expiration of sentence, on January 25, 1883. Myers does not appear on the criminal record so he either turned state's evidence and was released, or he managed to flee the region and was never captured.

Sources: *Calaveras Chronicle (CA)*: March 6, 1880. *Calaveras Prospect (CA)*: June 2, 1886, *Folsom Weekly Telegraph (CA)*: July 3, 1886; July 17, 1886. *Marysville Daily Appeal (CA)*: November 5, 1876; November 14–15, 1876; November 23, 1876; November 28, 1876; December 3, 1876; December 21, 1876; December 23–25, 1876. *Sacramento Daily Record-Union (CA)*: June 16–17, 1886; June 30, 1886; November 18, 1905. *Shasta Courier (CA)*: December 9, 1876; December 30, 1876; October 6, 1877; February 16, 1878; April 27, 1878. *Stockton Daily Evening Herald (CA)*: November 17, 1874; November 27–28, 1874; November 30, 1874. *Yreka Journal (CA)*: December 6, 1876; July 11, 1877. *Weekly Appeal (Marysville, CA)*: July 20, 1877; February 15, 1878; March 15, 1878; January 18, 1879; February 1, 1879; March 15, 1879. *Yreka Union (CA)*: July 14, 1877; September 22, 1877.

JOHN BROWN, APRIL 18, 1881

Warren "Doc" Dunham convinced Wells, Fargo to establish an office at Igo, he scheduled daily runs to the railroad connection at Anderson, and the Dunham & Leiter stage line began operations in September 1879. On Monday, April 18, 1881, the Igo to Anderson stagecoach, driven by Watt Gage, left Igo at 4:00 p.m. and had traveled four miles, to the old Champion house, when it was halted by a lone highwayman. The road agent, masked and with pistol in hand, stepped out from the roadside, stopped the horses, and commanded, "Give up that box!" As soon as the box lay on the roadway the road agent ordered Gage to drive on. A mile from the scene of the robbery Gage met Thad Jones, gave him the details of the robbery, and sent him back to Igo to sound the alarm, while he made the trip into Anderson in less than an hour. Dunham, with a man named Conger, went to the scene and two hundred yards off the roadway found the broken box, a sledgehammer, and an axle used as a pry bar, along with the waybills from which they learned that the road agent had removed $1,100 in currency, ten thousand shares of Chicago Mine stock, and some letters. From the detailed description of the road agent it was believed that he was the same man who had broken into the home of N. Beeves the previous Sunday, rifled a trunk for some coin, and then slept the night in a carpenter's shop. The description of the road agent also matched the lone highwayman who stopped the stagecoach from Laporte to Oroville on November 30, 1880.

Sheriff J. W. Smiley received the description of the man who had robbed the Igo stagecoach and information that the fugitive had been seen at the cabin of John Day and James Moore. On April 25 Smiley, with James Moore, traveled all night and most of the next day, arriving at Moore's cabin at 4:00 p.m. and finding Day at home. Smiley sent Day out to find and decoy the robber to the cabin while he and Moore lay down to rest, but they fell asleep. Some noise awoke Smiley, and he raised up in bed to find the fugitive seated at the table. The road agent said to Day, "Come here, I want to see you," but he immediately turned and ran outside while trying to draw his revolver. Smiley commanded him to halt, but he continued to run and managed to free his pistol from its scabbard. Smiley, Day and Moore rushed out and the sheriff commanded a second time for the fleeing fugitive to halt, and when he would not comply the lawman ordered Day to shoot. Day fired one round, but it did not appear to take effect, so Sheriff Smiley said, "Shoot him, for God's sake!" Day fired a second time and the man fell onto his elbows with his revolver still in his hand.

The sheriff then advanced on his quarry and the man said, "I didn't think you sons of bitches would murder me." Smiley then commanded, "Disarm yourself or I will blow your brains out!" He had to repeat the order a second time before the man threw the revolver aside and said, "For God's sake, don't murder me," and "I am killed anyway." The man, who refused to identify himself, was taken to the cabin, and Smiley sent Day for the doctor. Moore gathered up the man's coat, the pockets of which contained some gold dust and $13.10 in coin. The doctor arrived and cut out the bullet, which had entered on the left side in the small of the back and perforated the bowels of the prisoner, but the ball had not passed through. The men constructed a litter and took their prisoner to the hospital at Weaverville, where he died at 11:00 p.m. on April 27 after lingering and suffering from infection for hours. The body was put in charge of Shasta County Sheriff Hull for identification and burial.

At the inquest the jury identified the deceased as Edward Wilson, but later it was determined by James B. Hume that he was John Brown, alias Wilson, J. W. Marshall, O'Neill, or "Old Jack Brown, the cell tender." Brown was well known to lawmen, as he had served three terms at San Quentin between 1854 and 1879. He had been free less than one year when he robbed his first stagecoach and less than two years before he was killed while resisting arrest.

Sources: *Palo Alto Pilot (Emmetsburg, IA)*: May 6, 1881. *Plumas National (CA)*: December 11, 1880. *Shasta Courier (CA)*: May 7, 1881.

J. L. RAGSDALE, MAY 24, 1882

At noon on Wednesday, May 24, 1882, the stagecoach from Yreka to Redding, driven by Horace Williams, was passing over the summit of Bass Hill in Shasta County, fourteen miles from its destination, when suddenly a lone highwayman, masked and armed with a rifle, stepped in front of the leaders and commanded, "Halt! Throw out that box!" Once the box lay on the roadway the command came for the driver to throw down the mail sacks, and Williams was then ordered to continue on. The box and mail sacks were later found only a few feet from the roadway, carefully gone through for valuables. As soon as the command came to continue Williams whipped up his team and hurried into Redding, where he sounded the alarm, and a posse was soon on the trail of the road agent. They returned empty-handed and then circulated a description of the robber. On Sunday, May 28, Anderson's constable Elmore arrested a man who gave the name J. L. Ragsdale, and whom the lawman believed to be the road agent, so he took his prisoner to Shasta and lodged him in jail. The robber's mask and gun were found in the bushes near Anderson and brought in for evidence, and the prisoner had a diary in which he was detailing his adventures. He documented the purchase of a gun and commented in writing to his girlfriend, "I am robbing for a living now, and doing pretty well."

The editor of the *Shasta Courier* thought he was "too green to be allowed to run free" and speculated that he would plead guilty to receive a lighter sentence. It seems he was correct as on Wednesday, June 7, Ragsdale, along with stagecoach robber Stonewall Jackson Arthur, were taken to San Quentin Prison by Undersheriff Kennedy. Ragsdale had been sentenced to only four years, and he registered as prisoner #10445 when he arrived on June 9, 1882. On August 30, 1883, Ragsdale tried to escape from prison by hiding under a pile of straw while employed outside the walls, but the ploy failed, and he was quickly secured behind the prison's walls. Ragsdale forfeited twelve months of his good time credit, awarded under the Goodwin Act, and though the record does not state the reason, it was almost certainly for his escape attempt. He was discharged on June 9, 1886, after serving his entire four-year sentence.

Sources: *Shasta Courier (CA)*: May 27, 1882; June 3, 1882; June 10, 1882.

GEORGE HARRIS, JUNE 26, 1882

At 3:00 a.m. Monday, June 26, 1882, the stagecoach from Yreka in Siskiyou County bound for Redding in Shasta County was ascending the grade from Reid's Ferry into Redding when driver Horace Williams heard the command, "Halt!" The masked road agent, armed with a six-shooter, then commanded the driver to "throw down that box," but Williams informed the robber that it was fastened to the stagecoach. The robber made a second demand and would not believe the driver until Williams got down and showed him that the box was firmly riveted to the coach. He did not ask for the mail sacks. The road agent, who appeared quite young, then asked if there were any passengers aboard. Upon learning that there was but one named Brigadier General Llewelyn Tozer, the robber became frightened and ordered Williams to continue without molesting the passenger, and he quickly fled into the brush. Williams hurried into Redding, sounded the alarm, and described the young man in detail and the description was circulated throughout the region.

On Tuesday a young man, who gave his name as John Harris, was arrested at Redding on suspicion of being the road agent, and he was taken to Shasta and lodged in jail. He said he had recently come from Chicago and had a gun, but he sold it. At his examination there was enough evidence to hold him for action by the grand jury. He was indicted on the charge of "assault to rob" and when brought into court for arraignment he corrected his name to George Harris and pled guilty, hoping to get a lighter sentence. He was successful and was sentenced to serve only one and a half years at San Quentin. He arrived at the prison on July 8, 1882, registering as prisoner #10475, and he was discharged by expiration of sentence on October 8, 1883, after serving only fifteen months.

Source: *Shasta Courier (CA)*: July 3, 1882.

Unknown, September 12, 1883

At 6:00 p.m. on Wednesday, September 12, 1883, the down stagecoach from Yreka to Redding was two miles above Shasta when a road agent, masked with a black veil and partly concealed in a ditch, brought his six-shooter to bear upon driver Charles McConnell and ordered him to halt. Once the coach was stopped the command, "Throw down that box," was given. McConnell called out that it was an iron box bolted inside the coach, but the robber said "Throw out the one under the seat." McConnell threw out the "Weaverville and Yreka" local express box, and it landed near the side of the road. The road agent then told the driver to continue on without asking for the mail or showing any interest in the passengers. The coach only went a short distance, as long as it took county treasurer Jackson to load his Winchester rifle, and he got out and he took up a position to wait for the robber to come out of the ditch after the box. Apparently the robber watched the coach to be sure it had left and realized he was outgunned, so after a considerable wait Jackson determined that the robber had fled under concealment of the ditch. He recovered the box, put it on the coach, and waited at the scene for the posse to arrive. The coach hurried into Shasta and reported the attempted robbery. Lawmen went to the scene but could find no clue to the robber's identity, nor a clear trail to follow after the boot tracks in the ditch came to an end. They brought an extra horse and Jackson rode back to Shasta with the posse.

Sources: *Sacramento Daily Union (CA)*: September 13, 1883. *Territorial Enterprise (Virginia City, NV)*: September 13, 1883.

Edward Glover, Owen Temple and John Williams, May 8, 1884

At 2:00 p.m. on Thursday, May 8, 1884, the down stage from Yreka to Redding, driven by Dave Curtis, was near Buckeye when it was stopped by two masked road agents, one armed with a pistol and the other a shotgun. They demanded the Wells, Fargo express box and then went through the passengers, but got very little for their risk. The coach continued on to Redding to sound the alarm, and the sheriff soon organized a posse of lawmen and volunteers to track the robbers. They were not successful in finding the road agents, but their description was circulated and several lawmen were certain they knew the identities of the road agents. After the robbery the two road agents—Owen Temple and John Williams—camped along the river while Edward Glover stole a boat from Indian Frank and took them supplies for their escape. Afterward Glover, with his share of the plunder, returned to Redding where he had been boarding at the Pennsylvania House for three weeks, while Temple and Williams floated downriver to Red Bluff. There they abandoned the boat and took to the rails, Williams disembarking at Marysville and Temple continuing on to Rocklin.

In mid–May Undersheriff John Reynolds arrested Owen Temple at Rocklin. His prisoner confessed his part in the robbery and "peached," or informed, on his fellow robbers, naming John Williams and Edward Glover. Williams was arrested in Marysville when he was pawning a stolen watch and was brought back to Shasta, and he also confessed. Glover, who was from Junction City in Trinity County and was well known throughout the region, was soon arrested at Redding and joined his partners in the Shasta County jail. During the week of June 7 the three men had their examination before Justice Knox, and they were held over for action by the grand jury. They were indicted on a charge of robbery, with Glover's trial scheduled first, and on June 16 he was tried and found guilty of robbery. The following day Temple and Williams, seeing the outcome for Glover, pled guilty in the hope of getting a lighter sentence. Glover was sentenced to serve five years while Temple and Williams were sentenced to serve six years. All three men arrived at San Quentin on June 22, 1884, Glover registering as prisoner #11294, Temple registering as prisoner #11295, and Williams registering as prisoner #11296. Glover's prison record notes he was discharged on September 9, 1886, but lists the reason for his release as "Died." Temple and Williams were both discharged, by expiration of sentence, on August 22, 1888.

Sources: *Republican Free Press (Redding, CA)*: May 24, 1884. *Shasta Courier (CA)*: May 10, 1884; May 31, 1884; June 7, 1884; June 21, 1884; June 28, 1884.

STONEWALL JACKSON ARTHUR AND THOMAS CHAMBERLAIN ARTHUR, MAY 26, 1884

On Monday, May 26, 1884, a "half-breed Indian" named Stonewall Jackson Arthur stopped and robbed the stagecoach from Alturas in Modoc County bound for Redding in Shasta County. The southbound stagecoach, driven by Edward Brackett, was between Morley's station and Round Mountain when the lone, masked and armed road agent appeared. He pointed his six-shooter at the driver and demanded the Wells, Fargo express box, and Brackett, who was unarmed, had no choice but to deliver. In the box was a pair of shoes of an unusually large size and $125 in currency, and the robber left the shoes behind. After the treasure box was thrown down the road agent gestured to Brackett to continue, and the driver hurried into Redding where he sounded the alarm.

Constable McComber organized a posse of three men, and they soon were on the track of the fugitive and found where he had camped to await the arrival of the stagecoach. The lawmen continued on the trail and the following day, Tuesday, arrived at Predmore's ranch and surrounded the house. Soon a young man appeared carrying supplies and they followed him. After going a short distance the fugitive road agent came out of the brush to collect his food. The posse men confronted him and he began to struggle with them; but they knocked him to the ground and took his pistol, so he was forced to surrender without further resistance. He was taken to Millville and from there Deputy Sheriff Reynolds took him to Shasta and lodged him in the county jail. He gave his name as Stonewall Jackson Arthur and confessed all the details of the robbery. He was well known to lawmen and for the past six months, since his return home from San Quentin Prison, he had been committing petty crimes and annoying his neighbors, but a case could not be worked up against him. They identified Stonewall Jackson's brother as the man who was aiding him in eluding arrest by bringing supplies, and Thomas Chamberlain Arthur soon joined his brother in jail, charged with being an accessory after the fact.

The two prisoners had their examinations and were held over for action by the grand jury. They were indicted, Stonewall for the robbery and Thomas as an accessory. They were tried and convicted of the charges on July 8, 1884. Stonewall was sentenced to serve a term of nine years and Thomas a term of two years at San Quentin. On Wednesday, July 9, Undersheriff Reynolds left for San Quentin with the two prisoners, and they arrived on July 11, Thomas registering as prisoner #11313 and Stonewall registering as prisoner #11314. Thomas was discharged on March 11, 1886, after serving one year and seven months, and his brother, Stonewall, was discharged four years later on June 11, 1890.

Sources: *Republican Free Press (Redding, CA)*: May 31, 1884. *Shasta Courier (CA)*: July 12, 1884.

UNKNOWN, JULY 29, 1884

At 1:00 a.m. on Tuesday morning, July 29, 1884, the stagecoach coming from Yreka to Redding was stopped by one man near Bass' station. He demanded the Wells, Fargo express box but did not ask for the mail or inquire about passengers. The box was thrown down, and then the road agent told the driver to continue on. After the coach was out of sight the robber broke open the box and discovered he had made a "water haul." With nothing lost but the cost of repairing the box, no reward was posted and there was no motivation to pursue the robber.

Sources: *Los Angeles Herald (CA)*: July 30, 1884. *Territorial Enterprise (Virginia City, NV)*: July 30, 1884.

UNKNOWN, SEPTEMBER 12, 1885; SEPTEMBER 15, 1885

On Saturday, September 12, 1885, the stagecoach from Alturas to Redding was twenty miles south of Millville when a lone, masked and armed road agent stepped out of hiding and ordered the driver to halt. The driver reined in his team, and the robber demanded that he throw down the Wells, Fargo express box. He did as told and the robber then told the driver to continue on. Lawmen could not find a clue or a trail, and they had abandoned the search by Monday. Constable Eckles arrested a suspicious character, charging him with the robbery, but the prisoner proved to be the wrong man and he was released.

At 8:00 p.m. on Tuesday, September 15, 1885, the stagecoach from Alturas to Redding had just reached the summit of Cow Creek Hill, twenty miles south of Millville near where the stagecoach had been robbed three days earlier, when two highwaymen stepped into the road and ordered the driver to rein in his team. The two men were masked and armed, so the driver had no choice but to obey. They told him to thrown down the Wells, Fargo express box, and he did, but they did not ask for the mail nor ask about passengers. As soon as they had the box they told the driver to continue on. Officers rode to the scene but could not find a clue to the robbers' identities nor a trail to follow, but they were sure one, or both, of the men had been involved in the robbery of September 12.

Sources: *Daily Alta California (San Francisco)*: September 12, 1885. *Sacramento Daily Union (CA)*: September 12, 1885; September 17, 1885.

LEE SYKES, OCTOBER 21, 1887

A. M. Goodenough had a ranch four miles from Redding. He was engaged in cutting and hauling wood to Redding and had employed Leslie Jones, Ed Beck and Lee Sykes to do the work; and he had hired Clara Wright to care for his invalid wife while he supervised operations. On October 18, 1887, Lee Sykes quit his job and said he was going to Idaho, but he took with him Beck's .45 caliber Colt improved model carrying a swedged ball. Instead, however, Sykes hid in the brush near the house and Beck provided him with food for three days. Sykes spent part of that time reconnoitering the stagecoaches passing on the northernmost of three roads between Redding and Bieber in Modoc County. On October 21, 1887, the northbound stagecoach left Redding at 5:00 p.m. with Palmer driving, George C. Henderson riding next to the driver, and a man named Williams the only passenger inside. The coach had traveled four miles and had topped a small grade onto level road, only one mile from the Goodenough residence, when Sykes, masked and armed with the revolver, stepped out and ordered the coach to halt. Sykes fired almost immediately and the bullet whizzed past Palmer, but it struck Henderson in the stomach, shredding his bowels, a mortal wound. Sykes fled as Palmer whipped up his team and took the stagecoach four miles into Loomis Corners, and a rider was sent into Redding to bring back a doctor. The doctor arrived but could do nothing for Henderson, and he died in excruciating pain at 6:00 a.m. the next morning. Lawmen at the scene could not find a trail to follow nor a clue to the identity of the robber. After Sykes murdered Henderson, he fled back to the Goodenough ranch, where Beck hid and fed him in the barn for four days. Sykes then left and went south still carrying Beck's pistol, and he assumed the alias Bob James.

On October 24 Wells, Fargo's chief detective James B. Hume arrived accompanied by Deputy Allison of Loomis Corners, and they spent five days investigating the entire region. He determined from all the facts that the road agent was not an Indian or half-breed and that he was familiar with the area and stage line route, but Hume was convinced he was a "green hand" at stagecoach robbery. The robber had tried to stop the up coach which never carried much money, while the down coach often carried considerable sums, and he shot immediately before he made a demand for the treasure box or mail. However, Hume had no better luck in finding a clue so the case went cold. On November 21, with the wood-hauling business at an end, Jones, Beck and Wright left the employ of Goodenough. Wright returned to her family home not far from Redding while Jones and Beck went into Redding and got drunk. Hume had posted circulars all about the town giving all the known facts of the case, and emphasizing the rewards posted. As Jones and Beck walked toward the depot, where Jones was going to board a train for Fresno, Beck tore down three circulars and stuffed them into his pocket. Jones asked, "Why did you do that?" and Beck replied, "I know who killed Henderson, and I harbored him in Goodenough's barn the first four nights after the murder." Then Beck would say no more, claiming he was afraid to talk. At the depot Jones invited Beck to accompany him to Fresno, and as Beck had no money, Jones bought his ticket. Throughout the ride Jones tried to get Beck to say more, but Beck would not speak about the matter again. In Fresno Jones contacted a deputy sheriff, a previous acquaintance, and asked him to question Beck on the Henderson murder, but the deputy said he had word they had just arrested the murderer in Oregon. Jones then dropped his inquiry.

In early March 1888 Jones wrote to Goodenough and told him of the remarks by Beck, so Goodenough wrote to Hume on March 10 requesting all of the reward if he could determine the murderer. Hume agreed to support Goodenough's claim, went to his ranch, and they discussed a strategy. Goodenough told Hume that he had found, in his haymow, evidence that someone had hidden there for days and among the refuse were items foreign to the supplies available on the ranch. Hume was then convinced that Sykes was the murderer he was after. They knew that Beck had stayed in touch with Wright and that he might know of Sykes' whereabouts, and they believed that Wright might also know where Sykes could be found. They were concerned that if they contacted Wright or Beck they might warn Sykes, so they developed a plan to have Jones write to them and try to get information, and on March 28 Jones agreed. Jones told Hume all he knew of Beck including his relatives living at Live Oak and about Beck's pistol, taken by Sykes. Jones said that Beck had ordered a main spring for his revolver from Ladd & Company in San Francisco, so when Hume returned home he went to the company and learned that Beck's pistol was identical to the one that had been used to murder Henderson.

Hume decided not to pursue Beck, as he felt sure Sykes would be warned, but he learned that Beck had embezzled a silver watch from Joseph Covey while working at the Goodenough ranch. He had an arrest warrant issued and enlisted the help of Fresno officer Fraser to watch for the opportunity to arrest Beck. On May 13 Fraser notified Hume that he had a horse-stealing case on the 16th, and he would subpoena Beck to testify. Beck arrived on the evening of the 15th, but all the hotels were filled so Fraser agreed to let Beck stay in his room. During the night he arrested Beck on the warrant, took him to Lathrop where he was met by Hume, and they took their prisoner to Sacramento. Beck then told everything about the Sykes affair, said that Sykes had come to his home in Fresno in December and stayed until May 1 using the alias Bob James, then left for Bakersfield and wrote to him on June 5 using the name W. R. Short, and Beck said he wrote back immediately. Beck said that the last time he saw Sykes he was wearing a coat and pantaloons made of the same material as his vest, so Hume confiscated Beck's vest and cut it into pieces to be used as samples to distribute to lawmen. Hume felt he had enough evidence so he telegraphed the district attorney in Redding and had him issue a complaint for murder and an arrest warrant for Sykes. Fraser then left for Bakersfield to search for Sykes while Hume took Beck to Redding.

When Hume and Beck arrived they learned that the grand jury had just indicted John Curtis for the murder of Henderson, and public opinion was very strong against Curtis. Hume had Beck repeat his story to the sheriff and the district attorney, and then they went to the Goodenough ranch where the haymow had been preserved where Sykes had hidden for four days. This finally convinced the Redding authorities, the complaint and warrant were issued for Sykes, and the murder charge against Curtis was dismissed. Fraser had no luck in Bakersfield, so Hume went there on July 1, talked with Wells, Fargo agent Alonzo Coons and with all the lawmen, and gave each man a swatch of cloth from Beck's vest. He was certain that Sykes would be in town for the July 4 celebrations and planned to look for him then, but he was called away on business. He asked Fraser to do the work, and though the officer agreed, he failed to make it to Bakersfield. On July 4 the officers were overwhelmed with celebrants and lawbreakers and found no time to look for Sykes, though they learned later he had been parading up and down the streets in a rowdy drunken mood.

On July 2, 1888, the stagecoach from Madera to Hildreth in Modoc County had been robbed three-quarters of a mile from its destination by one masked road agent brandishing a large-caliber revolver. On July 23 a man came into Bakersfield's Wells, Fargo office to send a saddle and valise to Hildreth; he wore a large-caliber revolver, and agent Coons was sure this was the Hildreth road agent. He took the saddle and valise and gave the man a receipt, as was the standard practice so he would not alert the man to his suspicions. The man then asked to open his valise to take out his coat, and when it was removed the cloth matched the piece of Beck's vest Coons had been given. As soon as the man left the office Coons found Kern County sheriff Dallas McCord and Constable Tibbitts and they quickly traced their man to the livery stable. They got the drop on him, took his revolver, placed him under arrest, and learned he was Lee Sykes. Hume and Sheriff Hopping of Shasta County were notified, and the sheriff went to Bakersfield and took the prisoner back to Redding. Beck had been in the jail there, but he was moved to the Tehama County jail at Red Bluff to prevent their talking to each other. Sykes had his preliminary hearing on August 23 and, after all the evidence was presented, was held over for action by the grand jury. Meanwhile Beck was moved to the Sacramento County jail where he would be kept until he was to testify against Sykes. However, on October 6, 1888, Sykes, on the advice of his attorneys in a deal to avoid the death penalty, pled guilty to the charge in the information. Judge Bell set the date for testimony, to determine the gravity of the crime for sentencing purposes, for October 10, and when the evidence concluded, Judge Bell sentenced Sykes to serve life imprisonment at San Quentin. Sykes arrived at the prison on October 15, 1888, and under the name R. L. Sykes registered as prisoner #13266. In October 1896 Sykes was very ill and he was sent to the sick ward, but on the 22nd he tried to escape because of the lax security in the hospital. Sykes only made it into the prison yard where he was discovered, captured, and returned to the hospital. Apparently his illness was not a ruse, however, as Sykes died on October 28, 1896.

Source: *Sacramento Daily Record Union (CA)*: October 13, 1888.

Unknown, July 27, 1888

At 10:00 p.m. on Friday, July 27, 1888, the stagecoach from Redding to Bieber had traveled forty-five miles, and the horses were walking at a slow pace nearing the top of a sharp hitch when driver Dan DeForrest heard the command, "Halt!" A lone road agent, masked and armed with a double-barreled shotgun, stepped into the road and said, "Throw out the box, mailbags, and the brass lock." DeForrest tried to dissuade the robber from molesting the U.S. mail, but the robber made the demand again and added, "or I will blow the top of your head off." All were thrown down and the robber then said, "Drive on." DeForrest continued on to his next station and from there the robbery was reported, but he could not give a good description of the road agent. Undersheriff Reynolds and Constable Crum rode to the scene but could find no clue to the robber's identity, nor a trail to follow for any distance. After a brief delay the amount stolen was given as $800, and Wells, Fargo offered a large reward for the arrest and conviction of the robber.

It took nearly a year after the posting of the reward before three men came forward and identified their neighbor William Donaldson as the road agent, and he was arrested. He had his preliminary hearing on August 30, 1889, and Justice Simonds immediately dismissed the charges, released Donaldson, and directed that key witness John Allen be arrested for perjury. Allen was soon joined in jail by N. J. Orr and George Jones, who had conspired to send Donaldson to prison so they could share the reward. All four men were hard cases, but Donaldson was innocent of the charge of stagecoach robbery. They were indicted, tried for perjury, convicted, and each was sentenced to serve two years in prison. On November 9, 1889, the three perjurers were lodged in the city jail to await transfer to San Quentin. The stagecoach robber was never identified.

Sources: *Daily Alta California (San Francisco)*: August 31, 1889; November 10, 1889. *Sacramento Daily Union (CA)*: July 30, 1888.

UNKNOWN, NOVEMBER 9, 1888

At 6:00 p.m. on Friday, November 9, 1888, the stagecoach from Weaverville to Redding had just entered the city limits with Perry Davis driving when a lone road agent, masked and armed, ordered him to stop, but Davis continued to drive. The road agent warned that he would shoot if Davis did not halt, so Davis reined in his team. On the boot with Davis were two passengers, and the road agent said, "Get down here, get right down!" Once the three men were standing beside the coach the robber handed Davis three caps and told Davis to go to the heads of his leaders and control them after he put a cap over the head of each passenger and himself. Once their heads were covered the robber took $100 from the passengers and then climbed up and threw down the Wells, Fargo express box and mailbags, and he started to go through them. Just then Bill Wilson drove up on his way into town to fetch a doctor, and the road agent told him, "Drive right up here." Wilson said he was in a hurry to get the doctor, but the robber replied, "Never mind, drive right here, get out, and put this cap on." The robber punctuated the order with his gun barrel, and Wilson did what he was told and joined the two passengers. The robber then took $65 and a watch from Wilson, but Wilson asked for the watch back. The robber said, "If I get a good haul from the box I might give the watch back." He returned to his work on the box and mailbags when John Craddock drove up on his way out of town, and the robber ordered, "Drive right up here, close to this [Wilson's] team, and put this cap on." After Craddock joined the others the robber took from him $15 and then returned to the express box and mailbags. Craddock complained that the cap was choking him, so the robber told him to push it up until he could get air, but just then Miss Eliza Welsh drove up on her way to her home in Shasta, and he had her drive up behind Craddock's rig. He told her to remain seated, assuring her that if she was quiet she would not be hurt. He finally finished with the mailbags and express box, taking out $240, and then calmly walked over the hill to their left. After a brief delay Davis asked, "Has that man gone?" and Miss Welsh said, "A man went over the hill." They pulled off the caps and quickly one passenger got into the rig with Welsh, Wilson and Craddock got into their rigs, Davis and his other passenger boarded the coach, and all headed into Redding. They reported the robbery, and posses were quickly organized and went out in several directions, but without any success.

Source: *Sacramento Daily Union (CA)*: November 10, 1888.

UNKNOWN, OCTOBER 24, 1889

At 11:00 p.m. on Thursday, October 24, 1889, the stagecoach from Bieber to Redding, with Palmer driving, was seven miles from its destination, just past Buzzard's Roost, when the coach was halted by a masked, armed road agent. He called for the express box and mail, but there was no mail aboard. As soon as the Wells, Fargo express box lay in the road the robber told the driver to move along, without asking about passengers. The driver hurried into Redding and reported the robbery, but by the time a posse was organized and rode to the scene, several hours had passed, and they could find no clue to the robber's identity nor a trail to follow so they collected the broken box and returned to town.

Source: *Sacramento Daily Union (CA)*: October 26, 1889.

FRANK WILLIAMS, NOVEMBER 28, 1889

A lone road agent robbed the stagecoach between Auburn and Forest Hill on September 2, 1889, and again on September 16, 1889, and this would later lead to some confusion when Henry Williamson was arrested at Auburn and accused of those robberies. Meanwhile, the lone road agent moved his operations to Oregon, and on November 13, 1889, he robbed the Roseburg to Coos Bay stagecoach at Looking Glass, and then on November 18 he robbed the Igo to Tinkville stagecoach after it crossed into Oregon. This road agent apparently felt he could not be caught if he continually moved his operations, so he next went south into Shasta County. At 6:00 p.m. on Thursday, November 28, 1889, the stagecoach from Shasta to Redding was a half mile from Middle Creek station when a lone bandit, masked and carrying a .45 caliber revolver and a sawed-off shotgun similar to those carried by Wells, Fargo messengers, halted the coach. The robber appeared slightly taller than average, middle aged, and very stout. He demanded the Wells, Fargo express box and mail, but stage line owner J. P. "Luke" Dow, riding next to driver Kenuff, said there was no treasure box. The road agent cursed him and, yelling out the alias Jack Bryant, insisted he knew his business and there was a box aboard, so it was thrown down. The road agent then ordered Dow and Kenuff to get down and told Dow to get the ax, but Dow claimed there was none. The road agent, growing angry, said he knew better and soon he had Kenuff chop open the box while Dow removed the mail pouches from the empty passenger compartment. Once the box was opened the robber told Dow and Kenuff to board and then ordered the driver to continue on. It was later reported the box contained only $2, but the value of the registered mail was thought to be substantial.

Dow described the road agent and said he wore a yellow rubber raincoat over his clothing as a disguise. The next morning Dow, with undersheriff Reynolds and Constable Crum went to the scene to investigate, and they followed a trail to Salt Creek a half mile from the robbery scene. Dow found the shotgun, blankets, the yellow rubber raincoat, and other supplies lying in plain view on a rock, giving the impression they had just missed their man by moments. However, they could not find a further trail nor a clue to the robber's identity. It appeared that the raincoat and other items had been purchased in San Francisco, so Dow forwarded them to detective Isaiah Lees to see if he could locate the seller, and Lees shared his information with police court bailiff Thomas Ryan. (See Nevada County for December 15, 1889.)

UNKNOWN, SEPTEMBER 25, 1890

On Thursday night, September 25, 1890, the northbound stagecoach from Redding in Shasta County to Cedarville in Modoc County had traveled twenty-five miles and reached Morley's station at 11:00 p.m. Two masked road agents, one large and the other short, ordered driver

Ed Brackett to halt, and they waved their pistols to emphasize their determination. One robber asked, "Are there any passengers?" and the answer was "No." The robber doing the talking then asked for the Wells, Fargo express box and government way-pouch, but when he asked for the mail the other robber told him to leave it alone, so it was not thrown out. One of the robbers used an ax stolen in the vicinity to break open the box, and he cut open the pouch, gathering $800 from both, then put all the envelopes and other papers back into the box and pouch and put them back onto the coach. The two men were quite composed and were believed to be "old hands at the business of highway robbery." There were no clues to their identities, so no one was ever prosecuted.

Source: *Sacramento Daily Union (CA)*: September 27, 1890.

UNKNOWN, MARCH 7, 1891; MARCH 19, 1891

At 7:30 p.m. on Saturday, March 7, 1891, a "treasure night," the Weaverville to Redding stagecoach was two miles from Redding when a lone, masked highwayman armed with a revolver appeared on a four-foot embankment above the road. He ordered driver Ed Graham to halt, and Graham reined in his team immediately. The road agent told him, "Drive up a little further," and the team started but pulled up. The road agent then shouted, "A little further or, God damn you, I'll shoot." Messenger Ward, who was seated next to Graham, took that opportunity to raise his shotgun, but the robber fired first and the bullet struck Graham on his right side under his arm, then ranged around until it lodged near the right nipple. The messenger's shotgun snapped, and after the misfire he dropped the shotgun into the road and drew his revolver. The robber's shot had frightened the team and they took off at a dead run, so Ward leaned back over the top of the stagecoach and fired at the robber, with no success. The robber took one more shot at the coach, but neither the messenger nor any of the four passengers were hit. The wild ride into Shasta damaged the coach, and after the doctor examined Graham's wound he said is was serious but not fatal. Lawmen would not allow anyone to go to the scene, as walking around in the dark could destroy any foot track evidence. When the scene was investigated after daybreak there were no clues to the identity of the robber.

On Thursday, March 19, the coach to Weaverville was not more than twenty yards from the spot of the robbery on March 7 when the same highwayman appeared, masked with a barley sack and brandishing his revolver as he stepped out from behind a tree. He pointed his pistol at driver Ed Brackett and told him to "throw out that box." Brackett threw down the Shasta box, but the robber seemed familiar with the stage line and called for the Weaverville box as well. As this was not a "treasure night," there was no messenger, but a lady passenger was riding atop and a male passenger was riding inside. The passengers were not molested and the robber did not ask for the mail. He then told Brackett to continue, and he whipped up his team. Lawmen went to the scene the next morning but could find no clue to the robber's identity.

Sources: *Daily Alta California (San Francisco)*: March 8, 1891; March 20, 1891. *Sacramento Daily Union (CA)*: March 8, 1891.

WILLIAM H. "BILL" HOWARD AND ABRAHAM "ABE" JONES, AUGUST 4, 1891; SEPTEMBER 1, 1891; SEPTEMBER 29, 1891; OCTOBER 19, 1891

At 8:00 p.m. on Tuesday, August 4, 1891, the stagecoach from Bieber to Redding was three miles from its destination when two masked and heavily armed road agents stepped out of hiding and ordered the driver to halt. He had no choice but to obey, and then one of the robbers demanded the express packages in care of Wells, Fargo, and these were thrown out. The robbers did not ask for the mail nor inquire if there were passengers aboard. Once they had all the packages they told the driver to continue into Redding, and he lost no time in getting into town and reporting the robbery. Lawmen went to the scene but all they could find were the remnants of the packages ripped open with their valuable contents stolen, so they collected the debris and delivered it to the Wells, Fargo office in Redding. Two days later Samuel Flint of the Railway Mail Service was notified of the robbery, but, as the U.S. mail was not disturbed, he took no action.

At 7:30 p.m. on Tuesday, September 1, 1891, the northbound stagecoach from Redding to Alturas, with two female passengers aboard, had only traveled three and a half miles from Redding when a lone highwayman, masked and armed with a shotgun, stepped into the road and ordered the driver to halt. He demanded the Wells, Fargo express box and it was thrown down. As soon as the box lay in the road the robber ordered the driver to continue on, without asking for the mail or inquiring about passengers. After the coach was out of sight, his partner, who had remained concealed in the brush, joined him, and they broke open the box and removed the valuable items it contained. As soon as word could be sent back, a posse was organized at Redding and they rode to the scene, but they could find no clue to the robbers' identities other than to confirm that there had been two men involved, and no trail to follow beyond the boot tracks in the road. They recovered the broken box and returned it to the Wells, Fargo office in Redding.

At 3:00 a.m. on Tuesday morning, September 29, 1891, the northbound stagecoach from Redding to Alturas, with no passengers aboard, had traveled fifteen miles and was near Stillwater when two masked road agents armed with six-shooters stepped into the road and halted the coach. They demanded the Wells, Fargo express boxes, and once the two boxes lay in the road they demanded the axe or a hammer carried on the coach. The driver had neither and gave them a monkey wrench, and they used that to break open the box and remove the valuables it contained. They had the mail sacks thrown down but did not molest them after a careful examination, and they returned the sacks and broken box to the coach. As soon as word reached Redding, a posse was organized and rode to the scene, but once again they could find no clue to the robbers' identities nor a trail to follow. Wells, Fargo would not divulge the amount in the box, but it was thought to be quite small, as there was no messenger aboard.

On Wednesday, October 7, 1891, the two road agents moved their operations north into Oregon and stopped the stagecoach from Linkville to Lakeview as it neared its destination. One man was armed with a shotgun and the other a pistol as they demanded the Wells, Fargo express box, and it was thrown down. As soon as they had the box they told the driver to continue into Lakeview. It was only minutes before he was able to report the robbery, and less than an hour after the road agents first appeared, a posse was at the scene, but they could not find a clue or a trail. Lawmen in California, and Wells, Fargo detective James Hume, encouraged them to make every effort to capture the robbers, but they had fled south into California. On Monday night, October 19, 1891, the northbound stagecoach from Redding to Alturas had traveled only six miles and was still two miles west of Millville when two masked road agents stepped out and ordered driver Alec Smith to halt. One robber was armed with a pistol and the other a double-barreled shotgun, so the driver had no choice but to obey. Once the coach had stopped, the robbers demanded the Wells, Fargo express box and mail, and for the first time they kept the mail sacks. They then ordered Smith to continue into Millville, and from there the robbery was reported. Lawmen from Millville and from Redding rode to the scene, including undersheriff Ross, and he deputized Charles Overholzer to accompany him. Early the next morning Ross and Overholzer found a trail to the river and it appeared that three road agents had crossed in a skiff, so they swam their horses across and continued to follow the trail of foot tracks for a considerable distance. Just after daybreak the trail ended where three men were camped in a field; two fit the description of the road agents, and all three were arrested. They took their prisoners—identified as William H. "Bill" Howard, Abraham "Abe" Jones and John "Jack" Rice—to Alturas and lodged them in jail. They were put aboard a stagecoach bound for Redding, with four officers to guard them, one officer inside and John Thacker on top, with two officers following in a buggy. Howard and Jones were coupled together with a bracelet over each man's boot, but as the stagecoach proceeded along, each man managed to removed his boot and then the bracelet. On Sunday night, November 1, when the coach stopped near Holcomb's station to water the horses, Howard and Jones each bolted out an opposite door and fled into the darkness of the dense woods. The officer inside, Caril, could not leave Rice unattended so he called to Thacker, and the detective fired two shots at the fleeing fugitives but did not manage to hit either man. It was too dark and there was too much cover to follow the escaped prisoners so the coach continued on, and they lodged Rice in the Redding jail.

The fugitives had neither arms nor horses, so it was believed they would go to the farm of Bill Howard's father, Cornelius. He was arrested as an accomplice to his son's crimes, and three men—Thomas Miles, O. P. Whitten, and S. A. Stewart—were posted in the back room of the house in case the son returned. Toward midnight Bill Howard rode up to the house, and the three deputies, hiding in the back room using a small candle for light, quickly blew out the flame and waited. The house was dark so Howard called to his father by name and said, "Father, strike a light; strike a light." When he got no response he entered the front room, the door to the back room was opened, and one of the officers said, "Throw up your hands!" Howard replied, "Go to Hell!" as he turned toward the open door to leave. The officers fired three times, and the fugitive fell dead. At the inquest on November 4 the jurors found that twenty-eight-year-old Howard was killed under the authority of Deputy U.S. Marshal John N. Thacker. The robber had nothing in his pockets when he "died with his boots on," but his clothing had been shredded when he crawled through brush and over rocks after escaping from the stagecoach, and the horse he was riding had been stolen at Oak Run earlier that night and was returned to its owner.

After his escape from the stagecoach Abe Jones avoided capture all day Monday, but on Tuesday, November 3, he was spotted by a small posse. When they ordered him to surrender he yelled back, "Take that!" and fired one shot from a stolen Winchester rifle, which killed the horse beneath a posse man. In the confusion he managed to escape again and it was believed he was heading for the house of Cornelius Howard, but he never showed there. On November 7, 1891, Cornelius Howard and John Rice were taken to San Francisco where they were indicted by the U.S. grand jury as accessories to the stagecoach robberies. The search for Jones continued until December 12, 1891, when he was recognized and captured at Alturas. The following day Deputy U.S. Marshal Maloney went to Alturas and took the prisoner to San Francisco, where he was indicted, and his trial was set for late January. The jurors in the first trial deadlocked over conviction and were dismissed. Jones' second trial was held in late February and the case went to the jurors on March 2, but again they deadlocked. His third trial began on May 3, 1892, and this time the jurors found him guilty of robbing the U.S. mail during the two October 1891 stagecoach robberies, and on May 23, 1892, Jones was sentenced to serve a term of twenty years at San Quentin. He was delivered across the bay that afternoon and registered as prisoner #14966. District attorney Garter then motioned the court to dismiss the indictments against Rice and Cornelius Howard. Rice, who had not been involved in the robberies but assisted the road agents afterward, had turned state's evidence, and Garter argued that there was not sufficient evidence against Cornelius Howard to get a conviction as an accessory after the fact. Judge Morrow agreed, dismissed the indictments, and both men were released. There is no record for Jones' imprisonment and release in the prison archives.

Sources: *Daily Alta California (San Francisco)*: September 2, 1891. *Los Angeles Herald (CA)*: September 30, 1891; May 24, 1892. *Sacramento Daily Union (CA)*: October 21, 1891. *San Francisco Call (CA)*: August 6, 1891; October 21, 1891; November 3, 1891; November 5, 1891; November 7, 1891; November 26, 1891; December 13, 1891; January 26, 1891; March 2, 1891; May 4, 1891; May 24, 1892.

Jonn Stevens and Unknown, October 22, 1891

No sooner had a band of two Shasta County road agents been jailed when two new road agents, perhaps inspired by the success of those others or notice of their recent absence from the road, took to the road. At 7:00 p.m. on Thursday, October 22, 1891, they stopped the Redding to Alturas stagecoach driven by Alec Smith when he was near Leighton, six miles from Redding. They were masked and armed, one with a shotgun and the other a revolver, and they demanded the Wells, Fargo express box and the mailbags. Once these were thrown onto the road they robbed the lone passenger, a lady, and took $5 from Smith before they told the driver to move along. They broke open the box and took out $200, but the amount they got from the mail was not known. Smith reported the robbery as soon as he got to the next location and confirmed that these were not the same two men who had robbed him on Monday night, who were then in jail. A posse was formed at Redding and they rode to the scene but could find no clue to the robbers' identities, nor a trail to follow, but on Monday, October 26, lawmen arrested a twenty-three-year-old man named Jonn Stevens and a sixteen-year-old boy named Frank Wedenberg. They worked on the boy and by that evening he confessed and told them where to find the box in a gulch a quarter mile northwest of the robbery scene, and inside the box, officers found a new pair of pants, a mohair duster, and the waybills. The boy insisted he was not involved in the robbery but said he assisted the two robbers afterward. Stevens' trial concluded in early November, and he was convicted of robbery and sentenced to serve ten years at San Quentin. Twenty-two-year-old Stevens arrived at the prison on November 10, 1891, and registered as prisoner #14717; he was "restored" on May 10, 1898, after serving six years six months.

Sources: *Los Angeles Herald (CA)*: October 27, 1891. *Sacramento Daily Union (CA)*: October 24, 1891. *San Francisco Call (CA)*: October 27, 1891.

Charles Ruggles and John Dexter Ruggles, May 10, 1892; May 14, 1892

At 6:00 p.m. on Tuesday, May 10, 1892, the stagecoach from Weaverville to Redding was on the river road one mile from Redding with John Boyce driving. Suddenly he noticed a road agent concealed in the grapevines along the road pointing a pistol at him while a second road agent stepped into the road carrying a shotgun, and the latter man ordered Boyce to halt. He told Boyce to throw out the Wells, Fargo express box, and Boyce complied. There was no messenger aboard, indicating that there would be little or no treasure, and the robber expressed no interest in the passengers or the mail. Once the box lay on the road the robber backed up thirty feet and told Boyce to drive on, but he kept the driver covered with his shotgun until the coach was out of sight. Boyce hurried into Redding and reported the robbery, and he described the robber who stood in the road: "He was dressed in a long linen duster buttoned below the knees and having linen pants on. He was masked with a light linen mask, which had three large black teeth painted on it at the mouth. The man was about five feet eight inches tall and weighed about one hundred sixty pounds." Marshal Eckels organized a posse of constables and started for the scene, but they returned without an arrest or a clue to follow up.

At 6:00 p.m. on Saturday, May 14, the stagecoach in the Shasta line was just approaching the summit of a long grade five miles north of Redding with John Boyce driving and passenger George Suhr sitting next to him. Wells, Fargo messenger Amos "Buck" Montgomery was riding on the back seat inside the coach. Suddenly a man armed with a shotgun, with a red bandana for a mask, appeared on a bank above the coach and said, "Pull up and throw out the express box," and Boyce threw the box onto the road. At the first command Montgomery took careful aim at the road agent and fired both barrels of his sawed-off shotgun, and the robber dropped to his knees. As Montgomery fired, the robber's partner, concealed in the brush, opened fire on the messenger with his rifle, and the first bullet struck him in the back, passed through, and lodged near his navel, and several more bullets struck the seat. The first robber had recovered sufficiently to fire his shotgun, loaded with buckshot, and Suhr received three buckshot in the calf of his right leg while the driver received five buckshot near his right knee and two in his left leg, and Boyce fell on the footboard. The robbers then ordered the coach to continue, and Suhr took the reins while Boyce worked the brake and they managed to get the coach under way. After the coach was out of sight the robber lying in the brush went to his partner's assistance, took along the box, and fled.

After the coach had gone a short distance they met Dr. Stevenson and his wife and the doctor took over the reins and drove two miles to Middle Creek, while his wife hurried into Redding to summon Dr. Lawry. Montgomery was taken to the Middle Creek hotel where Dr. Lawry did what he could to help the messenger rest easily. The boxes were supposed to have contained $20,000, and large posses were already out looking for the robbers, but when they learned that Montgomery had died hours after being shot, their efforts doubled. By the next morning rewards totaling $1,100 had been posted, and later that day Harry Page, Nick Cusick and Lloyd Carter stumbled onto the wounded robber in a canyon near the town of Shasta. He seemed near death from loss of blood, as he had been shot in the breast, body and limbs. He could speak, however, and told of how his companion had abandoned him, expecting him to crawl off and die, and his partner took all the treasure for himself. The wounded robber was taken into Redding where he lingered between life and death but still managed to tell many conflicting stories about the robbery. He was finally identified as twenty-two-year-old Charles Ruggles, the young son of a Fresno farmer. On May 18 it appeared he would recover, so that night he tried to commit suicide by tearing off his bandages in an effort to bleed to death, but his effort was discovered and he was saved.

As soon as Charles Ruggles was identified, lawmen suspected that his accomplice was his thirty-three-year-old brother John, an ex-convict. The Ruggles family had previously lived at Woodland, and they still had influential relatives there. It was believed that John would not return to his father's home, where he would expect officers to be waiting for him, but would go to Woodland. On June 14 John Ruggles went to a Woodland hardware store and bought cartridges for his revolver, and the clerk recognized him. The clerk told Deputy Sheriff Wycoff who then searched the town but could find no trace of the fugitive, but he kept a careful watch. At 7:30 p.m. on June 19 Ruggles was seen, but officers followed him for two hours waiting for just the right circumstance to make a capture without a fight. At 9:30 p.m. Ruggles went into the Opera Restaurant and took a seat. Wycoff went in and sat at the same table, but the officer was recognized and Ruggles shifted in his seat so he could reach his revolver. Wycoff immediately drew his revolver and covered Ruggles and ordered him to raise his hands, but Ruggles reached for his revolver and Wycoff fired, the bullet striking the fugitive in his neck. Ruggles was stunned for a moment but then again tried to draw his revolver, so Wycoff grabbed Ruggles and in the struggle took away his pistol, and then two officers came to Wycoff's assistance. Once Ruggles was restrained he was taken to a drug store where two doctors took charge and found that the bullet had struck the left side of his neck and ranged downward, it could not be traced, and it was thought to be a mortal wound. Ruggles was lodged in jail and a large bag of money was found on his person, and when he believed he was dying he gave the sheriff a confession he had written out previously. He said that he had shot Montgomery, and that he had abandoned his brother when he was certain he would die, and he took off with the money. Most of it had been buried soon after he left his brother, but he would not say where he had buried it. By June 23 John had recovered sufficiently to be moved to the jail at Redding for a touching reunion with his brother.

Charles had his preliminary hearing on June 30 and John had his hearing scheduled for July 28, but then their defense strategy leaked out and they were going to blame the entire affair on Montgomery, saying he had planned the robbery but it had gone awry. The citizens of Redding were outraged to hear that their respected, murdered neighbor was to be maligned in a local courtroom. On Saturday, July 23, there seemed to be something in the air, but there was no sign that there was any plan in play, though quite a number of determined men had come into Redding from the surrounding towns and farms. At 1:00 a.m., July 24, a party of forty men, some masked and all the others disguised in some manner, marched eastward three abreast down the hill to the courthouse. From Butte and West streets they marched across the square and entered the courthouse by the north entrance, and all was done so quietly that no one in the building knew what was happening until they captured the jailor and then lit their torches. The jailer was taken to the lower floor, the door to the sheriff's office was forced open, and the jailor was directed to give them the keys to the jail, but the jailor said they were locked in the safe. He was tied, blindfolded, and placed in a corner under guard while the men brought in sledges, drills and powder and forced an entrance through the side of the safe and then into the strong box. By 2:00 a.m. the keys had been secured and the jail doors were opened. When the men appeared before the cells, John Ruggles asked if they meant him harm, but his brother said nothing. John's cell door was opened first and he was told to come out, and he said, "Gentlemen, be lenient with my bother; he is innocent of this crime." He was ignored, and his struggles were overcome as his wrists were cuffed behind his back and he was dragged from his cell. Someone then said, "Let's get the other one out," and when Charles' cell door was opened he stepped out. Both men were dressed only in their pants, undershirts, and stockings as they were hurried out of the courthouse and across the square. They were marched through an alley and down a street two blocks until they were in front of the blacksmith shop, where a crossbeam had been laid between the sturdy limbs of two pine trees. Nooses were placed around their necks with the opposite ends thrown across the crossbeam, their ankles were bound, and Charles' wrists were tied behind his back. The leader of the lynching party then said, "If you want to make a statement, now is your time, and be damned quick about it." John said, "Gentlemen, spare him." John was then asked if he had anything to say about the murder of the Rodisino girl on the Cazadero stagecoach or the drover murdered in Siskiyou County, but he answered, "I know nothing of these affairs." He was then asked where the balance of the stolen treasure was buried and he said, "Spare Charley, and I will tell you." Another then spoke up and said, "Never mind the treasure; tell us if you want to; if not, say what you have to say quick." Charles had said nothing, and John would say no more, so a rope was tied over John's mouth to prevent an outcry, and the hanging ropes were drawn until the feet of each man dangled four feet above the ground. The loose ends were tied off and then the crowd dispersed. A half hour later Charles' face appeared distorted as the noose had cut deeply into the fold of his neck, but John's countenance in death showed no distress. Coroner Moody did not arrive until 9:00 a.m., and then the bodies were cut down and the inquest was held that afternoon.

Sources: *Los Angeles Herald (CA)*: May 31, 1892. *Sacramento Daily Union (CA)*: June 20, 1892; July 25, 1892. *San Francisco Call (CA)*: May 15, 1892; May 11, 1892; May 31, 1892; July 25, 1892.

UNKNOWN, MARCH 22, 1895

On Friday, March 22, 1895, just after dusk the stagecoach from Weaverville had just topped the last hill before entering Redding and driver Richard Heath snapped his whip to increase his speed to a gallop. Messenger Haskell was seated next to the driver, and three passengers were riding inside. Just then the command came from the right and just behind the coach, "Hold up!

Hold up! Hold up! Throw down that box." Haskell lifted his shotgun to the ready just as there were two quick reports from a pistol and the "ping" of two bullets, and the flash pinpointed the road agent in the heavy brush. Haskell then aimed at the flash and let loose both barrels from his shotgun as Heath whipped up the team and drove the coach, passengers, and the treasure out of danger. As soon as the coach was a short distance away Heath stopped and Haskell returned to the spot of the attempted robbery, but he could find no sign of the highwayman nor any clue to his identity. Haskell returned to the coach, the driver hurried into town, and the sheriff was notified of the attempted robbery. At the scene there were no clues nor a trail to follow.

Source: *San Francisco Call (CA)*: March 23, 1895.

HENRY "JACK BRADY" WILLIAMS, JULY 6, 1895; JULY 8, 1895

At 11:00 p.m. on Saturday, July 6, 1895, the westbound stagecoach from Bieber to Redding was thirty miles from its destination and had just started down the Bullskin grade when a short, heavyset road agent in a dark mask ordered the driver to halt. He ordered driver Jay Smith to throw down the two Wells, Fargo express boxes and the mailbags, and they were deposited onto the road. There were two passengers aboard, a man and a woman, but they were not molested, and the registered packages were not requested. Once the robber had his plunder he ordered Smith to move on. As soon as the coach was out of sight the robber broke open the boxes and took out $150, and he cut the straps of one mailbag and rifled the contents, but there was nothing of value inside so he left the other bag unmolested. A posse rode to the scene and collected the boxes and the mailbags and returned them to Redding, and the registered packages, which had remained on the coach, were secured at Oak Run. Marshal Gard and Sheriff Bogard, brother of the sheriff murdered by Jack Brady, and post office inspector McGarrey went to the scene, but all they could determine was that the road agent had fled in the direction of the little hamlet of Morley, four miles away. Another posse was led by Sheriff Houston with Constable Campbell, but they had no better luck, and all the lawmen were certain that the man they were after was Jack Brady.

On Monday morning, July 8, 1895, the stagecoach from Redding to Alturas, with Jay Smith driving, had traveled twenty-four miles, two miles from Morley's station, when a lone road agent, masked and armed, halted the coach and demanded the Wells, Fargo express box and the mail. These were thrown onto the road, and the robber then told the driver to move along. There were two passengers on board but they were not molested. The driver hurried to Morley's station and reported that the road agent was five feet six inches tall, heavyset, and resembled the fugitive Jack Brady. It was later learned that the road agent took $400 from the box, but the value of the mail was not known, or at least not disclosed. Posses went out in all directions to try to cut off the road agent's flight, but they failed to find him though the search continued.

On July 16 the last of the posse men returned to Redding and the chase was abandoned. Brady was spotted ten days later at Courtland and when he was surrounded he surrendered meekly, then insisted his real name was Henry Williams. He was not charged with the stagecoach robberies. In August 1895, as Williams, the defendant was tried for the March 30 murder of Sheriff James J. Bogard, and in November he was sentenced to serve a life term at San Quentin. In 1913, after serving eighteen years, Williams (Brady) was paroled, which outraged the citizens of Shasta County, but the governor would not rescind the parole. Williams, who then insisted his name was Henry Ury, lived nearly three decades and died while still on parole.

Sources: *Los Angeles Herald (CA)*: July 9, 1895. *Sacramento Daily Union (CA)*: July 9–11, 1895; August 1, 1895. *San Francisco Call (CA)*: July 9, 1895; July 11, 1895; July 17, 1895

Unknown, August 18, 1896

At 3:00 a.m. on Tuesday, August 18, 1896, the southbound stagecoach from Bieber to Redding, with Jasper Hampton driving, was twenty-five miles from its destination near the hamlet of Morley when a lone road agent, masked and armed with a shotgun, stepped out from behind a tree and halted the coach. The robber demanded the Wells, Fargo express box, but there was none aboard, so he demanded the mail. Hampton threw down the way-pouch but saved the through-pouch, which contained all the registered packages, and the robber then told him to drive on without asking about passengers. As the coach was leaving Hampton looked back and saw the robber, with the sack slung across his shoulder, leisurely strolling down the road in the opposite direction. A posse rode to the scene but could find no clues, and the pursuit was abandoned. On August 20 the mail sack was found some distance from the road, with the top cut off and the letters rifled, but nothing had been opened or taken when the robber realized he had the way-pouch. Everything was gathered and taken into town to be made up for a fresh start. After the sack was found, Sheriff T. J. Houston rode to the place and from there took up the trail again, but he had no better luck with the new starting place.

Sources: *Los Angeles Herald (CA)*: August 19, 1896. *Sacramento Daily Union (CA)*: August 19, 1896. *San Francisco Call (CA)*: August 19, 1896; August 21, 1896.

Unknown, June 25, 1897

At 9:00 p.m. on Friday, June 25, 1897, the stagecoach from the rail depot to the town of Keswick, a distance of one mile, was traveling through an area where there was thick chaparral along the roadside. Suddenly someone called to the driver to rein in his horse and he stopped, thinking he had a passenger. A masked, armed road agent then appeared and asked, "What have you in the stage?" J. McMeekin, the driver who was a deputy sheriff, replied, "That!" as he drew his revolver and fired a shot at the robber. The road agent yelled out in pain and ran into the brush, but as it was pitch black, McMeekin did not follow. Instead he returned to town and delivered the mail and express box and quickly organized a posse. He directed them to the scene of the attempted robbery, and they began searching the area for the road agent and found evidence that he had been wounded. A check of the town found that a particular rough character, who had been loitering about, was nowhere to be seen, and it was believed he was the road agent. That suspicious character had been hanging around the Wells, Fargo office and saw that the driver carried a considerable amount of money on that trip. After searching for some time, the robber could not be found.

Source: *San Francisco Call (CA)*: June 26, 1897.

Unknown, December 21, 1902; June 9, 1903

On Tuesday, December 16, 1902, a "footpad" with a handkerchief over his head and another across his mouth and chin robbed two men near Keswick, brandishing a small revolver. At 9:30 a.m. on Sunday, December 21, 1902, the stagecoach from Redding to Weaverville, with driver James Wilson handling the four-horse team, was climbing the steep grade to an altitude of two thousand feet, four miles above Shasta, with seven passengers aboard: Miss Rebecca "Becky" Martinez, Mr. Fritz C. Meckel and his bride returning from their honeymoon, Frank Woods, C. C. Braton, William Jackson, and S. M. Fleming. The horses were traveling at a slow rate struggling in the deep mud when a lone road agent, masked with a handkerchief over his head and another over his mouth and chin, suddenly appeared and with a small cocked pistol pointed at Wilson's head ordered the driver to "Stop!" He ordered the passengers to get out and form a line and then made each man remove his coat and vest, and the ladies had to remove their coats, and he had them throw the garments onto the ground and then place their money, watches and jewelry on top of their clothing. The robber began to collect his plunder when Robert Carson of Shasta, with his nine-year-old daughter, drove up in a buggy and tried to pass the coach, thinking it had broken down. The road agent pointed his revolver at Carson and told him to stay where he was, and he stayed and watched the proceedings. Once the robber had gone through the garments and collected his plunder, he ordered Wilson to throw down the Wells, Fargo express boxes, and as soon as they were in the road he ordered the passengers to board and he told Wilson to drive on. Before boarding, passenger Meckel asked the robber to return his watch as it had been a gift from his mother, and the robber returned it with the remark, "I once had a mother and any gift from her was appreciated." S. M. Fleming then said his watch was a gift from his wife, and it was returned. The driver was not molested, and the road agent did not ask for the mail pouches. The coach and Carson's buggy then continued, and just as they rounded a bend the robber fired two shots into the air, then fled up the mountainside carrying the two express boxes. Wilson whipped up his team and hurried into Whiskeytown where he telephoned Sheriff Behrens in Redding and described the road agent as slim built, five feet eight inches tall. The sheriff, with undersheriff Richardson and Wells, Fargo messenger Daniel Haskell, rode to the scene, followed a trail for one hundred yards, and recovered the broken boxes in a small gulch. The boxes had been blown open with a small piece of dynamite placed in each lock, and the robber left behind the pouch holding the waybills and two packages of jewelry addressed to A. Fetzer at Weaverville. An inventory of his loot included $120 from the passengers, as well as watches, rings, and brooches, but the amount in the boxes was not reported. Miss Martinez had dropped her money in the coach, and Woods had dropped his watch and money down his pant leg, saving it from the robber. That evening Haskell struck out on his own to search for the robber while the posse, with bloodhounds, continued on the trail of the lone road agent heading toward Muletown. He managed to elude capture and identification, so the lawmen returned to Redding empty-handed and waited for some development in the case.

At 5:30 p.m. on Tuesday, June 9, 1903, the stagecoach from Weaverville to Redding, driven by James Wilson, was halted past the old town of Shasta. There were eight passengers aboard and the coach was traveling at a rapid gait when it reached the four-mile post on the Camden turnpike, and Mrs. H. C. Ferris of French Gulch called to the driver that she thought she heard an order to halt. Wilson thought she had imagined the order, so he continued until there were two shots fired and both his leaders collapsed dead. Two road agents, one tall the other small, then appeared, with one coming from each side of the road, and the taller one covered Wilson while the smaller robber demanded the Wells, Fargo express boxes. As soon as the two boxes were thrown down the road agent giving the orders told the passengers to get out and form a line. The smaller robber then went to each and, holding a sack, ordered them to deposit their money, watches, and jewelry, and they contributed as follows: M. Getz, $125; Ed M. Lynn, $40 and a gold watch; E. H. Hoag, $30; B. Carter, $50 and a watch; George Jinamini, $22 and a watch; Fred Condon, $45; Mrs. Ferris, $45; D. McCurdy, $7 in silver, but he saved $75 by putting it in his shoe before stepping out; and driver Wilson, a gold watch. Once the smaller road agent finished with the passengers he left them standing and called for the mail sacks; they were thrown down and cut open, and the registered mail pouches were taken. Each road agent then lifted an express box onto his shoulder and they backed into the brush and fled. As the passengers were boarding, a prospector happened along and Wilson sent him back to Shasta to telephone the officers in Redding, where Deputy Richardson organized a posse of twenty deputies and rode to the scene, and they found the robbers' trail heading west toward Clear Creek. In Redding, Wells, Fargo reported that there was little in the boxes, but they believed the robbers had expected to intercept the gold shipment from the Lappin mine, which was about $5,000 in gold. On June

12 a report from the Mount Shasta mine superintendent, Harry Paige, said that two suspicious men were seen at a tunnel in the Happy Jack group of mining claims and they had slipped into the tunnel when they thought they were spotted. A posse rode there but the men had already slipped away. By June 13 Deputy George Wiley, with half-breed trackers Dick Zedecker and Frank Marsh, had taken up the trail from a point near the mining tunnel using bloodhounds. Later that day the trackers were combing the area around Brandy Creek when they found two rifle cartridges and an unopened package of Cayenne pepper, dropped by accident. The items were found on the trail the men were following, two clear sets of foot tracks, but the tunnel sighting reported by Paige turned out to be a "wild goose chase," as there was no evidence anyone had been in the tunnel for some time.

As the investigation continued, suspicion focused on two men—ex-convicts George Dalton, alias George Davis, and James Barry. On September 9 officer John P. Colford of Marysville was in Chico and he happened onto Dalton, arrested him and turned him over to the marshal at Chico. It was not long, however, before these two suspects were cleared and no one was arrested for the robbery.

Sources: *Los Angeles Herald (CA)*: December 22, 1902; June 13, 1903. *San Francisco Call (CA)*: December 22, 1902; June 10–11, 1903; June 14, 1903; September 10, 1903.

UNKNOWN, OCTOBER 9, 1905

On Monday, October 9, 1905, the stagecoach from Redding to Delamar, with no passengers aboard, left town at 7:00 a.m. carrying a payroll of $10,000 for the employees of the Bully Hill smelter and mine. Wells, Fargo messenger Daniel N. "Dan" Haskell was riding atop as far as Delamar to protect the treasure. As the coach rolled down a small incline a mile and a quarter from Bear Valley, three miles west of the Pit River bridge, an unmasked man with a rifle stepped out from behind an improvised shield made of barrel staves, fifteen feet ahead of the coach, and shouted, "Halt! Throw up your hands." Driver Durfor ignored the command and whipped up his horses, and the robber began shooting. The first bullet struck Haskell in his abdomen and the second went through his left foot, but he returned fire with both barrels of his sawed-off scattergun. Haskell then pulled his revolver and aimed, but before he could fire, a third bullet from the robber struck the cylinder and disabled Haskell's revolver; that bullet would have struck Haskell in his head had it not been deflected by his pistol. Durfor continued to whip his team forward, and the robber chased after the coach on foot for one hundred yards, firing at Durfor and Haskell all the while. One bullet pierced the letter sack and another the paper sack holding the U.S. mail, but no more bullets struck Haskell or Durfor and they quickly drove out of range of the robber's rifle. Durfor, as he held the reins in one hand, then took hold of Haskell who was weakening, and held the messenger on the seat. They hurried into Bear Valley, and Marion Gregory left immediately for the Pit River bridge to telephone Delamar and Redding. Posses were organized at each end of the route and they started out for the scene. Dr. White started out from Redding for Bear Valley with Mrs. Haskell and Wells, Fargo express agent R. G. Dunn, and they returned to Redding with the wounded man that night. By the next morning it seemed Haskell might recover, but late in the day he weakened and fell into a "deep sleep" from which he never awoke, and he was pronounced dead at 7:45 p.m. The coroner convened a jury, and driver Durfor testified that the robber resembled teamster George Cody. Haskell was buried on October 13, the same day his replacement arrived in Redding.

Evidence at the scene first indicated that two men were involved, but why the second man, from concealment, had not become involved when the shooting began was a mystery. There was a cord one hundred yards long stretching from the place of concealment to the improvised shield, and Undersheriff Behrens later said that it appeared the lone road agent had wedged a rifle or shotgun among the rocks and tied the cord to the trigger, planning to pull the cord and make it seem as if there was a second man covering the driver. However, events happened so quickly that he did not have time to pull the cord, but he collected up the second weapon before leaving. Behrens, after he returned to town on the 10th, said the posse was on the robber's trail heading toward the Pit River while a second posse was on the other side of the river hoping to cut off the robber if he crossed over, and said that they would take bloodhounds to the scene the next day. Lawmen and Wells, Fargo detectives were persistent in their efforts to find the murderer of messenger Haskell. On October 11 George Cody was detained and questioned, but he proved he was nowhere near the scene of the robbery and was released. On October 12 a lone hunter was held and questioned by a posse, but he proved an alibi and was released, and a report was received that the road agent, carrying his rifle, had been seen near tunnel number 9 by a train crew, but that man could not be found. Rumors then circulated that the road agent had been captured and quietly taken to Red Bluff to avoid a lynching, but this proved false. On November 4 John Wilson was arrested, but he proved himself innocent and was released. On November 23 J. Swinney and C. George were arrested and taken to Redding for questioning, but the following day they proved an alibi and were released. The investigation continued for five months when C. C. "Con" Hardwick and Charles Whitescarbor were arrested, questioned, and released. Several lawmen had, from the beginning, been suspicious of a quarter-breed Indian named Popejoy but it was not until June 12, 1906, that he was arrested and questioned about the murder, and he provided an alibi which proved to be true and he was released. Nearly four years later, on July 4, 1909, James A. Roberts was arrested for Haskell's murder, questioned and investigated, and he was also proved innocent of that crime and released. There were no more clues forthcoming, and though everyone involved kept looking for the right man, there was never anyone identified as the murderer of Dan Haskell.

Sources: *San Francisco Call (CA)*: October 10–13, 1905; November 5, 1905; November 24–25, 1905; June 12, 1906; July 4, 1909.

Sierra County

UNKNOWN, SEPTEMBER 6, 1858

In Marysville there was reportedly a woman who persisted in wearing men's clothing, drinking whiskey, and gambling, and doing nearly all things masculine. In late August "Dutch Kate" had lost $2,000 playing cards at Marysville, and she was desperate to earn a new stake. At 3:00 a.m. on Monday morning, September 6, 1858, the stagecoach left Forest City for Nevada City with ten passengers aboard, among them a gold buyer named Nichols, and everyone knew that Nichols left every Monday with the purchases he had made the previous week. On this trip he was carrying $15,000 in gold dust for his employer Langston & Company at Downieville. Nichols did not put his gold dust in the company express box but instead hid the sack beneath the back seat inside the passenger compartment. Shortly after leaving town the coach reached the top of a hill, where the horses were walking slowly and spent, when three masked "men" armed with pistols ran out of the bushes and commanded driver William Wilson, "Halt! Throw down that box." Wilson reined in his team, and then the robber on the left took a position in front of the nigh-wheeler while the other took up a position behind the off-wheeler, directly beneath the driver. Upon demand Wilson threw down the mailbag, and then upon a second command he threw down the Langston & Company treasure box. The man behind the off-wheeler then demanded the bag that was hidden under the back seat but Wilson said he knew nothing of it, and then the third "man" in position near the coach door replied, "All right." The leader either believed that Nichols' sack was inside the treasure box, or the other robber who had spoken had already secured it, as he told Wilson to drive on. Wilson immediately whipped up the team and they galloped off, and it was not until daylight that Wilson learned that the sack of gold dust had not been stolen. At Cold Springs Nichols crawled out of the stagecoach with the sack of gold dust in hand, and when the coach reached Nevada City, he telegraphed his company headquarters the details of the robbery. In return Nichols received a telegram stating that, with the gold dust in his possession, the robbers had got nothing from the box. The driver later insisted that the third "man," who had said "All right," was Dutch Kate, and she had missed her chance to earn a share of the $15,000. However, there is no record of Dutch Kate being arrested or prosecuted, and the identities of the other two road agents remained a mystery.

Source: *Sacramento Daily Union (CA)*: September 9, 1858.

JOSE MACHADO, TRINIDAD NUNEZ AND UNKNOWN, JULY 26, 1877

On July 26, 1877, the coach from Marysville to Downieville, driven by Dave Quadlin, was halted by three Mexican road agents when four miles north of Camptonville. On board were seven passengers, including A. M. Crocker of San Francisco and Isaac Elias of Downieville who rode on top with the driver, and inside were Antonio Macon with his wife and two daughters, and one Chinaman. The robbers demanded the Wells, Fargo express box, but there was none aboard. The two road agents "went through" Macon, an Italian, taking $40, and from the Chinaman they took $22. They did not molest the mother and daughters, the driver, or the passengers riding on top. A posse was soon in the field and tracked the three men to a point near San Juan, where they captured two while the third road agent made his escape. The two prisoners identified themselves as Jose Machado and Trinidad Nunez, and they were lodged in the Sierra County jail; at their examination they were held over to answer to the grand jury. In early October the two defendants were indicted and tried, and they were found guilty of the robbery after only a half hour of jury deliberations. Sentencing was postponed so that their attorney, F. D. Soward, could argue a motion for a new trial, but the motion was denied. Machado, the leader of the road agents, was then sentenced to serve fourteen years while Nunez was sentenced to serve eight years at San Quentin. Both men arrived at the prison on October 18, 1877, with Machado registering as convict #7834 and Nunez registering as convict #7833. Nunez was discharged, by expiration of sentence, on February 17, 1883, while Machado was discharged on August 18, 1886, after serving less than nine years. Neither man would "peach," or inform, on the third robber, so he was never identified.

Sources: *The Daily Appeal (Marysville, CA)*: July 27, 1877; July 28, 1877; October 10, 1877.

WILLIAM SMITH, JUNE 29, 1881; AUGUST 15, 1881

On November 1, 1879, William Smith carefully selected a position on the road between Carson City and Aurora in Douglas County, Nevada, for the purpose of robbing the stagecoach. As the stagecoach approached, Smith discovered a carriage a few hundred yards in the rear of the coach. Fearing interference, he allowed the stagecoach to pass unmolested, but he stopped the carriage and robbed the occupant, a Mr. Kilgore, of a valuable gold watch and a small sum of money. He was tracked down, arrested and, using the name Charles P. Weibusch, convicted of robbery, but he had confessed his intention when he robbed Kilgore. He arrived at the Nevada State Prison on December 17, 1879, and registered as prisoner #117, serving a term of five years, and he was pardoned and released on April 12, 1881. He had not been given the opportunity to execute his plan to rob a stagecoach, so he went to California looking for just such an opportunity. On June 29, 1881, William Smith, alias Charles P. Weibusch, took up a position along the road four miles south of Sierraville in Sierra County where he planned to capture the stagecoach bound for Truckee in Nevada County. While waiting in ambush, Sol Rousseau appeared with a light wagon and six passengers. The robber stood them all up in a line out of sight of the road for one and a half hours, until the stagecoach from Sierra Valley arrived. This coach contained four passengers, all of whom were ordered to get down and join the others, except for driver, G. Q. Buxton, who was obliged to deliver and break open the Wells, Fargo express box with a rock and hand out the contents. While this was going on two other vehicles approached and the driver in each was ordered to get down and "mingle with the audience." At the close of the afternoon's performance, Smith had thirteen men, sixteen horses, and four vehicles "under the control of his little shotgun." On August 15, 1881, Smith set up a similar ambush at the same place and again stopped and robbed the Sierraville stagecoach bound for Truckee. Once again he made the driver break open the box and dump out the contents before he ordered him to continue on. In neither robbery did Smith molest the passengers nor ask for the mail. (See Calaveras County on December 29, 1881.)

JOHN MARSHALL, GEORGE B. SAYLOR AND JAMES MARTIN, AUGUST 13, 1883; OCTOBER 15, 1883

On Monday, August 13, 1883, the stagecoach from Sierra Valley to Truckee driven by G. Q. Buxton, the proprietor of the stage line, was stopped near the Little Truckee River in Sierra County. The two masked highwaymen demanded the Wells, Fargo treasure box, one pointing a shotgun and the other a revolver at Buxton. He threw out the box, and the road agents then went through the passengers, five men and one woman, and collected another $60. They kept the box, which contained $976 in gold dust, and sent Buxton on his way. The two men decided to return to the "states" and visit family, so they went to Omaha where they were arrested when they tried to sell the dust. After a careful, but flawed, investigation by the Nebraska authorities, no charges were filed and they were released. Once their money ran out Marshall returned to California while his partner struck out for Baltimore, Maryland.

On Monday, October 15, 1883, the stagecoach from Sierra Valley to Truckee was stopped by two road agents when it was near Cooley's station. Both road agents were masked and armed with six-shooters, which they brandished as they demanded the Wells, Fargo express box. G. Q. Buxton, the same driver robbed on August 13, threw down the box and they required him to get down from his seat and break it open. After they removed the gold dust from the box they went through the passengers, taking their money and jewelry, in all collecting $300.

Lawmen were soon on the trail of the road agents and on Sunday, October 21, the first road agent was captured by Captain Charles Aull at Wadsworth, and he gave the name John Marshall, but he used aliases William Simpson and Robinson. The prisoner had on his person some of the gold dust taken from the stagecoach and the jewelry taken from the passengers. Marshall was well known to the lawmen as he had robbed the Forbestown stagecoach in 1874; but Wells, Fargo detective James B. Hume had made a deal in that case to recover the treasure and the charge was reduced to grand larceny for stealing the shotgun he used to stop the stagecoach, and he was sentenced to serve only three years at San Quentin. Marshall, on the promise from Aull that he would intercede to see he did not get a life sentence, gave a full confession, naming George B. Saylor as his partner in the August 13 robbery. The second road agent from the October 15 robbery was soon arrested on the information provided by Marshall and he gave the name James

Martin, and he was new to the business. Marshall and Martin were lodged in the Oroville jail, and when taken into court, both men pled guilty. Marshall was given a sentence of fifteen years, and Martin was sentenced to a term of five years at San Quentin. Both men arrived at the prison on November 1, 1883, where Martin registered as convict #11013 and Marshall registered as convict #11014. Martin was discharged, by expiration of sentence, on June 1, 1887, and Marshall was discharged on April 1, 1893, after serving two-thirds of his sentence.

The search for Saylor continued, and on January 19 the *Mountain Messenger* reported, "George B. Saylor was recently arrested in Baltimore, Maryland and will arrive in Colfax on Tuesday on his way to jail in Downieville." The sheriff of a Pennsylvania county, where Saylor's well-to-do father lived, was sent to arrest the fugitive but, by mistake, arrested George's brother. George then fled to Baltimore, Maryland, and prepared to board a ship for Europe, but a Baltimore detective arrested him before he could board and started the road agent on the train for California. Saylor, who was then only twenty years old, arrived on Tuesday, January 22, 1884, and freely admitted the crime, but said he was induced by Marshall to rob the stagecoach. He was taken before Judge Howe for his examination where he confessed, pled guilty, and was ordered to return on Monday, January 28, for sentencing. Saylor was given a term of seven years and arrived at San Quentin on February 2, 1884, registering as convict #11118. Saylor was discharged on November 3, 1888, after serving only four years and nine months.

Sources: *Mountain Messenger (Downieville, CA)*: August 18, 1883; October 20, 1883; November 3, 1883; January 19, 1884; January 26, 1884; February 2, 1884.

UNKNOWN, SEPTEMBER 20, 1886

On Monday, September 20, 1886, the regular stagecoach from Sierraville to Truckee was stopped by two road agents, masked and armed. They demanded the Wells, Fargo express box, but the driver told them that he had none aboard, as the Wells, Fargo office at Sierraville had been discontinued. One of the road agents climbed up and checked the boot and, finding that the driver told the truth, told him to move on. There were no passengers aboard and there was no mention of mail. It was reported that the two men were known and would soon be in custody, but there were no rewards posted so the motivation to capture them was lacking, and it appears no one was charged with the robbery.

Sources: *Daily Alta California (San Francisco)*: September 21, 1886. *Sacramento Daily Union (CA)*: September 21, 1886. *Territorial Enterprise (Virginia City, NV)*: September 23, 1886.

JOHN SANSOME, JUNE 28, 1887

On Tuesday, June 28, 1887, the stagecoach from Forest City was nearing the Mountain House when driver Thomas Davis heard a command to halt. As he turned his head he saw a heavyset man wearing a mask standing above him on a dirt bank. The man, without further hesitation, fired his shotgun, and one pellet cut the driver's whip at the handle, another buckshot took off Davis' left thumb, and a third buckshot pellet struck passenger Ben Treloar in his right knee, shattering it. The shot frightened the horses and they took off at a run, leaving the road agent behind, but Davis kept control of the team and safely took the coach to Mountain House. The two wounded men were taken off the coach and sent to the county seat at Downieville for medical treatment, while the robbery attempt was reported to lawmen who started from Downieville and Forest City in pursuit. A large force of men were deputized and issued rifles, and they began scouring the countryside for any sign of the road agent, but to no avail. The following day Davis had the stump of his left thumb amputated at his hand, and Treloar had his right leg amputated above the knee. Davis was expected to recover but Treloar's condition was considered serious; it was believed he might not survive, but he rallied and recovered. The posse at the scene of the shooting could find no clue to the robber's identity, nor a clear trail to follow for any distance. On August 11 the same robber would rob a stagecoach near Michigan Bluff. (See also Placer County on August 11, 1887.)

Sources: *Daily Alta California (San Francisco)*: June 30, 1887. *Los Angeles Herald (CA)*: June 29, 1887. *Sacramento Daily Union (CA)*: June 30, 1887.

UNKNOWN, NOVEMBER 8, 1888

At 11:00 a.m. on Thursday, November 8, 1888, the Greene, Cole, & Company stagecoach from Downieville to Camptonville, driven by C. F. Johnson, had just reached the summit of Dutch Hill, near Nigger Tent in Sierra County, when a road agent with a red silk mask and a musket stepped out of hiding and ordered a halt. Johnson reined in his four-horse team and the road agent, a small man, then demanded that he throw out the mail pouches and the Wells, Fargo express boxes, and he received two boxes and three pouches. There were two passengers aboard, a Mr. Leek and a Mr. Chapman, but they were not molested. As soon as the robber had his plunder on the roadway he ordered the driver to continue, and Johnson whipped up his team and hurried to the next station to make his report. In the two boxes was a gold bar and coin valued at $2,500, but there was no estimate of the value of the mail and packages. It was the policy of the company to have a messenger aboard when the treasure was valued at more than $2,500, but there may have been some confusion with treasure split between the two boxes so there was no shotgun messenger on that trip. The boxes were found later near the scene, broken open and the contents rifled, and everything that had no value to the road agent had been left behind. It was gathered up and delivered to the Wells, Fargo office in Camptonville. The mail pouches had been carried off and were not recovered. Wells, Fargo's chief detective James B. Hume arrived on November 9 to investigate, and before he left for San Francisco at noon on November 13 he had concluded that the robber "was local talent." He had left some clothing which was identified as from that part of the county, but still he was never identified.

Sources: *Sacramento Daily Union (CA)*: November 10, 1888; November 13, 1888. *Territorial Enterprise (Virginia City, NV)*: November 10, 1888.

UNKNOWN, NOVEMBER 7, 1892

On Monday, November 7, 1892, the stagecoach running between Downieville and Sierra City was halted by a lone road agent, masked and armed, who demanded the Wells, Fargo express box. It was thrown down, and the robber immediately told the driver to continue on. The driver hurried into Sierra City and reported the robbery, but the box had contained nothing of value so there was no reward posted and no motivation to pursue the road agent.

Source: *Los Angeles Herald (CA)*: November 9, 1892.

UNKNOWN, JULY 3, 1902

At 10:00 a.m. on Friday, July 3, 1902, the stagecoach from Truckee to Sierraville driven by owner A. L. Richardson reached the top of Sage Hen Hill, just over the line in Sierra County, when a lone road agent armed with a rifle stepped out and pointed his weapon at Richardson's head. The driver reined in his team, and the robber then ordered him down and had his ten passengers step out and line up along the roadside. He told them he would not rob them but wanted only the Wells, Fargo treasure box. Richardson told him there was no treasure box, as he carried it only as far as Overton and had dropped it off. The robber checked the boot and found nothing, and while he was preoccupied, one of the passengers pulled out a pistol. The robber saw the movement and he jumped down and fled into the woods empty-handed. At Sierraville the attempted robbery was reported and officers went out to pursue the road agent, but they were not able to find a trail to follow or any clue to his identity.

Source: *Los Angeles Herald (CA)*: July 4, 1902.

Siskiyou County

ALEXANDER CONDREY, ELI KELLY AND INDIAN BILLY, OCTOBER 16, 1876

A lone road agent began operating in the Shasta area, and this prompted the *Shasta Courier* to comment, "Four stage robberies within fifteen miles of Shasta inside of four weeks is pretty rough." The first robbery by this "lone" road agent was on October 16, 1876, actually in Siskiyou County, when the stagecoach from Scott's Bar in Siskiyou County bound for Fort Jones in Trinity County was stopped a few miles from Scott's Bar and robbed of $1,250 in gold belonging to A. B. Carlock. The robber, armed with a double-barreled shotgun, had blackened his face so it seemed that identification would have been difficult. However, on October 18 Indian Billy was arrested at Scott's River, and as soon as he was behind bars he confessed to his part in the robbery and named his accomplices. He said the robbery was planned by Alexander Condrey, but he did not go with him and the Kelly brothers. The Kelly brothers remained in hiding, in case there was resistance, while Indian Billy disguised himself and stopped the coach. After they had the plunder they returned to Condrey, who divided the gold dust and gave each man his share. On October 19 the *Daily Alta California* newspaper reported that Alexander Condree (*sic*) and the Kelly brothers had been arrested at Oak Bar. One of the Kelly brothers was exonerated and released, but the other three men were tried in December. Condrey, Indian Billy, and Eli Kelly were convicted of robbery, and in early January 1877 they were sentenced to serve terms at San Quentin: Condrey to serve ten years, Kelly to serve eight years, and Indian Billy to serve five years. All three men arrived at the prison on January 7, with Alex Condrey registering as prisoner #7332, Kelly registered as prisoner #7331, and Indian Billy registered as prisoner #7330. Indian Billy died in prison on December 19, 1878, and Condrey and Kelly were discharged on August 6, 1880, after serving three years seven months.

Source: *Daily Alta California (San Francisco)*: October 20, 1876.

WILLIAM BARBER AND WILLIAM "JOE" BLANCHARD, JULY 18, 1877

On July 11, 1877, William Barber and William Blanchard, or John "Joe" Blanchard, robbed a sheep ranch on the McCloud River and took $300 in property, including a needle gun and a double-barreled shotgun, in preparation for robbing a stagecoach. On Wednesday, July 18, the northbound California & Oregon stagecoach from Redding, driven by Tom Tyndall, was one and a half miles north of Soda Springs in Siskiyou County when the two road agents stepped out of the brush and halted the coach. They were masked, one wielding the stolen needle gun and the other the stolen double-barreled shotgun. There was only one passenger aboard, and he was riding atop with the driver. The road agents ordered them to throw off the express box and mail sacks. The passenger threw out the mail sacks while the driver controlled his team, and Tyndall then informed the road agents that the box was chained to the coach and could not be thrown down. One of the robbers next ordered the driver and passenger to step down and had Tyndall take his place at the heads of the leaders to control the team. They demanded the tool sack, and it was delivered; they found nothing inside they could use, so one robber took the ax belonging to the stage and chopped open the box while the other guarded the driver and passenger with the shotgun. They took out everything including some letters and $600, then decided they had done well enough with the treasure box and ordered the passenger to put the mail sacks back onto the coach without opening them. They asked for nothing from the passenger except his labor and cooperation. They finally ordered the two men to board and continue on their way. The driver hurried into Sisson's station and reported the robbery.

Siskiyou County deputy sheriff John Hendricks of Yreka, Charles Carroll, and Richard Hubbard, with two Indian trackers, went to the scene of the robbery and took the track of the two robbers "through some of the roughest country ever traveled." The Indians, Sisson's "Indian Jim" and Bob Pitt's "Indian Charley" trailed the two men for forty miles to a point six miles from Trinity Center, near Bard & Morton's ranch on the fork of the Trinity River. The two men had concealed their camp in a deep, brushy gulch where, on Saturday afternoon, July 21, the two road agents were cornered. The lawmen got the drop on them, but one, later identified as Blanchard, immediately turned and started to run. He was ordered to halt, but when he continued to try to make his escape, Carroll shot him with a load of buckshot. The pellets took effect in the small of Blanchard's back and traveled to his hips. The wound was thought to be a mortal one, so Blanchard was left in the care of Carroll while Hendricks took Barber to Marysville and lodged him in jail. All the money from the stagecoach holdup was recovered, except $6, and the guns stolen from the sheep ranch and used in the robbery were also found with the two men.

Barber, once behind bars, began to talk, and he said he first met Blanchard at Reno, Nevada, a year earlier and they had been together, robbing and stealing, ever since. Wells, Fargo's chief detective James Hume interrogated the prisoners and Blanchard claimed to be a French-Canadian while Barber admitted he was a longtime resident of Ventura County, California, and each man confessed all the details of the robbery. Four days after Blanchard was wounded, his condition had improved and it was thought he would recover, but he suddenly took a turn for the worse and died on the evening of July 24.

Barber was examined before a justice of the peace and held over for action by the grand jury. He was indicted and tried in Siskiyou County in October and easily convicted on the evidence, testimony, and his confession. He was sentenced to serve a term of fifteen years at San Quentin, arriving at the prison on October 17, 1877, and registering as prisoner #7831. Barber was discharged on March 17, 1887, after serving less than ten years.

Sources: *Marysville Appeal (CA)*: July 20, 1877; July 24, 1877; July 26–27, 1877. *Sacramento Daily Union (CA)*: July 19, 1877; July 23, 1877. *Shasta Courier (CA)*: July 23, 1877; August 4, 1877. *Territorial Enterprise (Virginia City, NV)*: July 21, 1877.

THOMAS JACKSON, ANDREW MARSH AND MARTIN TRACY, SEPTEMBER 7, 1878

Thirty-year-old Thomas Jackson entered San Quentin on November 7, 1865, convicted of "assault to murder." He spent sixteen months before being released by expiration of sentence. In less than a year he was back in prison serving an eight-year term, this time for a robbery in Alameda County. Again he received no executive clemency and was released by expiration of sentence on September 23, 1874. Within a few months Jackson committed a burglary in San Mateo County, was captured, convicted, and sentenced to serve five years, arriving at the prison on March 18, 1875. California's Governor William Irwin, this time, commuted his sentence to four and a half years, and he was released on July 8, 1878. While in prison Jackson met Martin Tracy, a man serving his second term in prison—the first a three-year sentence for grand larceny and the second a term of three years for burglary. Once released the two ex-convicts rendezvoused and went on a spree, but as their funds ran low they began planning to rob a stagecoach when they met Andrew "Andy" Marsh and decided they could use three men for the job. Marsh was also an ex-convict who had learned the shoemaking trade in prison, but after a while working at his newfound trade he was ready for action and some easy money.

The trio headed north into Siskiyou County, an area where they were not known. After they sized up the situation they set up their ambush along the Yreka to Redding stagecoach route, four hundred yards below the summit of the Scott Mountain grade. Here the horses would be walking at a slow pace and would be relatively spent from the hard pull up the steep incline. The stagecoach approached at 3:30 a.m., so the three men pulled over their heads flour sacks with eyeholes cut in them. They had with them an "improved" Winchester model '76, a double-barreled shotgun, and each man had a six-shooter revolver. They suddenly stepped out in front of the horses, Jackson with the rifle and Tracy with the shotgun, and Marsh brandished his revolver, and they pointed their weapons at driver Charlie Williams. They ordered Williams, who was alone on the seat, to halt, and then Tracy and Jackson stepped up to the four-horse team on each side and grabbed the reins of the leaders, while Marsh stepped up to the driver and told him to raise his hands. The driver shifted the whip and reins to his right hand and raised his left, then said to the robber, "Lower your pistol, I have no arms." The robber, seeing he had the driver under his control, lowered his pistol. The driver's comment was meant to alert Wells, Fargo's messenger John E. Reynolds, who was riding inside with the treasure box, and give him time to react. Reynolds took but a moment before he pushed his shotgun out the window and shot Marsh in the chest and neck, causing gaping wounds which resulted in instant death, though the road agent's pistol discharged when he jerked his hand in a death grip. Jackson and Tracy, seeing Marsh killed, began their retreat while firing wildly at the driver and coach, mortally wounding the nigh-wheeler. Reynolds could not reload fast enough to shoot at the retreating road agents before they disappeared into the brush and the team, startled by the gunfire, bolted and ran seventy-five yards before the nigh (left) wheeler fell dead, peppered with buckshot. James Hume, Wells, Fargo's chief detective, asked that the horse not be destroyed or buried until all the shot was removed, and he saved the buckshot as evidence.

The dead wheeler was unhitched and the coach continued to the next station with three horses. As soon as the robbery was reported, and the description of the robbers circulated, a posse led by Jack Conant was on the trail of the two fleeing robbers, but the two men with Conant abandoned him. At Sisson's station Conant hired Indian tracker Sisson Jim, and Dick Hubbell also joined his posse, now again consisting of three men, as they headed toward Picayune Lake. The posse heard a shot after dark and realized it was the two fugitives hunting for food, and at dawn they captured the two fugitives without resistance. Jackson gave his name as Charles Brown while Tracy said he was Charles Mitchell, and the two were taken to Callahan's stagecoach station. The posse collected everything the men had with them, including a supply of buckshot. The body of Marsh had also been taken to Callahan's station but had been buried before the arrival of his two confederates. The two prisoners were taken to Yreka and lodged in jail. Tracy, while in jail, was diagnosed with heart disease and moved from the iron cell to a more comfortable wooden one, but he attempted to escape and was moved back to an iron cell.

Jackson hired Elijah Steele, an attorney of some renown, for his defense, but it was all for naught as the evidence against him was conclusive. The trial began on December 17, and Jackson's past prison experiences were read in court. Hume introduced the buckshot removed from the dead stage horse and the buckshot collected when the men were arrested, showing it was the same in size, weight, and appearance—a rudimentary attempt at introducing ballistics evidence. The case went to jury and on December 24, 1878, the *Sacramento Daily Union* reported the defendant had been convicted, and it took only five minutes to deliberate and convict Jackson of the "attempt to rob" charge. Jackson was sentenced to serve ten years in prison and arrived on December 31, 1878. He was released on June 30, 1885, by expiration of sentence. Tracy, seeing the outcome for Jackson, pled guilty to the attempted robbery in January 1879 and, for his cooperation, received a reduced sentence of five years, arriving at the prison on January 19, 1879. He was released, by expiration of sentence, on August 14, 1882, after serving three years seven months. However, Tracy was not yet finished with his criminal career, and three months later he was back in prison for a fourteen-year term, convicted of a first-degree burglary in Contra Costa County.

Sources: *Daily Alta California (San Francisco, CA)*: January 3, 1868. *Daily Evening Bulletin (San Francisco, CA)*: January 2, 1868. *Marysville Daily Appeal (CA)*: September 3, 1904. *Oroville Weekly Union Record (CA)*: July 15, 1865. *Redding Independent (CA)*: September 12, 1878. *Sacramento Daily Union (CA)*: December 25, 1878. *Shasta Courier (CA)*: September 14, 1878. *Yreka Journal (CA)*: September 11, 1878; September 18, 1878; September 25, 1878; October 9, 1878; November 27, 1878. *Yreka Union (CA)*: September 14, 1878; September 21, 1878; November 30, 1878; December 21, 1878; December 28, 1878.

CHARLES E. "BLACK BART" BOLTON, AUGUST 31, 1881

Bolton had been having good luck in California, but perhaps he believed that lawmen might be getting close or he believed he might do better in Oregon. On September 16, 1880, Bolton crossed the boundary into Oregon and stopped the stagecoach from Roseburg bound for Yreka in Siskiyou County, California. He chose that date as he had a bright moon to work under, and he had planned the robbery for the nighttime hours. When the coach was still two miles north of the state border, the road agent halted driver Nort Eddings, pointed his shotgun at the driver, and demanded the express box and mail sacks. Eddings threw out the mail but said the box was bolted in the rear boot. This time the robber was prepared and, with the proper tools, broke open the box without removing it and extracted more than $1,000 in gold dust and coin, and he also found a considerable amount of currency. The usual pursuit did not lead to the robber, and Bolton had done so well in Oregon he repeated the robbery on September 23, this time stopping driver George Chase and again finding more than $1,000. As usual, there were no clues to help identify the road agent. On November 20 Bolton closed out his 1880 endeavors with the robbery of the stagecoach traveling from Redding in Shasta County to Roseburg, Oregon, perhaps hoping for another good haul from an Oregon coach. Joe Mason, the driver, was halted and the mail sacks and treasure box were demanded. The mail was thrown out but Mason said the box was too heavy for one man to lift. When the road agent mounted the wheel to help lift the box, Mason took a swing with a hatchet and nearly hit Bolton in the head. The robber fell backward to avoid the blow and fled, and Mason hurried on, leaving the mail behind. Bolton returned after the stagecoach left, and later another stagecoach recovered the slashed mail sacks and the mail Bolton had not taken. The post office, in a rare disclosure, reported that the mail contained little of value.

Perhaps this close call in November 1880 had its effect, because Bolton did not appear again until August 31, 1881, when he returned to California and stopped the stagecoach from Roseburg, Oregon, bound for Yreka, California, when nine miles from its destination in Siskiyou County. There was a small fire beside the road, providing enough light for the nighttime work, and when driver John Sullaway came abreast of it a masked road agent wielding a shotgun stepped into the road and ordered him to stop. The mailbags were thrown out on demand but the box was fastened to the coach, so Sullaway was ordered to dismount and hold the leaders. Bolton broke open the box with an ax and found very little for his trouble, and then Sullaway was sent on his way. (See Calaveras County on November 3, 1883.)

Unknown, September 10, 1893; September 12, 1893

On Sunday, September 10, 1893, the northbound stagecoach from Ager to Klamath Falls, Oregon, had traveled only ten miles when it was halted by a lone road agent, masked and armed. He ordered the driver to step down and had the three passengers step out, and then told them to walk down the road some distance and not look back. After the party of four had gone a safe distance and stopped, the road agent broke open the express box and then went through the mail pouches in the driver's boot. When he did not find the registered mail pouch he called the driver back and asked him, "Where is the brass lock?" The driver replied, "This is Sunday, we don't carry a through-mail pouch on Sundays." The driver was sent back to the passengers and the road agent, after finishing his work in the driver's boot, went to the hind boot and unbuckled the cover, and when he saw the through-pouch he sang out, "You are the damnedest liar I ever saw!" While ripping open and rifling through the registered mail, the robber whistled "Yankee Doodle" loud enough to be heard by the passengers, and when he finished with that task he called the driver and passengers back and told them to remove their coats and hats, lay them on the ground, then throw their money at his feet. One of the passengers, while the robber was busy with the mails, had transferred a valuable purse from his pocket to his hat and saved it, and another passenger had converted his money to greenbacks in Ager and had hidden them into the lining of his hat, and he too saved most of his money. The robber did not molest the driver and the three passengers gave up only small amounts, which prompted the robber to complain, "For traveling men you carry very little money." The road agent collected the money from the ground and gave each passenger $2.50 for expenses, and then ordered, "Load up and move on." As the passengers boarded he backed away from the coach and then invited them to visit him at his mountain home "anytime you should come into the vicinity." From the express box, mail, packages, and passengers he collected about $600. The robbery was reported and the robber was described as medium height and build with light hair and blue eyes, he spoke with a German accent, and he wore new oilcloth pantaloons, similar to those stolen during a burglary of a store in Ager the previous Thursday. A posse rode to the scene, but there was no report of an arrest.

Two days later on Tuesday, September 12, 1893, the same road agent appeared nine miles north of Ager and, aiming his Martin-Henry rifle at the driver, ordered him to halt. As soon as the coach had stopped he ordered the driver and three passengers—two Chinamen and a sick hostler on his way to the doctor—to walk a distance ahead of the coach and stop. He followed along and said he thought it best to go through the Chinamen, and one contributed $55 and the other $35, but one had hidden a $20 gold piece under his arm as he stepped out of the coach and it was not found. The robber asked the hostler his occupation several times, but he was deaf so the driver answered for him, and the robber remarked he never robbed a poor or a sick man, and the hostler saved $140. The robber then returned to the coach and found the express box unlocked and empty. The mails were not molested, but the road agent returned a dirty sack containing letters and papers he had taken on Sunday saying, "I have no use for them." He then told the driver not to mention the robbery at the next post office in Bogus, three-quarters of a mile ahead, and then he departed. The driver was certain that it was the same road agent, as he had the same rifle and the same Colt pistol, but this time he also had a Smith & Wesson hammerless pistol tucked in his belt. Wells, Fargo's detective John N. Thacker was dispatched to investigate, even though the company had suffered no loss. An agent for the company said they had no clue to the robber's identity, but suspected he was an old hand at the business.

Source: *San Francisco Call (CA)*: September 13–14, 1893.

UNKNOWN, OCTOBER 2, 1894

At 10:00 a.m. on Tuesday, October 2, 1894, the stagecoach from Fort Jones to Yreka, with eight passengers aboard, had just reached the divide at the foot of the grade near Etna when a masked road agent armed with "a wicked looking revolver" stepped out and commanded, "Halt and hands up!" Driver Dan Cawley stopped his coach and the robber demanded that he throw down the Wells, Fargo express box, and once it lay in the road the robber told Cawley to move on. The road agent was not interested in the mail nor the passengers, and it was supposed that by some means he had learned that there was considerable treasure in the box. The robbery was reported and the posse that rode to the scene found and recovered the broken box, but little more to help in the investigation. Rewards were posted but never paid as the robber was never identified.

Sources: *Los Angeles Herald (CA)*: October 3, 1894. *San Francisco Call (CA)*: October 3, 1894.

UNKNOWN, NOVEMBER 21, 1894

On Wednesday afternoon, November 21, 1894, the stagecoach from Klamath Falls, Oregon, was two miles from its destination of Ager when a lone road agent, masked and armed, stepped out from the side of the road and ordered the driver to rein in his team. He told the driver to throw out the Wells, Fargo express box, and it was thrown down. There were two passengers on board but they were not molested, and the robber did not ask for the mail. He told the driver to move on, and after the coach pulled out he lifted the box and carried it into the brush. There was a road crew working nearby but none of the men were armed, so all they could do was watch while the coach was robbed. At Ager the robbery was reported, and it was determined that there was nothing of value in the box. Still, a posse rode to the scene, collected the broken box, and returned to town without a clue to the robber's identity.

Source: *Sacramento Daily Union (CA)*: November 23, 1894.

WILLIAM HENRY HORRALL, APRIL 3, 1897; JUNE 27, 1897; SEPTEMBER 27, 1897

On Saturday, April 3, 1897, the stagecoach between Shovel Creek, Oregon, and Ager in Siskiyou County was stopped south of the boundary by a lone, masked highwayman, armed with a double-barreled shotgun, who stepped out into the road and ordered the driver to rein in his team. He demanded the Wells, Fargo treasure box, and as soon as it was thrown down he told the driver to continue on. He did not ask about passengers nor did he ask for the mail. There was little treasure in the box, but still a posse rode to the scene, returned empty-handed, and waited for some break in the case. On Sunday, June 27, the stagecoach from Fort Jones to Yreka was nine miles from Yreka, in Siskiyou County, when the same road agent, again masked and carrying the same shotgun, stepped out from behind a rock and ordered the driver to halt. He called for the Wells, Fargo express box and broke it open, but again he got little for his trouble, and then he had the driver move along without bothering the passengers or asking for the mail. Lawmen again came up empty-handed at the scene and continued their wait for a break in the case, and Wells, Fargo, annoyed by the pesky robber, assigned detective John Thacker to the case.

On Monday, September 27, the same road agent struck again. When the stagecoach bound for Fort Jones reached the same place in the road as the previous two robberies, the road agent stepped from behind his familiar rock, shotgun in hand, and halted the coach. He called for the Wells, Fargo express box, and as soon as it lay in the road he told the driver to move on, without asking about passengers or calling for the mail pouches. There were four passengers aboard including two businessmen, a priest, and an Indian girl. The girl took the time to carefully examine the robber, who was disguised and had his boots muffled with barley sacks, but she later gave lawmen a good description. After the coach was out of sight the robber broke open the express box and took out $50, including a $20 U.S. gold certificate with a Garfield vignette, a denomination and type of bill quite rare in northern California. Lawmen went to the scene but could find no clue to the robber's identity nor a trail to follow. Perhaps the unique bill was planted, because Thacker immediately had a man begin searching the stores and financial institutions throughout the area. Messenger Daniel N. Haskell found the gold note, bought it, and shipped it to detective Thacker. The detective backtracked the $20 note to a store where the clerk, in checking his records, found that a man had bought supplies and had them shipped to "F. W. Lloyd at Delta," forty miles north of Redding. Thacker with Wells, Fargo detective Jennings went to Delta, contacted Shasta County deputy sheriff Stewart, and learned that thirty-five-year-old William Henry Horrall, sometimes misspelled "Harrall" or "Harald," lived there with his wife, whose maiden name was Lloyd, their two-year-old daughter, and a newborn baby. Horrall fit the description of the stagecoach robber exactly, and the boot tracks they found about the Horrall house matched the boot tracks at the robbery scene. Thacker wired the Siskiyou County sheriff for a warrant for Horrall's arrest, and Deputy W. A Radford was given the paperwork and sent to assist detectives Thacker and Jennings and Deputy Stewart.

At 8:30 a.m. on Thursday, October 14 deputies Stewart and Radford, with Detective Jennings, went up the hill from the railroad depot 150 yards to the front door of the Horrall house. Thacker and Jennings held back while the two lawmen went to the front door to make the arrest. Stewart was slightly in front, he knocked, and Mrs. Horrall opened the door. "Is Mr. Horrall in?" Stewart asked, and she replied, "Yes, he is inside." Horrall then walked to the front door and Stewart, who was well known by Horrall, said, "This is Mr. Radford." Horrall shook hands with Radford, and the lawman said, "I would like to see you a moment," and motioned with his head for Horrall to step outside. Horrall, still holding on to Radford's right hand, replied, "All right, I'm ready for you." Horrall at that moment pulled Radford off balance as he reached into his waistband with his left hand and came out with a .38 caliber revolver, which he placed against the officer's breast and fired once. The bullet pierced Radford's heart, and penetrated all the way through his body, lodging just under the skin on his back.

As Radford collapsed, Stewart pulled his revolver and struck Horrall on the head, expecting to knock him senseless, but Horrall fired again and this bullet struck Deputy Stewart just above the left knee. Stewart then opened fire, and the first of four shots pierced Horrall's heart, the second broke his right arm above the elbow, the third shattered his wrist, and as he was falling a fourth bullet struck him in the shoulder and came out his neck. Horrall's wife and daughter were only two feet away during the entire gunfight, but neither was hurt, and their newborn baby was only feet away and unhurt. The body of Radford was taken to the waiting room of the railroad depot and laid out to await an inquest, which was conducted with expedience, and then the body was put aboard a freight train which had been held over, and his remains were shipped to Yreka where his widow and four children awaited his arrival. Radford was buried at Yreka on October 17, 1897. Horrall's inquest was held in the front room of his house while his wife and children remained next door at her mother's house. After the inquest Horrall's body was put on the Oregon Express and shipped to Redding for burial by the county, as Mrs. Horrall said she could not bear the expense.

Sources: *Los Angeles Herald (CA)*: October 15, 1897. *Middletown Daily Argus (NY)*: September 27, 1897. *San Francisco Call (CA)*: October 15–16, 1897. *San Francisco Chronicle (CA)*: September 26, 1897; October 15–16, 1897.

UNKNOWN, APRIL 13, 1897

At 4:00 p.m. on Tuesday, April 13, 1897, the stagecoach from Yreka to Etna was halfway up the grade on the north side of Forest House Mountain, and just rounding a sharp curve ten miles south of Yreka, when a lone road agent, masked and armed with a rifle, stepped out from behind a large rock and ordered driver Frank Hovey to rein in his team. He told Hovey to throw out the Wells, Fargo express box and the mail, and as soon as they lay on the road he told Hovey to move on. There were five passengers on board, one a woman, but they were not molested. Hovey reached Fort Jones at 6:00 p.m. and he telegraphed back to Yreka detailing the robbery and describing the road agent as five feet ten inches tall, wearing dark clothing, a slouch hat, and a white mask. Express agent F. E. Wadsworth went with the deputy to the scene and arrived just after 7:00 p.m. but they could find no clue to the robber's identity nor a trail to follow. Wadsworth reported that there had only been $50 in the box, but he believed the robber had expected to find a shipment of bullion consigned to the bank of A. B. Carlock at Fort Jones.

Sources: *Sacramento Daily Union (CA)*: April 14, 1897. *San Francisco Call (CA)*: April 14, 1897.

UNKNOWN, AUGUST 22, 1901

On Thursday morning, August 22, 1901, the stagecoach from Klamath Falls, Oregon, to Ager, California, in Siskiyou County was ten miles east of its destination when several highwaymen appeared, masked and armed, and ordered the driver to halt. They demanded that he throw out the Wells, Fargo express box and the mail pouches, and after he followed their order they told him to continue into Ager. There was no mention of passengers. The driver got to his destination as quickly as possible and reported the robbery, and lawmen rushed to the scene. After investigating they could find no clue to the robbers' identities nor a trail to follow.

Sources: *Los Angeles Herald (CA)*: August 22, 1901. *San Francisco Call (CA)*: August 22, 1901.

UNKNOWN, JULY 6, 1908

On Monday, July 6, 1908, the Scott Valley stagecoach running between Yreka and Etna in Siskiyou County had gone to the railroad depot to pick up a large shipment being sent by Wells, Fargo, but the train was late so the stagecoach started without the treasure. When the coach reached Robbers' Rock on Forest Home mountain at 4:30 p.m. an armed white man, masked and with gunnysacks muffling his feet, stepped into the road and ordered the driver to halt. There was no messenger aboard because the treasure had not been loaded, but there were passengers. A "quarter-breed Indian" covered the driver and passengers with his rifle from behind a large rock while the man at the coach went through the passengers and took their watches and $300, but he did not molest the driver. He then called for the Wells, Fargo express box, and when it lay on the ground he fetched his ax and broke it open. He seemed surprised to find little of value inside, but he added the contents to his plunder, and then he told the driver to continue without asking for the mail sacks. When the coach reached the next station the driver reported the robbery, and Sheriff Howard and Deputy Geney started for the scene, while two other posses started out to try to intercept the robbers or cut their trail. The sheriff's best guess was that the pair would try to make it to the railroad at Gazelle and then head south, and it was stated that "escape is impossible."

However, the robbers just seemed to disappear, and no one was arrested for the robbery.

Source: *Los Angeles Herald (CA)*: July 7, 1908.

Sonoma County

UNKNOWN, FEBRUARY 16, 1871

At 4:00 a.m. on Thursday, February 16, 1871, a stagecoach was near Cloverdale, eighteen miles north of Healdsburg, when three men, masked and "muffled up," appeared with two on one side and one on the other side of the road. Two men grabbed the reins of the leaders while the third man pointed his pistol at the head of the driver and told him to halt. The driver asked, "What do you want?" and the man with the pistol said, "We want the express box." The driver pulled the Wells, Fargo express box from beneath his seat and threw it onto the road, and as soon as it came to rest the man with the pistol told him to "drive on," as the two at the head of the horses released their grasp and stepped aside. They had not been interested in robbing the passengers and did not ask about the mail. As soon as the coach was under way, the three robbers went to work and soon had the box busted open, and they removed the contents and fled. When the coach reached Cloverdale the robbery was reported, a posse was organized, and they rode to the scene. They recovered the broken box but could find no clue to the robbers' identities nor a trail to follow.

Source: *Sacramento Daily Union (CA)*: February 18, 1871.

UNKNOWN, JULY 12, 1871

At 10:00 p.m. on Wednesday, July 12, 1871, the northbound stagecoach from Healdsburg to Cloverdale was five miles from its destination when four road agents stepped into the road and two grabbed the reins of the leaders. They ordered the driver to throw down the Wells, Fargo express box, and as soon as it lay in the road they ordered him to continue on. The passengers were not molested, and they did not ask for the mail. A posse was organized to arrive at the site at daybreak the next day and they recovered the broken box, but they could find no clue to the robbers' identities nor a trail to follow.

Source: *Daily Alta California (San Francisco)*: July 14, 1871.

ELISHA "BIG FOOT" ANDRUS, JOHNNY BROWN, LODI BROWN, BILLY CURTIS, JOHN HOUX, TOM JONES AND "RATTLE JACK," AUGUST 12, 1871; AUGUST 16, 1871; OCTOBER 10, 1871

During the early months of 1871 there had been a rash of stagecoach holdups in Sonoma and Mendocino County. While the loot from any individual robbery was small, the largest being only $1,500, the accrued plunder was a staggering loss for Wells, Fargo. The robbers selected a spot where the coach would be moving at a slow pace, and they would step out from the side of the road, guns in hand. John Houx was suspected, arrested several times and lodged in the Mendocino County jail, but the lawmen could not work up a case against him so each time he was released. His "gang" consisted of Elisha "Big Foot" Andrus, brothers Lodi and Johnny Brown, Tom Jones and Billy Curtis, and at least one other. Houx, Andrus, and Lodi Brown were bad men with reputations to match, but Johnny Brown, Jones and Curtis had good reputations, despite their continued association with bad company. On Saturday, August 12, 1871, Houx, Brown and several other members of the gang stopped the Cloverdale to Healdsburg stagecoach, but when they found it was occupied by four heavily armed hunters they declined to make any demands and rode off.

On Wednesday evening, August 16, 1871, the southbound stagecoach from Cloverdale to Petaluma, with C. L. "Sandy" Woodworth at the reins, left Cloverdale with messenger Charles D. Upton riding next to him and fourteen passengers aboard, nine inside and five on top. Several of the passengers were armed, as they anticipated another robbery. At 9:00 p.m. the stagecoach had slowed for a steep grade north of Healdsburg when four masked men—Houx, Andrus, Lodi Brown, and one unidentified gang member—suddenly appeared from both sides of the road and covered those on top with shotguns, rifles, and pistols. They called for the driver to stop and fired once into the air. Without a moments hesitation Woodworth whipped up his team and the coach lurched forward at a rapid pace. The robbers fired after the fleeing coach and one buckshot hit the driver in the cheek and another cut his whip, but he continued to urge on the team. Upton returned fire at the robbers, and passenger Myers F. Truett shoved his shotgun out a window and fired both barrels. Lodi Brown and the unnamed robber were wounded, the latter, known as "Rattle Jack," seriously. Another passenger riding atop, B. S. Coffman, tried to pull his pistol but was shot in the arm and slumped back against Woodworth. Then, as the robbers continued a withering fusillade after the coach, Coffman was hit in the face with eighteen buckshot and Henry P. Benton, another passenger riding atop, was shot through the stomach with a rifle ball. The coach was then out of rifle range, so the robbers hurried to their horses and fled. The badly wounded robber only made it a short distance before he declared that he was dying and begged to be killed. Houx and Andrus accommodated their partner, reportedly put a noose around his neck so it would appear he had been lynched, and threw the body in the Russian River. The stagecoach continued to the first ranch they encountered and had the wounded passengers taken inside. Benton died the following day, but Coffman, whose wounds were thought fatal, fully recovered. Wells, Fargo posted a $3,500 reward and the state added $1,000. Stephen Venard, a renowned road agent killer, was sent to Sonoma County to investigate. He met with Healdsburg deputy William B. Reynolds who said he was certain the guilty parties were Houx and his gang, but he cautioned that there was not enough evidence and Houx would again elude indictment. Venard went undercover and learned that Billy Curtis had recently withdrawn from the gang. The lawmen gave him a promise of immunity so Curtis rejoined the gang as an agent for Venard and Reynolds.

On October 10 Houx, Curtis and several others robbed the Healdsburg stagecoach at McDonald's house and took $925 from Wells, Fargo's treasure box. Curtis then got word to Reynolds that Houx and company were going to rob Sheriff D. C. Crockett of Mendocino County's taxes when the lawman took them to Ukiah. Houx, for some reason, was suspicious and rode from Cloverdale to Healdsburg to see what Reynolds was doing, but found him at home with his family. Houx decided that everything was in place for his plan to rob the sheriff, so he headed for Cloverdale. As soon as Houx left, Reynolds telegraphed Venard at Cloverdale and then with his brother, Hedge Reynolds, started north. When Houx reached Cloverdale he was met by Curtis and Venard, who invited him for a drink. Just as he raised his glass he found himself looking down the barrel of Venard's pistol, who announced, "You are arrested. Throw up your hands or you're a dead man." The Reynolds brothers arrived a few minutes later, and the town was sealed to prevent any of Houx's friends from riding out to warn the other gang members. Venard told Houx of the evidence against him and offered him immunity if he would identify the murderer of Benton. He put the blame on Lodi Brown and Andrus but would not disclose the name of the dead road agent, and he implicated Johnny Brown and Tom Jones in several robberies. He also told Venard where Andrus could be found. Curtis and the Reynolds boys rode to the Jones farm and arrested Tom Jones. Both road agents were then placed under a strong guard, and all the lawmen and Curtis rode to the home of Houx's ex-wife. They arrived at 10:00 p.m. and surrounded the house, but they waited for daylight and when they went in at dawn Andrus was not there. The ex–Mrs. Houx told them that Andrus and Lodi Brown were at a deserted cabin on the headwaters of Dry Creek, ten miles north of Cloverdale, and that Johnny

Brown was at the home of Houx's father. At the Houx ranch a dog barked and Lodi Brown appeared at the door heavily armed. Reynolds approached and said, "I will have to disarm you," and then did so without incident.

In Cloverdale the three road agents were loaded into a stagecoach and taken to McDonald's station while Venard, Curtis and William Reynolds started for Andrus' cabin, and along the way they met a rancher familiar with the country who took them within a mile of their destination. They went up the canyon afoot until they saw fresh sign and heard voices. In a few minutes Lodi Brown walked down the trail and was captured. Venard asked, "Where is Bigfoot?" and Brown answered "He's up the canyon about three hundred yards getting dinner," and then warned, "You'll never take him unless you kill him."

Venard and Reynolds hid while Curtis walked Brown down the canyon, fired his rifle into the air and, threatening Brown, forced him to call out, "Bill, I've killed a big buck. Come and help me pack him in." As Andrus came down the trail he was suddenly confronted by two lawmen armed with shotguns and ordered to "unbuckle your pistol, drop it, and step aside." They secured their prisoners and then went to their camp to search for plunder or evidence. They found the ax used to break open the treasure boxes, Bigfoot's oversized shoes, and a mask. They took their prisoners to McDonald's and then continued on with the five road agents to the jail at Ukiah, arriving just before midnight, November 10, 1871. They were then removed to Sonoma County's jail at Santa Rosa.

Houx, the leader and worst of the lot, turned state's evidence and was released in consideration of his cooperation and testimony. After his release he returned to Missouri where he died of smallpox several years later. The case against Tom Jones was weak, as he was only charged with informing the gang when there were large Wells, Fargo shipments, and he was released after his preliminary hearing. Johnny Brown was indicted for several robberies, pled guilty and received a sentence of three years. He arrived at San Quentin on January 19, 1872, and registered as prisoner #5093; he was discharged on August 12, 1874, after serving two years seven months.

Andrus and Lodi Brown were charged with Benton's murder, but they were both allowed to plead guilty to second-degree murder and each received a sentence of thirty years. Both men arrived at San Quentin on February 19, 1872, and Brown registered as prisoner #5156 while Andrus registered as prisoner #5157. Brown was pardoned on January 6, 1880, after serving eight years, but his release was conditioned upon his leaving the state. He went to New Mexico where he became involve in a fracas and was killed. In May 1876 Andrus had his sentence commuted to twenty-five years, sometimes a precursor to an early pardon, and he had been promised a further commutation to ten years. At 8:00 p.m. on Wednesday, August 6, 1879, Andrus was seated on a low bureau in the dormitory cell he shared with thirty-seven other prisoners, talking to prisoner Brownlee. He had previously had a disagreement with cell mate John Maguire, #8064, over the transfer of two cell mates after Andrus reported them for minor violations, but Maguire later said they argued over remarks derogatory to Irish Roman Catholics. Maguire approached several times but turned without saying a word and walked away. On his third approach he grabbed Andrus and cut his throat from ear to ear, nearly severing his head from his body. Brownlee jumped up and yelled, "My God! Jim, what have you done?" Andrus struggled to his feet but immediately collapsed and bled to death in seconds. The knife, when found, turned out to be a shoe knife with a six-inch blade taken from the prison's shoe factory.

Sources: *Marin County Journal (CA)*: November 25, 1871; March 9, 1872. *Mendocino Democrat (Ukiah, CA)*: November 17, 1871; November 24, 1871; February 29, 1872; May 16, 1872. *Mendocino Press (Ukiah, CA)*: November 16, 1871. *Russian River Flag (Healdsburg, CA)*: May 16, 1872; January 1, 1880; January 15, 1880. *Sacramento Daily Union (CA)*: October 11, 1871; November 18, 1871; August 8, 1897. *San Francisco Chronicle (CA)*: August 6, 1880. *San Francisco Daily Alta (CA)*: August 18, 1871; July 12, 1872. *San Francisco Examiner (CA)*: December 29, 1889. *Territorial Enterprise (Virginia City, NV)*: November 24, 1871.

HENRY B. MITCHELL, DECEMBER 25, 1871

Late on December 25, 1871, when the stagecoach from Petaluma to Cloverdale was just below Geyserville in Sonoma County, and about 150 yards from William Ellis' ranch, a boy of about sixteen years stepped from behind a tree with a gun in his hand. He signaled for the driver, "Doc" Curtis, to halt but Curtis, did not see the gun at first and thought it was someone wanting a ride into town. However, when Curtis asked what he wanted, the boy waved his pistol and told him, "Throw out that box." This was immediately done, and Curtis was ordered to continue on. There was one passenger aboard but he was not molested. As soon as the stagecoach reached Healdsburg, Curtis reported the robbery to Deputy Sheriff William Reynolds who, with his brother Hedge, accompanied Curtis to the scene. They found the box thirty paces from where it had been dropped, and it had been cut open. It was too dark to track the robber, so the lawman took the box back to town and there found that the letter pouch, which had been inside the box, had not been molested, though one letter not inside the pouch and addressed to Sheriff Potter, was torn open. There was no money or valuables in the box, so the road agent had made a "water haul."

The next morning a small posse went to the scene and carefully circled the area for several miles but could not find a track of man or horse. The morning of December 26 the road agent, an Indian boy giving the name Harvey Bell, went to the ranch of Daniel Sink and there told a worker that it was he who had robbed the stagecoach. The employee told Sink what the boy had said, and Sink immediately started for Cloverdale and had a warrant issued by the justice of the peace. A Mr. Crawford was deputized to make the arrest, as the boy had at times lived with Sink and he declined to arrest him. The two men returned to the Sink ranch, and Crawford arrested Bell. On the way to town the boy confessed that he had done the work alone and had no gun but had pointed, as if it were a gun, a redwood picket he tore from a fence. He said he got the notion to rob a stagecoach because he had heard the Brown brothers, with whom he had lived recently until they were jailed, talking about the several stagecoaches they had robbed. He then offered to take Crawford to a certain place in a canyon where one of the express boxes had been cut open and the valueless contents, such as a box of type for the *Mendocino Press,* was scattered about. He also said that when another stagecoach was robbed below Truett's ranch, one of the road agents, whom he knew as "Rattle Jack," was mortally wounded, and he offered to show the grave. He told Crawford that the Browns had said it was Truett's shot which killed Rattle Jack.

Bell, once he was in jail, disclosed that his true name was Henry B. Mitchell. He was indicted and tried in early January 1872 and found guilty, and on January 15 he was sentenced to serve one year in prison. The light sentence was probably due to his youth, willingness to confess, and his cooperation with the lawmen. He arrived at San Quentin Prison on January 19, 1872, and was released by expiration of sentence on November 25, 1872, just eleven months after holding up the stagecoach. Mitchell would serve two more terms in San Quentin. Consumption (tuberculosis) was not understood, though it was, at times, epidemic in the prison and the close proximity of inmates meant it was easily spread. Many men died of the disease, and Mitchell probably succumbed to consumption on July 27, 1878, while serving his final term.

Sources: *Sonoma Democrat (CA)*: December 30, 1871; January 13, 1872.

CHARLES E. "BLACK BART" BOLTON, AUGUST 3, 1877; JULY 22, 1880; NOVEMBER 24, 1882; APRIL 12, 1883

At 6:00 a.m. Friday, August 3, 1877, the stagecoach driven by Ash Wilkinson left Point Arenas for Duncan's Mills in Sonoma County. By mid-afternoon the stage was ascending a steep grade near the Russian river, and was still several hours from its destination, when a masked road agent (Charles Bolton), wielding a shotgun, stepped in front of the leaders. He demanded the express box and mail sacks, and they were thrown out. There was no further delay, and driver Wilkinson was waved on. The road agent took from the box $300 in coin and a check, which was later destroyed because cashing it could identify the robber. This was the robbery where the road agent first left that famed note for lawmen and newspaper editors, and the one where he established an alias:

> I've labored long for bread,
> For honor and for riches,
> But on my corns too long you've tread,
> You fine haired Sons of Bitches.
> Black Bart, the P O 8

Bolton had adopted the sobriquet "Black Bart" used by Bartholomew Graham, a fictional desperado created in 1871 by William H. Rhodes for his tale "The Summerfield Case." Beneath this brief poem, Black Bart wrote, "Driver, give my respects to our old friend, the other driver. I really had a notion to hang my old disguise hat on his weather eye." Once again lawmen were clueless and the road agent disappeared from the highways again for nearly a year.

At 9:00 a.m. on Thursday, July 22, 1880, stagecoach driver Martin McClennan, on the Point Arenas to Duncan's Mills run, was stopped by a masked road agent brandishing a double-barreled shotgun when four miles from Henry's Hotel. The robber demanded the express box, but when he found it securely bolted into the coach floor, he settled for the mail sacks and gestured for McClennan to continue on. Lawmen once again found no clue to the robber's identity.

On Friday, November 24, 1882, Bolton, in his final adventure for that year, returned to Sonoma County and stopped the stagecoach from Lakeport to Cloverdale driven by Dick Crawford. He ordered the driver to unhitch the team and escort his passengers down the road a safe distance while he attacked the iron box bolted inside the stagecoach. There was probably not much plunder realized in either of his last two robberies for 1882, since the amount stolen was not even sufficient to report. There were no clues nor a trail to follow for any distance.

Once again Black Bart took off the winter months, but on Thursday, April 12, 1883, the stagecoach from Lakeport to Cloverdale, driven by Bill Connibeck, was five miles from its destination when Bolton appeared and followed his well-established protocol in securing two treasure boxes and the mail sacks, reportedly profiting less than $50 in all. Lawmen at the scene were again frustrated. (See Calaveras County on November 3, 1883.)

UNKNOWN, FEBRUARY 9, 1885

At 8:30 p.m. on Monday, February 9, 1885, the stagecoach for Cloverdale was climbing Heald's Hill, near the city limits of its destination, when two road agents, masked and armed, appeared and halted the coach. They demanded the Wells, Fargo express box, and it was thrown down. They then ordered the driver to continue, and after the coach was out of sight they broke open the box but there is no published record of the contents. A posse went to the scene but could not find a clue to the robbers' identities nor a trail to follow for any distance.

Sources: *Daily Alta California (San Francisco)*: February 3, 1885; February 11, 1885.

UNKNOWN, MARCH 26, 1885; APRIL 7, 1885; APRIL 18, 1885

On Thursday, March 26, 1885, the stagecoach from Mendocino bound for Cloverdale was stopped when nearing its destination. The lone highwayman demanded the Wells, Fargo express box and mail, and these were thrown down. The robber did not ask about passengers and ordered the driver to continue into town. A posse went to the scene but could find no clue to the robber's identity.

At midnight on Tuesday, April 7, 1885, the stagecoach from Mendocino was still twenty miles north of its destination at Cloverdale when a lone road agent stepped into the road, ordered the driver to rein in his team, and fired his revolver. The shot frightened the horses and they took off at a run, leaving the road agent behind. The startled horses took off with such a jolt that the driver lost his whip, but he made it into Cloverdale safely. Once again the posse that rode to the scene could find no clue to the robber's identity.

On Saturday, April 18, 1885, the stagecoach from Mendocino bound for Cloverdale was stopped and robbed by a lone, masked road agent when it was just a few miles from its destination. The following day lawmen from Cloverdale went to the scene and began a systematic search of the area, and they found the treasure box, unopened, hidden in the brush not far from the robbery scene. They could find no clue to the robber's identity, so they returned to town and delivered the box to the Wells, Fargo office.

Sources: *Daily Alta California (San Francisco)*: April 11, 1885; April 21, 1885. *Sacramento Daily Union (CA)*: March 28, 1885.

UNKNOWN, MAY 8, 1885

On Friday night, May 8, 1885, the northbound stagecoach from Mendocino to Cloverdale was nine miles from its destination and two miles past the Mountain House going down a grade. Suddenly two men, masked and armed with rifles, appeared on each side of the road. One was standing on a dirt bank which put him on a level with driver James Romaine and messenger Henry C. Ward, while the other was standing on the opposite edge of the road. When the coach was abreast of them the man on the bank yelled, "Halt! Halt!" and Ward told the driver to rein in his team. However, the road agent standing on the bank immediately began shooting, so Ward returned his rifle fire with one barrel from his Wells, Fargo scattergun, but the blast had no effect. Before Ward could cock his second load the robber in the road fired on Ward, striking him in the right hand, disabling him. The shooting frightened the horses and while the exchange of shots distracted the robbers, the team took off at a dead run, with the driver keeping a tight control and urging them on. The shots by the man on the bank were so close that both the driver and messenger had powder burns on their faces. The *Daily Alta California* newspaper remarked that this was the fourth attempt to rob the same stagecoach in the same vicinity, the first three having been successful, but this was the first where a messenger was aboard. Messenger Ward was well known west of the Rockies and had been employed by Wells, Fargo for over twenty-five years; he had withstood attacks on many occasions and had never given up a treasure box. There were no clues to the robbers' identities.

Source: *Daily Alta California (San Francisco)*: May 10, 1885.

GEORGE WILSON AND CHARLES COLE, AUGUST 4, 1886

On Wednesday, August 4, 1886, the Ukiah to Cloverdale stagecoach was three and a half miles north of Cloverdale on the Ukiah Road when two masked, armed road agents halted the coach and demanded the Wells, Fargo treasure box. The driver threw down the box and then was told to continue on his route. He whipped up his team and hurried into Cloverdale where he reported the robbery. Wells, Fargo detective John N. Thacker went to Cloverdale and with H. C. Ward and George Frazier rode to the scene and found the robbers' trail. They followed the tracks to Lower Lake where they were joined by Peter Smith, and then the posse continued on to Sulphur Creek where they captured the two road agents on Saturday night, August 7. They gave the names George Cole and A. Wilson, and they were taken to Santa Rosa on August 10 and lodged in jail. Later that day they had their examination before Justice Sewell and corrected their names to George Wilson, alias Thomas Paul, and Charles Cole, and they were held over for action by the grand jury. On August 17 they were brought into court for their arraignment, confessed and pled guilty, and they waived time so they were immediately sentenced to serve ten years at San Quentin. Wilson arrived at the prison on August 18, 1886, and registered as prisoner #12222, but he was granted a new trial, again convicted, and sentenced to serve ten years, and he arrived at Folsom Prison on December 21, 1887, where he registered as prisoner #1553. Cole arrived at San Quentin on August 18, 1886, where he registered as prisoner #12223. On July 21, 1888, Wilson was pardoned by Governor Robert Waterman, and he was discharged the following day. On December 18, 1890, Governor Waterman commuted Cole's sentence to seven years, and he was discharged the following day.

Sources: *Daily Alta California (San Francisco)*: August 18, 1886. *Sacramento Daily Union (CA)*: August 11, 1886; August 18, 1886.

JOSEPH FREY AND EUGENE PREUS, APRIL 28, 1888

In April 1888 Joseph Frey, a German immigrant, had been in the United States several months, had found a good job, and was living with his brother-in-law Eugene Preus in San Francisco. In mid–April Preus told Frey to quit his job and go with him to find better-paying work, and both men then quit their jobs and headed for Cloverdale. Early Saturday morning, April 28, they started afoot for Lakeport, but they had gone only a few miles when Preus told Frey that he intended to rob the stagecoach. Preus gave Frey two revolvers and Preus had three, one a heavy .44 caliber revolver. Preus made up masks and told his brother-in-law that he would do all the talking, and Frey was to display his weapon and keep watch to prevent interference when he demanded the treasure box. Then Preus selected a spot a short distance from town and they hid. At 1:30 p.m. the stagecoach from Lakeport to Cloverdale was a quarter mile past the tollgate on Geysers Springs Road, four miles east of Cloverdale, when Preus and Frey appeared and Preus ordered the driver to halt, then demanded the Wells, Fargo treasure box, and it was thrown down. As soon as the box lay in the road Preus told the driver to continue on, and they took the box and fled while the coach hurried into Cloverdale.

The robbery was reported and thirty-three-year-old Constable Albert "Ab" P. Crigler deputized Samuel Allen, and they started from Cloverdale for the scene. They followed a clear trail to a point near Sulphur Creek known as Profilo Rock, and at 5:30 p.m. the lawmen suddenly came upon the two road agents, who had arrived there only minutes earlier. Crigler ordered them to throw up their hands but they ran into the rocks, and Preus yelled out he would rather die than surrender as he fired a single shot from his .44 caliber revolver. The bullet pierced Crigler's heart, killing him instantly, and Allen immediately returned fire with his .44 caliber Winchester rifle. Allen called again for their surrender and Frey threw down the revolver he held in his hand, but when Allen turned to see Crigler's condition Frey grabbed up the revolver and fired at Allen, and Preus took a shot at Allen's head. Allen then returned fire at both men but he did not know if he had hit either of the robbers, and when he did not see them he thought they had slid down the steep precipice and escaped. Dusk was nearing and he did not want to chase two armed and desperate road agents alone in the dark, so he took Crigler's body back to Cloverdale. It was decided that the search, with a reinforced posse, would start again in the morning. When the posse returned to Profilo Rock they found that Preus had been killed by a bullet through his left eye penetrating into his brain, and he had fallen over the cliff. There was also blood evidence that proved the second robber had been hit, but also tracks where he had walked away. The posse recovered the battered treasure box, five pistols, a musket, and a mask and took the robber's dead body into Cloverdale. A description of the second man was circulated, and on April 30 Frey was arrested just south of Santa Rosa still in possession of the plunder: one gold and three silver watches. He confessed to being the second robber, through a German translator, named his brother-in-law, and the following morning he had his preliminary hearing. All the evidence that had been gathered was presented and three witnesses testified for the prosecution, while Frey testified on his own behalf, and he was held over for action by the grand jury on a charge of murder with no bail. Frey testified that when Allen returned fire he was hit in the right arm and collapsed unconscious. When he revived he could not find Preus, and Allen had left with the body of Crigler, so he started for Santa Rosa. Frey was tried for the murder of Crigler and convicted, but because he did not fire the fatal shot he was sentenced to serve only twenty-five years at San Quentin. Frey arrived at the prison on September 1, 1888, and registered as prisoner #13219. On May 20, 1892, Governor Henry H. Markham commuted Frey's sentence to five years and three months, and with good time credits he was released three days later after serving only three years nine months.

Sources: *Daily Alta California (San Francisco)*: May 1, 1888. *Los Angeles Herald (CA)*: April 29, 1888; May 2, 1888. *Sacramento Daily Record-Union (CA)*: May 1, 1888.

UNKNOWN, DECEMBER 4, 1888

At 5:30 p.m. on Tuesday, December 4, 1888, the stagecoach from Mendocino to Cazadero was eight miles from its destination with Jim Bland driving and stage line owner John Allman riding on top. The coach was behind schedule and driving very fast trying to make up time, and though they were among the heavy timber in Deep Creek Gulch where it was very dark, Allman told Bland not to stop and light the lamps, that he would do it at the next watering place. Suddenly the leaders swerved to one side of the road with a snort, and a voice called out, "Halt!" In the dim light Allman could just make out the silhouette of a man standing in the road with his gun leveled at himself and Bland. The coach stopped, and the man said, "Throw out that box and the mail. Be quick about it." After the box and mail pouches were thrown down he told the driver to get down and remove the logs that had been placed in the road to stop the coach. Then he had the driver board and told him to move on. There were five passengers in the coach but the robber did not seem interested in robbing them; it could have been caution as without the lamps lit he could not see what they were doing. As soon as he was given the order, Bland whipped up his team and hurried to the next watering place, lit the lamps, and then went into Cazadero where the robbery was reported. A man came into town shortly after the stagecoach and reported that the mail was scattered all over the road, so the posse that rode to the scene collected it and the slashed pouch and brought it to the postmaster. Allman said he did not believe there was anything in the box, but there was probably a substantial sum in the registered mail packages. The posse could not find a clue to the robber's identity, nor a trail to follow.

Source: *Daily Alta California (San Francisco)*: December 6, 1888.

Stanislaus County

DAN MCCARTY AND JOHN WEISENSTEIN, APRIL 27, 1882

Dan McCarty had served a year at San Quentin Prison for a stagecoach robbery in Merced County on May 7, 1877. After his release on June 15, 1878, he remained a law-abiding citizen, or at least he was not arrested for any crimes, until early 1882 when he met John Weisenstein. His new partner was seven years his senior, thirty-two years old, and he was game to find a way to make quick, easy money. McCarty related his experience robbing a stagecoach, emphasizing that he now knew what he had done wrong and he knew how to correct it, and he mentioned that when he was caught and convicted, the time he served was minimal. For some unknown reason the two road agents figured that the stagecoaches on Thursdays carried the heaviest treasure and set their sights on the stagecoach from Hills Ferry in Stanislaus County to Banta in San Joaquin County. On Thursday evening, April 27, they stepped into the road, masked and armed, halted the coach and demanded the Wells, Fargo treasure box. As soon as the box was delivered they ordered the driver to continue on, and he hurried into Banta to report the robbery, but lawmen responding to the scene could find no clue to the identities of the road agents nor a trail to follow. Emboldened by their success in stopping their first stagecoach, but disappointed in the small amount of plunder they had to share, they moved their operation to the Coast Line stage route between Soledad and San Luis Obispo. (See San Luis Obispo County on May 18, 1882.)

CHARLES M. CARTER AND JOSEPH FRANKLIN HARVEY, MAY 17, 1892

Charles M. Carter and Joseph Franklin Harvey were out of work and hungry when they met at Orland. They went across the mountains and finally reached Healdsburg, and there Carter proposed that they rob a store for food, clothing, guns and ammunition, but they could not find the right opportunity. They then went to Fort Ross, and while Harvey waited on the road two miles out, Carter went into town and burglarized a store and stole a Winchester rifle, a double-barreled shotgun, cigars and whiskey, but he took no food or clothing. Harvey, who was twenty-four years old, later insisted that twenty-year-old Carter convinced him that they must rob a stagecoach, so they made up masks. On Tuesday, May 17, 1892, they lay in wait for the stagecoach between Cazadero and Point Arenas. When the coach was near Seaview, eight miles above Cazadero, Carter suddenly jumped out and grabbed the reins of a leader and with his right hand pointed the stolen Winchester rifle at the driver and ordered him to stop. Once the team was reined in Harvey appeared with the double-barreled shotgun and ordered the passengers to step out, lined them up, and robbed them of $70.65. Carter would later say that they examined the Wells, Fargo treasure box and mailbags but determined there was nothing of value inside, but the driver would report they did not ask for the mail nor the box and they never saw them. The passengers were ordered to board and then the driver was told to continue on. At the next stop lawmen were notified, and a description was given of the two men. By that evening Harvey had been arrested on a train near Black's station, and on Thursday, May 19, Carter was arrested making his way from Guerneville to Santa Rosa. Both men were lodged in the Santa Rosa jail and charged with robbery, and on the morning of May 25 the two prisoners were taken before Justice Brown, they confessed, and they were held over for trial. However, it was determined that the charge should be "attempting to steal the U.S. mail," despite the testimony of the stagecoach driver, which was a federal matter. On May 31, the two prisoners were taken before U.S. Commissioner Sawyer and held over for the U.S. grand jury with bail set at $5,000. They pled guilty hoping for a lighter sentence, and this was a successful strategy. In early June, Judge Sawyer sentenced both men to serve terms of two years at Folsom Prison, and both men arrived on June 14, 1892, where Carter registered as prisoner #2667 and Harvey as prisoner #2668. Both men were released on February 11, 1894, after serving twenty months.

Sources: *Los Angeles Herald (CA)*: May 26, 1892. *Sacramento Daily Union (CA)*: May 18, 1892. *San Francisco Call (CA)*: May 25, 1892; May 31, 1892.

Tehama County

ZISKA CALMEZ, BILLY CULLEN, BILLY FUGATE, JOHNNY GRANT AND MILTON SHEPARDSON, AUGUST 21, 1871; SEPTEMBER 26, 1871

On August 21, 1871, four masked road agents, three armed with Henry rifles, stepped out of the brush twenty miles north of Red Bluff in Tehama County and ordered stagecoach driver Ed Lynch, "Hold, and hand down the Wells, Fargo treasure boxes!" The horses could not proceed because the men had stretched a rope across the road, so the driver had no choice but to comply. The driver had the presence of mind to hand down the smaller box, but then the other boxes were demanded. When Lynch said there were no others, one robber said, "You are a damned liar," and climbed up on the wheel. He pulled out the other boxes and threw them down on the road. There was one passenger aboard but he was not molested, and the driver was ordered to continue on. The coach hurried into Red Bluff and the alarm was sounded. At the scene were found boot and mule tracks where the plunder had been packed on a mule and carried away, but the trail was lost and the robbers were not captured.

On September 26, 1871, they reappeared at the same place along the road to Red Bluff and Lynch was again driving, and he delivered the boxes. The robbers took $60 from the Wells, Fargo box sent to Yreka and $240 from the box for Shasta. The amount was so small that they went through the passengers and collected $160, and Wells, Fargo offered a reward of $500 for the arrest and conviction of each robber. A posse was able to track the men, but three made a clean getaway. The lawmen captured Billy Cullen and Johnny Grant as well as five horses, the pack mule, four Henry rifles, and a camping outfit. Those that escaped included Milton Shepardson, Billy Fugate and Ziska Calmez. Cullen and Grant were tried, convicted, and sentenced to serve seven-year sentences at San Quentin. Fugate was captured next, and as soon as he was behind bars he "peached," or informed, on the others and pled guilty on September 15, 1874. He had been promised an early release, and while he was being transported to prison, Governor Newton Booth granted a pardon and he was released when he arrived at the prison.

On Friday, July 12, 1872, the topless stage wagon from Canyon City to The Dalles, Oregon, driven by Ad Edgar, reached Antelope Canyon at 6:30 p.m., a half hour before sunset. Suddenly three men, thoroughly disguised with masks of blue cloth, stepped out of the brush on the right side. After the mail sacks were thrown down, the road agent ordered the driver to continue on. The coach continued to Ward's station and from there hurried on to the Dalles, arriving on Saturday evening. Several men holding a grudge used the opportunity to arrest and prosecute four innocent men for the robbery. They perjured themselves and the four men were convicted, but Ad Edgar, Sheriff J. M. Boyd of Baker County, and Wells, Fargo's agent H. C. Page were certain the four men were innocent and kept a watch for any clue that would lead them to the guilty parties. Frank Johnson was serving a term at the Oregon penitentiary when he encountered Sheriff Boyd, who was at the prison on other business several years later. He told the lawman that a man named Homily, whose real name was Milton Shepardson, along with T. D. Phelps and Charles Darnell, were the men who had robbed the Canyon City stagecoach. According to Johnson, after dividing the plunder Shepardson had gone to Lewiston, Montana; Phelps went to his ranch near Dayton; Washington, and Darnell went to Iowa Hill in Placer County, California. Boyd was soon on their trail, arrested Darnell, and took him to Portland. He next went after Phelps, then hinted that Shepardson was in jail and was about to inform on his confederates, and Phelps made a detailed confession and later turned state's evidence to gain his release. Shepardson was arrested by Baker County, Oregon, deputy sheriff William Harper at Sparta, Oregon, and he was charged with the robbery of a Shasta County, California, stagecoach on the night of August 21, 1871, when five road agents shared $4,300 in gold bullion and coin. Shepardson was not charged in the September 26, 1871, robbery of the same stagecoach at the same place. His defense was that he was in Oregon during the period before, during, and after the robbery and proved his alibi through false testimony. He was tried three times, acquitted after his third trial, and released. On January 26, 1876, Deputy U.S. Marshal Boyd arrested Shepardson in his Colusa, California, hotel room, and the prisoner was extradited to Portland.

Shepardson's trial was called in the U.S. circuit court on June 21, 1876, and he was confronted with his alibi testimony in the California case, where he proved he was in Oregon at the time of the Canyon City stagecoach robbery. He was tried by Judge M. P. Deady who directed the jury to return a verdict of not guilty because conviction was barred by the statute of limitations. Still, the evidence was sufficient to gain the release of the four innocent men. Shepardson was then arrested for a stagecoach robbery in Baker County, Oregon, which occurred in 1873, and this crime was not barred by the statute of limitations. He was convicted and sentenced to serve ten years in the Oregon state penitentiary. He arrived at the prison on November 13, 1876, and registered as prisoner #693. He served his time as a model prisoner and was released on August 23, 1883. He lived a law-abiding life thereafter, or at least was never again convicted of a crime, and died at his home in Peanut, California, on November 14, 1915.

Sources: *Daily Oregonian (Portland, OR)*: July 16, 1872; July 22–23, 1872; July 25, 1872; July 27, 1872; August 21–24, 1872; August 26, 1872; February 7, 1876. *Gold Hill Daily News (NV)*: January 15, 1874. *Idaho Statesman (Boise, ID)*: November 16, 1872; February 8, 1876; February 10, 1876. *Shasta Courier (CA)*: April 10, 1875; May 22, 1875; February 12, 1876; April 1, 1876; July 8, 1876; September 23, 1876.

UNKNOWN, JULY 12, 1889

On July 11, 1889, an $800 payroll for the Sierra Lumber Company was withdrawn at the bank in Red Bluff in Tehama County to be sent to Champion Mill, and this was given to the stagecoach driver the following day. Apparently an aspiring road agent saw the withdrawal and decided to rob the stagecoach. At 8:00 a.m. on Friday, July 12, Bressler's stagecoach was eight miles from town, at a point called the Hog's Back, when a road agent appeared wearing a sack with eyeholes for a mask and brandishing a pistol. Instead of stopping the coach as ordered, the driver whipped up his team and drove the stagecoach, and the treasure, out of danger. After the coach passed, the road agent fired one shot after it, slightly wounding one of the horses, but none of the passenger nor the driver were hurt. When the stagecoach reached Champion Mill the attempted robbery was reported, and soon posses were out from Champion Mills and from Red Bluff, but they failed to identify the robber or find a trail to follow.

Source: *Sacramento Daily Union (CA)*: July 13, 1889.

Trinity County

UNKNOWN, AUGUST 16, 1859

On Tuesday, August 16, 1859, the stagecoach from Yreka to Trinity was near the mouth of Coffee Creek in Trinity County when four men, masked and armed, jumped out from the side of the road and tried to grab the reins of the leaders. Driver Dan Hooker saw them in time to whip up his team and drive out of danger. They did not fire on the coach as it was filled with passengers, and quite probably they did not want to turn an attempted robbery into murder. No reward was posted and no pursuit was made.

Source: *Sacramento Daily Union (CA)*: August 16, 1859.

Tulare County

ALBERT HEUSE DOWNER AND UNKNOWN, OCTOBER 18, 1873; NOVEMBER 22, 1873

On Saturday, October 18, 1873, the stagecoach from Visalia left for Tulare on schedule at 9:00 p.m. with Winn Thoms driving, and Sam Caruthers riding atop on the left. Inside was Caruthers' brother Bob, John Ridgeway with his wife and two small children, a Mr. Howard, and two other passengers unidentified in the record. When the stagecoach had traveled only one and a half miles south of Visalia, in Tulare County, two men suddenly sprang in front of the coach and, with guns in hand, ordered the driver to rein in his team. The appearance of the masked men was so sudden it startled the leaders, and they turned into the wheelers, nearly upsetting the coach. The road agents demanded the Wells, Fargo express box, but before Thoms regained control of his team, one of the robbers, "in a savage tone with a cocked revolver near his [Thoms'] person," made a second demand. Thoms complied and the robbers then ordered the passengers to pass out their valuables, or they would be removed from the coach, tied, and searched. The passengers, in consideration of the women and children, handed out $85, bringing the total to $600 when the $515 in the express box was added to the plunder. Thoms was then ordered to continue on, and he drove at a rapid pace. As soon as he could, he sent word back to Visalia and lawmen rushed to the scene of the robbery, but they could find no clue to the identity of the road agents. They found the treasure box, broken open and emptied, and returned it to the Wells, Fargo office in Visalia. The express company then posted a reward of $250 for the arrest and conviction of each road agent, and a quarter of any part of the plunder recovered. While there was no definite clue to the identity of the robbers, lawmen thought it was the same men who had burglarized Frenchy's Cabin near Wagy's Mill shortly before the stagecoach robbery. Lawmen had pursued the burglar into Stockton, but he eluded capture and it was supposed he had returned to Visalia to rob the stagecoach.

On Saturday, November 22, the stagecoach bound for Tulare left Visalia at 9:00 p.m. When the coach reached the same place it had been robbed six weeks earlier, the horses suddenly came to an abrupt stop. A lone road agent then leveled his revolver at the driver and demanded the Wells, Fargo express box. Thoms, again driving, delivered the box, and when the robber determined that there was only one passenger aboard, a woman, he ordered Thoms to continue on. The coach could not proceed, however, until the road agent removed a large rail he had placed across the road, unseen by Thoms but the reason the horses had stopped. The box, which contained $67 in coin, was found later at the same place the previous box had been broken open, and it was returned to Wells, Fargo.

Officers had, since a burglary at Frenchy's Cabin and the first stagecoach robbery, been interested in a man who gave his name as John Bell. Later in the evening, after the second stagecoach was robbed, officers found a man loitering about Keener's Stable in the south part of Visalia. They did not recognize him as "John Bell," and he convinced them he was a harmless drunk. Soon afterward a horse belonging to a Mr. McCloud was stolen and the horse thief fled toward King's River. A posse was soon on his trail and they recovered the stolen horse; then a mile and a half further along the trail they captured the fugitive. They found in his pockets $67 in coins in the exact denominations of the coins stolen from the coach, and the watch stolen from Frenchy's Cabin when it was burglarized. The prisoner gave his name as Albert Heuse Downer, often misspelled "Downen," "Downey," or "Downing." On Friday, November 28, Downer was arraigned before Judge N. O. Bradley. Winn Thoms identified him as one of the two road agents on October 18 and the lone highwayman on November 22. Downer was held over to answer to the grand jury, bail set in the sum of $5,000, and he was remanded to the county jail.

On February 19, 1874, the *Visalia Delta* reported that Downer "has got tired of cell life" and tried to escape through the wooden floor from the second-floor jail to the first floor. The walls were lined with iron, so he began burning through the wooden flooring, starting the flame by rubbing together two pieces of wood, and using lint from his bedding for kindling. He was nearly through the floor when discovered. Downer was indicted and tried, and on March 4 he was found guilty of robbing the stagecoach on October 18, 1873, and of burglarizing Frenchy's Cabin, but the jury could not agree on the second stagecoach robbery charge. On March 19, 1874, the *Visalia Delta* reported, "And the Court sentenced him to the Penitentiary for 22 years: 20 years for stage robbery and 2 years for house-breaking."

Downer arrived at San Quentin on March 16, 1874, and registered as prisoner #5923. On October 1, 1878, Downer, who had been doing the laundry for families within the "dead lines" of the prison, passed through the gates with his laundry basket to deliver the clean laundry and, when near the commissary building, changed into a fashionable suit, lit a cigar, and sauntered past six guards. When he arrived at the last guard he stopped to speak of the weather, and said, "Well, I've been waiting a long time for this." The guards recognized him, but seeing his dress and demeanor thought his time was up and he had been released, and it was an hour before his escape was reported. The warden offered a reward of $50 for his capture, and his description was circulated throughout the area. Downer made his way to Nevada County, California, and remained free until he was captured by G. W. Giffen on December 11, 1878. On September 12, 1884, Governor George Stoneman commuted Downer's sentence to ten and a half years, and four days later he was discharged by expiration of sentence. He was convicted of a robbery in Santa Clara County and arrived at the prison on October 17, 1885, to serve seven years, but two were added for an escape, and he was discharged on December 18, 1892. He then served two years at the Washington state penitentiary at Walla Walla and was discharged August 28, 1895. He arrived in Denver, Colorado, two months later and began a spree of more than fifty highway robberies and became known as the "Lone Highwayman." He was arrested on October 19, 1896, and confessed to the robberies and several murders committed during those robberies. He was convicted of murder in the first degree and sentenced to die, but his sentence was commuted to life in prison at the Colorado state penitentiary.

Sources: *National Police Gazette:* December 5, 1896. *San Francisco Chronicle (CA)*: October 3, 1878. *Visalia Weekly Delta (CA)*: October 23, 1873; December 4, 1873; March 12, 1874.

UNKNOWN, APRIL 26, 1881

On Tuesday, April 26, 1881, the down stagecoach from Laporte to Oroville, with Fred Morse driving, was one mile below Woodville when two road agents, masked with flour sacks and armed with double-barreled shotguns, stepped out from a large pine tree and ordered Morse to halt. They ordered out the three passengers—one man, and one woman with her child—but they were not molested. The road agents then called for the Wells, Fargo express box and the mail pouch and they broke open the box using tools they had brought with them, but there was nothing of value inside. They were disappointed to find there was no iron safe inside the passenger compartment, as the tools they brought would have been more than capable of busting it open. They next hefted and shook the mailbag, but it was too light to warrant cutting it open. Morse asked that the mail, box and waybills be returned to the coach, and the robbers lifted them aboard. They ordered the passengers to board, and as soon as they were seated they told Morse to move along. The driver whipped up his team and left the two frustrated robbers standing on the side of the road watching the coach depart. There were no clues to the robbers' identities at the scene, nor a trail that could be followed for any distance. With nothing stolen and no one hurt, there was little motivation to continue the investigation.

Source: *Sacramento Daily Union (CA)*: April 27, 1881.

Tuolumne County

UNKNOWN, APRIL 23, 1860; MAY 8, 1860

In early 1860 there had been a number of break-ins at cabins in the vicinity of Chinese Camp and Big Oak Flat, but no one had come under suspicion. Two men had been loitering about the town for some time, and they approached the Wells, Fargo watchman and recruited him into their scheme to steal the express box from the stagecoach when the box was heavy with treasure. The watchman was included in their planning and once he had all the details he alerted agent Miller of the scheme, and it was decided that they would proceed with the shipment to capture the men in the act. Six men were employed to hide nearby when the box was loaded and at 1:00 a.m. on Monday, April 23, 1860, a heavy express box was loaded onto the stagecoach from Chinese Camp to Big Oak Flat, but there were no passengers aboard. Miller and the watchman then conspicuously stepped into the house for a drink. The two footpads then snuck up to the coach, and one climbed aboard and removed the box. They had carried it just ten yards when a half dozen men ran forward from their hiding places and fired a dozen shots at the footpads. The two men then disappeared into the darkness, leaving the express box behind, but neither man was wounded. The men who had come to the rescue, with Miller and the watchman, began searching for sign and, using a lantern, spent several hours tracking the pair to a cabin a mile from town. Inside they found one of the men and arrested him, and upon searching the cabin they found a number of revolvers with ammunition, knives, slungshots, "jimmys," "billys," goods recently stolen from cabins, ample provisions for several men for an extended period, and an assortment of other burglar's tools. The men discussed lynching their prisoner but decided to let the law take its course. The tracks of the second road agent, determined to be an ex-convict by comments of the prisoner, headed from the cabin toward the American River, so a small party went in pursuit but returned empty-handed. The prisoner was charged with burglary.

At 3:00 a.m. on Tuesday, May 8, 1860, the stagecoach from Big Oak Flat had just reached

Moccasin Creek, a few miles from Chinese Camp, when three road agents, fully disguised, yelled to the driver, "Stand and deliver!" One road agent had a revolver but each of the others had a sawed-off shotgun. Driver Robinson, also owner of the stage line, reined in his horses, and the robbers immediately unhitched them and took them to the side of the road. A passenger named Hitchcock was riding atop and three more passengers were riding inside. The robbers took the Wells, Fargo express box, broke it open using an ax and a crowbar they had brought along, and took out $650. They next demanded the "private purses" of the passengers, but as each presented his money it was returned. Hitchcock, who had $700 in his pockets, handed over $13 which was returned with the comment, in French, "*le jeu ne vent pas la chan, delle.*" One of the inside passengers handed out $22.50 which was also returned, that robber saying that to take it would jeopardize his reputation as a highwayman. None of the passengers was searched and no valuables were taken from them. The robbers then hitched the horses and told Robinson to continue on. As soon as the coach reached Chinese Camp the robbery was reported to the Wells, Fargo agent and he began an investigation, but the robbers were not identified except that one was recognized as the robber missed at the cabin in April.

Sources: *Daily Alta California (San Francisco)*: April 28, 1860. *Sacramento Daily Union (CA)*: May 9, 1860.

UNKNOWN, AUGUST 31, 1864

At 3:00 p.m. on Wednesday, August 31, 1864, the southbound stagecoach from Sonora to Coulterville was three miles beyond Don Pedro's Bar when three masked road agents, armed with double-barreled shotguns, stepped out of the bushes in front of the coach and ordered the driver to halt. One robber covered the driver while the other two ordered out the inside passenger and then climbed into the passenger compartment and began working on the iron safe. It took them forty minutes to bust the safe open, and after they took out the money they destroyed the waybill so that the amount they stole could not be known immediately. They then ordered the passenger to board but did not rob him, nor the driver or passenger riding atop, and then they ordered the driver to continue on. The robbers had disguised themselves and their language to appear as Mexicans, but the ruse failed and they were known to be Americans. Tuolumne County sheriff Bourland was at that time transporting an insane person to the asylum, but at the Crimea House he was notified of the robbery. He left his ward with a passenger, who delivered him to the asylum without incident, while the sheriff went in pursuit of the road agents. The sheriff believed he knew the identities of the three road agents, but apparently he guessed wrong as no arrests followed.

Source: *Sacramento Daily Union (CA)*: September 1, 1864.

RAMON RUIZ, DECEMBER 1, 1875

Ramon Ruiz had been a member of the Ysidro Pardillo gang, but when they bungled a simple stagecoach robbery he struck out on his own. On Wednesday night, December 1, 1875, Ruiz rode up behind the Sonora to Copperopolis stagecoach in Tuolumne County, a few miles from its destination. As he came abreast of driver Jack Gibbons he ordered him to halt. Ruiz was not masked, but he brandished his pistol in a threatening manner and ordered, "Put out your lights," and they were extinguished. Next he commanded, "Throw down the box." The driver tried to convince Ruiz that the box was light and carried little or nothing of value, but Ruiz accepted no excuses and the box was delivered. The coach was waved on and Ruiz then went to work breaking open the box, and he took out $600 in gold coin and dust. Gibbons gave a detailed description to Tuolumne County sheriff Ben K. Thorn, who recognized the robber as Ruiz.

Wells, Fargo offered their standard reward and a portion of the plunder recovered. Sheriff Thorn tracked Ruiz to a cabin near Telegraph City in Calaveras County. On December 9, 1875, the lawman broke in on Ruiz and surprised the unarmed bandit before he could get hold of his pistols. Ruiz, after he was in jail, informed on the gang and by December 29 Pardillo, Antone Valacca and Jose Maria were behind bars, and soon all of the members of the Pardillo gang were either killed or were captured, convicted, and sentenced to prison terms.

In April 1876 Ruiz was convicted of the October 12, 1875, robbery and sentenced to serve only four years, in consideration of his cooperation with lawmen. He arrived at San Quentin on July 25, 1876, and was released on July 25, 1879, upon expiration of his sentence with credited time off for good behavior. As Ruiz exited the prison he was arrested by Tuolumne Sheriff Tyron M. Yancey for the December 1, 1875, stagecoach robbery. He was convicted and received another two-year sentence, arriving at the prison on October 14, 1879, and being released on June 14, 1881. After his second release Ruiz tried horse stealing again but managed to elude capture. In November 1881 the Sonora to Milton stagecoach was robbed and Ruiz was arrested and questioned, but he proved an alibi and was released. He again tried horse stealing and ended in prison once more, this time for a four-year term. When he was released he went to Baja, California, and opened a butcher shop. It soon became apparent he was selling more beef than he bought legally, so when a mob of ranchers came to put an end to the rustling, Ruiz fled. Narrowly missing a lynching seemed to have quite an effect on Ruiz and he "went straight" thereafter. He became a tamale vendor in the Angel's Camp area. In the summer of 1899 he caught a serious chest infection and, medical knowledge and skill being rudimentary in those primitive days, was able to do little to cure the malady. On August 31, 1899, Ruiz suddenly collapsed on the street of Angel's Camp and died. (See Calaveras County on November 7, 1874.)

UNKNOWN, NOVEMBER 15, 1876

At 3:30 a.m. on Wednesday, November 15, 1876, the stagecoach from Sonora to Milton had reached Brown's Flat when three masked road agents stepped out of hiding and ordered the driver to halt. After the coach was stopped one robber took a position at the nigh (left) fore wheel and covered the driver and passenger Captain L. E. Lyons with his double-barreled shotgun. The driver asked, "What do you want?" and the robber replied he wanted the treasure box. Meanwhile the second road agent, with revolver in hand, went round and tried to climb into the passenger compartment, but one of the three passengers inside asked him, "What do you want?" and he hesitated as he replied, "the treasure box." The third robber stood at the space between the nigh side horses and also covered the driver and Lyons with his shotgun. The second man seemed off balance and as he tried to climb aboard his pistol discharged, and the man holding the shotgun at the nigh side wheel staggered back as if wounded. The shot frightened the horses and they started off at a gallop, leaving behind all three road agents, and the driver applied his whip and continued for two miles before he stopped and checked on his passengers. As the coach passed, the third robber fired his shotgun in the direction of the driver's seat, but he was "out of line" with the driver and passenger Lyons by the time he was able to fire and he missed his mark, and the man with the pistol fired at the coach several times as well. No one was hit, but the covering on the back of the coach was riddled with buckshot and the standard that secured the covering was cut in two by a bullet. The coach continued into Milton where the robbery attempt was reported and a posse was organized. When they arrived at the scene the robbers had fled, leaving no trail nor a clue to their identities, nor did the posse find any blood evidence that one of the robbers had been wounded.

Source: *Stockton Herald (CA)*: November 15, 1876.

CHARLES BARNWELL, DICK BOLTER, EUGENE "JOSH" THAYER AND PEDRO YBARRA, JANUARY 16, 1878

During the latter part of 1877 Wells, Fargo & Company suffered so many losses along stagecoach routes in Tuolumne County that they stood nearly $20,000 in the red. They threatened to discontinue service in the county but had not taken any action as 1878 began, perhaps hoping that lawmen would now be motivated to put an end to the highway robberies to keep the company operating in their county. On January 16, 1878, after 4:00 p.m. four masked and armed road agents halted the stagecoach from Sonora to Milton when it was near Columbia. They demanded the Wells, Fargo treasure box, which was thrown down, and the robbers broke it open and took out $4,600 before ordering the driver to continue on. The driver hurried into Milton and sounded the alarm. Soon three men were in jail for the crime—Jack White, Newt Taylor, and Jesus Rendone, but Wells, Fargo's chief detective James B. Hume believed these men were innocent. Hume was put in charge of the investigation and, assisted by Calaveras County sheriff Ben K. Thorn, soon had a new suspect identified—Pedro Ybarra—but they lacked the evidence to make an arrest. They continued investigating, and their perseverance paid off when they interviewed Fabiana Soto, a soiled dove whose paramour was Josh Thayer. She confided to the lawmen that Thayer and Ybarra had committed the stagecoach robbery in the company of Dick Bolter and Charles Barnwell. She also directed them to the place behind her house where the men had buried $1,200, and then told them where $2,000 had been buried under the steps to Ybarra's house; but the remaining $1,400 was never recovered.

The four men were arrested and lodged in the jail at Sonora. Under close questioning, Bolter "peached," or informed, on his friends, giving all the details of the robbery, and Barnwell agreed to testify against Thayer and Ybarra in return for his release. When the road agents came to trial, Bolter and Barnwell testified against Thayer and Ybarra, and in consideration of turning state's evidence, they were released as promised. In late May the two defendants were found guilty as charged in the indictments. Thayer was sentenced to serve eight years at San Quentin; he arrived on June 5, 1878, and registered as prisoner #8296. Thayer was pardoned by Governor George C. Perkins on January 6, 1883, and discharged four days later. Ybarra was sentenced to serve a life term, and he also arrived at San Quentin on June 5, 1878, and registered as prisoner #8297. He was pardoned by Governor George Stoneman on February 27, 1884, and was discharged on March 3, 1884, after serving less than six years.

Sources: *Tuolumne Independent (Sonora, CA)*: February 2, 1878. *Calaveras Chronicle (CA)*: February 2, 1878.

CALVIN BRAGG AND FRANK ROLFE, FEBRUARY 2, 1882

During the early morning hours of February 2, 1882, the stagecoach "which plies between Sonora, Chinese Camp, and Copperopolis," with no passengers aboard, was halted when it was five miles from Chinese Camp. Two masked road agents, with feet muffled to cover their tracks, appeared suddenly from the roadside, covered the driver with double-barreled shotguns, and ordered him to rein in his team. The robbers demanded the Wells, Fargo treasure box, and it was thrown down. One robber took a sledgehammer and cold chisel and opened the box, taking out $286. When told to continue on, the driver whipped up his team and hurried to the next station. Calaveras County sheriff Benjamin K. Thorn was notified, and he was soon on the trail of the robbers. Thorn, with Deputy William Hendricks of Milton, returned on February 10 without prisoners, but reported that Sheriff Yancey of Tuolumne County, with a large posse, was trailing the robbers and, if he had no better luck, Thorn would again take the trail. However, neither Thorn nor Yaney found the robbers.

On February 16 Captain Charles Aull and Deputy Sheriff Whitlock of Fresno got onto the track of the robbers after they learned the two men had stopped two days at Jim White's place near the Fresno slough, but left for Hollister by way of Big Pinoche and Tres Pinos Canyons. The lawmen followed and that night were joined by L. C. Davis of Los Banos. They arrived at the Big Pinoche store at daybreak and found that the fugitives were only a few hours ahead of them. They hurried over the ridge into Tres Pinos canyon and after going ten miles overtook their quarry, heading toward Hollister in a light wagon. They were taken completely by surprise and, though heavily armed, were arrested without resistance. Captain Aull, who had worked as a guard at San Quentin, recognized both as ex-convicts, one giving the name Frank Rolfe and the other Joe Hampton, though it was later learned his real name was Calvin Bragg. On February 25 at 1:00 p.m. the two prisoners were safely lodged in the jail at Sonora.

The men had their examination and were held over for action by the grand jury. They were indicted, and Rolfe was tried in late March, with Bragg testifying against him. Rolfe was easily convicted and the defendant, who had a long prison record, was sentenced to serve a life term. He managed to escape from the Sonora jail during the first days of April but was recaptured the same day and arrived at San Quentin on April 8, 1882. On July 17, 1908, Rolfe's life sentenced was commuted, and he was discharged. Bragg was tried in late April and also convicted of the robbery, but his previous prison record was not as impressive as Rolfe's, he had cooperated in testifying against Rolfe, and he was sickly, so he was only sentenced to serve five years. Bragg arrived at Folsom, to keep him away from Rolfe, on May 3, 1882. Bragg died in the prison hospital on October 8, 1882.

Sources: *Calaveras Chronicle (CA)*: February 11, 1882; February 25, 1882. *Sacramento Daily Union (CA)*: February 3, 1882.

LEE BROWN, JULY 2, 1896; OCTOBER 6, 1896

Just before daybreak on Thursday morning, July 2, 1896, the stagecoach from Sonora to Knight's Ferry was one mile from Crabtrees, seven miles from its destination, when a lone road agent sprang from behind a large rock into the road near the heads of the leaders. He had his cocked revolver in his hand, pointed it at driver Andy Shine, and said, "Hold up there. Drop that box." He then called for the mailbags, and two bags were thrown down—one from Jamestown and the other from Chinese Camp—but Shine managed to slide a third bag under his seat. As soon as the plunder lay on the road the robber told Shine to proceed, declining to molest passenger Dr. Pegg. Shine whipped up his team and hurried into Knight's Ferry, where the local deputy and constable were notified and dispatches were sent to Sheriff Yancey. The robber was described as hatless with a black mask over his face, wearing a jumper and blue overalls; he was of medium height and about 150 pounds. The express box had no valuable contents, but the value of the contents of the two mailbags was estimated at several hundred dollars. A posse rode to the scene and recovered the busted box and the mail that was left behind, but there was no clue to the road agent's identity nor a trail to follow for any distance.

At 1:30 a.m. on Tuesday, October 6, 1896, the stagecoach from Chinese Camp to Knight's Ferry had reached Crimea Hill, halfway way between Chinese Camp and Cloudman, when a lone, masked road agent appeared at the side of the road. He pointed his revolver at driver Fred Johnson and commanded him to halt. Once the coach was stopped the road agent demanded the Wells, Fargo express box and the mailbags, and as soon as they lay on the road he told Johnson to move on. There were four passengers aboard—three men and one woman—but they were not molested. The amount in the box was not immediately known but the next morning postmaster John Curtin drove to the scene and gathered the mailbag and the mail which had been scattered about, and he was able to confirm that one registered package containing $65 was taken, as well as several packages from the box, the contents unknown, and he recovered the busted box. Deputies Lee Price of Sonora and James Donohue of Jamestown had already ridden to the scene and started on the trail of the robber, foot tracks made by moccasins. At Dom Pedro's Bar the robber threw away his moccasins, crossed the river, and continued along the La Grange Dam for ten miles, until he arrived in the town of La Grange where he bought a pair of shoes. From there he continued until he reached an abandoned tunnel on the banks of the Tuolumne River, and on October 7 he was captured inside the tunnel. The deputies took their prisoner to Sonora, and by that night he was safely lodged in jail. When first captured he denied being the robber, but while on his way to Sonora he said his name was Lee Brown and he confessed to the robbery. Brown, a twenty-five-year-old German, had only $5 in his pockets though it was known by then that there was more than $100 in the express box. He said he had sunk a parcel in the Tuolumne River, but would not describe the contents nor where it had been sunk. There appears no record of prosecution, and Brown does not appear on the rolls of the state prison.

Sources: *Sacramento Daily Union (CA)*: October 7–8, 1896. *San Francisco Call (CA)*: July 3, 1896; October 8, 1896.

"Black Kid," May 17, 1900

Between 8:00 and 9:00 p.m. on Thursday, May 17, 1900, the southbound stagecoach from Chinese Camp heading for Yosemite Valley was stopped at Big Oak Flat with five male passengers aboard. When the coach reached Moffitt's bridge a lone highwayman stepped out of hiding and leveled his gun at the driver's head and ordered him to stop. The driver reined in the team and the road agent told the passengers to come out and pile their money in the road, and this was done in minutes. As soon as all had contributed, the robber ordered them back into the coach and told the driver to continue on. Just then the northbound stagecoach appeared, driven by William Walton, and the robber told the driver of the first coach to wait. Once he had stopped the second coach he told the first driver he could then drive on. He went through the four male passengers in the second coach in the same manner, not molesting the two women aboard. In neither case did he ask for the mail nor for the treasure box, and Wells, Fargo later insisted that there was little or no treasure aboard either coach. After making his second collection the road agent told the passengers to board, and as soon as they were seated he told the driver to move on. From the first coach the road agent had collected $125, with $40 the most paid by one man, and he got $110 from the four men in the second coach. Though only one robber was seen there was a strong sense by all that there was at least a second man in hiding with his gun aimed at them.

Sheriff Price organized a posse and took bloodhounds to the scene where they started in pursuit, and the stage company posted a $200 reward for the capture of the robber. On May 18 Constable James Swatzel arrested two men who had come to Oakdale on the Sierra railway, and the man named Michael Kelley answered the description of the road agent—medium build, stoop shouldered, with blue eyes. They had little money and no weapons, and they proved they were in Jamestown at the time of the robbery and were released. One passenger said he was sure Kelley was the road agent, so Kelley and his partner Charles Molloy were kept under surveillance. No arrests followed, however, and lawmen waited for a break in the case. (See Madera County on June 2, 1900.)

Yuba County

THOMAS J. HODGES, BILL GRISTY, NED CONVERY, MONTAGUE LYON, JUAN ROCHER AND BOB CARR, AUGUST 12, 1856

Gold was discovered at Sutter's Mill in Coloma on January 24, 1848, and by 1849 the rush was on. Men from around the world flooded into California in search of riches. Mining, it turned out, was a lonely business, and homesick miners could hardly wait for some word from home to distract them from their daily routine. Mail was slow to arrive, if it arrived at all, at these isolated "boom" towns of tents and temporary buildings. Alexander Todd joined in the search for gold but soon learned that mining was a tough business, and few struck it rich for all the work and time they put in. Todd offered to bring in the mail which was piled high at the post office in San Francisco, and he employed pack trains and a water route. While this seemed the perfect scenario for a road agent to operate, there were no robberies in those early days and Todd later explained, "An express man on the road was almost exempt from interference because everybody was interested, and if an express man had been attacked, and his assailant discovered, punishment would have been very speedy.... An express man though carrying large sums of money, bore almost a charmed life in those days." In June 1849 the first stage line in California, the Maurison & Company Express and Mail Line from Stockton to the Stanislaus mines, was established, and the "coaches" were spring or dead axle wagons pulled by teams of two or four mules or horses. The first stagecoaches arrived by ship on June 24, 1850, and the next shipment of Concord stagecoaches did not arrive until 1851. Finally roads were established, though they were often little more than a worn track of wagon wheels, and stagecoaches began to replace pack trains and freight wagons, but no one had tried to stop and rob a stagecoach during those early years.

Thomas J. Hodges was arrested in 1851 for breaking into a cabin, and to protect his respectable family in Rome, Tennessee, he adopted an alias from an Auburn thief of small renown—Tom Bell. Twenty-one-year-old Bell was convicted and sentenced to a term on the *Waban,* a 268-ton prison bark anchored at Angel Island in San Francisco Bay across from Point San Quentin. He had not been in prison long when he managed to escape by feigning illness, but he was soon captured and returned to complete his sentence. In late 1854 he escaped again, this time with six men whom he would later enlist into his gang. One of these men, serving time as Bill White though his real name was Bill Gristy, would become his first lieutenant and close friend, but would eventually betray Bell. Bell and Gristy enlisted Ned Convery, alias Connor, and Jim Smith who had escaped prison with the gang leader. They added to their rolls Montague Lyon, known as "Monte Jack," and he brought with him Juan Rocher, alias Juan Fernandez. "English" Bob Carr also joined the ranks.

On August 5, 1856, two men on horseback rode in front of the stagecoach on the road near the Waukesha House in El Dorado County, stopping the coach. They were not masked but had pistols in their hands as they rode along the side of the coach and looked in, but they made no demands, were not recognized, and they leisurely rode on. This was, perhaps, a test run for the robbery to follow. On the morning of August 12, 1856, Sam Langston's Express Company stagecoach pulled out of Camptonville for Marysville with John Greer, sometimes spelled Gear, driving and Bill Dobson riding as shotgun messenger. Between Dobson's legs was the Wells, Fargo express box containing $100,000 in gold dust. A gold-dust dealer from Camptonville named Rideout, the major contributor to the treasure in the box, had elected to ride his horse ahead of the stagecoach to avoid the dust kicked up by the coach's wheels and horses. The stagecoach stopped at the California House twenty-five miles from Marysville where Smith Sutton, disguised as a miner, got off. He was Bell's chief spy in Camptonville and confirmed that the treasure was aboard.

The coach pulled out at 1:00 p.m. with Rideout still in the lead. Bell mounted and rode down a wash to collect his men, and they rode hard to get ahead of the stagecoach. Just before 4:30 p.m. Rideout came to the fork in the road to Marysville, only minutes ahead of the coach, and decided to take the alternate, slightly longer high road where many large trees offered shade on that warm afternoon. The fork was only a few miles from town and the trip looked like it would soon come to an end without any untoward event, so Rideout relaxed in his saddle. However, the gold dust dealer had not ridden more than a hundred yards when Monte Jack, "English" Bob Carr, and Juan Rocher rode out of the brush and covered him with their revolvers. They ordered Rideout to dismount and took his horse and he started toward the ravine, intending to climb down to the stage road and hitch a ride on the coach, when the men called him back and went through his empty pockets, then ordered him down to the road where he intended going anyway. The three men sat on their mounts, one holding the reins of Rideout's horse, and watched their victim struggle through the heavy brush.

As soon as Rideout got to the stage road he heard the coach coming, and was about to wave at the driver to stop when Tom Bell, Bill Gristy and Ned Convery rode out of the brush on the other side of the road and covered Greer and Dobson with revolvers, and Bell ordered "Halt!" The three men who had taken Rideout's horse were then riding as hard as they could through the heavy brush of the ravine, as they were supposed to be on the opposite side of the coach covering the two stage men, and this proved to be their downfall. Dobson could have made no move if covered from two sides, but with all three targets on one side of the coach he did not hesitate and opened fire with his rifle, and several armed passengers joined in the fracas with their revolvers. Convery was wounded slightly and unhorsed, so the other two men retreated into the brush pulling their wounded companion with them. The stagecoach proceeded on at a run as the three horse thieves arrived on the scene and fired after the coach. In their haste to try a second time to stop the stagecoach, they dropped the reins to Rideout's horse, and he swung into the saddle and raced after the coach. Dobson, though wounded in his arm, swung around as the three newcomers fired after the fleeing coach and the messenger shot Rocher out of his saddle, or at least the horse bolted and threw its rider. In all, over forty shots were exchanged in less than a minute, but not one of the robbers was seriously wounded.

When Rideout caught up with the coach, Greer told him to ride ahead and sound the alarm. The driver said they would take stock of the situation when they were safe in Marysville. The town was quickly alerted so everyone was on the street when the coach arrived, but the passengers had already determined that in addition to Dobson's arm wound, John Campbell had received a grazing shot to his forehead and another man had been shot in both legs. Worst of all, the Negress wife of the town barber, Mrs. Tilghman, had been shot through the brain and killed instantly. In addition, the crowd learned that a white male passenger and four Chinese male passengers had fled from the coach when it was attacked and were probably still stumbling through the brush on the outskirts of town. The robbers had not thought to wear masks, and from the description it was clear that it was the Bell gang, led by Bell himself.

Robbery was one thing, murder another, and throughout northern California citizens demanded that the Bell gang be rounded up and hanged or imprisoned. In Sacramento, detectives Robert Harrison and Daniel Gay were assigned to capture and destroy the Bell gang, and they were not to undertake any other tasks until they succeeded. Captain Bill King of the Marysville police swore in a posse and started on the robbers' trail. King was so persistent that Bell wrote him a letter in which he tried to trade information on other crimes and criminals and offered a monetary bribe; he challenged the lawman, "Catch me if you can." He suggested that he would consider an armistice and he took that opportunity to deny a killing which had been attributed to him. In September, Detective Harrison and his new partner J. M. Anderson of Marysville captured a member of the Bell gang named Tom Brown. Brown could not tell them anything about

Bell, but he disclosed where five members of the gang were camped. The detectives made their plans and enlisted the help of Captain A. J. Barclay and an unnamed butcher known for being a crack shot. They went to the camp near the Mountaineer House, arriving at night. The plan was for the prisoner to go ahead of the two detectives and open the flap, then greet the men inside. The detectives would then jump in and cover the fugitives with their double-barreled shotguns. The other two posse men would remain outside and draw a bead on the tent with rifles and, if there was any shooting, riddle the tent with bullets. All went well until George Walker grabbed a pistol from the table when told to surrender and replied, "No, never!" He was killed instantly with a load of buckshot in his chest, and the detectives, knowing that the tent would be shot to pieces in seconds, fell to the floor. This gave Bill Gristy the chance to escape under the side of the tent, and he got away though he suffered a severe wound to his scalp. Nicanora Rodriguez tried to follow but was shot in the hip. Meanwhile Anderson covered Brown, Adolph Newton and a Mexican, known only as Domingo, with his shotgun still fully loaded in both barrels, which prevented a further breakout. The posse, though disappointed with Gristy's escape, took to jail Brown, Newton, Rodriguez and Domingo and brought in the dead body of Walker, declaring it a good night's work.

Meanwhile Monte Jack had been hiding at the ranch of a man named Ramirez, and when a posse went there to capture him the Mexican resisted and was shot dead, which allowed Monte Jack to escape. Two days later word came that a number of gang members were in custody at the Oregon House, and when the posse arrived and sorted through the prisoners three more of Bell's gang were jailed, but not one of importance. The next day five more of Bell's men were captured and jailed by Captain Calloway of Marysville, and Jack Phillips of the Mountaineer House was arrested for harboring fugitives and providing Bell's men with intelligence on potential victims. Placer County sheriff Henson was the next to encounter gang members and nearly captured Bell. He got word that some of the gang was at the Franklin House near Auburn, and when the sheriff arrived with his posse he found Bell, Ned Convery and Perry "Texas" Owens mounted. A gunfight followed in which Convery was killed, but Bell and Owens fled. The two fugitives knew they had to hide for a few weeks until winter set in, when the cold and heavy rains might discourage the posses searching for them. Bell established a base camp and sent out word to Bill Gristy to join him. He also sent for Elizabeth Hood and her three daughters to come and keep house, and then hired two brothers named Farnsworth, too old to be gang members, to chop wood, tend the animals and do the other chores necessary to the upkeep of a frontier farm.

Gristy had been active robbing travelers with a Mexican partner, so when he got word to join Bell he started out bringing along the Mexican. When the pair got as far as Knight's Ferry, not far from Firebaugh's Ferry, they decided to go into the sleepy little farming community and have a good meal. They were in an area of California where the Bell gang had never operated and were sure they would not be recognized, but they had just sat down to dinner when they were arrested. It was a remarkable coincidence that Major T. W. Lane, a close friend of the Angel Island prison warden, was in town. He had visited the prison two years earlier and recognized Gristy as Bill White, before he had escaped from that institution, and knew him to be a member of the Bell gang. After a night in the stone jailhouse, Gristy and the Mexican were ready to negotiate, so after Gristy told all about Bell's hideout, he was sent north to stand trial while the Mexican was held as a guide. Plans were perfected and the posse started for a farm six miles above Firebaugh's Ferry. When they arrived they found that a posse had been camped there for a day and Bell had not appeared. They camped the week but when no other gang members showed by Saturday, October 4, they broke camp and started for their respective homes, Sheriff Mulford's posse heading for Stockton in San Joaquin County and Major Lane's posse heading for Knight's Ferry.

Robert Price, a member of Lane's posse, started for his home in Sonora by another route and, upon crossing the river to take the road northeast, saw a man hiding in the brush. His suspicious actions alerted Price, and he turned his horse and headed after the Lane posse. They returned to the place at 11:00 a.m. and found a tall, slender man relaxing in his saddle while talking with a mounted Mexican. They got the drop on him and asked his name, an unnecessary question when they saw his distinct features. Judge Belt said, "I believe that you are the man we have been looking for," and Bell replied, "Very probably." They tied their prisoner's hands and took him to Firebaugh's Ferry, arriving at 4:00 p.m. Lane then sent a man after Sheriff Mulford. Bell admitted his identity and the men discussed the events leading up to his capture, and he asked for the opportunity to tell all before they hanged him, but the men talked it over and refused his offer. Bell then asked for time to write to Mrs. Hood and to his mother, and paper, pen and ink were provided. The men, now concerned that Sheriff Mulford might arrive and demand custody, discussed their next move, and men went out to prepare a rope. It was nearly 5:00 p.m. when Bell finished the two letters and he was asked if he was ready, and he replied that he was since his life was now worth nothing. He was asked to identify others in his gang, but he declined to inform on them. He blamed drink and gambling for his end as he walked the fifty feet to the sturdy sycamore tree, where the noose awaited, but he took one last swig of whiskey when it was offered. As they put the noose over his head and adjusted it he began to pray in a low tone, and the men simply marched away holding the loose end. Tom Bell was pulled up, and the loose end was tied off to the tree trunk. Without a drop to dislocate his vertebrae the condemned man slowly strangled to death. Sheriff Mulford and his posse arrived ten minutes after Bell was dead and were present when the body was cut down and buried in an unmarked grave.

Jack Phillips was tried as an accessory and served two years in prison. Bill Gristy was returned to prison on his original sentence but was pardoned in 1858 in consideration of his cooperation with lawmen. Smith was in and out of prison the rest of his life, but Perry Owens was released for lack of evidence. All the other members of Bell's gang managed to flee the region or blend with the general population and were not heard of again.

Sources: American Medical Association Historical Register of Physicians. Oren Arnold, "The West's First Stage Robbery," *True Western Adventure*, vol. 1, 1957. Joseph H. Jackson, *Bad Company*, Lincoln, University of Nebraska Press, 1977. Clair Huffaker, "The First Stagecoach Robbery," SAGA, February 1956. National Archives Records Administration. *Old Military and Civilian Records: Veterans Roster for the Mexican American War*. William B. Secrest, *Perilous Trails, Dangerous Men*, Clovis, CA, Quill Driver Books, 2001.

UNKNOWN, AUGUST 31, 1859

On Sunday, August 31, 1859, the stagecoach from Shasta to Marysville was nearing its destination, and traveling at a rapid gait, when several road agents stepped into the road and ordered the driver to rein in his team. The driver, instead, whipped up the horses and took his coach out of danger. He acted so quickly that the robbers had no time to react or try some other way to stop the coach. No posse was organized and no pursuit was undertaken.

Source: *Sacramento Daily Union (CA)*: September 3, 1859.

UNKNOWN, AUGUST 16, 1865

At daybreak on Wednesday, August 16, 1865, the stagecoach from Laporte to Oroville had only traveled a short distance when it came to a barricade across the road made of fencing torn up from a nearby field. The coach came to a halt and five road agents, masked and armed with shotguns, appeared and demanded that driver Wheeler throw down the Rutherford & Company express box. Once it lay in the road several robbers covered Wheeler while the others broke open the box and took out the contents, thought to be of little value as the box had been quite light. The robbers returned the box to the coach and told Wheeler to drive on, and as soon as the coach was under way they ran into the woods. A posse was organized at Laporte and they rode to the scene, but there were no clues to the robbers' identities nor a clear trail to follow.

Source: *Sacramento Daily Union (CA)*: August 17, 1865.

CHARLES "ORMSTEAD" THURMAN, LOUIS J. DREIBELBIS AND UNKNOWN, JUNE 23, 1873

On June 23, 1873, the regular stagecoach, driven by Johnny Sharp, left Downieville at 3:00 a.m. bound for Marysville in Yuba County. There were four passengers aboard: Daniel Kime riding atop with Mrs. Ashcraft, W. T. Day, and a little girl inside. The stagecoach was carrying in Wells, Fargo's express box $2,800 in gold coin, gold dust, and a gold bar. At 1:00 p.m. the coach was twenty-one miles east of its destination, near the Oregon House, when three men slid down an embankment and took their places in front of the horses. The men were masked, their feet were muffled, and they were armed with shotguns, which they pointed at Sharp and Kime as they ordered the stagecoach to halt. The driver had no choice but to rein in his team, and then the demand for the treasure box was made. While Sharp handled the team, Kime delivered the box, and one of the road agents told the passengers, who seemed agitated, "Don't be frightened, we will not disturb you." Sharp wanted to start out again as soon as the box was delivered, but one of the robbers said, "Hold on where you are!" Two of the men covered Sharp and Kime with their shotguns as the horses became restive, but Sharp held them firmly, and the third robber broke open the box with three blows from a large rock. The contents were removed and the broken box was returned to the coach before Sharp was ordered to continue on. Kime and Sharp were certain one of the robbers was Louis J. Dreibelbis, a local desperado. Sharp whipped up his team and hurried into Marysville, where he reported the robbery. Wells, Fargo offered a reward of $500 for each road agent and one-fourth of any treasure recovered, and posses went out in search of the robbers but no arrests followed. James B Hume, Wells, Fargo's chief detective, was assigned to the case but did not make any progress until another stagecoach was robbed in Nevada County on July 27, 1873. (See Nevada County on July 27, 1873.)

AUSTIN N. SMITH, APRIL 14, 1875

At 10:30 a.m. on April 14, 1875, the stagecoach from Camptonville to Marysville, driven by Johnny Sharp, was three and a half miles northeast of the Fountain House ascending the Oregon Hill in Yuba County, which required the horses to walk at a slow pace. On the upper side of the road was a grove of mountain spruces, and from this stand of timber a road agent suddenly appeared. He wore no coat or boots but was masked with a handkerchief, with eyeholes cut in it, pulled over his head. He stepped off the steep embankment onto the road and leveled his double-barreled shotgun at the head of Sharp and ordered him to rein in his team. He demanded the Wells, Fargo express box, adding, "Throw it out damned quick, as I am in a hurry!" Sharp responded, "Don't hurry, you'll get it presently." The road agent kept his shotgun pointed at the driver while he awaited delivery of the box and at one point called out to imaginary confederates, "Keep back there, I need no assistance." Inside the stagecoach were ten passengers, four females and six males, and they were fidgeting about, afraid that at any moment they would lose their driver or be ordered to "pungle" for their valuables, but none could give aid as they were unarmed. The women included Mrs. William Edgar and Mrs. David E. Williams and her two daughters, and when the men began to scramble about, hiding their purses, Mrs. Williams' oldest daughter advised her to cover her gold necklace with her shawl. However at that moment one of the women, overcome with fright, screamed, so the road agent assured them, "Don't fear, ladies, no harm will be done you." Within a moment the treasure box lay on the ground and Sharp was ordered to continue on to Marysville, but the road agent kept the coach covered with his shotgun until it reached a sharp turn sixty yards ahead. Just before the coach passed out of sight of the robbery scene, Sharp turned and saw the road agent grab the box and scramble up the embankment in the direction from which he had come. The road agent went about thirty yards, broke the box open with a hatchet, and removed the contents. The box was found by Sharp two days later, with two packages of letters, an empty watch box, and the waybills still inside, and the hatchet used to break open the box lay nearby. These items were all gathered up and taken to Marysville, but the money from the box, nearly $6,000, was missing.

Rewards were posted for the arrest and conviction of the road agent and also one-fourth of the value of any treasure recovered. The promise of substantial rewards put many men on the trail of the road agent, but it was the jealousy of a Chico man, over his "woman of ill repute," that was the robber's undoing. The road agent had told a soiled dove that he "had a stage robbery put up, and I will make my big strike," and they made plans to leave Chico together once he had the treasure. The prostitute shared the story of her impending good fortune, and the jealous rival called upon U.S. Marshal Mart Casad and gave him the details. Casad went to the house of ill repute and captured his man—a well-known San Quentin ex-convict named Austin N. Smith. Smith had arrived in Chico on April 17, had been courting his soiled dove, and had been flashing a purse filled with gold.

Quickly evidence began to accumulate against Smith. First came Herman Thomas, the owner of the hatchet, who identified the tool and Smith as the man who had taken it. The hatchet seemed to worry the prisoner, and he told officers, "Don't you suppose that if I had committed the robbery I would take the precaution to put that hatchet out of the way?" Next the clothes Smith wore during the robbery were found, which had been described by Mrs. Williams' daughter, and these were brought in for evidence. A man named George Williams, not related to the women passengers, came forward and said that Smith had approached him on March 12 to join in a robbery of the Downieville stagecoach in company with John Clark, a San Quentin escapee, but Williams declined to take part. Smith's examination was held on April 29 and 30 and Smith blamed John Clark, denying any part in the robbery, but Clark was too tall and did not fit the general description of the robber, while Smith was the exact size and build. The large number of witnesses included Herman Thomas, George Williams, driver Johnny Sharp, several passengers, and others. Smith was held over to answer to the grand jury, which easily returned a true bill (indictment). During the first week of May 1875, on the advice of his attorney, Smith pled guilty and told where they could find the remainder of the plunder, and on May 4 James Hume arrived in Chico with all of the stolen treasure not spent. Smith said of his plea, "Mr. Murphy advised me to compromise the case as the evidence was sure to convict me, and told me I wouldn't get over four years as he, Murphy, was assured by the Court. (Smith) adopted the suggestion and directed officers to the place where the treasure was concealed on condition that one-fourth (the reward for recovery) should be turned over ... to (his attorney) as a fee." However, when Smith came into court he was sentenced to serve eighteen years in prison, and he learned that his attorney had no understanding with the court. The reward money was being held in trust for the convicted robber, so he turned it over to Wells, Fargo on the understanding that his attorney would get no part of it. On May 10 Smith was taken across San Francisco Bay to San Quentin and he registered as prisoner #6522. On May 30, 1876, Governor William Irwin commuted his sentence to seventeen years, something which suggested that his long term of imprisonment would be further shortened at a later date. However, on the morning of September 17, 1879, Smith was killed by fellow prisoner Peter Gibson while in the prison yard.

Sources: *The Weekly Appeal (Marysville, CA)*: April 23, 1875; April 30, 1875; May 14, 1875.

YSIDRO PARDILLO, JOAQUIN OLIVERA, JOSE LENARIS, ANTONE VALACCA, JOSE MARIA, ANTONE SAVAGE, MITCHELL RATOVICH, MITCHELL BROWN, RAMON RUIZ, AUGUST 3, 1875; OCTOBER 5, 1875

Ysidro Pardillo, sometimes Isador Pardillo, formed a gang and divided it into two sections, each with its own area to work. Pardillo's band consisted of Jose Lenaris, Red Antone, and Kokimbo. They robbed the Sonora to Milton stagecoach on November 7, 1874, and again on March 23, 1875. Ramon Ruiz was released from prison on July 8, 1875, and he joined Pardillo's section of the gang. On August 3, 1875, Pardillo, with Ruiz and Lenaris, robbed the stagecoach from Laporte in Yuba County to Oroville in Plumas County, and on October 5 the same three men stopped and robbed the stagecoach from Marysville in Yuba County to Downieville in Sierra County. They would then join the two factions to rob the Sonora to Milton stagecoach in Calaveras County on October 12, but that affair was a fiasco, as the driver of the only stagecoach on the route that day convinced them another stagecoach followed with the treasure box, so they waved him on. (See Calaveras County on November 7, 1874.)

UNKNOWN, DECEMBER 22, 1875

On Wednesday, December 22, 1875, the stagecoach from Downieville to Marysville was near Dobbin's ranch when three masked and heavily armed road agents ordered the driver to halt. They demanded the Wells, Fargo express box and made the driver wait while they broke it open, but there was no money inside so they put the broken box back onto the coach. They then ordered the two passengers to step out and line up, and they took from a Chinaman $165 and from the American $200, but they did not molest the driver. As soon as they were certain they had all the plunder they were going to find, they ordered the passengers to board and sent the coach on its way. A posse was organized at Marysville and they rode to the scene, but they could find no clue to the robbers' identities.

Source: *Los Angeles Herald (CA)*: December 23, 1875.

UNKNOWN, JANUARY 21, 1876

On Friday, January 21, 1876, Silas Canady, who ran a stage line between Brown's Valley and Marysville, drove his express wagon into Marysville and went directly to the Wells, Fargo office. He picked up $815.50 for F. W. Schaaf, a merchant in Brown's Valley, put it into a bag, and hid it in the bed of his wagon. At 8:00 p.m. he was three miles from his destination when he was hailed by two men, and he was at a point where he was often hailed by people wanting to place an order for his next trip or to hitch a ride into Brown's Valley. He did not suspect anything until a masked road agent thrust a shotgun in his face and ordered him to get down from his wagon. He got down and was covered by the first man while the second man searched the wagon bed and found the bag of money and, holding it aloft, said, "This is a pretty good night's work." Satisfied, they made Canady unhitch his team and drive off the horses, and when they were sure the horses had run beyond the point of easy recovery, they walked off into the darkness. Canady walked into Brown's Valley and reported the robbery, and it was not until January 27 that he recovered his team. There were no clues to the identity of the road agents, so no one was arrested.

Source: *Marysville Weekly Appeal (CA)*: January 28, 1876.

Unknown, February 1, 1876

On Tuesday, February 1, 1876, the stagecoach from Marysville to Camptonville was two miles from its destination when it was stopped by road agents and the Wells, Fargo express box was demanded. Once they had the box they broke it open but found little inside, so they ordered the passengers to step out and form a line. One man went through their pockets, and in all they collected $220. They ordered the passengers to board and then told the driver to continue on. He hurried into Camptonville and reported the robbery, and a posse was quickly organized and rode to the scene, but they could find no clue to the robbers' identities.

Source: *Sacramento Daily Union (CA)*: February 3, 1876.

Henry "Liverpool" Norton and "Doc" Johnson, June 21, 1876

Henry "Liverpool" Norton and John Doe had robbed a stagecoach in Butte County on June 20, 1876. The following day, Tuesday, June 21, Johnny Sharp was driving the stagecoach from Downieville to Marysville and at 2:00 p.m. he had reached the foot of Stanfield Hill in Yuba County, eighteen miles from Marysville and a short distance below Charley Smith's place, when he saw two men about one hundred yards from the stagecoach on his right running toward the road. They were partially unclothed and disguised, and George Hackett, the company's messenger who was on Sharp's left, was alerted by the driver. Hackett immediately raised his rifle and the two men, seeing the movement, started to run away. Hackett dismounted and took up a foot pursuit which lasted several hundred yards, but he could not find them. Instead he came upon their clothes lying where they had been discarded when they disrobed and donned their disguises. There was also a carpet sack which contained the package of gold dust taken from the Laporte coach the previous day, and valued at $640. The two road agents had disappeared into a thicket of underbrush and the guard could not keep them in view, so rather than take the risk of being ambushed he gathered up their clothing and carpet sack and returned to the coach, which was waiting in the road. Upon searching the clothes Hackett found two gold watches and a considerable amount of coin, also from the previous day's robbery. Hackett gave the articles to the driver to be taken into Marysville, and he started out again after the robbers, with a volunteer from among the passengers joining him. Sharp hurried into town and sounded the alarm, and soon the sheriff had organized a posse and he was also on their trail.

Hackett and his volunteer, thinking that the road agents would return for their clothes and plunder, hid in the underbrush to watch for them, and within twenty minutes they saw a man in the nearby underbrush heading for the place Hackett had found the clothes. The man had a pistol in his hand, but he was covered with Hackett's shotgun and made to drop it and surrender, and he was taken to a nearby farmhouse. James B. Hume, Wells, Fargo's chief detective, was already in the area investigating the robbery of the Laporte stagecoach, and upon learning of the arrest he went to the farmhouse and drove Hackett and his prisoner into Marysville, arriving at 2:00 a.m. Thursday. The robber was well known to lawmen throughout the region as "Liverpool," and it was soon known that his partner was "Doc" Johnson, alias "Snapping Andy." Posses from Butte and Yuba counties were out looking for Johnson, but he had fled the area and was not heard of again.

"Liverpool" was soon identified as Henry Norton. He had his picture taken and then he was lodged in jail to await his examination, and he was held over to answer to the grand jury. Norton was indicted in July and brought into court on July 13, when he pled guilty and was sentenced to serve fifteen years at San Quentin. He arrived at the prison on July 15, 1876, and registered as prisoner #7072. Norton managed to escape from prison on August 10, 1878, but was recaptured in two days. On September 6, 1880, Norton was transferred to the more secure facility at Folsom and registered as prisoner #130. In late December 1885, Governor George Stoneman commuted his sentence and he was discharged on December 23, 1885.

Sources: *Sacramento Daily Union (CA)*: June 22, 1876. *The Weekly Appeal (Marysville, CA)*: June 30, 1876; July 14, 1876; July 21, 1876.

JOE BROWN, TOM BROWN AND CHARLES "RED" FRAZIER, NOVEMBER 13, 1876

After robbing a Shasta stagecoach on November 3, Tom Brown and his brother Joe recruited Charles "Red" Frazier, who worked on a ranch in the vicinity, and he agreed to provide fresh horses, and the Browns planned the next robbery for the stagecoach from Downieville in Sierra County to Marysville in Yuba County. The Browns hid along the road to Marysville on November 13 and stepped out when the coach came into view. They were masked, with guns in hand, and ordered the driver to halt. They were about to demand the treasure box and mail sack as the stage was coming to a halt when Henry Scammon, a Downieville banker, stuck his pistol out the window and fired at the two robbers. He missed them, but he was seriously wounded with the return fire, and several of the robbers' shots killed a stage horse. Once the shooting ceased, the Brown brothers demanded the treasure box and mails and, upon receiving them, immediately broke open the box with an ax and, seeing it contained treasure, left it until they concluded their business. They went through the passengers taking all their money and jewelry, getting about $450. They then allowed the dead horse to be cut free and sent the coach on its way. The take from the box was small, so they supplemented it with gold dust from the Shasta robbery in making their escape. The Browns fled to Norco, California, where they stole fresh horses and headed into Nevada. The son of the horses' owner, Charles Wilson, with a Mexican tracker and Deputy Sheriff Alonzo Dolliver, followed the two road agents to Susanville where they organized an eleven-man posse and continued in pursuit. They cornered the horse thieves in a corral near Deep Holes Springs in Nevada and, blockading the exit, forced the two men to abandon the stolen stock and flee on foot. Joe Brown, after running about one hundred yards, was shot through the calf of his leg by Wilson, who carried a Henry rifle, and collapsed from the wound, and Tom surrendered to avoid the same fate. Once both brothers were arrested they were searched and the plunder from the stagecoaches was found: $170 in gold dust and $100 in coin—the first time the posse men knew they were after bigger game than horse thieves. Although the brothers begged to be released and offered bribes to allow them to escape, they were taken to Chico and lodged in jail. Joe was in terrible agony and begged to be killed, and on December 5, 1876, he succumbed to his wound and infection.

James Hume was brought in and he told Tom of the overwhelming evidence against him, and Tom then "peached," or informed, on Dave Tye and Charles Frazier to get a reduced sentence. Brown was indicted, and in January 1877 he was tried and convicted. He was sentenced to serve a ten-year prison term at San Quentin, arriving on January 13, 1877, as prisoner #7336. Dave Tye was also convicted of the November 3 robbery and he was sentenced to serve seven years, arriving on March 8, 1877, as prisoner #7431. Tye served out his entire term and was released by expiration of sentence on December 5, 1881, and then pardoned to restore his rights. Frazier was convicted of being an accessory to both robberies and sentenced to serve seventeen years in prison, arriving on April 6, 1878, where he was registered as prisoner #8121. Frazier's late arrival was due to several escapes from the Marysville jail—first on June 1, 1877, and again on February 26, 1878. Frazier was pardoned by Governor George Stoneman on March 16, 1883, after serving only five years. (See Shasta County on May 27, 1877.)

GEORGE N. RUGG AND EPH. H. WHITE, JULY 31, 1877

On July 2, 1871, Kirkendall's fast freight team was halted at a point below Corbett's station, and one of many passengers was robbed before help arrived and scared off the road agents. On July 9 a treasure box was removed from the stagecoach coming from Helena, Montana, bound for Corrine, Utah. The investigation was going nowhere until George N. Rugg was arrested and he "peached," or informed, on W. H. Heinsman and Donald McLean. Rugg, to secure his release, testified against them at trial and then pled guilty; he was convicted, immediately pardoned, and released. Rugg went to Marysville, California, and led a law-abiding life for four years, but he was determined to be a road agent so he joined forces with E. H. "Eph" White.

On July 31, 1877, the stagecoach bound for Downieville from Marysville in Yuba County, driven by Johnny Sharp, had only traveled a mile and a half from town on the lower road, about 150 yards from H. L. McCoy's place near a wooden bridge, when two road agents, one armed with a shotgun and the other with a Colt revolver and a shotgun, stopped the coach. One robber told the passengers to step out, saying, "Every damned one of you to the last man." Once everyone was standing in the road the robber with the pistol ordered Sharp to deliver the Wells, Fargo express box, but Sharp replied that it was empty. The robber then told him again to throw it out, and he did. The robber took an ax and broke open the box, spilled the contents, and kicked the items about until he finally picked up one item, but there seemed little of value inside. He went through the passengers taking everything of value, including a silver "5 groschen" German coin carried by G. Schottler as a good luck "pocket piece." The passengers, which included Schottler, B. P. Hugg, J. H. Hart, Pat Elmore, Lawrence "Irish Jimmy" McCarrell, Samuel D. Johns, G. Shotier, and a Mr. Lyons, were ordered aboard and Sharp was told to continue on. The coach hurried into town and Sharp sounded the alarm.

Officer H. L. McCoy and George Hackett, a Wells, Fargo messenger, started for the scene and found two sets of boot tracks confirming there were just two men, with one set of two tracks coming from town and the other set of two going in the direction of town. Both tracks were quite distinctive because of the pattern of nails and tacks in the heels and defects in the soles. The lawmen followed the tracks to the wooden bridge and from there into a levee coming from town, and then into town as far as Eleventh Street. It was clear that one set of two tracks were made after the stage passed as they were on top of the wheel ruts and the other before the stage passed as the wheel ruts obliterated those two sets of tracks, and McCoy recorded the design of the boot tracks for later evidence. The investigation continued, and evidence began to point to White and Rugg. Both men had been seen on the road several times in the days before the robbery, seeming to reconnoiter a place to commit the robbery.

Finally on August 3 McCoy arrested White in Trickle's Saloon, and soon afterward he arrested Rugg, who was then working as a driver for the competing stage line from Marysville to Colusa. McCoy took their boots and matched the design with that of the tracks at the robbery scene, and found they were identical. He also took their property and found in Rugg's pocket a silver "five groschen" coin. Their examination was set for August 16, and among those who testified were E. Brow who had made the boots for White and Rugg a week before the robbery, Albert Metz who had sold each man a shotgun, several men who had seen the two road agents looking over the road just days before the robbery, and driver Sharp who identified them by size and appearance. Along with a number of other witnesses and the physical evidence, there was enough to hold them for the grand jury, and Judge C. M. Gorham set their bail at $5,000.

On the first Sunday in October, Rugg and prisoner Juan Sancho, another robber, tried to escape from the jail. The prisoners had braided a twenty-five-foot rope from their woolen blankets, which they were going to use to scale the outer wall, and they had made a pole from several broom handles to throw up to secure the rope. The prisoners were turned out of their cells into the yard at 8:00 a.m. so the cells could be cleaned, and the deputies, as was their practice, absented themselves from the yard as the wall was believed to be unscalable. However, the sheriff had word of the escape attempt and had his men take up positions for observation and also outside the wall. As soon as the guards were out of the yard, Rugg and Sancho went to work. They tried several times to toss the pole up on the northeast corner and then the southeast corner of the wall to secure the rope and climb out, but every effort failed. Finally the officers had seen enough and returned to lock the prisoners in their cells and confiscate the escape equipment. Rugg and White were convicted of stagecoach robbery, and each was sentenced to serve six years at San Quentin. Rugg arrived at the prison on November 8, 1877, and registered as prisoner #7868. Rugg died in the prison hospital on July 26, 1880. White arrived at San Quentin on November 12, 1877, and registered as prisoner #7874. He was released, by expiration of sentence, on January 12, 1882.

Sources: *Daily Appeal (Marysville, CA)*: October 11, 1877. *Helena Daily Herald (MT)*: July 11–12, 1871; July 19, 1871. *Weekly Appeal (Marysville, CA)*: August 10, 1877; August 17, 1877.

UNKNOWN, OCTOBER 7, 1880

At 11:00 a.m. on Thursday, October 7, 1880, the down stage from Laporte to Marysville was five miles from Brownville when two masked road agents, one armed with a rifle and the other a double-barreled shotgun, stepped from the side of the road and halted the coach. They ordered the passengers out and had them form a line, and then the man with the rifle collected their money, watches and jewelry while the man with the shotgun covered them and the driver. When he finished he told them to board, and then he called for the driver to throw out the Wells, Fargo express box, but did not ask for the mail. As soon as the box lay in the road he told the driver to continue on. The driver whipped up his team and took the coach into Brownville, where he reported the robbery and a posse was quickly organized. The lawmen and citizens rode to the scene but all they could find was the busted box, and they took it back to town. Later it was determined there had been $160 in the box.

Source: *Sacramento Daily Union (CA)*: January 1, 1881.

UNKNOWN, DECEMBER 15, 1881

On December 15, 1881, a road agent, trying to copy the style of Black Bart to mislead lawmen, stopped the stagecoach from Downieville to Marysville when it was four miles north of Dobbins Ranch in Yuba County. The man stepped from behind a tree and then stepped back to keep partly concealed, pointed his shotgun at driver George Sharpe, and commanded, "Throw down that box or I'll blow your damned head off!" The polite request and demeanor of the real "Black Bart" were absent, but there were other discrepancies in the modus operandi as the robber used a different style of shotgun, used profanity rather freely throughout the affair, and wore a different type of mask. The road agent must have been disappointed when he found the box was empty and there was very little in the mails. The only thing consistent with Bolton's methods was that he did not molest the passengers, five Chinamen riding inside, nor the small boy riding atop.

The newspaper must have criticized this copycat's failure to represent himself as Black Bart, and may even have published a primer for him to follow. On December 27, 1881, this same road agent stopped and robbed the stagecoach from North San Juan to Smartsville when it was four miles north of its destination in Nevada County. The robber again made a "water haul" and apparently retired when it became apparent his crimes did not pay.

Sources: *Sacramento Daily Union (CA)*: December 17, 1881; December 28, 1881.

Charles E. "Black Bart" Bolton, July 13, 1882

On Thursday, July 13, 1882, the stagecoach between Laporte in Plumas County bound for Oroville in Butte County, driven by George H. Helm, was on the down grade into Strawberry Valley when a lone road agent, masked and armed with a shotgun, stepped from the side of the road. The robber, Charles Bolton, took up a position in front of the leaders, bringing them to a halt. Wells, Fargo messenger George Hackett immediately fired one load from his double-barreled shotgun at the robber who then tried to conceal himself behind one of the leaders, but one arm stuck out and Hackett took careful aim and shot at the exposed arm. The robber then started to run away but fell after going only a few feet. He quickly got up and went on, but again he fell before reaching the bushes on the side the road; then he managed to arise once more and scramble into the brush. Hackett dismounted and recovered the robber's bloodstained hat and his mask, which he had dropped, and it showed several buckshot holes, so Hackett was certain he had hit his mark. One buckshot, it would later be learned, had grazed Bolton's temple. The road agent had not returned Hackett's shots, but Helms and Hackett were concerned that the man might have confederates nearby. Helm whipped up the team and took the coach, at top speed, into Strawberry Valley where Hackett telephoned Laporte with the news. There were no passengers aboard, but Wells, Fargo was shipping more than $30,000 in treasure on that trip, so it appeared the robber was well informed. From Laporte a posse was organized and headed for the scene of the robbery, but though it was almost certain the robber had been wounded, he could not be found. This was the only time Bolton tried to take in a stagecoach with a messenger aboard, and he learned a lesson.

The stagecoach continued on toward Oroville, and when it was two miles above Boston Ranch, Hackett saw a coat fluttering from behind a tree, and almost at the same instant he saw the glistening from a gun barrel. Looking closer he saw a masked man standing nearly behind the tree, so he raised his shotgun and fired the load from one barrel. The robber fired his shotgun at the same moment, and two of the robber's buckshot struck Hackett in the face, causing minor wounds. The robber then ran out across the road and up a hill while Hackett took careful aim. However, when he tried to fire his second load, the shell misfired and he missed a sure chance to dispatch the aspiring road agent. This robber was not captured.

Source: *Weekly Mercury (Oroville, CA)*: July 14, 1882.

George Tesker, March 21, 1887

On Monday, March 21, 1887, the stagecoach from Marysville to Camptonville was ten miles from its destination when a lone highwayman, unmasked and dressed in a black coat and wearing blue overalls and a blue shirt, halted the coach. He pointed his rifle at driver David Quadlin and ordered him to throw down the Wells, Fargo express box, and this was done. He then ordered the passengers, five men and one woman, to pass out their money and valuables, but Quadlin said, "These are needy men, just looking for work." The road agent then told them to keep their money and ordered Quadlin to move along. He broke open the express box but found it was empty. As soon as the coach reached Camptonville, Quadlin described the road agent's clothing and said he was "five feet eight inches high, dark complected, with blue eyes and a black moustache and goatee." Thomas Labadie, who lived near the Dobbins Ranch not far from Marysville, listened intently and intended to begin searching for the robber the next morning, hoping to earn the reward that would be offered by the Wells, Fargo company. At 6:00 a.m. Tuesday a young man answering the description of the road agent in every detail approached Labadie's house and asked for breakfast, and while he was waiting for the meal to be prepared he talked of looking for work in the area. After he ate he arose to leave, but Labadie told him he was under arrest. The young man was disarmed, tied with ropes, and taken into town where he was delivered to Sheriff Inlow. He insisted, to Labadie and later to the sheriff, that he had nothing to do with the stagecoach robbery. A preliminary examination was held in the Justice Court on the evening of March 23 and the defendant was positively identified by Quadlin as the road agent. After hearing the testimony, and being held over for trial, he said he was George Tesker, sometimes reported as Tuscan, twenty-three years old, and this was his first criminal offense. He claimed he was driven to the crime because he had been out of work for eight months. The following day Wells, Fargo's chief detective James B. Hume arrived and upon seeing the prisoner said he had served a previous two-year sentence at San Quentin under the name C. H. Adkson. It was also suggested that he had "robbed a stagecoach in Nevada a short time ago," but there had been no such robbery in the past four years. On Saturday, April 9, the prisoner was brought into court at Marysville where he confessed and pled guilty, and Judge Keyser sentenced him to serve eleven years at San Quentin. The following day Sheriff Inlow delivered his prisoner to the prison to start serving his time. George Tesker arrived at the prison on April 11, 1887, and registered as prisoner #12488. The record shows that the prisoner had been previously registered as C. H. Adkson #11591 sentenced to serve two years for an assault with a deadly weapon in Sierra County and released on October 22, 1886. On his current conviction Tesker was released on May 11, 1894, after serving seven years and one month.

Sources: *Daily Alta California (San Francisco)*: March 22, 1887. *Los Angeles Herald (CA)*: March 25, 1887. *Sacramento Daily Union (CA)*: March 24, 1887; April 11, 1887. *Territorial Enterprise (Virginia City, NV)*: March 25, 1887.

GEORGE GODFREY, ROBERT W. HOWARD AND JOHN REILLY, EARLY JANUARY 1908

In early January 1908 Robert W. Howard, driver of the mail stagecoach out of Marysville, met with George Godfrey and John Reilly to discuss robbing the mail. They decided to wait for a day when the pouches were very heavy and there were no passengers aboard. When the day came, Godfrey and Reilly went out on the road and waited for the coach to pass, and Howard continued until he reached a quiet, isolated place and then stopped to wait for his accomplices. Godfrey and Reilly stepped out of the bushes and Godfrey asked, "Is everything according to schedule?" Howard said it was and got down, and Reilly was to strike him a blow hard enough to leave a mark; then Howard was to roll in the dust to bolster their story of an attack by road agents. However, Reilly balked because Howard was so much bigger than he was, and Godfrey then said, "Aw, well, I'll do the hitting." Howard said, "Be careful," and Godfrey replied, "Aw! Don't be skeered." Godfrey then struck Howard so hard that it knocked him unconscious, and the two men then rolled Howard's lifeless body in the road until he was covered in dust. Godfrey and Reilly took the mail sacks and fled, and when Howard regained consciousness he drove his coach into the next station and reported the robbery. "Nobody wuz to know nuthin' no siree," Godfrey had promised, and Howard was expected to get sympathy "from the horror stricken populace." However, after everything settled, Howard went to Bakersfield and met with Godfrey and Reilly and asked for his share. Godfrey told him they had hidden the mailbags and that someone must have found and stole them. Howard asked, "What do I get out of this?" and Godfrey replied, "a sore head." That made Howard so mad he rushed to the postal inspectors and told them every detail of the scheme. All three men were arrested, and on January 12 they appeared before Commissioner Heacock and were held over for the U.S. grand jury in San Francisco and taken there. Howard never saw any part of the $400 stolen from the mail. Howard and Reilly were to be tried in early April but they pled guilty to "larceny from the mail," and Reilly was sentenced to serve five years on April 6 while Howard was sentenced to the same term on April 8. Godfrey delayed the proceedings as long as he could, and on September 15 he also pled guilty to "larceny from the mail," and he was sentenced to serve five years. There is no record of Howard in the prison archive, so perhaps he was pardoned and released in return for his cooperation; but twenty-three-year-old Reilly arrived at San Quentin on March 18, 1908, and registered as prisoner #22743, though there is no record of his release. Twenty-one-year-old Godfrey arrived at San Quentin on September 23, 1908, and registered as prisoner #23081; the only notation on his record was that he was transferred to the Leavenworth, Kansas, federal prison on January 24, 1910.

Sources: *San Francisco Call (CA)*: January 22, 1908; April 9, 1908; September 16, 1908.

Appendix: Stagecoach Robberies Listed Chronologically

The information presented shows the date a robbery occurred, (the county where it took place), the starting point of the route and the next town or "home station" following the robbery. Where "at" is used, it indicates the actual location of the robbery.

August 5, 1856 (El Dorado)—at Waukesha House
August 12, 1856 (Yuba)—Camptonville to Marysville
February 17, 1857 (Calaveras)—Murphy's to Cherokee Flat
February 25, 1857 (Plumas)—Marysville to Rabbit Creek
May 3, 1858 (Nevada)—Nevada City to Auburn
July 6, 1858 (Placer)—Michigan Bluff to Yankee Jim
September 6, 1858 (Sierra)—Forest City to Nevada City
November 1, 1858 (Placer)—Rattlesnake Bar to Folsom
August 10, 1859 (Shasta)—Angel's Camp to San Andreas
August 16, 1859 (Trinity)—Yreka to Coffee Creek
August 31, 1859 (Yuba)—Shasta to Marysville
November 8, 1859 (Placer)—at Todd's Valley
January 16, 1860 (Calaveras)—Murphy's Camp to Stockton
April 23, 1860 (Tuolumne)—Chinese Camp to Big Oak Flat
May 8, 1860 (Tuolumne)—Big Oak Flat to Chinese Camp
May 28, 1860 (Placer)—Iowa Hill to Sacramento
June 9, 1860 (Butte)—Marysville to Shasta
November 10, 1863 (El Dorado)—Georgetown to Folsom
November 17, 1863 (Amador)—Fiddletown to Folsom
May 30, 1864 (Mariposa)—at Coulterville
June 7, 1864 (El Dorado)—at Georgetown
June 30, 1864 (El Dorado)—Carson City, NV to San Francisco
July 6, 1864 (Santa Clara)—San Jose to Los Angeles
July 9, 1864 (Santa Clara)—Los Angeles to San Jose
August 5, 1864 (Santa Clara)—Pacheco Pass to Visalia
August 31, 1864 (Tuolumne)—Sonora to Coulterville
August 16, 1865 (Yuba)—Laporte to Oroville
November 20, 1865 (Calaveras)—San Andreas to at Valley Springs
May 6, 1866 (Nevada)—North San Juan to Nevada City
May 16, 1866 (Nevada)—North San Juan to Nevada City
December 1, 1866 (Nevada)—Nevada City to Marysville
January 5, 1867 (Calaveras)—Murphy's Camp to Copperopolis
January 5, 1867 (Amador)—Irish Hill to Forest Home
November 18, 1867 (Nevada)—Lake City to Moore's Flat
December 2, 1867 (Amador)—Ione to Jackson
October 18, 1869 (Santa Barbara)—at Santa Barbara
October 21, 1869 (Los Angeles)—Los Angeles to San Francisco
November 7, 1869 (San Diego)—Fort Yuma to San Diego
December 2, 1869 (Santa Barbara)—Los Angeles to Santa Barbara
April 5, 1870 (Calaveras)—Murphy's to Stockton
April 19, 1870 (Amador)—Fiddletown to Ione
June 4, 1870 (Monterey)—Stone's Station to San Luis Obispo

July 14, 1870 (Monterey)—San Luis Obispo to Salinas
August 8, 1870 (Amador)—Volcano to Jackson
November 11, 1870 (Amador)—Jackson to Mokelumne Hill
January 17, 1871 (Calaveras)—Stockton to San Andreas
January 23, 1871 (Calaveras)—Stockton to San Andreas
February 16, 1871 (Sonoma)—Cloverdale to Healdsburg
May 5, 1871 (Monterey)—North San Juan to Los Angeles
July 12, 1871 (Sonoma)—Healdsburg to Cloverdale
August 11, 1871 (Santa Clara)—Visalia to Gilroy
August 12, 1871 (Sonoma)—Cloverdale to Healdsburg
August 16, 1871 (Sonoma)—Cloverdale to Petaluma
August 21, 1871 (Tehama)—Red Bluff to Shasta
September 26, 1871 (Tehama)—Shasta to Red Bluff
October 10, 1871 (Sonoma)—at Healdsburg
November 14, 1871 (Santa Clara)—Visalia to Gilroy
November 28, 1871 (El Dorado)—Georgetown to Auburn
December 25, 1871 (Sonoma)—Petaluma to Cloverdale
January 6, 1872 (Calaveras)—Milton to San Andreas
March 5, 1872 (Calaveras)—San Andreas to Milton
March 9, 1872 (Calaveras)—San Andreas to Milton
April 20, 1872 (Monterey)—Gilroy to Hollister
May 1, 1872 (Amador)—Jackson to Volcano
February 26, 1873 (Fresno)—at Firebaugh's Ferry
June 23, 1873 (Yuba)—Downieville to Marysville
July 27, 1873 (Nevada)—Nevada City to Grass Valley
August 18, 1873 (Calaveras)—Mokulumne Hill to Mokulumne Station
September 12, 1873 (Placer)—Forest Hill to Auburn
October 10, 1873 (Shasta)—Yreka to Redding
October 18, 1873 (Tulare)—Visalia to Tulare
November 22, 1873 (Tulare)—Tulare to Visalia
February 25, 1874 (Kern)—at Coyote Holes
April 1, 1874 (Santa Clara)—Santa Clara to Santa Cruz
April 28, 1874 (Santa Clara) Santa Clara to Santa Cruz
April 28, 1874 (Santa Clara)—San Jose to Santa Clara
August 8, 1874 (Calaveras)—San Andreas to Milton
August 11, 1874 (Monterey)—Salinas to Monterey
August 29, 1874 (San Bernardino)—San Bernardino to Spadra
October 21, 1874 (Calaveras)—West Point to Mokelumne Hill
November 7, 1874 (Calaveras)—Sonora to Milton
January 15, 1875 (Kern)—Lone Pine to Bakersfield
February 16, 1875 (Shasta)—Shasta to Redding
February 22, 1875 (San Diego)—San Diego to Julian
March 1, 1875 (Calaveras)—Mokelumne Hill to Lodi
March 17, 1875 (Kern)—Bakersfield to Panamint Springs
March 23, 1875 (Calaveras)—Sonora to Milton
April 14, 1875 (Yuba)—Camptonville to Marysville
April 16, 1875 (Nevada)—Grass Valley to Colfax
April 28, 1875 (Inyo)—at Cerro Gordo
May 3, 1875 (Amador)—Ione to Galt
May 28, 1875 (San Luis Obispo)—Soledad to Paso de Robles
July 6, 1875 (Amador)—Fiddletown to Latrobe
July 26, 1875 (Calaveras)—Sonora to Milton
August 3, 1875 (Yuba)—Oroville to Laporte
August 17, 1875 (Plumas)—Quincy to Oroville
August 31, 1875 (Monterey)—Soledad to Lowe's Station
October 4, 1875 (Kern)—Bakersfield to Sumner
October 5, 1875 (Yuba)—Downieville to Laporte
October 9, 1875 (Lake)—Calistoga to Lower Lake
October 12, 1875 (Calaveras)—Sonora to Milton
October 19, 1875 (Shasta)—Redding to Yreka
October 22, 1875 (Monterey)—Soledad to Paso de Robles
November 30, 1875 (Kern)—Caliente to San Fernando
December 1, 1875 (Calaveras)—Sonora to Copperopolis
December 4, 1875 (Kern)—Caliente to Kernville
December 4, 1875 (Kern)—Los Angeles to Caliente
December 7, 1875 (Kern)—Kernville to Walker's Basin
December 17, 1875 (Nevada)—North San Juan to Marysville
December 22, 1875 (Nevada)—Marysville to North San Juan
December 22, 1875 (Yuba)—Downieville to Marysville
December 28, 1875 (Nevada)—Marysville to San Juan
January 10, 1876 (Amador)—Fiddletown to Latrobe
January 17, 1876 (El Dorado)—Georgetown to Auburn
January 21, 1876 (Yuba)—at Brown's Valley
January 28, 1876 (Butte)—Chico to railroad depot
January 31, 1876 (Amador)—Jackson to Drytown
February 1, 1876 (Yuba)—Marysville to Camptonville
February 4, 1876 (Placer)—Forest Hill to Auburn

April 5, 1876 (Placer)—Forest Hil to Auburn
June 2, 1876 (Shasta)—Cottonwood to Yreka
June 20, 1876 (Butte)—Laporte to Oroville
June 21, 1876 (Yuba)—Downieville to Marysville
June 27, 1876 (Plumas)—Oroville to Laporte
July 22, 1876 (Calaveras)—San Andreas to Angel's Camp
September 11, 1876 (Amador)—Jackson to Latrobe
October 12, 1876 (Kern)—Mojave to Darwin
October 16, 1876 (Siskiyou)—Scott's Bar to Fort Jones
October 17, 1876 (Placer)—Georgetown to Auburn
October 24, 1876 (Shasta)—Shasta to Redding
November 3, 1876 (Shasta)—Reid's Ferry to Buckeye
November 3, 1876 (Shasta)—Yreka to Redding
November 6, 1876 (Shasta)—Shasta to Weaverville
November 8, 1876 (Shasta)—Shasta to Weaverville
November 11, 1876 (Shasta)—Yreka to Redding
November 13, 1876 (Yuba)—Downieville to Marysville
November 15, 1876 (Tuolumne)—Sonora to Milton
December 28, 1876 (Calaveras)—Murphy's to Milton
January 6, 1877 (Kern)—Darwin to Mojave
January 19, 1877 (Nevada)—San Juan to Marysville
January 20, 1877 (Los Angeles)—Newhall to Ventura
January 22, 1877 (Shasta)—Shasta to Redding
February 2, 1877 (Calaveras)—Murphy's to Milton
February 5, 1877 (Amador)—at Spring Mountain House
February 10, 1877 (Inyo)—Mojave to Darwin
February 14, 1877 (Inyo)—Mojave to Darwin
February 24, 1877 (Calaveras)—Sonora to Milton
March 6, 1877 (San Diego)—Indian Wells to San Bernardino
March 9, 1877 (Los Angeles)—Anaheim to San Diego
March 26, 1877 (Santa Barbara)—Santa Barbara to Oak Grove
March 31, 1877 (Santa Barbara)—Santa Barbara to Oak Grove
April 14, 1877 (Monterey)—Soledad to San Luis Obispo
May 7, 1877 (Merced)—Los Banos to Gilroy
May 27, 1877 (Shasta)—Roseburg, OR to Redding
June 12, 1877 (Napa)—Calistoga to Lakeport
July 18, 1877 (Siskiyou)—Redding to Soda Springs
July 26, 1877 (Sierra)—Marysville to Downieville
July 31, 1877 (Yuba)—Marysville to Downieville
August 3, 1877 (Calaveras)—Milton to Sonora
August 3, 1877 (Sonoma)—Point Arenas to Duncan's Mills
August 27, 1877 (Los Angeles)—Soledad to Newhall
August 28, 1877 (San Diego)—Los Angeles to San Diego
August 31, 1877 (Calaveras)—Milton to Sonora
January 16, 1878 (Nevada)—Murphy's to Milton
January 16, 1878 (Tuolumne)—Sonora to Milton
July 25, 1878 (Plumas)—Quincy to Oroville
July 30, 1878 (Plumas)—Laporte to Oroville
September 7, 1878 (Siskiyou)—Yreka to Redding
October 2, 1878 (Mendocino)—Arcata to Ukiah
October 3, 1878 (Mendocino)—Covelo to Ukiah
January 14, 1879 (Plumas)—Quincy to Oroville
February 22, 1879 (Calaveras)—Mokelumne Hill to Camanche
June 21, 1879 (Butte)—Laporte to Oroville
September 1, 1879 (Nevada)—Eureka to Nevada City
October 11, 1879 (Mendocino)—Ukiah to Eureka
October 25, 1879 (Shasta)—Redding to Roseburg, OR
October 27, 1879 (Modoc)—Redding to Alturas
December 3, 1879 (Monterey)—San Luis Obispo to Soledad
March 30, 1880 (Monterey)—San Luis Obispo to Soledad
April 29, 1880 (Calaveras)—San Andreas to Milton
May 6, 1880 (Amador)—Jackson to Ione
May 15, 1880 (Placer)—Forest Hill to Auburn
May 24, 1880 (Calaveras)—Murphy's to Milton
May 24, 1880 (El Dorado)—Georgetown to Placerville
July 22, 1880 (Sonoma)—Point Arenas to Duncan's Mills
July 26, 1880 (Nevada)—Spenceville to Wheatland
August 6, 1880 (Placer)—Auburn to Forest Hill
September 1, 1880 (Shasta)—Redding to Weaverville
September 11, 1880 (Placer)—Georgetown to Auburn
September 22, 1880 (Placer)—Auburn to Forest Hill
September 30, 1880 (Nevada)—Nevada City Marysville
October 7, 1880 (Yuba)—Laporte to Marysville
October 11, 1880 (Shasta) Lakeview to Redding
October 30, 1880 (Nevada)—Nevada City to North San Juan
November 1, 1880 (Placer)—Georgetown to Auburn
November 29, 1880 (Inyo)—Bishop Creek to Independence
November 30, 1880 (Butte)—Laporte to Oroville
December 10, 1880 (Nevada)—Truckee to Sierraville
December 11, 1880 (Inyo)—Benton to Darwin
January 5, 1881 (Alameda)—Walnut Creek to Oakland
April 18, 1881 (Shasta)—Igo to Inderson

April 26, 1881 (Tulare)—Laporte to Oroville
May 27, 1881 (Placer)—Dutch Flat depot to Dutch Flat
June 10, 1881 (Mendocino)—Eureka to Ukiah
June 29, 1881 (Sierra)—Sierraville to Truckee
July 19, 1881 (Monterey)—San Luis Obispo to Soledad
August 15, 1881 (Sierra)—Sierraville to Truckee
August 16, 1881 (Napa)—Aetna Springs to St. Helena
August 25, 1881 (San Luis Obispo)—San Luis Obispo to San Jose
August 31, 1881 (Siskiyou)—Roseburg, OR to Yreka
October 8, 1881 (Shasta)—Redding to Yreka
October 11, 1881 (Shasta)—Lakeview, OR to Redding
November 7, 1881 (Calaveras)—Sonora to Milton
December 11, 1881 (Monterey)—San Luis Obispo to Soledad
December 15, 1881 (Yuba)—Downieville to Marysville
December 27, 1881 (Nevada)—North San Juan to Marysville
December 29, 1881 (Calaveras)—Milton to Sonora
December 29, 1881 (San Luis Obispo)—Santa Barbara to San Luis Obispo
January 2, 1882 (San Luis Obispo)—San Luis Obispo to Santa Barbara
January 8, 1882 (Santa Barbara)—San Luis Obispo Santa Barbara
January 13, 1882 (Monterey)—at Soledad
January 26, 1882 (Mendocino)—Ukiah to Cloverdale
February 2, 1882 (Tuolumne)—Sonora to Chinese Camp
April 27, 1882 (Stanislaus)—Hills Ferry to Banta
May 18, 1882 (San Luis Obispo)— Soledad to San Luis Obispo
May 24, 1882 (Shasta)—Yreka to Redding
May 25, 1882 (Butte)—Chico to Susanville
May 25, 1882 (San Luis Obispo) Soledad to San Luis Obispo
June 14, 1882 (Mendocino)—Little Lake to Ukiah
June 26, 1882 (Shasta)—Yreka to Redding
July 13, 1882 (Yuba)—Laporte to Oroville
September 17, 1882 (Shasta)—Yreka to Redding
November 24, 1882 (Sonoma)—Lakeport to Cloverdale
April 12, 1883 (Sonoma)—Lakeport to Cloverdale
May 9, 1883 (Placer)—Dutch Flat to railroad depot
June 23, 1883 (Amador)—Jackson to Ione
August 13, 1883 (Mariposa)—Wawona to Yosemite
August 13, 1883 (Sierra)—Sierraville to Truckee
September 12, 1883 (Shasta)—Yreka to Redding
October 15, 1883 (Sierra)—Sierraville to Truckee
November 3, 1883 (Calaveras)—Sonora to Milton
December 27, 1883 (Inyo)—Bishop Creek to R. R. Depot
February 26, 1884 (Calaveras)—Sonora to Milton
March 23, 1884 (Lake)—Calistoga to Lower Lake
May 5, 1884 (Mendocino)—Cloverdale to Ukiah
May 7, 1884 (Fresno)—Fresno to Yosemite
May 8, 1884 (Shasta)—Yreka to Redding
May 26, 1884 (Shasta)—Alturas to Redding
July 29, 1884 (Shasta)—Yreka to Redding
September 11, 1884 (Butte)—Laporte to Oroville
September 22, 1884 (Santa Barbara)—Santa Maria to Guadalupe
October 9, 1884 (Mendocino)—Cloverdale to Mendocino
October 17, 1884 (Calaveras)—Milton to Sonora
October 23, 1884 (San Joaquin)—Banta to Grayson
November 29, 1884 (Lake)—Cloverdale to Lakeport
December 4, 1884 (Mendocino)—Lakeport to Ukiah
December 19, 1884 (Calaveras)—Sonora to Milton
January 24, 1885 (Mendocino)—Ukiah to Little Lake
February 2, 1885 (Calaveras)—Sonora to Milton
February 9, 1885 (Sonoma)—Cloverdale to Mendocino
March 26, 1885 (Calaveras)—Sonora to Stockton
March 26, 1885 (El Dorado)—Placerville to at Shingle Springs
March 26, 1885 (Sonoma)—Mendocino to Cloverdale
April 7, 1885 (Sonoma)—Mendocino to Cloverdale
April 14, 1885 (Amador)—Plymouth to Sacramento
April 16, 1885 (San Mateo)—San Mateo to Pescadero
April 18, 1885 (Sonoma)—Mendocino to Cloverdale
May 8, 1885 (Sonoma)—Mendocino to Cloverdale
May 22, 1885 (Mariposa)—Madera to Yosemite
August 19, 1885 (Calaveras)—Sonora to Milton
September 12, 1885 (Shasta)—Alturas to Redding
September 15, 1885 (Shasta)—Alturas to Redding
September 23, 1885 (Nevada)—North San Juan to Nevada City
October 8, 1885 (Napa)—Lakeport to Calistog
November 19, 1885 (Amador)—Ione to Jackson
December 3, 1885 (Mariposa)—Merced to Coulterville
January 5, 1886 (Mendocino)—Cloverdale to Mendocino City
January 12, 1886 (Calaveras)—Milton to Funk Hill
January 26, 1886 (Mendocino)—Cloverdale to Ukiah
June 5, 1886 (San Joaquin)—Hill's Ferry to Banta
August 4, 1886 (Sonoma)—Ukiah to Cloverdale
September 6, 1886 (Mendocino)—Cloverdale to Ukiah
September 20, 1886 (Sierra)—Sierraville to Truckee

October 11, 1886 (Plumas)—Gibsonville to Reno, NV
November 20, 1886 (Calaveras)—San Andreas to Valley Springs
December 4, 1886 (Plumas)—Oroville to Quincy
March 21, 1887 (Yuba)—Marysville to Camptonville
April 5, 1887 (Placer)—Auburn to Forest Hill
April 19, 1887 (Mendocino)—Ukiah to Cloverdale
June 28, 1887 (Sierra)—Forest City to at Mountain House
August 11, 1887 (Placer)—Michigan Bluff to Auburn
October 14, 1887 (El Dorado)—at Auburn
October 21, 1887 (Shasta)—Redding to Bieber
March 23, 1888 (Napa)—Calistoga to mines
April 28, 1888 (Sonoma)—Lakeport to Cloverdale
June 23, 1888 (Lake)—Lakeport to Calistoga
July 2, 1888 (Mariposa)—Madera to Hildreth
July 21, 1888 (San Luis Obispo)—Templeton to San Luis Obispo
July 27, 1888 (Shasta)—Redding to Bieber
October 24, 1888 (Mariposa)—Coulterville to Merced
November 3, 1888 (Santa Barbara)—Santa Barbara to Los Olives
November 8, 1888 (Sierra)—Downieville to Camptonville
November 9, 1888 (Sierra)—Weaverville to Redding
November 20, 1888 (Mendocino)—Eureka to Ukiah
December 4, 1888 (Mendocino)—Mendocino City to Ingram
December 4, 1888 (Sonoma)—Mendocino City to Cazadero
March 12, 1889 (San Luis Obispo)—Gilroy to Santa Margarita
April 1, 1889 (Calaveras)—Murphy's Camp to Milton
June 15, 1889 (Placer)—Auburn to Forest Hill
July 12, 1889 (Tehama)—Red Bluff to Champion Mill
July 31, 1889 (Calaveras)—Sonora to Milton
August 29, 1889 (Lassen)—at Susanville
September 2, 1889 (Mono)—Bodie to Hawthorne
September 2, 1889 (Placer)—Auburn to Forest Hill
September 5, 1889 (Mendocino)—Ukiah to Cahto
September 10, 1889 (Plumas)—Quincy to Oroville
September 16, 1889 (Placer)—Forest Hill to Auburn
October 24, 1889 (Shasta)—Bieber to Redding
November 28, 1889 (Shasta)—Shasta to Redding
December 2, 1889 (Mariposa)—Merced to Mariposa
December 12, 1889 (Placer)—Auburn to Forest Hill
December 15, 1889 (Nevada)—Downieville to Nevada City
February 26, 1890 (Merced)—Mariposa to Merced
April 7, 1890 (Placer)—Michigan Bluff to Auburn
April 10, 1890 (Placer)—at Auburn
May 15, 1890 (Mariposa)—Merced to Mariposa
June 6, 1890 (Mendocino)—at Ukiah
June 25, 1890 (Lake)—Napa to Harbin Springs
July 14, 1890 (Calaveras)—Mokelumne Hill to Valley Springs
September 1, 1890 (Lassen)—Leigan to Susanville
September 8, 1890 (El Dorado)—Georgetown to Auburn
September 24, 1890 (Lassen)—Lompoc to Los Alamos
September 25, 1890 (Shasta)—Redding to Cedarville
October 12, 1890 (Mendocino)—Ukiah to Willits
March 7, 1891 (Shasta)—Weaverville to Redding
March 19, 1891 (Shasta)—Weaverville to Redding
August 4, 1891 (Shasta)—Bieber to Redding
September 1, 1891 (Shasta)—Redding to Alturas
September 25, 1891 (Butte)—Chico to Powellton
September 27, 1891 (Butte)—Chico to Powellton
September 29, 1891 (Shasta)—Redding to Alturas
October 19, 1891 (Shasta)—Redding to Alturas
October 22, 1891 (Shasta)—Redding to Alturas
November 12, 1891 (Amador)—Sacramento to Plymouth
November 15, 1891 (Mendocino)—Eureka to Ukiah
January 7, 1892 (Calaveras)—Mokelumne Hill to Valley Springs
February 7, 1892 (Calaveras)—Mokelumne Hill to Valley Springs
April 30, 1892 (Calaveras)—Stockton to San Andreas
May 10, 1892 (Shasta)—Weaverville to Redding
May 14, 1892 (Shasta)—Shasta to Redding
May 17, 1892 (Stanislaus)—Cazadero to Point Arenas
June 17, 1892 (Calaveras)—Valley Springs to San Andreas
July 22, 1892 (San Joaquin)—Stockton to Robert's Island
November 7, 1892 (Sierra)—Downieville to Sierra City
February 16, 1893 (Amador)—Ione to Jackson
March 9, 1893 (Mendocino)—Gualala to Ukiah
June 15, 1893 (Amador)—Ione to Jackson
July 31, 1893 (San Benito)—San Benito to Hernandez Valley
September 10, 1893 (Siskiyou)—Ager to Klamath Falls, OR
September 12, 1893 (Siskiyou)—Ager to Klamath Falls, OR
November 15, 1893 (Mendocino)—at Ukiah
March 7, 1894 (Calaveras)—Milton to Angel's Camp
April 16, 1894 (Calaveras)—Milton to Angel's Camp

May 2, 1894 (Calaveras)—Milton to Sonora
May 6, 1894 (Calaveras)—Angel's Camp to Milton
May 19, 1894 (Calaveras)—Angel's Camp to Milton
August 2, 1894 (Nevada)—Truckee to Tahoe
September 14, 1894 (Mendocino)—Ukiah to Idaho
October 2, 1894 (Siskiyou)—Fort Jones to Yreka
October 11, 1894 (Lake)—Lakeport to Ukiah
October 30, 1894 (Nevada)—North Bloomfield to Nevada City
November 21, 1894 (Siskiyou)—Klamath Falls, OR to Ager
February 16, 1895 (Plumas)—Oroville to Forbestown
March 22, 1895 (Shasta) Weaverville to Redding
May 7, 1895 (Lake)—Calistoga to Lakeport
June 15, 1895 (Mendocino)—Ukiah to Anderson Valley
July 6, 1895 (Shasta)—Redding to Bieber
July 8, 1895 (Shasta)—Redding to Alturas
August 1, 1895 (Merced) Coulterville to Merced
August 31, 1895 (Calaveras)—Angel's Camp to Milton
October 1, 1895 (Merced)—Coulterville to Merced
October 1, 1895 (Modoc)—Chico to Bidwell
October 7, 1895 (Mariposa)—Merced to Mariposa
December 31, 1895 (Mendocino)—Harris to Ukiah
January 15, 1896 (Mendocino)—at Robber's Pass
June 18, 1896 (Madera)—at Raymond
June 22, 1896 (San Mateo)—Half Moon Bay to San Mateo
July 2, 1896 (Tuolumne)—Sonora to Knight's Ferry
August 18, 1896 (Shasta)—Bieber to Redding
August 28, 1896 (Kern)—Kernville to Caliente
October 6, 1896 (Tuolumne)—Chinese Camp to Knight's Ferry
December 4, 1896 (Santa Barbara)—Los Alamos to Lompoc
December 17, 1896 (El Dorado)—Auburn to Georgetown
December 18, 1896 (El Dorado)—Auburn to Georgetown
April 3, 1897 (Siskiyou)—Shovel Creek, OR to Ager
April 13, 1897 (Siskiyou)—Yreka to Etna
June 25, 1897 (Shasta)—Railroad depot to Keswick
June 27, 1897 (Siskiyou)—Yreka to Fort Jones
September 26, 1897 (Mendocino)—Ukiah to Booneville
September 27, 1897 (Siskiyou)—Yreka to Fort Jones
September 30, 1897 (Calaveras)—Angels' Camp to Milton
December 25, 1897 (Mendocino)—Ukiah to Laytonville
March 5, 1898 (Santa Barbara)—Santa Barbara to Los Olivos
June 4, 1898 (Santa Barbara)—Santa Ynez to Santa Barbara
February 7, 1899 (Amador)—Jackson to Ione
February 9, 1899 (Santa Barbara)—San Marcos Rancho to Santa Barbara
March 24, 1899 (Calaveras)—Stockton to Angel's Camp
September 14, 1899 (Napa)—Calistoga to Clear Lake
September 19, 1899 (Marin)—Bolinas to San Rafael
March 2, 1900 (Napa)—Calistoga to Clear Lake
March 12, 1900 (Calaveras)—San Andreas to Mokelumne Hill
March 19, 1900 (Calaveras)—Milton to Copperopolis
May 17, 1900 (Tuolumne)—Chinese Camp to Yosemite Valley
June 2, 1900 (Madera)—Grub Gulch to Yosemite
September 15, 1900 (Nevada)—Nevada City to Downieville
May 30, 1901 (Kern)—Mojave to Eighteen-Mile House
July 3, 1901 (Placer)—Forest Hill to Auburn
July 16, 1901 (Mendocino)—Ukiah to Potter Valley
July 23, 1901 (Mendocino)—Mendocino City to Cazadero
August 1, 1901 (Mendocino)—Ukiah to Potter Valley
August 3, 1901 (Placer)—Colfax to Forest Hill
August 9, 1901 (Calaveras)—San Andreas to Sheep Ranch
August 14, 1901 (Napa)—Calistoga to Clear Lake
August 22, 1901 (Siskiyou)—Klamath Falls, OR to Ager
August 26, 1901 (Mendocino)—Ukiah to Mendocino
November 15, 1901 (Butte)—Chico to West Branch
December 21, 1901 (Mendocino)—at Willits
July 3, 1902 (Sierra)—Truckee to Sierraville
July 20, 1902 (Colusa)—Colusa to Bartlett Springs
September 2, 1902 (Sacramento)—Sacramento to Walnut Grove
December 21, 1902 (Shasta)—Redding to Weaverville
January 3, 1903 (Napa)—Calistoga to Clear Lake
February 13, 1903 (Mendocino)—Ukiah to Mendocino City
March 10, 1903 (Amador)—Ione to Jackson
March 24, 1903 (Mendocino)—Ukiah to Mendocino City
April 11, 1903 (Nevada)—Nevada City Downieville

April 27, 1903 (Napa)—Calistoga to Oathill
June 9, 1903 (Shasta)—Weaverville to Redding
July 6, 1903 (Colusa)—Colusa to Bartlett Springs
August 27, 1903 (Napa)—Calistoga to Oat Hill
November 14, 1904 (El Dorado)—Georgetown to Auburn
April 29, 1905 (Santa Clara)—San Jose to Mount Hamilton
August 15, 1905 (Madera)—Wawona to Raymond
August 17, 1905 (San Mateo) Half Moon Bay to San Mateo
October 9, 1905 (Shasta)—Redding to Delamar
July 7, 1906 (Madera)—Yosemite to Ahwahnee
July 10, 1906 (El Dorado)—Tahoe stagecoach
September 2, 1906 (Madera)—Wawona to Yosemite
April 24, 1907 (Amador—Sacramento to Plymouth
June 19, 1907 (Madera)—Raymond to Wawona
June 24, 1907 (Madera)—Madera to Yosemite
July 27, 1907 (Mendocino)—Ukiah to Witter Springs
January ___, 1908 (Yuba)—at Marysville
January 15, 1908 (Mendocino)—Ukiah to Potter Valley
January 15, 1908 (Mendocino)—Ukiah to Lakeport
July 6, 1908 (Siskiyou)—Yreka to Etna
June 23, 1909 (Nevada)—Nevada City to Downieville
September 9, 1912 (Modoc)—Fort Bidwell to High Grade
July 25, 1913 (Butte)—Blairsden to Gold Lake

Bibliography

Arnold, Oren. "The West's First Stage Robbery." *True Western Adventure* 1 (1957).
Beebe, Lucius, and Charles Clegg. *U.S. West: The Saga of Wells, Fargo.* New York: E. P. Dutton, 1949.
Block, Eugene B. *Great Stagecoach Robberies of the West.* Garden City, NY: Doubleday, 1962.
Boessenecker, John. *Badge and Buckshot: Lawlessness in Old California.* Norman: University of Oklahoma Press, 1988.
California State Archives: Prisoner Records of San Quentin and Folsom Prisons.
County Court Records, County of Amador, December 5–6, 1876; County Court Records, County of Amador, December 22–23, 1876.
Franklin, Philip L. *Stagecoach: Wells, Fargo and the American West.* New York: Free Press, 1997.
Hoag, Maury. *Stagecoaching on the California Coast: The Coastline Stage from Los Angeles to San Juan.* McKinleyville, CA: Fithian, 2001.
Huffaker, Clair. "The First Stagecoach Robbery." SAGA, February 1956.
Jackson, Joseph H. *Bad Company.* Lincoln: University of Nebraska Press, 1939.
Jackson, W. Turrentine. "Wells Fargo Staging Over the Sierra." *California Historical Society Quarterly,* June 1970.
Loomis, Noel M. *Wells, Fargo: An Illustrated History.* New York: Clarkson N. Potter, 1968.
Moody, Ralph. *Stagecoach West.* Lincoln: University of Nebraska Press, 1998.
People of the State of California vs. Charles Tadman and Charles Thompson. Justice Court Records, County of Amador, September 18–19, 1876.
Robertson, Dale. *Wells, Fargo, the Legend.* Millbrae, CA: Celestial Arts, 1975.
Secrest, William B. *California Badmen: Mean Men with Guns.* Sanger, CA: World Dancer, 2007.
_____. *California Desperadoes: Stories of Early California Outlaws in Their Own Words.* Clovis, CA: World Dancer, 2000.
_____. *Perilous Trails, Dangerous Men.* Clovis, CA: Quill Driver Books, 2002.
_____. "Steven Venard, Nevada County Pioneer." *Nevada (County) Historical Society Quarterly* 21 (December 1967).
_____. "When the Ghost Met Steve Venard," *Old West Magazine,* Fall 1968.
Wilson, R. Michael. *Great Stagecoach Robberies of the Old West.* Guilford, CT: TwoDot, 2007.
_____. *Wells, Fargo & Co. Stagecoach and Train Robberies, 1870–1884.* Jefferson, NC: McFarland, 2010.

Newspapers

Amador Dispatch (CA)
Amador Ledger (CA)
Bakersfield Courier Californian (CA)
Belmont Courier (NV)
Calaveras Chronicle (CA)
Calaveras Prospect (CA)
Calaveras Weekly Citizen (CA)
Carson City Appeal (NV)
Carson Tribune (NV)
Chico Daily Enterprise (CA)
Chronicle (Auburn, CA)
Cloverdale Reveille (Santa Rosa, CA)
Courier Californian (Bakersfield)
Daily Alta California (San Francisco)
Daily Appeal (Marysville, CA)
Daily Californian (Bakersfield)
Daily Patriot (San Jose, CA)
Daily Tribune (Salt Lake City, UT)
Decatur Daily Review (IL)
Denver Republican (CO)
Dispatch Democrat (Ukiah, CA)
Downieville Messenger (CA)
Eureka Daily Sentinel (CA)
Evening Bulletin (San Francisco, CA)
Evening Expositor (Fresno, CA)
Evening Herald (Stockton, CA)
Evening Mail (Stockton, CA)

Folsom Telegraph (CA)
Free Press (Bodie, CA)
Fresno Expositor (CA)
Fresno Weekly Republican (CA)
Genoa Weekly Courier (NV)
Gilroy Advocate (CA)
Gold Hill Daily News (NV)
Grass Valley Daily Union (CA)
Helena Daily Herald (MT)
Herald (San Jose, CA)
Humboldt Times (CA)
Idaho Statesman (Boise, ID)
Independent (Helena, MT)
Independent (Stockton, CA)
Inyo Independent (Independence, CA)
Janesville Daily Gazette (WI)
Kern County Weekly Courier (Bakersfield, CA)
Los Angeles Herald (CA)
Los Angeles News (CA)
Los Angeles Star (CA)
Marin County Journal (CA)
Mariposa Gazette (CA)
Marysville Appeal (CA)
Marysville Democrat (CA)
Marysville Herald (CA)
Mendocino Beacon (CA)
Mendocino Democrat (CA)
Mendocino Dispatch (CA)
Mendocino Dispatch-Democrat (CA)
Mendocino Press (Ukiah, CA)
Merced Express (CA)
Middletown Daily Argus (NY)
Morning Tribune (San Luis Obispo, CA)
Mountain Democrat (Placerville, CA)
Mountain Messenger (Downieville, CA)
Mountain Messenger (Sierra County, CA)
Napa Daily Register (CA)
National Police Gazette (NY)
Nevada Transcript (Nevada City, CA)
Oregonian (Portland)
Oroville Mercury (CA)
Oroville Weekly Union Record (CA)
Pacific Rural Press (CA)
Pacific Sentinel (Santa Cruz, CA)
Palo Alto Pilot (Emmetsburg, IA)
Placer Herald (Auburn, CA)
Placerville Mountain Democrat (CA)
Plumas National (CA)

Red Bluff Beacon (OR)
Red Bluff Sentinel (CA)
Redding Independent (CA)
Redding Republican Free Press (CA)
Republican Free Press (Redding, CA)
Rocky Mountain News (Denver, CO)
Russian River Flag (Healdsburg, CA)
Sacramento Bee (CA)
Sacramento Bulletin (CA)
Sacramento Daily Union (CA)
Sacramento Record-Union (CA)
Salinas City Index (CA)
San Andreas Independent (CA)
San Bernardino Guardian (CA)
San Diego Union Tribune (CA)
San Francisco Call (CA)
San Francisco Chronicle (CA)
San Francisco Examiner (CA)
San Francisco Police Gazette (CA)
San Joaquin Republican (CA)
San Joaquin Valley Argus (CA)
San Jose Herald (CA)
San Jose Mercury (CA)
San Jose Patriot (CA)
San Juan Prospector (Del Norte, CO)
San Luis Obispo Tribune (CA)
Santa Cruz Daily Echo (CA)
Santa Cruz Sentinel (CA)
Santa Maria Times (CA)
Sausalito News (CA)
Shasta Courier (CA)
Silver State (Winnemucca, NV)
Sonoma Democrat (CA)
Stanislaus News (CA)
Stockton Herald (CA)
Stockton Independent (CA)
Territorial Enterprise (Virginia City, NV)
Transcript (Nevada City, CA)
Tuolumne Independent (Sonora, CA)
Ukiah City Press (CA)
Ukiah Republican Press (CA)
Union Democrat (Sonora, CA)
Visalia Weekly Delta (CA)
Walker Lake Bulletin (CA)
Weekly Mercury (Oroville, CA)
Weekly News (Milledgeville, GA)
Yreka Journal (CA)
Yreka Union (CA)

Index

Abbey, William 130
Abrogast, __ 145
Ackerman, Charles 56
Adams, __ (judge) 76
Adams, __ (sheriff) 74
Adams, A.C. (driver) 191
Adams, C.P. (W, F & Co. agent) 82
Adams, George (road agent) 124–125
Adams, John H. (sheriff) 61–62, 187
Adams Express 3, 9
Adkson, C.H. 259
Aetna Springs, CA 128
Ager, CA 224–225, 227
Ahart, Peter 151
Ahwahnee, CA 90–92
Ainslie, Joseph (driver) 113
Alameda, CA 46
Alamosa, CO 43
Aldridge, Albert "A.E." (road agent) 47–48
Aldridge, Leonard "C.A." (road agent) 47–48
Alexander Valley, CA 111
Allen, __ 68
Allen, __ (constable) 130–133
Allen, John 139, 203
Allen, John (aka John D. Gundlack; road agent) 192–193
Allen, S.A. (aka Sol White; road agent) 75, 162
Allen, Samuel (deputy) 103, 234
Allen, Y. (deputy) 103
Allison, __ (deputy) 200
Allman, John 235
Almaden, CA 54
Almy, Daniel (driver) 31
Aloff, Abraham 56
Alta Express 3
Altaville, CA 39, 53, 56–57, 140
Alturas, CA 119, 199–200, 206–208, 211
Amador City, CA 13
Anaheim, CA 87
Anderson, J.M. (detective) 248
Anderson, CA 101–102, 107, 190, 194–197

Andrus, Elisha "big foot" (road agent) 228–230
Angel Island, CA 247
Angellotti, __ (judge) 93
Angel's Camp, CA 29–30, 32, 37, 39, 43–44, 49, 52–56, 188, 243
Angel's Creek, CA 46
Antelope Canyon, OR 237
Arcata, CA 98
Armstrong, J.W. 182
Arrison, Walter A. (aka George Henderson; road agent) 165
Arroyo Grande, CA 174
Arthur, Stonewall J. 197, 199
Arthur, Thomas C. 199
Ashcraft, __ (Mrs.) 251
Ashland, OR 195
Atwood, Oscar F. (deputy) 45
Auburn, CA 7, 33, 63–64, 66–68, 136, 149–151, 154–160, 189, 204, 249
Aull, Charles (warden) 21
Aull, Charles (W, F & Co. detective) 26, 81, 126, 141, 179, 217, 245
Aurora, NV 151–152, 154, 162, 216
Austin,__ (road agent) 161
Ayer, __ (justice of the peace) 89

Backbone House, CA 136
Bailey, A.J. 151
Bailey, Frank (driver) 142
Baja, CA 243
Baker, Charles (road agent) 71, 102
Baker, George (aka H.W. Hanlon; road agent) 61–63
Bakersfield, CA 75–77, 79, 86, 92, 201–202, 259
Balch, Billy (driver) 70
Baldwin, Barry (U.S. marshal) 110
Baltimore, MD 217–218
Ban, __ (officer) 175–176
Banks, __ (messenger) 49
Banshee (stagecoach) station, CO 43
Banson, George (driver) 115
Banta, CA 171–172, 174, 236
Barber, William (road agent) 220–221

Barclay, Capt. A.J. 249
Barkley, __ (marshal) 25
Barnett, John R. 111
Barns, Samuel 121
Barnwell, Charles (road agent) 244
Barr, __ 53–54
Barrett, Parker H. 111
Barry, Dan (driver) 163
Barry, James 214
Bartlett, Washington (California governor) 42
Bartlett Springs, CA 58–59
Bartolomo, Constanso 118
Bass Hill, CA 192, 196
Bass (stagecoach) station, CA 199
Baumen, __ 89
Bear Valley, CA 214
Beck, Ed 200–202
Beeves, N. 196
Behrens, __ (undersheriff) 213, 214
Belden, David (judge) 74
Bell, __ (constable) 190
Bell, __ (judge) 202
Bell, Harvey see Mitchell, Henry B.
Bell, John see Downer, Albert
Bell, Theodore A. (attorney/deputy) 83–84
Bell, Tom see Hodges, Thomas J.
Bellville, NV 152
Belshaw, M.W. 73
Belt, __ (judge) 250
Bennett, __ (constable) 175–176
Benson, James (road agent) 40–42
Benson, John (road agent) 40–42
Benson, Patrick 41
Benton, Henry P. 229
Benton, CA 71
Berdans, CA 28
Bernard, A.P. (driver) 76
Bernie Hill, CA 67
Berry, David E. (driver) 36
Berryessa Valley, CA 83
Berryhill, F.D. 111
Bertelotte, E. 177
Bevano, Fernando (driver) 97
Bichard, W. 169
Bickford, L.D. (constable) 193

271

Index

Bidwell's Bar, CA 165
Bieber, CA 200, 202–205, 211–212
Bierer, Amos (road agent) 52–55
Big Meadows, CA 84
Big Oak Flat, CA 90, 241, 246
Big Pinoche, CA 245
Big Trees, CA 95, 195
Billings, J. (division agent) 152
Bine, __ (Mrs.) 81
Bine, Leon 81
Birk, James E. (aka James Burkley; road agent) 81
Bishop, Wertemer 91
Bishop Creek, CA 70–71
Bixler, John S. (road agent) 88
Black, __ (deputy) 173
Black Bart see Bolton, Charles E.
Black Kid (road agent) 89–90, 92, 246
Blackmore, __ (driver) 97
Black's Crossing, CA 133
Black's (railroad) station, CA 236
Blair, Eugene (driver) 61–62
Blairsden, CA 29
Blanchard, William (road agent) 220–221
Bland, Jim (driver) 235
Blasdel, Henry G. (NV governor) 136
Blewett, L. 55
Blocker, Tom (driver) 96
Bloodworth, William (road agent) 170
Bludworth, H. (deputy) 75
Blue Lakes, CA 112, 115
Boardman, John 15
Bodie, CA 129, 151–152
Boehmer, A.J. 29
Bogard, __ (sheriff) 211
Bogard, James J. (sheriff) 211
Boggs, John C. (sheriff) 156
Bogus, CA 224
Boles, Charles E. see Bolton, Charles E.
Bolinas, CA 93
Bolter, Dick (road agent) 244
Bolton, Charles E. (aka Black Bart; aka Charles E. Boles; road agent) 19, 26, 36–39, 98–99, 119, 139, 143, 163, 191–192, 223, 231–232, 258
Bona, Dan (deputy) 24
Bonher, Louis R. (road agent) 136
Booneville, CA 56, 101, 110–111, 115
Booth, Newton (CA governor) 63, 178, 237
Borax Lake, CA 74
Borondas, CA 175
Boston Ranch, CA 258
Boulder Creek, CA 126
Bouldware, John (road agent) 61–63
Bourland, __ (sheriff) 242
Bovee, C.H. 145
Bowen, __ (messenger) 25
Bowes, __ (sheriff) 75
Bowman, __ (deputy) 62
Boyce, John (driver) 208
Boyd, __ 117

Boyd, __ (deputy) 238
Boyd, J.M. (sheriff) 237
Boyle, Charlie (road agent) 93–94
Brackett, Edward (driver) 199, 205
Bradford, __ (justice of the peace) 84
Bradford's (stagecoach) station, CA 127
Bradley, Lewis R. (Nevada governor) 83
Bradley, N.O. (judge) 240
Brady, Jack see Williams, Henry
Bragg, Calvin (aka Joe Hampton; road agent) 244–245
Brandy Creek, CA 214
Branham, Benjamin (sheriff) 69
Brannan, John M. (road agent) 76
Brantiheidt, Ernest 79
Brastow, S.D. (W, F & Co. superintendent) 77
Braton, C.C. 212
Brawn, William (road agent) 82–83
Brazier, Thomas R. (road agent) 93–94
Breckenridge, R.N. (road agent) 83–84
Brewster, Lewis (driver) 192
Briarre, Frank (prison guard) 144
Bridgeport, CA 140
Briggs, __ 79
Briggs, __ (driver) 86
Brison, Thomas (road agent) 176–177
Britton, George 137
Brockway, S.W. (judge) 62
Bronaugh, __ (sheriff) 155
Brophy, Thomas (road agent) 171
Brow, E. 256
Brown, __ (Dr.) 74
Brown, __ (justice of the peace) 236
Brown, Billy 185
Brown, Charles (road agent) 50
Brown, Charles see Jackson, Thomas
Brown, John (aka Edward Wilson; road agent) 26, 29–30, 195–196
Brown, Johnny (road agent) 228–230
Brown, Joseph (road agent) 194, 255
Brown, Lee (road agent) 245–246
Brown, Lodi (road agent) 228–230
Brown, Mitchell (road agent) 35, 70, 253
Brown, Thomas (road agent) 194–195, 248–249, 255
Browning, Henry (road agent) 29–30
Brownlee, __ (deputy) 62
Brownlee, __ 230
Brownlee, Robert (undersheriff) 83–84
Brown's Flat, CA 243
Brown's Valley, CA 253
Brownville, CA 257
Brumer, William 57

Bryan, Ab (road agent) 40–42
Bryan, Ed (driver) 167
Bryant, Jack see Williams, Frank
Buckeye, CA 189, 192–193, 198
Bucknell, "Bunt" (driver) 112
Buena Vista, CA 23
Bugbee, Edward (road agent) 161
Bunny, __ (Miss) 54
Burch, Charles D. 190
Burger, John 101
Burke, __ (constable) 126
Burke, Alexander (constable) 107, 109
Burke, Ira (driver) 159–160
Burkley, James see Birk, James E.
Burns, Daniel 121
Burns, Samuel L. (road agent) 121–122
Burus' Ferry, CA 46
Bush, Charles A. (road agent) 170–171
Bushyhead, Ned (deputy) 88, 171
Butler, John (sheriff) 158
Butler, W. (driver) 24
Buxton, G.Q. (driver) 217
Buzzard's Roost, CA 204

Cady, Frank P. (sheriff) 84–85
Cahto, CA 104
Cajon Pass, CA 168
Caliente, CA 76–77, 79
California House, CA 247
Calistoga, CA 80–83, 127–133
Callahan's (stagecoach) station, CA 222
Calloway, __ (police captain) 249
Calmez, Ziska (road agent) 237–238
Cal's English, CA 99
Camanche, CA 36, 42, 45
Cambridge, W. (driver) 124, 151, 154
Campbell, __ (constable) 211
Campbell, Bert (driver) 118
Campbell, Edward (driver) 177
Campbell, John 248
Camptonville, CA 156, 216, 219, 247, 251, 254, 258
Canady, Silas (driver) 253
Candelaria, NV 152
Canebreak (stagecoach) station, CA 75
Canyon City, OR 237
Cape Horn Mills, CA 50, 159
Capella, CA 109
Captain Ingram's Partisan Rangers 61
Carbondale, CA 24
Caril, __ (officer) 207
Carlock, A.B. 220, 227
Carlton, Albert A. see Tubbs, Albert A.
Carmen Hill, CA 52–54
Carothers, T.L. (U.S. commissioner) 110
Carr, Bob (road agent) 247–250
Carr, Peter (road agent) 185–186
Carroll, Charles 221

Index

Carroll, James P. (constable) 173
Carson, Robert 213
Carson City, NV 41, 61, 63, 68, 151–154, 162, 216
Carter, __ (sheriff) 141
Carter, B. 213
Carter, Charles M. (road agent) 236–237
Carter, J.S. 96
Carter, Lloyd 209
Caruthers, Bob 239
Caruthers, Sam 239
Casad, Mart (U.S. marshal) 25, 252
Casey, James (road agent) 171–172
Cassenelli, Louis (driver) 58
Castle, Charles (road agent) 75–76
Cathay, Jim 118
Cawley, Dan (driver) 225
Cazaderim CA 236
Cazadero, CA 113, 210, 235
Cedarville, CA 204
Centerville, CA 98
Central Hill, CA 41
Cerro Gordo, CA 70, 74
Champion Mill, CA 238
Chandler, William (road agent) 190–191
Chaparral House, CA 36
Chapman, __ 27
Chapman, __ 219
Chapman, Frank (road agent) 192–193
Chase, George (driver) 223
Chavez, Clodoveo (road agent) 68, 73–78
Cherokee Bob (road agent) 30
Cherokee Flat, CA 29
Cherry, L.S. (constable) 128
Chicago, IL 159, 166, 197
Chico, CA 24–28, 119–120, 193, 214, 252, 255
Chinese Camp, CA 46, 94, 241–242, 244–246
Chinn, __ (justice of the peace) 130
Cinnabar, CA 190
C.L. Cady's Express 8
Clark, B.F. (road agent) 167–169
Clark, John (road agent) 149, 188–189
Clark, John 252
Clark's (stagecoach) station, CA 95
Claughton, Benjamin F. (road agent) 121–122
Clear Creek, CA 213
Clear Lake, CA 130–132
Clements, Bob (road agent) 27–28, 138
Clendenning, John (road agent) 61–63
Clendenning, William W. 62
Cliff, William (driver) 121
Cline, P. 75
Clipper Gap, CA 157
Cloudman, CA 245
Cloverdale, CA 71, 81, 98, 100–106, 107, 111, 228–234
Coal Valley (stagecoach) station, NV 152

Coan, __ (deputy) 160
Coburn, George 130
Cody, George 214–215
Coffee Creek, CA 239
Coffey, __ (detective) 153
Coffman, B.S. 229
Coffroth, __ (attorney) 25
Cohn, H.S. 45
Cold Springs, CA 216
Cole, Charles (road agent) 233
Colfax, CA 137, 149, 154, 156–157, 160, 218
Colford, John P. (officer) 214
Collins, J.C. (road agent) 67–68
Collins, Jim (deputy) 119
Collins, John C.P. (aka John Patterson; road agent) 140–142
Coloma, CA 3, 138, 247
Colorado Springs, CO 33, 43
Colton, William (driver) 57
Columbia, CA 244
Colusa, CA 59, 238, 256
Colwell, Victor J. (road agent) 93
Comanche, CA 21
Comptche, CA 113–114
Conant, Jack 222
Condon, Fred 213
Condrey, Alexander (road agent) 220
Conley, __ (judge) 89
Connelly, Ed 52
Conner, William (driver) 131–132
Connibeck, Bill (driver) 232
Connor, C. 128
Connors, Tom (road agent) 195
Conroy, William C. (sheriff) 67
Convery, Ned (road agent) 247–250
Conway, John (deputy) 85
Cook, __ (deputy) 180
Cook, Frank (driver) 182
Cook, George (driver) 113
Cook, R.D. (Mrs.) 109
Cool, CA 68
Cooley, __ (justice of the peace) 57–58
Cooley's (stagecoach) station, CA 217
Coons, Alonzo (W, F & Co. agent) 96, 202
Cooper, Charlie (road agent) 32–33
Cooper, Sam (driver) 134
Coos Bay, OR 204
Copperopolis, CA 31, 35–37, 40–41, 45, 48, 54, 58, 242, 244
Corbett, William (road agent) 101
Corbett's (stagecoach) station, CA 256
Corcoran, __ (judge) 97
Corrine, UT 256
Cory, __ (Dr.) 74
Cottonwood, CA 191
Coulterville, CA 93–96, 98, 117–119, 242
Course Gold, CA 92
Courtland, CA 211, 167
Covelo, CA 26, 98
Covey, Joseph 201
Cow Creek Hill, CA 200

Coyne, __ (sheriff) 171
Coyote Holes (stagecoach) station, CA 73, 75
Crabtrees, CA 245
Craddock, John 203
Craig, __ 73
Crawford, __ (deputy) 231
Crawford, Dick (driver) 232
Creamer, Charley (driver) 192
Crescent, CA 166
Crigler, Albert P. (constable) 234
Crimea House, CA 46, 242, 245
Crippin, Clarence (driver) 65–66
Criswell, __ 184
Critchfield, __ (justice of the peace) 108
Crocker, A.M. 216
Crockett, D.C. (sheriff) 229
Crockett, Henry (driver) 160
Crooks, CA 92
Cross, George 62
Crough, __ (undersheriff) 71
Crow, John 111
Crowley, __ (chief of police) 153
Crum, __ (constable) 202, 204
Crum, Jim (road agent) 43–44
Crystal Springs, CA 176–177
Cucovich, Michael (road agent) 173
Cuff, L.C. (road agent) 175–176
Cullen, Billy (road agent) 237
Culverhouse, Jerry (driver) 190
Cummings, __ 159
Cummings, George W. (aka Henry Rivers; road agent) 105
Cummings, William F. 140–141
Cuneo, Madeline 45
Cunningham, Thomas (sheriff) 45, 50, 56, 172–173
Curtin, John (postmaster) 245
Curtis, Billy (road agent) 228–230
Curtis, Dave (driver) 198
Curtis, "Doc" (driver) 231
Curtis, Frank (deputy) 186
Curtis, John 201–202
Cushman, John (driver) 20
Cusick, Nick 209
Cutler, Billy (driver) 32–33

Daily, Matthew (driver) 149–150
Dalles, OR 237
Dalton, __ (priest) 141–142
Dalton, George 214
Dalzell's (stagecoach) station, NV 151
Daniels, Lew M. (driver) 105
Darden, J.B. 180
Dark Gulch, CA 113
Darling, Louis 40
Darnell, Charles (road agent) 237–238
Darwin, CA 70–71, 78–79, 87
Davidson, __ (judge) 138
Davidson, Bill (W, F & Co. agent) 135
Davidson, M. 34
Davis, __ 169
Davis, __ (driver) 73
Davis, __ (sheriff) 142

Index

Davis, Edgar L. (road agent) 112
Davis, H.G. (constable) 40
Davis, John N. "J.L." (road agent) 112
Davis, L.C. 245
Davis, Perry (driver) 203
Davis, Thomas (driver) 218–219
Davisville, CA 166
Day, Bert (driver) 68
Day, D.W.H. (Gen.) 164
Day, John 196
Day, W.T. 251
Dayton, WA 238
Deady, M.P. (judge) 238
Deal, __ (constable) 50
Dean, __ (sheriff) 164
De Camp, __ (deputy) 53
Deep Creek Gulch, CA 235
Deep Holes Springs, NV 255
DeForest, Dan (driver) 202
de Haven, __ (judge) 112, 114
De la Cuesta, __ (deputy) 182
De Lacy, Charles W. (or C.W.) see Taylor, George F.
De Lacy, George see Driscoll, James
Delamar, CA 214
Delaney, Michael (road agent) 32
De Lano, Rose 31
Del Norte, CO 43–44
Delta, CA 226
Demerest, James 190
Denver, CO 155, 240
Dependener, __ (deputy) 160
Devil's Gate toll house, NV 136
De Witt, Charles 180
Diaz, E. 87
Dingman, Charles (road agent) 44
Dobbins Ranch, CA 257
Dobson, Bill (messenger) 247–248
Dodds, J.G. 160
Dodsworth, M. 149
Doebler, __ (officer) 25
Doherty, Dan 80
Dollar, James R. (road agent) 127–128
Dolliver, Alonzo (deputy) 255
Domingo 249
Don Pedro's Bar, CA 242
Donaldson, William 203
Donohue, Fred 111
Donohue, James (deputy) 246
Donohue, R.E. (sheriff) 115–116
Donovan, Michael 129
Dorsey, __ 178
Dorsey, Charles (aka Charles H. Thorn; road agent) 49–50, 140–142, 159, 166
Doty's Flat, CA 35
Douglas, __ (officer) 194
Dow, __ (deputy) 103
Dow, J.P. 204
Dowdle, W.E. (road agent) 52–55
Downer, Albert H. (aka John Bell; road agent) 239
Downey, Joseph (driver) 146
Downieville, CA 138, 143, 145–146, 215–216, 218–219, 251–257
Dreibelbis, Louis J. (road agent) 27, 137–138, 251

Driscoll, James W. (aka George De Lacy; road agent) 11–12, 147–148
driver (defined) 6
Dry Creek, CA 229
Drytown, CA 17, 24, 64
Duffy, Martin 45
Dufrene's (stagecoach) station 23–24
Duggan, __ (driver) 77
Duncan's Mills, CA 231–232
Dunham, Warren 195–196
Dunlap, D.A. (sheriff) 130–133
Dunlevy, Michael 166
Dunn, R.G. (W, F & Co. agent) 214
Durfor, __ (driver) 214
Duryea, W.H. 34
Dusty Bend, CA 132
Dutch Flat, CA 155–156
Dutch Hill, CA 219
Dutch Kate 215–216
Dutton, Robert 133
Dwyer, John (road agent) 101

Eagle Bird Hill, CA 161
Earl, William L. (road agent) 124
Early, Bill see Thurman, Charles
East, Jim 44
Eaton, __ (Mrs.) 92
Eaton, Francis S. 92
Eberhardt, __ 31
Eckles, __ (constable) 193, 200, 208
Eddings, Nort (driver) 223
Edgar, Ad (driver) 237
Edgar, William (Mrs.) 251
Edith, __ (Miss) 109
Edwards, Harry (road agent) 186–187
Egan, __ (judge) 88
Ehrenberg, AZ 170
Eighteen-Mile House, CA 80
Elias, Isaac 216
Elizabeth Lake, CA 86
Elkhorn (stagecoach station), CA 53, 55
Ellinitos, CA 171
Ellis, James W. 165
Elmore, __ (constable) 197
Elmore, Pat 256
Elroy, __ (sheriff) 177
Emery, Henry (or Harry) 106
Emigrant Gap, CA 146
Engles, Frederick 94
English, Lawrence B. (road agent) 83–84
Eproson, Jackson 40
Eschbacher, W.F. 145
Etna, CA 225, 227
Etna Springs, CA 83
Eureka, CA 99–100, 104, 106, 140
Evans, William (road agent) 20–22

Fairburn, CA 21
Fairfield, CA 59
Falkenberry, James A. (road agent) 13–14
Farmington, CA 40
Farnsworth __ (bros.) 249
Farnsworth, __ (Miss) 97

Farnsworth, Walter (driver) 90
Farrel, Thomas 126
Fellows, Dick see Perkins, Richard
Ferguson & Biggs California Laundry 38
Ferris, H.C. (Mrs.) 213
Ferry Hill, CA 171
Fessenfield, William 73
Fick, H.L. (constable) 158
Fickas, __ 132
Fiddletown, CA 11, 14, 16–17, 64
Fife, __ 190
Finch, __ (constable) 172
Finchley, T.W. (driver) 28
Finley, G. (driver) 152
Finley, James W. (road agent) 58–59
Finn, __ 17
Finn, Robert (road agent) 133–136
Finney, __ 110
Finney, "Lish" 111
Firebaugh's Ferry, CA 68, 249–250
Fisher, Joseph 167
Fitzgerald, Jack (detective) 90
Fleck, Thomas 28
Fleming, S.M. 212–213
Fletcher, Fred (driver) 120
Flint, __ (postal inspector) 181
Flint, Samuel 206
Foff, __ (constable) 133
Folsom, CA 11, 60, 64, 147
Forbestown, CA 26–27, 138, 166, 217
Ford, __ (Alta Express agent) 147
Forest City, CA 215, 218
Forest Hill, CA 7, 33, 144, 149–151, 154, 15–158, 160, 189, 204
Forest Home, CA 12, 19
Forest House Mountain, CA 227
Formsbee, A. 91
Forse, Harry (driver) 98
Forse, Thomas (driver) 99
Forsythe, William (deputy) 104
Fort Bidwell, CA 119–120
Fort Bragg, CA 114
Fort Brown, CA 112–113
Fort Jones, CA 220, 224–225, 227
Fort Ross, CA 236
Fort Yuma, CA 169
Foster, A.H. (driver) 89–90
Fountain House, CA 251
Fowler, Alexander (driver) 98
Foxen, Nick (deputy) 181
Franklin House, CA 249
Franks, John C. (sheriff) 124–126
Fraser, __ (officer) 201–202
Frazier, Charles 194–195
Frazier, Charles (road agent) 255
Frazier, George 233–234
Frazier, William (deputy) 103–104
Fredericks, William (road agent) 97
Freer, __ (judge) 165
French Camp, CA 45, 173
French Gulch, CA 213
Fresno, CA 46, 69, 95, 201, 209, 245
Fresno Flats, CA 46–47, 95, 119
Frey, John 20
Frey, Joseph (road agent) 234–235

Index

Froom, Wesley (driver) 179–180
Frost, C.A.S. 116
Fugate, Billy (road agent) 237
Fulkerth, __ (deputy) 172
Fuller, __ (detective) 11
Fulton, M.J. 148
Fulwider, Theodore 109
Funk Hill, CA 36–38, 48–49

Gaffney, L.L. (driver) 145
Gage, Watt (driver) 196
Gainesville, GA 44
Galeni, Louis 115
Galt, CA 15, 105
Gamble, Joseph W. 62
Garcia, __ 74
Gard, __ (marshal) 211
Gardner, John (driver) 83–84
Garter, __ (attorney) 207
Garvey, __ (sheriff) 41
Gately, H.H. 62
Gator, J.E. 111
Gay, Daniel C. (officer) 25, 30, 148, 248
Gazelle, CA 227
Geney, __ (deputy) 227
Genoa, NV 61, 182
Gentry, Albert (deputy) 134–135
Gentry, R.B. (sheriff) 134–135
George, C. 215
George, "Greek" 74
Georgetown, CA 60, 63–68, 150, 154–155
Getchell, __ (deputy) 52
Getchell, D.B. (sheriff) 146
Getz, M. 213
Geyserville, CA 111, 231
Gibbons, Jack D. (driver) 35, 42, 242
Gibson, Ed (detective) 90
Gibson, Frank J. 170–171
Gibson, Peter 252
Gibsonville, CA 163
Gil, Jose M. (road agent) 124
Gill, George 72
Gillespie, Bright (driver) 89, 91–92
Gillett, Frederick (road agent) 78–79
Gillette, James (CA governor) 22
Gilroy, CA 68, 116–117, 123, 175–176, 184–185
Gimletville, CA 163
Glasby, Alban H. (road agent) 61–63
Glover, Edward (road agent) 198–199
Godfrey, George (driver/road agent) 259–260
Gold Lake, CA 29
Goldner, H. (justice of the peace) 18
Goldstein, H. 183
Goleta, CA 182
Gonzales, A.S. (road agent) 125
Gonzales, Romulo (road agent) 68
Gonzales, CA 125
Goodenough, A.M. 200–202
Goodwin, __ (deputy) 50–51
Gorham, C.M. (judge) 256
Goss, Frank 22

Gossin, Cal (driver) 12–13
Gottschalk, C.V. (judge) 39, 43, 57
Gould, __ (deputy) 62
Grace, __ (deputy) 115
Graham, Bartholomew 232
Graham, Ed (driver) 205
Grant, James (road agent) 61, 183–184
Grant, James O. 4
Grant, Johnny (road agent) 237
Grass Valley, CA 32, 64, 137–138, 149–150, 156
Grauss, Ben (constable) 130–132
Graves, __ (deputy) 54, 123
Graves, Hugh 180
Grayson, CA 171
Greeley, Burton (road agent) 46–47
Green Camp, CA 29
Greenlee, __ (Mrs.) 130
Greenville, CA 166
Greenwood, CA 60, 63–67
Greer, John (driver) 247–248
Gregg, __ (sheriff) 71
Gregory, Marion 214
Gregory, U.S. (sheriff) 22–24
Grewell, __ 185
Gridley, P.D. 83
Griffen, G.W. 240
Griffith, Elijah 22
Grimes, Frank (driver) 171
Gristy, Bill (aka Bill White; road agent) 247–250
Grizzly Bear House, CA 151
Grofette, John (driver) 146
Groshong, Hiram (deputy) 103
Grub Gulch, CA 88–90, 92
Guadalupe, CA 179–180
Gualala, CA 106
Guerneville, CA 81, 236
Gunckel, W.F. (Dr.) 126
Gundlack, John D. see Allen, John
Gwin, Wash (driver) 127

Hackett, George (messenger) 166, 254, 256, 258
Haggin, J.B. 52
Haight, Henry H. (California governor) 13
Half Moon Bay, CA 177
Halfway House, CA 114–115, 123
Hall, __ (deputy) 18
Halleck, John (deputy) 191
Hall's (stagecoach) station, CA 18
Halmer, J. (driver) 81
Ham, __ (judge) 84
Hamilton, Albert P. (aka Henry Tarlton; road agent) 10, 15–16, 43, 65, 149–150, 185–186
Hampton, Jasper (driver) 212
Hampton, Joe see Bragg, Calvin
Handy, Philo (undersheriff) 109
Hankins, __ 164
Hanlon, H.W. see Baker, Charles
Hannah, __ (judge) 72
Hansley, __ (sheriff) 92
Hanson, John 174
Harbin Springs, CA 81–82
Hardwick, C.C. 215

Harmon, __ 25
Harniss, T.C. (road agent) 71–72
Harper, William (deputy) 238
Harrington, Frank 111
Harrington, James (road agent) 32–33
Harris, __ (sheriff) 185
Harris, George (road agent) 197
Harris, "Happy Jack" (driver) 29
Harris, Len (officer) 64, 156
Harris (stagecoach) station, CA 109
Harrison, Harry (sheriff) 93
Harrison, Robert (detective) 248
Hart, __ (judge) 59
Hart, J.H. 256
Hart, Samuel (road agent) 194–195
Hartman, William P. (Dr./coroner) 191
Harvey, Joseph F. (road agent) 236–237
Haskell, __ (Mrs.) 214
Haskell, Daniel N. (messenger) 210–211, 213–214, 226
Hatch, __ (messenger) 115
Hatch, C.C. 170
Hatch, H.T. (deputy) 109
Hatfield, Nat 134
Havilah, CA 75, 79
Hawkeye, CA 30
Hawthorne, CA 120
Hayes, Rutherford B. (U.S. president) 171
Hays, John (road agent) 81, 149, 188–189
Heacock, __ (U.S. commissioner) 112, 259
Head, __ 17
Head, __ (judge) 176
Heald's Hill, CA 232
Healdsburg, CA 103, 228–229, 231, 236
Heap, Charles W. (road agent) 119–120
Heath, Richard (driver) 210–211
Heinsman, W.H. 256
Helena, MT 144, 256
Helm, __ (Mrs.) 59
Helm, George H. (driver) 258
Henderson, Devin (constable) 45
Henderson, George see Arrison, Walter A.
Henderson, George C. 200–201
Hendricks, Joe (road agent) 194–195
Hendricks, John (deputy) 195, 221
Hendricks, Lee 56
Hendricks, William (deputy) 244
Hendricks, William (messenger) 54
Henry, Sam 135
Hensley, __ (constable) 96
Henson, __ (sheriff) 249
Henson, Rufus 128
Hepburn, James (Dr.) 36
Herbert, John M. (road agent) 69
Hereford, Hugh 101
Hernandez Valley, CA 167
Hertz, Louis 180
Hicks, __ (sheriff) 181–182

Index

Higgs, George (road agent) 163–164
High Grade mining camp, CA 120
Hilbert, J.H. (sheriff) 67
Hildreth, CA 96, 202
Hill, Henry C. (road agent) 84
Hill, Raymond (driver) 112–113
Hill, S.H. (justice of the peace) 69
Hill, William H. (driver) 63
Hill's Ferry, CA 172, 174, 236
Hilton, George W. (road agent) 107–108
Hipkins, __ (driver) 15
Hitchcock, __ 242
Hoadley, Milo 40
Hoag, E.H. 213
Hodges, Preston 62
Hodges, Thomas J. (aka Tom Bell; road agent) 7, 247–250
Hodson, CA 58
Hoffman, __ (judge) 96
Hoffman, George L. 68
Hogan, Mike (driver) 138–140, 143
Hog's Back, CA 238
Holbrook, E.E. (sheriff) 167
Holcomb's (stagecoach) station, CA 207
Holladay Overland Mail & Express Company 9
Hollister, __ 183
Hollister, CA 123, 245
home station (defined) 5
Homily, __ see Shepardson, Milton
Hood, Elizabeth 249–250
Hooker, Dan (driver) 239
Hooper, Jimmy (driver) 173
Hopkins, __ (constable) 18
Hopland, CA 104, 106
Hopping, __ (judge) 194
Hopping, __ (sheriff) 202
Hornitos, CA 97, 118
Horrall, __ (Mrs.) 226
Horrall, William H. (road agent) 225–226
Horsetown, CA 147
Hot Springs, CA 108
Houston, T.J. (sheriff) 211–212
Houx, John (road agent) 228–230
Hovey, Frank (driver) 227
Howard, __ 239
Howard, __ (deputy) 82
Howard, __ (sheriff) 227
Howard, Cornelius 207
Howard, Robert W. (road agent) 259–260
Howard, Theodore (driver) 109
Howard, William H. (road agent) 205–207
Howe, __ (judge) 218
Hower, __ (deputy) 133
Hoyman, George J.A. (road agent) 67–68
Hoyt's crossing, CA 134
Hubbard, Richard 221
Hubbell, Dick 222
Hugg, B.P. 256
Hughes, G.W. (deputy) 109
Hughes & Keys (railroad) station 117
Hull, __ (sheriff) 194, 196

Hume, James B. (sheriff) 63–64
Hume, James B. (W, F & Co. detective) 21, 26, 37, 41, 46, 52, 64, 67, 77–79, 81, 99, 125, 138, 140–141, 151, 153–155, 157–159, 162, 165, 194, 196, 200–202, 206, 217, 219, 221–223, 244, 251–252, 254–255, 259
Hume, T.T. 54
Hunnefauth, __ 134
Hunt, H.S. (road agent) 190–191
Hunter & Company Express 9
Huntley, __ (sheriff) 142

Igo, CA 195–196, 204
Independence, CA 70–71
Indian Billy (road agent) 220
Indian Charley 221
Indian Frank 198
Indian (Sisson) Jim 221–222
Indian Wells, CA 78, 170
Ingram, John 62, 101
Ingram, Rufus H. (road agent) 61–63
Ingram, CA 104
Inlow, __ (sheriff) 259
Inspiration Point, CA 94
Ione, CA 13–15, 19–23, 40, 65, 115, 195
Iowa Hill, CA 148, 238
Irish Hill, CA 12
Irwin, William (CA governor) 41, 75, 117, 186, 193, 222, 252
Iseberg, Andy 28
Isham, Henry F. 167
Ivans, John (road agent) 113–114

Jackson, __ 198
Jackson, __ (deputy) 23–24
Jackson, F. (messenger) 56–57
Jackson, George see Lester, George
Jackson, Thomas (aka Charles Brown; road agent) 221–223
Jackson, William 212
Jackson, CA 13–17, 19–20, 22–24, 35, 40, 65, 115, 162
James, Bob see Sykes, Lee
James, Jeff 49
Jamestown, CA 245–246
Jamison, __ (messenger) 108
Jamison, Al (driver) 187
Jarboe, Henry I. 62
Jennings, __ (W, F & Co. detective) 226
Jenny Lind, CA 31, 33
Jinamini, George 213
Joachimsen, __ (judge) 144
Johns, Samuel D. 256
Johnson, __ 16
Johnson, __ (marshal) 131–132
Johnson, __ (officer) 25
Johnson, __ (officer) 169
Johnson, __ (sheriff) 82
Johnson, __ (W, F & Co. detective) 13
Johnson, A.J. (Miss) 177
Johnson, Al 114
Johnson, C.F. (driver) 219

Johnson, "Doc" (road agent) 26, 254
Johnson, Frank 237–238
Johnson, Frank T. (sheriff) 106–107
Johnson, Fred (driver) 245
Johnson, George 155
Johnson, J.L. (deputy) 109–110, 114–115
Johnson, J.R. (sheriff) 109–111
Johnson, Richard (aka Richard McMahon; road agent) 167–169
Jolon, CA 124
Jones, __ (detective) 153
Jones, __ (road agent) 52
Jones, Abraham (road agent) 205–207
Jones, E.K. 101
Jones, George 203
Jones, James (road agent) 162
Jones, J.M. (sheriff) 91–92
Jones, Leslie 200–201
Jones, Stanton P. 155
Jones, Stanton T. (road agent) 43–44
Jones, Thad 196
Jones, Tom (road agent) 228–230
Jones, William C. (road agent) 151–154
Jose, William (road agent) 163–164
Jule, Peter 177
Julian, CA 170
Junction City, CA 41, 198

Kean, P.H. (justice of the peace) 39, 47
Keener, John (road agent) 52–55
Keith, Frank 154
Kellett, Frank (road agent) 118–119
Kelley, __ 246
Kelley, __ (driver) 48
Kellogg, CA 128
Kelly, __ (constable) 21, 23
Kelly, Eli (road agent) 220
Kendall, __ 21
Kenna, __ (sheriff) 160
Kennedy, Robert (undersheriff) 193, 197
Kent, C.A. (road agent) 49
Kenuff, __ (driver) 204
Kern, CA 87
Kernville, CA 78–80
Keswick, CA 111, 212
Ketchum, __ (judge) 166
Keyser, __ (judge) 259
Kilgore, __ 216
Kilgore's (stagecoach) station, NV 162
Kimble, I.W. (constable) 64
Kime, Daniel 251
King, Bill (police captain) 248
Kingston, CA 73
Kirk, George (driver) 118–119
Klamath Falls, OR 224–225, 227
Knight's Ferry, CA 245, 249
Knights of the Golden Circle 61–62
Knight's Valley, CA 82, 133
Knox, __ (justice of the peace) 198
Kokimbo see Maria, Jose

Kopp, Lillie 19
Kossuth Hill, CA 55

La Graciosa, CA 179
La Grange, CA 119, 246
La Plana, CA 13
Labadie, Thomas 258–259
Ladd, W.J. (driver) 75
Lake, C.G. (justice of the peace) 29–30
Lake, John 76
Lake City, CA 136–137
Lake Vera, CA 146
Lakeport, CA 81–83, 101, 116, 127, 129, 232, 234
Lakeview, OR 192, 206
Lambert, Charles (driver) 106
Lance, J.A. 98
Lander, Eugene (deputy) 168
Lane, Thomas M. (undersheriff) 41, 117
Lane, T.W. (Maj.) 249–250
Langerman, Will (driver) 120
Laporte, CA 26–27, 162–163, 196, 241, 250–251, 253–254, 257–258
Larue, __ (sheriff) 74
Last Chance (stagecoach) station, CA 192
Lathrop, CA 16, 45, 201
la Tour, Ed (constable) 119
Latrobe, CA 17
Lawrence, KS 61
Lawry, __ (Dr.) 209
Lawson, Douglas 95
Laytonville, CA 112
Leach, __ (constable) 156
Leard, __ (deputy) 111
Leavenworth, KS 260
Lee, Eddie (road agent) 149, 188–189
Lee, Frank 170
Lee, Harvey H. (road agent) 69
Lee, James H. (deputy) 134–135
Lee, Perron (road agent) 67
Leek, __ 219
Lees, Isiah (police captain) 141–144, 204
Lees, J.W. (officer) 25
Leesville, CA 58–59
Leighton, CA 208
Leiva, Abdon (road agent) 68
Lemos, John A. 59, 115
Lenaris, Jose (road agent) 35, 70, 253
Leonard, __ 25
Leonard, __ (constable) 90
Leonard, Al 167
Lerda, __ (priest) 74
Leroy, Billy see Pond, Arthur
Lester, George (aka George Jackson; road agent) 27–28, 137–138
Levy, Charles 71
Lewis, __ (driver) 55
Lewiston, MT 238
Lexington, CA 186
Liegan, CA 85
Lierly, __ (constable) 180
Linden, CA 45
Linkville, OR 206

Little Lake, CA 99, 102
Littlefield, __ 89
Lloyd, F.W. 226
Lloyd, Jack T. 70
Lodi, CA 36
Lompoc, CA 85, 181
Lone Pine, CA 70, 75, 86–87
Long, __ (U.S. marshal) 144
Long, Jim 119
Looking Glass, OR 204
Loomis Corners, CA 200
Lopez, Manuel 73
Lopez, Rafael 87
Lord, __ (W, F & Co. detective) 147
Los Alamos, CA 178
Los Angeles, CA 73, 77, 81, 85–86, 122, 167, 169–171, 178, 181, 183, 185
Los Banos, CA 116, 245
Los Olives, CA 181–182
Lost Chance Gulch, CA 123
Love, __ (constable) 13
Love, W. (deputy) 21
Lovelace, "Colonel" (driver) 43
Loveless, Seth (sheriff) 66
Low, Frederick F. (CA governor) 62–63, 135
Lower Lake, CA 80, 234
Lower Springs, CA 190
Lowe's (stagecoach) station, CA 123
Loyed, __ (Mrs.) 51
Lucas, __ (Dr.) 163
Luddy, __ (messenger) 19
Lugo, Chico see Sotello, Santos
Lupton, J.C. (deputy) 41
Lutgen, C.F. 87–88
Lynch, Ed (driver) 237
Lynch, James (road agent) 47–48
Lynn, Ed M. 213
Lyon, Montague (road agent) 247–250
Lyons, __ 256
Lyons, L.E. (Capt.) 243
Lytle, G. Brett see Perkins, Richard

Maben, __ (marshal) 166
Machado, Jose (road agent) 216
Mack, T.A. (constable) 118–119
Macon, Antonio (Mr. & Mrs.) 216
Madera, CA 69, 90, 92, 95–96, 202
Madill, Matt 96
Magee, Thomas (messenger) 41
Maguin, __ (Mrs.) 81
Maguire, John 230
Mairs, Arlie F. (road agent) 71–72
Majors, John (driver) 133
Malaga, CA 28
Mammoth City, NV 152
Manning, Charles (road agent) 71, 102
Mansfield, Joseph (sheriff) 177
Mantle, John (detective) 170–171
Maria, Jose (aka Kokimbo; road agent) 35, 70, 243, 253
Mariposa, CA 89, 94–95, 97–98, 117
Mariposa Big Trees, CA 89
Mariposa Creek, CA 46

Markham, H.H. (CA governor) 50, 69, 235
Marlett, Ella 64
Marsh, Andrew (road agent) 221–223
Marsh, Frank (deputy) 214
Marshal, __ (officer) 173
Marshall, J. 44
Marshall, John (road agent) 217–218
Martell's (stagecoach) station, CA 22–23
Martin, __ (deputy) 146–147
Martin, Dick 45
Martin, James W. (aka William Robinson; road agent) 24, 217–218
Martin, Jerome 92
Martin, John (road agent) 103
Martin, John H. 95
Martin, Owen (road agent) 24–25
Martin, Thomas 38
Martinez, Rebecca (Miss) 212–213
Marysville, CA 24, 39, 136, 138–140, 142–143, 161, 166, 189, 195, 198, 214–216, 221, 247–249, 250–259
Mason, Joe (driver) 223
Massachusetts Hill, CA 155
Mastick, G.H. (Mrs.) 58
Mathews, __ (justice of the peace) 168
Mattel, Charles 182
Mauriata, Crocopolo (road agent) 184–185
Maxey, "Captain" 24
May, __ (justice of the peace) 187
May, __ (Mrs.) 157
May, __ (undersheriff) 160
May, Reuben 173
Mayfield, __ (deputy) 168
Mayfield, CA 33, 126
McCarrell, Lawrence 256
McCarty, Dan (road agent) 116–117, 174–175, 236
McClellan, __ (sheriff) 27
McClelland, Felix 51
McClennan, Martin (driver) 232
McCloud, __ 240
McClure, Nelson (deputy) 109–110
McCoffrey, Patrick 43
McComber, __ (constable) 199
McConnell, Charles (driver) 198
McConnell, Reason E. (driver) 22–23, 33, 37–39, 56–57
McCord, Dallas (sheriff) 96, 202
McCoy, C.F. (Rev.) 130
McCoy, H.L. (deputy) 117, 256
McCurdy, D. 213
McDonald's (stagecoach station) House, CA 229–230
McDuffee, __ (officer) 175–176
McDuffie, James Y. 25
McFarland, W.E. (driver) 186
McGarrey, __ (postal inspector) 211
McGarvey, __ (judge) 108
McGee, Thomas (messenger) 17
McIntyre, Hattie 140

278　　　　　　　　　　　　　　　　Index

McKay, Joe *see* Miller, Harry
McKee, Frank 134
McKenzie, George S. (sheriff) 82
McKiernan, Charley 186
McKinney, __ (driver) 136–137
McKune, __ (judge) 25
McLean, Donald 256
McMahon, Richard{en *see* Johnson, Richard
McManus, __ (judge) 78
McMeekin, J. (driver) 212
McNemar, John (messenger) 190–191
McNichols, __ 23
McQuade, __ (sheriff) 46
Meacham, Joel (driver) 163
Mead, __ (sheriff) 142
Mead, Willard (driver) 34
Meadow Lake, CA 135
Meagher, __ (priest) 141
Meckel, Fritz C. (Mr. & Mrs.) 212–213
Melton, Ben (deputy) 115
Mendocino City, CA 71, 101–102, 104, 113–114, 232–233, 235
Menhall, Thomas 116
Merced, CA 95–98, 117–119
Merritt, C.W. (W, F & Co. agent) 180
messenger (defined) 6
Messer, M.N. 27
Metz, Albert 256
Meyer, Arthur (driver) 145
Meyers, __ (judge) 157
Meyers, Charles 111
Meyers, Charles (road agent) 95
Meyers, James 138
Meyers, J.B. (constable) 43
Meyers, Jerome (chief of police) 77
Meyers, Martin (road agent) 166
Michigan Bluff, CA 63, 147, 149, 157, 159, 219
Middle Creek (stagecoach) station, CA 204, 209
Middleton, __ (sheriff) 25
Middletown, CA 80, 82–83
Miles, Thomas (deputy) 207
Milledgeville, GA 44
Miller, __ (W, F & Co. agent) 241
Miller, Bill (road agent) 43–44
Miller, George B. 106
Miller, Harry (aka Joe McKay; road agent) 106, 181
Miller, Henry 68
Miller, Joaquin 106
Miller, L. (driver) 35
Miller's (stagecoach) station, CA 23
Millerton, CA 73
Millford, CA 85
Millville, CA 119, 199–200, 206
Milton, CA 19, 33–37, 39–49, 52–56, 58, 65, 70, 140, 159, 243–244, 253
Miner, Ezra W. (road agent) 32–33, 43–44, 154
Minges, __ 118
Mirabel, CA 83

Mitchell, __ (deputy) 67
Mitchell, Arthur 96
Mitchell, Charles *see* Tracy, Martin
Mitchell, Henry B. (aka Harvey Bell; road agent) 231
Moccasin Creek, CA 242
Modesto, CA 41, 172
Mojave, CA 70, 78–80, 86
Mokelumne (stagecoach) station 34
Mokelumne Hill, CA 14, 23, 33–34, 36, 40, 50–52, 57
Mokelumne River, CA 22
Molloy, Charles 246
Montejos, Refugio 73
Monterey, CA 123
Montgomery, Amos (messenger) 208–210
Moody, __ (Dr./coroner) 210
Mooney, Joseph (aka Joe Morgan; road agent) 81
Moore, __ 184
Moore, __ (driver) 11
Moore, Charles 83
Moore, Fred (driver) 166
Moore, George W. (road agent) 133–136
Moore, James 196
Moore, James R. (sheriff) 98–99
Moore's Flat, CA 136–137, 140, 159
Moran, Tom 90
Moreno, Teodoro (road agent) 68
Morgan, Joe *see* Mooney, Joseph
Morley's (stagecoach) station, CA 211–212, 204
Mormon Island, CA 65
Moro, Peter (road agent) 57
Morris, __ (deputy) 62
Morrison, Jack (driver) 100
Morrison's (stagecoach) station, CA 137
Morrow, __ (judge) 207
Morse, Fred (driver) 27, 241
Morse, Harry (W, F & Co. detective) 38
Mount Hamilton, CA 187–188
Mountain Charley 187
Mountain House, CA 65, 218, 233, 249
Mountain View, CA 126
Muir, __ 159
Muletown, CA 13, 213
Mulford, __ (sheriff) 249–250
Mullerson, T.J. 47
Mulligan, Joe (driver) 46–47
Mulvane, Charles 140
Murphy, __ (attorney) 252
Murphy, __ (Miss) 185
Murphy, Eugene (road agent) 171–172
Murphy, Robert (road agent) 56–57
Murphy's Camp, CA 29–32, 39, 43, 47, 49, 54, 140
Murphy's Creek, CA 32
Murray, Jim (driver) 157
Myers, Jim (driver) 124–126
Myers, Martin (road agent) 195
Myer's Creek, CA 135

Naciemento, CA 173
Nance, T.C. (deputy) 180
Napa, CA 64, 81–83, 129–133
Napa (CA) Insane Asylum 11
Nash, __ (marshal) 130–131
Nasrelli, Mike 56
Natividad, CA 121
Nelson, Ed (driver) 27
Nevada City, CA 129, 133–136, 140–143, 145–146, 215–216
New Orleans, LA 44, 141
New York, NY 44
Newell, A. 187
Newhall, CA 86–88
Newton, Adolph 249
Nichols, __ 215–216
Nicholson, J.R. (messenger) 96
Nigger Tent, CA 145, 219
Norco, CA 255
Norman, Thomas (sheriff) 23
North, John 165
North American House 31, 33–34
North Bloomfield, CA 145
North Branch, CA 52
North San Juan, CA 133, 142–143, 257
Norton, Henry (road agent) 26, 254
Nunes, Francisco (road agent) 148
Nunez, Trinidad (road agent) 216
Nye, Joe (constable) 172

Oak Bar, CA 220
Oak Grove, CA 179
Oak Hill, CA 83
Oak Run, CA 207, 211
Oakdale, CA 246
Oakland, CA 11
Oaks, __ (sheriff) 174
Oates, __ (detective) 175–176
Oathill, CA 132
Oats, __ (driver) 28
Odum, W.H. 41
Ogden, Hattie 59
Ohio City, CO 43
Oldham, David (road agent) 107–108
Olivas, Francisco *see* Sotello, Francisco
Olivera, Joaquin (road agent) 35, 70, 253
Olsen, O. 177
Omaha, NE 217
O'Meara, Roger (road agent) 16, 19, 43, 65, 141
O'Neil, Charles P. (officer) 30, 148
Oregon House, CA 251
Orland, CA 236
Ornbaum, Nute 101
Ornbaum, William F. (deputy) 112–113, 115
Oroville, CA 25–27, 138, 159, 161, 163–166, 196, 218, 241, 250, 253, 258
Orr, James (driver) 60
Orr, N.J. 203
Orr Hot Springs, CA 113
Orton, Bob (sheriff) 186
Ostander, __ (attorney) 118

Index

Overholzer, Charles (deputy) 206
Overmeyer, Q.A. (messenger) 114–115
Overton, CA 220
Owens, Perry 249–250
Owens River, CA 73
Owsley, Harry (driver) 114

Pacheco, Romualdo (California governor) 64
Pacheco Pass, CA 117, 184
Pacific Express 3
Pacific House, CA 68
Paddock, __ 182
Page, Frank 63
Page, Frank (judge) 154
Page, Harry 209
Page, H.C. (W, F & Co. agent) 237
Page, Bacon & Company 9
Paige, Harry 214
Palafos Hill, CA 55
Palermo, CA 166
Palmer, Albert R. (driver) 83, 130–131, 200, 204
Palmer, James R. (road agent) 125
Panama, CA 86
Panamint Junction, CA 78
Panamint Springs, CA 75
Pardillo, Ysidro (road agent) 35, 70, 242–243, 253
Parker, __ (constable) 27, 59
Parker, __ (deputy) 22–23
Parks, Daniel (road agent) 40–42
Parron, Al (driver) 187
Pasco, __ (sheriff) 110
Paso de Robles, CA 173
Passmore, __ (sheriff) 78
Patterson, __ (deputy) 13
Patterson, __ (road agent) 24–25
Patterson, John see Collins, John C.P.
Patton, Joseph 183
Paul, Robert H. (messenger/deputy) 86–87
Paul, Thomas (road agent) 99
Payne, Ed (driver) 119
Pea Ridge, CA 89
Peanut, CA 238
Pegg, __ (Dr.) 245
Penobscot, CA 67
Perkins, George C. (California governor) 76, 99–100, 128, 189, 193, 244
Perkins, Richard (aka Dick Fellows; aka G. Brett Lytle; road agent) 77, 125–126, 174, 178–179
Perrin, J. (constable) 13
Perrin, Joseph (sheriff) 138
Perry, Ned (driver) 19
Pescadero, CA 126, 176
Petaluma, CA 140, 229, 231
Peters, __ (constable) 155–156
Peters, Tommy (driver) 168
Phelps, T.D. (road agent) 237–238
Philadelphia, PA 141
Phillips, Dave (driver) 23
Phillips, Ellery (driver) 119–120
Phillips, Jack 249–250

Philpott, Budd (driver) 127
Picayune Lake, CA 222
Pierce, Isiah (road agent) 186–187
Pike, J.M. (W, F & Co. detective) 37
Pilot Hill, CA 151
Pine Grove, CA 15
Pioneer Stage Line 9
Pit River (bridge), CA 214–215
Placerville, CA 61–65, 66–67, 94, 183–184
Plato (stagecoach) station, CA 121
Pleasant Valley, CA 95
Pledger, Isaac 173
Plymouth, CA 16–17, 19–20, 24
Podesta, Peter (driver) 22
Point Arena, CA 106, 231–232, 236
Point San Quentin, CA 247
Pond, Arthur (aka Billy Leroy; road agent) 43–44, 155
Poole, A.W. (ex-sheriff) 123–124
Poole, Thomas (road agent) 61–63
Pope Valley, CA 133
Popejoy 215
Porter, __ 32
Porter, __ (California assistant governor) 127
Portland, OR 238
Potter, __ (marshal) 62
Potter, A.W. (deputy) 134–135
Potter Valley, CA 112–113, 115–116
Powell, Frank (driver) 144, 158
Powellton, CA 28
Powers, Ed (officer) 132
Prage, __ (judge) 106
Pratt, Charles (road agent) 17, 64–65
Predmore, __ 199
Prescott, William (road agent) 95
Prescott, AZ 170
Preus, Eugene (road agent) 234–235
Price, __ (sheriff) 246
Price, Lee (deputy) 246
Price, Robert 249–250
Pridham, __ (W, F & Co. agent) 168
Profilo Rock, CA 234
Prouty, R.A. (sheriff) 89, 91–92
Putah Creek, CA 132

Quadlin, David (driver) 26, 216, 258
Quantrill, William C. 61
Quigley, Tuck (driver) 130
Quillei, __ (Mrs.) 20
Quincy, CA 159, 161, 163–166
Quinton, Edward 27

Rabbit Creek, CA 161
Radcliffe, Clinton (driver) 19–21
Radford, W.A. (deputy) 226
Raggio, Babe (driver) 51
Raggio, Louis (driver) 55, 74
Ragsdale, J.L. (road agent) 196–197
Rameriz, __ 249
Randolph, Patrick J. 106–107
Ranney, George (constable) 62
Ratovich, Mitchell (road agent) 35, 70, 253
Rattle Jack (road agent) 228–230
Rattlesnake Bar, CA 147

Ratto, Joe 22
Rattray, B.F. (Rev.) 46
Ray, H. 34
Raymon, Dan F. 165
Raymond, __ (Mr. & Mrs.) 73
Raymond, CA 88–90, 92
Read, __ (judge) 119
Rector, Charles 101
Red Antone see Valacca, Antone
Red Bluff, CA 21, 189, 198, 202, 237–238
Red Gate, CA 182
Red Rock Canyon, CA 79
Reddick, __ (justice of the peace) 40
Redding, CA 97, 119, 144, 149, 188, 190–210, 211–215, 220, 222–223, 226
Redfield, __ 184
Redwood City, CA 176
Reed, Andy (driver) 96
Reed, Ira H. (judge) 40
Reed, Justin (driver) 132
Reese, Cornelius (driver) 156
Reid's Ferry, CA 193, 197
Reig, George 86
Reilly, John (road agent) 259–260
Rendone, Jesus 244
Rennick, Clay (driver) 113, 115
Reno, NV 38, 154, 163, 221
Reservoir House, CA 47
Reynard, Paul (driver) 116–117
Reynolds, __ (deputy) 62
Reynolds, Hedge 229
Reynolds, John (driver) 191
Reynolds, John (undersheriff) 198–199, 202, 204
Reynolds, John E. (messenger) 195, 222
Reynolds, William B. (deputy) 155, 229, 231
Reynold's Ferry, CA 35, 37
Reynolds, Todd & Company Express 9
Rhodes, William H. 232
Rice, Fannie (Miss) 109
Rice, John 206–207
Richardson, __ (undersheriff) 213
Richardson, A.L. (driver) 219–220
Richmond, George (driver) 178
Rideout, __ 247–248
Ridgeway, John (Mr. & Mrs.) 239
Riley, James see Starling, George
Ringer, George W. (road agent) 13–14
Rising River, CA 193
Rivers, Henry see Cummings, George W.
road agent (defined) 6–7
Roberts, James A. 215
Robert's Island, CA 173
Robertson, John A. 62
Robinson, __ 89
Robinson, __ (driver) 242
Robinson, Kite 137
Robinson, William see Martin, James W.
Rocher, Juan (road agent) 247–250
Rock Creek, CA 145

Index

Rocklin, CA 198
Rodden, __ (judge) 93
Rodisino, Jennie 51–52
Rodisino, John 52
Rodisino, Louisa 51–52, 210
Rodriguez, Nicanora 249
Rogers, J.T. (attorney) 99
Rogers, William (road agent) 81
Rogers, William (sheriff) 62
Rolfe, Frank (road agent) 244–245
Rolleri, James 37
Rollins, __ (Mrs.) 27
Romaine, James (driver) 233
Romargi, __ (madame) 140
Romero, Francisco 86–87
Rooks, Frank 21
Roon, John 106
Roosen, Ralph 177
Rose, N.H. 180
Roseburg, OR 119, 191, 195, 204, 223
Ross, __ (jailor) 162
Ross, __ (undersheriff) 206
Ross, Frank H. (sheriff) 188
Ross' (stagecoach) station, CA 93, 193
Round Mountain, CA 192
Rousseau, Sol (driver) 217
Rowland, William (sheriff) 74
Rucker, __ (Maj.) 90
Rugg, George N. (road agent) 256–257
Ruggles, Charles (road agent) 208–210
Ruggles, John D. (road agent) 208–210
Ruiz, Ramon (road agent) 35, 70, 242–243, 253
Russell, James (deputy) 88
Russell, William (driver) 107
Russell, William (road agent) 127–128
Rust, __ (judge) 24
Rutherford, John (road agent) 179–181
Rutherford & Company Express 3
Ryan, E.B. 137
Ryan, Martin (road agent) 48–49
Ryan, Thomas (court bailiff) 144, 204

Sacramento, CA 19–20, 24–25, 38, 44, 147–148, 167, 184, 189, 201
Sage Hen Hill, CA 219
St. Helena, CA 82, 128–129
St. Louis, MO 9, 41, 65, 141
St. Louis Ravine, CA 164
Salem, OR 106
Salinas, CA 122–125, 175
Salt Spring Valley House 31
San Andreas, CA 19, 29–34, 38–39, 40–43, 45, 47–48, 50–52, 57–58, 188
San Benito, CA 167
San Bernardino, CA 168, 170
San Diego, CA 86–88, 169–171
San Felix (stagecoach) station, CA 176

San Francisco, CA 4, 9, 16, 25, 33, 38, 45, 56, 58, 61, 74–76, 85, 90, 105, 111, 114, 122, 124, 133, 141, 144, 153, 158, 169, 172, 186, 189–190, 201, 204, 207, 216, 219, 234, 259
San Francisquito Canyon, CA 86
San Joaquin, CA 148, 172, 185
San Jose, CA 61–62, 69, 74, 126, 174, 183–184, 186–188
San Juan, CA 39, 122, 138–140, 216
San Juan Capistrano, CA 87–88
San Juan Ridge, CA 156
San Luis Obispo, CA 121–126, 174–175, 178–179, 236
San Mateo, CA 126, 177
San Rafael, CA 93
Sancho, Juan 256–257
Sansome, John (road agent) 32, 157, 218
Santa Barbara, CA 126–127, 174, 178–179, 181–182
Santa Clara, CA 74, 126, 186–187
Santa Cruz, CA 126, 186–187
Santa Margarita, CA 175
Santa Maria, CA 179–180
Santa Rosa, CA 106, 109, 230, 234–236
Santa Ynez, CA 182
Santos, J.C. 177
Savage, Antone (road agent) 35, 70, 253
Sawyer, __ (officer) 173
Sawyer, __ (U.S. commissioner) 105–196, 236
Sawyer, Lorenzo (judge) 122
Saylor, George B. (road agent) 217–218
Scammon, Henry 255
Scapucino, Serafino 15
Schaaf, F.W. 253
Schalten, Louis (driver/road agent) 71–72
Schneider, Antoine 166
Schneider, John (road agent) 109–110
Schottler, G. 256
Schwoerer, Al (driver) 55
Scofield, James (deputy) 97
Scott, __ (deputy) 62
Scott, Bob (driver) 137, 150
Scott Valley, CA 190
Scott's Bar, CA 220
Scovel, H.H. 182
Seaview, CA 236
Seawell, __ (undersheriff) 101
Secord, __ (constable) 131
Secord, George (driver) 156
Selby, Thomas (road agent) 121–122
Senter, __ (deputy) 62
Seven-Mile House, CA 101
Seven Wells, CA 169
Sewards, CA 109
Sewell, __ (justice of the peace) 234
Seymour, __ (W, F & Co. detective) 147
Shallenberger, W.M. 20

Shanks, George (aka Jack Williams; road agent) 133–136
Shannon, Peter W. 112
Sharp, __ 111
Sharp, Johnny (driver) 251, 254, 256
Sharp, Milton A. (road agent) 21, 52, 151–154
Sharpe, George (driver) 257
Shasta, CA 25, 97, 190, 193–194, 197–199, 203–205, 209, 213, 220, 250, 255
Shaw, Ed B. 153–154
Shaw, Frank (driver) 88
Shearer, __ (sheriff) 59
Sheep Ranch mine 51–52
Sheep Ranch (stagecoach) station, CA 58
Shelford, Peter (deputy) 103–104
Shepardson, Milton (aka Homily, __; road agent) 237–238
Shine, __ (U.S. marshal) 114
Shine, John (driver) 36, 245
Shingle Springs, CA 65–66
Shinn, George (road agent) 49–50, 159, 166
Shore, M.P. 73
Short, W.R. see Sykes, Lee
Shotier, G. 256
Shovel Creek, OR 225
Sierra City, CA 29, 219
Sierraville, CA 142, 217–220
Simonds, __ (justice of the peace) 203
Simpson, __ (detective) 173
Sinclair, John (road agent) 32
Sink, Daniel 231
Sisson's (stagecoach) station, CA 221–222
Six-Mile House, CA 134
Skelton, Ed (driver) 91
Skelton, Tom (driver) 89–90
Slum Gullion Pass, CO 43
Smartsville, CA 139, 142–143, 257
Smiley, J.W. (sheriff) 196
Smith, __ 155–156
Smith, Alec (driver) 206, 208
Smith, Austin N. (road agent) 251–252
Smith, Charlie 114
Smith, C.V. (driver) 121
Smith, Dick (driver) 179
Smith, Edward (driver) 17
Smith, George H. (driver) 87–88
Smith, James P. (road agent) 64–65
Smith, Jay (driver) 211
Smith, J.H. (sheriff) 112–114
Smith, Jim 247
Smith, John (driver) 98
Smith, Joseph (road agent) 176–177
Smith, J.P. (driver) 186
Smith, Peter (road agent) 171–172, 234
Smith, Sam (driver) 40–41
Smith, William (aka Charles P. Weibusch; road agent) 45, 216–217
Smith's Creek, CA 187
Smithson, James (driver) 192

Index

Snelling, CA 118
Soap Lake, CA 184
Soda Springs, CA 220
Soledad, CA 88, 123–126, 173–175, 236
Somerset House, CA 62
Sonora, CA 35–37, 40–42, 44–49, 53, 70, 94, 159, 242–246, 249, 253
Sotello, Francisco (aka Francisco Olivas; road agent) 79, 86–87
Sotello, Santos (aka Chico Lugo) 79, 86–87
Soto, Fabiana 244
Soward, F.D. (attorney) 216
Spadra, CA 167
Sparta, OR 238
Spaulding, H.R. (justice of the peace) 109
Spence, J. 146
Spenceville, CA 142
Sprague, __ (sheriff) 26
Spring Mountain House, CA 18, 40
Springe, Heinz 116
Springsteen, __ (Dr.) 84
Spurr, __ (constable) 131–133
Squire, Eugene 164
stagecoach (defined) 5
Standley, J.M. (sheriff) 101–103, 105–106, 108–112
Stanfield Hill, CA 254
Stanford, Charles 108
Stanislaus, CA 40
Staples, Joseph M. (deputy) 62
Starbird, __ (deputy) 188
Starke, Gus (deputy) 168
Starkey, Joel (deputy) 109–110
Stark's (stagecoach) station, CA 75
Starling, George (aka James Riley; road agent) 66
Starr, James E. (road agent) 58
Steele, Elijah (attorney) 222
Stevens, __ (Mrs.) 115
Stevens, Ernest (driver) 89, 94
Stevens, John (road agent) 208
Stevens, Thomas 66
Stevenson, __ (Dr.) 209
Stewart, __ 96
Stewart, __ (deputy) 226
Stewart, James (deputy) 168
Stewart, Nat (sheriff) 182
Stewart, S.A. (deputy) 207
Stiff, Newton 130
Stiles, W.C. (Dr./coroner) 135
Stillwater, CA 206
Stockgoff, Neil (driver) 116
Stockton, __ (sheriff) 147
Stockton, CA 12, 22, 30, 32, 38, 45, 48, 51, 56, 148, 172–173, 187, 239, 249
Stockyard, Ed (deputy) 119
Stoll, Lillie 54
Stone, Appleton W. (police captain) 38, 164
Stone, Jack (road agent) 90–92
Stoneman, George (CA governor) 165, 195, 240, 244, 255
Storni, Peter (deputy) 182

Stover, Nat C. (road agent) 27, 137–138
Stowell, Frank 182
Strawberry Valley, CA 258
Strickland, P.G. (stage line agent) 190
Stringham, Clark (driver) 18, 44–45
Stutzman, N.G. (road agent) 175–176
Suhr, George 208
Suisun, CA 59
Sullaway, John (driver) 223–224
Sullivan, __ (justice of the peace) 110
Sullivan, James (messenger) 14
Sulphur Creek, CA 234
Sulphur Springs, GA 44
Summit House, CA 117
Sumner, CA 76
Sunny Creek, CA 21
Supulveda, Bartola (road agent) 184–185
Surface, __ (deputy) 13
Susanville, CA 27, 84–85, 255
Sutter's Mill, CA 3, 9
Sutton, John (road agent) 171
Sutton, Smith 247
Swain, C.W. 21
Swatzel, James (constable) 246
Sweeney, J.J. 171
Sweet, Jack 90–91
Sweet, William (driver) 79–80
swing station (defined) 5
Swinney, J. 215
Sykes, Lee (aka Bob James; aka W.R. Short; road agent) 96, 200–202
Sylva, Jackson (deputy) 186

Taber, __ (marshal) 148
Tadmen, Charles (road agent) 15, 17–18
Tahoe, CA 68
Tahoe City, CA 145
Tait, __ (justice of the peace) 43
Tapia, Jose (road agent) 86–87
Tarlton, Henry see Hamilton, Albert P.
Tatum, John (road agent) 88–89
Taylor, George F. (aka Charles W. [C.W.] De Lacy; road agent) 11–12, 148
Taylor, Newt 244
team (defined) 5–6
Tehachapi Mountains, CA 79, 87
Telegraph City, CA 35, 243
Temple, __ (justice of the peace) 97
Temple, Owen (road agent) 198–199
Templeton, CA 175–176
Tesker, George (road agent) 258–259
Thacker, John N. (W, F & Co. detective) 38, 54, 59, 71, 84, 108, 115, 129, 156, 172, 177, 207, 224–226, 233–234
Thayer, Eugene (aka Josh Thayer; road agent) 244

Thayer, Josh see Thayer, Eugene
Thirteen-Mile House, CA 61
Thomas, Barry (road agent) 121–122
Thomas, George (road agent) 103
Thomas, Herman 252
Thomas, J.R. (undersheriff) 112
Thompson, Charles (road agent) 17–18, 149, 188–189
Thompson, "Cyclone" (driver) 120
Thompson, David (road agent) 43
Thompson, James (road agent) 179–181
Thoms, Winn (driver) 239–240
Thorn, __ (Dr.) 74
Thorn, Benjamin K. (sheriff) 21, 52, 35, 37–38, 41, 45–47, 50, 52, 58, 195, 242–244
Thorn, Charles H. see Dorsey, Charles
Thornburgh, Lark 180
Thurman, Charles (aka Bill Early; aka Ormstead Thurman; road agent) 27, 66–67, 93–94, 137–138, 251
Thurman, Ormstead see Thurman, Charles
Thurman, W.B. (sheriff) 90
Tibbitts, __ (constable) 96, 202
Tice, __ (W, F & Co. route agent) 54
Tickner, H.C. (stage line agent) 190
Tickner, H.L. (W, F & Co. agent) 151
Tilghman, __ (Mrs.) 248
Timbuctoo, CA 139
Tinkville, CA 204
Todd, __ (Dr.) 74
Todd, Alexander 247
Todd's Valley, CA 148
Tombstone, AZ 140
Toney, John A. (road agent) 192–193
Tovey, Mike (messenger) 20–22, 51, 71, 152–154
Tower House, CA 191
Townsend, __ (driver) 174
Tozer, Llewelyn (brigadier general) 197
Tracy, Martin (road agent) 221–223
Tracy, Thomas (road agent) 155
Treatwell, __ (judge) 172
Treaty of Guadalupe Hidalgo 3
Treloar, Ben 218–219
Tres Pinos, CA 68, 73–74
Tres Pinos Canyon, CA 245
Trinity, CA 239
Trinity Center, CA 190
Troop F, 4th Cavalry 90
Truckee, CA 143, 145, 217–219
True, J.N. (deputy) 83–84
Truett, Myers F. 229
Truman, Ben 85–86
Tubbs, Albert A. (aka Albert A. Carlton; road agent) 11
Tucker, J.L. 166
Tulare, CA 239
Tulare Lake, CA 86–87
Tunnell, Henry C. 180
Tunnell, James 180

Turner, Archie (driver) 92
Turner, Clifford 132
Turner, J.N. 163
Tuttle, R.A. 91
Tye, David (road agent) 194, 255
Tyler, Eugene (road agent) 116–117
Tyler's (stagecoach) station, CA 81
Tyndall, Tom (driver) 220–221
Tyrrel, Jeremiah (sheriff) 11

Ukiah, CA 26, 56, 98–106, 107–116, 229–230, 233
Upper Lake, CA 115
Upton, Charles D. (messenger) 229
Ury, Henry{en see Williams, Henry

Valacca, Antone (aka Red Antone; road agent) 35, 70, 243, 253
Valentine, John J. (W, F & Co. superintendent) 162–163, 169
Vallecito, CA 29
Valley Springs, CA 49–52
van Eaton, J.D. (deputy) 62
Van Duren, C. 126
Vasquez, Tiburcio (road agent) 68, 73–74, 184–185
Venard, Stephen (deputy) 64, 129, 134–136, 155, 229
Venice, CA 22
Ventura, CA 86–87
Vincent, __ 168
Virginia City, NV 136
Visalia, CA 54, 184–185, 239–240
Vogan, John (sheriff) 18
Volcano, CA 14–15, 18
von Schmidt, A.W. (Col.) 161–162
Voss, __ 113

Wadsworth, F.E. (W, F & Co. agent) 227
Wadsworth, CA 217
Waldin, David (road agent) 29–30
Wales, James (deputy) 78
Walker, __ (sheriff) 147
Walker, __ (W, F & Co. agent) 164
Walker, George 249
Walker, John (driver) 125
Walker's Basin, CA 78
Walker's (stagecoach) station, CA 170
Walla Walla, WA 240
Walnut Creek, CA 11
Walnut Grove, CA 167
Walton, William (driver) 246
Waltrip, Nathan (driver) 98
Ward, Henry C. (messenger) 205, 233–234
Ward's (stagecoach) station, OR 237
Ware, Thomas 38
Warfield, __ (sheriff) 118
Warnock, __ (W, F & Co. detective) 13
Washburn, Frank (driver) 56–57
Waterman, Robert (CA governor) 234
Waters, __ (undersheriff) 146–147

Watkins, James E.G. (road agent) 63–64
Watson, Charles W. (road agent) 161
Watson, Charley (driver) 61–62
Watsonville, CA 124, 184
Wattenberger's Resort, CA 116
Waukesha House, CA 60, 247
Wawona, CA 88, 90, 92, 94
Weaverville, CA 190, 192–193, 196, 203, 205, 208, 210, 212–213
Weber House 31
Wedenberg, Frank 208
Weibusch, Charles P. see Smith, William
Weir, Joseph 130
Weise, __ (deputy) 111
Weisenstein, John (road agent) 174–175, 236
Welden, T.J. (deputy) 105
Wellborn, __ (justice) 181
Wellington's (stagecoach) station, NV 151–152
Wellock, James (road agent) 75–76
Welsh, Elza (Miss) 203
Wending, CA 115
Wesson, Fred (driver) 52–55
Wesson, G.F. 41
West, Charles 107
West, Harry or Henry see Wise, Henry I.
West, Joseph 59
West Branch, CA 28
West Point, CA 34
Westfall, Herman "Henry" (road agent) 56–57
Westville, CA 160
Weybright, __ 128
Wheatland, CA 142
Wheeler, __ (driver) 250
Wheeler, __ (W, F & Co. agent) 99
Wheeler, Norman (constable) 24
Whiskeytown, CA 213
White, __ (Dr.) 214
White, Bill see Gristy, Bill
White, Eph. H. (road agent) 256–257
White, Jack 244
White, Samuel (road agent) 148
White, Sol see Allen, S.A.
Whitescarbor, Charles 215
Whiting, __ (deputy) 193
Whitlock, __ (deputy)
Whitten, O.P. (deputy) 207
Whittier Springs, CA 108
Wilbur, W.C. 107
Wilcox, __ (Capt.) 90
Wiley, __ (deputy) 18
Wiley, George (deputy) 214
Wilkinson, Ash (driver) 231–232
Willard, Henry 106
Williams, __ 27, 200
Williams, __ (road agent) 14–15
Williams, Charles 69
Williams, Charlie (driver) 222
Williams, David E. (Mrs.) 251
Williams, Frank (aka Jack Bryant;

road agent) 97, 143–144, 158, 204
Williams, George 252
Williams, Henry (aka Henry Ury; aka Jack Brady; road agent) 211
Williams, Horace (driver) 192, 196–197
Williams, Jack see Shanks, George
Williams, John (deputy) 83–84
Williams, John (driver) 58–59
Williams, John (road agent) 198–199
Williamson, Charlie (road agent) 75
Williamson, Henry 158, 204
Willis, __ (deputy) 62
Willis, John 28
Willits, CA 99, 102, 105, 109, 112–114
Wilson, Bill 203
Wilson, Charles 255
Wilson, Charles (road agent) 155
Wilson, Edward see Brown, John
Wilson, Fred 23
Wilson, George (road agent) 17, 64–65, 233
Wilson, James (driver) 212–213
Wilson, James (road agent) 183–184
Wilson, John 215
Wilson, William (driver) 215–216
Winans, Robert 139
Winchell, __ (undersheriff) 66, 74
Winchell, Ned (driver) 161
Wise, Henry I. (aka Harry or Henry West; road agent) 85
Witter Spring, CA 115
Witthouse, __ (deputy) 69
Woodbridge, CA 32
Woodland, CA 23, 209
Woodruff, Harry (deputy) 185
Woodruff, Tom (messenger) 153
Woods, Frank 212
Woods, H.W. (attorney) 78
Woodville, CA 241
Woodworth, C.L. (driver) 229
Wool Rock, CA 116
Wright, Clara 200–201
Wright, John A. (road agent) 18, 39–40, 140
Wycoff, __ (deputy) 209

Yager, __ (deputy) 168
Yancey, Tyron M. (sheriff) 243–245
Yankee Jim, CA 147
Ybarra, Pedro (road agent) 244
Yeates, __ (sheriff) 26
Yeates, James H. (sheriff) 163
Yosemite, CA 88–89, 91–92, 94–95
Yosemite Valley, CA 69
Yreka, CA 149, 188, 190–193, 194–199, 221–223, 225–227, 237, 239

Zedecker, Dick (deputy) 214
Zumwalt, I.G. (attorney) 59

www.ingramcontent.com/pod-product-compliance
Lightning Source LLC
Chambersburg PA
CBHW081543300426
44116CB00015B/2741